At a Glance Chapter Summary

The At a Glance chapter summary ties everything together and helps you stay on course! First, the Key Points recap the chapter content for each Learning Objective. Second, the related Key Learning Outcomes list all of the expected student performance capabilities that come from completing each objective. In case you need further practice on a specific outcome, the last column references the related Example Exercises. In addition, the At a Glance grid guides you from the Key Learning Outcomes to the page reference in the textbook where the material is covered.

At a Glance 13

1 Describe and illustrate the accounting for share dividends, share splits, and share repurchase transactions.

Key Points	Key Learning Outcomes	Page	Example Exercises
A corporation may issue share dividends, split shares, and repurchase outstanding shares, for a variety of reasons.	• Describe a share dividend.	660	
	• Journalize a share dividend.	662	13-1
	• Prepare the shareholders' equity section of the balance sheet.	662	13-2 13-3
	• Describe a share split.	664	
	• Identify the reasons a corporation might repurchase its shares.	666	
	• Journalize a share repurchase transaction	667	13-4

2 Describe and illustrate the corporate income statement and earnings per share.

Key Points	Key Learning Outcomes	Page	Example Exercises
A corporate income statement differs from partnership and sole proprietorship income statements in that it includes income taxes expense. Corporations that prepare their financial statements under IFRS will also report earnings per share at the bottom of their income statement. Corporations that use ASPE are not required to report earnings per share.	• Prepare a corporate income statement.	668	13-5
	• Calculate earnings per share for corporations preparing financial statements under IFRS.	670	13-6

End-of-chapter Practice Exercises parallel the Example Exercises for further reinforcement and self-study. If you struggle with a Practice Exercise, you can return to the Example Exercise to see a model solution.

PE 13-3
Shareholders' equity

EE 13-3 p. 666

Winston Corporation had the following balances in its shareholders' equity accounts as at May 31, 2015:

Retained earnings	$268,000
Common shares, unlimited authorized, 40,000 issued and outstanding	215,000
$2.50 preferred shares, unlimited authorized, 2,000 issued and outstanding	86,000

On June 18, 2015, the board of directors declared a 4:1 share split.

Prepare the Shareholders' Equity section of the balance sheet for Winston Corporation on June 19, 2015.

ACCOUNTING

Second Canadian Edition

Carl S. Warren
Professor Emeritus of Accounting
University of Georgia, Athens

James M. Reeve
Professor Emeritus of Accounting
University of Tennessee, Knoxville

Jonathan E. Duchac
Professor of Accounting
Wake Forest University

Sheila F. Elworthy
Vice President of Learning
CA School of Business

Tana M. Kristjanson
Instructor, School of Business
Camosun College

Barrie E. Tober
Professor and Coordinator of Accounting
Niagara College

NELSON EDUCATION

NELSON / EDUCATION

Accounting, Volume 2, Second Canadian Edition

by Carl S. Warren, James M. Reeve, Jonathan E. Duchac,
Sheila F. Elworthy, Tana M. Kristjanson, and Barrie E. Tober

**Vice President, Editorial
Higher Education:**
Anne Williams

Senior Acquisitions Editor:
Amie Plourde

Acquisitions Editor:
Rod Banister

Executive Marketing Manager:
Sean Chamberland

Technical Reviewer:
Ross Meacher

Developmental Editor:
Lisa Berland

**Photo Researcher/Permissions
Coordinator:**
Natalie Barrington

**Senior Content Production
Manager:**
Imoinda Romain

Production Service:
Integra Software Services Pvt. Ltd.

Copy Editor:
Mariko Obokata

Proofreader:
Margaret DeWind

Indexer:
Jeanne Busemeyer, Hyde Park
Publishing Services

Manufacturing Manager:
Joanne McNeil

Design Director:
Ken Phipps

Managing Designer:
Franca Amore

Interior Design Modifications:
Greg Devitt Design

Cover Design:
Liz Harasymczuk

Cover Image:
Roy Ooms/Masterfile

Compositor:
Integra Software Services Pvt. Ltd.

Printer:
R.R. Donnelley

Library and Archives Canada
Cataloguing in Publication

Accounting / Carl S. Warren ...
[et al.]. — 2nd Canadian ed.

Includes indexes.
Contents: v. 1. Chapters 1–10 —
v. 2. Chapters 11–17.

ISBN 978-0-17-650973-6 (v. 1).—
ISBN 978-0-17-650974-3 (v. 2)

1. Accounting—Textbooks.
I. Warren, Carl S

HF5636.A315 2013
657'.044   C2012-905659-6

ISBN-13: 978-0-17-650974-3
ISBN-10: 10: 0-17-650974-7

BRIEF CONTENTS

VOLUME 1

VOLUME 2

CONTENTS

11 Accounting for Partnerships 561

12 Corporations: Organization, Share Transactions, and Shareholders' Equity 613

16 *Statement of Cash Flows* 813

17 *Financial Statement Analysis* 869

THE AUTHOR TEAM

Carl S. Warren

Dr. Carl S. Warren is Professor Emeritus of Accounting at the University of Georgia, Athens. Dr. Warren has taught classes at the University of Georgia, University of Iowa, Michigan State University, and University of Chicago. Professor Warren focused his teaching efforts on principles of accounting and auditing. He received his Ph.D. from Michigan State University and his B.B.A. and M.A. from the University of Iowa. During his career, Dr. Warren published numerous articles in professional journals, including *The Accounting Review, Journal of Accounting Research, Journal of Accountancy, The CPA Journal*, and *Auditing: A Journal of Practice & Theory.* Dr. Warren has served on numerous committees of the American Accounting Association, the American Institute of Certified Public Accountants, and the Institute of Internal Auditors. He has also consulted with numerous companies and public accounting firms. Warren's outside interests include playing handball, golfing, skiing, backpacking, and fly-fishing.

James M. Reeve

Dr. James M. Reeve is Professor Emeritus of Accounting and Information Management at the University of Tennessee. Professor Reeve taught on the accounting faculty for 25 years, after graduating with his Ph.D. from Oklahoma State University. His teaching effort focused on undergraduate accounting principles and graduate education in the Master of Accountancy and Senior Executive MBA programs. Beyond this, Professor Reeve is also very active in the Supply Chain Certification program, which is a major executive education and research effort of the College. His research interests are varied and include work in managerial accounting, supply chain management, lean manufacturing, and information management. He has published over 40 articles in academic and professional journals, including the *Journal of Cost Management, Journal of Management Accounting Research, Accounting Review, Management Accounting Quarterly, Supply Chain Management Review*, and *Accounting Horizons*. He has consulted or provided training around the world for a wide variety of organizations, including Boeing, Procter & Gamble, Norfolk Southern, Hershey Foods, Coca-Cola, and Sony. When not writing books, Professor Reeve plays golf and is involved in faith-based activities.

Jonathan E. Duchac

Dr. Jonathan Duchac is the Merrill Lynch and Co. Professor of Accounting and Director of the Program in Enterprise Risk Management at Wake Forest University. He earned his Ph.D. in accounting from the University of Georgia and currently teaches introductory and advanced courses in financial accounting. Dr. Duchac has received a number of awards during his career, including the Wake Forest University Outstanding Graduate Professor Award, the T.B. Rose award for Instructional Innovation, and the University of Georgia Outstanding Teaching Assistant Award. In addition to his teaching responsibilities, Dr. Duchac has served as Accounting Advisor to Merrill Lynch Equity Research, where he worked with research analysts in reviewing and evaluating the financial reporting practices of public companies. He has testified before the U.S. House of Representatives, the Financial Accounting Standards Board, and the Securities and Exchange Commission; and has worked with a number of major public companies on financial reporting and accounting policy issues. In addition to his professional interests, Dr. Duchac is the Treasurer of The

Special Children's School of Winston-Salem, a private, nonprofit developmental day school serving children with special needs. Dr. Duchac is an avid long-distance runner, mountain biker, and snow skier. His recent events include the Grandfather Mountain Marathon, the Black Mountain Marathon, the Shut-In Ridge Trail run, and NO MAAM (Nocturnal Overnight Mountain Bike Assault on Mount Mitchell).

Sheila F. Elworthy

Dr. Sheila Elworthy, C.A., is the Vice President of Learning at the CA School of Business (CASB), the professional school for aspiring chartered accountants in western Canada. Dr. Elworthy has taught introductory, intermediate, and advanced accounting, and general business courses for 20 years at Camosun College in Victoria, B.C.; University of Victoria in Victoria, B.C.; Eastern Institute of Technology in Napier, New Zealand; and in the Executive Certified Management Accounting (ECMA) program. Her professional interest in successful learning processes for accounting students extends from the introductory stages in college and university settings through to the successful completion of the students' chosen designation. Dr. Elworthy received her M.B.A. from the Richard Ivey School of Business in London, Ontario, and her Doctor of Education from Simon Fraser University in Burnaby, B.C. In 1984, Dr. Elworthy qualified as a Chartered Accountant in Ontario. In addition to her professional pursuits, Dr. Elworthy is active in Big Brothers Big Sisters, currently serving as a member of the board and of the Fund Development Committee and previously as the Treasurer and the Chair of the Finance Committee. Sheila is also a founding member of the CPA Professional Education Program Working Group, tasked with the design of the national program for Canadian accounting education and accreditation. Her personal interests include spending time with her husband and her three children, playing bridge, cycling, kayaking, and skiing.

Tana M. Kristjanson

Tana M. Kristjanson, C.A., C.F.E., is an instructor in the School of Business at Camosun College, in Victoria, B.C. She has also taught accounting at North Island College in Courtenay, B.C.; Vancouver Island University (formerly Malaspina College) in Nanaimo, B.C.; in the Certified Management Accounting (CMA) program; and the Chartered Accountant School of Business (CASB). Ms. Kristjanson currently teaches introductory and intermediate courses in financial accounting and auditing and has developed a college-level fraud awareness course. She is an investigator for the Professional Conduct and Ethics Committee of the Institute of Chartered Accountants of B.C. Her professional interests focus on the use of reflection and student feedback as mechanisms to improve teaching. She is currently working on her Masters of Education at Simon Fraser University. Ms. Kristjanson spent five years in public practice working on reviews, audits, and taxes for clients such as not-for-profits, businesses, and Native Councils. She became a Chartered Accountant in 2004. Her personal interests include hiking, travelling, and spending time with her husband, friends, and family.

Barrie E. Tober

Barrie E. Tober, C.M.A, is a professor in the School of Business and Management at Niagara College, Niagara-on-the-Lake, Ontario, where she teaches introductory financial accounting, managerial accounting, and operations management. She is also the program coordinator for the two- and three-year accounting diplomas at Niagara College. She has taught managerial accounting, advanced financial accounting, and accounting information systems at Brock University in St. Catharines, Ontario. Professor Tober completed her B.Comm at the University of Windsor, received her C.M.A. designation in 1992, and earned a Master of Accountancy degree from Brock in 2005. Prior to becoming a full-time professor, she spent eight years working in public accounting and two years as a consultant for new entrepreneurs in the Business Development Centre at Niagara College. Her personal interests include camping and travelling with her husband and four children.

PREFACE

In the second Canadian edition of *Accounting*, we have continued with the tradition of focusing on the changing needs of accounting students and their instructors by utilizing feedback from student reviews, an Editorial Advisory Board, and other reviewers. Accounting faculty from all over the country contributed to our book development process in a direct and creative way. Many of the features and themes in this text reflect the suggestions and feedback received from both instructors and students.

Textbooks play an invaluable role in the teaching and learning environment at postsecondary institutions. Designed for today's students, this text uses a high-impact writing style that emphasizes topics in a concise and clearly written manner. Direct sentences, concise paragraphs, numbered lists, and step-by-step calculations provide students with an easy-to-follow structure for learning accounting. This is achieved without sacrificing content or rigour.

Walkthrough of Pedagogical Features

Accounting, Second Canadian Edition, is unparalleled in pedagogical innovation. Our goal is to provide a logical framework and pedagogical system that cater to how today's students study and learn. Our student surveys and review board of accounting faculty from across Canada significantly influenced the textbook presentation. Here is a preview of the important features that are used throughout the textbook:

After studying this chapter, you should be able to:

1 Describe why companies invest in debt and equity securities.

Why Companies Invest	Investing Cash in Current Operations
	Investing Cash to Earn Additional Revenue
	Investing Cash for Strategic Reasons

2 Describe and illustrate the accounting for non-strategic investments.

Accounting for Non-Strategic Investments	Accounting for Held-for-Trading Investments	EXAMPLE EXERCISE 15-1 (page 764) EXAMPLE EXERCISE 15-2 (page 765)
	Accounting for Held-to-Maturity Investments, Loans, and Receivables	EXAMPLE EXERCISE 15-3 (page 769)
	Purchase of Bonds at a Discount or Premium	EXAMPLE EXERCISE 15-4 (page 770) EXAMPLE EXERCISE 15-5 (page 771)
	Accounting for Available-for-Sale Investments	EXAMPLE EXERCISE 15-6 (page 773)

3 Describe and illustrate the accounting for strategic investments.

Accounting for Strategic Investments	Classifications of Strategic Investments	
	Accounting for Investments in Associates	EXAMPLE EXERCISE 15-7 (page 779)
	Accounting for Joint Ventures	
	Accounting for Business Combinations	
	Reporting of Investments	
	Financial Analysis and Interpretation	EXAMPLE EXERCISE 15-8 (page 780)

APPENDIX 1 Accounting for Non-Strategic Investments Using International Financial Reporting Standards (IFRS) 9

For the chapter *At a Glance*, turn to page 785.

Guiding Principles System

Students can easily locate the information they need to master course concepts with the Guiding Principles System (GPS). At the beginning of every chapter, this innovative system plots a course through the chapter content by displaying the chapter objectives, major topics, and related Example Exercises. The GPS reference to the chapter At a Glance summary completes this proven system.

Clear Objectives and Key Learning Outcomes

Describe and illustrate the accounting for non-strategic investments.

To help guide students, the authors provide clear chapter objectives and important learning outcomes. All aspects of the chapter materials relate back to these key points and outcomes, which keeps students focused on the most important topics and concepts to help them succeed in the course.

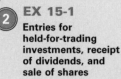

2 **EX 15-1**

Entries for held-for-trading investments, receipt of dividends, and sale of shares

✔ c. Gain on sale of investments, $10,385

On March 13, Android Corporation acquired 4,500 shares of the 100,000 outstanding Tannis Inc. common shares at $32 per share plus Brokerage Fees of $250. On August 16, a cash dividend of $1.20 per share was received. On December 8, 1,500 shares were sold at $39 per share, less Brokerage Fees of $115.

Record the entries for (a) the purchase of shares, (b) the receipt of dividends, and (c) the sale of 1,500 shares. These shares were classified as held-for-trading investments.

Example Exercises

Example Exercises were developed to reinforce concepts and procedures in a bold, new way. Similar to following the instructor's example in the classroom, students follow the authors' example to see how to complete accounting applications as they are presented in the text. This feature also provides a list of Practice Exercises that parallel the Example Exercises to provide students with the practice they need. In addition, the Practice Exercises also include references back to the Example Exercises so that students can easily cross-reference when completing homework.

See the example of the application being presented.

Follow along as the authors work through the Example Exercise.

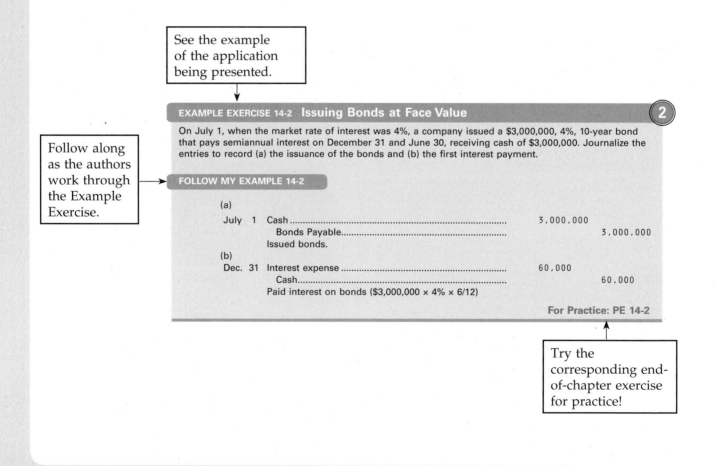

EXAMPLE EXERCISE 14-2 Issuing Bonds at Face Value   **2**

On July 1, when the market rate of interest was 4%, a company issued a $3,000,000, 4%, 10-year bond that pays semiannual interest on December 31 and June 30, receiving cash of $3,000,000. Journalize the entries to record (a) the issuance of the bonds and (b) the first interest payment.

FOLLOW MY EXAMPLE 14-2

(a)
July	1	Cash	3,000,000	
		Bonds Payable		3,000,000
		Issued bonds.		

(b)
Dec.	31	Interest expense	60,000	
		Cash		60,000
		Paid interest on bonds ($3,000,000 × 4% × 6/12)		

For Practice: PE 14-2

Try the corresponding end-of-chapter exercise for practice!

At a Glance Chapter Summary

The At a Glance summary grid ties everything together and helps students stay on course. First, the Key Points recap the chapter content for each Learning Objective. Second, the related Key Learning Outcomes list all the expected student performance capabilities that result from completing each objective. The Key Learning Outcomes are referenced by page number in the next column, to guide students to the related content in the chapter. For students needing further practice on a specific outcome, the last column references the related Example Exercise. Through this intuitive grid, all of the chapter pedagogy links together in one cleanly integrated summary.

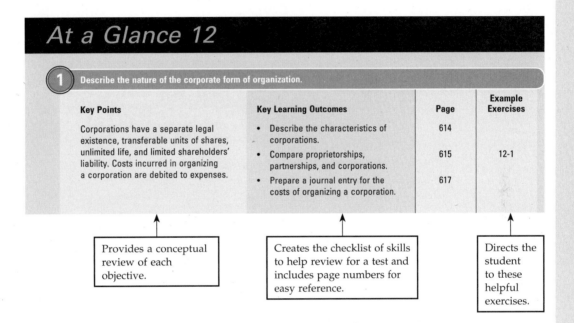

At a Glance 12

1 Describe the nature of the corporate form of organization.

Key Points	Key Learning Outcomes	Page	Example Exercises
Corporations have a separate legal existence, transferable units of shares, unlimited life, and limited shareholders' liability. Costs incurred in organizing a corporation are debited to expenses.	• Describe the characteristics of corporations.	614	
	• Compare proprietorships, partnerships, and corporations.	615	12-1
	• Prepare a journal entry for the costs of organizing a corporation.	617	

Provides a conceptual review of each objective.

Creates the checklist of skills to help review for a test and includes page numbers for easy reference.

Directs the student to these helpful exercises.

Practice Exercises

The Example Exercises direct students to the Practice Exercises. These Practice Exercises parallel the Example Exercises and provide the opportunity for further reinforcement and course mastery. Students who have difficulty with the Practice Exercises can return to the Example Exercises to see a model solution.

**2 PE 14-2
Issuing bonds at face value**

On January 1, when the market rate of interest was 5% for similar bonds, a company issued a $15,000,000, 5%, 10-year bond that pays semiannual interest on June 30 and December 31, receiving cash of $15,000,000. Journalize the entries to record (1) the issuance of the bonds and (2) the first interest payment.

EE 14-2 p. 712

Real-World Chapter Openers

Chapter openers relate the accounting and business concepts in the chapter to familiar companies and activities in students' lives. These openers employ examples of real companies and provide invaluable insight into real business practices. Several of the openers focus on familiar companies, such as Facebook, Shoppers Drug Mart, Tim Hortons, and Potash Corp. of Saskatchewan.

Corporations: Additional Share Transactions, Income Statement, and Accounting Changes

CHAPTER
13

SHOPPERS DRUG MART

In 1962, Shoppers Drug Mart, a company founded by pharmacist Murray Koffler, opened its first store in the Shoppers World Plaza in Toronto, Ontario. Since then, Shoppers Drug Mart has continually expanded, opening its 1,000th store in 2007. By 2011, the company had more than 1,200 stores across Canada. Shoppers Drug Mart is the leader in Canada's retail drug store marketplace, claiming the number-one ranking as a provider of pharmacy products and services. Shoppers Drug Mart offers 7,500 of its own private-label brands, such as Life Brand, Quo, Simply Food, and Nativa. Ten million customers participate in the Shoppers Optimum loyalty card program, whereby customers collect points that can be cashed in for products. On November 21, 2001, Shoppers Drug Mart had its initial public offering (IPO) of shares at $18 per share. Ten years later, those shares were trading at $42 a share.

In 2011, Shoppers Drug Mart repurchased more than five million shares for $206.8 million. Why would Shoppers Drug Mart buy back its shares? And,

equally importantly, if you were Shoppers Drug Mart's accountant, how would you have accounted for that transaction?

In Chapter 12, basic accounting transactions for corporations were introduced, such as forming a corporation, issuing shares for cash or in exchange for other assets, and recording cash dividends. In addition, Chapter 12 illustrated the Shareholders' Equity section of a balance sheet and the statement of changes in equity.

Chapter 13 describes additional share transactions that a corporation may engage in, such as Shoppers Drug Mart's share repurchase, issuing share dividends, and share splits. We will also explain some of the items that may appear on a corporation's income statement, such as discontinued operations and earnings per share. By the end of this chapter, you will know how to account for Shoppers Drug Mart's share repurchase. You will also have some ideas about what might have caused Shoppers Drug Mart to make the repurchase. Shoppers Drug Mart's 2011 financial statements and selected notes are shown in Appendix C.

NEL

Morning Java Financial Statements

Beginning in Chapter 6, "Inventories," and continuing through Chapter 15, "Investments," chapters contain excerpts from the full financial statements for Morning Java, a coffee company. These statements show students the big picture of accounting by providing a consistent reference point for users who want to see a set of financial statements and how each chapter topic relates to the different financial statements. The financial statements were crafted by the authors to be consistent with the presentation in each chapter and are prepared using Accounting Standards for Private Enterprises (ASPE) in Volume 1 and International Financial Reporting Standards (IFRS) in Volume 2. Any significant differences in financial statement presentation when using ASPE or IFRS are mentioned. The Morning Java statements in Appendix A of each volume follow this same pattern. In Appendix A of Volume 1, the ASPE version of the statements is presented with IFRS differences pointed out. In Appendix A of Volume 2, the IFRS version of the statements is presented with ASPE differences pointed out.

User-Friendly Design

Based on students' testimonials of what they find most useful, this streamlined presentation includes a wealth of helpful resources without the clutter. Some exhibits use computerized spreadsheets to better reflect the changing environment of business. Visual learners will appreciate the generous number of exhibits and illustrations used to convey concepts and procedures.

Exhibit 4

Dividends to Cumulative Preferred Shares

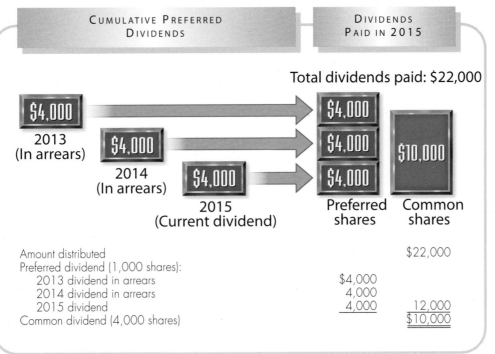

| | CUMULATIVE PREFERRED DIVIDENDS | | DIVIDENDS PAID IN 2015 | |

Total dividends paid: $22,000

	Preferred shares	Common shares
Amount distributed		$22,000
Preferred dividend (1,000 shares):		
2013 dividend in arrears	$4,000	
2014 dividend in arrears	4,000	
2015 dividend	4,000	12,000
Common dividend (4,000 shares)		$10,000

Financial Records Colour Coding

Accounting, Second Canadian Edition, introduces a new colour scheme to help students learn to identify the different types of accounting records.

Financial statements →

Kelly Consulting
Income Statement
For the Month Ended December 31, 2015

Revenues:		
Fees earned		$17,500
Expenses:		
Salaries expense.	$1,620	
Rent expense	1,600	
Supplies expense	550	
Utilities expense	330	
Depreciation expense	330	
Total expenses.		4,430
Net income.		$13,070

Trial balances →

Kelly Consulting
Post-Closing Trial Balance
December 31, 2015

	Debit Balances	Credit Balances
Cash.	19,170	
Accounts Receivable.	3,100	
Supplies	850	
Prepaid Rent	3,200	
Office Equipment.	14,500	
Accumulated Depreciation		330
Accounts Payable.		800
Salaries Payable		120
Unearned Fees.		2,500
Kelly Pitney, Capital		37,070
	40,820	40,820

T accounts →

ALLOWANCE FOR DOUBTFUL ACCOUNTS

			Jan. 1	Balance	30,000
Total accounts written off $26,750	Jan. 21	6,000			
	Feb. 2	3,900			
	⋮	⋮			
			Dec. 31	Unadjusted balance	3,250

Journals, bank reconciliations, charts of accounts, and worksheets →

Journal
Page *2*

Date		Description	Post. Ref.	Debit	Credit
2015					
Dec	30	Accounts Receivable	1020	1,500	
		Fees Earned	4010		1,500
		Services provided on account.			
	30	Kelly Pitney, Withdrawals	3020	6,000	
		Cash	1010		6,000
		Owner withdrawal.			

Financial Analysis and Interpretation

The Financial Analysis and Interpretation, or FAI, section at the ends of Chapters 4 to 16 introduces relevant key ratios used throughout the textbook. Students connect with the business environment as they learn how stakeholders interpret financial reports. This section covers basic analysis tools that students will use again in Chapter 17, "Financial Statement Analysis." Furthermore, a related Example Exercise has been added after each FAI in this edition, and students can test their proficiency with these tools through special activities and exercises at the end of each chapter. To ensure a consistent presentation, a unique icon is used for both the section and in the margin beside related end-of-chapter materials.

FINANCIAL ANALYSIS AND INTERPRETATION

The dividend yield indicates the rate of return to shareholders in terms of cash dividend distributions. Although the dividend yield can be computed for both preferred and common shares, it is more often computed for common shares. This is because most preferred shares have a stated dividend rate or amount. In contrast, the amount of common dividends normally varies with the profitability of the corporation.

The dividend yield is computed by dividing the annual dividends paid per common share by the market price per share at a specific date, as shown below.

$$\text{Dividend Yield} = \frac{\text{Annual Dividends per Share}}{\text{Market Price per Share}}$$

To illustrate, the market price of Shaw Communications Inc. common shares was $19.37 as at the close of business, June 27, 2012. During the past year, Shaw Communications Inc. has paid dividends of $0.90 per common share. Thus, the dividend yield of Shaw Communications Inc. common share is 4.65% ($0.90/$19.37). Because the market price of a corporation's shares will vary from day to day, its dividend yield will also vary from day to day. Fortunately, the dividend yield is provided in the newspaper listings of market prices and by most Internet quotation services, such as from Yahoo!'s Finance website.

The recent dividend yields for some selected companies are as follows:

Company	Dividend Yield (%)
Enerflex Systems Income Fund	2.29
General Motors Corporation	None
Hewlett-Packard Development Company	2.73
Power Financial Corporation	5.51
Research In Motion	None
Suncor Energy Ltd.	1.88
Toronto-Dominion Bank	3.68

As can be seen, the dividend yield varies widely across firms. Growth companies often do not pay dividends but, instead, reinvest their earnings in research and marketing, which is the case with Research In Motion, the Canadian maker of BlackBerry® smartphones.

Integrity, Objectivity, and Ethics in Business

In each chapter, these cases help students develop their ethical compass. Often coupled with related end-of-chapter activities, these cases can be discussed in class, or students can consider the cases as they read the chapter. Both the section and related end-of-chapter materials are indicated with a unique icon for a consistent presentation.

INTEGRITY, OBJECTIVITY, AND ETHICS IN BUSINESS

ACCURATELY REPORTING OPERATING RESULTS

How can financial statements best predict the future? By separating out items such as discontinued operations that are not expected to recur.

In 2010, Shaw Communications Inc. began exploring the opportunity to add wireless networking to the complement of products and services offered to its customers. In 2011, after investing much research and more than $90 million into the initiative, Shaw Communications determined it was not economically feasible to enter into competition in the wireless networking market.

This decision to discontinue construction of the wireless network resulted in losses of $89.3 million in 2011 and $1 million in 2010. Each loss was recognized as a *loss from discontinued operations*.

If these losses had been included in the regular operating results, Shaw Communications would have appeared to have had an unusually bad year in 2011, when, in fact, its income from operations was almost $30 million higher in 2011 than in 2010. Financial statements must accurately disclose the reality of what happened if the users of those statements are to rely on them.

Critical Thinking

Boxed critical thinking features in each chapter present samples of the ambiguities, risks, and uncertainties that students may encounter in their accounting practice. Using a question and answer format, this feature helps students develop their ability to consider multiple factors and use their judgment in applying accounting concepts to realistic and ambiguous situations. The critical thinking icon is also used in end-of-chapter materials to indicate the need for analysis or deeper thinking.

CRITICAL THINKING

Employers often say their employees are their most valuable asset. **Does an employee meet the definition of an asset?**

An employee meets two of the three essential characteristics of an asset: (1) an employee contributes to future cash flows, and (2) the event giving rise to the benefit has already occurred—the employee has been hired. The third essential characteristic, however, is not met: the business cannot control access to the benefit because an employee has the right to resign at any time. Thus, an employee does not appear on the financial statements as an asset, despite what many employers say!

Mid-Chapter Illustrative Problem and Solution

A problem and its solution illustrate one or more concepts from the first half of the chapter. Students are thus able to apply their knowledge early in the chapter.

MID-CHAPTER ILLUSTRATIVE PROBLEM

On March 1, 2015, Apex Corporation, a wholesaler of mountain-climbing equipment, issued $1,000,000, three-year, 4% bonds at an effective interest rate of 5%, receiving cash of $972,459.37. Interest on the bonds is payable semiannually on August 31 and February 28 or 29. The fiscal year of the company is the calendar year.

Instructions

1. Journalize the cash proceeds from the sale of the bonds.
2. Prepare a bond discount amortization table for the bonds.
3. Journalize the August 31, 2015, entry to record payment of interest and amortization of the bond discount, using the effective interest method.
4. Journalize the December 31, 2015, adjusting entry pertaining to the bond.
5. Journalize the February 29, 2016, entry pertaining to the bond.

MID-CHAPTER ILLUSTRATIVE SOLUTION

1.

2015				
Mar.	1	Cash	972,459.37	
		Discount on Bonds Payable	27,540.63	
		Bonds Payable		1,000,000.00
		Issued $1,000,000 bonds payable at a discount.		

End-of-Chapter Illustrative Problem and Solution

A solved problem models one or more of the chapter's assignment problems so that students can apply the modelled procedures to end-of-chapter materials.

Market-Leading End-of-Chapter Material

Students need to practise accounting so that they can understand and use it. To give students the greatest possible advantage in the real world, *Accounting*, Second Canadian Edition, goes beyond presenting theory and procedure by including comprehensive end-of-chapter material.

New to the Second Canadian Edition

Textbooks continue to play an invaluable role in the teaching and learning environments. Continuing our focus from the previous edition, we reached out to accounting instructors in an effort to improve the textbook presentation. Our research indicated a need to remain current in the areas of emerging topics and trends, while continuing to look for ways to make the book more accessible to students. The results of the collaboration with instructors from across Canada are reflected in the following major improvements to the second Canadian edition.

Accounting Standards for Private Enterprise (ASPE) and International Financial Reporting Standards (IFRS)

Today's accounting educators face the challenge of teaching introductory accounting in an environment that uses more than one set of corporate accounting standards. Based upon feedback from instructors, we have organized the volumes so that Volume 1 emphasizes ASPE and discusses the IFRS differences, while Volume 2 includes both ASPE and IFRS treatments. We feel this approach will allow students to learn both accounting treatments without being overly confused or overwhelmed. In Volume 1, Appendix A presents the ASPE version of the financial statements for our fictitious company, Morning Java, with IFRS differences pointed out. In Volume 2, both IFRS versions of the financial statements for Morning Java are presented, with ASPE differences pointed out.

The Accounting Equation and the Accounting Cycle

To help students understand that a transaction ultimately affects the accounting equation, T accounts are now shown for each journal entry in Chapters 2 and 3.

Also, an image of the accounting cycle has been referenced throughout Chapters 2 to 4, to ensure that students know where they are working in the accounting cycle and how each step relates to prior and subsequent steps.

Additional Example and Practice Exercises

Example Exercises and Practice Exercises were developed to reinforce concepts and provide students with opportunities to practise the chapter content. This edition adds more Example Exercises and Practice Exercises for chapter material and for the Financial Analysis and Interpretations (FAIs).

Critical Thinking

A new feature of *Accounting*, Second Canadian Edition, is the introduction of Critical Thinking boxes, designed with the assistance of Dr. Susan Wolcott, CMA, CPA, Ph.D. These boxes allow students to explore ambiguous accounting issues or accounting treatments. This feature gives students the opportunity to use the conceptual framework to resolve situations that have more than one correct answer.

End-of-Chapter Exercises and Problems

This edition increases the number of end-of-chapter exercises and problems by 30% over the previous edition. Many of the end-of-chapter materials have been updated for both fictitious and real-world companies. The longer questions are now shorter in response to feedback that they were too time-consuming, and the number of questions has increased substantially.

Chapter-by-Chapter Enhancements

The following specific content changes can be found in *Accounting,* Second Canadian Edition.

Volume 1

Chapter 1: Introduction to Accounting and Business

- The chapter opener features Facebook.
- Subtotals have been removed from the accounting equation analysis throughout the chapter.
- The continuing case study and longer problems are shorter.
- Discussions have been added on the Chartered Professional Accountant (CPA) designation and the merger of the accounting professions.
- Definitions have been added for assets and liabilities.
- More of the conceptual framework elements are discussed.
- New end-of-chapter exercises and problems have been added.

Chapter 2: Analyzing Transactions

- T accounts have been added to help students better understand the accounting equation.
- A new table summarizes common transaction terminology and the related accounts to be debited or credited.
- The steps of the accounting cycle are emphasized and each step is tied to the accounting cycle.
- Prepaid insurance and unearned revenue are introduced to lead to better flow when introducing adjusting entries in the next chapter.
- New end-of-chapter exercises and problems have been added.

Chapter 3: The Adjusting Process

- T accounts are used to describe and illustrate adjusting entries.
- The chapter features five new exhibits summarizing the five types of adjusting entries, as a reference for identifying the differences between adjusting entries and the journal entries required.
- The continuing problem is shorter.
- The coverage of depreciation is more comprehensive and introduces the calculations for straight-line depreciation.
- New end-of-chapter exercises and problems have been added.

Chapter 4: Completing the Accounting Cycle

- The steps of the accounting cycle are emphasized, and each step is tied to the accounting cycle.
- A new Example Exercise and Practice Exercise correspond with the new FAI, Working Capital and Current Ratio.
- New end-of-chapter exercises and problems have been added.

Chapter 5: Accounting for Merchandising Businesses

- Chapter 5 from the first Canadian edition, "Accounting Systems," has moved to Appendix E, in response to reviewer feedback on the best way to treat this material. Accounting Systems for Merchandisers, which was an appendix to "Accounting for Merchandising Businesses" in the previous edition, now forms part of Appendix E.
- Treatment under ASPE is presented, and the IFRS differences are identified and discussed.
- Coverage, exercises, and problems for Appendix 2 now allow instructors to teach PST only, PST and GST, or HST only. The accounting treatment of refund entries has also been added.
- Problems are shorter.
- A new Financial Analysis and Interpretation box features gross profit and gross margin using the real-world retailer Le Château.
- A new Example Exercise and Practice Exercise correspond with the new FAI.
- New end-of-chapter exercises and problems have been added.

Chapter 6: Inventories

- The steps have been added for calculating the moving weighted average cost using the perpetual inventory method.
- The discussion of the periodic inventory system has moved to Appendix 2 to be consistent with Chapter 5.
- A new Example Exercise and Practice Exercise correspond with the FAI.
- Treatment of inventories under ASPE is presented, and the IFRS differences are identified and discussed.
- New end-of-chapter exercises and problems have been added.

Chapter 7: Internal Control and Cash

- A new discussion addresses the responsibilities of internal and external auditors.
- An example of an online bank statement is presented to be consistent with statements that students are familiar with.
- The steps for completing a bank reconciliation have been condensed.
- New end of chapter exercises and problems have been added.

Chapter 8: Receivables

- Content and exercises address the percent of receivables allowance method.
- Problems now show more than one allowance method used throughout the year.
- Merchandise transactions have been added to reinforce inventory chapter coverage.
- Treatment under ASPE is presented, and the IFRS differences are identified and discussed.
- A new Example Exercise and Practice Exercise correspond with the FAI.
- New end-of-chapter exercises and problems have been added.

Chapter 9: Property, Plant, and Equipment and Other Long-Term Assets

- Discussion of impairment losses for long-term assets has been expanded, and more related exercises have been added.
- The discussion on goodwill has been updated to reflect recent changes in accounting standards.

- A new discussion addresses the revaluation model.
- New problems have been added that require balance sheet preparation for consecutive years.
- Content and exercises on lump-sum purchases have been added.
- The discussion of depreciation for partial years is simplified.
- T accounts have been added to illustrate the impact of property, plant, and equipment disposals on account balances.
- Treatment under ASPE is presented, and the IFRS differences are identified and discussed.
- A new Financial Analysis and Interpretation features return on assets, using the real-world company WestJet Airlines Ltd.
- A new Example Exercise and Practice Exercise correspond with the FAI.
- New end-of-chapter exercises and problems have been added.

Chapter 10: Current Liabilities and Payroll

- Discussion has been expanded on different types of liabilities such as accrued liabilities and unearned revenues.
- An explanation of Harmonized Sales Tax (HST) and examples of HST have been added.
- The discussion of discounted notes payable has been omitted.
- Provisions have been added to the chapter content.
- Updated payroll calculations now include excerpts of payroll charts supplied by Canada Revenue Agency (CRA).
- Federal and provincial income taxes are now shown separately throughout the chapter.
- New Example Exercises and Practice Exercises have been added to calculate gross pay and deductions and record remittance of payroll deductions.
- The material has been rearranged to show single employee information all together.
- New end-of-chapter exercises and problems have been added.

Volume 2
Chapter 11: Partnerships

- New Example Exercises and Practice Exercises have been added for recording closing entries, division of income when allowances exceed net income, and partner withdrawals.
- The Mid-Chapter Illustrative Problem is shorter.
- The asset revaluation Example Exercise now includes an allowance for doubtful accounts to be consistent with examples used in exercises and problems.
- The same partnership scenario is used throughout the chapter.
- More of the examples and exercises now show an unequal division of profits to better reflect real-world scenarios.
- The balance sheet presentation for partnerships has been added.
- The liquidation section has been rearranged to embed the journal entries within the explanation of the steps.
- The coverage on characteristics of corporations has been moved to Chapter 12.
- New end-of-chapter exercises and problems have been added.

Chapter 12: Corporations: Organization, Share Transactions, and Shareholders' Equity

- The chapter opener features Leon's Furniture Limited.
- The characteristics of corporations have been moved to this chapter from Chapter 11.
- New Example Exercises and Practice Exercises compare the three business forms, closing entries for corporations, and the statement of changes in equity.
- A more detailed discussion has been added on retained earnings, including closing entries.
- A discussion has been added on other comprehensive income and accumulated other comprehensive income.
- The discussion on common and preferred shares rights and privileges has been expanded.
- The option of recording cash dividends to a cash dividends account and closing it to retained earnings at year-end has been added.
- The presentation of shareholders' equity has been reorganized to cover IFRS first in this chapter, and Morning Java's equity is shown under both IFRS and ASPE for comparison purposes.
- The FAI has been expanded to discuss the industry comparison between the returns on common shareholders' equity for Bank of Montreal and for Royal Bank of Canada.
- The statement of shareholders' equity has been omitted.
- New end-of-chapter exercises and problems have been added.

Chapter 13: Corporations: Additional Share Transactions, Income Statement, and Accounting Changes

- The chapter opener features Shoppers Drug Mart.
- New Example Exercises and Practice Exercises address share splits.
- The explanation of weighted average common shares has been expanded to include share splits and share dividends.
- The Mid-Chapter Illustrative Problem has been expanded.
- An example has been added to demonstrate the "tax effect" on discontinued operations.
- Extraordinary items have been omitted.
- An example has been added to show the accounting treatment for correction of an error.
- Objective 5 has been revised to address the statement of comprehensive income.
- New end-of-chapter exercises and problems have been added.

Chapter 14: Long-Term Liabilities: Bonds and Notes

- The chapter opener features WestJet Airlines Ltd.
- The Mid-Chapter Illustrative Problem is shorter.
- IFRS is used, and the differences under ASPE are discussed.
- A new Example Exercise shows the issuing of bonds at face value.
- The coverage of financing corporations is simplified and now opens the chapter.
- New problems address adjusting entries, the effective interest method of bond amortization, bond retirement, and financial statement presentation.
- New problems integrate current liabilities from Chapter 11 with long-term liabilities transactions.
- New T accounts illustrate the impact of bond redemptions on the general ledger accounts.

- A new Example Exercise and Practice Exercise correspond with the FAI.
- New end-of-chapter exercises and problems have been added.

Chapter 15: Investments

- The chapter opener features Shaw Communications Inc.
- The chapter has been reorganized to enable students to understand and apply the current standard. A new appendix describes the upcoming changes affecting investments for corporations reporting under IFRS.
- Chapter material has been updated to reflect current IFRS.
- A new discussion addresses the effective method and the straight line method of amortizing bond discounts and premiums.
- The direct valuation method of tracking investments has been added.
- For comparison purposes, Morning Java investments are illustrated for IFRS and ASPE.
- New end-of-chapter exercises and problems have been added.

Chapter 16: Statement of Cash Flows

- A new Example Exercise and Practice Exercise correspond with the FAI.
- Cash flows are presented using IFRS, with a discussion of the differences under ASPE.
- New end-of-chapter exercises and problems have been added.

Chapter 17: Financial Statement Analysis

- The chapter opener features Potash Corporation of Saskatchewan, Inc.
- The problems are shorter and critical thinking questions have been added.
- New end-of-chapter exercises and problems have been added.

Appendices

The complete annual report of Leon's Furniture Limited and the partial report of Shoppers Drug Mart illustrate financial statements prepared according to IFRS.

Custom Publishing

Nelson Education Ltd. is pleased to offer instructors greater flexibility in the choice of material covered in their textbooks by offering the opportunity to customize the textbook resources. If you are an instructor who is interested in selecting an alternative organization, adding or omitting chapters from what is currently presented in the two volumes, or other variations on this textbook, please contact your Nelson Sales and Editorial Representative to discuss the options available to you.

Online Support: Homework Management for Students and Instructors

Aplia

Founded in 2000 by economist and Stanford professor Paul Romer, Aplia is an educational technology company dedicated to improving learning by increasing student effort and engagement. Currently, Aplia products have been used by more than a million students at more than 1,300 institutions.

For students, Aplia offers a way to stay on top of coursework by working through regularly scheduled homework assignments that increase their practice time and provide prompt feedback. Interactive tools and additional content further increase students' engagement and understanding.

For instructors, Aplia offers high-quality, auto-graded assignments that ensure students apply effort on a regular basis throughout the term. These assignments can easily be customized to suit individual teaching schedules. To ensure consistency between the Aplia course and the textbook, the Aplia course for *Accounting*, Second Canadian Edition, was prepared by two of the textbook authors, Sheila Elworthy and Tana Kristjanson.

To help improve the homework system, a Technology Advisory Board provided competitive reviews and direction for the development of the Aplia course. The following people were members of the Technology Advisory Board:

Jerry Aubin	Anu Goel	Cheryl Wilson
Algonquin College	*Seneca College*	*Durham College*
Tamara Ebl	Kerry Hendricks	Julie Wong
Okanagan College	*Fanshawe College*	*Dawson College*
Deirdre Fitzpatrick		
George Brown College		

For more information, please contact your Nelson Education sales and editorial representative or go to **www.aplia.com/accounting**.

Instructor Support

When it comes to supporting instructors, Nelson Education Ltd. is unsurpassed. *Accounting*, Second Canadian Edition, continues this tradition with powerful print and digital ancillaries aimed at facilitating greater course successes.

Nelson Education Teaching Advantage

The Nelson Education Teaching Advantage (NETA) program delivers research-based instructor resources that promote student engagement and higher-order thinking to enable the success of Canadian students and educators.

Instructors today face many challenges. Resources are limited, time is scarce, and a new kind of student has emerged: one who balances school with work, has gaps in his or her basic knowledge, and is immersed in technology in a way that has led to a completely new style of learning. In response, Nelson Education has gathered a group of dedicated instructors to advise us on the creation of richer and more flexible ancillary materials that respond to the needs of today's teaching environments.

Instructor's Resource CD

Key instructor ancillaries are provided on the Instructor's Resource CD (ISBN 0-17-666107-7), providing instructors with the ultimate tool for customizing lectures and presentations.

(Downloadable web versions are also available at **www.warren2ce.nelson.com**.) The following NETA items are available on the IRCD:

Enriched Instructor's Manual The Enriched Instructor's Manual was written by one of the textbook authors, Barrie Tober. It is organized according to the textbook chapters and addresses eight key educational concerns, including typical stumbling blocks students face and how to address them. Other features include at least two alternative lesson plans per chapter, activities for large and small classes, exploration of learning objectives, and opportunities for students to interact with the material in different ways.

Test Bank The Test Bank was written by Maria Belanger of Algonquin College. It includes more than 2,800 multiple-choice questions written according to NETA guidelines for effective construction and development of Bloom's higher-order questions. Also included are true/false questions and problems. The test bank provides a grid for each chapter that correlates each question to the chapter's objectives and a ranking of difficulty. Test bank files are provided both online and in Word for easy editing.

The Computerized Test Bank by ExamView® includes all the questions from the test bank. The easy-to-use ExamView software is compatible with Microsoft Windows and Mac OS. Create tests by selecting questions from the test bank, modifying these questions as desired, and add new questions you write yourself. You can administer quizzes online and export tests to WebCT, Blackboard, and other formats.

Solutions Manual Prepared by the authors of this textbook, the Solutions Manual contains answers to all exercises, problems, and activities in the textbook. As always, the solutions are author-written and have been verified multiple times for numerical accuracy and consistency with the core text.

NETA Presentation Microsoft PowerPoint lecture slides for every chapter have been created by Sheila Elworthy and Tana Kristjanson, authors of the textbook. Each chapter contains objectives followed by a thorough outline of the chapter that together provide an entire lecture model. Exhibits from each chapter, such as Example Exercises, have been recreated as PowerPoint slides to create a powerful, customizable tool. NETA principles of clear design and engaging content have been incorporated throughout.

Image Library This resource consists of digital copies of figures, short tables, and photographs used in the book. Instructors may use these files to create their own PowerPoint presentations.

Instructor Excel® Templates Prepared by Paul Elworthy, these templates provide the solutions for the problems and exercises that have Enhanced Excel® templates for students. By using these files, instructors can see the solutions in the same format as the students. All problems with accompanying templates are marked in the book with an icon. These templates are available for download at **www.warren2ce.nelson.com** and are on the IRCD.

DayOne Day One—Prof InClass is a PowerPoint presentation that you can customize to orient your students to the class and their text at the beginning of the course.

TurningPoint® Another valuable resource for instructors is TurningPoint® classroom response software customized for *Accounting,* Second Canadian Edition. Now you can author, deliver, show, access, and grade, all in PowerPoint—with no toggling back and forth between screens! JoinIn on Turning Point is the only classroom response software tool that gives you true PowerPoint integration. With JoinIn, you are no longer tied to your computer. You can walk about your classroom as you lecture, showing slides and collecting and displaying responses with ease. There is simply no easier or more effective way to turn your lecture hall into a personal, fully interactive experience for your students. If you can use PowerPoint, you can use JoinIn on TurningPoint! (Contact your Nelson publishing representative for details.)

Student Support

Students come to accounting with a variety of learning needs. *Accounting*, Second Canadian Edition, offers a broad range of supplements in both printed form and easy-to-use technology. We refined our entire supplement package around the comments instructors have provided about their courses and teaching needs.

Working Papers for Exercises and Problems Prepared by the authors of this textbook, the traditional working papers include problem-specific forms for preparing solutions for Exercises, A & B Problems, the Continuing Problem, and the Comprehensive Problems from the textbook. These forms, with preprinted headings, provide a structure for the problems, which helps students get started and saves them time. Additional blank forms are included.

 Enhanced Excel® Templates Prepared by Paul Elworthy, these templates are provided for selected long or complicated end-of-chapter exercises and problems and provide assistance to students as they set up and work through the problem. Certain cells are coded to display a red asterisk when an incorrect answer is entered, which helps students stay on track. Selected problems that can be solved using these templates are designated by an icon.

Product Companion Website The companion site at **www.warren2ce.nelson .com** provides students with a wealth of introductory accounting resources, including Interactive Quizzes to test their understanding, Crossword Puzzles, Flashcards, Online Glossary, and downloadable Enhanced Excel® templates for selected exercises and problems in the text. The Interactive Quizzes were prepared by Maria Bergeron of Algonquin College.

Acknowledgments

Throughout our development of *Accounting*, Second Canadian Edition, we had the privilege to work alongside our Editorial Advisory Board and Technology Advisory Board. Nelson Education Ltd. brought these talented and creative individuals together to serve on the boards to help guide the direction of the textbook. Through countless reviews, phone calls, emails, and an intensive meeting in Toronto, their comments and feedback had a profound impact on the presentation and core themes of this text. We are forever indebted to our advisory board members for the contribution to this textbook: Maria Belanger

Maria Belanger
Algonquin College

David Fleming
George Brown College

Darlene Lowe
Grant MacEwan University

Darla Lutness
NAIT

Pina Salvaggio
Dawson College

David Van Rijt
St. Clair College

Harvey Willows
Centennial College

We also thank our Technology Advisory Board, mentioned earlier, for their contributions:

Jerry Aubin
Algonquin College

Anu Goel
Seneca College

Cheryl Wilson
Durham College

Tamara Ebl
Okanagan College

Kerry Hendricks
Fanshawe College

Julie Wong
Dawson College

Deirdre Fitzpatrick
George Brown College

Courtesy of Barrie Tober

Our thanks also go to Susan K. Wolcott, of WolcottLynch Associates, for her analysis of the critical thinking components in *Accounting* and for her recommendations for how *Accounting* can support and develop critical thinking among students.

We want to take this opportunity to thank the following reviewers for their perspectives and feedback on textbook use:

Karina Brassard
Champlain College

Shelley Johnson
Okanagan College

David Sale
Kwantlen Polytechnic University

Walt Burton
Okanagan College

Gerry La Rocca
Vanier College

Pina Salvaggio
Dawson College

Derek Cook
Okanagan College

Darlene Lowe
Grant MacEwan University

Elaine Sonberg
Dawson College

Paul Griffin
Humber College

Karen Matthews
Okanagan College

Dan Wong
SAIT Polytechnic

Ken Hartford
St. Clair College

Doug Ringrose
Grant MacEwan University

Kerry Hendricks
Fanshawe College

We also want to thank the following people who made significant contributions to our previous Canadian edition.

Adrian Fontenla
Okanagan College

Amy Greene
triOS College

Barbara Likar
Sprott Shaw Community College

Barbara Moore
triOS College

Betty Cook
CompuCollege

Cynthia Lone
Red River College

Dan Wong
SAIT Polytechnic

Dave Fleming
George Brown College

David Mills
SAIT Polytechnic

Debbie Musil
Kwantlen Polytechnic University

Don Hutton
Durham College

Don Smith
Georgian College

Doug MacDonald
CompuCollege

Doug Mann
Georgian College

Doug Ringrose
MacEwan College

Douglas Leatherdale
Georgian College

Geoff Stephenson
Olds College

Glenn Ankrom
CDI College

Glen Stanger
Douglas College

Graeme Gomes
Everest College

Heather Martin
Nova Scotia Community College

Ian Hutchinson
Acadia University

Jerry Aubin
Algonquin College

Joan Wallwork
Kwantlen Polytechnic University

Joe Pidutti
Durham College

Joy Atkinson
NSCC/CompuCollege

Kim Dyck
Red River College

Maria Belanger
Algonquin College

Patrick Hamilton
Nova Scotia Community College

Penny Parker
Fanshawe College

Raymond Leung
University of the Fraser Valley

Rhonda Fenner
University College of the North

Susan Johnston Emberly
Maritime Business College

Traven Reed
Canadore College

Vanessa Oltmann
Vancouver Island University

Sheila and Tana would like to thank the following Camosun College instructors who approached them personally with very helpful suggestions:

Stu Berry

Leelah Dawson

Barbara Edwards

Amy Hoggard

Jolene Kendrew

Michelle Lysak

Keri Norrie

Alison Parker

Jennifer Reed

Stephen Scott

Lyle Widdifield

Thanks also to Diane McDonald and Shan Thomas, who provided guidance on technical accounting issues.

We also thank all those involved in helping us through this entire writing process. Specifically, we thank our Acquisitions Editor, Rod Banister, who provided answers and direction to countless questions; Amie Plourde, Senior Acquisitions Editor; Lisa Berland, Developmental Editor; our Copy Editor, Mariko Obokata; and Sean Chamberland, Executive Marketing Manager; Dave Stratton, Marketing Manager; and Imoinda Romain, Senior Content Production Manager.

Combatting Errors

Over the years, we have all used books where we have encountered problems with errors. One of our goals with *Accounting*, Second Canadian Edition, was to minimize the possibility that errors would slip through. Many people have been involved in checking this textbook for errors and ensuring its accuracy, and we believe it is as free of mistakes as we can make it. Any that remain are, of course, the responsibility of the authors. We would like to thank Ross Meacher, C.A., for the detailed accuracy check that he performed on our text, the assignment materials, and the accompanying Solutions Manual. If by chance you do identify what you believe to be an error, please report your findings to kristjansontextbook@camosun.bc.ca.

Conclusion

Mastering introductory accounting can be a daunting task for many students. Through careful planning and execution of our development plan, we feel that this textbook will help your students master the course and assist you with the challenging task of teaching introductory accounting. If you have any thoughts or suggestions, please email us at kristjansontextbook@camosun.bc.ca, barrietober@gmail.com, or sheilaelworthy@ gmail.com. Our goal is to produce the best possible textbook by recognizing that change is the only constant, and by actively seeking innovative methods to provide the best possible accounting textbook for Canadian students and instructors.

Sheila Elworthy
Tana Kristjanson
Barrie Tober
January 2013

Accounting for Partnerships

HANSON CULVER CONSTRUCTION

When a partnership is formed, partners may choose to draw up a document called a partnership agreement. The purpose of this agreement is to set parameters for running the partnership. The agreement can outline income division, decision-making processes, steps for disagreement resolution, and sale to outsiders. If a partnership is formed without an agreement, income will be divided equally, regardless of the amount of time or skill each partner devotes to the partnership. Also, if a partnership seeks legal counsel to resolve differences, the courts will decide how assets should be shared.

The importance of the partnership agreement was apparent to Ron Culver when he and his partner disagreed about the dissolution of their construction business, Hanson Culver Construction. They had been working together for five years, and both individuals had invested time and money into the successful business. When Ron decided to leave the country and the partnership, he and his partner disagreed about the dissolution process. Although the company had little equity, Ron believed that the business had considerable value because of its excellent reputation

in the community. His partner refused to pay Ron his share of this intangible asset, forcing Ron to either sue or leave empty-handed. Ron decided not to sue, and so he departed with his tools, after investing five years of his time into the partnership.

How could these problems have been avoided? Although a partnership agreement wouldn't necessarily have prevented the partnership breakup, details of how to proceed with the partnership dissolution would have been discussed and documented by the partners in advance of their problems. David Hanson continued to run the company on his own, and it continued to be profitable for more than 15 years. Ron received no compensation for his part in the development of the business.

The three major forms of business entities discussed in this text are proprietorships, partnerships, and corporations. We have already introduced proprietorships. Partnerships will be discussed in this chapter, along with characteristics of proprietorships, for comparison purposes. Corporations will be discussed in the next two chapters.

After studying this chapter, you should be able to:

1 Describe the characteristics of proprietorships and partnerships.

Proprietorships and Partnerships	Proprietorships	
	General Partnerships	
	Limited Partnerships and Limited Liability Partnerships (LLPs)	
	Comparing Proprietorships and Partnerships	

2 Describe and illustrate the accounting for forming a partnership and for dividing the net income and net loss of a partnership.

Forming and Dividing Income of a Partnership	Forming a Partnership	EXAMPLE EXERCISE 11-1 (page 565)
	Dividing Income	EXAMPLE EXERCISE 11-2 (page 567)
		EXAMPLE EXERCISE 11-3 (page 569)
		EXAMPLE EXERCISE 11-4 (page 570)
		EXAMPLE EXERCISE 11-5 (page 571)

3 Describe and illustrate the accounting for partner admission and withdrawal.

Partner Admission and Withdrawal	Admitting a Partner	EXAMPLE EXERCISE 11-6 (page 575)
		EXAMPLE EXERCISE 11-7 (page 578)
	Withdrawal of a Partner	EXAMPLE EXERCISE 11-8 (page 580)
	Death of a Partner	

4 Describe and illustrate the accounting for liquidating a partnership.

Liquidating Partnerships	Gain on Sale of Assets	
	Loss on Sale of Assets	EXAMPLE EXERCISE 11-9 (page 584)
	Loss on Sale of Assets—Capital Deficiency	EXAMPLE EXERCISE 11-10 (page 587)

5 Prepare the statement of changes in partnership equity.

Statement of Changes in Partnership Equity		

For the chapter *At a Glance*, turn to page 589.

Proprietorships and Partnerships

Describe the characteristics of proprietorships and partnerships.

As discussed on page 8 in Chapter 1, the three most common legal forms for organizing and operating a business are as follows:

1. Proprietorships
2. Partnerships
3. Corporations

In this section, the characteristics of proprietorships and partnerships are described. The characteristics of and the accounting for corporations are described in Chapters 12 and 13.

Proprietorships

A proprietorship is a business owned by a single individual. The most common type of proprietorships are professional service providers, such as lawyers, architects, realtors, and physicians.

Characteristics of proprietorships include the following:

1. Ease of formation: *Simple.* There are no legal restrictions or forms to file.
2. Legal liability: *No limitation.* The owner is personally liable for any debts or legal claims against the business. Thus, creditors can take the personal assets of the owner if the business debts exceed the owner's investment in the business.
3. Taxation: *Not taxable.* The income of a proprietorship is not subject to income tax. Instead, the business's income or loss is "passed through" to the owner's personal tax return.
4. Life of entity: *Limited life.* When the owner dies or retires, the proprietorship ceases to exist.
5. Access to capital: *Limited.* The ability to raise capital is typically limited to what the owner provides personally or through borrowing.
6. Ease of transfer of ownership: *Difficult.* A proprietor must find a buyer in order to transfer ownership of the business.
7. Form of payment to owners: *Withdrawals.* Payments to owners take the form of withdrawals.

General Partnerships

A **partnership** is an association of two or more persons who own and manage a business for profit. Partnerships are less widely used than proprietorships.

Characteristics of a **general partnership** include the following:

1. Ease of formation: *Moderately complicated.* A partnership requires only an agreement between two or more persons to organize. However, because the **partnership agreement** includes matters such as amounts to be invested, limits on withdrawals, distributions of income and losses, and admission and withdrawal of partners, a lawyer is often used in drawing up the agreement.
2. Legal liability: *No limitation.* The partners are personally liable for any debts or legal claims against the partnership. Therefore, creditors can take the personal assets of the partners if the business debts exceed the partners' investment in the partnership. A **limited partnership,** which will be discussed later in this chapter, offers some protection for partners.
3. Taxation: *Not taxable.* Similar to a proprietorship, the income or loss of a partnership is "passed through" to the partners' individual income tax returns. However, partnerships must still report revenues, expenses, and income or loss annually to Canada Revenue Agency (CRA).
4. Life of entity: *Limited.* When a partner dies or retires, the partnership ceases to exist. However, the partnership agreement can often be amended, allowing the business to continue operating without the need to form a new partnership or prepare a new partnership agreement.
5. Access to capital: *Limited.* The ability to raise capital is limited to what the partners can provide from personal resources or through borrowing.
6. Ease of transfer of ownership: *Moderate.* As will be discussed later in this chapter, a partner can sell his or her interest in the partnership to the existing partners or to a new partner.
7. Form of payment to owners: *Withdrawals.* Similar to a proprietorship, payments to partners take the form of withdrawals.

Note: A partnership is a nontaxable entity that has a limited life and unlimited liability.

In addition to the above characteristics, some unique aspects of partnerships are as follows:

1. *Co-ownership of partnership property.* The property invested in a partnership by a partner becomes the joint property of all the partners. When a partnership is dissolved, each partner's share of the partnership assets is the balance in his or her capital account.

2. *Mutual agency.* **Mutual agency** means each partner is an agent of the partnership and may act on behalf of the entire partnership. Thus, any liabilities created by one partner become liabilities of all the partners.

3. *Participation in income.* Net income and net loss are distributed among the partners according to their partnership agreement. If the partnership agreement does not provide for distribution of income and losses, then income and losses are divided equally among the partners.

In Canada, a partnership may take three forms: a general partnership, as previously described, a limited partnership, and a limited liability partnership (LLP).

Limited Partnerships and Limited Liability Partnerships (LLPs)

A limited partnership offers limited liability to partners who, in most cases, provide some funding but are not involved in the day-to-day operations of the partnership. In such a legal form, at least one *general partner* operates the partnership and has unlimited liability. The remaining partners are considered *limited partners. The accounting for a limited partnership is the same as for a general partnership.*

A **limited liability partnership (LLP)** is a relatively new form of business entity available in some provinces and all territories to professionals, such as lawyers and accountants. An LLP protects partners from malpractice or negligence claims caused by the work of one of the partners. Although all partners are still liable for other partnership debts, debts that arise because of the specific work of one partner are paid by that partner personally. The accounting for an LLP is the same as for a general partnership.

Comparing Proprietorships and Partnerships

Exhibit 1 summarizes the previously discussed characteristics of proprietorships and partnerships.

Exhibit 1

Characteristics of Proprietorships and General Partnerships

Organizational Form	Ease of Formation	Legal Liability	Taxation	Life of Entity	Access to Capital	Ease of Transfer of Ownership	Form of Payment to Owners
Proprietorship	Simple	No limitation	Nontaxable entity (owner pays personal tax on earnings)	Limited	Limited	Difficult	Withdrawals
General Partnership	Moderate	No limitation	Nontaxable entity (owners pay personal tax on earnings)	Limited	Limited	Moderate	Withdrawals

② **Forming and Dividing Income of a Partnership**

Describe and illustrate the accounting for forming a partnership and for dividing the net income and net loss of a partnership.

Most of the day-to-day accounting for a partnership is similar to that illustrated in earlier chapters. However, the formation, division of net income or net loss, dissolution, and liquidation of partnerships give rise to unique transactions.

In the remainder of this chapter, the unique transactions for partnerships are described and illustrated.

Forming a Partnership

In forming a partnership, the investments of each partner are recorded in separate entries. The assets contributed by a partner are debited to the partnership asset accounts. If any liabilities are assumed by the partnership, the partnership liability accounts are credited. Each partner's capital account is credited for the net amount.

To illustrate, assume that Lara Greguric and Mike Belfry, owners of competing hardware stores, agree to combine their businesses in a partnership, Dundas Hardware, on January 1, 2014. Greguric agrees to contribute the following:

Cash	$ 7,400	Office equipment	$2,500
Accounts receivable	16,300	Allowance for doubtful accounts	1,500
Inventory	28,700	Accounts payable	2,600
Store equipment	5,400		

Belfry agrees to contribute the following:

Accounts receivable	$18,300	Office supplies	1,500
Inventory	12,500	Allowance for doubtful accounts	5,000
Store equipment	22,000	Accounts payable	8,300

The entry to record the assets and liabilities contributed by Greguric is as follows:

2014					
Jan.	1	Cash		7,400	
		Accounts Receivable		16,300	
		Inventory		28,700	
		Store Equipment		5,400	
		Office Equipment		2,500	
		Allowance for Doubtful Accounts			1,500
		Accounts Payable			2,600
		Lara Greguric, Capital			56,200
		Formation of partnership.			

In the preceding entry, the noncash assets and liabilities are recorded at values agreed upon by the partners. These values are normally based on current market values, which may differ from their carrying values.

To illustrate, the store equipment contributed by Belfry has a carrying value of $22,000 (cost of $30,000 less accumulated depreciation of $8,000), but the partners agree that its market value is $19,300. The partners also feel that some of Belfry's inventory is old and overvalued by $1,500. The contributions of Belfry would be recorded as follows:

Jan.	1	Accounts Receivable		18,300	
		Inventory		11,000	
		Store Equipment		19,300	
		Office Supplies		1,500	
		Allowance for Doubtful Accounts			5,000
		Accounts Payable			8,300
		Mike Belfry, Capital			36,800
		Formation of partnership.			

EXAMPLE EXERCISE 11-1 *Journalize Partners' Original Investment* ②

Reese Howell and Shelley Baker decided to form a partnership. Reese Howell contributed equipment, inventory, and $34,000 cash. The equipment had a carrying value of $23,000 and a market value of $29,000. The inventory had a carrying value of $60,000, but had a market value of only $15,000 because of obsolescence. The partnership also assumed a $12,000 note payable owed by Howell that was used originally to purchase the equipment.

(continued)

Baker contributed equipment, inventory, and $8,000 cash to the partnership. The equipment had a carrying value of $33,000 and a market value of $18,000. The inventory had a market value of $40,000. Provide the journal entries for Howell's and Baker's contributions to the partnership.

FOLLOW MY EXAMPLE 11-1

Cash	34,000	
Inventory	15,000	
Equipment	29,000	
Notes Payable		12,000
Reese Howell, Capital		66,000
Cash	8,000	
Equipment	18,000	
Inventory	40,000	
Shelly Baker, Capital		66,000

For Practice: PE 11-1

CRITICAL THINKING

What are some of the risks of forming a partnership?
It is possible that some of the partners will not get along or will not do their share of the work. Because of the *mutual agency* characteristic, which is unique to partnerships, it is also possible for one partner to cause all the partners to lose money by entering into an unprofitable arrangement.

How can these risks be minimized?
These risks can be reduced by drawing up a partnership agreement, setting joint goals and objectives, and working together before forming the partnership.

Dividing Income

Income or losses of the partnership are divided *equally* if no partnership agreement exists or the partnership agreement does not specify how the division is to occur. Most partnership agreements, however, do specify how income or losses are to be divided.

Common methods of dividing partnership income are based on the following:

Note:

3:2 ratio

=

$\frac{3}{5}, \frac{2}{5}$ **fractions**

=

60%, 40% percentages

1. Services of the partners
2. Services and investments of the partners

Dividing Income—Services of Partners One method of dividing partnership income is based on the services provided by each partner to the partnership. These services are often recognized by partner salary allowances. Such allowances reflect differences in partners' abilities and time devoted to the partnership. Because partners are not employees, such allowances are recorded as divisions of net income and are credited to the partners' capital accounts.

To illustrate, assume that the partnership agreement of Lara Greguric and Mike Belfry provides for the following:

	Monthly Salary Allowance	Remaining Income
Lara Greguric	$5,000	60%
Mike Belfry	4,000	40%

The division of the remaining income or loss can be expressed as a ratio (6:4), as a percentage (60%, 40%), or as a fraction (6/10, 4/10).

The division of income may be reported at the bottom of the partnership income statement. Using this format, the division of $150,000 of net income would be reported on the bottom of the partnership income statement as follows:

	L. Greguric	M. Belfry	Total
Net income...			$150,000
Division of net income:			
Annual salary allowance	$60,000	$48,000	$108,000
Remaining income	25,200	16,800	42,000
Net income	$85,200	$64,800	$150,000

The division of net income may also be reported as a separate statement accompanying the balance sheet and the income statement or in a statement of partnership capital.

The closing entries for revenue and expense accounts are the same as those for proprietorships, discussed in Chapter 4. The net income division is recorded as a closing entry. Net income division is separate from cash withdrawals. The entry for closing Income Summary and dividing net income is as follows:

Dec.	31	Income Summary	150,000	
		Lara Greguric, Capital		85,200
		Mike Belfry, Capital		64,800
		To close Income Summary account.		

If Greguric and Belfry withdraw funds from the partnership throughout the year, the withdrawals are debited to their withdrawals accounts. At the end of the year, the withdrawals account debit balances are closed to the partners' capital accounts. The fiscal year-end for partnerships, like proprietorships, is December 31, since partnership income "passes through" to the partners who file taxes on a calendar-year basis. To illustrate, assume that Greguric and Belfry withdrew funds equal to their salary allowances in January. The entry for the withdrawal is as follows:

Jan.	31	Lara Greguric, Withdrawals	5,000	
		Mike Belfry, Withdrawals	4,000	
		Cash		9,000
		Monthly withdrawal of funds.		

If Greguric and Belfry withdrew funds equal to their salary allowances each month, then the entry for closing their withdrawal accounts is as follows:

Dec.	31	Lara Greguric, Capital	60,000	
		Mike Belfry, Capital	48,000	
		Lara Greguric, Withdrawals		60,000
		Mike Belfry, Withdrawals		48,000
		To close withdrawals accounts.		

EXAMPLE EXERCISE 11-2 Dividing Partnership Net Income—Closing Entries   ②

John Lee and Brett Young's partnership agreement provided a salary allowance of $80,000 and $75,000 to each partner, respectively, with any remaining net income to be divided equally. During the year, both partners withdrew $6,000 per month.

a. Determine the division of $200,000 net income for the year.

b. Provide journal entries to close (1) the Income Summary account and (2) the withdrawals accounts for the two partners.

(continued)

FOLLOW MY EXAMPLE 11-2

a.

	J. Lee	B. Young	Total
Annual salary allowance	$ 80,000	$75,000	$155,000
Remaining income	22,500	22,500	45,000
Net income	$102,500	$97,500	$200,000

b. (1)

Income Summary	200,000	
John Lee, Capital		102,500
Brett Young, Capital		97,500
To close the Income Summary account.		

(2)

John Lee, Capital	72,000	
Brett Young, Capital	72,000	
John Lee, Withdrawals		72,000
Brett Young, Withdrawals		72,000
To close the withdrawals accounts.		

For Practice: PE 11-2

Dividing Income—Services of Partners and Investments A partnership agreement may divide income based not only on services but also on the amount invested by each partner. In doing so, the partnership may pay interest on the capital balance of each partner. In this way, partners with more invested in the partnership are rewarded by receiving more of the partnership income. One such method of dividing partnership income would be as follows:

1. Partner salary allowances
2. Interest on capital investments
3. Any remaining income divided

To illustrate, assume that the partnership agreement for Greguric and Belfry provides for the following:

1.

	Monthly Salary Allowance
Lara Greguric	$5,000
Mike Belfry	4,000

2. Interest of 3% on each partner's capital balance as at January 1, 2014.

Capital, Lara Greguric, January 1	$56,200
Capital, Mike Belfry, January 1	36,800

3. Remaining income: 60% to Greguric, 40% to Belfry.

The $150,000 net income for the year is divided as follows:

Net income $150,000

Division of net income:

	L. Greguric	M. Belfry	Total
Annual salary allowance	$60,000	$48,000	$108,000
Interest allowance	1,686*	1,104**	2,790
Remaining income	23,526†	15,684‡	39,210
Net income	$85,212	$64,788	$150,000

*3% × $56,200.

**3% × $36,800.

†($150,000 − $108,000 − $2,790) × 60%

‡($150,000 − $108,000 − $2,790) × 40%

The entry for closing Income Summary and dividing net income is as follows:

Dec.	31	Income Summary	150,000	
		Lara Greguric, Capital		85,212
		Mike Belfry, Capital		64,788
		To close Income Summary account.		

If Greguric and Belfry withdrew funds equal to their salary allowances each month, then the entry for closing their withdrawals accounts into their capital accounts would be the same as shown on page 567.

EXAMPLE EXERCISE 11-3   Dividing Partnership Net Income   ⟨2⟩

Sarah Stephen and Xavier Williams formed a partnership, dividing income as follows:

1. Annual salary allowance to Stephen of $42,000.
2. Interest of 4% on each partner's capital balance on January 1.
3. Any remaining net income will be shared by Stephen and Williams in a ratio of 1:3.

Stephen and Williams had $20,000 and $150,000 in their January 1 capital balances, respectively. Net income for the year was $240,000.

   How much net income should be distributed to Williams?

FOLLOW MY EXAMPLE 11-3

	Sarah Stephen	Xavier Williams	Total
Annual salary	$42,000	$ 0	$ 42,000
Interest.	800*	6,000**	6,800
Remaining income.	47,800†	143,400‡	191,200
Total distributed to Williams	$90,600	$149,400	$240,000

*$20,000 × 4%.
**$150,000 × 4%.
†($240,000 − $42,000 − $6,800) × 1/4.
‡($240,000 − $42,000 − $6,800) × 3/4.

For Practice: PE 11-3

Dividing Income—Allowances Exceed Net Income   In the preceding example, the net income is $150,000. The total of the salary ($108,000) and interest ($2,790) allowances is $110,790. Thus, the net income exceeds the salary and interest allowances. In some cases, however, the net income may be less than the total of the allowances. In this case, the remaining net income to divide is a *negative* amount. This negative amount is divided among the partners as though it were a net loss.

   To illustrate, assume the same salary and interest allowances as in the preceding example, but the net income is $100,000. In this case, the total of the allowances of $110,790 exceeds the net income by $10,790 ($100,000 − $110,790). This amount is divided between Greguric and Belfry. The final division of net income between Greguric and Belfry is as follows:

Net income...$100,000

Division of net income:

	L. Greguric	M. Belfry	Total
Annual salary allowance	$60,000	$48,000	$108,000
Interest allowance	1,686	1,104	2,790
Total	61,686	49,104	110,790
Deduct excess of allowances over income	6,474*	4,316**	10,790
Net income	$55,212	$44,788	$100,000

*($100,000 − $108,000 − $2,790) × 60%
**($100,000 − $108,000 − $2,790) × 40%

The entry for closing Income Summary and dividing net income is as follows:

Dec.	31	Income Summary	100,000	
		Lara Greguric, Capital		55,212
		Mike Belfry, Capital		44,788
		To close Income Summary account.		

EXAMPLE EXERCISE 11-4   Dividing Partnership Net Income—Allowances Exceed Net Income

2

Use the information supplied in EE 11-3 for Sarah Stephen and Xavier Williams, except for net income. Assume the partnership had net income for the year of $40,000, instead of $240,000.

How much net income should be distributed to Stephen? Prepare the journal entry to close the Income Summary account.

FOLLOW MY EXAMPLE 11-4

	Sarah Stephen	Xavier Williams	Total
Annual salary allowance......................	$42,000	$ 0	$42,000
Interest......................................	800	6,000	6,800
Total...	42,800	6,000	48,800
Deduct excess of allowances over net income ...	2,200*	6,600**	8,800
Net income (loss)...........................	$40,600	$ (600)	$40,000

*($40,000 − $42,000 − $6,800) × ¼
**($40,000 − $42,000 − $6,800) × ¾

Dec. 31	Income Summary	40,000	
	Xavier Williams, Capital	600	
	Sarah Stephen, Capital		40,600
	To close the Income Summary account.		

For Practice: PE 11-4

Dividing Income in Event of Net Loss In the event of a net loss, the amount deducted from the total allowances is the sum of the net loss and the allowances, divided according to the sharing ratio.

To illustrate, assume the same salary and interest allowances as in the preceding example, but the net loss is $7,000. The division of net income between Greguric and Belfry is as follows:

Net loss .... $(7,000)

Division of net loss:

	L. Greguric	M. Belfry	Total
Annual salary allowance	$60,000	$48,000	$108,000
Interest allowance	1,686	1,104	2,790
Total	61,686	49,104	110,790
Difference between allowances and loss	70,674*	47,116	117,790
Net income (loss)	$ (8,988)	$ 1,988	$ (7,000)

*(−$7,000 − $108,000 − $2,790) × 60%

The entry for closing Income Summary and dividing net loss is as follows:

Dec.	31	Lara Greguric, Capital	8,988	
		Mike Belfry, Capital		1,988
		Income Summary		7,000
		To close Income Summary account.		

EXAMPLE EXERCISE 11-5 Dividing Partnership Net Income in Event of Net Loss ②

Use the information supplied in EE 11-3 for Sarah Stephen and Xavier Williams, except for net income. Assume the partnership had a net loss for the year of $30,000, instead of net income of $240,000.

How much net income should be distributed to Stephen? Prepare the journal entry to close the Income Summary account.

FOLLOW MY EXAMPLE 11-5

	Sarah Stephen	Xavier Williams	Total
Annual salary allowance.....................	$42,000	$ 0	$ 42,000
Interest...........................	800	6,000	6,800
Total...........................	42,800	6,000	48,800
Differences between allowances and loss	19,700*	59,100	78,800
Net income (loss)........................	$23,100	$(53,100)	$(30,000)

*(−$30,000 − $42,000 − $6,800) × 1/4

Dec. 31	Xavier Williams, Capital	53,100	
	Sarah Stephen, Capital		23,100
	Income Summary		30,000
	To close the Income Summary account.		

For Practice: PE 11-5

MID-CHAPTER ILLUSTRATIVE PROBLEM

On January 1, Brian Barrington and Gregory Paul decided to combine Brian's carpentry expertise and Gregory's business skills in a partnership. Brian contributed the following items to the partnership: cash, $1,000; accounts receivable with a market value of $8,000; equipment with a carrying value of $3,400 (cost of $15,000 and accumulated depreciation of $11,600) and a market value of $5,000; and accounts payable of $4,000. Gregory

(continued)

invested cash equal to the value of Brian's investment. The partners decided to provide a salary allowance of $48,000 to Brian, to credit each partner with 6% of their January 1 capital balances, and to split the remainder equally.

a. Journalize the partnership's entry to record Brian's investment.
b. Journalize the partnership's entry to record Gregory's investment.
c. Determine the division of income for the two partners, assuming net income of $100,000.
d. Provide the journal entry to close the Income Summary account at the end of the year, assuming net income of $100,000.
e. Provide the journal entry to close the withdrawals accounts at the end of the year, assuming Brian withdrew his salary allowance and Gregory withdrew $12,000.

MID-CHAPTER ILLUSTRATIVE SOLUTION

a.

Jan.	1	Cash		1,000	
		Accounts Receivable		8,000	
		Equipment		5,000	
		Accounts Payable			4,000
		Brian Barrington, Capital			10,000
		Formation of partnership—Brian's investment.			

b.

		Cash		10,000	
		Gregory Paul, Capital			10,000
		Formation of partnership—Gregory's investment.			

c.

	B. Barrington	G. Paul	Total
Annual salary allowance	$48,000	$ –	$ 48,000
Interest allowance	600	600	1,200
Remaining income	25,400	25,400	50,800
Net income	$74,000	$26,000	$100,000

d.

Dec.	31	Income Summary		100,000	
		Brian Barrington, Capital			74,000
		Gregory Paul, Capital			26,000
		To close the Income Summary account.			

e.

	31	Brian Barrington, Capital		48,000	
		Gregory Paul, Capital		12,000	
		Brian Barrington, Withdrawals			48,000
		Gregory Paul, Withdrawals			12,000
		To close the withdrawals accounts.			

3 Partner Admission and Withdrawal

Describe and illustrate the accounting for partner admission and withdrawal.

Many partnerships provide for admitting new partners and for partner withdrawals by amending the existing partnership agreement. In this way, the business may continue operating without the need to form a new partnership and prepare a new partnership agreement. In any case, existing partners must consent to the admission of a new partner.

Exhibit 2

Two Methods for Admitting a Partner

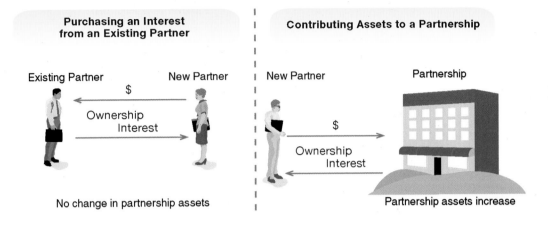

| | **Purchasing an Interest from an Existing Partner** | **Contributing Assets to a Partnership** |

Admitting a Partner

As shown in Exhibit 2, a person may be admitted to a partnership by either of the following:

1. Purchasing an interest from one or more of the existing partners
2. Contributing assets to the partnership

When a new partner is admitted by *purchasing an interest* from one or more of the existing partners, the total assets and the total owners' equity of the partnership are not affected. The capital (equity) of the new partner is recorded by transferring capital (equity) from the existing partners.

When a new partner is admitted by *contributing assets* to the partnership, the total assets and the total owners' equity of the partnership are increased. The capital (equity) of the new partner is recorded as the amount of assets contributed to the partnership by the new partner.

Purchasing an Interest from Existing Partners When a new partner is admitted by purchasing an interest from one or more of the existing partners, the transaction is between the new and existing partners acting as individuals. The admission of the new partner is recorded by transferring partners' equity amounts from the capital accounts of the selling partners to the capital account of the new partner.

To illustrate, assume that on June 1, Lara Greguric and Mike Belfry each sell 20% (one-fifth) of their partnership equity of Dundas Hardware to Marion Coome for cash of $16,000 and $11,200, respectively. On June 1, also assume that the partnership had net assets of $136,000, and Greguric and Belfry had capital balances of $80,000 and $56,000, respectively. This transaction is between Greguric, Belfry, and Coome. The only entry required by Dundas Hardware is to record the transfer of one-fifth of the existing partners' capital to Coome, as shown below.

2015					
Jun.	1	Lara Greguric, Capital		16,000*	
		Mike Belfry, Capital		11,200**	
		Marion Coome, Capital			27,200
		Admission of Coome to partnership—purchase			
		of interest.			
		*$80,000 × 20%			
		**$56,000 × 20%			

The effect of the transaction on the partnership accounts is shown in the following diagram:

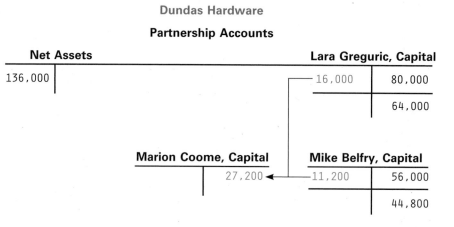

Dundas Hardware

Partnership Accounts

Net Assets	Lara Greguric, Capital
136,000	16,000 ‖ 80,000
	64,000

Marion Coome, Capital	Mike Belfry, Capital
27,200 ◄ 11,200	56,000
	44,800

After Coome is admitted to Dundas Hardware, the total partners' equity is still $136,000. Coome has a 20% interest ($27,200/$136,000) and the original partners have an 80% interest (($64,000 + $44,800)/$136,000) in the new partnership.

Even though Coome has a one-fifth (20%) interest in the partnership, she may not be entitled to a one-fifth share of the partnership net income. The division of the net income or net loss is made according to the new or amended partnership agreement.

The preceding entry is not affected by the amount paid by Coome for the one-fifth interest. For example, if Coome had paid $30,000 in total to Greguric and Belfry instead of $27,200, the entry would still be the same. This is because the transaction is between Greguric, Belfry, and Coome, not between Coome and the partnership. Any gain or loss by Greguric and Belfry on the sale of their partnership interest is theirs as individuals and does not affect the partnership.

Contributing Assets to a Partnership When a new partner is admitted by contributing assets to the partnership, the total assets and the total partners' equity of the partnership are increased. This is because the transaction is between the new partner and the partnership.

To illustrate, assume that instead of purchasing a one-fifth ownership in Dundas Hardware directly from Lara Greguric and Mike Belfry, Marion Coome contributes $27,200 cash to Dundas Hardware for ownership equity of $27,200. The entry to record this transaction is as follows:

Jun.	1	Cash	27,200	
		Marion Coome, Capital		27,200
		Admission of Coome to partnership—		
		contribution of assets.		

The effect of the transaction on the partnership accounts is shown in the following diagram:

Dundas Hardware

Partnership Accounts

Net Assets	Lara Greguric, Capital
136,000	80,000
27,200	
163,200	

Marion Coome, Capital	Mike Belfry, Capital
↑	
27,200	56,000

After the admission of Coome, the net assets and total partners' equity of Dundas Hardware increase to $163,200, of which Marion Coome has a $27,200 interest. In contrast, in the prior example, the net assets and total partners' equity of Dundas Hardware did not change from $136,000.

Revaluation of Assets Before a new partner is admitted, the balances of a partnership's asset accounts should be stated at current values. If necessary, the accounts should be adjusted. Any net adjustment (increase or decrease) in asset values is divided among the capital accounts of the existing partners similar to the division of income.

To illustrate, assume that in the preceding example the carrying value of accounts receivable is $24,000, with an Accounts Receivable balance of $28,000 and an Allowance for Doubtful Accounts balance of $4,000. The partners feel the allowance should be increased by $3,000 to more accurately reflect the current market value of the receivables. Using the income allocation formula of their partnership agreement, the revaluation is recorded as follows:

Jun.	1	Lara Greguric, Capital	1,800	
		Mike Belfry, Capital	1,200	
		Allowance for Doubtful Accounts		3,000
		Revaluation of partnership assets.		

Failure to adjust the partnership accounts for current values before admission of a new partner may result in the new partner sharing in asset gains or losses that arose in prior periods.

EXAMPLE EXERCISE 11-6 Revaluing and Contributing Assets to a Partnership ③

Blake Nelson invested $45,000 in the Lawrence & Kerry partnership for ownership equity of $45,000. Prior to the investment, land was revalued to a market value of $260,000 from a carrying value of $200,000. Lynne Lawrence and Tim Kerry share net income in a 1:2 ratio.

a. Provide the journal entry for the revaluation of land.

b. Provide the journal entry to admit Nelson.

FOLLOW MY EXAMPLE 11-6

a. Land..	60,000	
Lynne Lawrence, Capital..		20,000*
Tim Kerry, Capital...		40,000**
*$60,000 × 1/3.		
**$60,000 × 2/3.		
b. Cash..	45,000	
Blake Nelson, Capital		45,000

For Practice: PE 11-6

Partner Bonuses A new partner may pay existing partners a bonus to join a partnership. In other cases, existing partners may pay a new partner a bonus to join the partnership.

Bonuses are usually paid because of higher-than-normal profits the new or existing partners are expected to contribute in the future. For example, a new partner may bring special qualities or skills to the partnership. Celebrities such as actors, musicians, or sports figures often provide name recognition that is expected to increase a partnership's profits.

Exhibit 3

Partner Bonuses

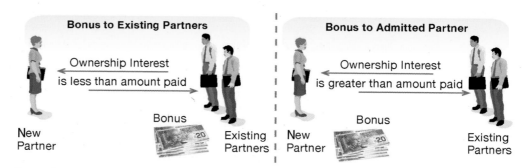

Source: Currency images used with the permission of the Bank of Canada.

Partner bonuses are illustrated in Exhibit 3. Existing partners receive a bonus when the ownership interest received by the new partner is less than the amount paid. In contrast, the new partner receives a bonus when the ownership interest received by the new partner is greater than the amount paid.

To illustrate, assume that on June 1, 2015, the partnership of Lara Greguric and Mike Belfry is considering a new partner, Marion Coome. After the assets of the partnership have been adjusted to current market values, the capital balances of Greguric and Belfry are as follows:

Lara Greguric, Capital	$ 78,200
Mike Belfry, Capital	54,800
Total owners' equity *before* admitting Coome	$133,000

No Bonus If the new partner pays the existing partners the exact price of the ownership interest received, then no bonus is generated for either party. To illustrate, assume Greguric and Belfry agree to admit Coome to the partnership for $33,250 on June 1, in return for a one-fifth equity in the partnership. In exchange for $33,250, Greguric and Belfry agree to each give Coome 10% of the partnership income or losses, so the income allocation is 50%, 30%, and 20%, respectively. In this case, no bonus is paid, calculated as follows:

Lara Greguric, Capital	$ 78,200
Mike Belfry, Capital	54,800
Coome's contribution	33,250
Total owners' equity after admitting Coome	166,250
Coome's equity interest after admission	× 1/5
Marion Coome, Capital	$ 33,250
Coome's contribution	$ 33,250
Marion Coome, Capital	33,250
Bonus	$ 0

The entry to record the admission of Coome to the partnership is as follows:

Jun.	1	Cash	33,250	
		Marion Coome, Capital		33,250
		Admission of Coome to partnership—contribution of assets.		

Bonus to Existing Partners Assume Greguric and Belfry agree to admit Coome to the partnership for $40,000. In return, Coome will receive a one-fifth equity in the partnership and will share with Greguric and Belfry in partnership income as in the prior example. In this case, Coome is paying Greguric and Belfry a $5,400 bonus to join the partnership, computed as follows:

Lara Greguric, Capital	$ 78,200
Mike Belfry, Capital	54,800
Coome's contribution	40,000
Total owners' equity after admitting Coome	173,000
Coome's equity interest after admission	× 1/5
Marion Coome, Capital	$ 34,600
Coome's contribution	$ 40,000
Marion Coome, Capital	34,600
Bonus	$ 5,400

The $5,400 bonus paid by Coome increases Greguric's and Belfry's capital accounts. It is distributed to the capital accounts of Greguric and Belfry according to their income-sharing ratio.[1] Since Greguric's and Belfry's shares of profit and loss were 60% and 40%, respectively, before Coome's admission, the entry to record the admission of Coome to the partnership is as follows:

Jun.	1	Cash	40,000	
		Marion Coome, Capital		34,600
		Lara Greguric, Capital		3,240
		Mike Belfry, Capital		2,160
		Admission of Coome to partnership—contribution of assets.		

Bonus to Admitted Partner Existing partners may also agree to pay the new partner a bonus to join a partnership. Assume Greguric and Belfry agree to admit Coome to the partnership for $25,000 in return for a one-fifth equity in the partnership and a 20% share in partnership income or losses. In this case, a bonus is paid to the admitting partner, Coome, calculated as follows:

Lara Greguric, Capital	$ 78,200
Mike Belfry, Capital	54,800
Coome's contribution	25,000
Total owners' equity after admitting Coome	158,000
Coome's equity interest after admission	× 1/5
Marion Coome, Capital	$ 31,600
Coome's contribution	$ 25,000
Marion Coome, Capital	31,600
Bonus	$ 6,600

The $6,600 bonus paid to Coome decreases Greguric's and Belfry's capital accounts. The cost of the bonus is distributed to the capital accounts of Greguric and Belfry according to their income-sharing ratio. Since Greguric's and Belfry's shares of profit and loss were 60% and 40%, respectively, before Coome's admission, the entry to record the admission of Coome to the partnership is as follows:

Jun.	1	Cash	25,000	
		Lara Greguric, Capital	3,960	
		Mike Belfry, Capital	2,640	
		Marion Coome, Capital		31,600
		Admission of Coome to partnership—contribution of assets.		

1 Another method used to record the admission of partners attributes goodwill rather than a bonus to the partners. This method is discussed in advanced accounting textbooks.

EXAMPLE EXERCISE 11-7   Partner Bonus   ③

Lowman has a capital balance of $45,000 after adjusting assets to fair market value. Conrad contributes $26,000 to receive a 30% interest in a new partnership with Lowman.
    Determine the amount and recipient of the partner bonus.

FOLLOW MY EXAMPLE 11-7

Equity of Lowman	$ 45,000
Conrad's contribution..	26,000
Total equity after admitting Conrad............................	71,000
Conrad's equity interest...	× 30%
Conrad's equity after admission.................................	$ 21,300
Conrad's contribution..	$ 26,000
Conrad's equity after admission.................................	21,300
Bonus paid to Lowman..	$ 4,700

For Practice: PE 11-7

Withdrawal of a Partner

As shown in Exhibit 4, a partner may retire or withdraw from a partnership by taking either of the following actions:

1. Selling his or her partnership interest to the existing partners
2. Selling his or her partnership interest to the partnership

If the withdrawing partner's interest is sold to *existing partners*, the sale of the partnership interest is between the partners as individuals. The only entry on the partnership's records is to debit the capital account of the partner withdrawing and to credit the capital account of the partner or partners buying the additional interest.

If the withdrawing partner's interest is sold to the *partnership*, the assets and the owners' equity of the partnership are reduced by the purchase price. Before the sale, the asset accounts should be adjusted to current values. The net amount of the adjustment should be divided among the capital accounts of the partners according to their income-sharing ratio. If insufficient partnership cash is available to pay the withdrawing partner, a liability may be created (credited) for the amount owed the withdrawing partner.

Selling an Interest to Existing Partners   When a retiring partner's interest is sold to one or more of the existing partners, the transaction is between the partners acting as individuals. The retirement is recorded by transferring partners' equity amounts

Exhibit 4

Two Methods for Retiring or Withdrawing from a Partnership

Sell the Interest to Existing Partners	Sell the Interest to the Partnership
Existing Partner —$→ Retiring Partner ←Ownership Interest	Retiring Partner ←$— Partnership Ownership Interest→
No change in partnership assets	Partnership assets decrease

from the capital accounts of the departing partner to the capital accounts of the existing partner or partners.

To illustrate, assume that on November 15, 2015, Lara Greguric decides to retire from the partnership. After the assets of the partnership have been adjusted to current market values, the capital balances of Greguric, Belfry, and Coome are as follows:

Lara Greguric, Capital	$ 82,500
Mike Belfry, Capital	66,000
Marion Coome, Capital	42,500
Total owners' equity before Greguric retires	$191,000

Belfry and Coome agree to each pay Greguric $40,000 for equal rights to her partnership share. This transaction is between Greguric, Belfry, and Coome. The only entry required by the partnership is to record the transfer of capital as shown below.

Nov.	15	Lara Greguric, Capital	82,500	
		Mike Belfry, Capital		41,250
		Marion Coome, Capital		41,250
		Retirement of Greguric from partnership—sale to partners.		

The assets of the partnership remain unchanged after the transaction, and the only change is in the partners' capital account balances. The preceding entry is not affected by the amount paid by Belfry and Coome to Greguric. For example, if Belfry and Coome had paid $90,000 to Greguric instead of $80,000, the entry would still be the same. This is because the transaction is between Belfry, Coome, and Greguric, not between Greguric and the partnership.

Selling an Interest to the Partnership
When a departing partner's interest is sold to the partnership, the total assets and the total partners' equity of the partnership is decreased. Selling an interest to the partnership can result in (a) no bonus paid, (b) a bonus paid to the remaining partners, or (c) a bonus paid to the retiring partner.

No Bonus
If the partnership pays the retiring partner the exact price of the ownership interest, then no bonus is generated for either party.

To illustrate, using the preceding example, assume Greguric is offered $82,500 upon her retirement. In this case, no bonus is paid, and the entry to record Greguric's withdrawal from the partnership is as follows:

Nov.	15	Lara Greguric, Capital	82,500	
		Cash		82,500
		Retirement of Greguric from partnership—sale to partnership.		

Bonus to Remaining Partners
A retiring partner may be willing to accept less than the amount in his or her capital balance because the partnership has limited resources to make the payment or the departing partner is anxious to leave. Assume Lara Greguric agrees to a payment of $80,000. In this case, a bonus is paid to the remaining partners, calculated as follows:

Lara Greguric, Capital	$82,500
Cash paid to retire Lara Greguric	80,000
Bonus to remaining partners	$ 2,500

Assuming a profit-sharing ratio of 50%, 30%, and 20% to Greguric, Belfry, and Coome, respectively, the bonus is split over the remaining partners' shares. Belfry will receive 30/50ths of the bonus (30/(30 + 20)) and Coome will receive 20/50ths (20/(20 + 30)) of the bonus. The entry to record withdrawal from the partnership is as follows:

Nov.	15	Lara Greguric, Capital	82,500	
		Cash		80,000
		Mike Belfry, Capital		1,500*
		Marion Coome, Capital		1,000
		Retirement of Greguric from partnership—sale to partnership.		
		*$2,500 × 30/50		

Bonus to Retiring Partner A partnership may be willing to pay more than a partner's capital balance when it wants to encourage a partner to leave. Assuming Lara Greguric is offered $90,000 upon retirement, the journal entry to record her withdrawal from the partnership is as follows:

Nov.	15	Lara Greguric, Capital	82,500	
		Mike Belfry, Capital	4,500*	
		Marion Marion Coome, Capital	3,000	
		Cash		90,000
		Retirement of Greguric from partnership—sale to partnership.		
		*$7,500 × 30/50		

EXAMPLE EXERCISE 11-8 **Withdrawal of Partner with Bonus**   ③

On June 30, Joanne Kyne decided to retire from the partnership of Wilson, Kyne, Rose, and Jack. The partnership decided to buy her out. After the assets of the partnership had been adjusted to current market values, the capital balances of Wilson, Kyne, Rose, and Jack were $112,000, $80,000, $60,000, and $80,000, respectively. Prepare the journal entry to record Kyne's retirement, assuming Kyne accepts payment of $83,000 and the partners shared net income and losses equally.

FOLLOW MY EXAMPLE 11-8

June	30	Kyne, Capital	80,000	
		Wilson, Capital	1,000*	
		Rose, Capital	1,000	
		Jack, Capital	1,000	
		Cash		83,000
		To record Kyne's retirement.		
		*($83,000 − $80,000) × 1/3		

For Practice: PE 11-8

Death of a Partner

When a partner dies, the partnership accounts should be closed as at the date of death. The net income for the current period should then be determined and divided among the partners' capital accounts. The asset accounts should also be adjusted to current values and the amount of any adjustment divided among the capital accounts of the partners.

After the income is divided and any assets revalued, an entry is recorded to close the deceased partner's capital account. The entry debits the deceased partner's capital account for its balance and credits a liability account, which is payable to the deceased's estate. The remaining partner or partners may then decide to continue the business or liquidate it.

4 Liquidating Partnerships

Describe and illustrate the accounting for liquidating a partnership.

When a partnership goes out of business, it sells the assets, pays the creditors, and distributes the remaining cash or other assets to the partners. This winding-up process is called the **liquidation** of the partnership. Although *liquidating* refers to the payment of liabilities, it also includes the entire winding-up process.

When the partnership goes out of business and the normal operations are discontinued, the accounts should be adjusted and closed as they would be at the end of an accounting year. The only accounts remaining open will be the asset, contra asset, liability, and partners' equity accounts.

The steps in the liquidation process are as follows:

Note: In liquidation, cash is distributed to partners according to their capital balances.

Step 1. Sell the partnership assets.

Step 2. Divide any gains or losses from the sale of assets to the partners' capital accounts based on their income-sharing ratio.

Step 3. Pay the claims of creditors using the cash from step 1.

Step 4. Distribute the remaining cash to the partners based on the balances in their capital accounts.

To illustrate, assume that Greguric, Belfry, and Coome decide to liquidate their partnership. On April 9, 2015, after discontinuing business operations of the partnership and closing the accounts, the following trial balance is prepared:

Dundas Hardware Post-Closing Trial Balance April 9, 2015	Debit Balances	Credit Balances
Cash	9,600	
Accounts Receivable	28,400	
Inventory	66,000	
Equipment	75,000	
Accumulated Depreciation—Equipment		17,000
Accounts Payable		9,000
Lara Greguric, Capital		75,000
Mike Belfry, Capital		52,200
Marion Coome, Capital		25,800
	179,000	179,000

Greguric, Belfry, and Coome share income and losses in a ratio of 5:3:2 (50%, 30%, 20%). To simplify, assume that all noncash assets are sold in a single transaction.

Gain on Sale of Assets

Step 1: Sale of Partnership Assets Assume that Greguric, Belfry, and Coome sell the noncash assets on April 12 for $160,000, realizing a gain of $7,600 ($160,000 − ($28,400 + $66,000 + $75,000 − $17,000)). The entry to record the sale of assets is as follows:

Apr.	12	Cash	160,000	
		Accumulated Depreciation—Equipment	17,000	
		Accounts Receivable		28,400
		Inventory		66,000
		Equipment		75,000
		Gain on Sale of Assets		7,600
		Sold partnership assets.		

Step 2: Division of any Gain or Loss

The gain of $7,600 is allocated to Greguric, Belfry, and Coome in the income-sharing ratio of 5:3:2. Thus, the partner capital accounts are credited as follows:

Greguric	$3,800 ($7,600 × 50%)
Belfry	2,280 ($7,600 × 30%)
Coome	1,520 ($7,600 × 20%)

The entry to record the division of the gain is as follows:

Apr.	12	Gain on Sale of Assets	7,600	
		Lara Greguric, Capital		3,800
		Mike Belfry, Capital		2,280
		Marion Coome, Capital		1,520
		Divided gain on sale of assets.		

Step 3: Payment of Liabilities

The next step in the liquidation is to pay any liabilities. The payment of $9,000 to creditors is recorded as follows:

		Accounts Payable	9,000	
		Cash		9,000
		Paid liabilities.		

Step 4: Distribution of Cash to Partners

The remaining cash of $160,600 ($9,600 + $160,000 − $9,000) is distributed to the partners according to their capital balances as follows:

Greguric	$78,800 ($160,600 × 50%)
Belfry	54,480 ($160,600 × 30%)
Coome	27,320 ($160,600 × 20%)

The distribution would be recorded as follows:

		Lara Greguric, Capital	78,800	
		Mike Belfry, Capital	54,480	
		Marion Coome, Capital	27,320	
		Cash		160,600
		Distributed cash to partners.		

A **statement of partnership liquidation**, which summarizes the liquidation process, is shown in Exhibit 5.

Exhibit 5

Statement of Partnership Liquidation: Gain on Sale of Assets

Dundas Hardware
Statement of Partnership Liquidation
For Period April 10–30, 2015

	Cash +	A/R +	Inv. +	Equip. –	Accum Deprec'n =	A/P +	Capital Greguric (50%) +	Belfry (30%) +	Coome (20%)
Balances before sale of assets	$ 9,600	$28,400	$66,000	$75,000	$17,000	$9,000	$75,000	$52,200	$25,800
Sale of assets and division of gain	+160,000	–28,400	–66,000	–75,000	–17,000		+ 3,800	+ 2,280	+ 1,520
Balances after sale of assets	169,600	0	0	0	0	9,000	78,800	54,480	27,320
Payment of liabilities	– 9,000					–9,000			
Balances after payment of liabilities	160,600	0	0	0	0	0	78,800	54,480	27,320
Cash distributed to partners	–160,600						–78,800	–54,480	–27,320
Final balances	$ 0	$ 0	$ 0	$ 0	$ 0	$ 0	$ 0	$ 0	$ 0

Steps 1–2 → Sale of assets and division of gain
Step 3 → Payment of liabilities
Step 4 → Cash distributed to partners

As shown in Exhibit 5, the *cash is distributed to the partners based on the balances of their capital accounts*. These balances are determined after the gain on sale of assets has been divided among the partners and the liabilities paid. The *income-sharing ratio should not be used as a basis for distributing the cash to partners*.

Loss on Sale of Assets

Assume that Greguric, Belfry, and Coome sell the assets on April 12 for $140,000, realizing a loss of $12,400 ($140,000 – ($28,400 + $66,000 + $75,000 – $17,000)).

Step 1: Sale of Partnership Assets The entry to record the sale of assets is as follows:

Apr.	12	Cash	140,000	
		Accumulated Depreciation—Equipment	17,000	
		Loss on Sale of Assets	12,400	
		Accounts Receivable		28,400
		Inventory		66,000
		Equipment		75,000
		Sold partnership assets.		

Step 2: Division of any Gain or Loss The loss of $12,400 is allocated to Greguric, Belfry, and Coome in the income-sharing ratio of 5:3:2. Thus, the partner capital accounts are debited as follows:

Greguric	$6,200 ($12,400 × 50%)
Belfry	3,720 ($12,400 × 30%)
Coome	2,480 ($12,400 × 20%)

The entry to record the division of the loss is as follows:

Apr.	12	Lara Greguric, Capital	6,200	
		Mike Belfry, Capital	3,720	
		Marion Coome, Capital	2,480	
		Loss on Sale of Assets		12,400
		Divided loss on sale of assets.		

Step 3: Payment of Liabilities The next step in the liquidation is to pay any liabilities. The payment of $9,000 to creditors is recorded as follows:

Accounts Payable	9,000	
Cash		9,000
Paid liabilities.		

Step 4: Distribution of Cash to Partners The remaining cash of $140,600 ($9,600 + $140,000 − $9,000) is distributed to the partners according to their capital balances as follows:

Greguric	$68,800 ($140,600 × 50%)
Belfry	48,480 ($140,600 × 30%)
Coome	23,320 ($140,600 × 20%)

The distribution would be recorded as follows:

Lara Greguric, Capital	68,800	
Mike Belfry, Capital	48,480	
Marion Coome, Capital	23,320	
Cash		140,600
Distributed cash to partners.		

The steps in liquidating the partnership, with the $12,400 loss, are summarized in the statement of partnership liquidation shown in Exhibit 6.

Exhibit 6

Statement of Partnership Liquidation: Loss on Sale of Assets

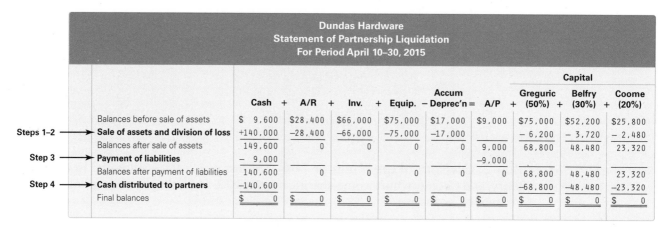

	Cash +	A/R +	Inv. +	Equip.	− Deprec'n =	A/P +	Greguric (50%) +	Belfry (30%) +	Coome (20%)
Balances before sale of assets	$ 9,600	$28,400	$66,000	$75,000	$17,000	$9,000	$75,000	$52,200	$25,800
Steps 1–2 → **Sale of assets and division of loss**	+140,000	−28,400	−66,000	−75,000	−17,000		− 6,200	− 3,720	− 2,480
Balances after sale of assets	149,600	0	0	0	0	9,000	68,800	48,480	23,320
Step 3 → **Payment of liabilities**	− 9,000					−9,000			
Balances after payment of liabilities	140,600	0	0	0	0	0	68,800	48,480	23,320
Step 4 → **Cash distributed to partners**	−140,600						−68,800	−48,480	−23,320
Final balances	$ 0	$ 0	$ 0	$ 0	$ 0	$ 0	$ 0	$ 0	$ 0

Table title (within image): Dundas Hardware / Statement of Partnership Liquidation / For Period April 10–30, 2015 — Capital columns: Greguric (50%), Belfry (30%), Coome (20%)

EXAMPLE EXERCISE 11-9 Liquidating Partnerships

④

Prior to liquidating their partnership, Todd and Gentry had capital accounts of $150,000 and $50,000, respectively, noncash assets of $220,000, and liabilities of $20,000. Todd and Gentry share income and loss in a ratio of 5:3. The assets of the partnership were sold for $200,000. Determine the amounts received by Todd and Gentry as a final distribution from the liquidation of the partnership.

(continued)

FOLLOW MY EXAMPLE 11-9

	Cash	+	Noncash assets	=	A/P	+	Capital Todd (5/8)	+	Gentry (3/8)
Balances before sale of assets	$ 0		$ 220,000		$ 20,000		$ 150,000		$ 50,000
Sale of assets and division of loss	+200,000		−220,000				−12,500		−7,500
Balances after sale of assets	200,000		0		20,000		137,500		42,500
Payment of liabilities	−20,000				−20,000				
Balances after payment of liabilities	180,000		0		0		137,500		42,500
Cash distributed to partners	−180,000						−137,500		−42,500
Final balances	$ 0		$ 0		$ 0		$ 0		$ 0

For Practice: PE 11-9

Loss on Sale of Assets—Capital Deficiency

The share of a loss on sale of assets may be greater than the balance in a partner's capital account. The resulting debit balance in the capital account is called a **deficiency**. It represents a claim of the partnership against the partner.

To illustrate, assume that Greguric, Belfry, and Coome sell the assets on April 12 for $12,400, realizing a loss of $140,000 ($12,400 − ($28,400 + $66,000 + $75,000 − $17,000)).

Step 1: Sale of Partnership Assets

The entry to record the sale of assets is as follows:

Apr.	12	Cash		12,400	
		Accumulated Depreciation—Equipment		17,000	
		Loss on Sale of Assets		140,000	
		Accounts Receivable			28,400
		Inventory			66,000
		Equipment			75,000
		Sold partnership assets.			

Step 2: Division of any Gain or Loss

The loss of $140,000 is allocated to Greguric, Belfry, and Coome in the income-sharing ratio of 5:3:2. Thus, the partner capital accounts are debited as follows:

Greguric	$70,000 ($140,000 × 50%)
Belfry	42,000 ($140,000 × 30%)
Coome	28,000 ($140,000 × 20%)

The entry to record the division of the loss is as follows:

Apr.	12	Lara Greguric, Capital		70,000	
		Mike Belfry, Capital		42,000	
		Marion Coome, Capital		28,000	
		Loss on Sale of Assets			140,000
		Divided loss on sale of assets.			

Step 3: Payment of Liabilities The next step in the liquidation is to pay any liabilities. The payment of $9,000 to creditors is recorded as follows:

Accounts Payable	9,000	
Cash		9,000
Paid liabilities.		

Step 4: Distribution of Cash to Partners The share of the loss allocated to Coome, $28,000 (20% × $140,000), exceeds the $25,800 balance in her capital account. This $2,200 deficiency represents an amount that Coome owes the partnership. Assuming that Coome pays the deficiency, the cash of $15,200 ($9,600 + $12,400 + $2,200 − $9,000) is distributed to the partners according to their capital balances as follows:

Greguric	$ 5,000
Belfry	10,200
Coome	0

The distribution would be recorded as follows:

Lara Greguric, Capital	5,000	
Mike Belfry, Capital	10,200	
Cash		15,200
Distributed cash to partners.		

The steps in liquidating the partnership, with the $140,000 loss, are summarized in the statement of partnership liquidation shown in Exhibit 7.

If the deficient partner does not pay the partnership the deficiency, there will not be sufficient partnership cash to pay the remaining partners in full. Any uncollected deficiency becomes a loss to the partnership and is divided among the remaining partners' capital balances based on their income-sharing ratio. The cash balance will then equal the sum of the capital account balances. The cash can then be distributed to the remaining partners, based on the balances of their capital accounts.

To illustrate, assume that in the preceding example Coome could not pay her deficiency. The deficiency would be allocated to Greguric and Belfry based on their

Exhibit 7

Statement of Partnership Liquidation: Loss on Sale of Assets—Capital Deficiency

								Capital		
						Accum		Greguric	Belfry	Coome
	Cash +	A/R +	Inv. +	Equip.	−Deprec'n=	A/P +	(50%) +	(30%) +	(20%)
Balances before sale of assets	$ 9,600	$28,400	$66,000	$75,000	$17,000	$ 9,000	$75,000	$52,200	$25,800
Sale of assets and division of loss	+12,400	−28,400	−66,000	−75,000	−17,000		−70,000	−42,000	−28,000
Balances after sale of assets	22,000	0	0	0	0	9,000	5,000	10,200	−2,200
Payment of liabilities	− 9,000					− 9,000			
Balances after payment of liabilities	13,000	0	0	0	0	0	5,000	10,200	−2,200
Receipt of deficiency	+2,200								+2,200
Balances	15,200						5,000	10,200	0
Cash distributed to partners	−15,200						−5,000	−10,200	0
Final balances	$ 0	$ 0	$ 0	$ 0	$ 0	$ 0	$ 0	$ 0	$ 0

Dundas Hardware
Statement of Partnership Liquidation
For Period April 10–30, 2015

Steps 1–2 →
Step 3 →
Step 4 →

income-sharing ratio of 5:3. The remaining cash of $13,000 would then be distributed to Greguric ($3,625) and Belfry ($9,375) as shown below.

	Capital Balances Before Deficiency	Allocated Deficiency	Capital Balances After Deficiency
Greguric	$ 5,000	$(1,375)*	$ 3,625
Belfry	10,200	(825)**	9,375
Coome	(2,200)	2,200	0
Total	$13,000		$13,000

*$1,375 = [$2,200 × (5/8)]

**$825 = [$2,200 × (3/8)]

The entries to allocate Coome's deficiency and distribute the cash are as follows:

Allocation of deficiency:

Lara Greguric, Capital	1,375	
Mike Belfry, Capital	825	
Marion Coome, Capital		2,200
Allocated deficiency to capital accounts.		

Distribution of cash to partners:

Lara Greguric, Capital	3,625	
Mike Belfry, Capital	9,375	
Cash		13,000
Distributed cash to partners.		

EXAMPLE EXERCISE 11-10 Liquidating Partnerships—Deficiency   (4)

Prior to liquidating their partnership, Short and Bain had capital accounts of $20,000 and $80,000, respectively, noncash assets of $110,000, and $10,000 of liabilities. Short and Bain share income and loss equally. The assets were sold for $40,000. Determine the amount of Short's deficiency. Determine the amount distributed to Bain, assuming Short is unable to satisfy the deficiency.

FOLLOW MY EXAMPLE 11-10

	Cash	+	Noncash assets	=	A/P	+	Capital Short (50%)	+	Bain (50%)
Balances before sale of assets	$ 0		$ 110,000		$ 10,000		$ 20,000		$ 80,000
Sale of assets and division of loss	+40,000		−110,000				−35,000		−35,000
Balances after sale of assets	40,000		0		10,000		−15,000		45,000
Payment of liabilities	−10,000				−10,000				
Balances after payment of liabilities	30,000		0		0		−15,000		45,000
Allocation of deficiency							15,000		−15,000
Balances	30,000		0		0		0		30,000
Cash distributed to Bain	−30,000						0		−30,000
Final balances	$ 0		$ 0		$ 0		$ 0		$ 0

For Practice: PE 11-10

Statement of Changes in Partnership Equity

Prepare the statement of changes in partnership equity.

Reporting changes in partnership capital accounts is similar to the reporting of changes for a proprietorship. The primary difference is that each partner has a capital account. The changes in partner capital accounts for a period of time are reported in a **statement of changes in partnership equity**.

Exhibit 8 illustrates a statement of changes in partnership equity for Investors Associates, a partnership of Dan Cross and Kelly Baker. Each partner's capital account is shown as a separate column. The partner capital accounts may change as the result of capital additions, net income, or withdrawals.

The year-end balances for each partners' capital account will appear on the partnership balance sheet. To illustrate, the balance sheet for Investors Associates would be prepared as follows:

Exhibit 8

Statement of Changes in Partnership Equity

Investors Associates Statement of Changes in Partnership Equity For the Year Ended December 31, 2015	Dan Cross, Capital	Kelly Baker, Capital	Total Partnership Capital
Balance, January 1, 2015	$245,000	$365,000	$610,000
Capital additions	50,000		50,000
Net income for the year	40,000	80,000	120,000
Less partner withdrawals	(5,000)	(45,000)	(50,000)
Balance, December 31, 2015	$330,000	$400,000	$730,000

Investors Associates Balance Sheet December 31, 2015					
Assets			**Liabilities**		
Current assets:			Current liabilities:		
Cash		$ 20,000	Accounts payable		$ 54,400
Accounts receivable, net		135,000	Loans payable		104,600
		155,000			
			Total liabilities		159,000
Property, plant, and equipment:					
Equipment	$900,000				
Less accumulated			**Partnership equity:**		
depreciation	166,000	734,000	**Dan Cross, capital**	$330,000	
			Kelly Baker, capital	400,000	730,000
			Total liabilities and		
Total assets		$889,000	partnership equity		$889,000

At a Glance 11

1 · Describe the characteristics of proprietorships and partnerships.

Key Points	Key Learning Outcomes	Page	Example Exercises
The characteristics of proprietorships and partnerships are summarized in Exhibit 1.	• Identify the characteristics of proprietorships and partnerships.	562	

2 · Describe and illustrate the accounting for forming a partnership and for dividing the net income and net loss of a partnership.

Key Points	Key Learning Outcomes	Page	Example Exercises
When a partnership is formed, accounts are debited for contributed assets and credited for assumed liabilities, and the partner's capital account is credited for the net amount. The net income of a partnership may be divided among the partners on the basis of services rendered, interest earned on the capital account balance, and the income-sharing ratio.	• Journalize the initial formation of a partnership and establish partner capital.	565	11-1
	• Determine and journalize the income or loss distributed to each partner under various income-sharing arrangements.	566	11-2 11-3 11-4 11-5

3 · Describe and illustrate the accounting for partner admission and withdrawal.

Key Points	Key Learning Outcomes	Page	Example Exercises
A new partner may be admitted to a partnership by either purchasing an interest from an existing partner or by contributing assets to the partnership. Partnership assets should be restated to current values prior to admission or withdrawal of a partner. A partner may withdraw from a partnership by selling his or her interest to a partner or to the partnership.	• Distinguish between partner admission through purchase from an existing partner or through contribution to the partnership.	573	11-6
	• Prepare for partner admission by revaluing assets to approximate current values.	575	11-6
	• Determine partner bonuses.	575	11-7
	• Journalize retirement of a partner with a bonus.	578	11-8

4 · Describe and illustrate the accounting for liquidating a partnership.

Key Points	Key Learning Outcomes	Page	Example Exercises
A partnership is liquidated by (1) the sale of assets, (2) the division of gain or loss on sale of assets to the partners' capital accounts, (3) the payments to creditors, and (4) the distribution of the remaining cash according to the partners' capital account balances.	• Apply the four steps of liquidating a partnership for either a gain or loss on sale of assets.	581	11-9
	• Apply the four steps of partnership liquidation when there is a partner deficiency.	585	11-10

5 Prepare the statement of changes in partnership equity.

Key Points	Key Learning Outcomes	Page	Example Exercises
A statement of changes in partnership equity reports the changes in partnership equity from capital additions, net income, and withdrawals. The final capital account balances will appear on the partnership balance sheet.	• Prepare a statement of changes in partnership equity.	588	

GLOSSARY

deficiency – The debit balance in the owner's equity account of a partner. (p. 585)

general partnership – A form of partnership in which partners are personally liable for any debts or legal claims against the business. (p. 563)

limited liability partnership (LLP) – A form of partnership that protects partners from malpractice or negligence claims caused by the work of one of their partners. (p. 564)

limited partnership – A form of partnership that offers limited liability to one or more partners for any debts

or legal claims against the business and at least one general partner has unlimited liability. (p. 563)

liquidation – The winding-up process when a partnership goes out of business. (p. 581)

mutual agency – The characteristic of general partnerships whereby each partner is an agent of and may act on behalf of the partnership. (p. 564)

partnership – An unincorporated business form consisting of two or more persons conducting business as co-owners for profit. (p. 563)

partnership agreement – The formal written contract creating a partnership. (p. 563)

statement of changes in partnership equity – A summary of the changes in each partner's capital in a partnership that have occurred during a specific period of time. (p. 588)

statement of partnership liquidation – A summary of the liquidation process whereby cash is distributed to the partners based on the balances in their capital accounts. (p. 582)

END-OF-CHAPTER ILLUSTRATIVE PROBLEM

Radcliffe, Sonders, and Towers, who share in income and losses in the ratio of 2:3:5, decided to discontinue operations as at April 30, 2015, and liquidate their partnership. After the accounts were closed on April 30, 2015, the following trial balance was prepared:

Radcliffe, Sonders, and Towers Post-Closing Trial Balance April 30, 2015		
	Debit Balances	**Credit Balances**
Cash..	5,900	
Accounts receivable, net	35,000	
Inventory	74,900	
Accounts payable		26,800
Radcliffe, Capital		14,600
Sonders, Capital		27,900
Towers, Capital		46,500
	115,800	115,800

Between May 1 and May 18, the noncash assets were sold for $27,400, and the liabilities were paid.

Instructions

1. Assuming that the partner with the capital deficiency pays the entire amount owed to the partnership, prepare a statement of partnership liquidation.
2. Journalize the entries to record (a) the sale of the assets, (b) the division of loss on the sale of the assets, (c) the payment of the liabilities, (d) the receipt of the deficiency, and (e) the distribution of cash to the partners.

Solution

1.

	Radcliffe, Sonders, and Towers Statement of Partnership Liquidation For Period May 1–18, 2015				Capital		
	Cash +	A/R +	Inventory =	Accounts Payable +	Radcliffe (20%) +	Sonders (30%) +	Towers (50%)
Balances before sale of assets	$ 5,900	$35,000	$74,900	$26,800	$14,600	$27,900	$46,500
Sale of assets and division of loss	+27,400	−35,000	−74,900		−16,500	−24,750	−41,250
Balances after sale of assets	33,300	0	0	26,800	(1,900)	3,150	5,250
Payment of liabilities	−26,800			−26,800			
Balances after payment of liabilities	6,500	0	0	0	(1,900)	3,150	5,250
Receipt of deficiency	+ 1,900				+ 1,900		
Balances	8,400	0	0	0	0	3,150	5,250
Cash distributed to partners	− 8,400					− 3,150	− 5,250
Final balances	$ 0	$ 0	$ 0	$ 0	$ 0	$ 0	$ 0

2. a.

Cash	27,400	
Loss on Sale of Assets	82,500	
Accounts Receivable		35,000
Inventory		74,900

b.

Radcliffe, Capital	16,500	
Sonders, Capital	24,750	
Towers, Capital	41,250	
Loss on Sale of Assets		82,500

c.

Accounts Payable	26,800	
Cash		26,800

d.

Cash	1,900	
Radcliffe, Capital		1,900

e.

	Sonders, Capital		3,150	
	Towers, Capital		5,250	
	Cash			8,400

EYE OPENERS

1. What are the main advantages of (a) proprietorships and (b) partnerships?
2. Emily Gordon and Grace Cheung joined together to form a partnership. Is it possible for them to lose an amount greater than the amount of their investment in the partnership? Explain.
3. What are the major features of a partnership agreement?
4. In the absence of an agreement, how will the net income be distributed between Ethan Arnold and Tessa Winthrop, partners in the firm of A and W Environmental Engineering?
5. Josiah Barlow, Patty DuMont, and Owen Maholic are contemplating the formation of a partnership. According to the partnership agreement, Barlow is to invest $60,000 and devote one-half time, DuMont is to invest $40,000 and devote three-fourths time, and Maholic is to make no investment and devote full time. Would Maholic be correct in assuming that because he is not contributing any assets to the firm, he is risking nothing? Explain.
6. As a part of the initial investment, a partner contributes delivery equipment that had originally cost $50,000 and on which accumulated depreciation of $37,500 had been recorded. The partners agree on a valuation of $10,000. How should the delivery equipment be recorded in the accounts of the partnership?
7. All partners agree that $150,000 of accounts receivable invested by a partner will be collectible to the extent of 90%. How should the accounts receivable be recorded in the general ledger of the partnership?
8. During the current year, Marsha Engles withdrew $4,000 monthly from the partnership of Engles and Cox Water Management Consultants. Is it possible that her share of partnership net income for the current year might be more or less than $48,000? Explain.
9. a. What accounts are debited and credited to record a partner's cash withdrawal in lieu of salary?
   b. The articles of partnership provide for a salary allowance of $6,000 per month to partner C. If C withdrew only $4,000 per month, would this lesser amount affect the division of the partnership net income?
   c. At the end of the fiscal year, what accounts are debited and credited to record the division of net income among partners?
10. Explain the difference between the admission of a new partner to a partnership (a) by purchase of an interest from another partner and (b) by contribution of assets to the partnership.
11. Why is it important to state all partnership assets in terms of current prices at the time of the admission of a new partner?
12. Why might a partnership pay a bonus to a newly admitted partner?
13. In the liquidation process, (a) how are losses and gains on sale of assets divided among the partners, and (b) how is cash distributed among the partners?

PRACTICE EXERCISES

PE 11-1
② Journalize partner's original investment

EE 11-1 p. 565

Josh Beach and Craig Fox decided to form a partnership. Josh Beach contributed land, inventory, and $24,000 cash. The land had a carrying value of $65,000 and a market value of $114,000. The inventory had a carrying value of $60,000 and a market value of $56,000. The partnership also assumed a $50,000 note payable owed by Beach that was used originally to purchase the land.

Craig Fox contributed inventory with a carrying value of $100,000 and a market value of $94,000 and $50,000 cash.

Provide the journal entries for Beach's and Fox's contributions to the partnership.

PE 11-2
② Dividing partnership net income—closing entries

EE 11-2 p. 567

Jane McDonald and Dave Ward's partnership agreement provided a salary allowance of $60,000 and $50,000 to each partner, respectively, with any remaining net income to be divided equally. During the year, both partners withdrew $4,000 per month.
a. Determine the division of $160,000 net income for the year.
b. Provide journal entries to close (1) the Income Summary account and (2) the withdrawals accounts for the two partners.

PE 11-3
② Dividing partnership net income

EE 11-3 p. 569

Brandon Smithson and Lakendra Mooney formed a partnership, dividing income as follows:
1. Annual salary allowance to Mooney of $53,000.
2. Interest of 5% on each partner's capital balance on January 1.
3. Any remaining net income will be shared by Smithson and Mooney in a 3:1 ratio.
Smithson and Mooney had $50,000 and $150,000, respectively, in their January 1 capital balances. Net income for the year was $240,000.

How much net income should be distributed to Mooney?

PE 11-4
② Dividing partnership net income— allowances exceed net income

EE 11-4 p. 570

Use the information supplied in PE 11-3 for Brandon Smithson and Lakendra Mooney but assume that the partnership had net income of $61,000 for the year instead of net income of $240,000.

How much net income should be distributed to Mooney? Prepare the journal entry to close the income summary account.

PE 11-5
② Dividing partnership net income—in event of net loss

EE 11-5 p. 571

Use the information supplied in PE 11-3 for Brandon Smithson and Lakendra Mooney but assume that the partnership had a net loss of $10,000 for the year instead of net income of $240,000.

How much net income or loss should be distributed to Mooney? Prepare the journal entry to close the income summary account.

PE 11-6
③ Revaluing and contributing assets to a partnership

EE 11-6 p. 575

Brandon Tarr invested $64,000 in the Garmon and Miller partnership for ownership equity of $64,000. Prior to the investment, equipment was revalued to a market value of $45,000 from a carrying value of $33,000. Jordon Garmon and Kali Miller share net income in a 2:1 ratio.
a. Provide the journal entry for the revaluation of equipment.
b. Provide the journal entry to admit Tarr.

PE 11-7
Partner bonus

Maples has a capital balance of $65,000 after adjusting assets to fair market value. Baker contributes $25,000 to receive a 30% interest in a new partnership with Maples.

Determine the amount and recipient of the partner bonus.

EE 11-7 p. 578

PE 11-8
Withdrawal of partner with bonus

On September 15, Jackie Landall decided to retire from the partnership of Kitchener, Landall, and Page. The partnership decided to buy her out. After the assets of the partnership had been adjusted to current market values, the capital balances were $67,200, $89,400, and $48,000, respectively. Prepare the journal entry to record Landall's retirement, assuming Landall accepts payment of $85,000 and the partners share net income and losses equally.

EE 11-8 p. 580

PE 11-9
Liquidating partnerships

Prior to liquidating their partnership, Penn and Ryan had capital accounts of $160,000 and $100,000, respectively, noncash assets of $275,000, and liabilities of $15,000. These partnership assets were sold for $250,000. Penn and Ryan share income and losses equally. Determine the amount received by Penn as a final distribution from liquidation of the partnership.

EE 11-9 p. 584

PE 11-10
Liquidating partnerships—deficiency

Prior to liquidating their partnership, Min and Alvarez had capital accounts of $120,000 and $200,000, respectively, noncash assets of $320,000, and no liabilities. The partnership assets were sold for $60,000. Min and Alvarez share income and losses equally.

a. Determine the amount of Min's deficiency.
b. Determine the amount distributed to Alvarez, assuming Min is unable to satisfy the deficiency.

EE 11-10 p. 587

EXERCISES

EX 11-1
Record partners' original investment

Gwen Delk and Alliesha Johnson decide to form a partnership by combining the assets of their separate businesses. Delk contributes the following assets to the partnership: cash, $13,000; accounts receivable of $136,000; allowance for doubtful accounts of $8,400; inventory of $90,000; and equipment with a cost of $155,000 and accumulated depreciation of $100,000.

The partners agree that $6,000 of the accounts receivable are completely worthless and are not to be accepted by the partnership, that $10,200 is a reasonable allowance for the uncollectibility of the remaining accounts, that the inventory is to be recorded at the current market price of $84,700, and that the equipment is to be valued at $69,500.

Johnson contributes the following assets to the partnership: cash, $130,000; accounts receivable of $76,500; allowance for doubtful accounts of $3,600; inventory of $37,000; and equipment with a cost of $72,000 and accumulated depreciation of $14,000.

The partners agree that Johnson's allowance for doubtful accounts should be increased to $5,000, that the inventory is to be recorded at the current market value of $33,000, and that the equipment is to be valued at $52,500.

Provide the journal entries for Delk's and Johnson's contributions to the partnership.

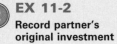

EX 11-2
Record partner's
original investment

Brandi Bonds and Sam Stakes form a partnership by combining assets of their former businesses. The following balance sheet information is provided by Bonds, sole proprietorship:

Cash		$ 40,000
Accounts receivable	$75,000	
Less: Allowance for doubtful accounts	4,100	70,900
Equipment	$70,000	
Less: Accumulated depreciation—equipment	43,000	27,000
Land		180,000
Total assets		$317,900
Accounts payable		$ 22,500
Notes payable		65,000
Brandi Bonds, capital		230,400
Total liabilities and owner's equity		$317,900

Bonds obtained appraised values for the land and equipment as follows:

Land	$250,000
Equipment	21,000

An analysis of the accounts receivable indicated that the allowance for doubtful accounts should be increased to $6,000.

Journalize the partnership's entry for Bonds's investment.

EX 11-3
Dividing partnership
income

✔ b. Haskett,
$240,000

Dave Haskett and Brenda Humphrys formed a partnership, investing $240,000 and $80,000, respectively. Determine their participation in the year's net income of $320,000 under each of the following independent assumptions:

(a) no agreement concerning division of net income;
(b) divided in the ratio of original capital investment;
(c) interest at the rate of 15% allowed on original investments and the remainder divided in a ratio of 2:3;
(d) salary allowances of $50,000 and $70,000, respectively, and the balance divided equally;
(e) allowance of interest at the rate of 15% on original investments, salary allowances of $50,000 and $70,000, respectively, and the remainder divided equally.

EX 11-4
Dividing partnership
income

✔ c. Haskett,
$208,800

Determine the income participation of Haskett and Humphrys according to each of the five assumptions as to income division listed in Exercise 11-3, if the year's net income is $480,000.

EX 11-5
Dividing partnership
income

✔ d. Humphrys,
$65,000

Determine the income participation of Haskett and Humphrys according to each of the five assumptions as to income division listed in Exercise 11-3, if the year's net income is $110,000.

EX 11-6
Dividing partnership
net loss

Casey Fisher and Logan Baylor formed a partnership in which the partnership agreement provided for salary allowances of $40,000 and $35,000, respectively. Determine the division of a $20,000 net loss for the current year.

② EX 11-7

Dividing partnership income

✔ a. Gillis, –$2,080

The partnership of McGillivray, Gillis, and Newton had the following transactions in 2015:

Feb. 1. The partnership was formed with the following amounts invested by the partners:
McGillivray invested $10,000 cash and equipment valued at $12,000.
Gillis invested $5,000 cash and inventory with a carrying value of $16,000 and a market value of $13,000.
Newton invested $10,000.

Jun. 10. The partners invested an additional $5,000 each.

Oct. 31. Newton received a salary allowance of $25,000. (The full salary allowance for the year was not paid due to concerns about cash flow).

Dec. 31. The partnership reported net income of $33,600.

a. Determine the division of income among the three partners, assuming that the partnership agreement specifies that the partners receive 4% interest on their year-end capital balance, that Newton receives a salary allowance of $40,000, and that any remaining income or loss is shared in a ratio of 3:2:1.

b. Prepare the journal entry to close the net income and withdrawals to the individual partner equity accounts.

---

② EX 11-8

Dividing partnership income

✔ a. Bowman, $106,800

Ben Bowman and Savannah Mapes formed a limited liability partnership with a partnership agreement that provided a salary allowance of $75,000 and $60,000 to each partner, respectively. In addition, the partnership agreement specified an income-sharing ratio of 3:2. The two partners withdrew amounts equal to their salary allowances.

a. Determine the division of $188,000 net income for the year.

b. Provide journal entries to close (1) the income summary and (2) the withdrawals accounts for the two partners.

---

② EX 11-9

Dividing partnership income

✔ a. Bowman, $54,000

Use the information supplied in Exercise 11-8 for Ben Bowman and Savannah Mapes.

a. Determine the division of $100,000 net income for the year.

b. Provide journal entries to close (1) the income summary and (2) the withdrawals accounts for the two partners.

---

② ⑤ EX 11-10

Dividing partnership income and statement of changes in partnership equity

✔ a. Wilson, $268,600

Intermedia LLP has three partners: Sheila Frances, Lindsey Wilson, and Maureen Culver. On January 1, 2015, the three partners had equity of $200,000, $50,000, and $120,000, respectively. Sheila Frances contributed an additional $50,000 to Intermedia LLP on June 1, 2015. Lindsey Wilson received an annual salary allowance of $115,600 during 2015. The partners' equity accounts are also credited with 12% interest on each partner's January 1 capital balance. Any remaining income is to be shared in a ratio of 4:3:3 among the three partners. The net income for Intermedia LLP for 2015 was $650,000. The salary and interest allowances were distributed to the partners.

a. Determine the division of income among the three partners.

b. Prepare the journal entry to close the net income and withdrawals to the individual partner equity accounts.

c. Prepare a statement of changes in partnership equity for 2015.

---

③ EX 11-11

Admitting new partners

✔ b. $50,000

Lia Wu and Becca Sims are partners who share in the partnership's income equally and have capital balances of $150,000 and $62,500, respectively. Wu, with the consent of Sims, sells one-third of her interest to Kara Oliver. What entry is required by the partnership if the sales price is (a) $40,000? (b) $60,000?

EX 11-12
Admitting new partners

Diana de Courcey and Leah Kalleen are partners who share in the partnership's income equally and have capital balances of $62,500 and $150,000, respectively. Gary Daniel will receive a one-third equity in the partnership and will share equally with de Courcey and Kalleen in partnership income and losses. What entry is required by the partnership if Daniel pays (a) $80,000? (b) $120,500?

EX 11-13
Admitting new partners who buy an interest and contribute assets

✔ b. Shaw, $96,000

The capital accounts of Barbara Shaw and Jane O'Halloran have balances of $120,000 and $100,000, respectively. Juan Rohon and Marco Galen are to be admitted to the partnership. Rohon buys one-fifth of Shaw's interest for $40,000 and one-fourth of O'Halloran's interest for $30,000. Galen contributes $50,000 cash to the partnership, for which he is to receive an ownership equity of $50,000.

a. Journalize the entries to record the admission of (1) Rohon and (2) Galen.
b. What are the capital balances of each partner after the admission of the new partners?

EX 11-14
Admitting new partner who contributes assets

✔ b. Flores, $60,000

After the tangible assets have been adjusted to current market prices, the capital accounts of Travis Harris and Keelyn Kidd have balances of $60,000 and $90,000, respectively. Felix Flores is to be admitted to the partnership, contributing $45,000 cash to the partnership, for which he is to receive an ownership equity of $60,000. All partners share equally in income.

a. Journalize the entry to record the admission of Flores, who is to receive a bonus of $15,000.
b. What are the capital balances of each partner after the admission of the new partner?

EX 11-15
Admitting new partner with bonus

✔ b. (2) Bonus paid to Koster, $15,000

Excel Medical LLP consists of two doctors, Douglass and Finn, who share in all income and losses of the partnership according to a 2:3 income-sharing ratio. Dr. Lindsey Koster has been asked to join the partnership. Prior to admitting Koster, the assets of Excel Medical, LLP, were revalued to reflect their current market values. The revaluation resulted in medical equipment being increased by $25,000. Prior to the revaluation, the equity balances for Douglass and Finn were $240,000 and $275,000, respectively.

a. Provide the journal entry for the asset revaluation.
b. Provide the journal entry for the bonus under the following independent situations:
   1. Koster purchased a 30% interest in Excel Medical LLP for $310,000.
   2. Koster purchased a 25% interest in Excel Medical LLP for $160,000.

EX 11-16
Admitting new partner with bonus

✔ b. (1) Bonus paid to Harris, $4,600

P. Whyte and M. Cunningham are partners in Green Earth Consultants. Whyte and Cunningham share the partnership's income equally. L. Harris will be admitted to the partnership. Prior to the admission, equipment was revalued downward by $16,000. The capital balances of each partner are $100,000 and $139,000, respectively, prior to the revaluation.

a. Provide the journal entry for the asset revaluation.
b. Provide the journal entry for Harris's admission under the following independent situations:
   1. Harris purchased a 20% interest for $50,000.
   2. Harris purchased a 30% interest for $125,000.

EX 11-17
Partner bonuses, statement of changes in partnership equity

✔ Wilson capital, Dec. 31, 2015, $83,400

The partnership of Angel Investor Associates began operations on January 1, 2015, with contributions from two partners as follows:

Jen Wilson	$45,000
Teresa McDonald	55,000

The following additional partner transactions took place during the year:

1. In early January, Jaime Holden is admitted to the partnership by contributing $25,000 cash for a 20% interest.
2. Net income of $160,000 was earned in 2015. In addition, Jen Wilson received a salary allowance of $30,000 for the year. The three partners agree to an income-sharing ratio equal to their capital balances after admitting Holden.
3. The partners' withdrawals are equal to half of the increase in their capital balances from income and salary allowances.

Prepare a statement of changes in partnership equity for the year ended December 31, 2015.

---

③ EX 11-18

Withdrawal of partner

✔ a. Candace Heraghty, Capital, $43,000

Candace Heraghty, Joe Chew, and Chris Kilgour have run a successful partnership for a number of years, sharing income 3:2:1, respectively. On December 31, Joe Chew decided to leave the partnership. After the assets of the partnership have been adjusted to current market values, the capital balances of Heraghty, Chew, and Kilgour are as follows:

Candace Heraghty, Capital	$122,000
Joe Chew, Capital	86,000
Chris Kilgour, Capital	54,000

Provide the journal entry for Chew's departure under the following independent situations:

a. Heraghty and Kilgour agree to each pay Chew $40,000 for equal rights to his partnership share.
b. Heraghty and Kilgour agree to each pay Chew $50,000 for equal rights to his partnership share.

---

③ EX 11-19

Withdrawal of partner

✔ a. Jeff Hanning, Capital, $61,560

Andy Heel has decided to retire from the partnership of Heel, Hanning, and Paull LLP on May 31, 2015. The partners have shared income equally. After the assets of the partnership have been adjusted to current market values, the capital balances of Heel, Hanning, and Paull, LLP, are as follows:

Andy Heel, Capital	$307,800
Jeff Hanning, Capital	429,788
Les Paull, Capital	386,500

Provide the journal entry for Heel's departure under the following independent situations:

a. Hanning agrees to pay Heel $62,000 for a 20% right to his partnership share and Paull agrees to pay Heel $248,000 for an 80% right to his partnership share.
b. Paull agrees to pay Heel $300,000 for full rights to his partnership share.

---

③ EX 11-20

Withdrawal of partner with bonus

✔ b. Heather Catte, Capital, $1,600

Heather Catte, Joe Collins, and Chris Gilgan have run a successful partnership for a number of years, sharing income 4:2:1, respectively. On September 30, Joe Collins decided to leave the partnership. After the assets of the partnership have been adjusted to current market values, the capital balances of Catte, Collins, and Gilgan are as follows:

Heather Catte, Capital	$32,000
Joe Collins, Capital	26,000
Chris Gilgan, Capital	22,000

Provide the journal entry for Collins' departure under the following independent situations:

a. The partnership offers Collins $26,000 upon his retirement.
b. The partnership offers Collins $24,000 upon his retirement.
c. The partnership offers Collins $28,000 upon his retirement.

EX 11-21

Partner income and withdrawal of partner journal entries

✔ b. Andrew Morris, Capital, $33,500

Terry Constantino, Carissa Alton, and Andrew Morris have run a successful partnership for a number of years, sharing income 4:2:2, respectively. Carissa Alton has decided to leave the partnership. After the assets of the partnership have been adjusted to current market values, the capital balances of Constantino, Alton, and Morris are as follows:

Terry Constantino, Capital	$102,000
Carissa Alton, Capital	66,000
Andrew Morris, Capital	72,000

The partnership offers Alton $60,000 upon her retirement.

a. Provide the journal entry for Alton's departure on July 10, 2015.
b. Provide the journal entry to close the income summary account at the end of 2015, assuming net income of $100,500 was earned for the remainder of the year, after the books were closed on July 10, 2015, to record Alton's retirement.

EX 11-22

Partner income and withdrawal of partner journal entries

✔ c. $112,800

Elena Oprescu, Xiru Wang, Reg Miller, and Kendra Batty have capital balances of $25,000, $30,000, $20,000, and $20,000, respectively. They share income or loss on a 4:4:1:1 basis and Oprescu and Wang each receive a monthly salary allowance of $8,000. Xiru Wang decided to leave the partnership on March 31, 2015, at which point the partnership had earned net income of $400,000.

a. Determine the division of income among the four partners.
b. Provide the journal entries to close the net income and withdrawals to the individual partner equity accounts on March 31, 2015.
c. Determine the balance in Wang's capital account after the March 31, 2015, closing entries have been recorded.
d. Provide the journal entry for Wang's departure on March 31, 2015, assuming the partnership offers Wang $120,000.

EX 11-23

Statement of changes in partnership equity, admitting new partner

✔ a. 3:7

The statement of changes in partnership equity for PQR Partners is shown below.

PQR Partners
Statement of Changes in Partnership Equity
For the Years Ended December 31, 2015 and 2016

	Pat Peters, Capital	Jessie Quan, Capital	Randy Reed, Capital	Total Partnership Capital
Balance, Jan. 1, 2015	$450,000	$310,000		$ 760,000
Net income for 2015	90,000	210,000		300,000
Balance, Dec. 31, 2015	540,000	520,000		1,060,000
Reed contribution	6,000	14,000	$270,000	290,000
Net income for 2016	100,000	220,000	80,000	400,000
Less partner withdrawals	(32,000)	(48,000)	(50,000)	(130,000)
Balance, Dec. 31, 2016	$614,000	$706,000	$300,000	$1,620,000

a. What was the income-sharing ratio in 2015?
b. What was the income-sharing ratio in 2016?
c. How much cash did Randy Reed contribute to PQR Partners for his interest?
d. Why do the partner capital accounts of Pat Peters and Jessie Quan have positive entries for Randy Reed's contribution?
e. What percentage interest of PQR Partners did Randy Reed acquire?

EX 11-24

Distribution of cash upon liquidation

✔ a. $4,000 loss

Pryor and Lester are partners, sharing gains and losses of the partnership equally. They decide to terminate their partnership. Prior to the sale of assets, their capital balances are $12,000 and $8,000, respectively. After all noncash assets are sold and all liabilities are paid, there is a cash balance of $16,000.

a. What is the amount of the gain or loss on the sale of assets?
b. How should the gain or loss be divided between Pryor and Lester?
c. How should the cash be divided between Pryor and Lester?

4 **EX 11-25**

Distribution of cash upon liquidation

Jason Bradley and Abdul Barak, with capital balances of $26,000 and $35,000, respectively, decide to liquidate their partnership. After selling the noncash assets and paying the liabilities, there is $76,000 of cash remaining. If the partners share income and losses equally, how should the cash be distributed?

✔ Bradley, $33,500

---

4 **EX 11-26**

Liquidating partnerships—capital deficiency

Matthews, Williams, and Shen share equally in their partnership's net income and net losses. After the partnership sells all assets for cash, divides the losses on the sale of assets, and pays the liabilities, the balances in the capital accounts are as follows: Matthews, $28,000 Cr.; Williams, $62,500 Cr.; Shen, $18,000 Dr.

a. What term is applied to the debit balance in Shen's capital account?
b. What is the amount of cash on hand?
c. Journalize the transaction that must take place for Matthews and Williams to receive cash in the liquidation process equal to their capital account balances.

✔ b. $72,500

---

4 **EX 11-27**

Distribution of cash upon liquidation

Bianca Houston, Jana Alsup, and KeKe Cross arranged to import and sell orchid corsages for a university dance. They agreed to share equally the net income or net loss of the venture. Houston and Alsup advanced $250 and $380 of their own respective funds to pay for advertising and other expenses. After collecting for all sales and paying creditors, the partnership has $1,020 in cash.

a. How should the money be distributed?
b. Assuming that the partnership has only $540 instead of $1,020, do any of the three partners have a capital deficiency? If so, how much?

✔ a. Houston, $380

---

4 **EX 11-28**

Liquidating partnerships— capital deficiency

Hilliard, Downey, and Petrov are partners sharing income 3:2:1. After the firm's loss from liquidation is distributed, the capital account balances were Hilliard, $24,000 Dr.; Downey, $90,000 Cr.; and Petrov, $64,000 Cr. If Hilliard is personally bankrupt and unable to pay any of the $24,000, what will be the amount of cash received by Downey and Petrov upon liquidation?

---

4 **EX 11-29**

Statement of partnership liquidation

After closing the accounts on July 1, prior to liquidating the partnership, the capital account balances of Dover, Goll, and Chamberland are $35,000, $50,000, and $22,000, respectively. Cash, inventory, and liabilities total $55,000, $92,000, and $40,000, respectively. Between July 1 and July 29, the inventory is sold for $74,000, the liabilities are paid, and the remaining cash is distributed to the partners. The partners share net income and loss in a ratio of 3:2:1. Prepare a statement of partnership liquidation for the period July 1–29, 2015.

---

4 **EX 11-30**

Statement of partnership liquidation

Brazier, Moore, and Jonah are partners of Bright Sales LLP, sharing income and losses in a ratio of 2:2:1, respectively. The partners decide to liquidate the partnership. The capital account balances prior to liquidation and the sale of assets, on May 1, 2015, are as follows:

Brazier	$15,000
Moore	35,000
Jonah	22,000
Total	$72,000

✔ b. Jonah, capital $21,200

In winding up operations during the month of May, accounts receivable with a carrying value of $94,000 are sold for $90,000, and liabilities of $30,000 are satisfied. Prior to liquidation, the LLP has a cash balance of $8,000.

a. Prepare a statement of partnership liquidation.
b. Provide the journal entry for the final cash distribution to partners.

2
5

EX 11-31
Partnership entries and statement of changes in partnership equity

✔ b. Abdel-Raja, capital, Dec. 31, $114,000

The capital accounts of Hossam Abdel-Raja and Aly Meyer have balances of $90,000 and $65,000, respectively, on January 1, 2015, the beginning of the current fiscal year. On April 10, Abdel-Raja invested an additional $10,000. During the year, Abdel-Raja and Meyer withdrew $48,000 and $39,000, respectively, and net income for the year was $124,000. The articles of partnership make no reference to the division of net income.

a. Journalize the entries to close (1) the income summary account and (2) the withdrawals accounts.

b. Prepare a statement of changes in partnership equity for the current year for the partnership of Abdel-Raja and Meyer.

PROBLEMS SERIES A

2

PR 11-1A
Entries and balance sheet for partnership

✔ 3. Schmidt net income, $47,200

On January 1, 2015, Kevin Schmidt and David Cohen form a partnership. Schmidt agrees to invest $12,000 cash and inventory valued at $32,000. Cohen invests certain business assets at valuations agreed upon, transfers business liabilities, and contributes sufficient cash to bring his total capital to $80,000. Details regarding the carrying values of the business assets and liabilities and the agreed valuations follow:

	Cohen's Ledger Balance	Agreed-Upon Valuation
Accounts Receivable	$18,400	$14,900
Allowance for Doubtful Accounts	800	1,000
Inventory	21,400	28,600
Equipment	36,000	35,000
Accumulated Depreciation—Equipment	12,000	
Accounts Payable	6,500	6,500
Notes Payable	4,000	4,000

The partnership agreement includes the following provisions regarding the division of net income: interest of 10% on original investments, salary allowances of $36,000 (Schmidt) and $22,000 (Cohen), and the remainder equally.

Instructions

1. Journalize the entries to record the investments of Schmidt and Cohen in the partnership accounts.

2. Prepare a balance sheet as at January 1, 2015, the date of formation of the partnership of Schmidt and Cohen.

3. After adjustments and the closing of revenue and expense accounts at December 31, 2015, the end of the first full year of operations, the income summary account has a credit balance of $84,000, and the withdrawals accounts have debit balances of $30,000 (Schmidt) and $25,000 (Cohen). Journalize the entries to close the income summary account and the withdrawals accounts at December 31, 2015.

3

PR 11-2A
Dividing partnership income

✔ 1. f. Drury net income, $92,900

Desmond Drury and Ty Wilkins have decided to form a partnership. They have agreed that Drury is to invest $20,000 and that Wilkins is to invest $30,000. Drury is to devote full time to the business, and Wilkins is to devote one-half time. The following plans for the division of income are being considered:

a. Equal division.
b. In the ratio of original investments.
c. In the ratio of time devoted to the business.
d. Interest of 10% on original investments and the remainder in the ratio of 3:2.
e. Interest of 10% on original investments, salary allowances of $34,000 to Drury and $17,000 to Wilkins, and the remainder equally.
f. Plan (e), except that Drury is also to be allowed a bonus equal to 20% of the amount by which net income exceeds the salary allowances.

Instructions

For each plan, determine the division of the net income under each of the following assumptions: (1) net income of $150,000 and (2) net income of $66,000. Present the data in tabular form, using the following columnar headings:

	$150,000		$66,000	
Plan	Drury	Wilkins	Drury	Wilkins

PR 11-3A

Dividing partnership income and statement of changes in partnership equity

✔ 1. Wang, $109,923

Artemis LLP has four partners, with equity balances on January 1, 2015, as follows:

Sam Frances	$115,800
Lynn Madson	120,500
Mike Wang	88,700
Deirdre Manis	75,000

Sam Frances contributed an additional $100,000 to Artemis LLP on June 1, 2015. Lynn Madson received an annual salary allowance of $115,600 during 2015. The partners' equity accounts are also credited with 5% interest on each partner's January 1 capital balance. Any remaining income is to be shared in a ratio of 4:3:2:1 among the partners. The net income for Artemis LLP for 2015 was $663,040. The salary and interest allowances were distributed to the partners during the year.

Instructions

1. Determine the division of income among the four partners.
2. Prepare the journal entries to close the net income and withdrawals to the individual partner equity accounts.
3. Prepare a statement of changes in partnership equity for 2015.
4. Identify the amount of partnership income that Lynn Madson will report on her 2015 personal tax return. Why might this amount be different from the amount of cash she withdrew from the partnership during 2015?

PR 11-4A

Dividing partnership loss and statement of partnership equity

✔ 1. Alexis, $3,334

Louis, Alexis, and Donald LLP had equity balances on January 1, 2015, as follows:

Sandra Louis	$106,700
Amelia Alexis	58,400
Alex Donald	46,200

Louis and Alexis received annual allowances of $40,000 each, and the partners' equity accounts were credited 6% interest on their January 1 capital balance. Any remaining income is to be shared in a ratio of 2:1:1. The partnership had a net loss of $68,002 for 2015. The salary and interest allowances were distributed to the partners during the year.

Instructions

1. Determine the division of income among the three partners.
2. Prepare the journal entries to close the net loss and withdrawals to the individual partner equity accounts.
3. Prepare a statement of changes in partnership equity for 2015.

PR 11-5A

Financial statements for partnerships

✔ 2. Dec. 31 capital—Weekley, $181,875

The ledger of Ken White and Alex Weekley, lawyers, contains the following accounts and balances after adjustments have been recorded on December 31, 2015:

(continued)

	Debit Balances	Credit Balances
Cash	24,200	
Accounts Receivable	41,300	
Supplies	6,700	
Equipment	500,000	
Accumulated Depreciation—Equipment		240,600
Accounts Payable		3,400
Salaries Payable		5,200
Ken White, Capital		125,000
Ken White, Withdrawals	50,000	
Alex Weekley, Capital		160,000
Alex Weekley, Withdrawals	60,000	
Professional Fees		562,200
Salaries Expense	312,300	
Depreciation Expense	81,700	
Adminstrative Expenses	20,200	
	1,096,400	1,096,400

The balance in Weekley's capital account includes an additional investment of $20,000 made on April 5, 2015.

Instructions

1. Prepare an income statement for the current fiscal year, indicating the division of net income as shown on page 570. The articles of partnership provide for salary allowances of $60,000 to White and $75,000 to Weekley, allowances of 5% on each partner's capital balance at the beginning of the fiscal year, and equal division of the remaining net income or net loss.
2. Prepare a statement of changes in partnership equity for 2015.
3. Prepare a balance sheet as at the end of 2015.

---

③ PR 11-6A

Admitting new partner

✔ 1. Jordan Cates, Capital, $11,750 Cr.

Jordan Cates and LaToya Orr have operated a successful firm for many years, sharing net income and net losses of the partnership equally. Caleb Webster is to be admitted to the partnership on June 1 of the current year, in accordance with the following agreement:

a. Assets and liabilities of the old partnership are to be valued at their carrying values as at May 31, except for the following:
  - Accounts receivable amounting to $2,000 are to be written off, and the allowance for doubtful accounts is to be increased to 5% of the remaining accounts.
  - Inventory is to be valued at $63,870.
  - Equipment is to be valued at $90,000.
b. Webster is to purchase $30,000 of the ownership interest of Orr for $37,500 cash and to contribute $35,000 cash to the partnership for a total ownership equity of $65,000.
c. The income-sharing ratio of Cates, Orr, and Webster is to be 2:1:1.

The post-closing trial balance of Cates and Orr as at May 31 follows.

Cates and Orr
Post-Closing Trial Balance
May 31, 2015

	Debit Balances	Credit Balances
Cash	9,400	
Accounts Receivable	21,400	
Allowance for Doubtful Accounts		500
Inventory	58,600	
Prepaid Insurance	3,500	
Equipment	95,000	
Accumulated Depreciation—Equipment		25,700
Accounts Payable		14,700
Notes Payable		12,000
Jordan Cates, Capital		75,000
LaToya Orr, Capital		60,000
	187,900	187,900

Instructions

1. Journalize the entry as at May 31 to record the revaluations. The balance in the accumulated depreciation account is to be eliminated.
2. Journalize the additional entries to record the remaining transactions relating to the formation of the new partnership. Assume that all transactions occur on June 1.
3. Present a balance sheet for the new partnership as at June 1, 2015.

---

③ PR 11-7A
Withdrawal of partner with bonus

✔ 2 (c). Culver, capital, $1,600 Dr.

Noni Fidler is to retire from the partnership of Fidler and Associates as at December 31, 2015. After closing the accounts, the capital balances of the partners are as follows: Noni Fidler, $245,000; Margot Hess, $125,000; and Susan Culver, $140,000. They have shared net income and net losses of the partnership in a ratio of 3:2:2. The partners agree that the inventory should be increased by $24,000, and the allowance for doubtful accounts should be increased by $5,800. Fidler agrees to accept a note for $200,000 in partial settlement of her ownership equity. The remainder of her claim is to be paid in cash.

Instructions

1. Provide the journal entry for the asset revaluation.
2. Provide the journal entry under the following independent situations:
   a. Fidler received cash of $52,800.
   b. Fidler received cash of $45,000.
   c. Fidler received cash of $56,000.
3. Provide the journal entries to close the income summary and the withdrawals accounts, on December 31, 2016, assuming income of $320,000 and monthly withdrawals of $10,000 by Hess and $8,000 by Culver.

---

④ PR 11-8A
Statement of partnership liquidation

✔ 2. (b) Kris Harken, Capital, $23,300 Dr.

After the accounts are closed on September 10, 2015, prior to liquidating the partnership, the capital accounts of Kris Harken, Brett Sedlacek, and Amy Eldridge are $31,000, $5,700, and $24,500, respectively. Cash and inventory total $7,800 and $61,400, respectively. Amounts owed to creditors total $8,000. The partners share income and losses in a ratio of 1:1:2. Between September 10 and September 30, the inventory is sold for $32,600, the partner with the capital deficiency pays his or her deficiency to the partnership, and the liabilities are paid.

Instructions

1. Prepare a statement of partnership liquidation, indicating (a) the sale of assets and division of loss, (b) the payment of liabilities, (c) the receipt of the deficiency (from the appropriate partner), and (d) the distribution of cash.
2. Assume the partner with the capital deficiency declares bankruptcy and is unable to pay the deficiency. Journalize the entries to (a) allocate the partner's deficiency and (b) distribute the remaining cash.

PR 11-9A

Statement of partnership liquidation

✔ 2 (a). Watkis, Capital, $4,000 Dr.

On June 3, 2015, the firm of Adams, Watkis, and Cooper decided to liquidate its partnership. The partners have capital balances of $14,000, $84,000, and $118,000, respectively. The cash balance is $29,000, the carrying value of accounts receivable totals $242,000, and liabilities total $55,000. The partners share income and losses of the partnership in a ratio of 1:2:2.

Instructions

1. Prepare a statement of partnership liquidation, covering the period June 3–29, 2015, for each of the following independent assumptions:
   a. Accounts receivable are sold for $220,000, the creditors are paid, and the remaining cash is distributed to the partners.
   b. Accounts receivable are sold for $132,000, the creditors are paid, the partner with the debit capital balance pays the amount owed to the firm, and the remaining cash is distributed to the partners.
2. Assume the partner with the capital deficiency in part (b) above declares bankruptcy and is unable to pay the deficiency. Journalize the entries to (a) allocate the partner's deficiency and (b) distribute the remaining cash.

PROBLEMS SERIES B

PR 11-1B

Entries and balance sheet for partnership

✔ 3. Walker net income, $36,400

On January 10, 2016, Jarius Walker and Rae King form a partnership. Walker agrees to invest $18,200 in cash and inventory valued at $48,800. King invests certain business assets at valuations agreed upon, transfers business liabilities, and contributes sufficient cash to bring her total capital to $60,000. Details regarding the carrying values of the business assets and liabilities and the agreed valuations follow:

	King's Ledger Balance	Agreed-Upon Valuation
Accounts Receivable	$25,300	$24,100
Allowance for Doubtful Accounts	1,500	1,800
Equipment	92,300	55,100
Accumulated Depreciation—Equipment	35,600	
Accounts Payable	15,000	15,000
Notes Payable	25,000	25,000

The partnership agreement includes the following provisions regarding the division of net income: interest on original investments at 10%, salary allowances of $22,500 (Walker) and $30,400 (King), and the remainder equally.

Instructions

1. Journalize the entries to record the investments of Walker and King in the partnership accounts.
2. Prepare a balance sheet as at January 10, 2016, the date of formation of the partnership of Walker and King.
3. After adjustments and the closing of revenue and expense accounts at December 31, 2016, the end of the first full year of operations, the income summary account has a credit balance of $80,000, and the withdrawals accounts have debit balances of $22,500 (Walker) and $30,400 (King). Journalize the entries to close the income summary account and the withdrawals accounts at December 31, 2016.

PR 11-2B

Dividing partnership income

✔ 1. f. Larson net income, $41,600

Larson and Amos have decided to form a partnership. They have agreed that Larson is to invest $150,000 and that Amos is to invest $50,000. Larson is to devote one-half time to the business, and Amos is to devote full time. The following plans for the division of income are being considered:

a. Equal division.
b. In the ratio of original investments.

c. In the ratio of time devoted to the business.
d. Interest of 12% on original investments and the remainder equally.
e. Interest of 12% on original investments, salary allowances of $32,000 to Larson and $64,000 to Amos and the remainder equally.
f. Plan (e), except that Amos is also to be allowed a bonus equal to 20% of the amount by which net income exceeds the salary allowances.

Instructions

For each plan, determine the division of the net income under each of the following assumptions: (1) net income of $105,000 and (2) net income of $180,000. Present the data in tabular form, using the following column headings:

	$105,000		$180,000	
Plan	Larson	Amos	Larson	Amos

PR 11-3B

②

⑤

Dividing partnership income and statement of changes in partnership equity

✔ 1. Estevan, $46,512

Ambiguity LLP has four partners, with equity balances on January 1, 2015, as follows:

Von Porter	$68,500
Elisse Rand	75,000
Ming Foo	49,900
David Estevan	35,460

Rand contributed an additional $50,000 to Ambiguity LLP on June 1, 2015. Porter received an annual salary allowance of $85,600 during 2015. The partners' equity accounts are also credited with 5% interest on each partner's January 1 capital balance. Any remaining income is to be shared in a ratio of 4:3:2:1 among the partners. The net income for Ambiguity LLP for 2015 was $544,433. The salary and interest allowances were distributed to the partners during the year.

Instructions

1. Determine the division of income among the four partners.
2. Prepare the journal entries to close the net income and withdrawals to the individual partner equity accounts.
3. Prepare a statement of changes in partnership equity for 2015.
4. Identify the amount of partnership income that Von Porter will report on his 2015 personal tax return. Why might this amount be different from the amount of cash he withdrew from the partnership during 2015?

PR 11-4B

②

⑤

Dividing partnership loss and statement of changes in partnership equity

✔ 1. George, $169

Funk, George, and Lafayette LLP had equity balances on January 1, 2015, as follows:

David Funk	$160,050
Nathan George	87,600
Princess Lafayette	69,300

George and Lafayette received annual allowances of $50,000 each, and the partners' equity accounts were credited 8% interest on their January 1 capital balance. Any remaining income is to be shared in a ratio of 2:1:1. The partnership had a net loss of $102,000 for 2015. The salary and interest allowances were distributed to the partners during the year.

Instructions

1. Determine the division of income among the three partners.
2. Prepare the journal entries to close the net loss and withdrawals to the individual partner equity accounts.
3. Prepare a statement of changes in partnership equity for 2015.

PR 11-5B

Financial statements for partnership

✔ 2. Dec. 31 capital—Jones, $87,250

The ledger of Shizuka Kikuchi and Kilmeny Jones, lawyers, contains the following accounts and balances after adjustments have been recorded on December 31, 2015:

	Debit Balances	Credit Balances
Cash	32,000	
Accounts Receivable	42,300	
Supplies	1,500	
Equipment	249,100	
Accumulated Depreciation—Equipment		81,900
Accounts Payable		4,800
Salaries Payable		3,200
Shizuka Kikuchi, Capital		120,000
Shizuka Kikuchi, Withdrawals	45,000	
Kilmeny Jones, Capital		75,000
Kilmeny Jones, Withdrawals	65,000	
Professional Fees		340,300
Salaries Expense	146,800	
Depreciation Expense	19,000	
Adminstrative Expenses	24,500	
	625,200	625,200

The balance in Jones's capital account includes an additional investment of $10,000 made on August 10, 2015.

Instructions

1. Prepare an income statement for 2015, indicating the division of net income as shown on Page 568. The articles of partnership provide for salary allowances of $40,000 to Kikuchi and $50,000 to Jones, allowances of 10% on each partner's capital balance at the beginning of the fiscal year, and equal division of the remaining net income or net loss.
2. Prepare a statement of changes in partnership equity for 2015.
3. Prepare a balance sheet as at the end of 2015.

PR 11-6B

Admitting new partner

✔ 3. Total assets $333,000

Sadhil Rao and Lauren Sails have operated a successful firm for many years, sharing net income and net losses of the partnership equally. Paige Hancock is to be admitted to the partnership on May 1 of the current year, in accordance with the following agreement:

a. Assets and liabilities of the old partnership are to be valued at their carrying values as at April 30, except for the following:
   - Accounts receivable amounting to $2,800 are to be written off, and the allowance for doubtful accounts is to be increased to 5% of the remaining accounts.
   - Inventory is to be valued at $65,480.
   - Equipment is to be valued at $194,000.
b. Hancock is to purchase $55,000 of the ownership interest of Sails for $60,000 cash and to contribute another $30,000 cash to the partnership for a total ownership equity of $85,000.
c. The income-sharing ratio of Rao, Sails, and Hancock is to be 2:1:1.

The post-closing trial balance of Rao and Sails as at April 30 is as follows:

Rao and Sails
Post-Closing Trial Balance
April 30, 2015

	Debit Balances	Credit Balances
Cash	7,500	
Accounts Receivable	38,400	
Allowance for Doubtful Accounts		1,400
Inventory	59,000	
Prepaid Insurance	2,200	
Equipment	165,000	
Accumulated Depreciation—Equipment		51,700
Accounts Payable		9,000
Notes Payable		10,000
Sadhil Rao, Capital		110,000
Lauren Sails, Capital		90,000
	272,100	272,100

Instructions

1. Journalize the entry as at April 30 to record the revaluations. The balance in the accumulated depreciation account is to be eliminated.
2. Journalize the additional entries to record the remaining transactions relating to the formation of the new partnership. Assume that all transactions occur on May 1.
3. Present a balance sheet for the new partnership as at May 1, 2015.

PR 11-7B

Withdrawal of partner with bonus

✔ 2. (c) Donald, $4,000 Cr.

Sandra Brox is to retire from the partnership of Brox and Associates as at December 31, 2015. After closing the accounts, the capital balances of the partners are as follows: Sandra Brox, $144,600; Amelia Donald, $105,000; and Alex Caesar, $95,000. They have shared net income and net losses of the partnership in a ratio of 4:2:1. The partners agree that the inventory should be decreased by $1,550, and the allowance for doubtful accounts should be increased by $3,000. Brox agrees to accept a note for $100,000 in partial settlement of her ownership equity. The remainder of her claim is to be paid in cash.

Instructions

1. Provide the journal entry for the asset revaluation.
2. Provide the journal entry under the following independent situations:
    a. Brox received cash of $42,000.
    b. Brox received cash of $45,000.
    c. Brox received cash of $36,000.
3. Provide the journal entries to close the income summary and the withdrawals accounts on December 31, 2016, assuming net income of $240,000 and monthly withdrawals of $7,000 by Donald and $5,000 by Caesar.

PR 11-8B

Statement of partnership liquidation

✔ 2. (a) Whitney Lacy, Capital, $3,000 Dr.

After the accounts are closed on July 3, 2015, prior to liquidating the partnership, the capital accounts of Whitney Lacy, Eli Oliver, and Marc Dussault are $28,200, $7,800, and $37,200, respectively. Cash and accounts receivable total $5,800 and $82,400, respectively. Amounts owed to creditors total $15,000. The partners share income and losses in a ratio of 2:1:1. Between July 3 and July 29, the accounts receivable are sold for $33,200, the partner with the capital deficiency pays his deficiency to the partnership, and the liabilities are paid.

Instructions

1. Prepare a statement of partnership liquidation, indicating (a) the sale of assets and division of loss, (b) the payment of liabilities, (c) the receipt of the deficiency (from the appropriate partner), and (d) the distribution of cash.
2. Assume the partner with the capital deficiency declares bankruptcy and is unable to pay the deficiency. Journalize the entries to (a) allocate the partner's deficiency and (b) distribute the remaining cash.

PR 11-9B

Statement of partnership liquidation

✔ 2. (b) Dorr, Capital $33,500 Dr.

On October 1, 2015, the firm of Orson, Dorr, and Killough decided to liquidate its partnership. The partners have capital balances of $48,000, $63,000, and $11,000, respectively. The cash balance is $9,000, the carrying value of the equipment totals $155,000, and liabilities total $42,000. The partners share income and losses of the partnership in a ratio of 2:2:1.

1. Prepare a statement of partnership liquidation, covering the period October 1–30 2015, for each of the following independent assumptions:
   a. The equipment is sold for $195,000, the creditors are paid, and the remaining cash is distributed to the partners.
   b. The equipment is sold for $85,000, in cash, the creditors are paid, the partner with the debit capital balance pays the amount owed to the firm, and the remaining cash is distributed to the partners.
2. Assume the partner with the capital deficiency in part (b) above declares bankruptcy and is unable to pay the deficiency. Journalize the entries to (a) allocate the partner's deficiency and (b) distribute the remaining cash.

SPECIAL ACTIVITIES

SA 11-1

Partnership agreement

Group Project

Dustin Edwards, CA, and Daylan Hayes, CA, are sole owners of two accounting practices that operate in the same building. The two accountants agree to combine assets and liabilities of the two businesses to form a partnership. The partnership agreement calls for dividing income equally between the two accountants. After several months, the following conversation takes place between the two accountants:

Edwards: I've noticed that your client load has dropped over the past couple of months. When we formed our partnership, we were seeing about the same number of clients per week. However, now our client records show that you have been seeing about half as many clients as I have. Are there any issues that I should be aware of?

Hayes: There's nothing going on. When I was working on my own, I was really putting in the hours. One of the reasons I formed this partnership was to enjoy life a little more and scale back a little bit.

Edwards: I see. Well, I find that I'm working as hard as I did when I was on my own yet making less than I did previously. Essentially, you're sharing in half of my billings, and I'm sharing in half of yours. Because you are working much less than I am, I end up on the short end of the bargain.

Hayes: Well, I don't know what to say. An agreement is an agreement. The partnership is based on a 50/50 split. That's what a partnership is all about.

Edwards: If that's so, then it applies equally well on the effort end of the equation as on the income end.

Discuss whether Hayes is acting in an ethical manner. How could Edwards renegotiate the partnership agreement to avoid this dispute?

SA 11-2

Dividing partnership income

Rahmel Becker and Heather Morrow decide to form a partnership. Becker will contribute $300,000 to the partnership, whereas Morrow will contribute only $30,000. However, Morrow will be responsible for running the day-to-day operations of the partnership, which are anticipated to require about 45 hours per week. In contrast, Becker will only work five hours per week for the partnership. The two partners are attempting to determine a formula for dividing partnership net income. Becker believes the partners should divide income in the ratio of 7:3, favouring Becker, who provides the majority of the capital. Morrow believes the income should be divided 7:3, favouring Morrow, who provides the majority of effort in running the partnership business.

How would you advise the partners in developing a method for dividing income? Is there a method that will recognize the differing investments of time and money by the two partners?

SA 11-3
Partnership agreement

Kelly Herron has agreed to invest $200,000 into an LLP with Michelle Moss and Dan Kim. Moss and Kim will not invest any money but will provide effort and expertise to the LLP. Moss and Kim have agreed that the net income of the LLP should be divided so that Herron is to receive a 10% preferred return on her capital investment prior to any remaining income being divided equally among the partners. In addition, Moss and Kim have suggested that the operating agreement be written so that all matters are settled by majority vote, with each partner having a one-third voting interest in the LLP.

If you were providing Kelly Herron counsel, what might you suggest in forming the final agreement? Can you think of some decisions that should not be settled by majority rule? What are some factors that Herron should consider when deciding whether the division of income is fair?

SA 11-4
Negotiating income-sharing ratio

Group Project

Sixty-year-old Jasmine Howard retired from her computer consulting business in Toronto and moved to Halifax. There she met 27-year-old Dawn Patel, who had just graduated from Dalhousie University with an associate degree in computer science. Jasmine and Dawn formed a partnership called J&D Computer Consultants. Jasmine contributed $25,000 for startup costs and devoted one-half time to the business. Dawn devoted full time to the business. The monthly withdrawals were $2,000 for Jasmine and $4,000 for Dawn.

At the end of the first year of operations, the two partners disagreed on the division of net income. Jasmine reasoned that the division should be equal. Although she devoted only one-half time to the business, she contributed all of the startup funds. Dawn reasoned that the income-sharing ratio should be 2:1 in her favour because she devoted full time to the business and her monthly withdrawals were twice those of Jasmine.

1. Can you identify any flaws in the partners' reasoning regarding the income-sharing ratio?
2. Discuss some of the factors that should be considered when dividing income among partners.
3. What division of income would you recommend?

Corporations: Organization, Share Transactions, and Shareholders' Equity

Courtesy of Leon's Furniture Limited

LEON'S FURNITURE LIMITED

If you purchase a share from Leon's, you own a small interest in the company. You may request a Leon's share certificate as an indication of your ownership.

As you may know, Leon's is one of Canada's most successful home furnishings retailers. Leon's opened for business in 1909 with one store in Welland, Ontario. In 1969, Leon's incorporated, which means the business became a separate legal entity from its owners. The retailer's 1974 expansion into Laval, Quebec, added store number 10 and marked its first venture outside of Ontario. Leon's opened six new home furnishings superstores in 2011 for a total of 75 outlets located in every province except British Columbia, and more stores are planned for 2012. Leon's head office is located in Toronto, Ontario.

Purchasing a share from Leon's may be a great gift idea for the "hard-to-shop-for" person. However, a share certificate represents more than just a picture that you can frame. In fact, the share certificate is a document that reflects legal ownership of the future financial prospects of Leon's. In addition, if you are a shareholder, the share certificate represents your claim against the assets and earnings of the corporation.

If you are purchasing Leon's shares as an investment, you should analyze Leon's financial statements, management behaviour in the past, and management's plans for the future. For example, Leon's management is expecting increased sales as a result of the six new stores added in 2011. The company recognizes consumers' hesitancy to spend their hard-earned dollars on new home furnishings in a slow economy and plans to execute a strong marketing campaign. According to its 2011 annual report, included in Appendix B, Leon's plans to continue renovation and expansion throughout Canada and has four new stores already planned for 2012/13. Do these plans influence how much you would be willing to pay for Leon's shares? You might also want to know whether Leon's plans to pay cash dividends or whether management is considering issuing additional shares.

In this chapter, we describe and illustrate the nature of corporations, including the accounting for shares and dividends. This discussion will aid you in making decisions such as whether to buy Leon's shares.

After studying this chapter, you should be able to:

1 Describe the nature of the corporate form of organization.

Nature of a Corporation	Characteristics of a Corporation	
	Comparing Proprietorships, Partnerships, and Corporations	EXAMPLE EXERCISE 12-1 (page 616)
	Forming a Corporation	

2 Describe the three main sources of shareholders' equity.

Shareholders' Equity	Retained Earnings	
	Accumulated Other Comprehensive Income	EXAMPLE EXERCISE 12-2 (page 620)

3 Describe and illustrate the characteristics of shares, classes of shares, and entries for issuing shares.

Contributed Capital	Characteristics of Shares	
	Classes of Shares	
	Issuing Shares for Cash	
	Issuing Shares for Other Assets	EXAMPLE EXERCISE 12-3 (page 623)

4 Describe and illustrate the accounting for cash dividends.

Accounting for Cash Dividends	Cash Dividends	EXAMPLE EXERCISE 12-4 (page 625)
	Dividend Distribution	EXAMPLE EXERCISE 12-5 (page 628)

5 Describe and illustrate the reporting of shareholders' equity.

Reporting Shareholders' Equity	Shareholders' Equity in the Balance Sheet	EXAMPLE EXERCISE 12-6 (page 629)
	Reporting Shareholders' Equity, Using IFRS	EXAMPLE EXERCISE 12-7 (page 630)
	Reporting Retained Earnings, Using ASPE	EXAMPLE EXERCISE 12-8 (page 631)
	Reporting Shareholders' Equity for Morning Java	
	Financial Analysis and Interpretation	EXAMPLE EXERCISE 12-9 (page 634)

For the chapter *At a Glance*, turn to page 635.

Nature of a Corporation

Describe the nature of the corporate form of organization.

Most large businesses are organized as corporations. As a result, corporations generate more than 70% of the total business dollars in Canada. Although we tend to think of corporations as large businesses, many small businesses in Canada are incorporated. Most small corporations are private corporations, owned by only a few **shareholders**, who sell their **shares**, their units of ownership interest, privately.

Characteristics of a Corporation

A corporation is a form of legal entity that is distinct and separate from the individuals who create and operate it. As a legal entity, a corporation may acquire, own, and dispose of property in its own name. It may also incur debts and enter into contracts. Most importantly, a corporation can sell shares of ownership without affecting the corporation's operations or continued existence.

Characteristics of a corporation include the following:

1. Ease of formation: *Complex.* A corporation requires an agreement among the owners, who are called shareholders. The agreement, called the articles of incorporation, includes information regarding the rules and regulations, types of shares to be issued, and the rights of each type of share. A lawyer is normally consulted when forming a corporation.

2. Legal liability: *Limited.* The shareholders have limited liability because the creditors of a corporation usually may not go beyond the assets of the corporation to satisfy their claims. Thus, the financial loss that a shareholder may suffer is limited to the amount invested.

3. Taxation: *Taxable.* The corporation is taxable as a separate identity. A separate corporate tax return is filed.

4. Life of entity: *Unlimited.* The corporation has an unlimited life because it has a separate legal existence from its owners.

5. Access to capital: *Unlimited.* The corporation form is designed to make it easy to raise capital, through the issuance of ownership shares.

6. Ease of transfer of ownership: *Simple.* The shareholders of a public company can transfer their shares to other shareholders through stock markets, such as the Toronto Stock Exchange. Shareholders of a private company, however, may have a more difficult time finding a buyer for their shares since there is no organized market.

7. Form of payment to owners: *Dividends.* The shareholders, who are the owners, receive distributions of the corporation's earnings, known as dividends.

Comparing Proprietorships, Partnerships, and Corporations

Exhibit 1 summarizes the characteristics of proprietorships discussed in the early chapters, partnerships discussed in Chapter 11, and corporations.

One of the distinguishing characteristics of a corporation is that, unlike proprietorships and partnerships, a corporation is subject to taxes. Tax is charged at two levels: at the corporate level on income and at the individual level on dividends received by shareholders. Although the two taxes appear to result in double taxation, dividends

Exhibit 1

Characteristics of Proprietorships, General Partnerships, and Corporations

Organizational Form	Ease of Formation	Legal Liability	Taxation	Life of Entity	Access to Capital	Ease of Transfer of Ownership	Form of Payment to Owners
Proprietorship	Simple	No limitation	Nontaxable entity (owner pays personal tax on earnings)	Limited	Limited	Difficult	Withdrawals
General Partnership	Moderate	No limitation	Nontaxable entity (owners pay personal tax on earnings)	Limited	Limited	Moderate	Withdrawals
Corporation	Complex	Limited liability	Taxable (corporation pays corporate tax on earnings)	Unlimited	Unlimited	Simple	Dividends

presently receive a dividend tax credit, which essentially removes the impact of double taxation.

Canada Revenue Agency (CRA) requires tax to be paid on a calendar-year basis for proprietorships and partnerships, so these business entities typically use December 31 as their year-end. Corporations are not restricted by CRA and can choose any date for their year-end, often selecting a year-end during a less busy time of year.

The shareholders control a corporation by electing a *board of directors*. This board meets periodically to establish corporate policies. It also selects the chief executive officer (CEO) and other officers to manage the corporation's day-to-day affairs. Exhibit 2 shows the organizational structure of a corporation.

Exhibit 2

Organizational Structure of a Corporation

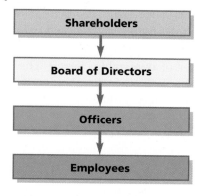

INTEGRITY, OBJECTIVITY, AND ETHICS IN BUSINESS

THE RESPONSIBLE BOARD

Accounting scandals, such as those involving Enron, WorldCom, and Nortel, have highlighted the roles of boards of directors in executing their responsibilities. For example, 18 of Enron's former directors and their insurance providers have settled shareholder litigation for $168 million, of which $13 million is to come from the directors' personal assets. Board members are now on notice that their directorship responsibilities are being taken seriously by shareholders. The directorship responsibilities of board members are vital to the success of the business and, if not fulfilled, create potential liabilities for the board of directors.

EXAMPLE EXERCISE 12-1 Comparing Proprietorships, General Partnerships, and Corporations

1. Rex Luther operates Rex Luther Custom Upholstery and claims the business income on his personal income tax return.
2. Sally Somers and Tom Thompson operate ST Home Renovations Ltd. and receive annual dividends from the company.
3. Kas Masterson and Chad Broker are fully liable for the debt of We Paint While You Relax.
4. Crompton's Plumbing Ltd. has an unlimited life.

For each scenario above, state whether the business is a sole proprietorship, a general partnership, or a corporation.

FOLLOW MY EXAMPLE 12-1

1. Sole proprietorship—One owner claims the business income personally.
2. Corporation—All owners receive dividends.
3. General partnership—Both owners are fully liable for the company's debt.
4. Corporation—The company has an unlimited life.

For Practice: PE 12-1

Forming a Corporation

Articles of incorporation are required to form a corporation. They are filed in each of the provinces and territories where the company plans to conduct business, and may be filed federally if the corporation intends to operate in most of the provinces and territories. The **articles of incorporation** contain the rules and regulations that govern the conduct of the company shareholders and directors. They also state the number and type of shares that a corporation is authorized to issue.

Costs may be incurred in organizing a corporation. These costs include legal fees, taxes, licence fees, and promotional costs. These costs are expensed.

Note: Corporations have a separate legal existence, transferable units of ownership, and limited shareholder liability.

Forming a Corporation—Illustration

To illustrate, assume that John Daly and Jennifer Fernwood decide to establish a corporation for their computer animation company, DFI Ltd. They have been running their business as a partnership but want to expand. Incorporating will allow them to attract capital through sales of shares. They decide to use August 31 as their year-end. On September 1, 2015, John and Jennifer pay $1,200 to a lawyer who helps them to complete the incorporation process, recording the transaction as follows:

2015					
Sep.	1	Legal Expenses		1,200	
		Cash			1,200
		Paid legal fees of organizing the corporation.			

CRITICAL THINKING

Why might a sole proprietor or partnership choose to incorporate? Is there any downside to incorporating?

Incorporating definitely incurs a cost. First is the initial cost to incorporate, followed by the costs of additional paperwork and annual filings. Incorporating reduces the owners' personal liability, can make it easier to secure financing, and typically makes it easier to sell the business. A sole proprietor or partnership needs to decide whether these expected benefits of incorporating outweigh the costs.

INTEGRITY, OBJECTIVITY, AND ETHICS IN BUSINESS

NOT-FOR-PROFIT, OR NOT?

Corporations can be formed for not-for-profit purposes by making a request to Canada Revenue Agency. These corporations, such as Big Brothers, Big Sisters, and The Salvation Army, may still engage in activities that result in income or profit, but these profits are exempt from tax. Forming businesses inside a tax-exempt organization that competes with profit-making (and hence, tax-paying) businesses is very controversial. For example, should the local YMCA receive a tax exemption for providing services similar to those of a local health club business?

2 Shareholders' Equity

Describe the three main sources of shareholders' equity.

In proprietorships and partnerships, the equity section of the balance sheet is called *owner's equity,* or *partners' equity,* and typically includes capital accounts only. The sole proprietorship NetSolutions, for example, included the capital account *Chris Clark, Capital.* The equity section in a corporation is called **shareholders' equity**. For corporations, the equity section is divided into, and reported by, its three main sources:

1. Capital contributed to the corporation by the shareholders, called **contributed capital**, *paid-in capital,* or *share capital.* When shares are sold by the corporation, the amount received is reported as contributed capital.

2. Net income retained in the business, called **retained earnings**.

3. Accumulated gains or losses resulting from transactions such as revaluation of assets to fair value, called **accumulated other comprehensive income.**

Exhibit 3 contrasts the Owner's Equity section of NetSolutions' balance sheet at December 31, 2015, from Chapter 5, with the Shareholders' Equity section of DFI Ltd., a corporation, at August 31, 2016. The differences on the balance sheet are mainly in the equity section.

Retained Earnings

The Retained Earnings balance is a corporation's cumulative net income that has not been distributed as dividends. **Dividends** are distributions of a corporation's earnings to shareholders, similar to *withdrawals for sole proprietorships or partnerships*. Detailed accounting for dividend distributions is discussed later in this chapter and again in Chapter 13. Briefly, dividends are recorded with a debit, either directly to the retained earnings account or to a temporary account called Dividends.

Closing Entries for a Corporation   As discussed in Chapter 4, some sole proprietorships close their revenues and expenses directly to the capital account. A corporation using this method would close its revenues and expenses directly to Retained Earnings.

Exhibit 3

NetSolutions
Balance Sheet (Partial)
December 31, 2015

Owner's Equity

Chris Clark, Capital	211,200
Total liabilities and owner's equity	$261,560

DFI Ltd.
Balance Sheet (Partial)
August 31, 2016

Shareholders' Equity

Contributed capital:		
$1.25 preferred shares, 500,000 authorized,		
30,000 issued and outstanding	$1,200,000	
Common shares, unlimited authorized,		
40,000 issued and outstanding	420,000	
Total contributed capital	1,620,000	
Retained earnings	154,400	
Accumulated other comprehensive income	27,000	
Total shareholders' equity		1,801,400
Total liabilities and shareholders' equity		$2,222,571

For corporations that use an income summary account, the net income or loss for a period and the dividends recorded in the dividends account are transferred to Retained Earnings through the closing entries. To illustrate, assume DFI Ltd. uses an income summary account, earned net income of $203,900 in its first year of operation, and paid out $49,500 in dividends to shareholders during the first year.

DFI Ltd. would close sales and expenses to Income Summary, using the same method covered in Chapter 4, leaving a credit balance in Income Summary of $203,900. The Income Summary is transferred to Retained Earnings as follows:

2016				
Aug.	31	Income Summary	203,900	
		Retained Earnings		203,900
		Closed income summary account to retained earnings.		

If the retained earnings account is used to record dividends, no additional entry is necessary. If the dividends account is used during the year, it will have a debit balance. DFI Ltd. would transfer the balance in the dividends account to Retained Earnings as follows:

2016				
Aug.	31	Retained Earnings	49,500	
		Dividends		49,500
		Closed dividends account to retained earnings.		

Since this is the first year of operations for DFI Ltd., the ending balance in the retained earnings account is a credit of $154,400 ($203,900 − $49,500).

Most companies generate net income. In addition, most companies do not pay out all of their net income in dividends. As a result, Retained Earnings normally has a credit balance. However, in some cases, a debit balance in Retained Earnings may occur. A debit balance in Retained Earnings is called a **deficit**. Such a balance often results from cumulated net losses. In the Shareholders' Equity section, a deficit is deducted from contributed capital in determining total shareholders' equity.

The balance of Retained Earnings does not represent surplus cash or cash left over for dividends. This is because cash generated from operations is normally used to improve or expand operations. As cash is used, its balance decreases; however, the balance of the retained earnings account is unaffected. As a result, over time the balance in Retained Earnings becomes less and less related to the balance of Cash.

Accumulated Other Comprehensive Income

Accumulated other comprehensive income is an equity account that corporations reporting under International Financial Reporting Standards (IFRS) use to track increases and decreases in other comprehensive income. Gains or losses resulting from transactions such as revaluation of assets to fair value are not recognized in net income or net loss because the transaction to generate the gain or loss has yet to occur. Once the transaction occurs, when the assets are sold, any gain or loss is recognized in income. In the meantime, the temporary gain or loss from revaluation will be recorded as **other comprehensive income** and closed to Accumulated Other Comprehensive Income at year-end. Other comprehensive income originated with the adoption of IFRS and does not exist for Accounting Standards for Private Enterprises (ASPE). This topic will be discussed further, with examples, in Chapter 15. Contributed capital will be discussed further in the next section.

Other comprehensive income is closed to Accumulated Other Comprehensive Income through the year-end closing entries. Assume DFI Ltd. recorded an unrealized gain on available-for-sale investments of $27,000 that would be included in other comprehensive income. DFI Ltd. would close its other comprehensive income account at year-end with the following entry:

2016 Aug.	31	Other Comprehensive Income	27,000	
		Accumulated Other Comprehensive Income		27,000
		Closed other comprehensive income to accumulated other comprehensive income.		

EXAMPLE EXERCISE 12-2 Closing Entries for Corporations   2

Barkley Books Corp. is a retailer of new and used books. During 2015, Barkley Books earned $239,000 in revenue, incurred $120,000 of expenses, and paid $40,000 in dividends. Barkley Books recorded a gain in other comprehensive income of $32,000 as a result of revaluation of assets.

Journalize the closing entries for Barkley Books Corp. on December 31, 2015, assuming it uses an income summary and a dividends account.

FOLLOW MY EXAMPLE 12-2

Dec. 31	Income Summary	119,000	
	Retained Earnings		119,000
	Closed the income summary account.		
Dec. 31	Retained Earnings	40,000	
	Dividends		40,000
	Closed the dividends account.		
Dec. 31	Other Comprehensive Income	32,000	
	Accumulated Other Comprehensive Income		32,000
	Closed the other comprehensive income account.		

For Practice: PE 12-2

---

3   # Contributed Capital

Describe and illustrate the characteristics of shares, classes of shares, and entries for issuing shares.

The three main sources of shareholders' equity are contributed capital, retained earnings, and, for businesses reporting under IFRS, accumulated other comprehensive income. The main source of contributed capital is from issuing shares.

Characteristics of Shares

The number of shares that a corporation is authorized to issue is stated in its articles of incorporation. The term *issued* refers to the shares distributed to the shareholders. A corporation may re-acquire some of the shares that it has issued. The shares remaining in the hands of shareholders are called **outstanding shares**. Often, the number of shares issued and outstanding is identical, and so the shares in the hands of shareholders are called **issued and outstanding shares**. The articles of incorporation for many Canadian companies allow them to issue an unlimited number of common shares.

Upon request, corporations may issue share certificates to shareholders to document their ownership. Printed on a share certificate are the name of the company, the name of the shareholder, and the number of shares owned. The share certificate may also indicate an initial nominal dollar amount assigned to each share, called **par** value. Because the Canada Business Corporations Act and most provincial and territorial acts require shares to be issued without par value, par value shares will not be dealt with in this text. Some corporations have stopped issuing share certificates except on special request. In these cases, the corporation maintains records of ownership.

Classes of Shares

Common Shares

Every corporation is required to have at least one class of **common shares**, which includes voting rights. When a corporation has more than one class of common shares, they are listed separately, such as Class A common shares and Class B common shares. Each common share in a specified class has equal rights. For example, if Jim owns 10 Class A shares of a corporation and Sandra owns 30 Class A shares of the same corporation, Jim has 10 votes and Sandra has 30 votes.

Some corporations establish a share structure that allows different classes of common shares to have different voting rights. Danier Leather, for example, has two classes of common shares: multiple and subordinate. The multiple-voting shareholders are entitled to 10 votes for every share they own, while the subordinate voting shareholders are entitled to one vote per share.

Common shareholders are considered owners of the corporation. A shareholder who owns only one share is still considered an owner of the corporation. If Sandra owns 30 shares and the corporation has 40 shares issued in total, Sandra owns 75% (30/40) of the corporation and has control over any company decisions or policies. Any shareholder owning 50% plus one share of all outstanding shares has more voting rights than all the other shareholders combined, giving that shareholder full control over all corporate decisions.

Common shares have a right to receive dividends when they are declared, and they have a preemptive right when new common shares are issued. The **preemptive right** allows a shareholder to maintain a proportionate share of the new share issue. To illustrate, if Jim owns 25% (10/40) of the current shares outstanding, his preemptive rights allows him an option to purchase 25% of the new share issue. If Jim chooses not to purchase more shares, those shares can then be sold to others.

Share rights normally vary with the class of share. When only one class of share is issued, it is called common shares. Each common share has equal rights. Common shares typically offer the right to vote on matters concerning the corporation and the right to share in distributions of earnings.

Although common shareholders also technically have the right to share in assets on liquidation, bondholders, secured creditors, and preferred shareholders are paid first. For this reason, common shareholders are considered to have a *residual interest* in the company, which means they receive what remains after others have been paid.

Preferred Shares

A corporation may also issue one or more classes of share with various preference rights, such as preference to dividends, called **preferred shares**. The dividend rights of preferred shares are normally stated as dollars per share. For example, a preferred share with a $4 per share annual dividend would be described as $4 Preferred shares, or Preferred shares, $4. When dividends are declared, the owner of 55 shares would receive $220 (55 shares × $4).

Note: The two primary classes of contributed capital are common shares and preferred shares.

Because preferred shareholders have first rights (preference) to any dividends, they have a greater chance of receiving dividends than common shareholders. However, because dividends are normally based on earnings, a corporation cannot guarantee dividends even to preferred shareholders. Preferred shares are also often non-voting shares.

In addition to the above preferences, preferred shares may be given preferences to assets if the corporation goes out of business and is liquidated. However, the claims of creditors must be satisfied first. Preferred shareholders are next in line to receive any remaining assets, followed by the common shareholders.

Special Share Features

Other features that may be attached to preferred shares include cumulative dividends, participating dividends, the ability to convert, and the ability to call. Cumulative shares will be discussed later in the chapter. Owners of **participating preferred shares** have the right to receive their dividend preference, and they share with the common shareholders in any excess dividends declared. **Convertible preferred shares** may be converted to common shares at the option of the purchasing investor. These shares would be traded for the corporation's common shares at the conversion rate stated in the share issue. **Callable preferred shares,** also referred to as *redeemable preferred shares*, may be called in and cancelled at the option of the issuing corporation. The corporation will pay the shareholders for the shares called in at a call price stated in the share issue.

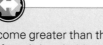

CRITICAL THINKING

Why might preferred shareholders choose to convert their shares to common?

Preferred dividend rates are fixed when the shares are initially issued. At the time of issue, these diviend rates may be higher than the rates the common shareholders are receiving. As the business grows and becomes prosperous, the common dividend rate may become greater than the preferred dividend rate, enticing preferred shareholders to convert their shares to common shares. Also, because common shareholders hold the voting rights in a corporation, preferred shareholders who want to have more input into the management of the corporation may choose to convert their preferred shares to common shares.

Issuing Shares for Cash

A separate account is used for recording the amount of each share class issued to investors in a corporation. For example, assume that DFI Ltd.'s articles of incorporation allow it to issue up to 500,000 $1.25 preferred shares and an unlimited number of common shares. On September 28, 2015, DFI Ltd. sold 30,000 $1.25 preferred shares for $40 per share and 30,000 common shares for $10 per share.

The entry to record the sale of shares is as follows:

2015				
Sep.	28	Cash	1,500,000	
		Preferred Shares		1,200,000*
		Common Shares		300,000**
		Sold 30,000 preferred and 30,000 common shares.		
		*(30,000 × $40)		
		**(30,000 × $10)		

This entry is recorded when the shares are initially issued by the corporation. The shares may be issued directly to the shareholders, or they may be sold to an independent brokerage house or investment banker, which then sells them to the public. Private corporations can control who purchases (or sells) their shares through a restriction of share transfer in the articles of incorporation, but public corporations cannot enforce the same control. After the shares are initially sold, they may continue to be traded in the marketplace. Shares of public corporations are traded through stock markets such as the Toronto Stock Exchange. Since the corporation is not involved in the subsequent trading of its shares in the marketplace, these trades do not affect the company's equity.

The market price of the shares is determined by investors, not by the company. Based on the company's past performance and plans for the future, investors determine a reasonable price for the shares.

Issuing Shares for Other Assets

When shares are issued in exchange for assets other than cash, such as land, buildings, and equipment, the assets acquired should be recorded at their fair market value. Sometimes the market value is difficult to confirm; in such cases, the fair market price of the shares issued is used. By choosing the more reliable value, the corporation ensures the transaction meets the qualitative characteristics of verifiability and reliability.

To illustrate, assume that on October 15, 2015, DFI Ltd. acquired land with a fair market value that cannot be determined. In exchange, DFI Ltd. issued 10,000 common shares. If the shares have a market price of $12 per share, the transaction is recorded as follows:

2015				
Oct.	15	Land	120,000	
		Common Shares		120,000
		Issued 10,000 common shares, valued at $12 per share, for land.		

EXAMPLE EXERCISE 12-3 Entries for Issuing Shares ③

On February 6, Sampson Corporation issued for cash 25,000 common shares at $40 per share. On March 21, Sampson issued 2,000 $3 preferred shares for $62 per share. On April 3, Sampson issued 15,000 common shares in exchange for land with a fair market value of $720,000.

Journalize the entries to record the February 6, March 21, and April 3 transactions.

FOLLOW MY EXAMPLE 12-3

Feb.	6	Cash	1,000,000	
		Common Shares		1,000,000
		Issued 25,000 common shares at $40 per share.		
Mar.	21	Cash	124,000	
		Preferred Shares		124,000
		Issued 2,000 preferred shares at $62 per share.		
Apr.	3	Land	720,000	
		Common Shares		720,000
		Issued 15,000 common shares in exchange for land.		

For Practice: PE 12-3

Accounting for Cash Dividends

Describe and illustrate the accounting for cash dividends.

When a board of directors declares a cash dividend, it authorizes the distribution of cash to shareholders. In order to distribute dividends, financial statements, and other reports, a corporation must keep track of its shareholders. Large public corporations normally use a financial services company for this purpose. In such cases, the financial institution is referred to as a *transfer agent* or *registrar*.

Cash Dividends

A cash distribution of earnings by a corporation to its shareholders is a **cash dividend**. Although dividends may be paid in other assets, cash dividends are the most common.

Three conditions for a cash dividend are as follows:

1. Sufficient retained earnings
2. Sufficient cash
3. Formal action by the board of directors

There must be a sufficient (large enough) balance in Retained Earnings to declare a cash dividend. That is, the balance of Retained Earnings must be large enough that the dividend does not create a deficit (debit balance) in the retained earnings account. However, a large Retained Earnings balance does not necessarily mean that cash is available to pay dividends because the balances of Cash and Retained Earnings are unrelated.

Even if there are sufficient retained earnings and cash, a corporation's board of directors is not required to pay dividends. For example, a corporation may be planning for a large expansion in the near future and thus may choose to forego paying a dividend, preferring instead to reserve cash for the expansion. Nevertheless, many corporations pay quarterly cash dividends to ensure their shares continue to be attractive to investors. *Special* or *extra* dividends may also be paid when a corporation experiences higher-than-normal profits.

Three dates included in a dividend announcement are as follows:

1. Date of declaration
2. Date of record
3. Date of payment

The **date of declaration** is the date the board of directors formally authorizes the payment of the dividend. On this date, the corporation incurs the liability to pay the amount of the dividend.

The **date of record** is the date the corporation uses to determine which shareholders will receive the dividend. During the period of time between the date of declaration and the date of record, the share price is quoted as selling *cum-dividends*. This means that share purchases settled before the date of record will receive the dividend.[1]

The **date of payment** is the date the corporation will pay the dividend to the shareholders who owned the shares on the date of record. During the period of time between the record date and the payment date, the share price is quoted as selling *ex-dividends*. This means that since the date of record has passed, any new investors will not receive the dividend.

As mentioned earlier, two options exist when recording the dividend on the date of declaration. One option is to debit the cash dividends account, allowing the corporation to easily track the dividends paid during the year. The second option is to record the debit directly to the retained earnings account since dividends reduce the retained earnings of the corporation.

To illustrate, assume that on March 1, 2016, DFI Ltd. declares the cash dividends shown below with a date of record of April 10 and a date of payment of May 2.

	Dividend per Share	Total Dividends
Preferred shares, 30,000 shares outstanding	$1.25	$37,500
Common shares, 40,000 shares outstanding	$0.30	12,000
Total		$49,500

On March 1, the declaration date, DFI Ltd. records the following entry:

2016					
Mar.	1	Retained Earnings (or Cash Dividends)		49,500	
		Dividends Payable—Preferred			37,500
		Dividends Payable—Common			12,000
		Declared cash dividends.			

On April 10, the date of record, no entry is necessary. This date merely determines which shareholders will receive the dividends.

On May 2, the date of payment, DFI Ltd. records the payment of the dividends as follows:

2016					
May	2	Dividends Payable—Preferred		37,500	
		Dividends Payable—Common		12,000	
		Cash			49,500
		Paid cash dividends.			

---

1 Share transactions take three days to settle so dividends on shares traded 1 or 2 business days prior to the date of record will be paid to the seller of the shares.

If the cash dividends have not been paid by the end of the period, Dividends Payable will be reported on the balance sheet as a current liability. If the cash dividend account is used, a closing entry is required at year-end to close cash dividends to retained earnings, shown earlier in the chapter.

EXAMPLE EXERCISE 12-4 Entries for Cash Dividends　　　　　　　　　　　　④

The important dates related to a cash dividend of $62,000 on a corporation's common shares are June 20, July 15, and August 1. Journalize the entries required on each date.

FOLLOW MY EXAMPLE 12-4

Jun.	20	Retained Earnings (or Cash Dividends)	62,000	
		Dividends Payable		62,000
		Declared cash dividends.		
Jul.	15	No entry required.		
Aug.	1	Dividends Payable..	62,000	
		Cash..		62,000
		Paid cash dividends.		

For Practice: PE 12-4

DIVIDEND DATES

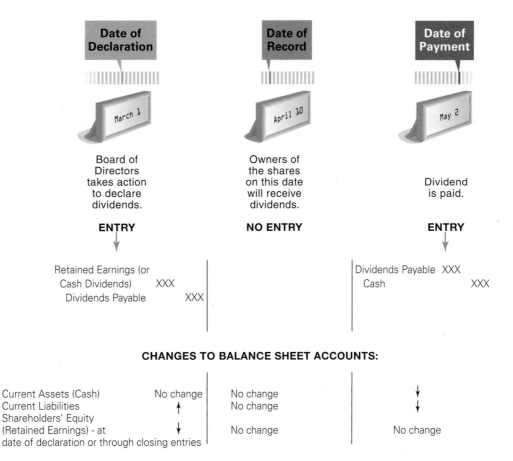

	Date of Declaration	Date of Record	Date of Payment
	March 1	April 10	May 2
	Board of Directors takes action to declare dividends.	Owners of the shares on this date will receive dividends.	Dividend is paid.
	ENTRY	**NO ENTRY**	**ENTRY**

| Retained Earnings (or Cash Dividends)　XXX | | Dividends Payable　XXX | |
| Dividends Payable　XXX | | Cash　XXX | |

CHANGES TO BALANCE SHEET ACCOUNTS:

	Declaration	Record	Payment
Current Assets (Cash)	No change	No change	↓
Current Liabilities	↑	No change	↓
Shareholders' Equity (Retained Earnings) - at date of declaration or through closing entries	↓	No change	No change

MID-CHAPTER ILLUSTRATIVE PROBLEM

In March 2014, Bonnie Enterprises Inc. received its approved articles of incorporation granting the right to issue an unlimited number of common shares and 10,000, $3 preferred shares. Bonnie Enterprises uses a cash dividends account. During the fiscal year ended February 28, 2015, the following transactions occurred:

2014

Mar. 19   Issued 45,000 common shares at $2 per share.

19   Gave the corporation's promoters 3,000 common shares for their services in getting the corporation organized. The promoters valued the services at $6,500.

Aug. 31   Exchanged 50,000 common shares for machinery with a fair market value of $87,500 and a book value of $60,000.

Dec. 15   Issued 2,000 preferred shares at $70 per share.

30   Declared a dividend of $15,000, with a record date of January 30, payable on February 28, 2015.

2015

Jan. 30   Record date of dividends payable.

Feb. 28   Payment date of dividends.

28   Closed the Income Summary account for net income of $55,000 for the year.

28   Closed the Cash Dividends account.

Instructions

Prepare journal entries to record the selected transactions.

MID-CHAPTER ILLUSTRATIVE SOLUTION

2014				
Mar.	19	Cash	90,000	
		Common Shares		90,000
		Issued 45,000 common shares for cash, $2 per share.		
	19	Promotion Expenses	6,000*	
		Common Shares		6,000
		Issued 3,000 common shares in exchange for promotions. *The more verifiable amount is the common share value, since they traded today at $2 each.		
Aug.	31	Machinery	87,500	
		Common Shares		87,500
		Issued 50,000 common shares in exchange for machinery.		
Dec.	15	Cash	140,000	
		Preferred Shares		140,000
		Issued 2,000 preferred shares at $70 per share.		
	30	Cash Dividends	15,000	
		Dividends Payable—Preferred (2,000 × $3)		6,000
		Dividends Payable—Common ($15,000 − $6,000)		9,000
		Declared cash dividends.		
2015				
Jan.	30	No entry required.		
Feb.	28	Dividends Payable—Preferred	6,000	
		Dividends Payable—Common	9,000	
		Cash		15,000
		Paid cash dividends.		

(continued)

Feb.	28	Income Summary	55,000	
		Retained Earnings		55,000
		Closed income summary account.		
	28	Retained Earnings	15,000	
		Cash Dividends		15,000
		Closed cash dividends account.		

Dividend Distribution

As mentioned earlier in the chapter, the payment of dividends is authorized by the corporation's board of directors. When authorized, the directors are said to have *declared* a dividend.

The board of directors is not required to declare dividends. If the retained earnings account is in a deficit position, the board of directors cannot declare a dividend. If the corporation is planning a large expansion, it may choose to keep the cash in the business instead of paying it out to the shareholders. When the board of directors declares a cash dividend, the preferred shareholders will receive their dividend entitlement first. The common shareholders will receive only those dividends declared in excess of the preferred dividend entitlement.

Some preferred shares have a cumulative preference attached to them. Owners of **cumulative preferred shares** have a right to receive regular dividends that were not declared in prior years. Cumulative preferred share dividends that have not been declared are said to be **in arrears**. Preferred dividends in arrears must be paid before any common share dividends are paid. Dividends in arrears are not considered a liability to the corporation because the issuance of dividends is at the discretion of the board of directors. Instead, dividends in arrears are normally disclosed in the notes to the financial statements. Dividends are only a liability when declared. If dividends are not declared, noncumulative preferred shares and common shares have no claim to future dividend declarations.

To illustrate, assume that a corporation, organized on January 1, 2013, issued the following shares during its first year:

1,000 $4 cumulative preferred shares

4,000 common shares

Also assume that the corporation paid no dividends in 2013 and 2014. In 2015, the corporation paid dividends of $22,000.

The owners of the cumulative preferred shares are entitled to receive $4,000 (1,000 shares × $4) each year in dividends. Exhibit 4 shows how the $22,000 of dividends paid in 2015 is distributed between the preferred and common shareholders.

Exhibit 4

Dividends to Cumulative Preferred Shares

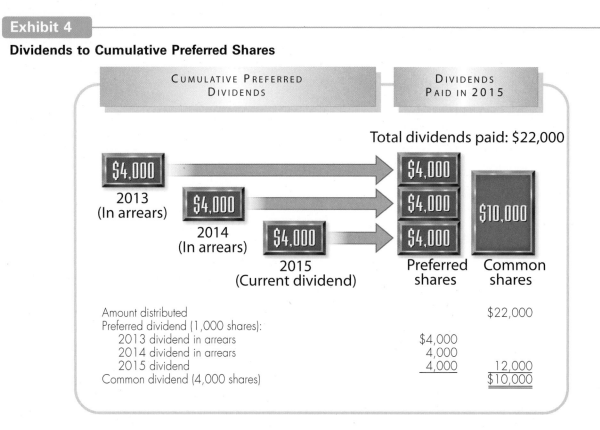

		Preferred shares	Common shares
Amount distributed			$22,000
Preferred dividend (1,000 shares):			
2013 dividend in arrears		$4,000	
2014 dividend in arrears		4,000	
2015 dividend		4,000	12,000
Common dividend (4,000 shares)			$10,000

EXAMPLE EXERCISE 12-5   Dividends Distribution   ④

Sandpiper Company has 20,000 shares of $1 cumulative preferred shares and 100,000 common shares. The following amounts were distributed as dividends:

Year 1	$10,000
Year 2	45,000
Year 3	80,000

Determine the distribution of dividends.

FOLLOW MY EXAMPLE 12-5

Cumulative preferred shares are entitled to receive $20,000 (20,000 shares × $1) annually.

	Year 1	Year 2	Year 3
Amount distributed	$10,000	$45,000	$80,000
Preferred dividend (20,000 shares)	10,000	30,000*	20,000
Common dividend (100,000 shares)	$ 0	$15,000	$60,000
*($10,000 arrears + $20,000 current)			

For Practice: PE 12-5

⑤ **Reporting Shareholders' Equity**

Describe and illustrate the reporting of shareholders' equity.

As mentioned in Chapter 1, publicly accountable enterprises prepare their financial statements using IFRS; private enterprises use either IFRS or ASPE. Similar to proprietorships and partnerships, corporations adopting ASPE compile four statements: the income statement, the balance sheet, the cash flow statement, and the statement of retained earnings. Corporations adopting IFRS also produce these statements; however, they use different titles. The income statement is referred to as a Statement of

Comprehensive Income, the balance sheet is called the Statement of Financial Position, the statement of retained earnings is a Statement of Changes in Equity, and the cash flow statement is the Statement of Cash Flows. Private enterprises using ASPE may also prepare a statement of changes in equity rather than, or in addition to, a statement of retained earnings.

Shareholders' Equity in the Balance Sheet

An example of the Shareholders' Equity section of a balance sheet is shown in Exhibit 3 on page 618. The following conventions are used when completing the equity section:

1. Shares are listed in order of preference in terms of receipt of dividends: preferred shareholders are listed before common shareholders because they are paid their dividends before the common shareholders are paid.
2. The rights and privileges of the various classes of shares should be reported. Examples include the number of shares authorized, the number of shares issued and outstanding, dividend and liquidation preferences, conversion rights, and redemption rights. Such information may be disclosed on the face of the balance sheet or in the notes to the financial statements.

Significant changes in shareholders' equity during a period may also be presented in a statement of changes in equity or in the notes to the financial statements.

EXAMPLE EXERCISE 12-6 Reporting Shareholders' Equity   5

Using the following accounts and balances, prepare the shareholders' equity section of the balance sheet for Forward Corporation's March 31, 2015, year-end.

Common shares (30,000 issued, unlimited authorized)	$ 1,500,000
$2.25 preferred shares (10,000 issued, 50,000 authorized)	1,000,000
Retained earnings	4,395,000
Dividends declared and paid	250,000
Total assets	10,000,000

FOLLOW MY EXAMPLE 12-6

Forward Corporation
Balance Sheet (partial)
March 31, 2015

Shareholders' Equity

Contributed Capital:	
$2.25 preferred shares, 50,000 authorized, 10,000 issued and outstanding	$ 1,000,000
Common shares, unlimited authorized, 30,000 issued and outstanding	1,500,000
Total contributed capital	2,500,000
Retained earnings	4,395,000
Total shareholders' equity	6,895,000
Total liabilities and shareholders' equity	$10,000,000

For Practice: PE 12-6

Reporting Shareholders' Equity, Using IFRS

For corporations using IFRS, a **statement of changes in equity** is required. This statement is normally prepared in a column format with separate columns for major shareholders' equity classifications. Changes in shares, retained earnings, and accumulated other comprehensive income are described in the left-hand column. Exhibit 5 illustrates a statement of changes in equity for DJK Toys Ltd., a publicly traded corporation.

Exhibit 5

Statement of Changes in Equity

	Preferred Shares	Common Shares	Retained Earnings	Accum. Other Comprehensive Income	Total
DJK Toys Ltd.					
Statement of Changes in Equity					
For the Year Ended August 31, 2016					
Balance, Sept. 1, 2015	$1,710,000	$25,140,000	$11,945,000	$1,008,000	$39,803,000
Net income			7,580,400		7,580,400
Dividends on preferred shares			(119,700)		(119,700)
Dividends on common shares			(1,508,400)		(1,508,400)
Unrealized gain on available-for-sale investments				146,300	146,300
Balance, Aug. 31, 2016	$1,710,000	$25,140,000	$17,897,300	$1,154,300	$45,901,600

EXAMPLE EXERCISE 12-7 Statement of Changes in Equity   5

Mark's Construction Ltd. has a December 31 year-end, and it began 2015 with the following balances:

Accumulated Other Comprehensive Income	$750,500
Common Shares	832,000
Retained Earnings	456,789
Preferred Shares	381,658

During the year, the company issued 20,000 preferred shares at $17 per share and 10,000 common shares at $8 per share. The net income for the year was $924,600, and the company paid out $150,000 in preferred dividends and $70,000 in common dividends. There were no changes to accumulated other comprehensive income.

Prepare a statement of changes in equity for Mark's Construction Ltd. for 2015.

FOLLOW MY EXAMPLE 12-7

Mark's Construction Ltd.
Statement of Changes in Equity
For the Year Ended December 31, 2015

	Preferred Shares	Common Shares	Retained Earnings	Accumulated Other Comprehensive Income	Total
Balance, January 1, 2015	$381,658	$832,000	$ 456,789	$750,500	$2,420,947
Net income			924,600		924,600
Issuance of shares	340,000	80,000			420,000
Dividends on preferred shares			(150,000)		(150,000)
Dividends on common shares			(70,000)		(70,000)
Balance, December 31, 2015	$721,658	$912,000	$1,161,389	$750,500	$3,545,547

For Practice: PE 12-7

Reporting Retained Earnings, Using ASPE

Changes in retained earnings for private corporations adopting ASPE are reported using any one of the following:

1. A separate statement of retained earnings
2. A combined income and retained earnings statement
3. A statement of changes in equity

Changes in retained earnings may be reported in a separate statement of retained earnings. When a separate **statement of retained earnings** is prepared, the beginning balance of retained earnings is reported. The net income is then added (or net loss is subtracted), and any dividends are subtracted to arrive at the ending balance of retained earnings for the period.

To illustrate, a statement of retained earnings for Morning Java, a private enterprise, is shown in Exhibit 6.

Exhibit 6

Statement of Retained Earnings

Morning Java
Statement of Retained Earnings
For the Year Ended December 31, 2015

Retained earnings, January 1, 2015			$ 806,700
Net income		$421,600	
Less dividends:			
Preferred	$30,000		
Common	44,000	74,000	
Increase in retained earnings			347,600
Retained earnings, December 31, 2015			$1,154,300

EXAMPLE EXERCISE 12-8   Statement of Retained Earnings   ⑤

Dry Creek Cameras Inc. reported the following results for the year ended March 31, 2015:

Retained earnings, April 1, 2014	$3,338,500
Net income	461,500
Cash dividends declared	200,000

Prepare a statement of retained earnings for the fiscal year ended March 31, 2015.

FOLLOW MY EXAMPLE 12-8

Dry Creek Cameras Inc.
Statement of Retained Earnings
For the Year Ended March 31, 2015

Retained earnings, April 1, 2014		$3,338,500
Net income	$461,500	
Less dividends declared	200,000	
Increase in retained earnings		261,500
Retained earnings, March 31, 2015		$3,600,000

For Practice: PE 12-8

Changes in retained earnings may also be reported in combination with the income statement. This format emphasizes net income as the link between the income statement and ending retained earnings. Because this format is not often used, we do not illustrate it.

Reporting Shareholders' Equity for Morning Java

To demonstrate the differences between financial statements prepared under IFRS and ASPE, we will examine the Shareholders' Equity of Morning Java, as at December 31, 2015, using both reporting methods. Morning Java's full set of financial statements prepared using IFRS and ASPE is available in Appendix A.

Morning Java is planning to expand its operations to various locations around the world, with financing coming from foreign banks. The foreign banks will require the financial statements to be prepared using IFRS.

In the first statement below, Morning Java prepared its statements using IFRS. The company recognized a gain due to the revaluation of its assets that was recorded in other comprehensive income and was closed to accumulated other comprehensive income at year-end. The statement of changes in equity includes a column for accumulated other comprehensive income.

	Preferred Shares	Common Shares	Retained Earnings	Accum. Other Comprehensive Income	Total
Morning Java International Statement of Changes in Equity For the Year Ended December 31, 2015					
Balance, January 1, 2015	$350,000	$2,075,000	$ 806,700	$ 0	$3,231,700
Net income			421,600		421,600
Dividends on preferred shares			(30,000)		(30,000)
Dividends on common shares			(44,000)		(44,000)
Issuance of additional common shares		275,000			275,000
Unrealized gain on revaluation of land and building...................				44,800	44,800
Balance, December 31, 2015	$350,000	$2,350,000	$1,154,300	$44,800	$3,899,100

Morning Java's statement of changes in equity reported using ASPE is shown below. Under ASPE, Morning Java did not revalue its assets so the column for accumulated other comprehensive income is omitted. Under ASPE, Morning Java has the option to prepare either the statement of changes in equity or the statement of retained earnings, as shown in Exhibit 6. Companies reporting under ASPE would not prepare both.

	Preferred Shares	Common Shares	Retained Earnings	Total
Morning Java Statement of Changes in Equity For the Year Ended December 31, 2015				
Balance, January 1, 2015	$350,000	$2,075,000	$ 806,700	$3,231,700
Net income			421,600	421,600
Dividends on preferred shares			(30,000)	(30,000)
Dividends on common shares			(44,000)	(44,000)
Issuance of additional common shares		275,000		275,000
Balance, December 31, 2015	$350,000	$2,350,000	$1,154,300	$3,854,300

Below is the equity section of the statement of financial position for Morning Java International, prepared using IFRS.

Morning Java International
Statement of Financial Position (Partial)
December 31, 2015

Liabilities and Shareholders' Equity

Shareholders' Equity:

$5 preferred shares (6,000 shares authorized, issued, and outstanding)		$ 350,000
Common shares (50,000 shares authorized, 45,000 shares issued and outstanding)		2,350,000
Accumulated other comprehensive income		44,800
Retained earnings		1,154,300
Total shareholders' equity		$3,899,100
Total liabilities and equity		$6,214,500

Under ASPE, Morning Java would prepare the shareholders' equity section of the balance sheet shown below. Note the difference between the two equity sections. Under IFRS, the equity is $44,800 higher than under ASPE. Again, this difference is the result of the accumulated other comprehensive income being included under IFRS but not under ASPE.

Morning Java
Balance Sheet (Partial)
December 31, 2015

Shareholders' Equity

Contributed capital:	
$5 preferred shares (6,000 shares authorized, issued, and outstanding)	$ 350,000
Common shares (50,000 shares authorized, 45,000 shares issued and outstanding)	2,350,000
Total contributed capital	2,700,000
Retained earnings	1,154,300
Total shareholders' equity	3,854,300
Total liabilities and shareholders' equity	$6,169,700

FINANCIAL ANALYSIS AND INTERPRETATION f·a·i

The amount of net income is one measure of a company's profitability. However, net income by itself does not take into consideration the amount of money invested to generate that profit. A ratio that helps investors evaluate the net income as a return on investment is **return on common shareholders' equity**. This ratio measures the efficiency of the company in generating profit for every dollar invested by common shareholders.

The return on common shareholders' equity is calculated as follows:

Return on Common Shareholders' Equity

$$= \frac{\text{Net Income} - \text{Preferred Dividends}}{\text{Average Common Shareholders' Equity}}$$

(*continued*)

Because preferred shareholders rank ahead of the common shareholders in their claim on earnings, any preferred dividends, either declared or in arrears, are subtracted from net income when computing the return to common shareholders. If preferred shares are noncumulative and not declared, they are not deducted. The return on common shareholders' equity for Morning Java International when reporting under IFRS would be calculated as follows:

($421,600 − $30,000) ÷ [($3,549,100* + $2,881,700*) ÷ 2] = 12.2%

*The $350,000 preferred shareholders' equity is deducted from the total shareholders' equity to calculate the average *common* shareholders' equity.

It is difficult to determine whether this ratio signifies a good performance without having another company's ratio for comparison.

Return on common shareholders' equity can be used to compare a company's current performance with its prior years' results or to compare one company's results to that of another. For example, the following data are available for recent years for Bank of Montreal and Royal Bank of Canada (all numbers are in millions):

Bank of Montreal	2011	2010	2009
Net income	3,266	2,810	
Shareholders' equity	28,123	21,880	20,197
Preferred dividends	144	136	

Royal Bank of Canada			
Net income	4,852	5,223	
Shareholders' equity	36,894	34,138	32,093
Preferred dividends	258	258	

The return on common shareholders' equity can be calculated as follows:

Bank of Montreal

2011 = ($3,266 − $144) ÷ [($28,123 + $21,880) ÷ 2]
  = 12.5%
2010 = ($2,810 − $136) ÷ [($21,880 + $20,197) ÷ 2]
  = 12.7%

Royal Bank of Canada

2011 = ($4,852 − $258) ÷ [($36,894 + $34,138) ÷ 2]
  = 12.9%
2010 = ($5,223 − $258) ÷ [($34,138 + $32,093) ÷ 2]
  = 15.0%

Because banking does not involve much investment in assets, the industry average for this ratio is high, relative to more capital-intensive industries. Bank of Montreal and Royal Bank of Canada both have relatively high ratios.

We can compare one company's performance with another company in the same industry. For example, when considering the return on common shareholders' equity alone, Bank of Montreal appears to be performing better than Royal Bank of Canada with a 1.57% [(12.7% − 12.5%) ÷ 12.7%] decrease in its ratio versus a 14% [(15% − 12.9%) ÷ 15.0%] decrease in the Royal Bank of Canada's ratio. Further analysis reveals that the Bank of Montreal had a 16.3% [($3,266 − $2,810) ÷ $2,810] increase in net income, while its return on common shareholders' equity decreased 1.57% because of the increased number of shares outstanding in 2011. Royal Bank of Canada had a 7.1% [($4,852 − $5,223) ÷ $5,223] decrease in net income, while its return on common shareholders' equity decreased 14%. Using this comparison, Bank of Montreal appears to be performing better than Royal Bank of Canada.

EXAMPLE EXERCISE 12-9 **Return on Common Shareholders' Equity** ⑤

Custodial Contractors Ltd.'s shareholders' equity balance on January 1, 2015, was $25,430. It reported the following account balances as at December 31, 2015:

Net income	$15,389
Shareholders' equity	26,765
Preferred dividends paid	1,500

Calculate the return on common shareholders' equity at December 31, 2015.

FOLLOW MY EXAMPLE 12-9

$$\text{Return on common shareholders' equity} = \frac{\text{Net Income} - \text{Preferred Dividends}}{\text{Average Common Shareholders' Equity}}$$

$$= \frac{(\$15,389 - \$1,500)}{(\$25,430 + \$26,765)/2}$$

$$= \$13,889/\$26,097.50$$

$$= 53.2\%$$

For Practice: PE 12-9

At a Glance 12

1 Describe the nature of the corporate form of organization.

Key Points	Key Learning Outcomes	Page	Example Exercises
Corporations have a separate legal existence, transferable units of shares, unlimited life, and limited shareholders' liability. Costs incurred in organizing a corporation are debited to expenses.	• Describe the characteristics of corporations.	614	
	• Compare proprietorships, partnerships, and corporations.	615	12-1
	• Prepare a journal entry for the costs of organizing a corporation.	617	

2 Describe the three main sources of shareholders' equity.

Key Points	Key Learning Outcomes	Page	Example Exercises
The three main sources of shareholders' equity are (1) capital contributed by the shareholders and others, called *contributed capital*, (2) net income retained in the business, called *retained earnings*, and (3) for corporations that prepare financial statements using IFRS, accumulated gains or losses resulting from transactions such as revaluation of assets to fair value, called *accumulated other comprehensive income*. Corporations using a separate dividends account close Dividends to Retained Earnings at the year-end.	• Describe what is meant by contributed capital.	617	
	• Describe what is meant by net income retained in the business.	618	
	• Describe what is meant by accumulated other comprehensive income.	618	
	• Prepare a simple shareholders' equity section of the balance sheet.	618	
	• Journalize closing entries for a corporation.	618	12-2

3 Describe and illustrate the characteristics of shares, classes of shares, and entries for issuing shares.

Key Points	Key Learning Outcomes	Page	Example Exercises
The main source of contributed capital is from issuing common and preferred shares. Shares issued for cash are recorded by debiting Cash and crediting the class of share issued. When shares are issued in exchange for assets other than cash, the assets acquired are recorded at their fair market value.	• Describe the characteristics of common and preferred shares, including rights to dividends.	621	
	• Journalize the entry for common and preferred shares issued for cash.	622	12-3
	• Journalize the entry for common and preferred shares issued in exchange for other assets.	622	12-3

4 **Describe and illustrate the accounting for cash dividends.**

Key Points	Key Learning Outcomes	Page	Example Exercises
The entry to record a declaration of cash dividends debits Retained Earnings (or Cash Dividends) and credits Dividends Payable.	• Journalize the entries for the declaration and payment of cash dividends.	623	12-4
	• Determine the distribution of dividends between common and preferred shares.	627	12-5

5 **Describe and illustrate the reporting of shareholders' equity.**

Key Points	Key Learning Outcomes	Page	Example Exercises
An example of the shareholders' equity section of a balance sheet is shown in Exhibit 3. A statement of changes in equity, as shown in Exhibit 5, is mandatory for corporations reporting under IFRS, but optional for corporations reporting under ASPE. Corporations reporting under ASPE may report changes in retained earnings in a statement of retained earnings, as shown in Exhibit 6.	• Prepare the shareholders' equity section of the balance sheet.	629	12-6
	• Prepare a statement of changes in equity for a corporation using IFRS.	629	12-7
	• Prepare a statement of retained earnings for a corporation using ASPE.	631	12-8
	• Calculate the return on common shareholders' equity	633	12-9

GLOSSARY

accumulated other comprehensive income – An equity account used to track increases and decreases in other comprehensive income. (p. 618)

articles of incorporation – The rules and regulations that govern the conduct of the company shareholders and directors. (p. 617)

callable preferred shares – Shares that may be called in and cancelled at the option of the issuing corporation. (p. 621)

cash dividend – A cash distribution of earnings by a corporation to its shareholders. (p. 623)

common shares – The shares outstanding when a corporation has issued only one class of shares. (p. 621)

contributed capital – Capital contributed to a corporation by shareholders and others. (p. 617)

convertible preferred shares – Shares that may be converted to common shares at the option of the purchasing investor. (p. 621)

cumulative preferred shares – Shares that have a right to receive regular dividends that were not declared (paid) in prior years. (p. 627)

date of declaration – The date the board of directors authorizes the payment of a dividend. (p. 624)

date of payment – The date the corporation will pay the dividend to shareholders. (p. 624)

date of record – The date the corporation uses to determine which shareholders will receive a dividend. (p. 624)

deficit – A debit balance in the retained earnings account. (p. 619)

dividends – Distributions of a corporation's earnings to shareholders. (p. 618)

in arrears – Cumulative preferred share dividends that have not been paid in prior years. (p. 627)

issued and outstanding shares – The shares in the hands of shareholders when no shares have been reacquired. (p. 620)

other comprehensive income – A temporary gain or loss resulting from transactions such as revaluation of assets to fair value, which is closed to accumulated other comprehensive income at year-end. (p. 619)

outstanding shares – The shares in the hands of shareholders. (p. 620)

par – The monetary amount printed on a share certificate. (p. 620)

participating preferred shares – Shares that entitle shareholders to receive their dividend preference and to share their dividend preference and to share with the common shareholders in any excess dividends declared. (p. 621)

preemptive right – Shareholders' entitlement to maintain their proportionate share of a new share issue. (p. 621)

preferred shares – A class of shares with preferential rights over common shares. (p. 621)

retained earnings – Net income retained in a corporation. (p. 618)

return on common shareholders' equity – Net income per dollar invested by common shareholders. (p. 633)

shareholders – The owners of a corporation. (p. 614)

shareholders' equity – The owners' equity in a corporation. (p. 617)

shares – Units of ownership interest in a corporation. (p. 614)

statement of changes in equity – A summary of the changes in the shareholders' equity in a corporation that have occurred during a specific period of time. (p. 629)

statement of retained earnings – A summary of the changes in the retained earnings in a corporation for a specific period of time, such as a month or a year. (p. 631)

ILLUSTRATIVE PROBLEM

Ashton Corporation is a lighting fixture wholesaler located in Manitoba. At January 1, 2015, the start of its current fiscal year, Ashton had the following equity balances:

Common shares, 40,000 issued, unlimited authorized	$800,000
$1 preferred shares, 10,000 issued, 50,000 authorized	150,000
Retained earnings	225,700

During 2015, Ashton Corporation completed the following selected transactions:

Feb.	3.	Issued 2,500 of its common shares at $26 per share.
May	1.	Declared a semiannual dividend of $13,750 to shareholders of record on May 31, payable on June 15.
Jun.	15.	Paid the cash dividends.
Sep.	23.	Issued 1,000 preferred shares at $18 per share.
Nov.	1.	Declared semiannual dividends of $14,750 to shareholders of record on November 30, payable on December 30.
Dec.	30.	Paid the cash dividends.
	31.	Recorded the closing entries for the year; net income was $300,000.

Instructions

1. Journalize the entries to record the transactions for Ashton Corporation. Omit explanations.
2. Prepare the statement of changes in equity for 2015.
3. Prepare the shareholders' equity section of the balance sheet as at December 31, 2015.

(continued)

Solution

1.

2015				
Feb.	3	Cash	65,000	
		Common Shares		65,000
May	1	Retained Earnings (or Cash Dividends)	13,750	
		Dividends Payable—Preferred		10,000*
		Dividends Payable—Common		3,750**
		*(10,000 × $1)		
		**($13,750 − $10,000)		
Jun.	15	Dividends Payable—Preferred	10,000	
		Dividends Payable—Common	3,750	
		Cash		13,750
Sep.	23	Cash	18,000	
		Preferred Shares		18,000
Nov.	1	Retained Earnings (or Cash Dividends)	14,750	
		Dividends Payable—Preferred		11,000*
		Dividends Payable—Common		3,750**
		*(11,000 × $1)		
		**($14,750 − $11,000)		
Dec.	30	Dividends Payable—Preferred	11,000	
		Dividends Payable—Common	3,750	
		Cash		14,750
	31	Income Summary	300,000	
		Retained Earnings		300,000
	31	Retained Earnings	28,500	
		Cash Dividends		28,500

Note: This entry is required only if the cash dividends account is used when dividends are declared.

2.

Ashton Corporation Statement of Changes in Equity For the Year Ended December 31, 2015				
	Preferred Shares	**Common Shares**	**Retained Earnings**	**Total**
Balance, January 1, 2015	$150,000	$800,000	$225,700	$1,175,700
Net income			300,000	300,000
Dividends on preferred shares			(21,000)	(21,000)
Dividends on common shares			(7,500)	(7,500)
Issuance of shares	18,000	65,000		83,000
Balance, December 31, 2015	$168,000	$865,000	$497,200	$1,530,200

3.

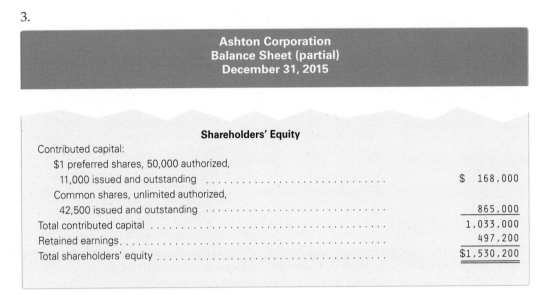

Ashton Corporation
Balance Sheet (partial)
December 31, 2015

Shareholders' Equity

Contributed capital:

$1 preferred shares, 50,000 authorized,
11,000 issued and outstanding .... $ 168,000

Common shares, unlimited authorized,
42,500 issued and outstanding 865,000

Total contributed capital 1,033,000

Retained earnings................................... 497,200

Total shareholders' equity $1,530,200

EYE OPENERS

1. Why are most large businesses organized as corporations?
2. What is the board of directors' role in a corporation?
3. Describe the shareholders' liability to creditors of a corporation.
4. Name at least four differences between partnerships and corporations.
5. The retained earnings balance for Alpha Corporation was $100,000 at the start of the fiscal year. The company earned net income of $125,000, and dividends of $25,000 were declared but unpaid at year-end. Determine the ending retained earnings balance for the year.
6. A stockbroker advises a client to "buy preferred shares. With that type of share, you will never have to worry about losing the dividends." Is the broker right?
7. What factors influence the market price of a corporation's shares?
8. (a) What are the three conditions required for the declaration and payment of a cash dividend? (b) The dates related to the declaration of a cash dividend are February 16, March 18, and April 17. Identify each date.
9. A corporation with both preferred and common shares outstanding has a substantial credit balance in its Retained Earnings account at the beginning of the current fiscal year. Although net income for the current year is sufficient to pay the preferred dividend of $125,000 each quarter and a common dividend of $300,000 each quarter, the board of directors declares dividends only on the preferred shares. Suggest possible reasons for not paying the dividends on the common shares.
10. In what part of the balance sheet is a declared but unpaid cash dividend reported?
11. Nova Corporation, organized on January 1, 2015, had 3,000 $2 cumulative preferred shares and 5,000 common shares issued and outstanding. Nova Corporation paid no dividends in 2015 and 2016. In 2017, the corporation paid dividends of $50,000. Determine the distribution of the dividend between the preferred and common shareholders.
12. What is the primary advantage of combining the statement of retained earnings with the income statement?
13. When is a statement of changes in equity normally prepared?

PRACTICE EXERCISES

① PE 12-1

Comparing proprietorships, general partnerships, and corporations

EE 12-1 p. 616

1. Sami Tokar and Janet Locher will not be responsible for income tax on their $350,000 business income this year.
2. When Carm Cassman and Carl Donker receive funds from their business for personal use, the withdrawals account is used.
3. Jonathan and Jeffrey Pasher are both equally liable for all the debts of their business.
4. When Francis Barker opened Barker's Chips she was not aware that she would be required to personally pay the business income taxes.

For each scenario, state whether the business is a sole proprietorship, a general partnership, or a corporation.

---

① PE 12-2

Closing entries for corporations

EE 12-2 p. 620

Cornerstone Fitness Inc. is a health and wellness centre. During 2015, Cornerstone Fitness earned $326,000 in revenue, incurred $98,000 of expenses, and paid $32,000 in dividends. Cornerstone Fitness recorded a gain in other comprehensive income of $28,500 as a result of revaluation of assets.

Journalize the closing entries for Cornerstone Fitness Inc. on December 31, 2015, assuming it uses an income summary and a dividends account.

---

③ PE 12-3

Entries for issuing shares

EE 12-3 p. 623

On October 15, Crimson Pottery Corporation issued for cash 400,000 common shares at $4.50 per share. On November 6, Crimson Pottery issued 15,000 $1 preferred shares for $32 per share. On December 21, Crimson Pottery issued 13,000 common shares in exchange for equipment with a fair market value of $61,750.

Journalize the entries to record the October 15, November 6, and December 21 transactions.

---

④ PE 12-4

Entries for cash dividends

EE 12-4 p. 625

The important dates related to a cash dividend of $246,500 on a corporation's common shares are July 31, August 12, and August 28. Journalize the entries required on each date.

---

④ PE 12-5

Dividends distribution

EE 12-5 p. 628

Taiwanese Company has 5,000 $1.60 cumulative preferred shares and 10,000 common shares. The following amounts were distributed as dividends:

Year 1	$15,000
Year 2	5,000
Year 3	62,000

Determine the distribution of dividends.

---

⑤ PE 12-6

Reporting shareholders' equity

EE 12-6 p. 629

Using the following accounts and May 31, 2015 balances, prepare the Shareholders' Equity section of the balance sheet for Able Corporation Ltd. as at May 31, 2015. There are 70,000 common shares authorized, and 63,000 shares are issued and outstanding; 10,000 preferred shares are authorized, and 6,000 shares are issued and outstanding.

Common shares	$4,725,000
Retained earnings	2,032,800
$10.50 preferred shares	600,000
Dividends declared and paid in 2015	204,750
Total assets	12,500,000

⑤ PE 12-7
Statement of changes in equity

Happy Rupert's Pets Ltd. has a November 30 year-end, and it began the year 2015 with the following balances:

Retained Earnings	$346,190
Accumulated Other Comprehensive Income	257,387
Common Shares	386,021
Preferred Shares	157,350

EE 12-7 p. 630

During the year, the company issued 10,000 preferred shares at $22 per share and 30,000 common shares at $7 per share. The net income for the year was $524,568, and it paid out $23,000 in preferred dividends and $15,000 in common dividends. The company recorded an unrealized gain on investments of $13,587 in other comprehensive income.

Prepare a statement of changes in equity for Happy Rupert's Pets Ltd. for 2015.

---

⑤ PE 12-8
Statement of retained earnings

Hornblower Cruises Ltd. reported the following results for the year ended October 31, 2015:

Retained earnings, November 1, 2014	$1,500,000
Net income	475,000
Cash dividends declared	350,000

EE 12-8 p. 631

Prepare a statement of retained earnings for the fiscal year ended October 31, 2015.

---

⑤ PE 12-9
Return on common shareholders' equity

f·a·i

Barker Inc.'s shareholders' equity balance on January 1, 2015, was $32,645. It reported the following account balances as at December 31, 2015:

Net income	$21,340
Shareholders' equity	37,830
Preferred dividends paid	7,000

Calculate the return on common shareholders' equity at December 31, 2015.

EE 12-9 p. 634

EXERCISES

① EX 12-1
Advantages and disadvantages of incorporation

Janice Rockover has been operating her flower shop as a sole proprietorship for five years. She is currently trying to decide between three options: continuing as a sole proprietorship, taking on a partner in her flower shop, and incorporating the business. Janice has come to you for advice about the advantages and disadvantages of incorporating compared with the other two options. How would you advise Janice?

① EX 12-2
Comparing sole proprietorships, partnerships, and corporations

1. Michael and Matthew will each pay their share of income tax on the business income when they file their personal income tax returns.
2. Sharon is responsible for all the debts of the business.
3. Emily and John are liable only for the amount of money they have invested in their business.
4. When Peter and Sandy withdraw business funds for personal expenses, it is recorded as a withdrawal.
5. Jonathan is an owner of the company. When he needed extra cash to purchase a new home, he sold his ownership in the business on the stock market.
6. Although Joshua was at risk of losing only his own investment in the company, when he decided to pursue other interests, he needed the permission of the remaining owners to sell his share of the business.

For each scenario, state whether the business is a sole proprietorship, a partnership, or a corporation.

① EX 12-3
Entries for organization costs

Cassandra and Jefferson decided to incorporate their partnership. On March 28, they paid a lawyer $1,500 to file the articles of incorporation. On April 3, they paid a local advertising firm $3,750 to promote their new corporation.

Journalize the entries on March 28 and April 3.

② EX 12-4
Closing entries for corporations

During 2015, Emmerson Construction Ltd. earned $387,456 in revenue, incurred $219,364 in expenses, and declared cash dividends of $50,000.

Journalize the closing entries for Emmerson Construction Ltd. on December 31, 2015.

② EX 12-5
Closing entries for corporations

Computer Consultants Inc., a software installation company, earned revenues of $529,463 in 2015, incurred expenses of $693,502, declared cash dividends of $25,000, and recognized a gain on the revaluation of assets of $129,346.

Journalize the closing entries for Computer Consultants Inc. as at December 31, 2015.

③ EX 12-6
Entries for issuing shares

On February 10, Peerless Rocks Inc., a marble contractor, issued for cash 40,000 common shares at $34 per share, and on May 9, it issued for cash 100,000 $5 preferred shares at $70 per share.

Journalize the entries for February 10 and May 9.

③ EX 12-7
Issuing shares for assets other than cash

On January 30, Lift Time Corporation, a wholesaler of hydraulic lifts, acquired land in exchange for 18,000 common shares with a current market price of $15 per share. The land was appraised at $295,000. Journalize the entry to record the transaction.

③ EX 12-8
Selected share transactions

Rocky Mountain Sounds Corp., an electric guitar retailer, was organized by Cathy Dewitt, Melody Leimbach, and Mario Torres. The charter authorized 250,000 common shares. The following transactions affecting shareholders' equity were completed during the first year of operations:

a. Issued 10,000 shares to Cathy Dewitt for $400,000 cash.
b. Issued 750 shares to Mario Torres for $28,000 in marketing services provided in connection with the organization of the corporation and issued 20,000 shares to Mario Torres for $750,000 cash.
c. Purchased land and a building from Melody Leimbach. The building is mortgaged for $400,000 for 20 years at 7%, and the mortgage note had accrued interest of $7,000 at the time of the purchase. It is agreed that the land is to be priced at $125,000 and the building at $600,000 and that Melody Leimbach's equity will be exchanged for 8,400 shares. The corporation agreed to assume responsibility for paying the mortgage note and the accrued interest.

Journalize the entries to record the transactions.

④ EX 12-9
Dividend distribution per share

East Coast Pool and Spa Ltd., a retailer of pools and spas, had 24,000 $2.50 preferred shares and 100,000 common shares. During 2015, the company declared $110,000 in dividends.

Determine the distribution of dividends on each class of share and calculate the dividends per share paid in 2015 to each class of share.

④ EX 12-10
Dividend distribution per share

On May 1, 2015, Welland Fisheries Inc. declared $235,000 in dividends, to be paid on July 3 to shareholders of record on June 5. On June 5, 30,000 $4 preferred shares and 46,000 common shares were outstanding.

Determine the distribution of dividends on each class of share and calculate the dividends per share paid in 2015 to each class of share.

EX 12-11

④ Dividend distribution per share

Ridge Crest Inc., a developer of construction equipment, has shares outstanding as follows: 25,000 $2 cumulative preferred shares and 72,000 common shares. During its first four years of operations, the following amounts were distributed as dividends: first year, $40,000; second year, $50,000; third year, $78,000; fourth year, $122,000. Determine the distribution of dividends on each class of share for each of the four years, and calculate dividends paid per share for common and preferred shares.

EX 12-12

④ Dividend distribution per share

Michelangelo Inc., a software development firm, has shares outstanding as follows: 20,000 $0.25 cumulative preferred shares and 25,000 common shares. During its first four years of operations, the following amounts were distributed as dividends: first year, $3,000; second year, $4,000; third year, $30,000; fourth year, $80,000. Determine the distribution of dividends on each class of share for each of the four years, and calculate dividends paid per share for common and preferred shares.

EX 12-13

③ Issuing shares

Norwest Products Inc., a wholesaler of office products, was organized on January 20 of the current year, with an authorization of 175,000 $1.50 preferred shares and unlimited common shares. The following selected transactions were completed during the first year of operations:

Jan. 20. Issued 250,000 common shares for $2,250,000 cash.
     26. Issued 1,000 common shares to a lawyer in payment of $9,000 legal fees for organizing the corporation.
Feb. 6. Issued 32,000 common shares in exchange for land, buildings, and equipment with fair market prices of $90,000, $278,000, and $80,000, respectively.
Mar. 30. Issued 45,000 preferred shares at $48 per share for cash.
May   5. Declared a $125,000 cash dividend to be paid on July 15 to shareholders of record on June 20.
Dec. 31. Prepared closing entries for the dividends and for $538,356 net income.

Instructions

1. Journalize the transactions.
2. Prepare a statement of retained earnings for the year.
3. Prepare the shareholders' equity section of the balance sheet as at December 31.

EX 12-14

④ Entries for cash dividends

The important dates related to a cash dividend of $365,850 on a corporation's common shares are April 1, May 1, and June 3. The corporation does not use the cash dividends account.

Journalize the entries required on each date.

EX 12-15

④ Entries for cash dividends

The important dates related to a cash dividend of $69,500 on a corporation's common shares are May 3, June 17, and August 1. The corporation does not use the cash dividends account. Journalize the entries required on each date.

EX 12-16

⑤ Reporting shareholders' equity

The following accounts and their balances were selected from the unadjusted trial balance of REO Ltd., a freight forwarder, at October 31, 2015, the end of the current fiscal year:

Common shares, 80,000 shares issued and outstanding	$ 490,000
Retained earnings	3,150,000
$2 preferred shares, 7,500 shares issued and outstanding.....	750,000
Accumulated other comprehensive income (loss)	(25,000)

Prepare the shareholders' equity section of the balance sheet for REO Ltd. as at October 31, 2015. There are 250,000 common shares authorized and 20,000 preferred shares authorized.

EX 12-17
Reporting shareholders' equity

Race Car Ltd. retails racing products for BMWs, Porsches, and Ferraris. The following accounts and their balances appear in the ledger of Race Car Inc. on April 30, 2015, the end of the current fiscal year:

Common shares, 40,000 shares issued and outstanding	$ 520,000
Retained earnings	3,900,000
$2 preferred shares, 30,000 shares issued and outstanding. . . .	1,500,000
Accumulated other comprehensive income	145,000
Land purchased in exchange for 10,000 common shares	125,000

Prepare the shareholders' equity section of the balance sheet for Race Car Ltd. as at April 30, 2015. There are 200,000 common shares authorized and 50,000 preferred shares authorized.

EX 12-18
Statement of changes in equity

Kroker Plumbing Ltd., a plumbing installation company, began the year with the following balances:

Accumulated other comprehensive income	$136,000
Retained earnings	845,945
Common shares	780,000
Preferred shares	300,000

The following selected transactions affected the equity during the year:

Net income reported	$264,947
Loss due to the revaluation of assets	28,000
Preferred shares issued	110,000
Common shares issued	253,000
Dividends paid	
Preferred	30,000
Common	25,000

Prepare a statement of changes in equity for the fiscal year ended October 31, 2015.

EX 12-19
Statement of changes in equity

My Fair Lady Inc. sells ladies' fashions. The following balances were as at March 1, 2015:

Accumulated other comprehensive income	$ 253,967
Retained earnings	2,374,286
Common shares	1,230,000
Preferred shares	750,000

The following selected transactions affected the equity during the year:

Net loss reported	$732,002
Gain due to the revaluation of assets	42,540
Preferred shares issued	200,000
Common shares issued	730,000
Dividends paid	
Preferred	120,000
Common	43,000

Prepare a statement of changes in equity for the fiscal year ended February 29, 2016.

EX 12-20
Statement of retained earnings

Bancroft Corporation, a manufacturer of industrial pumps, reported the following results for the year ended January 31, 2015:

Retained earnings, February 1, 2014	$3,175,500
Net income	415,000
Cash dividends declared—common	75,500
Cash dividends declared—preferred	140,000

Prepare a statement of retained earnings for the fiscal year ended January 31, 2015.

⑤ EX 12-21
Statement of retained earnings

Sandy Corporation, a manufacturer of chemical compounds, reports the following results for the year ended October 31, 2015:

Retained earnings, November 1, 2014	$796,750
Net loss	215,000
Cash dividends declared—common	15,000
Cash dividends declared—preferred	30,000

Prepare a retained earnings statement for the fiscal year ended October 31, 2015.

---

⑤ EX 12-22
Shareholders' equity section of balance sheet

List the errors in the following shareholders' equity section of the balance sheet prepared as at the end of the current year:

Shareholders' Equity

Contributed capital:	
Preferred $3 shares (10,000 shares authorized and issued)	$ 2,380,000
Retained earnings	1,143,000
Accumulated other comprehensive income	48,000
Dividends payable	227,000
Total contributed capital	3,798,000
Common shares (250,000 shares authorized,	
180,000 shares issued)	12,075,000
Organizing costs	(18,000)
Total shareholders' equity	$15,855,000

---

⑤ EX 12-23
Statement of changes in equity

Time Travel Ltd. reported the following accounts and their balances as at April 1, 2015, the beginning of the current fiscal year:

Common shares, unlimited authorized,	
40,000 shares issued and outstanding	$1,150,000
Retained earnings	980,000
$2 preferred shares, unlimited authorized,	
30,000 shares issued and outstanding	210,000

The company reported the following results for the year:

Net income	120,000
Dividends declared	80,000
Common shares issued, 10,000	300,000
Preferred shares issued, 5,000	40,000

Instructions

1. Journalize the share issuances and year-end closing entries.
2. Prepare a statement of changes in equity for the year ended March 31, 2016.

---

⑤ EX 12-24
Statement of changes in equity

Brighttime Business Centre Ltd. reported the following accounts and their balances as at January 1, 2015, the beginning of the current fiscal year:

Common shares, unlimited authorized,	
180,000 shares issued and outstanding	$14,040,000
Retained earnings	1,550,000
$3 preferred shares, 50,000 authorized,	
30,000 shares issued and outstanding	5,250,000
$1.50 preferred shares, unlimited authorized,	
10,000 shares issued and outstanding	875,000
Dividends payable	135,000

The company reported the following results for the year:

Net loss	76,000
Dividends declared	150,000

Instructions

1. Journalize the closing entries at year-end.
2. Prepare a statement of changes in equity for the year ended December 31, 2015.

Why would a company declare dividends in a year it recorded a net loss?

EX 12-25
Return on common shareholders' equity

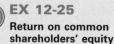

Glibwater Refining Ltd., a water refining corporation, reported the following account balances for 2016, 2015, and 2014:

	2016	2015	2014
Net income	$ 1,532,487	$ 985,743	$ 895,234
Shareholders' equity	12,548,687	11,562,357	9,854,217
Preferred dividends	69,523	69,523	50,258

Instructions

1. Calculate the return on common shareholders' equity for 2016 and 2015.
2. Has the ratio improved or declined over the years? Do you have enough information to determine whether Glibwater Refining is performing to standard? If you do not have enough information, what additional information is needed to make this determination?

EX 12-26
Return on common shareholders' equity

Archibald's Trucking Inc., a moving company, reported the following account balances for 2016, 2015, and 2014:

	2016	2015	2014
Net income	$ 782,569	$ 657,235	$ 548,756
Shareholders' equity	7,587,456	6,025,368	3,958,745
Preferred dividends	43,000	43,000	43,000

Instructions

1. Calculate the return on common shareholders' equity for 2016 and 2015.
2. Has the ratio improved or declined over the years? Do you have enough information to determine whether Archibald's Trucking is performing to standard? If you do not have enough information, what additional information is needed to make this determination?

PROBLEMS SERIES A

PR 12-1A
Dividends on preferred and common shares

✔ 1. Common dividends in 2012: $8,000

Bridger Bike Corp. manufactures mountain bikes and distributes them through retail outlets in Canada. Bridger Bike Corp. has declared the following annual dividends over a six-year period ended December 31 of each year: 2010, $5,000; 2011, $18,000; 2012, $45,000; 2013, $45,000; 2014, $60,000; and 2015, $67,000. During the entire period, the outstanding shares of the company comprised 10,000 $2 preferred shares and 25,000 common shares.

Instructions

Determine the total dividends declared on each class of share for each of the six years. No dividends were in arrears on January 1, 2010. Summarize the data in tabular form, using the following columnar headings:

Year	Total Dividends	Preferred Dividends	Common Dividends
2010	$ 5,000		
2011	18,000		
2012	45,000		
2013	45,000		
2014	60,000		
2015	67,000		

PR 12-2A

Share transactions for corporate expansion

Sheldon Optics produces medical lasers for use in hospitals. At the annual shareholders' meeting on December 7, the board of directors presented a plan for modernizing and expanding plant operations at a cost of approximately $5,300,000. The plan proposed (a) the corporation borrow $2,000,000, (b) 15,000 shares of the unissued preferred shares be issued through an underwriter, and (c) a building, valued at $1,850,000, and the land on which it is located, valued at $162,500, be acquired in accordance with preliminary negotiations by the issuance of 17,500 common shares. The plan was approved by the shareholders and accomplished by the following transactions:

Jan. 10. Borrowed $2,000,000 from Bank of Montreal, giving a 7% mortgage note.
   21. Issued 15,000 preferred shares, receiving $84.50 per share in cash.
   31. Issued 17,500 common shares in exchange for the land and the building, according to the plan.

No other transactions occurred during January.

Instructions

Journalize the entries to record the transactions.

PR 12-3A

Selected share transactions

✔ d. Cash dividends, $414,350

Coil Welding Corporation sells and services pipe welding equipment in the Maritimes. The following selected accounts appear in the ledger of Coil Welding Corporation on February 1, 2015, the beginning of the current fiscal year:

$0.50 preferred shares (50,000 shares authorized, 40,000 shares issued and outstanding)	$ 1,240,000
Common shares (1,000,000 shares authorized, 750,000 shares issued and outstanding)	9,750,000
Retained earnings	36,785,000

During the year, the corporation completed a number of transactions affecting shareholders' equity. Coil Welding uses a cash dividend account. The transactions are summarized as follows:

a. Issued 60,000 common shares in exchange for a building with a fair market value of $540,000.
b. Sold 7,500 preferred shares at $38 per share.
c. Issued 120,000 common shares at $15.025 per share, receiving cash.
d. Declared cash dividends. Common shares will receive $0.42 per share.
e. Recorded the closing entry for the income for the year of $3,900,000 and the dividends.

Instructions

1. Journalize the entries to record the transactions. Identify each entry by letter.
2. Prepare a statement of retained earnings for the year ended January 31, 2016.
3. Prepare the shareholders' equity section of the balance sheet as at January 31, 2016.

PR 12-4A

Statement of retained earnings

✔ d = $31,000

The partially completed statement of retained earnings information is given for Willy Wally's Chocolates Ltd. for four years.

	2016	2015	2014	2013
Beginning balance	$ a	$1,481,779	$ f	$568,432
Net income (loss)	b	(125,983)	652,423	i
Preferred dividends	60,000	62,000	g	25,000
Common dividends	28,000	d	23,000	12,000
Increase (decrease) in retained earnings	268,257	(218,983)	h	j
Ending balance	$ c	$ e	$1,481,779	$890,356

Instructions

Fill in the missing numbers.

PR 12-5A

Selected corporate transactions

✔ 3. Total shareholders' equity, $13,935,000

Karson's Nautical Ltd. produces shipping navigation equipment. The shareholders' equity accounts of Karson's Nautical Ltd., with balances on January 1, 2015, are as follows:

Common shares (750,000 shares authorized, 175,000 shares issued and outstanding)	$5,425,000
Retained earnings	5,700,000

The following selected transactions occurred during the year:

Jan. 6. Paid cash dividends of $0.20 per share. The dividend had been properly recorded when declared on November 29 of the preceding fiscal year.

Apr. 3. Issued 30,000 common shares for $960,000.

Nov. 7. Issued 35,000 common shares at $36 per share.

Dec. 30. Declared a $0.25-per-share dividend. Karson's Nautical does not use a cash dividends account.

     31. Recorded the closing entry for the income for the year of $650,000.

Instructions

1. Journalize the entries to record the transactions.
2. Prepare a statement of retained earnings for the year ended December 31, 2015.
3. Prepare the shareholders' equity section of the December 31, 2015, balance sheet.

PR 12-6A

Selected corporate transactions

✔ Sep. 1, Preferred dividends, $22,500

Eastwind Corporation manufactures and distributes leisure clothing. The shareholders' equity accounts, with balances on October 1, 2015, the beginning of the fiscal year, are as follows:

$1.50 preferred shares (400,000 shares authorized, 30,000 shares issued and outstanding)	$1,050,000
Common shares (unlimited shares authorized, 270,000 shares issued and outstanding)	3,240,000
Retained earnings	2,160,000

Selected transactions completed by Eastwind during the current fiscal year are as follows:

Mar. 1. Declared semiannual dividends on the preferred shares and $0.20 on the common shares to shareholders of record on March 31, payable on April 30. Eastwind does not use a cash dividends account.

Apr. 30. Paid the cash dividends.

Jul. 9. Issued 100,000 common shares at $14 per share.

Aug. 29. Issued an additional 70,000 common shares at $16 per share.

Sep. 1. Declared semiannual dividends on the preferred shares and $0.25 on the common shares to shareholders of record on September 30, payable on October 31.

     30. Recorded the closing entry for the income for the year of $1,305,000.

Instructions

1. Journalize the transactions.
2. Prepare the statement of retained earnings for the year ended September 30, 2016.
3. Prepare the shareholders' equity section of the balance sheet as at September 30, 2016.

PR 12-7A

Selected corporate transactions, statement of changes in equity

✔ Total shareholders' equity, April 30, 2016, $77,850,343

Phillips Electronics Inc. supplies television and audio equipment to consumers. The shareholders' equity account balances as at May 1, 2015, are shown below:

$4 preferred shares (1,000,000 authorized, 178,000 issued and outstanding)	$ 9,434,000
Common shares (unlimited authorized, 1,458,600 issued and outstanding)	33,548,000
Retained earnings	25,156,845
Accumulated other comprehensive income	0

Following are some selected transactions affecting the shareholders' equity during the year:

May   3.   Declared quarterly dividends of $235,000 to be paid July 31, to the shareholders of record on June 28. Phillips Electronics uses a cash dividends account.

Jul.   15.   Issued 32,000 preferred shares for $54 per share.
      31.   Paid the cash dividends.

Aug.   5.   Declared quarterly dividends of $346,000 to be paid October 31, to shareholders of record on September 24.

Oct.   31.   Paid the cash dividends.

Nov.   4.   Issued 400,000 common shares for $25 per share.

Nov.   7.   Declared quarterly dividends of $534,000 to be paid January 31, to shareholders of record on December 21.

Jan.   31.   Paid the cash dividends.

Feb.   15.   Declared quarterly dividends of $625,000 to be paid April 30, to shareholders of record on March 20.

Apr.   30.   Paid the cash dividends.
      Prepared the year-end closing entries for a loss of $365,923 and other comprehensive income of $89,421. Phillips Electronics uses the income summary account when preparing the closing entries.

Instructions

1. Journalize the transactions.
2. Prepare a statement of changes in equity.
3. Prepare the shareholders' equity section of the balance sheet as at April 30, 2016.

---

③
④
⑤

PR 12-8A

Selected transactions, statement of changes in equity

✔ Total shareholders' equity January 31, 2016, $11,791,475

Crombie Landscaping Inc. performs yard cleanup for homeowners in Oakville, Ontario. The shareholders' equity account balances at February 1, 2015, are shown below:

$2.20 cumulative preferred shares (1,000,000 authorized, 150,000 issued and outstanding)	$4,650,000
Common shares (750,000 authorized, 280,600 issued and outstanding)	1,683,600
Retained earnings	3,450,000
Accumulated other comprehensive income	54,670

The following are selected transactions during the year:

Feb.   21.   Paid the semiannual dividends of $200,000 declared and recorded properly in December 2014. No new preferred or common shares were issued during December, January, or February. Crombie Landscaping uses a cash dividends account.

Apr.   5.   Issued 40,000 preferred shares for $33 per share.

Jun.   15.   Declared semiannual dividends of $200,000 to be paid August 20, to shareholders of record on July 28.

Aug.   20.   Paid the cash dividends.

Nov.   4.   Issued 25,000 common shares for $16 per share.

Dec.   5.   Declared semiannual dividends of $300,000 to be paid February 16, 2016, to shareholders of record on January 24.

Jan.   15.   3,000 common shares were traded in the marketplace at $18 per share.

Jan.   31.   Prepared the year-end closing entries with net income of $735,950 and a loss in other comprehensive income of $2,745. Crombie Landscaping uses the income summary account when preparing the closing entries.

Instructions

1. Journalize the transactions.
2. Prepare a statement of changes in equity.
3. Prepare the shareholders' equity section of the balance sheet as at January 31, 2016.

5 **PR 12-9A**
Return on common shareholders' equity

✔ 2016 return on common shareholders' equity, 7.8%

Jefferson Manufacturing Ltd. produces custom furniture in the Ottawa area. The statement of changes in equity for the years ended December 31, 2015, and 2016 are shown below:

Jefferson Manufacturing Ltd.
Statement of Changes in Equity
For the Year Ended December 31, 2016

	Preferred Shares	Common Shares	Retained Earnings	Accum. Other Compre. Income	Total
Balance, January 1, 2016	$2,000,000	$14,820,000	$3,450,000	$32,651	$20,302,651
Net income			1,653,000		1,653,000
Dividends on preferred shares			(100,000)		(100,000)
Dividends on common shares			(75,000)		(75,000)
Issuance of shares		1,500,000			1,500,000
Unrealized gain on revaluation of assets				12,560	12,560
Balance, December 31, 2016	$2,000,000	$16,320,000	$4,928,000	$45,211	$23,293,211

Jefferson Manufacturing Ltd.
Statement of Changes in Equity
For the Year Ended December 31, 2015

	Preferred Shares	Common Shares	Retained Earnings	Accum. Other Compre. Income	Total
Balance, January 1, 2015	$2,000,000	$14,820,000	$2,276,420	$29,391	$19,125,811
Net income			1,423,580		1,423,580
Dividends on preferred shares			(150,000)		(150,000)
Dividends on common shares			(100,000)		(100,000)
Unrealized gain on revaluation of assets				3,260	3,260
Balance, December 31, 2015	$2,000,000	$14,820,000	$3,450,000	$32,651	$20,302,651

Instructions

1. Calculate the return on common shareholders' equity for 2016 and 2015.
2. Has the ratio improved or declined over the years? Do you have enough information to determine whether Jefferson Manufacturing is performing to standard? If you do not have enough information, what additional information is needed to make this determination?

PROBLEMS SERIES B

4 **PR 12-1B**
Dividends on preferred and common shares

✔ Common dividends in 2012: $16,500

Lone Star Theatre Ltd. owns and operates movie theatres throughout central Canada. Lone Star Theatre has declared the following annual dividends over a six-year period ended December 31 of each year: 2010, $7,500; 2011, $9,000; 2012, $30,000; 2013, $30,000; 2014, $40,000; and 2015, $48,500. During the entire period, the outstanding shares of the company comprised 10,000 $1 preferred shares and 50,000 common shares.

Instructions

Determine the total dividends declared on each class of share for each of the six years. No dividends were in arrears on January 1, 2010. Summarize the data in tabular form, using the following columnar headings:

Year	Total Dividends	Preferred Dividends	Common Dividends
2010	$ 7,500		
2011	9,000		
2012	30,000		
2013	30,000		
2014	40,000		
2015	48,500		

③ PR 12-2B

Share transactions for corporate expansion

On April 2, at the annual shareholders' meeting of Wild Things Corp., a meat processor, the board of directors presented a plan for modernizing and expanding plant operations at a cost of approximately $3,650,000. The plan proposed (a) a building, valued at $1,680,000, and the land on which it is located, valued at $420,000, be acquired in accordance with preliminary negotiations by the issuance of 65,000 common shares; (b) 21,000 preferred shares be issued through an underwriter; and (c) the corporation borrow $700,000. The plan was approved by the shareholders and accomplished by the following transactions:

Jun. 9. Issued 65,000 common shares in exchange for the land and the building, according to the plan.
      13. Issued 21,000 preferred shares, receiving $40 per share in cash.
      25. Borrowed $700,000 from Central Bank, giving an 8% mortgage note.

No other transactions occurred during June.

Instructions

Journalize the entries to record the transactions.

③④⑤ PR 12-3B

Selected share transactions

✔ 1e. Cash dividends, $82,000

The following selected accounts appear in the ledger of Okie Environmental Corporation on August 1, 2015, the beginning of the current fiscal year:

$1 preferred shares (40,000 shares authorized,	
20,000 shares issued and outstanding)	$1,100,000
Common shares (100,000 shares authorized,	
40,000 shares issued and outstanding)	3,150,000
Retained earnings	8,170,000

During the year, the corporation completed a number of transactions affecting shareholders' equity. Okie Environmental uses a cash dividends account. The transactions are summarized as follows:

a. Sold 8,000 preferred shares at $63 per share.
b. Issued 17,500 common shares for $81.214 per share.
c. Issued 10,000 common shares in exchange for a building with a fair market value of $800,000.
d. Declared dividends. Common shareholders will receive $0.80 per share.
e. Recorded the closing entry for the income for the year of $1,870,000, and the dividends.

Instructions

1. Journalize the entries to record the transactions. Identify each entry by letter.
2. Prepare a statement of retained earnings for the year ended July 31, 2016.
3. Prepare the shareholders' equity section of the balance sheet as at July 31, 2016.

⑤

PR 12-4B

Statement of retained earnings

✔ d = $1,023,828

The partially completed statement of retained earnings information is given for Crossman's Deli Ltd. for four years.

	2016	2015	2014	2013
Beginning balance	$ a	$ d	$ g	$925,478
Net income (loss)	238,945	e	h	258,475
Preferred dividends	55,000	82,000	36,000	i
Common dividends	17,000	31,000	24,000	10,000
Increase (decrease) in retained earnings	b	(89,451)	(118,125)	216,475
Ending balance	$ c	$ f	$1,023,828	$ j

Instructions

Fill in the missing numbers.

---

③
④
⑤

PR 12-5B

Selected corporate transactions

✔ 1. Dec. 30, Dividends payable, $121,050

Your Environment Ltd. manufactures household cleaning supplies. The shareholders' equity accounts of Your Environment Ltd., with balances on January 1, 2015, are as follows:

Common shares (1,000,000 shares authorized, 430,000 shares issued and outstanding)	$9,460,000
Retained earnings	8,230,000

The following selected transactions occurred during the year:

Jan. 7. Paid cash dividends of $0.13 per share. The dividend had been properly recorded when declared on November 30 of the preceding fiscal year.

Feb. 9. Issued 40,000 common shares for $960,000.

Jul. 1. Issued 14,200 common shares at $25.75 per share.

Dec. 30. Declared a $0.25-per-share dividend. Your Environment does not use a cash dividends account.

31. Recorded the closing entry for the income for the year of $732,000.

Instructions

1. Journalize the entries to record the transactions.
2. Prepare a statement of retained earnings for the year ended December 31, 2015.
3. Prepare the shareholders' equity section of the December 31, 2015, balance sheet.

---

③
④
⑤

PR 12-6B

Selected corporate transactions

✔ Nov. 15, cash dividends, $638,600

Konzo's Boating Corporation makes specialty sailboats in Ontario. The shareholders' equity accounts, with balances on April 1, 2015, the beginning of the fiscal year, are as follows:

$2.80 preferred shares (700,000 shares authorized, 150,000 shares issued and outstanding)	$ 5,250,000
Common shares (unlimited shares authorized, 1,250,000 shares issued and outstanding)	18,750,000
Retained earnings	3,040,000

Selected transactions completed by Konzo's Boating Corporation during the current fiscal year are as follows:

May 1. Declared semiannual dividends on the preferred shares and $0.26 on the common shares to shareholders of record on May 15, payable on June 1. Konzo's Boating does not use a cash dividends account.

Jun. 1. Paid the cash dividends.

Aug. 5. Issued an additional 34,000 preferred shares at $37 per share.

Sep. 10. Issued an additional 20,000 common shares at $13 per share.

Nov. 15. Declared semiannual dividends on the preferred shares and $0.30 on the common shares to shareholders of record on November 30, payable December 31.

Dec. 31. Paid the cash dividends.

Mar. 31. Recorded the closing entry for the income for the year of $2,950,000.

Instructions

1. Journalize the transactions.
2. Prepare the statement of retained earnings for the year ended March 31, 2016.
3. Prepare the shareholders' equity section of the balance sheet as at March 31, 2016.

---

③ ④ ⑤ PR 12-7B
Selected transactions, statement of changes in equity

✔ Total shareholders' equity, June 30, 2016, $28,616,523

Belinger Cooling Ltd. supplies and installs air conditioners to new homes. The shareholders' equity account balances as at July 1, 2015, are shown below:

$1.60 preferred shares (750,000 authorized, 200,000 issued and outstanding)	$ 8,400,000
Common shares (unlimited authorized, 750,000 issued and outstanding)	12,000,000
Retained earnings	3,057,823
Accumulated other comprehensive income	0

Following are some selected transactions affecting the shareholders' equity during the year:

Jul. 3. Declared quarterly dividends of $120,000 to be paid September 30, to shareholders of record on August 28. Belinger Cooling uses a cash dividends account.

Sep. 15. Issued 50,000 preferred shares for $48 per share.
     30. Paid the cash dividends.

Oct. 5. Declared quarterly dividends of $130,000 to be paid December 31, to shareholders of record on November 24.

Dec. 31. Paid the cash dividends.

Jan. 4. Issued 125,000 common shares for $20 per share.
      7. Declared quarterly dividends of $135,000 to be paid March 31, to shareholders of record on February 21.

Mar. 31. Paid the cash dividends.

Apr. 15. Declared quarterly dividends of $145,000 to be paid June 30, to shareholders of record on May 20.

Jun. 30. Paid the cash dividends.
          Prepared the year-end closing entries with net income of $734,800 and other comprehensive income of $53,900. Belinger Cooling uses the income summary account when preparing the closing entries.

Instructions

1. Journalize the transactions.
2. Prepare a statement of changes in equity.
3. Prepare the shareholders' equity section of the balance sheet as at June 30, 2016.

---

③ ④ ⑤ PR 12-8B
Selected transactions, statement of changes in equity

✔ Total retained earnings at July 31, 2016, $1,543,235

Veronica's Bears Ltd. manufactures teddy bears. The shareholders' equity account balances at August 1, 2015, are shown below:

$3.60 cumulative preferred shares (750,000 authorized, 75,000 issued and outstanding)	$2,100,000
Common shares (1,000,000 authorized, 460,000 issued and outstanding)	6,440,000
Retained earnings	1,354,000
Accumulated other comprehensive income	22,369

The following are selected transactions during the year:

Aug. 21. Paid the semiannual dividends of $160,000 declared and recorded properly in June. No new preferred or common shares were issued during June, July, or August. Veronica's Bears uses a cash dividends account.

Sep. 5. Issued 25,000 preferred shares for $29 per share.

Dec. 15. Declared semiannual dividends of $160,000 to be paid February 20, 2016, to shareholders of record on January 28.

(continued)

Feb. 20. Paid the cash dividends.

Mar. 4. Issued 75,000 common shares for $12 per share.

Jun. 5. Declared semiannual dividends of $240,000 to be paid August 16, to shareholders of record on July 24.

Jun. 15. 10,000 common shares were traded in the marketplace at $16 per share.

Jul. 31. Prepared the year-end closing entries with net income of $589,235 and a gain in other comprehensive income of $6,258. Veronica's Bears uses the income summary account when preparing the closing entries.

Instructions

1. Journalize the transactions.
2. Prepare a statement of changes in equity.
3. Prepare the shareholders' equity section of the balance sheet as at July 31, 2016.

PR 12-9B

Return on common shareholders' equity

Whitewater Adventurers Ltd. is a getaway resort in northern Ontario. The statement of changes in equity for the years ended December 31, 2015 and 2016, are shown below:

✔ 2016 return on common shareholders' equity, 12.5%

Whitewater Adventurers Ltd.
Statement of Changes in Equity
For the Year Ended December 31, 2016

	Preferred Shares	Common Shares	Retained Earnings	Accum. Other Compre. Income	Total
Balance, January 1, 2016	$750,250	$1,356,000	$1,434,000	$ 6,400	$3,546,650
Net income			486,000		486,000
Dividends on preferred shares			(100,000)		(100,000)
Dividends on common shares			(75,000)		(75,000)
Issuance of shares		275,000			275,000
Unrealized gain on revaluation of assets				12,560	12,560
Balance, December 31, 2016	$750,250	$1,631,000	$1,745,000	$18,960	$4,145,210

Whitewater Adventurers Ltd.
Statement of Changes in Equity
For the Year Ended December 31, 2015

	Preferred Shares	Common Shares	Retained Earnings	Accum. Other Compre. Income	Total
Balance, January 1, 2015	$750,250	$1,356,000	$ 956,000	$3,600	$3,065,850
Net income			653,000		653,000
Dividends on preferred shares			(100,000)		(100,000)
Dividends on common shares			(75,000)		(75,000)
Unrealized gain on revaluation of assets				2,800	2,800
Balance, December 31, 2015	$750,250	$1,356,000	$1,434,000	$6,400	$3,546,650

Instructions

1. Calculate the return on common shareholders' equity for 2016 and 2015.
2. Has the ratio improved or declined over the years? Do you have enough information to determine whether Whitewater Adventurers is performing to standard? If you do not have enough information, what additional information is needed to make this determination?

SPECIAL ACTIVITIES

SA 12-1
Board of directors' actions

Bernie Ebbers, the CEO of WorldCom, a major telecommunications company, was having personal financial troubles. Ebbers pledged a large stake of his WorldCom shares as security for some personal loans. When the price of WorldCom shares sank, Ebbers' bankers threatened to sell his shares in order to protect their loans. To avoid having his shares sold, Ebbers asked the board of directors of WorldCom to loan him nearly $400 million of corporate assets at 2.5% interest to pay off his bankers. The board agreed to lend him the money.

Comment on the decision of the board of directors in this situation.

SA 12-2
Issuing shares

Biosciences Unlimited Ltd. begins operations on January 2, 2015, with the issuance of 100,000 common shares at $50 per share. The only shareholders of Biosciences Unlimited Ltd. are Rafel Baltis and Dr. Oscar Hansel, who organized Biosciences Unlimited Ltd. with the objective of developing a new flu vaccine. Dr. Hansel claims that the flu vaccine, which is nearing the final development stage, will protect individuals against 90% of the flu types that have been medically identified. To complete the project, Biosciences Unlimited Ltd. needs $10,000,000 of additional funds. The local banks have been unwilling to loan the funds because of the lack of sufficient collateral and the riskiness of the business.

The following is a conversation between Rafel, the chief executive officer of Biosciences Unlimited Ltd., and Dr. Hansel, the leading researcher.

Rafel: What are we going to do? The banks won't loan us any more money, and we need $10 million to complete the project. We are so close! It would be a disaster to quit now. The only thing I can think of is to issue additional shares. Do you have any suggestions?

Oscar: I guess you're right. But if the banks won't loan us any more money, how do you think we can find any investors to buy shares?

Rafel: I've been thinking about that. What if we promise the investors that we will pay them 2% of net sales until they have received an amount equal to what they paid for the shares?

Oscar: What happens when we pay back the $10 million? Do the investors get to keep the shares? If they do, it'll dilute our ownership.

Rafel: How about, if after we pay back the $10 million, we make them turn in their shares for $100 per share? That's twice what they paid for it, plus they would have already received all their money back. That's a $100 profit per share for the investors.

Oscar: It could work. We get our money, but don't have to pay any interest, dividends, or the $50 until we start generating net sales. At the same time, the investors could get their money back plus $100 per share.

Rafel: We'll need current financial statements for the new investors. I'll get our accountant working on them and contact our lawyer to draw up a legally binding contract for the new investors. Yes, this could work.

In late 2015, the lawyer and the various regulatory authorities approve the new share offering, and 200,000 common shares are privately sold to new investors at $50 per share.

In preparing financial statements for 2015, Rafel Baltis and Emma Cavins, the controller for Biosciences Unlimited Ltd., have the following conversation:

Emma: Rafel, I've got a problem.

Rafel: What's that, Emma?

Emma: Issuing common shares to raise that additional $10 million was a great idea. But . . .

Rafel: But what?

Emma: I've got to prepare the 2015 annual financial statements, and I am not sure how to classify the common shares.

Rafel: What do you mean? It's equity.

Emma: I'm not so sure. I called the auditor and explained how we are contractually obligated to pay the new shareholders 2% of net sales until $50 per share is paid. Then we may be obligated to pay them $100 per share.

Rafel: So . . .

Emma: So the auditor thinks that we should classify the issuance of $10 million as debt, not shares! And if we put the $10 million on the balance sheet as debt, we will violate our other loan agreements with the banks. And if these agreements are violated, the banks may call in all our debt immediately. If they do that, we are in deep trouble. We'll probably have to file for bankruptcy. We just don't have the cash to pay off the banks.

1. Discuss the arguments for and against classifying the issuance of the $10 million of shares as debt.
2. Can you think of a practical solution to this classification problem?

SA 12-3

Interpret stock exchange listing

f·a·i

The following stock exchange data for Leon's Furniture Limited was taken from the Toronto Stock Exchange (TSX) website on June 21, 2012:

Leon's Furniture Limited (TSX: LNF)			
Last Trade:	10.95	Prev. Close:	10.95
$ Change:	0	% Change:	0
# of o/s shares:	69,974,017	52 wk. range:	10.55–13.08
Div. paid:	Quarterly	Indicated Annual Div. Rate:	$0.10
EPS:	$0.78		

a. If you owned 500 shares of Leon's, what amount would you receive as a quarterly dividend?
b. What are the net earnings for the year, assuming no preferred shares have been issued?
c. If you bought 500 shares of Leon's at the last trade price on June 21, 2012, how much would it cost, and who receives the money?

SA 12-4

Profiling a corporation

Group Project

Internet Project

Select a public corporation you are familiar with or one that interests you. Using the Internet, your school library, and other sources, develop a short profile (one to two pages) of the corporation. Include in your profile the following information:

1. Name of the corporation
2. Location of incorporation
3. Nature of its operations
4. Total assets for the most recent statement of financial position
5. Total revenues for the most recent income statement
6. Net income for the most recent income statement
7. Classes of shares outstanding
8. Market price of the shares outstanding
9. High and low price of the shares for the past year
10. Dividends paid for each class of shares during the past year

In groups of three or four, discuss each corporate profile. Select one of the corporations, assuming that your group has $100,000 to invest in its shares. Summarize why your group selected the corporation it did and how financial accounting information may have affected your decision. Keep track of the performance of your corporation's shares for the remainder of the term.

Note: A corporation's website provides a variety of information on the corporation and often includes the corporation's financial statements. In addition, the Toronto Stock Exchange website, **www.tmx.com**, includes links to the websites of many listed companies. Financial statements can also be accessed using SEDAR (System for Electronic Document Analysis and Retrieval), the electronic archives of financial statements filed with the Canadian Securities Administrators (CSA).

CSA documents can be retrieved using the SEDAR service at **www.sedar.com/ homepage_en.htm**. To obtain annual report information, select "Search Database," then select "Public Company." Enter the company name where it is indicated. When the list comes up, click on the document you are searching for, such as the "Audited annual financial statements."

SA 12-5
Share ownership

Carl and Janet recently received $5,000 bonuses from work and have been discussing buying shares as an investment opportunity. They are considering two different companies and have come to you for advice. Given the information below, how would you advise Carl and Janet?

	Capricorn Delivery Inc.	Universal Training Equipment Inc.
Share price	$ 10	$ 7.50
Current number of shares outstanding	1,200	10,000
Annual dividend rate	$ 1.75	$ 2.25

SA 12-6
Market price of shares

Dom Dominici is the founder of Dom's Pizzeria Inc. Dom has been watching the share price for Dom's Pizzeria rise steadily over the past three months. Dom is extremely excited during a conversation with the accountant for Dom's Pizzeria. They are only a few weeks away from releasing the company's annual report. Dom believes the results of the share price increase will have an astounding impact on the financial results of Dom's Pizzeria this year. If you were Dom's accountant, what would you tell him?

SA 12-7
Dividends per share

Refer to the financial statements for Morning Java at the end of this chapter or in Appendix A.

Answer the following questions:
1. How much was the preferred dividend per share?
2. How much was the common dividend per share?
3. Why did the shareholders receive different amounts?

SA 12-8
Market value of shares

Catherine has been approached by her brother Dirk, who has recently started a new corporation with their brother David. Thompson Brothers Inc. manufactures specialized equipment to aid in cleaning the underside of boats without removing them from the water. Dirk and David had been operating Thompson Brothers as a partnership for five years. The expansion to a corporation has required more money than they expected, and they have asked Catherine to purchase shares in their corporation. Catherine is trying to determine a fair price for the shares but is having difficulty. She has asked you to explain why she is unable to find out the current market price for Thompson Brothers Inc.

1. What might help Catherine determine a fair price?
2. What questions should you advise Catherine to ask her brothers?

Corporations: Additional Share Transactions, Income Statement, and Accounting Changes

SHOPPERS DRUG MART

In 1962, Shoppers Drug Mart, a company founded by pharmacist Murray Koffler, opened its first store in the Shoppers World Plaza in Toronto, Ontario. Since then, Shoppers Drug Mart has continually expanded, opening its 1,000th store in 2007. By 2011, the company had more than 1,200 stores across Canada. Shoppers Drug Mart is the leader in Canada's retail drug store marketplace, claiming the number-one ranking as a provider of pharmacy products and services. Shoppers Drug Mart offers 7,500 of its own private-label brands, such as Life Brand, Quo, Simply Food, and Nativa. Ten million customers participate in the Shoppers Optimum loyalty card program, whereby customers collect points that can be cashed in for products. On November 21, 2001, Shoppers Drug Mart had its initial public offering (IPO) of shares at $18 per share. Ten years later, those shares were trading at $42 a share.

In 2011, Shoppers Drug Mart repurchased more than five million shares for $206.8 million. Why would Shoppers Drug Mart buy back its shares? And, equally importantly, if you were Shoppers Drug Mart's accountant, how would you have accounted for that transaction?

In Chapter 12, basic accounting transactions for corporations were introduced, such as forming a corporation, issuing shares for cash or in exchange for other assets, and recording cash dividends. In addition, Chapter 12 illustrated the Shareholders' Equity section of a balance sheet and the statement of changes in equity.

Chapter 13 describes additional share transactions that a corporation may engage in, such as Shoppers Drug Mart's share repurchase, issuing share dividends, and share splits. We will also explain some of the items that may appear on a corporation's income statement, such as discontinued operations and earnings per share. By the end of this chapter, you will know how to account for Shoppers Drug Mart's share repurchase. You will also have some ideas about what might have caused Shoppers Drug Mart to make the repurchase. Shoppers Drug Mart's 2011 financial statements and selected notes are shown in Appendix C.

After studying this chapter, you should be able to:

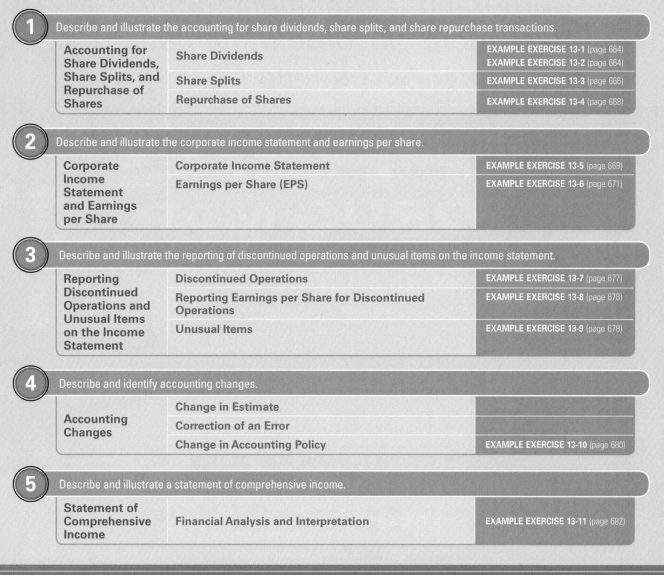

1 Describe and illustrate the accounting for share dividends, share splits, and share repurchase transactions.

Accounting for Share Dividends, Share Splits, and Repurchase of Shares	Share Dividends	EXAMPLE EXERCISE 13-1 (page 664) EXAMPLE EXERCISE 13-2 (page 664)
	Share Splits	EXAMPLE EXERCISE 13-3 (page 666)
	Repurchase of Shares	EXAMPLE EXERCISE 13-4 (page 668)

2 Describe and illustrate the corporate income statement and earnings per share.

Corporate Income Statement and Earnings per Share	Corporate Income Statement	EXAMPLE EXERCISE 13-5 (page 669)
	Earnings per Share (EPS)	EXAMPLE EXERCISE 13-6 (page 671)

3 Describe and illustrate the reporting of discontinued operations and unusual items on the income statement.

Reporting Discontinued Operations and Unusual Items on the Income Statement	Discontinued Operations	EXAMPLE EXERCISE 13-7 (page 677)
	Reporting Earnings per Share for Discontinued Operations	EXAMPLE EXERCISE 13-8 (page 678)
	Unusual Items	EXAMPLE EXERCISE 13-9 (page 678)

4 Describe and identify accounting changes.

Accounting Changes	Change in Estimate	
	Correction of an Error	
	Change in Accounting Policy	EXAMPLE EXERCISE 13-10 (page 680)

5 Describe and illustrate a statement of comprehensive income.

Statement of Comprehensive Income	Financial Analysis and Interpretation	EXAMPLE EXERCISE 13-11 (page 682)

For the chapter *At a Glance*, turn to page 683.

1

Describe and illustrate the accounting for share dividends, share splits, and share repurchase transactions.

Accounting for Share Dividends, Share Splits, and Repurchase of Shares

Share Dividends

In Chapter 12, cash dividends were described and illustrated. As discussed, dividends are distributions of a corporation's earnings to shareholders, similar to withdrawals for sole proprietorships or partnerships. When the board of directors declares that a dividend will be paid (on the date of declaration), a liability is incurred, which is to be paid to shareholders of record (shareholders as of the date of record), and the liability is discharged when the dividend is paid (on the date of payment).

In addition to cash dividends, a corporation can issue a **share dividend**, or **stock dividend**, which is a distribution of shares to shareholders. Share dividends are normally declared only on common shares and, thus, are issued only to common shareholders. Share dividends allow corporations to give shareholders a dividend without using cash. Reasons for a corporation issuing a share dividend are varied and may include the following:

- To satisfy the expectations of owners without spending cash.

  If a corporation normally pays a quarterly dividend, then shareholders expect to receive a disbursement each quarter. If adequate cash to pay a dividend is not available, issuing a share dividend provides the shareholder with something of value, without draining the corporation's working capital.

- To reduce the market price of the share.

  Issuing a share dividend increases the number of shares outstanding. Basic economics suggests that when supply increases, demand becomes satisfied, and thus, the market price of the shares declines. Because shares normally trade in blocks of 100, an investor would need $10,000 to purchase a block of shares with a market price of $100 per share. Reducing the market price can make a share more affordable and, thus, more attractive as an investment.

- To emphasize the permanent reinvestment of shareholders' equity.

  Issuing a share dividend can be a signal to the market that the money is better spent within the corporation than paid out as a cash dividend. A corporation is implicitly saying it has better use for the cash and can make a better return by investing the cash in the business than can the shareholder who would otherwise receive the cash dividend.

Similar to cash dividends, share dividends are declared by the board of directors (on the date of declaration), issued to shareholders of record (shareholders as at the date of record), and distributed to shareholders (on the date of distribution). The recording of a share dividend affects only shareholders' equity. Specifically, the amount of the share dividend is transferred from Retained Earnings to Contributed Capital. The amount transferred is normally the fair value (market price), on the date of declaration, of the shares issued in the share dividend. To illustrate, assume that the shareholders' equity accounts of Henderson Corporation as at December 15, 2015, are as follows:

Henderson Corporation
Balance Sheet (Partial)
December 15, 2015

Shareholders' Equity

Contributed capital:

$2.50 preferred shares, 150,000 issued and outstanding	$ 9,000,000
Common shares, 2,000,000 issued and outstanding	40,000,000
Total contributed capital	49,000,000
Retained earnings	26,600,000
Total shareholders' equity	$75,600,000

On December 15, Henderson Corporation declares a share dividend of 5% or 100,000 shares (2,000,000 shares × 5%) to be issued on January 10 to shareholders of record on December 31. The market price of the shares on December 15 (the date of declaration) is $31 per share. When recording a share dividend, the debit may be to Retained Earnings or Share Dividends, but not both. If the corporation wants to track the dividends distributed to the shareholders, it would use the share dividends account and prepare a closing entry at year-end to close the share dividends account to the retained earnings. This concept was discussed in Chapter 12. The entry to record the share dividend is as follows:

2015				
Dec.	15	Retained Earnings (or Share Dividends)	3,100,000	
		Common Share Dividend Distributable		3,100,000
		Declared 5%(100,000 shares) share dividend on		
		common shares with a market price of $31 per		
		share (5% × 2,000,000 shares × $31).		

If, at the end of the period, the common shares have not yet been issued, the *common share dividend distributable* account is reported in the Contributed Capital section of the balance sheet. Note that this treatment differs from that afforded a cash dividend—a declared but unpaid cash dividend is a current obligation that will require a future payment of cash, which meets the definition of a liability, and thus appears as a current liability on the balance sheet. Share dividends do not result in the future outflow of cash and do not meet the definition of a liability. The shareholders' equity accounts of Henderson Corporation as at December 31, 2015, are as follows:

Henderson Corporation
Balance Sheet (Partial)
December 31, 2015

Shareholders' Equity

Contributed capital:

$2.50 preferred shares, 150,000 issued and outstanding	$ 9,000,000
Common shares, 2,000,000 issued and outstanding	40,000,000
Common share dividend distributable	3,100,000
Total contributed capital	52,100,000
Retained earnings	23,500,000
Total shareholders' equity	$75,600,000

On January 10, 2016, the share dividend is distributed to shareholders by issuing 100,000 common shares. The issuance of the shares is recorded by the following entry:

2016				
Jan.	10	Common Share Dividend Distributable	3,100,000	
		Common Shares		3,100,000
		Issued share dividend of 100,000 common		
		shares.		

The shareholders' equity accounts of Henderson Corporation as at January 10, 2016, are as follows:

Henderson Corporation
Balance Sheet
January 10, 2016

Shareholders' Equity

Contributed capital:

$2.50 preferred shares, 150,000 issued
    and outstanding . . . . $ 9,000,000

Common shares, 2,100,000 issued
    and outstanding   43,100,000

    Total contributed capital   52,100,000

Retained earnings   23,500,000

Total shareholders' equity $75,600,000

A share dividend does not change the assets, liabilities, or total shareholders' equity of a corporation. Likewise, a share dividend does not change an individual shareholder's proportionate interest (equity) in the corporation. The share dividend does change the reporting of the shares because the number of shares outstanding has changed.

To illustrate, assume a shareholder owns 10,000 of Henderson's shares prior to the share dividend declaration. The impact of the share dividend on the number of shares issued and the shareholder's proportionate ownership are shown below.

	Before Share Dividend	**After Share Dividend**
Total common shares issued	2,000,000	2,100,000 [2,000,000 + (2,000,000 × 5%)]
Number of shares owned	10,000	10,500 [10,000 × (10,000 × 5%)]
Proportionate ownership	0.5% (10,000/2,000,000)	0.5% (10,500/2,100,000)

As illustrated by the Henderson example, a share dividend shifts value from retained earnings to contributed capital with no change to the total shareholders' equity.

Impact of Share Dividend on Equity:

	Before Share Dividend	**After Share Dividend**	**Change**
Total common shares issued	2,000,000	2,100,000	↑
Book value of common shares	$40,000,000	$43,100,000	↑
Retained earnings	$26,600,000	$23,500,000	↓
Total shareholders' equity	$75,600,000	$75,600,000	No change

1

EXAMPLE EXERCISE 13-1 **Entries for Share Dividends**

On August 1, 2015, Merlin Island Hoppers Corporation has the following capital account balances:

$2 preferred shares, 200,000 authorized,	
20,000 issued and outstanding..	$ 2,000,000
Common shares, unlimited authorized,	
300,000 issued and outstanding...	3,120,000
Total contributed capital..	5,120,000
Retained earnings...	10,000,000
Total shareholders' equity..	$15,120,000

On August 14, Merlin Island Hoppers declared a 4% share dividend to be issued October 15 to shareholders of record on September 1. The market price was $110 per share on August 14.
   Journalize the entries required on August 14, September 1, and October 15.

FOLLOW MY EXAMPLE 13-1

Aug. 14	Retained Earnings (or Share Dividends)..	1,320,000	
	Common Share Dividend Distributable.......................................		1,320,000
	Declared 4% (12,000 Shares) share dividend on		
	common shares with a market price of $110 per share		
	(300,000 × 4% × $110).		
Sept. 1	No entry required.		
Oct. 15	Common Share Dividend Distributable	1,320,000	
	Common Shares..		1,320,000
	Issued share dividend of 12,000 Common Shares.		

For Practice: PE 13-1

1

EXAMPLE EXERCISE 13-2 **Shareholders' Equity**

Using the information in Example Exercise 13-1, prepare the Shareholders' Equity section of the balance sheet for Merlin Island Hoppers Corporation as at October 15, 2015.

FOLLOW MY EXAMPLE 13-2

Merlin Island Hoppers Corporation
Balance Sheet (Partial)
October 15, 2015

Shareholders' Equity

Contributed Capital:	
$2 preferred shares, 200,000 authorized,	
20,000 issued and outstanding..	$ 2,000,000
Common shares, unlimited authorized,	
312,000 issued and outstanding..	4,440,000
Total contributed capital...	6,440,000
Retained earnings...	8,680,000
Total shareholders' equity..	$15,120,000

For Practice: PE 13-2

Share Splits

A **share split**, or **stock split**, is a process by which a corporation reduces the value of each common share by issuing a proportional number of additional shares. A "2-for-1 share split," for example, would require the issuance of an equal number of shares to the existing number of shares. A share split applies to all common shares, including the unissued shares. A share dividend, on the other hand, applies only to issued shares.

A major objective of a share split is to reduce the market price per share in order to attract more investors to purchase the shares and to broaden the types and numbers of shareholders.

To illustrate, assume that on June 30, 2015, Rosen Corporation's shares were trading at $150 per share. Rosen Corporation's equity account balances on that date were as follows:

Rosen Corporation
Balance Sheet (Partial)
June 30, 2015

Shareholders' Equity

Contributed capital:	
Common shares, 100,000 issued and outstanding	$10,000,000
Retained earnings	12,680,000
Total shareholders' equity	$22,680,000

The board of directors declared a 5-for-1 share split, meaning that each common share-holder will receive four additional shares for each share held. The average cost, or **book value**, of the individual outstanding common shares will be reduced as shown below.

Before: $10,000,000 ÷ 100,000 shares = $100 per share
After: $10,000,000 ÷ 500,000 shares = $20 per share

Because more shares are outstanding after the share split, the market price of the shares should decrease. For example, in the preceding example, five times as many shares are outstanding after the split. Because the shares were trading at $150 per share before the split, the market price would likely decrease to approximately $30 ($150/5). Share splits often have a buoyant effect on the market price of a share, and so Rosen's shares may trade at more than $30 per share. Other factors, such as expected future earn-ings of the company, would also be considered by existing and potential shareholders.

In addition, each Rosen Corporation shareholder owns the same total dollar amount of shares before and after the share split. For example, a shareholder who owned 25,000 shares before the split (total book value of $2,500,000) would own 125,000 shares after the split (total book value of $2,500,000). Only the number of shares and the book value per share have changed.

Note: A share split does not require a journal entry.

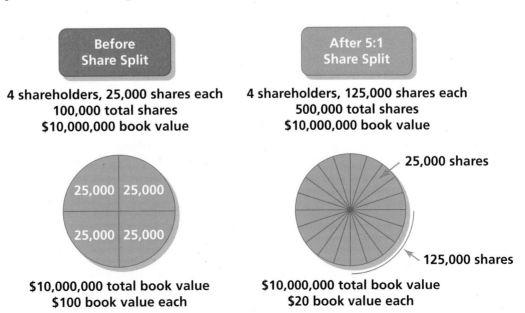

Before Share Split	After 5:1 Share Split
4 shareholders, 25,000 shares each	4 shareholders, 125,000 shares each
100,000 total shares	500,000 total shares
$10,000,000 book value	$10,000,000 book value

25,000 shares

125,000 shares

$10,000,000 total book value
$100 book value each

$10,000,000 total book value
$20 book value each

Share splits do not require a journal entry because only the book value and the number of shares outstanding have changed; however, the details of share splits are normally disclosed in the notes to the financial statements.

The board of directors may also declare a reverse share split. A reverse share split occurs when a corporation wants to increase the market price of its shares. A 1-for-10 share split, for example, would result in the issuance of one new share for 10 old shares. Decreasing the supply of shares in the marketplace should increase the demand, thereby causing an upward adjustment of the fair value (market price) of the shares.

EXAMPLE EXERCISE 13-3 Shareholders' Equity   (1)

Blackmore Corporation had the following balances in its shareholders' equity accounts as at October 31, 2015:

Retained earnings	$375,000
Common shares, unlimited authorized, 10,000 issued and outstanding	175,000
$1.50 preferred shares, unlimited authorized, 3,000 issued and outstanding	90,000

On November 14, the board of directors declared a 3:1 share split.
  Prepare the Shareholders' Equity section of the balance sheet for Blackmore Corporation as at November 15, 2015.

FOLLOW MY EXAMPLE 13-3

Blackmore Corporation
Balance Sheet (Partial)
November 15, 2015

Shareholders' Equity	
Contributed Capital:	
$1.50 preferred shares, unlimited authorized,	
3,000 issued and outstanding...	$ 90,000
Common shares, unlimited authorized,	
30,000 issued and outstanding...	175,000
Total contributed capital	265,000
Retained earnings...	375,000
Total shareholders' equity...	$640,000

For Practice: PE 13-3

Repurchase of Shares

A corporation may reacquire (repurchase) its own shares for a variety of reasons including the following:

1. to avoid a hostile takeover by an investor
2. to reduce future dividend payments
3. to support the market price of the shares

The Canada Business Corporations Act requires corporations to retire or cancel shares they repurchase from the shareholders. Shoppers Drug Mart disclosed that it had *purchased and cancelled* common shares in 2011. British Columbia and Nova Scotia permit corporations registered under their respective provincial corporations acts to hold repurchased shares in their Treasury. Because treasury shares are rare in Canada, we do not include a discussion about them in this textbook.

The *cost method* is normally used for recording the repurchase of shares. Using the cost method, the share capital account is debited for the average original issuance price of the shares. If the amount of cash paid to repurchase the shares is less than the average issue price, the difference is credited to **Contributed Capital from Retirement of Common Shares**. If the amount of cash paid is greater than the average issue price, the difference is debited to Contributed Capital from Retirement of Common Shares to the extent this account had a credit balance, or debited to retained earnings. Contributed capital from retirement of common shares cannot have a debit balance.

No dividends are paid on the repurchased shares. To do so would result in the corporation earning dividend revenue from itself. Also, the above transactions do not result in gains or losses because the transaction is nonoperational and doesn't meet the definition of a gain or loss. To illustrate, assume that on February 1, 2015, Insight Corporation has the following capital account balances:

Common shares, 20,000 shares authorized and issued	$500,000
Retained earnings	150,000
Total shareholders' equity	$650,000

On February 13, Insight Corporation repurchases and retires 1,000 common shares at $25 per share. The average price at which the shares were issued ($500,000/20,000 = $25) is equal to the purchase price, and so the entry to record the repurchase of shares is as follows:

2015				
Feb.	13	Common Shares	25,000	
		Cash		25,000
		Repurchased and retired 1,000 common shares		
		at $25 per share.		

On April 29, the corporation repurchases and retires 600 common shares for $20 per share. The repurchase price of $20 is less than the average price of $25 at which the shares were originally issued. The difference is credited to Contributed Capital from Retirement of Common Shares. If the Contributed Capital from Retirement of Common Shares account has a balance when the financial statements are prepared, that amount will be reported immediately following the common shares in the contributed capital portion of the Shareholders' Equity section. The entry to record the purchase is as follows:

2015				
Apr.	29	Common Shares (600 × $25)	15,000	
		Cash (600 × $20)		12,000
		Contributed Capital from Retirement of		
		Common Shares		3,000
		Repurchased and retired 600 common shares		
		at $20 per share.		

On October 4, the corporation repurchases and retires 1,200 common shares for $35 per share. The purchase price exceeds the $25 average issuance price. When shares are repurchased at a price that exceeds their issuance price, or average cost, the difference is debited to Contributed Capital from Retirement of Common Shares or the Retained Earnings account.

The entry to record the sale is as follows:

2015				
Oct.	4	Common Shares (1,200 × $25)	30,000	
		Contributed Capital from Retirement		
		of Common Shares	3,000	
		Retained Earnings	9,000	
		Cash		42,000
		Repurchased and retired 1,200 common shares		
		at $35 per share.		

Exhibit 1 summarizes the journal entries for share repurchases when shares are repurchased at various prices relative to their issuance cost.

Exhibit 1

1. When shares are repurchased for their average issuance cost:

Dr. Common Shares (# of repurchased shares × average cost)	xxx	
Cr. Cash (# of repurchased shares × repurchase price)		xxx

2. When shares are repurchased for less than their average issuance cost:

Dr. Common Shares (# of repurchased shares × average cost)	xxx	
Cr. Cash (# of repurchased shares × repurchase price)		xxx
Cr. Contributed Capital from Retirement of Common Shares		xxx

3. When shares are repurchased for more than their average issuance cost:

Dr. Common Shares (# of repurchased shares × average cost)	xxx	
Dr. Contributed Capital from Retirement of Common Shares (to lesser of difference or balance in account)	xxx	
Dr. Retained Earnings	xxx	
Cr. Cash (# of repurchased shares × repurchase price)		xxx

EXAMPLE EXERCISE 13-4 Repurchase of Shares ①

Buzz Off Corporation's shareholders' equity had the following account balances:

Common shares, unlimited authorized, 250,000 issued and outstanding	$2,500,000
Retained earnings	400,000

On May 3, Buzz Off Corporation reacquired and retired 3,200 common shares at $12 per share. On July 22, Buzz Off purchased and retired an additional 2,000 shares at $9 per share. On August 30, Buzz Off purchased and retired another 1,000 shares at $13 per share.

Journalize the transactions of May 3, July 22, and August 30.

FOLLOW MY EXAMPLE 13-4

May	3	Common Shares (3,200 × $10)...	32,000	
		Retained Earnings..	6,400	
		Cash (3,200 × $12)...		38,400
		Repurchased and retired 3,200 common shares at $12 per share.		
Jul.	22	Common Shares (2,000 × $10)...	20,000	
		Cash (2,000 × $9)...		18,000
		Contributed Capital from Retirement of Common Shares...		2,000
		Repurchased and retired 2,000 common shares at $9 per share.		
Aug.	30	Common Shares (1,000 × $10)...	10,000	
		Contributed Capital from Retirement of Common Shares	2,000	
		Retained Earnings..	1,000	
		Cash (1,000 × $13)...		13,000
		Repurchased and retired 1,000 common shares at $13 per share.		

For Practice: PE 13-4

---

② **Corporate Income Statement and Earnings per Share**

Describe and illustrate the corporate income statement and earnings per share.

Corporate Income Statement

An example of a corporate income statement is shown in Exhibit 2. A corporate income statement differs from income statements prepared for partnerships or sole proprietorships in a number of ways:

One major difference is income taxes.

Exhibit 2

Corporate Income Statement

Smith Corporation Income Statement For the Year Ended December 31, 2015		
Net sales.		$12,350,000
Cost of goods sold.		5,800,000
Gross profit.		6,550,000
Selling and administrative expenses.		5,240,000
Income from operations		1,310,000
Other revenues and expenses:		
Interest revenue.	$ 355,000	
Gain on sale of capital assets.	83,450	
Loss due to plant shutdown	(743,200)	
		304,750
Income before income taxes		1,005,250
Income taxes expense		301,575
Net income		$ 703,675
Earnings per share		$ 0.47

Income Taxes All business income is subject to federal and provincial or territorial income taxes. For sole proprietorships and partnerships, the owners declare the business income and pay the business taxes when they file their personal income tax returns. Thus, the category of income taxes expense does not exist on the income statements for sole proprietorships or partnerships.

As discussed in Chapter 12, corporations are separate legal entities from their owners and, as such, are responsible for their income taxes. The determination of income taxes owing is a detailed topic that will not be covered in this textbook. For illustrative purposes, we will use simple percentages to calculate the income taxes expense. In Exhibit 2, taxes have been calculated as 30% of income.

Another difference is earnings per share. Corporations that report using IFRS are required to show the earnings that are attributable to common shareholders. ASPE does not require the inclusion of earnings per share.

As discussed in Chapter 5, companies may choose to report their income using a single-step or a multiple-step income statement. This choice applies to sole proprietorships, partnerships, and corporations. Exhibit 2 is an example of a multiple-step income statement for a corporation, with revenues and expenses divided into categories. Later in the chapter we will introduce a category that may appear on a corporate income statement: discontinued operations.

EXAMPLE EXERCISE 13-5 Corporate Income Statement   2

Using the following accounts and balances, prepare the income statement for Fosters Equipment Ltd. for the year ended April 30, 2015, assuming a 30% tax rate. Ignore earnings per share.

Cost of goods sold	$5,000,000
Income taxes payable	235,677
Selling and administrative expenses.	2,355,000
Accrued liabilities.	237,000
Interest expense.	140,000
Prepaid insurance	5,670
Loss on sale of land	677,000
Unearned revenue	323,000
Net sales	9,500,400

(continued)

Fosters Equipment Ltd.
Income Statement
For the Year Ended April 30, 2015

Net sales		$9,500,400
Cost of goods sold		5,000,000
Gross profit		4,500,400
Selling and administrative expenses		2,355,000
Income from operations		2,145,400
Other revenues and expenses:		
Interest expense	$140,000	
Loss on sale of land	677,000	
		817,000
Income before income taxes		1,328,400
Income taxes expense		398,520*
Net income		$ 929,880**

*($1,328,400 × 30% = $398,520)

**Income taxes payable, accrued liabilities, prepaid insurance, and unearned revenue are balance sheet accounts.

For Practice: PE 13-5

Earnings per Share (EPS)

Earnings per share (EPS) is a measure of the profitability of the company as it relates to the owners, the common shareholders. Investors look for an EPS ratio to be increasing over a three- to five-year period, which indicates the company is operating more efficiently. Earnings per share is calculated as follows:

$$\text{Earnings per Share} = \frac{\text{Net Income} - \text{Preferred Dividends}}{\text{Weighted Average Number of Common Shares}}$$

Because preferred shareholders will be paid a dividend before any dividends are paid to common shareholders, their potential dividend for the year is subtracted from the numerator of the formula. Preferred dividends to be deducted include dividends declared during the year and the current year's undeclared dividends for cumulative preferred shares. Dividends in arrears from prior years, discussed in Chapter 12, are not deducted. The EPS ratio is rounded to the nearest whole cent.

Weighted Average Number of Common Shares When the number of common shares issued does not change during the year, the denominator is simply the number of shares issued and outstanding. When the number of common shares does change during the year, the **weighted average number of common shares** is calculated to recognize the portion of the year the shares were available to earn income. To illustrate this concept, assume ExpertTech Corporation had 100,000 common shares on January 1. No additional shares were issued until October 1, when an additional 1,000,000 shares were issued. The 1,000,000 shares issued in October were available to earn income for only three months, or 3/12 of the year. For nine months, or 9/12, of the year, only 100,000 shares were available to earn income. These shares would be weighted as follows:

100,000 shares × 9/12 (January 1–September 30)	75,000
1,100,000 shares × 3/12 (October 1–December 31)	275,000
Weighted average number of common shares	350,000

If ExpertTech Corporation earned $473,500 net income for the year and declared $50,000 in preferred dividends, its EPS would be calculated as follows:

$$\text{EPS} = \frac{\$473,500 - \$50,000}{350,000 \text{ shares}} = \$1.21 \text{ per share}$$

The number of common shares available to earn income during the year is also affected by share dividends, share splits, and shares that are repurchased and retired. When share dividends and share splits occur during the year, the number of shares outstanding is recalculated as if the share dividend or share split had occurred at the beginning of the year.

To illustrate the effect of share dividends on the weighted average number of common shares, assume ExpertTech Corporation began the year with 100,000 common shares outstanding, issued an additional 1,000,000 shares on October 1, and declared a 5% share dividend on October 15, to be issued on December 1 to shareholders of record on November 8. The weighted average number of common shares would be calculated as follows:

100,000 shares × 1.05 (5% share dividend) × 9/12 (January 1–September 30)	78,750
1,100,000 shares × 1.05 (5% share dividend) × 3/12 (October 1–December 31)	288,750
Weighted average number of common shares	367,500

The effect of a share split would be calculated in the same manner, by adjusting the number of outstanding shares prior to the split to include the effect of the share split.

Earnings per share are reported as *basic* earnings per share and *diluted* earnings per share. Diluted earnings per share take into consideration any preferred shares that have the option of converting to common shares. This topic is more appropriate for an intermediate accounting course and is not covered in this textbook.

EXAMPLE EXERCISE 13-6   Earnings per Share   ②

Conserve Corporation earned income of $1,350,000 for the fiscal year ended December 31. Conserve has 25,000 $2 preferred shares outstanding. Conserve started the year with 200,000 common shares, sold an additional 100,000 shares on April 1, declared a 2:1 share split on August 1, and issued an additional 75,000 shares on November 1. Calculate earnings per share for Conserve Corporation.

FOLLOW MY EXAMPLE 13-6

Weighted average number of common shares

200,000 shares × 2 (2:1 split) × 3/12 (January 1–March 31)	100,000
300,000 shares × 2 (2:1 split) × 7/12 (April 1–October 31)	350,000
675,000 shares × 2/12 (November 1–December 31)	112,500
Weighted average number of common shares	562,500

$$\text{Earnings per share} = \frac{\$1,350,000 - (\$2 \times 25,000)}{562,500} = \$2.31$$

For Practice: PE 13-6

CRITICAL THINKING

The chapter opener mentions that Shoppers Drug Mart repurchased more than 5 million shares in 2011. **What might have led to the repurchase of shares?**

Companies repurchase their own shares for a variety of reasons. They may be trying to avoid a hostile takeover by an investor, or they may want to reduce future dividend payments. Shoppers Drug Mart's annual report states its primary objective of capital management is to grow earnings for its investors. By repurchasing the shares, the company will reduce the dividends paid out in the year, thereby allowing the cash in the business to continue to grow. By increasing the company's earnings, and by reducing the number of outstanding shares, Shoppers Drug Mart's earnings per share will increase, making the company more attractive to future investors.

MID-CHAPTER ILLUSTRATIVE PROBLEM

Sherman's Sailboats Ltd. had the following selected shareholders' equity account balances as at December 31, 2015:

$5.50 preferred shares, 100,000 authorized	
25,000 issued and outstanding..	$2,500,000
Common shares, unlimited authorized	
548,600 issued and outstanding...	5,403,710
Retained earnings..	9,841,870

Additional account balances for Sherman's Sailboats Ltd. as at December 31, 2016 are as follows (all accounts have normal balances):

Cash (after transactions below have been recorded)............	$ 2,378,750
Accounts Receivable	8,090,500
Inventory	19,451,400
Supplies	3,723,900
Prepaid Expenses	620,360
Equipment..	24,571,240
Accumulated Depreciation	6,270,500
Accounts Payable	5,174,121
Salaries Payable	544,983
Long-term Debt, due 2021	10,000,000
Interest Revenue	53,560
Net Sales	72,960,496
Cost of Goods Sold	47,832,070
Interest Expense	550,000
Selling and Administrative Expenses	5,849,770

Sherman's Sailboats Ltd. uses an income summary account, cash or share dividends accounts to record all dividends, and its income tax rate is 25%. Below are selected transactions during 2016:

Mar. 31. Sherman's Sailboats repurchased and retired 50,000 common shares at $9.00 per share.

Aug. 31. Issued 75,000 common shares for $10.25 per share.

Oct. 15. The board of directors declared a 10% share dividend to be capitalized at the fair market value of $7.80, and distributed on December 1, to shareholders of record on November 15.

Dec. 1. The board of directors declared dividends on the preferred shares and a dividend of $0.25 on the common shares, to be paid January 15, 2017, to shareholders of record on December 20.

Dec. 31. Recorded an accrued liability for income taxes expense.

31. Closed the accounts on December 31, 2016.

Instructions

1. Journalize the transactions (including the cash dividend payment in 2017).
2. Prepare an income statement for the year ended December 31, 2016.
3. Prepare a statement of changes in equity for 2016.
4. Prepare a balance sheet as at December 31, 2016.

MID-CHAPTER ILLUSTRATIVE SOLUTION

1.

2016				
Mar.	31	Common Shares	492,500*	
		Contributed Capital from Retirement		
		of Common Shares		42,500
		Cash		450,000
		Repurchased and retired 50,000 common shares		
		*(50,000 shares × $5,403,710/548,600).		
Aug.	31	Cash	768,750	
		Common Shares		768,750
		Issued 75,000 common shares for $10.25 per share.		
Oct.	15	Share Dividends	388,908	
		Common Share Dividend Distributable		388,908
		Declared 10% common share dividend.		
		[(548,600 − 50,000) × 10% × $7.80]		
Dec.	1	Common Share Dividend Distributable	388,908	
		Common Shares		388,908
		Distributed common share dividend.		
Dec.	1	Cash Dividends	295,240	
		Dividends Payable—Preferred		137,500*
		Dividends Payable—Common		157,740**
		Declared cash dividends.		
		*($5.50 × 25,000 shares)		
		**[$0.25 × (548,600 − 50,000 + 75,000 + 57,360		
		shares)]		
Dec.	31	Income Taxes Expense	4,695,554	
		Income Taxes Payable		4,695,554
		To record income taxes payable.		
		[($53,560 + $72,960,496 − $47,832,070 − $550,000		
		− $5,849,770) × 25%]		
	31	Retained Earnings	684,148	
		Share Dividends		388,908
		Cash Dividends		295,240
		To close the dividend accounts.		
	31	Income Summary	14,086,662	
		Retained Earnings		14,086,662
		To close the income summary account.		
2017				
Jan.	15	Dividends Payable—Preferred	137,500	
		Dividends Payable—Common	157,740	
		Cash		295,240
		Paid the cash dividend.		

2.

Sherman's Sailboats Ltd. Income Statement For the Year Ended December 31, 2016		
Net sales...		$72,960,496
Cost of goods sold		47,832,070
Gross profit		25,128,426
Selling and administration expenses		5,849,770
Income from operations		19,278,656
Other revenues and expenses:		
Interest expense	$ 53,560	
Interest expense	(550,000)	
		496,440
Income before income taxes		18,782,216
Income taxes expense.............................		4,695,554
Net income		$14,086,662
Earnings per share................................		$ 23.65*
*[$14,086,662 − ($5.50 × 25,000)] / 589,710**		
**weighted average number of common shares		
548,600 shares × 1.10 (10% share dividend) × 3/12 (Jan. 1 – Mar. 31)		150,865
498,600 shares × 1.10 (10% share dividend) × 5/12 (Apr. 1 – Aug. 31)		228,525
573,600 shares × 1.10 (10% share dividend) × 4/12 (Sept. 1 – Dec. 31)		210,320
Weighted average number of common shares		589,710

3.

Sherman's Sailboats Ltd. Statement of Changes in Equity For the Year Ended December 31, 2016					
	Preferred Shares	Common Shares	Contributed Capital from Retirement of Common Shares	Retained Earnings	Total
Balance January 1, 2016	$2,500,000	$5,403,710	$ 0	$ 9,841,870	$17,745,580
Net income				14,086,662	14,086,662
Issuance of common shares		768,750			768,750
Common shares repurchased		(492,500)	42,500		(450,000)
Cash dividends on preferred shares				(137,500)	(137,500)
Cash dividends on common shares				(157,740)	(157,740)
Share dividends on common shares		388,908		(388,908)	0
Balance December 31, 2016	$2,500,000	$6,068,868	$42,500	$23,244,384	$31,855,752

4.

Sherman's Sailboats Ltd.
Balance Sheet
December 31, 2016

Assets			**Liabilities and Shareholders' Equity**		
Current assets:			Current liabilities:		
Cash	$ 2,378,750		Accounts payable	$5,174,121	
Accounts receivable	8,090,500		Salaries payable	544,983	
Inventory	19,451,400		Dividends payable	295,240	
Supplies	3,723,900		Income taxes payable	4,695,554	
Prepaid expenses	620,360		Total current liabilities		10,709,898
Total current assets		$ 34,264,910	Long-term liabilities:		
Property, plant, and equipment:			Long-term debt, due 2021		10,000,000
Equipment	24,571,240		Total liabilities		20,709,898
Less accumulated depreciation	6,270,500		**Shareholders' Equity**		
Total property, plant,			Contributed capital:		
and equipment		18,300,740	$5.50 preferred shares, 100,000 authorized,		
			25,000 issued and outstanding	2,500,000	
			Common shares, unlimited authorized,		
			630,960 issued and outstanding	6,068,868	
			Contributed capital from retirement		
			of common shares	42,500	
			Total contributed capital		8,611,368
			Retained earnings		23,244,384
Total assets		$ 52,565,650	Total liabilities and shareholders' equity		$52,565,650

Reporting Discontinued Operations and Unusual Items on the Income Statement

Describe and illustrate the reporting of discontinued operations and unusual items on the income statement.

Generally accepted accounting principles require that **discontinued operations** be reported separately on the income statement. This is because such items do not occur frequently and often are unrelated to current operations. Without separate reporting, users of the financial statements might be misled about current and future operations.

Discontinued Operations

A company may discontinue a segment of its operations by selling or abandoning the operations. For example, a retailer with both a retail division and an online sales division might decide to sell its product only online and, thus, discontinue selling its merchandise at its retail outlets (stores). Because the retail division will not be producing any income in the future, the net earnings from this division should be shown separately so projections about future earnings can be made.

Any gain or loss resulting from the operations of or sale of discontinued operations is reported on the income statement as a Gain (or loss) from Discontinued Operations. It is reported immediately following *Income from continuing operations.*

To clearly show the full impact of discontinuing operations, the gain or loss from discontinued operations is reported net of any tax effects. To understand what is meant by tax effects, consider how income taxes reduce the net income of the business, as shown in Exhibit 2. If a company reports a gain from the sale of discontinued operations, it will pay more income taxes as a result of the gain, ultimately reducing net income by the increased income taxes paid. The reverse is true if the corporation reports a loss from the sale. The loss will result in higher costs, thereby reducing the income, and ultimately reducing the income taxes paid. To illustrate, we compare one corporation's original results with a gain on sale and with a loss on sale, assuming a 20% income tax rate.

	Original results (no gain or loss)	$3,000 gain from original results	$2,000 loss from original results
Income before income taxes	$10,000	$13,000	$8,000
Income taxes expense	2,000	2,600	1,600
Net income	$ 8,000	$10,400	$6,400

As shown in the example, the original results produced net income of $8,000. When a gain of $3,000 was included (in the second column), net income increased by only $2,400 ($10,400 − $8,000) because of additional income taxes payable on the gain of $600 ($3,000 × 20%). The third column demonstrates the effect of a $2,000 loss. Net income decreased by only $1,600 ($6,400 − $8,000), not by the full amount of the $2,000 loss. The difference between the $2,000 loss and the $1,600 reduction in net income is considered a $400 tax savings.

To illustrate discontinued operations, assume that Jones Corporation produces and sells electrical products, hardware supplies, and lawn equipment. Because of lack of profits, Jones discontinues its electrical products operation and sells the remaining inventory and other assets at a loss of $145,000.

Assuming a tax rate of 31%, this loss would generate a tax savings of $44,950 ($145,000 × 31%), and Jones Corporation would report a net loss of $100,050 ($145,000 − $44,950). Exhibit 3 illustrates the reporting of the loss on discontinued operations.

In addition, a note accompanying the income statement should describe the operations sold, including such details as the date operations were discontinued, the date the assets were sold, and the effect (if any) on current and future operations.

Exhibit 3

Discontinued Operations in the Income Statement

Jones Corporation
Income Statement
For the Year Ended December 31, 2015

Net sales	$12,350,000
Cost of goods sold	5,800,000
Gross profit	6,550,000
Selling and administrative expenses	5,240,000
Income from continuing operations before income taxes	1,310,000
Income taxes expense ($1,310,000 × 31%)	406,100
Income from continuing operations	903,900
Loss on discontinued operations, net of tax savings of $44,950	100,050
Net income	$ 803,850

ACCURATELY REPORTING OPERATING RESULTS

How can financial statements best predict the future? By separating out items such as discontinued operations that are not expected to recur.

In 2010, Shaw Communications Inc. began exploring the opportunity to add wireless networking to the complement of products and services offered to its customers. In 2011, after investing much research and more than $90 million into the initiative, Shaw Communications determined it was not economically feasible to enter into competition in the wireless networking market.

This decision to discontinue construction of the wireless network resulted in losses of $89.3 million in 2011 and $1 million in 2010. Each loss was recognized as a *loss from discontinued operations*.

If these losses had been included in the regular operating results, Shaw Communications would have appeared to have had an unusually bad year in 2011, when, in fact, its income from operations was almost $30 million higher in 2011 than in 2010. Financial statements must accurately disclose the reality of what happened if the users of those statements are to rely on them.

EXAMPLE EXERCISE 13-7   Discontinued Operations   **3**

Random Retail Corp. reported the following balances for the year ended April 30, 2015:

Loss due to discontinuing its financial services division	$ 200,000
Income from continuing operations before income taxes	1,350,000

Assuming a 30% tax rate, prepare an income statement, starting from *Income from continuing operations before income taxes.*

FOLLOW MY EXAMPLE 13-7

Random Retail Corp.
Income Statement (partial)
For the Year Ended April 30, 2015

Income from continuing operations before income taxes	$1,350,000
Income taxes expense	405,000*
Income from continuing operations..	945,000
Loss on discontinued operations, net of tax savings of $60,000...................	140,000**
Net income	$ 805,000

* ($1,350,000 × 30%).
** [$200,000 − ($200,000 × 30%)].

For Practice: PE 13-7

Reporting Earnings per Share for Discontinued Operations

For corporations reporting using IFRS, basic and diluted earnings per share are disclosed for discontinued operations, either in the statement of comprehensive income or in the notes to the financial statements.[1] As discussed earlier, earnings per share is not required under ASPE, and this textbook does not cover diluted earnings per share. Earnings per share will be reported for *Income (loss) from continuing operations, Discontinued operations,* and *Net income (loss).*

To illustrate, a partial income statement for Jones Corporation is shown in Exhibit 4, using the data from Exhibit 3 and assuming the issued and outstanding shares consist of 100,000 $1 preferred shares and a weighted average number of common shares of 200,000.

---

1 *CICA Handbook-Accounting*, 2013, Part 1, IAS 33.68.

Exhibit 4

Income Statement with Earnings per Share

Jones Corporation Income Statement (Partial) For the Year Ended December 31, 2015	
Earnings per share:	
Income from continuing operations	$4.02*
Loss on discontinued operations	0.50**
Net income	$3.52

*[(903,900 − $100,000) ÷ 200,000].
** ($100,050 ÷ 200,000).

EXAMPLE EXERCISE 13-8 Earnings per Share   ③

Using the information from Example Exercise 13-7, determine the earnings per share for Random Retail Corp., assuming the following capital structure existed at year-end and no common shares were issued or repurchased throughout the year:

Contributed capital:
$1 preferred shares, 10,000 issued and outstanding	$ 500,000
Common shares, 150,000 issued and outstanding	1,500,000

FOLLOW MY EXAMPLE 13-8

Earnings per share:

Income from continuing operations [($945,000 − $10,000)/150,000]...........................	$6.23
Loss on discontinued operations ($140,000/150,000)	0.93
Net income [($805,000 − $10,000)/150,000]..	$5.30

For Practice: PE 13-8

Unusual Items

An **unusual item** is defined as an event or transaction that possesses one or more of the following characteristics:

- It is an atypical business transaction, such as a major equipment upgrade.
- It occurs infrequently, such as a loss due to a labour strike.
- It is a larger than normal transaction, such as a substantial inventory write-down.

Instead of including unusual items in *Income from operations*, they are often included in the *Other income and expense* category. Disclosing unusual items in this manner allows management to emphasize the infrequent, atypical, or large nature of the transaction; the relevance of the information is improved and shareholders are better equipped to make predictions about future earnings.

EXAMPLE EXERCISE 13-9 Classification of Income Statement Items   ③

Random Retail Corp. reported the following for the year ended April 30, 2015:

i. Gain due to settlement of lawsuit
ii. Loss due to flood at plant (floods occur infrequently at this location)
iii. Gain on sale of assets
iv. Loss on closure of retail line of business
v. Bad debt expense

(continued)

Determine whether each item should be classified as (a) a discontinued operation, (b) an unusual item, or (c) an operating item. Explain where and how each item should be reported on the income statement.

FOLLOW MY EXAMPLE 13-9

i. (b) An unusual item; include in Other income and expense category.
ii. (b) An unusual item; include in Other income and expense category.
iii. (c) An operating item; include in Operating expenses category. If the gain were larger than normal, it would be treated as an unusual item.
iv. (a) A discontinued operation; show net of taxes, after Income from continuing operations.
v. (c) An operating item; include in Operating expenses category.

For Practice: PE 13-9

 ## Accounting Changes

Describe and identify accounting changes.

Accounting changes occur for three main reasons:

1. a change in an estimate
2. a correction of an error
3. a change in accounting policy

Change in Estimate

Accounting involves many estimates, such as the expected useful life of an asset, the expected residual value of assets, and the size of warranty liabilities. If management decides to change an estimate to better reflect reality, the change is incorporated into the current and future years' financial results. This accounting treatment is referred to as a **prospective treatment**. No adjustment is made to the financial results for earlier years because accountants are expected to make their estimations to the best of their ability, so the estimates made in the past are valid and based on the information known at that time. If an accountant later has a better estimate of value, then the estimates are revised to ensure the relevance of the information. Estimates will change as reality and knowledge change.

Correction of an Error

An error may arise from a mathematical mistake or from a mistake in applying accounting principles. Such errors may not be discovered within the same accounting period in which they occur. In such cases, the effect of the error should not affect the current period's net income. Instead, the correction of the error is reported in the retained earnings statement. This accounting treatment is referred to as a **retroactive treatment**. Such corrections are reported as an adjustment to the beginning balance of retained earnings. The correction is also reflected in the prior year's comparative numbers.

To illustrate, assume the bookkeeper for Carine's Cove Corp. incorrectly recorded $24,000 as an asset, prepaid rent, when it should have been recorded as rent expense for 2015. The error was not discovered until the following year, at which time the accountant recorded the following entry:

2016				
Dec.	31	Retained Earnings	19,200	
		Income Taxes Payable	4,800	
		Prepaid Rent		24,000
		To correct 2015 error in rent expense recorded		
		as prepaid rent.		

When the 2016 financial statements are prepared, the opening balance in retained earnings must equal the closing balance shown in 2015. To reflect the correction, the retained earnings column in the statement of changes in equity will include a line item for *correction of prior period error* as follows:

Carine's Cove Corp. Statement of Changes in Equity For the Year Ended December 31, 2016			
	Common Shares	Retained Earnings	Total
Balance January 1, 2016	$500,000	$450,000	$ 950,000
Correction of prior period error		(19,200)	(19,200)
Net income		180,000	180,000
Cash dividends on common shares		(30,000)	(30,000)
Balance December 31, 2016	$500,000	$580,800	$1,080,800

Assuming comparative financial statements are prepared, the affected accounts for the prior period will also be restated to their correct amounts.

Change in Accounting Policy

Companies sometimes elect to change the method of accounting being used, such as switching from straight-line to double-declining-balance depreciation. This change may be the result of a change in regulations under ASPE or IFRS, or a managerial decision that a different accounting policy will lead to more relevant financial statements. Prior years' financial statements must be restated to allow for comparisons from year to year. The cumulative effect of the change on prior years' income is reported as an adjustment to the beginning balance of retained earnings, similar to the treatment of a prior year's error.

In some situations, a company may switch from straight-line to double-declining-balance depreciation as a result of a change in the expected consumption of the future economic benefits received from that asset. In such a case, what appears to be a change in accounting policy would be treated as a change in an estimate under IFRS, and prior years' financial statements would not require restatement.[2]

The following summarizes the treatment of accounting changes:

Change in estimate	Prospective treatment	Changes are applied to current and future periods only.
Correction of an error or Change in accounting policy	Retroactive treatment	Affected accounts in the prior period will be restated to reflect corrections. Retained earnings will require adjustment.

EXAMPLE EXERCISE 13-10 **Accounting Changes**   4

1. Identify whether each of the following items should be treated as (a) a correction of an error, (b) a change in accounting policy, or (c) a change in estimate.
2. Determine the correct accounting treatment for each transaction.
   i. In 2015, Opus Corporation decided that its farm equipment would last for five years longer than originally expected.
   ii. In 2015, Opus Corporation switched from the FIFO method to the weighted average method for its inventory costing.
   iii. Opus Corporation's accountant discovered that in 2011 a building had been expensed instead of capitalized.

(continued)

2 *CICA Handbook–Accounting*, 2013, IAS 8.38.

FOLLOW MY EXAMPLE 13-10

i. (c) A change in estimate
   Change the depreciation for 2015 and future years (prospective treatment).
ii. (b) A change in accounting policy
   Adjust the beginning balance of retained earnings (retroactive treatment).
iii. (a) A correction of an error
   Adjust the beginning balance of retained earnings (retroactive treatment).

For Practice: PE 13-10

CRITICAL THINKING

If the Allowance for Doubtful Accounts has a credit balance of $20,000 at the end of the year, has an error occurred?

No. Because accounting requires many estimates to be made, professional judgment is often needed. When establishing the allowance for doubtful accounts, an accountant estimates the ability of customers to honour their debts to the company. The estimate is based upon many factors, including past credit history, the nature of the industry, and the economy. Over time, adjustments or revisions to current and future bad debt expense may be necessary as better information is acquired.

⑤ Statement of Comprehensive Income

Describe and illustrate a statement of comprehensive income.

All corporations are required to prepare an income statement. Corporations that use IFRS are also required to prepare a statement of comprehensive income. These two statements can be presented separately or combined into one single statement of comprehensive income. If the two statements are presented separately, the statement of comprehensive income provides details regarding other comprehensive income and begins where the income statement ends, with net income. A combined statement of comprehensive income is shown below for Morning Java International. Examples of both types of statements presented separately can be found for Leon's Furniture Limited and Shoppers Drug Mart in Appendix B and C, respectively.

Morning Java, reporting under ASPE, would prepare an income statement with the same details presented here, but would stop at *Profit for the year*, excluding *Other comprehensive income*, and *Earnings per share*.

Morning Java International Statement of Comprehensive Income For the Year Ended December 31, 2015	
Sales (net)	$ 5,402,100
Cost of sales	(2,160,000)
Gross profit	3,242,100
Selling expenses	(1,654,700)
Administrative expenses	(954,000)
Loss on disposal of property, plant, and equipment	(23,000)
Other income	23,000
Share in profit of associates	57,000
Operating profit	690,400
Finance costs	(136,000)
Profit before income taxes	554,400
Income taxes expense	(132,800)
Net income	421,600
Other comprehensive income	
Gain on revaluation of properties	44,800
Total comprehensive income for the year, net of tax	$ 466,400
Earnings per share, basic	9.58

FINANCIAL ANALYSIS AND INTERPRETATION

The amount of net income is often used by investors and creditors when evaluating a company's profitability. However, net income by itself is difficult to use when comparing companies of different sizes. Thus, the profitability of companies is often expressed as earnings per share. Corporations whose shares are trading in a public market must report earnings per share on their income statements.

As discussed in this chapter, earnings per share is calculated as follows:

Earnings per Share =

$$\frac{\text{Net Income} - \text{Preferred Dividends}}{\text{Weighted Average Number of Common Shares}}$$

Earnings per share can be used to compare two companies with different net incomes. For example, the following data are available for a recent year for Molson Coors Brewing Co. and Brick Brewing Co. Limited, two companies in the Canadian brewery market:

	Molson Coors Brewing Co. (in thousands)	Brick Brewing Co. Limited (in thousands)
Net income	$674,000	$ 657
Preferred dividends	0.0	0.0
Weighted average number of common shares issued and outstanding	184,900	28,181

The earnings per share for both companies can be calculated as follows:

Molson Coors Brewing Co. $\dfrac{\$674,000}{184,900} = \$3.65$ per share

Brick Brewing Co. Limited $\dfrac{\$657}{28,181} = \$0.02$ per share

Although the net income for Molson Coors Brewing Co. greatly exceeds that of Brick Brewing Co. Limited, a brewery that operates primarily in Ontario, the calculation of earnings per share allows for comparison between the two companies. Molson's earnings per share are more than 180 times greater than Brick's. Not surprisingly, the share price of Molson (at $40.87 per share) is also greater than Brick's (at $1.42 per share), reflecting the superior earnings per share performance.

EXAMPLE EXERCISE 13-11 Earnings per Share

5

Evelyn's Books Inc. reported the following as at December 31, 2015:

Net income	$258,500
Preferred dividends declared	$ 43,000
Weighted average number of common shares	74,000

Calculate Evelyn's Books Inc.'s earnings per share for 2015.

FOLLOW MY EXAMPLE 13-11

$$\text{Earnings per share} = \frac{\text{Net Income} - \text{Preferred Dividends}}{\text{Weighted Average Number of Common Shares}}$$

$$= \frac{\$258,500 - \$43,000}{74,000}$$

$$= \$2.91 \text{ per share}$$

For Practice: PE 13-11

At a Glance 13

1 **Describe and illustrate the accounting for share dividends, share splits, and share repurchase transactions.**

Key Points	Key Learning Outcomes	Page	Example Exercises
A corporation may issue share dividends, split shares, and repurchase outstanding shares, for a variety of reasons.	• Describe a share dividend.	660	
	• Journalize a share dividend.	662	13-1
	• Prepare the shareholders' equity section of the balance sheet.	662	13-2 13-3
	• Describe a share split.	664	
	• Identify the reasons a corporation might repurchase its shares.	666	
	• Journalize a share repurchase transaction	667	13-4

2 **Describe and illustrate the corporate income statement and earnings per share.**

Key Points	Key Learning Outcomes	Page	Example Exercises
A corporate income statement differs from partnership and sole proprietorship income statements in that it includes income taxes expense. Corporations that prepare their financial statements under IFRS will also report earnings per share at the bottom of their income statement. Corporations that use ASPE are not required to report earnings per share.	• Prepare a corporate income statement.	668	13-5
	• Calculate earnings per share for corporations preparing financial statements under IFRS.	670	13-6

3 **Describe and illustrate the reporting of discontinued operations and unusual items on the income statement.**

Key Points	Key Learning Outcomes	Page	Example Exercises
Generally accepted accounting principles require that discontinued operations be reported separately on the income statement. These items are shown after income from continuing operations, net of taxes. For corporations preparing financial statements under IFRS, earnings per share must be calculated for *Income from continuing operations, Discontinued operations, and Net income.* Corporations using ASPE are not required to report earnings per share.	• Describe discontinued operations.	675	
	• Prepare an income statement containing discontinued operations.	676	13-7
	• Report earnings per share for discontinued operations for corporations preparing financial statements under IFRS.	677	13-8
	• Determine the classification of transactions as discontinued items, unusual items, and operating items.	678	13-9

(continued)

3 (continued)

Key Points	Key Learning Outcomes	Page	Example Exercises
Unusual items are financial transactions that are not typical of operations, are infrequent, or are larger than normal. Unusual items are reported in the Other income and expense section of the income statement.			

4 Describe and identify accounting changes.

Key Points	Key Learning Outcomes	Page	Example Exercises
Accounting changes occur due to three main reasons: (1) a change in an estimate, (2) a correction of an error, or (3) a change in accounting policy. A change in an estimate is included in the current and future year's financial results, with no adjustment made for prior years. Correction of an error from a prior accounting period and a change in accounting policy are handled in the same manner. The impact of the change on prior years' income is reported as an adjustment to the beginning balance of retained earnings.	• Define and give examples of the three types of accounting changes.	679	13-10
	• Describe the accounting treatment for each type of accounting change.	680	13-10

5 Describe and illustrate a statement of comprehensive income.

Key Points	Key Learning Outcomes	Page	Example Exercises
Corporations reporting using IFRS can report their profit or loss using an income statement or combined with other comprehensive income in a statement of comprehensive income.	• Discuss the components of a statement of comprehensive income.	681	
	• Analyze a corporations performance based on its earnings per share.	682	13-11

GLOSSARY

accounting changes – Accounting changes result from changes in estimates, corrections of errors, and changes in accounting policies. (p. 679)

book value – The average cost of the individual outstanding common shares. (p. 665)

contributed capital from retirement of common shares – A shareholders' equity account used for accounting for the difference between the original issue price and the repurchase price on retirement of shares. (p. 666)

discontinued operations – A segment of the business that a company is in the process of selling or abandoning. (p. 675)

earnings per share (EPS) – Net income per common share outstanding during a period. (p. 670)

prospective treatment – Adoption of accounting changes in current and future years' financial records. (p. 679)

retroactive treatment – A change in accounting that is reported in prior years' financial records. (p. 679)

share dividend – A distribution of shares to the common shareholders. (p. 660) Also known as a *stock dividend*.

share split – A reduction in the per-share value of common shares and the issuance of a proportionate number of additional shares. (p. 664) Also known as a *stock split*.

stock dividend – A distribution of shares to the common shareholders.

(p. 660) Also known as a *share dividend*.

stock split – A reduction in the per-share value of common shares and the issuance of a proportionate number of additional shares. (p. 664) Also known as a *share split*.

unusual item – A financial item that is not typical of operations, is infrequent, or is larger than normal. (p. 678)

weighted average number of common shares – When the number of outstanding shares has increased or decreased during the year, the determination of the average number of shares to recognize the portion of the year shares were available to earn income. Used in the calculation of earnings per share. (p. 670)

ILLUSTRATIVE PROBLEM

Brady Ltd. is a distributor of office products in the Maritimes. Brady Ltd. reports the following for the year ended March 31, 2015:

Income from continuing operations before income taxes	$500,000
Loss from discontinued operations, before taxes	90,000
Weighted average number of common shares	40,000
Number of $1.25 preferred shares outstanding at March 31, 2015	10,000
Tax rate	40%

Instructions

1. Prepare a partial income statement for Brady Ltd., beginning with income from continuing operations before income taxes.
2. Calculate the earnings per share for Brady Ltd.

Solution

Brady Ltd.
Income Statement (Partial)
For the Year Ended March 31, 2015

Income from continuing operations before taxes.	$500,000
Income taxes expense	200,000
Income from continuing operations	300,000
Loss from discontinued operations, net of tax savings of $36,000.	(54,000)
Net income.	$246,000
Earnings per share:	
Income from continuing operations	$7.19
[$300,000 – ($1.25 × 10,000)] ÷ 40,000	
Discontinued operations ($54,000) ÷ 40,000 · · · · · · · · · · · · · · · · ·	(1.35)
Net income [$246,000 – ($1.25 × 10,000)] ÷ 40,000	$5.84

EYE OPENERS

1. Can a share dividend be reported as a liability?
2. What is the main objective of a share split?
3. What is the main objective of a share dividend?
4. Why might a corporation reacquire its shares?
5. An owner of 500 common shares of Microshop Corporation receives a share dividend of five shares. (a) What is the effect of the share dividend on the shareholder's proportionate interest (equity) in the corporation? (b) How does the total equity of 500 shares before the share dividend compare with the total equity of 505 shares after the share dividend?
6. a) Where is a declared but unissued cash dividend reported on the balance sheet?
   b) Where is a declared but unissued share dividend reported on the balance sheet?
7. A corporation reacquires and retires 10,000 of its common shares for $450,000. These shares were originally issued for $500,000. (a) What effect does this transaction have on revenue or expense of the period? (b) What effect does this transaction have on shareholders' equity?
8. On January 1, Baker Ltd. had 100,000 common shares outstanding. Baker Ltd. issued 25,000 shares on May 1 and repurchased and retired 10,000 shares on October 1. What is the weighted average number of shares for the year ended December 31?
9. What is the definition of an unusual item?
10. A corporation reports a loss from discontinued operations for the current fiscal year. Identify the financial statement items for which earnings per share must be calculated, according to IFRS.
11. Tokyo Corporation decided to switch from the FIFO method to the weighted average cost method to determine cost of goods sold and ending inventory. Indicate how this change is reported on the Tokyo Corporation financial statements for the current period.
12. Japan Corporation discovered that a $2,000,000 expense for the prior year had been omitted from the financial statements. Indicate how this change is reported on the Japan Corporation financial statements for the current year.
13. Name the statement that corporations reporting under IFRS prepare to replace an income statement. How does this statement differ from an income statement?

PRACTICE EXERCISES

① PE 13-1
Entries for share dividends

EE 13-1 p. 664

On July 1, 2015, Hardy Drivers Ltd. has the following capital account balances:

$1.75 preferred shares, 50,000 authorized, 30,000 issued and outstanding	$ 700,000
Common shares, unlimited authorized, 450,000 issued and outstanding	2,030,000
Total contributed capital	2,730,000
Retained earnings	2,100,000
Total shareholders' equity	$4,830,000

On May 10, Hardy Drivers declared a 5% common share dividend to be issued July 10 to shareholders of record on June 10. The market price was $32.50 per share on May 10.

Journalize the entries required on May 10, June 10, and July 10.

① PE 13-2
Shareholders' equity

EE 13-2 p. 664

Using the information in Practice Exercise 13-1, prepare the Shareholders' Equity section of the balance sheet for Hardy Drivers Ltd. on July 10, 2015.

PE 13-3
Shareholders' equity

EE 13-3 p. 666

Winston Corporation had the following balances in its shareholders' equity accounts as at May 31, 2015:

Retained earnings	$268,000
Common shares, unlimited authorized, 40,000 issued and outstanding	215,000
$2.50 preferred shares, unlimited authorized, 2,000 issued and outstanding	86,000

On June 18, 2015, the board of directors declared a 4:1 share split.

Prepare the Shareholders' Equity section of the balance sheet for Winston Corporation on June 19, 2015.

PE 13-4
Repurchase of shares

EE 13-4 p. 668

Catcher Corp.'s shareholders' equity had the following account balances:

Common shares, unlimited authorized, 4,000,000 issued and outstanding	$ 24,500,000
Retained earnings	150,700,000

On July 3, Catcher Corp. reacquired and retired 52,000 common shares at $8 per share. On September 22, Catcher Corp. purchased and retired an additional 200,000 shares at $6 per share. On November 10, Catcher Corp. purchased and retired another 10,000 shares at $9 per share.

Journalize the entries to record the July 3, September 22, and November 10 transactions.

PE 13-5
Corporate income statement

EE 13-5 p. 669

Using the following accounts and balances, prepare the income statement for Diamond Mines Ltd. for the year ended June 30, 2015, assuming a 28% tax rate. Ignore earnings per share.

Selling and administrative expenses	$1,555,000
Interest expense	120,000
Accrued liabilities	400,000
Gain on sale of land	217,000
Cost of goods sold	4,850,000
Net sales	7,500,000

PE 13-6
Earnings per share

EE 13-6 p. 671

Point Pelee Parks Ltd. earned income of $6,732,000 for the fiscal year ended December 31. Point Pelee Parks has 180,000 $3 preferred shares issued and outstanding. Point Pelee Parks started the year with 900,000 common shares, sold an additional 200,000 shares on June 1, declared a 3:1 share split on August 31, and issued an additional 30,000 shares on December 1. Calculate earnings per share for Point Pelee Parks Ltd.

PE 13-7
Discontinued operations

EE 13-7 p. 677

Toys Unlimited Corp. reported the following results for the year ended March 31, 2015:

Loss due to discontinuing its manufacturing division	$ 1,300,000
Income from continuing operations before income taxes	10,350,000

Assuming a 25% tax rate, prepare a partial income statement, starting from Income from continuing operations before taxes.

PE 13-8
Earnings per share

EE 13-8 p. 678

Using the information from Practice Exercise 13-7, determine the earnings per share for Toys Unlimited Corp., assuming the following capital structure existed at year-end and no common shares were issued or repurchased throughout the year:

Contributed capital:	
$3 preferred shares, 100,000 issued and outstanding	$ 5,000,000
Common shares, 1,150,000 issued and outstanding	11,500,000

③ PE 13-9

**Classification of
income statement
items**

EE 13-9 p. 678

Toys Unlimited Corp. reported the following for the year ended March 31, 2015:

  i. Loss due to earthquake

  ii. Extremely large bad debt expense due to loan defaults

  iii. Gain on sale of equipment

  iv. Loss on closure of retail stores in Fredericton (the company has other retail locations)

  v. Loss on closure of all manufacturing operations (retail operations continue)

Determine whether each item above should be classified as (a) a discontinued operation, (b) an unusual item, or (c) an operating item. Explain where and how each item should be reported on the income statement.

---

④ PE 13-10

Accounting changes

EE 13-10 p. 680

1. Identify whether each of the following items should be treated as (a) a correction of an error, (b) a change in accounting policy, or (c) a change in estimate.
2. Determine the correct accounting treatment for each transaction.
    i. In 2015, Baker Corporation's accountant decided that the company's building would last for 10 years longer than originally anticipated.
    ii. Baker Corporation's bookkeeper discovered that insurance expense of $25,000 had not been recorded for 2013.
    iii. In 2015, Baker Corporation switched from the straight-line method to the double-declining-balance method for depreciation of the equipment to be consistent with calculating depreciation an all property, plant, and equipment.

---

⑤ PE 13-11

Earnings per share

f·a·i

EE 13-11 p. 682

Bronwyn Construction Ltd. reported the following as at December 31, 2015:

Net income	$735,920
Preferred dividends declared	$162,000
Weighted average number of common shares	130,000

Calculate Bronwyn Construction Ltd.'s earnings per share for 2015.

EXERCISES

① EX 13-1

**② Cash and share
dividends**

On January 1, 2015, Marxsman Ltd. has the following capital account balances:

$1 preferred shares, 500,000 authorized,	
124,000 issued and outstanding	$ 3,480,000
Common shares, unlimited authorized,	
2,180,000 issued and outstanding	12,640,000
Retained earnings	42,750,000

The following transactions occurred during the year ended December 31, 2015:

Jan. 1. Issued 150,000 common shares for $245,000.

Jun. 30. Declared a semiannual dividend of $254,000, payable on August 15 to the shareholders of record on July 15. Marxsman uses dividend accounts.

Aug. 15. Paid the dividend.

Oct. 31. Declared a share dividend of 5% to shareholders of record on November 15 to be issued on December 15. The market price of the common shares was $17 on the declaration date.

Dec. 15. Issued share dividend.

      31. Declared a semiannual dividend of $201,300, payable on February 15 to the shareholders of record on January 15.

      31. Prepared the closing entry for the net income of $2,078,000 for the year, and the dividends.

Instructions

1. Journalize the above transactions.

2. Prepare the Shareholders' Equity section of the statement of financial position for Marxman Ltd. as at December 31, 2015.
3. Calculate Marxsman's earnings per share for 2015.

EX 13-2

Share repurchase and share split

Carlsbad & Sons Inc. produces custom garden furniture. On March 1, 2015, it had the following capital account balances:

Retained earnings	$456,000
Common shares, unlimited authorized, 20,000 issued and outstanding	100,000
$2.50 preferred shares, 100,000 authorized, 2,000 issued and outstanding	50,000

Carlsbad & Sons uses dividend accounts to record all dividends, and its income tax rate is 25%. Below are selected transactions during the year ended February 29, 2016:

Mar. 31.   Carlsbad & Sons repurchased and retired 5,000 common shares at $4.00 per share.

Aug. 31.   Issued 25,000 common shares for equipment valued at $160,000. On this day, the common shares were trading at $6.50 per share.

Oct. 15.   The board of directors declared a 2:1 share split.

Dec. 1.   The board of directors declared annual dividends of $8,000 to be paid January 15, 2016, to shareholders of record on December 20.

Jan. 15.   Paid the cash dividend.

Feb. 29.   Closed the accounts on February 29, 2016. Net income was $230,000.

Instructions

1. Journalize the transactions.
2. Calculate earnings per share.
3. Prepare a Statement of Changes in Equity for 2016.
4. Prepare the shareholders' equity section of the statement of financial position as at February 29, 2016.

EX 13-3

Issuing shares and share dividends

Organic Health Inc. is a distributor of health food products in the Toronto area. The following account balances appear on the balance sheet of Organic Health Inc.: $2 preferred shares (100,000 shares authorized, 20,000 shares issued and outstanding), $2,000,000, Common shares (300,000 shares authorized, 100,000 shares issued and outstanding), $10,000,000, and Retained earnings, $45,000,000. The board of directors declared a 2% share dividend when the market price was $125 per share.

a. Journalize the entries to record (1) the declaration of the dividend and (2) the issuance of the share certificates.
b. Determine the following amounts before the share dividend was declared: (1) total contributed capital, (2) total retained earnings, and (3) total shareholders' equity.
c. Determine the following amounts after the share dividend was declared and closing entries were recorded at the end of the year: (1) total contributed capital, (2) total retained earnings, and (3) total shareholders' equity.

EX 13-4

Share splits

Carlo's Restaurant Corporation wholesales ovens and ranges to restaurants throughout Canada. Carlo's Restaurant Corporation, which had 80,000 common shares outstanding, declared a 3-for-1 share split (two additional shares for each share outstanding).

a. How many shares will be outstanding after the split?
b. If the common shares had a market price of $300 per share before the share split, what is the approximate market price per share after the split?

EX 13-5

Effect of cash dividend and share split

Indicate whether the following actions will (+) increase, (−) decrease, or (0) not affect Indigo Inc.'s total assets, liabilities, and shareholders' equity:

(continued)

		Assets	Liabilities	Shareholders' Equity
1	Declaring a cash dividend	_____	_____	_____
2	Paying the cash dividend declared in (1)	_____	_____	_____
3	Authorizing and issuing share certificates in a share split	_____	_____	_____
4	Declaring a share dividend	_____	_____	_____
5	Issuing share certificates for the share dividend declared in (4)	_____	_____	_____

EX 13-6

Selected dividend transactions, share split

Selected transactions completed by Carleton Aeronautic Supply Corporation during the current fiscal year were as follows:

Mar. 8. Split the common shares 4 for 1. After the split, 400,000 common shares were outstanding.

May. 3. Declared semiannual dividends of $2 on 20,000 preferred shares and $0.75 on the common shares to shareholders of record on June 5, payable on July 7. Carleton Aeronautic does not use a dividend account.

Jul. 7. Paid the cash dividends.

Oct. 2. Declared semiannual dividends of $2 on the preferred shares and $0.90 on the common shares (before the share dividend). In addition, a 3% common share dividend was declared on the common shares outstanding. The fair market value of the common shares is estimated at $42.

Dec. 5. Paid the cash dividends and issued the certificates for the common share dividend.

Journalize the transactions.

EX 13-7

Entries for repurchasing shares

Pictou Framing Ltd.'s Shareholders' Equity had the following account balances:

$2.25 preferred shares, 100,000 authorized, 5,000 issued and outstanding	$ 500,000
Common shares, unlimited authorized, 3,000,000 issued and outstanding	24,000,000
Contributed capital from retirement of common shares	120,000
Retained earnings	50,700,000

On June 30, 2015, Pictou Framing Ltd. reacquired and retired 52,000 common shares at $10 per share. On September 22, 2015, Pictou Framing Ltd. purchased and retired an additional 200,000 shares at $6 per share. On November 1, 2015, Pictou Framing Ltd. purchased and retired another 10,000 shares at $9 per share.

Journalize the entries to record the June 30, September 22, and November 1 transactions.

EX 13-8

Shareholders' equity

Using the information in Exercise 13-7, prepare the Shareholders' Equity section of the statement of financial position for Pictou Framing Ltd. as at November 1, 2015.

EX 13-9

Entries for repurchasing shares

MicroChip Corporation's Shareholders' Equity had the following account balances:

Common shares, 900,000 authorized, 400,000 issued and outstanding	$1,800,000
Retained earnings	750,000

On July 3, Best Corporation reacquired and retired 40,000 common shares at $5 per share. On September 12, Best Corporation purchased and retired an additional 20,000 shares at $4 per share. On November 11, Best Corporation purchased and retired another 30,000 shares at $7 per share.

Journalize the transactions of July 3, September 12, and November 11.

EX 13-10
Repurchase of shares

Valley Clothing Inc. had the following account balances on January 1, the start of its fiscal year:

Common shares, unlimited authorized, 100,000 issued and outstanding	$800,000
Retained earnings	400,000
Accumulated other comprehensive income	15,000

On October 3 of the current year, Valley Clothing Inc. reacquired and retired 10,000 common shares at $9 per share. On November 15, Valley Clothing Inc. purchased and retired an additional 5,000 shares at $6 per share. On December 22, Valley Clothing Inc. purchased and retired another 1,000 shares at $10 per share.

Journalize the transactions of October 3, November 15, and December 22.

EX 13-11
Repurchase of shares

Beaverhead Creek Inc. bottles and distributes spring water. In 2008, Beaverhead Creek was incorporated, and 100,000 common shares were issued for $70 per share. No share transactions have occurred until the current year. On March 4 of the current year, Beaverhead Creek reacquired and retired 5,000 common shares at $80 per share. On April 10, Beaverhead purchased and retired an additional 5,000 common shares at $65 per share and another 2,000 shares on November 30 at $75 per share.

a. Journalize the transactions of March 4, April 10, and November 30.
b. For what reasons might Beaverhead Creek have repurchased its shares?

EX 13-12
Earnings per share

Crystal Arts Ltd. had earnings of $240,000 for 2015. The company had 40,000 common shares outstanding during the year. In addition, the company issued 3,000 preferred shares at $75 per share on January 3, 2015. The preferred share has a dividend of $5 per share. No other transactions in either common or preferred shares occurred during 2015.

Determine the basic earnings per share for Crystal Arts Ltd.

EX 13-13
Earnings per share

Royal Bank of Canada is one of the largest commercial banks in Canada. Financial information for the bank for three recent years is as follows:

	Fiscal Years Ended (in millions)		
	2011	2010	2009
Net income	$4,852	$5,223	$3,858
Preferred dividends	$ 258	$ 258	$ 233
Common shares outstanding	1,431	1,421	1,399

a. Determine the earnings per share for fiscal years 2011, 2010, and 2009.
b. Is higher earnings per share a positive trend?
c. Evaluate the growth in earnings per share for the three years in comparison to the growth in net income for the three years.

EX 13-14
Earnings per share

Staples and OfficeMax compete in the retail office supply business. OfficeMax had a net income of $87 million for a recent year, whereas Staples had a net income of $985 million. OfficeMax had preferred dividends of $2 million. Staples had no preferred shares outstanding. The issued and outstanding common shares for each company were as follows:

	Common Shares (in millions)
OfficeMax	224
Staples	694

a. Determine the earnings per share for each company.
b. Evaluate the relative profitability of the two companies.

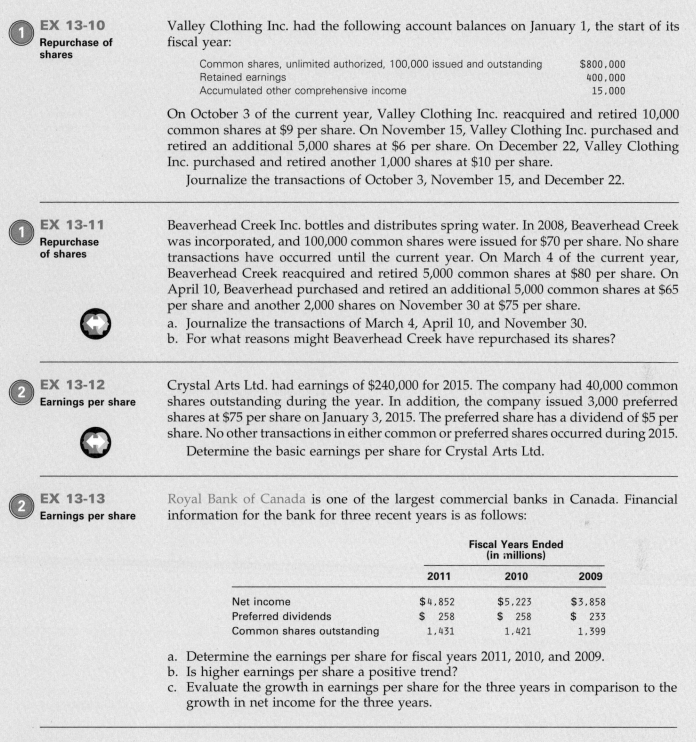

EX 13-15
Calculating tax effect

For each of the following items, determine the applicable income taxes using a tax rate of 30%. State whether the income taxes are additional taxes owing (O) or tax savings (S). Calculate the after-tax amount and state where the after-tax amount will be reported on the income statement: normal operations (NO), other revenues and expenses (ORE), discontinued operations (DO), or not applicable (NA).

	Original Value	Applicable Income Taxes	Taxes Owing (O) or Savings (S)	After-Tax Value	Income Statement Reporting
Payment on settlement of lawsuit	150,000				
Loss on discontinued operations	30,000				
Operating revenue	650,000				
Advertising expenses	120,000				
Gain on discontinued operations	65,000				
Cash dividends	120,000				
Interest revenue	8,000				

EX 13-16
Calculating tax effect

For each of the following items, determine the applicable income taxes using a tax rate of 25%. State whether the income taxes are additional taxes owing (O) or tax savings (S). Calculate the after-tax amount and state where the after-tax amount will be reported on the income statement: normal operations (NO), other revenues and expenses (ORE), discontinued operations (DO), or not applicable (NA).

	Original Value	Applicable Income Taxes	Taxes Owing (O) or Savings (S)	After-Tax Value	Income Statement Reporting
Share dividend	650,000				
Payment on account payable	23,000				
Interest expense	6,500				
Rent expense	64,000				
Loss on discontinued operations	950,000				
Rental income	98,000				
Gain on disposal of computer equipment	5,000				

EX 13-17
Multiple-step income statement and earnings per share

Toby Corporation reported the following for 2015 (all amounts are before taxes):

Sales, net	$14,600,000
Cost of goods sold	11,430,000
Selling and administrative expenses	225,000
Interest expense	15,000
Gain on sale of equipment	6,000
Loss from discontinued operations	80,000
Weighted average number of common shares	175,000
Number of $2 cumulative preferred shares outstanding	200,000

a. Assuming a 27% tax rate, prepare an income statement for the year ended December 31, 2015.
b. Determine earnings per share for (i) income from continuing operations, (ii) discontinued operations, and (iii) net income.

EX 13-18
Multi-step income statement and earnings per share, share issuance

Barks Bites Ltd. reported the following for 2015 (all amounts are before taxes):

Sales, net	$685,000
Cost of goods sold	458,000
Selling and administrative expenses	56,000
Interest expense	2,000
Gain on sale of equipment	4,000
Gain from discontinued operations	60,000
Number of $2.50 cumulative preferred shares outstanding	6,000
Number of common shares, January 1, 2015	75,000
Additional common shares issued on April 1, 2015	15,000

a. Assuming a 22% tax rate, prepare an income statement for the year ended December 31, 2015.

b. Determine earnings per share for (i) income from continuing operations, (ii) discontinued operations, and (iii) net income.

EX 13-19

Earnings per share

The net income reported on the income statement of Berkwood Ltd. was $500,000. Berkwood had 70,000 common shares and 4,000 $2 cumulative preferred shares outstanding throughout the current year. The income statement included a $20,000 gain arising from discontinued operations after applicable income taxes. Determine earnings per share for (a) income from continuing operations, (b) discontinued operations, and (c) net income.

EX 13-20

Earnings per share

The net income reported on the income statement of Rocky Corporation for the year ended May 31, 2015, was $6,530,000. The number of common shares outstanding at June 1, 2014, was 200,000, and the number of $3.50 cumulative preferred shares was 80,000. On September 1, 2014, Rocky issued 40,000 common shares. During fiscal 2015, Rocky discontinued one segment of its business, resulting in an after-tax loss of $110,000. Determine earnings per share for (a) income from continuing operations, (b) discontinued operations, and (c) net income.

EX 13-21

Earnings per share

Net income of $1,350,000 was reported on the income statement of Andy Boy Ltd. for the year ended July 31, 2015. The number of common shares outstanding as at August 1, 2014, was 350,000, and the number of $1.50 cumulative preferred shares was 60,000. On February 1, 2015, Andy Boy declared a 3:1 share split on the common shares. During fiscal 2015, Andy Boy discontinued a division of the company, resulting in a loss of $230,000 after taxes. Determine the earnings per share for (a) income from continuing operations, (b) discontinued operations, and (c) net income.

EX 13-22

Earnings per share

The net income reported on the income statement of Augustine Inc. for the year ended October 31, 2015, was $2,540,000. The number of common shares outstanding as at November 1, 2014, was 100,000, and the number of $1.50 cumulative preferred shares was 100,000. On May 1, 2015, Augustine repurchased and retired 20,000 common shares, and on May 15 it declared a 10% share dividend on the common shares. During fiscal 2015, Augustine discontinued a division of the company, resulting in a gain of $340,000 after taxes. Determine earnings per share for (a) income from continuing operations, (b) discontinued operations, and (c) net income.

EX 13-23

Discontinued operations

Apple Gardens Limited sells orchard supplies. In 2015, the company earned $1,346,000 from its Okanagan location and experienced a loss of $467,000 from the sale of its Ontario division (before taxes).

Assuming a 35% tax rate, prepare a partial income statement for the year ended December 31, 2015, starting from Income from continuing operations.

EX 13-24

Earnings per share

Using the data in Exercise 13-23, determine the earnings per share for Apple Gardens Limited for 2015, assuming Apple Gardens has 400,000 $1.25 preferred shares and 1,250,000 common shares outstanding for the entire fiscal year.

EX 13-25

Classification of income statement items

Classify each of the following items as either normally occurring (NO), discontinued operations (DO), or unusual (U).

a. Loss on the disposal of equipment considered to be obsolete because of the development of new technology.

(continued)

b. Uncollectible accounts expense.

c. Gain on disposal of property, plant, and equipment related to the closing of the retail division.

d. Gain on sale of land due to expropriation by the government.

e. Interest revenue on notes receivable.

f. Uninsured flood loss. (Flood insurance is unavailable because of periodic flooding in the area.)

g. Loss due to closing 3 of the 50 coffee shop outlets operated by the company.

---

(4) EX 13-26
Correction of a prior period error

In preparation for the December 31, 2015, year-end, Carolanne was reviewing the records of Holmes Ltd. She discovered a balance of $32,000 in accounts receivable that related to an account received in full in 2014. Upon further investigation, Carolanne discovered the 2014 journal entry to record receipt of the $32,000 had incorrectly been credited to Revenue, an error that had gone undetected in the 2014 financial statements. Holmes Ltd. pays income taxes at a rate of 22%.

Instructions

1. Journalize the entry to correct the error in 2015.
2. Explain how this correction will be reflected in the statement of changes in equity for the year ended December 31, 2015.

Assuming Holmes Ltd. prepares comparative financial statements, what other impact will this correction have on the financial statements for 2015?

---

(4) EX 13-27
Correction of prior period error

In preparation for the October 31, 2016, year-end, Frank was reviewing the records of Berkhout Holdings Ltd. In the Vehicle account, he discovered a balance of $18,000 relating to December 2014 vehicle repairs, which should have been recorded as vehicle maintenance expenses. This error had gone undetected in the 2015 financial statements. Berkhout Holdings Ltd. pays income taxes at a rate of 27%.

Instructions

1. Journalize the entry to correct the error in 2016.
2. Explain how this correction will be reflected in the statement of changes in equity for the year ended October 31, 2016.

Assuming Berkhout Holdings Ltd. prepares comparative financial statements, what other impact will this correction have on the financial statements for 2016?

PROBLEMS SERIES A

(1) (2) PR 13-1A
Selected share transactions

✔ b. Cash dividends, $318,500

Comp You Solutions Corp. is a national information technology consulting firm. The following selected accounts appear in the ledger of Comp You Solutions Corp. on April 1, 2015, the beginning of the current year:

$1.50 preferred shares (500,000 authorized, 56,000 shares issued and outstanding)	$2,550,000
Common shares (unlimited authorized, 550,000 shares issued and outstanding)	8,356,500
Retained earnings	4,358,000

Comp You Solutions Corp. uses dividend accounts. During the year, the corporation completed the following transactions that affected its shareholders' equity.

a. Sold 2,000 preferred shares at $52 per share.

b. Declared semiannual cash dividends of $0.75 per preferred share and $0.50 per common share.

c. Issued 100,000 common shares at $12 per share, receiving cash.

d. Paid the dividend declared in (b).

e. Declared a common share dividend of 5% when the market price of the common share was trading at $12.50.
f. Issued the share dividend.
g. Declared semiannual cash dividends of $0.75 per preferred share and $0.65 per common share.
h. Recorded closing entries. The net income for the year was $3,745,000.

Instructions

1. Journalize the entries to record the transactions. Identify each entry by letter.
2. Prepare a statement of changes in equity for the year ended March 31, 2016.
3. Prepare the Shareholders' Equity section of the statement of financial position for Comp You Solutions Corp. as at March 31, 2016.
4. Calculate the basic earnings per share for the year ended March 31, 2016, assuming a weighted average number of common shares of 673,750.

PR 13-2A

Selected share transactions

① ②

✔ Retained earnings June 30, 2016, $10,822,450

Rowing Regattas Ltd. is a national organization providing support to Canadian rowers. The following selected accounts appear in the ledger of Rowing Regattas Ltd. on July 1, 2015, the beginning of the current year:

$1.90 preferred shares (750,000 authorized,	
42,000 shares issued and outstanding)	$1,630,000
Common shares (unlimited authorized,	
400,000 shares issued and outstanding)	6,850,000
Retained earnings	5,432,000

Rowing Regattas Ltd. uses dividend accounts. During the year, the corporation completed the following transactions that affected its shareholders' equity.

a. Issued 50,000 common shares in exchange for an office building with a fair market value of $480,000.
b. Declared semiannual cash dividends of $0.95 per preferred share and $0.40 per common share.
c. Issued 5,000 preferred shares at $42 per share, receiving cash.
d. Paid the dividend declared in (b).
e. Declared a 3:1 common share split.
f. Declared semiannual cash dividends of $0.95 per preferred share and $0.50 per common share.
g. Recorded closing entries. The net income for the year was $6,330,000.

Instructions

1. Journalize the entries to record the transactions. Identify each entry by letter.
2. Prepare a statement of changes in equity for the year ended June 30, 2016.
3. Prepare the Shareholders' Equity section of the statement of financial position for Rowing Regattas Ltd. as at June 30, 2016.
4. Calculate the basic earnings per share for the year ended June 30, 2016, assuming a weighted average number of common shares of 1,325,000.

PR 13-3A

Selected share transactions and earnings per share

① ②

✔ Retained earnings, Apr. 30, $4,485,221

ITA Ltd. is a grocery store chain operating in the western provinces. The following selected accounts appear in the ledger of ITA Ltd. on May 1, 2015, the beginning of the current fiscal year:

$0.50 preferred shares (10,000,000 shares authorized,	
583,000 shares issued and outstanding)	$5,830,000
Common shares (unlimited authorized,	
35,760 shares issued and outstanding)	92,976
Retained earnings	1,027,855

ITA Ltd. does not use dividend accounts. During the year, the corporation completed the following transactions that affected its shareholders' equity.

May 2. Split the common shares 2 for 1.
     30. Sold 5,000 preferred shares for $55,000.

(continued)

Nov. 1. Declared semiannual dividends of $0.25 on the preferred shares and $0.10 on the common shares to shareholders of record on November 20, payable on December 20.

Dec. 20. Paid the cash dividends.

31. Repurchased 10,000 common shares at $1.435 per share.

Apr. 30. Declared semiannual dividends of $0.25 on the preferred shares and $0.10 on the common shares to shareholders of record on May 20, payable on June 20.

30. Recorded the closing entry for the income for the year of $3,766,020.

Instructions

1. Journalize the entries to record the transactions.
2. Prepare the Shareholders' Equity section of the statement of financial position as at April 30, 2016.
3. Calculate basic earnings per share for the year ended April 30, 2016.

PR 13-4A

Selected share transactions

✔ May 1, total dividends, $21,250

Ashton Corporation is a lighting fixture wholesaler located in Manitoba. The following selected accounts appear in the ledger of Ashton Corporation on January 1, 2013, the beginning of the current fiscal year:

$2 preferred shares (100,000 shares authorized, 10,000 shares issued and outstanding)	$1,000,000
Common shares (unlimited authorized, 40,000 shares issued and outstanding)	800,000

During its current fiscal year, Ashton Corporation completed the following selected transactions:

Feb. 3. Purchased and retired 2,500 of its common shares at $26 per share.

May 1. Declared a semiannual dividend on the 10,000 preferred shares and a $0.30 dividend on the common shares to shareholders of record on May 31, payable on June 15. Ashton Corporation does not use dividend accounts.

Jun. 15. Paid the cash dividends.

Sep. 28. Purchased and retired 1,000 shares at $18 per share.

Nov. 1. Declared semiannual dividends on the preferred shares and $0.30 on the common shares. In addition, a 5% share dividend was declared on the common shares outstanding, to be capitalized at the fair market price of $19 per share.

Dec. 1. Paid the cash dividends and issued the certificates for the common share dividend.

Instructions

Journalize the entries to record the transactions for Ashton Corporation.

PR 13-5A

Selected share transactions

✔ Nov. 30, Common shares, $493,000 Dr.

Alfred Art Ltd. sells native art to specialty stores in western Canada. The following selected accounts appear in the ledger of Alfred Art Ltd. at June 1, 2015, the beginning of the current fiscal year:

$0.60 preferred shares (5,000,000 shares authorized, 250,700 shares issued and outstanding)	$2,507,000
Common shares (unlimited authorized, 700,000 shares issued and outstanding)	3,451,000
Retained earnings	2,529,620

Selected transactions completed by Alfred Art Ltd. during the fiscal year ended May 31, 2016, were as follows:

a. On November 30, 2015, repurchased and retired 100,000 shares at $6 per share.

b. On December 1, 2015, declared semiannual dividends of $0.25 per common share (to shareholders of record on December 31, 2015, payable on January 15, 2016) and $0.30 per preferred share.

c. On February 25, 2016, repurchased and retired 100,000 shares at $4 per share.

d. On May 1, 2016, declared semiannual dividends of $0.32 per common share and $0.30 per preferred share (to shareholders of record on May 31, 2016, payable on June 30, 2016).

e. On May 31, 2016, declared a 5% share dividend on the common shares outstanding, when the shares had a fair market value of $4.50 per share, to shareholders of record on June 30, 2016, distributable on July 31, 2016.

Instructions

Journalize the selected transactions for the year ended May 31, 2016.

PR 13-6A

Income statement with discontinued operations

✔ Net income, $428,400

Branksome Retailing Inc. has the following account balances as at June 30, 2015, its year-end (all numbers are before tax):

Error discovered in 2013 financial statements (prepaid rent recorded incorrectly as rent expense)	32,600
Selling and administration expenses	253,000
Net sales	2,356,000
Gain on sale of building	28,750
Interest expense	12,050
Cost of goods sold	1,425,000
Income taxes expense	?
Payment made in settlement of a lawsuit, in October 2014	158,000
Effect of change in accounting policy	65,000
Interest revenue	2,500
Gain on discontinued operations	32,000
Weighted average number of common shares	135,000

Branksome Retailing pays income taxes at a rate of 25%. It has no outstanding preferred shares. Prepare an income statement for Branksome Retailing for the year ended June 30, 2015, including earnings per share.

PR 13-7A

Corporate financial statements

✔ Net Income, $1,281,890

After all the transactions for the year ended May 31, 2016, had been posted, the data below were taken from the records of Angelos Design Ltd. Assume all accounts have normal balances.

Cash	$ 160,000
Accounts receivable	3,090,500
Inventory	2,451,400
Supplies	723,900
Notes receivable	700,000
Equipment	5,100,000
Accumulated depreciation–Equipment	400,000
Accounts payable	2,250,810
Salaries payable	475,690
Income taxes payable	55,000
Dividends payable	235,210
Long-term debt, due 2022	500,000
$0.60 preferred shares, 5,000,000 authorized, 250,700 issued and outstanding	2,507,000
Common shares, unlimited authorized, 500,000 issued and outstanding	2,465,000
Contributed capital from retirement of common shares	93,000
Common share dividend distributable	112,500
Retained earnings	3,131,590
Gain on sale of equipment	53,560
Net sales	6,960,500
Cost of goods sold	2,732,070
Loss on discontinued operations	600,000
Tax savings on discontinued operations	180,000
Interest expense	350,000
Income taxes expense (regular operations)	729,300
Selling and administration expenses	1,500,800

(continued)

Instructions

a. Prepare a multiple-step income statement for the year ended May 31, 2016, including earnings per share. The weighted average number of common shares is 656,250. Preferred shareholders were paid their dividend entitlement during the year.

b. Prepare a balance sheet as at May 31, 2016.

---

4 PR 13-8A
Accounting Changes

✔ Retained
earnings, April 30,
2016, $8,327,700

Bronwyn Medical Labs Ltd. has the following balances in its shareholders' equity accounts as at April 30, 2015:

Retained earnings	$5,214,230
Common shares	5,236,500
Preferred shares	1,325,000
Accumulated other comprehensive income	325,000

During the fiscal year ended April 30, 2016, Bronwyn Medical Labs Ltd. issued preferred shares of $525,300, recorded net income of $3,562,310, a gain on revaluation of assets of $23,000, issued common shares of $1,235,000, declared a share dividend of $368,000, declared cash dividends of $235,000 on the preferred shares and $256,000 on the common shares, and discovered that $62,000 of revenue in March 2014 had been credited to accounts receivable in error. Bronwyn Medical Labs has a 32% income tax rate.

Instructions

1. Journalize the correction of the error from March 2014.
2. Prepare a statement of changes in equity for the year ended April 30, 2016.

PROBLEMS SERIES B

1 PR 13-1B
Selected share
transactions

2

✔ b. Common
shares, April 30,
2016, $16,511,500

Make a Dream Ltd. has the following selected account balances in the ledger as at May 1, 2015, the beginning of the current year:

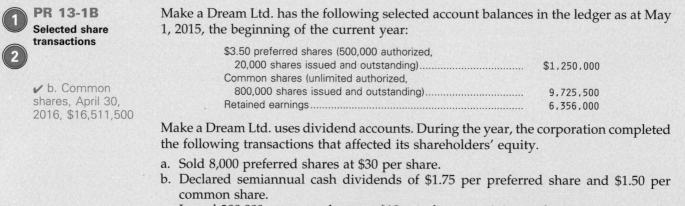

$3.50 preferred shares (500,000 authorized, 20,000 shares issued and outstanding)	$1,250,000
Common shares (unlimited authorized, 800,000 shares issued and outstanding)	9,725,500
Retained earnings	6,356,000

Make a Dream Ltd. uses dividend accounts. During the year, the corporation completed the following transactions that affected its shareholders' equity.

a. Sold 8,000 preferred shares at $30 per share.
b. Declared semiannual cash dividends of $1.75 per preferred share and $1.50 per common share.
c. Issued 300,000 common shares at $18 per share, receiving cash.
d. Paid the dividend declared in (b).
e. Declared a common share dividend of 6% when the market price of the common share was trading at $21.
f. Issued the share dividend.
g. Declared semiannual cash dividends of $1.75 per preferred share and $1.65 per common share.
h. Recorded closing entries. The net income for the year was $4,642,000.

Instructions

1. Journalize the entries to record the transactions. Identify each entry by letter.
2. Prepare a statement of changes in equity for the year ended April 30, 2016.
3. Prepare the Shareholders' Equity section of the statement of financial position for Make a Dream Ltd. as at April 30, 2016.
4. Calculate the basic earnings per share for the year ended April 30, 2016, assuming a weighted average number of common shares of 1,033,500.

PR 13-2B

Selected share transactions

✔ f. cash dividends, $591,250

The following selected account balances are in the ledger of Calhoon Junction Inc. on December 1, 2015, the beginning of the current year:

$2.90 preferred shares (1,000,000 authorized, 75,000 shares issued and outstanding)................................	$2,300,000
Common shares (unlimited authorized, 250,000 shares issued and outstanding).............................	3,650,000
Retained earnings..	6,582,000

Calhoon Junction Inc. uses dividend accounts. During the year, the corporation completed the following transactions that affected its shareholders' equity.

a. Issued 10,000 common shares in exchange for equipment with a fair market value of $600,000.
b. Declared semiannual cash dividends of $1.45 per preferred share and $0.80 per common share.
c. Issued 10,000 preferred shares at $68 per share, receiving cash.
d. Paid the dividend declared in (b).
e. Declared a 2:1 common share split.
f. Declared semiannual cash dividends of $1.45 per preferred share and $0.90 per common share.
g. Recorded closing entries. The net income for the year was $5,236,000.

Instructions

1. Journalize the entries to record the transactions. Identify each entry by letter.
2. Prepare a statement of changes in equity for the year ended November 30, 2016.
3. Prepare the Shareholders' Equity section of the statement of financial position for Calhoon Junction Inc. as at November 30, 2016.
4. Calculate the basic earnings per share for the year ended November 30, 2016, assuming a weighted average number of common shares of 510,000.

PR 13-3B

Selected share transactions and earnings per share

✔ Dec. 1, Retained earnings, $1,196,524.80

Max Corporation is a hardware store chain operating in the Atlantic provinces. The following selected accounts appear in the ledger of Max Corporation on June 1, 2015, the beginning of the current fiscal year:

$2.25 preferred shares (1,000,000 shares authorized, 75,000 shares issued and outstanding)	$ 3,750,000
Common shares (unlimited authorized, 3,054,930 shares issued and outstanding)	10,845,040
Retained earnings	3,076,400

Max Corporation does not use dividend accounts. During the year, the corporation completed the following transactions that affected its shareholders' equity.

Jun. 15. Split the common shares 3 for 1.
Jul. 30. Sold 11,000 preferred shares for $575,000.
Dec. 1. Declared semiannual dividends of $1.125 on the preferred shares and $0.12 on the common shares to shareholders of record on December 31, payable on January 31.
Jan. 1. Repurchased and retired 540,350 common shares at $4 per share.
31. Paid the cash dividends.
May 31. Declared semiannual dividends of $1.125 on the preferred shares and $0.13 on the common shares to shareholders of record on June 30, payable on July 30.
31. Recorded the closing entry for the income for the year of $4,785,029.

Instructions

1. Journalize the entries to record the transactions.
2. Prepare the Shareholders' Equity section of the statement of financial position as at May 31, 2016.
3. Calculate basic earnings per share for the year ended May 31, 2016.

PR 13-4B

Selected share transactions

✔ May 1, total dividends, $25,750

Berry Limited is a fruit wholesaler in Ontario. The following selected accounts appear in the ledger of Berry Limited on January 1, 2015, the beginning of the current fiscal year:

$0.50 preferred shares (100,000 shares authorized,	
15,000 shares issued and outstanding)	$ 100,000
Common shares (unlimited authorized,	
60,000 shares issued and outstanding)	1,200,000

During its current fiscal year, Berry Limited completed the following selected transactions:

Feb. 3. Purchased and retired 5,000 of its common shares at $18 per share.

May 1. Declared a semiannual dividend on the preferred shares and a $0.40 dividend on the common shares to shareholders of record on May 31, payable on June 15. Berry Limited does not use dividend accounts.

Jun. 15. Paid the cash dividends.

Sep. 28. Purchased and retired 5,000 shares at $22 per share.

Nov. 1. Declared semiannual dividends on the preferred shares and $0.30 on the common shares. In addition, a 3% share dividend was declared on the common shares outstanding, when the fair market price was $30 per share.

Dec. 1. Paid the cash dividends and issued the certificates for the common share dividend.

Instructions

Journalize the entries to record the transactions for Berry Limited.

PR 13-5B

Selected share transactions

✔ Nov. 25, Common shares, $739,500 Dr.

Diamond Trucking Ltd. is a trucking company operating in Ontario, Quebec, and the Atlantic provinces. The following selected accounts appear in the ledger of Diamond Trucking Ltd. at June 1, 2015, the beginning of the current fiscal year:

$0.90 preferred shares (5,000,000 shares authorized,	
376,050 shares issued and outstanding)	$3,760,500
Common shares (unlimited authorized,	
1,050,000 shares issued and outstanding)	5,176,500
Retained earnings	3,550,523

Selected transactions completed by Diamond Trucking Ltd. during the fiscal year ended May 31, 2016, were as follows:

a. On November 25, 2015, repurchased 150,000 shares at $5 per share.

b. On December 1, 2015, declared dividends of $0.375 per common share (to shareholders of record on December 31, 2015, payable on January 15, 2016) and $0.45 per preferred share.

c. On February 28, 2016, repurchased and retired 150,000 shares at $4 per share.

d. On March 1, 2016, declared dividends of $0.48 per common share and $0.45 per preferred share (to shareholders of record on March 31, 2016, payable on April 30, 2016).

e. On May 31, 2016, declared a 7.5% share dividend on the common shares outstanding, when the shares had a fair market value of $3 per share, to shareholders of record on June 30, distributable on July 31, 2016.

Instructions

Journalize the selected transactions for the year ended May 31, 2016.

PR 13-6B

Income statement with discontinued operations

✔ Income taxes expense, $492,346

Crookmonty Inc. has the following account balances as at November 30, 2015, its year-end (all numbers are before tax):

Effect of change in accounting policy	$ 36,000
Selling and administration expenses	178,000
Net sales	3,562,780
Gain on sale of land	78,000
Interest expense	14,000
Cost of goods sold	1,652,000
Income taxes expense	?
Losses due to tornado damage	42,000
Error discovered in 2013 financial statements	
(revenue recorded incorrectly as unearned revenue)	48,000
Interest revenue	3,600
Gain on discontinued operations	54,000
Weighted average number of common shares	236,000

Crookmonty Inc. pays income taxes at a rate of 28%. It has no outstanding preferred shares.

Prepare an income statement for Crookmonty Inc. for the year ended November 30, 2015, including earnings per share.

---

② ③ PR 13-7B

Corporate financial statements

✔ Net Income, $1,922,835

After all the transactions for the year ended May 31, 2016, had been posted the following data were taken from the records of Desmond Shipping Ltd. Assume all accounts have normal balances.

Cash	$ 240,001
Accounts receivable	4,635,750
Inventory	3,677,100
Supplies	1,085,850
Land	1,050,000
Equipment	7,650,000
Accumulated depreciation–Equipment	750,000
Accounts payable	3,376,215
Salaries payable	826,350
Income taxes payable	82,500
Dividends payable	529,223
Long-term debt, due 2022	750,000
$0.90 preferred shares, 5,000,000 authorized, 376,050	
issued and outstanding	3,760,500
Common shares, unlimited authorized, 750,000 issued and	
outstanding	3,697,500
Contributed capital from retirement of common shares	139,500
Common share dividend distributable	168,750
Retained earnings	4,258,163
Gain on sale of land	80,340
Net sales	10,440,750
Cost of goods sold	4,098,105
Loss on discontinued operation	900,000
Tax savings on discontinued operation	270,000
Interest expense	525,000
Income taxes expense (on regular operations)	1,093,950
Selling and administration expenses	2,251,200

Instructions

a. Prepare a multiple-step income statement for the year ended May 31, 2016, including earnings per share. The weighted average number of common shares is 1,007,813.

b. Prepare a balance sheet as at May 31, 2016.

---

④ PR 13-8B

Accounting Changes

✔ Retained earnings, October 31, 2016, $4,065,960

Capri Classic Inc. has the following balances in its shareholders' equity accounts as at October 31, 2015:

Retained earnings	$2,561,000
Common shares	985,000
Preferred shares	298,000
Accumulated other comprehensive income	32,000

(continued)

During the fiscal year ended October 31, 2016, Capri Classic Inc. issued preferred shares of $25,000, recorded net income of $1,582,000, a loss on revaluation of assets of $12,000, issued common shares of $138,000, declared a 3:1 share split, declared cash dividends of $32,000 on the preferred shares and $28,000 on the common shares, and discovered that $24,000 of rent expense in May 2014 had been debited to prepaid rent in error. Capri Classic Inc. has a 29% income tax rate.

Instructions

1. Journalize the correction of the error from May 2014.
2. Prepare a statement of changes in equity for the year ended October 31, 2016.

SPECIAL ACTIVITIES

SA 13-1
Accounting changes

Group Project

Discuss whether Baxter Company correctly reported the following items in its 2015 financial statements, assuming that all amounts are material. If you disagree with Baxter's reporting, indicate where and how the item should have been reported.

a. The company discovered a clerical error in the prior year's accounting records. As a result, the reported net income for 2014 was overstated by $2,000,000. The company corrected this error by restating the prior-year financial statements.

b. The company voluntarily changed its method of accounting for inventories from the FIFO method to the specific identification method. Both methods are acceptable under ASPE and IFRS. The cumulative effect of this change was reported as a separate component of income in the 2015 income statement.

c. In 2015, the company workers went on strike, resulting in an additional expense of $12,000,000. Because management wanted to highlight to shareholders that this expense is unlikely to occur every year, the expense was reported net of tax after income taxes expense.

d. The government expropriated some of Baxter's land, resulting in a gain of $700,000, which Baxter reported in its Other Income section on the income statement.

e. Baxter repurchased and retired common shares for $2 per share less than their issuance price. The difference, totalling $1,200,000, was recorded in Other Income as a gain on sale of shares.

SA 13-2
Dividends

Rainbow Designs Inc. has paid quarterly cash dividends since 2002. These dividends have steadily increased from $0.05 per share to the latest dividend declaration of $0.40 per share. The board of directors would like to continue this trend and is hesitant to suspend or decrease the amount of quarterly dividends. Unfortunately, sales dropped sharply in the fourth quarter of 2015 because of worsening economic conditions and increased competition. As a result, the board is uncertain whether it should declare a dividend for the last quarter of 2015.

On November 1, 2015, Rainbow Designs Inc. borrowed $1,200,000 from TD Bank to modernize its retail stores and to expand its product line in response to its competition. The terms of the 10-year, 6% loan require Rainbow Designs Inc. to do the following:

a. Pay monthly interest on the last day of the month.
b. Pay $120,000 of the principal each November 1, beginning in 2016.
c. Maintain a minimum current ratio (current assets/current liabilities) of 2.
d. Maintain a minimum balance (a compensating balance) of $60,000 in its TD Bank account.

On December 31, 2015, $300,000 of the $1,200,000 loan had been disbursed in modernization of the retail stores and in expansion of the product line. Rainbow Designs Inc.'s balance sheet as at December 31, 2015, is shown below.

Rainbow Designs Inc.
Balance Sheet
December 31, 2015

Assets

Current assets:			
Cash			$ 96,000
Marketable securities.................			900,000
Accounts receivable..................		$ 219,600	
Less allowance for doubtful accounts ..		15,600	204,000
Inventory.............................			300,000
Prepaid expenses.....................			10,800
Total current assets			1,510,800
Property, plant, and equipment:			
Buildings...........................	$2,280,000		
Less accumulated depreciation	516,000	1,764,000	
Equipment	1,104,000		
Less accumulated depreciation	264,000	840,000	
Land		360,000	
Total property, plant, and equipment...			2,964,000
Total assets			$4,474,800

Liabilities

Current liabilities:		
Accounts payable....................		$ 172,320
Notes payable (TD Bank)..............		120,000
Salaries payable		7,680
Total current liabilities..............		300,000
Long-term liabilities:		
Notes payable (TD Bank)..............		1,080,000
Total liabilities........................		1,380,000

Shareholders' Equity

Contributed capital:		
Common shares (100,000 shares		
authorized, 60,000 shares issued and outstanding)	$1,296,000	
Retained earnings	1,798,800	
Total shareholders' equity		3,094,800
Total liabilities and shareholders' equity		$4,474,800

The board of directors is scheduled to meet January 15, 2016, to discuss the results of operations for 2015 and to consider the declaration of dividends for the fourth quarter of 2015. The chair of the board has asked for your advice on the declaration of dividends.

1. What factors should the board consider when deciding whether to declare a cash dividend?
2. The board is considering the declaration of a share dividend instead of a cash dividend. Discuss the issuance of a share dividend from the point of view of (a) a shareholder and (b) the board of directors.

SA 13-3

Share structure and dividends

Refer to the financial statements for Shoppers Drug Mart in Appendix C at the back of the textbook, specifically Note 24.

1. What is the share structure for Shoppers Drug Mart?
2. Did its shares increase or decrease during the year?
3. What is the average issue price of the shares on December 31, 2010, and on December 31, 2011?
4. What dividends were paid to shareholders in 2011?
5. What dividends were declared by the board of directors during 2011?
6. Assuming no change in common shares between December 31, 2011, and January 13, 2012, what will be the amount of the dividend payment on January 13, 2012?
7. When is the next dividend payment to be made in 2012?

SA 13-4
Share price

Go to the website of the Toronto Stock Exchange at **tmx.com.** Search for Shoppers Drug Mart using its trading symbol, SC. Review the 30-day price history prior to June 29, 2012. Compare those prices to the 30-day price history prior to June 29, 2010. If you bought 1,000 shares of Shoppers Drug Mart at the opening price on June 29, 2010, and still owned those shares today, how much money would you have gained or lost, ignoring dividends?

SA 13-5
Share split

Theoretically, a 2:1 share split should cut the market price of a company's shares in half. On June 9, 2011, lululemon athletica inc. announced a 2:1 share split with shares traded on a post-split basis on the Toronto Stock Exchange, effective July 6, 2011.

Go to the website of the Toronto Stock Exchange at **tmx.com.** Search for lululemon athletica inc. using its trading symbol, LLL. Review the 30-day price history for the period prior to July 31, 2011. What was the effect of the share split on the market price of lululemon athletica inc. shares?

Long-Term Liabilities: Bonds and Notes

Larry MacDougal/TCP/The Canadian Press

Most of us don't have enough money in our bank accounts to buy a house or a car by simply writing a cheque. Just imagine if you had to save the complete purchase price of a house before you could buy it! To help us make these types of purchases, banks will typically lend us the money, as long as we agree to repay the loan with interest in small future payments. Loans such as this, or long-term debt, allow us to purchase assets such as houses and cars today, which benefit us over the long term.

The use of debt can also help a business reach its objectives. Most businesses need to borrow money to acquire the assets they will use to generate income. For example,

WestJet Airlines Ltd., a Canadian low-cost airline, uses debt to finance its expansion of routes and acquisition of new airplanes. Formed by three young men in 1996, WestJet has continually expanded, offering flights to more destinations and increasing the size and variety of its fleet of aircraft. WestJet currently offers scheduled service throughout its 71-city North American and Caribbean network.

Although debt can help companies like WestJet grow to achieve financial success, too much debt can be a financial burden that may even lead to bankruptcy. Just like individuals, businesses must manage debt wisely. In this chapter, we will discuss the nature of, accounting for, analysis of, and investments in long-term debt.

After studying this chapter, you should be able to:

1 Describe the characteristics and terminology of bonds payable, and the potential impact of borrowing on earnings per share.

Nature of Bonds Payable	Bond Characteristics and Terminology	
	Financing Options for Corporations	
	Advantages of Issuing Bonds	
	Disadvantages of Issuing Bonds	EXAMPLE EXERCISE 14-1 (page 709)
	Proceeds from Issuing Bonds	

2 Journalize entries for bonds payable.

Accounting for Bonds Payable	Bonds Issued at Face Value	EXAMPLE EXERCISE 14-2 (page 712) EXAMPLE EXERCISE 14-3 (page 713)
	Bonds Issued at a Discount	EXAMPLE EXERCISE 14-4 (page 714)
	Amortizing a Bond Discount	EXAMPLE EXERCISE 14-5 (page 716) EXAMPLE EXERCISE 14-6 (page 717)
	Adjusting Entry for Interest Expense	
	Bonds Issued at a Premium	EXAMPLE EXERCISE 14-7 (page 721)
	Amortizing a Bond Premium	EXAMPLE EXERCISE 14-8 (page 722) EXAMPLE EXERCISE 14-9 (page 723)
	Bond Redemption	EXAMPLE EXERCISE 14-10 (page 726)

3 Describe and illustrate the accounting for installment notes.

Installment Notes	Issuing an Installment Note	
	Annual Payments	EXAMPLE EXERCISE 14-11 (page 729)

4 Describe and illustrate the reporting and analysis of long-term liabilities.

Reporting of Long-Term Liabilities	Financial Analysis and Interpretation	EXAMPLE EXERCISE 14-12 (page 730)

APPENDIX 1 Present Value Concepts and Pricing Bonds Payable

For the chapter *At a Glance*, turn to page 735.

1 Nature of Bonds Payable

Describe the characteristics and terminology of bonds payable, and the potential impact of borrowing on earnings per share.

A **bond** is a form of an interest-bearing note that a corporation may issue as a way to borrow on a long-term basis. The relationship of the bondholder to the issuer of the bond (the corporation) is similar to the relationship between a landlord and a tenant. The bondholder (the landlord) gives the corporation (the tenant) use of the money (the apartment). Over the life of the bond, the corporation (the tenant) will pay interest (rent) for use of the money (the apartment). At the end of the bond's life, the initial amount of money (the apartment) lent to the corporation (the tenant) will be returned to the bondholder (the landlord). Because bondholders are creditors of the corporation, their claims on the corporation's assets rank ahead of those of the owners, the shareholders. An example of a bond is shown in Exhibit 1.

Corporate bonds normally differ in face values, interest rates, interest payment dates, and maturity dates. Bonds also differ in other ways, such as whether corporate assets are pledged in support of the bonds.

Exhibit 1

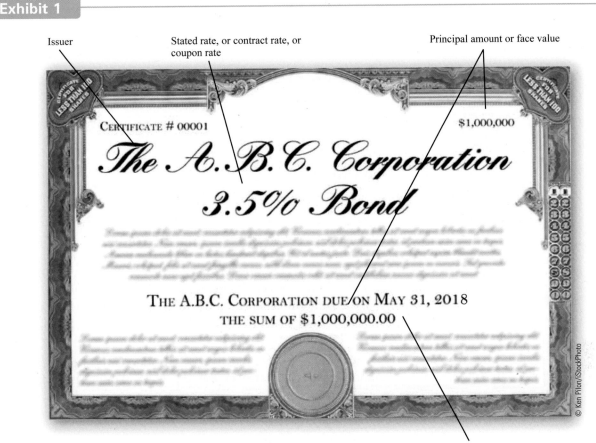

Issuer

Stated rate, or contract rate, or coupon rate

Principal amount or face value

Maturity date

Bond Characteristics and Terminology

The underlying contract between the company issuing bonds and the bondholders is called a **bond indenture**. A bond issue is normally divided into a number of individual bonds. Usually, the face value of each bond is $1,000 or a multiple of $1,000. The **face value**, or principal, is the amount due at the maturity date of the bonds. The interest on bonds may be payable annually, semiannually, or quarterly. Most bonds pay interest semiannually.

The price of a bond is quoted as a percentage of the bond's face value. For example, a $1,000 bond quoted at 98 or at 98% or at 0.98 could be purchased or sold for $980 ($1,000 × 0.98). Likewise, bonds quoted at 109 or at 109% or at 1.09 could be purchased or sold for $1,090 ($1,000 × 1.09).

When all bonds of an issue mature at the same time, they are called *term bonds*. If the bonds mature over several dates, they are called *serial bonds*. For example, one-tenth of an issue of $1,000,000 bonds, or $100,000, may mature 16 years from the issue date, another $100,000 in the 17th year, and so on.

Bonds that may be exchanged for other securities, such as common shares, are called *convertible bonds*. Convertible bonds offer purchasers the option of exchanging the bonds for shares in the corporation. This feature is attractive to bondholders and allows the corporation to pay a lower rate of interest on the bonds. Because these liabilities (bonds) can be exchanged for equity (shares), the accounting for convertible bonds is complex and will be covered in a more advanced accounting course.

Bonds that a corporation may redeem before maturity are called *callable bonds*. Bonds that the purchaser may redeem before maturity are called *redeemable bonds*. Bonds issued on the basis of the general credit of the corporation are called *debenture bonds*.

Why would an investor buy a corporation's bond instead of buying its common shares?

A bond offers a guaranteed return on the investment in the form of interest. Investors can sell the bond and receive their principal investment back with little risk that the price will vary from what they paid initially. In contrast, the purchase of a share does not offer a guaranteed return, and its selling price is likely to fluctuate more than the price of a bond. In exchange for this higher risk, a share gives the investor the opportunity to earn future profits should the company be profitable. Because of the risk/return tradeoff, a bond, which is less risky than a share, offers a lower rate of return than a common share.

Financing Options for Corporations

Corporations finance their operations using the following:

1. Debt—a corporation can issue bonds or notes payable or make purchases on account (accounts payable). The issuance of bonds or notes payable requires the corporation to pay interest on the debt.

2. Equity—a corporation can issue common or preferred shares. The corporation may choose to pay dividends to the shareholders, but is not required to do so.

3. Debt and equity—a corporation can use a combination of debt and equity. The corporation's use of this combination requires it to pay interest, and possibly dividends, on the debt and shares.

In deciding which option to choose, a corporation would consider many factors, including the impact on the shareholders, as calculated by the impact on earnings per share.

Advantages of Issuing Bonds

The advantages of issuing bonds instead of shares include the following:

1. *No impact on ownership*—bondholders have no ownership of the corporation. In contrast, when a corporation issues additional common shares to finance its operations, those additional shares reduce the percentage ownership of the existing shareholders.

2. *Tax-deductible interest*—interest paid on bonds is tax-deductible, whereas dividends are paid out of after-tax income. Assuming a 30% tax rate, $100,000 in bond interest has an after-tax cost of $70,000, whereas a $100,000 dividend would cost the corporation $100,000.

3. *Positive impact on earnings per share*—issuing bonds can result in an increase to earnings per share. If a corporation can use bonds to generate a return that is higher than the interest cost of the bonds, then the earnings per share will increase.[1]

To illustrate, assume the following data for Highland Corporation:

1. Earnings before interest and income taxes are $1,000,000.
2. The tax rate is 30%.
3. Highland Corporation has 100,000 outstanding common shares.

Highland Corporation is planning to expand its operations and is considering the following funding plans:

Plan 1: Sell 40,000 common shares at the current market price of $100 each
Plan 2: Issue $4,000,000 5% bonds
Plan 3: Sell 20,000 common shares and issue $2,000,000 5% bonds

The effect of these options on Highland's net income and earnings per share is shown in Exhibit 2.

---

1 The higher earnings per share are due to a finance concept known as *leverage*. This concept is discussed further in Chapter 17.

Exhibit 2

Impact on EPS—$1,000,000 Earnings

	Plan 1	Plan 2	Plan 3
Common shares @ $100 each	$ 4,000,000	–	$ 2,000,000
5% bonds..................................	–	$ 4,000,000	2,000,000
Total	$ 4,000,000	$ 4,000,000	$ 4,000,000
Earnings before interest and income taxes	$ 1,000,000	$ 1,000,000	$ 1,000,000
Deduct interest on bonds	–	200,000	100,000
Income before income taxes	1,000,000	800,000	900,000
Deduct income taxes........................	300,000	240,000	270,000
Net income............................	700,000	560,000	630,000
Number of common shares outstanding.........	÷ 140,000	÷ 100,000	÷ 120,000
Earnings per share........................	$ 5.00	$ 5.60	$ 5.25

Disadvantages of Issuing Bonds

1. *Mandatory interest payments*—a corporation must make interest payments on the bonds issued. If the interest payments are not made, the bondholders can seek court action and force the company into bankruptcy. In contrast, a corporation is not legally obligated to pay dividends on common or preferred shares.

2. *Mandatory principal repayment*—at maturity, the **principal** amount of the bond must be repaid. In contrast, the amount received for sale of a share is not repaid.

3. *Negative impact on earnings per share*—if the return generated by the additional financing is less than the cost of the bonds, financing with bonds will decrease earnings per share.

To illustrate, the effect of earnings of $500,000 rather than $1,000,000 is shown in Exhibit 3.

Exhibit 3

Impact on EPS—$500,000 Earnings

	Plan 1	Plan 2	Plan 3
Common shares @ $100 each	$ 4,000,000	–	$ 2,000,000
5% bonds..................................	–	$ 4,000,000	2,000,000
Total	$ 4,000,000	$ 4,000,000	$ 4,000,000
Earnings before interest and income taxes	$ 500,000	$ 500,000	$ 500,000
Deduct interest on bonds	–	200,000	100,000
Income before income taxes	500,000	300,000	400,000
Deduct income taxes........................	150,000	90,000	120,000
Net income............................	350,000	210,000	280,000
Number of common shares outstanding.........	÷ 140,000	÷ 100,000	÷ 120,000
Earnings per share........................	$ 2.50	$ 2.10	$ 2.33

EXAMPLE EXERCISE 14-1   Financing with Bonds versus Shares   ⓵

Greenfield Co. is planning a new business, which is expected to generate $750,000 income before interest and income taxes. Greenfield is considering the following alternative plans for financing its expansion:

	Plan 1	Plan 2
Issue common shares, at $10 per share	$3,000,000	$1,000,000
Issue 5% bonds	–	$2,000,000

(continued)

Determine the earnings per share under the two alternative financing plans, assuming an income tax rate of 30%.

FOLLOW MY EXAMPLE 14-1

	Plan 1	Plan 2
Earnings before interest and income taxes	$750,000	$750,000
Deduct interest on bonds	–	100,000
Income before income taxes	750,000	650,000
Deduct income taxes	225,000	195,000
Net income	525,000	455,000
Number of common shares outstanding	÷300,000	÷100,000
Earnings per share	$ 1.75	$ 4.55

For Practice: PE 14-1

Proceeds from Issuing Bonds

When a corporation issues bonds, the proceeds received for the bonds depend on the following:

1. The principal amount, or face value, of the bonds, which is the amount due at the maturity date
2. The interest rate on the bonds
3. The market rate of interest

The principal amount and the interest rate on the bonds are identified in the bond indenture. The interest rate to be paid on the face value of the bond is called the **stated rate**, **contract rate**, or **coupon rate**.

The **market rate of interest**, sometimes called the **effective rate of interest**, is the rate determined from sales and purchases of similar bonds. The market rate of interest is affected by a variety of factors, including investors' expectations of current and future economic conditions.

Often a bond's stated rate of interest differs from the market rate of interest. Because a few months may be needed to put together and to sell a bond offering, the market rate could change from the rate in place when the bond was originally structured. The purchasers of the bond will act prudently, by bidding the price of the bond up or down to eventually pay a price that gives them a return on the bond equal to the prevailing market interest rate.

By comparing the market and stated rates of interest, the selling price of a bond can be determined as being equal to, less than, or more than the bond's face value, as shown below.

If: Market Rate > Contract Rate	If: Market Rate = Contract Rate	If: Market Rate < Contract Rate
Less than $1,000	$1,000	More than $1,000
Then: Selling Price < Face Value	**Then:** Selling Price = Face Value	**Then:** Selling Price > Face Value
Sold at a DISCOUNT	Sold at FACE VALUE	Sold at a PREMIUM

If the market rate equals the contract rate, bonds will sell at their face value.

If the market rate is greater than the contract rate, the bonds will sell for less than their face value. The face value of the bonds less the selling price is called a **discount**.

A bond sells at a discount because buyers are not willing to pay the full face amount for bonds whose contract rate is lower than the market rate.

If the market rate is less than the contract rate, the bonds will sell for more than their face value. The selling price of the bonds less the face amount is called a **premium**. A bond sells at a premium because buyers are willing to pay more than the face value for bonds whose contract rate is higher than the market rate.

INTEGRITY, OBJECTIVITY, AND ETHICS IN BUSINESS

RISK VERSUS RETURN

The market rate of interest for a bond is influenced by many factors, including the interest rate offered by bonds of a similar risk, the returns available in the stock market, and the credit quality of the issuer. The inverse relationship between risk and return explains, for example, the lower interest rates offered on Government of Canada bonds, compared with corporate bonds, such as Bombardier Inc. bonds. A five-year Government of Canada bond pays 2.7% interest, whereas Bombardier bonds need to pay 6.75% to attract investors. The government bonds can pay less interest as they are a safer investment than the Bombardier bonds.

 ## Accounting for Bonds Payable

Journalize entries for bonds payable.

Bonds may be issued at their face value, at a discount, or at a premium. When bonds are issued at less or more than their face value, the discount or premium must be amortized over the life of the bonds. A corporation may redeem bonds before their maturity date.

Bonds Issued at Face Value

If the market rate of interest is equal to the stated rate of interest, the bonds will sell for their face value or a price of 100. To illustrate, assume that on January 1, 2014, Muskoka Communications Ltd. issued the following bonds:

Face value..................	$100,000
Stated rate..................	6%
Interest paid semiannually on June 30 and December 31.	
Term of bonds	5 years
Market rate	6%

Because the stated rate and the market rate are the same, the bonds will sell at their face value, or par. The entry to record the issuance of the bonds is as follows:

2014					
Jan.	1	Cash		100,000	
		Bonds Payable			100,000
		Issued $100,000 bonds payable at face value.			

Every six months (on June 30 and December 31) after the bonds are issued, interest of $3,000 ($100,000 × 6% × ½) is paid. The first interest payment on June 30, 2014, is recorded as follows:

2014					
Jun.	30	Interest Expense		3,000	
		Cash			3,000
		Paid six months' interest on bonds.			

At the maturity date, the payment of the principal of $100,000 is recorded as follows:

2018				
Dec.	31	Bonds Payable	100,000	
		Cash		100,000
		Paid bond principal at maturity date.		

EXAMPLE EXERCISE 14-2   Issuing Bonds at Face Value   ②

On July 1, when the market rate of interest was 4%, a company issued a $3,000,000, 4%, 10-year bond that pays semiannual interest on December 31 and June 30, receiving cash of $3,000,000. Journalize the entries to record (a) the issuance of the bonds and (b) the first interest payment.

FOLLOW MY EXAMPLE 14-2

(a)

July	1	Cash...	3,000,000	
		Bonds Payable..		3,000,000
		Issued bonds.		

(b)

Dec.	31	Interest expense	60,000	
		Cash..		60,000
		Paid interest on bonds ($3,000,000 × 4% × 6/12)		

For Practice: PE 14-2

Bonds Issued between Interest Dates If bonds are sold between interest dates, the amount of interest earned to date is calculated and added to the selling price. To illustrate, assume that the Muskoka Communications Ltd. bonds in the prior example were sold on March 1, 2014, at par value. The bondholder will receive six months' interest on the interest payment date of June 30, even though the bonds have been owned for only four months (March 1 to June 30), as indicated by the time line shown below.

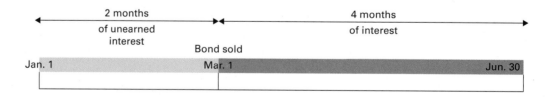

To reduce the interest received to four months' interest, the purchaser of the bonds will pay for the bonds plus two months' interest as follows:

2014				
Mar.	1	Cash	101,000[1]	
		Bonds Payable		100,000
		Interest Payable		1,000
		Issued $100,000 bonds payable at face value,		
		plus two month's accrued interest.		
		[1]$100,000 + ($100,000 × 6% × 2/12)		

The interest payment on June 30, 2014, is recorded as follows:

2014					
Jun.	30	Interest Expense	2,000		
		Interest Payable	1,000		
		Cash			3,000
		Paid six months' interest on bonds.			

EXAMPLE EXERCISE 14-3   Bonds Issued between Interest Dates   2

On May 1, a company issued at face value a $1,200,000, 3%, five-year bond that pays semiannual interest on March 31 and September 30. Journalize (a) the sale of the bond and (b) the interest payment on September 30.

FOLLOW MY EXAMPLE 14-3

(a)

May	1	Cash	1,203,000[1]	
		Bonds Payable..		1,200,000
		Interest Payable..		3,000
		Issued $1,200,000 bonds payable at face value, plus one month's accrued interest.		

[1]$1,200,000 + ($1,200,000 × 3% × 1/12).

(b)

Sep.	30	Interest Expense	15,000[2]	
		Interest Payable..	3,000	
		Cash		18,000[3]
		Paid interest on bonds.		

[2]($1,200,000 × 3% × 5/12).

[3]($1,200,000 × 3% × 6/12).

For Practice: PE 14-3

Bonds Issued at a Discount

If the market rate of interest is more than the stated rate, the bonds will sell for less than their face value. This is because investors are not willing to pay the principal amount for bonds that pay a lower stated rate than the rate they could earn on similar bonds (market rate). The price that investors are willing to pay for the bonds depends on present value concepts. Present value concepts, including the computation of bond prices, are described and illustrated in the Appendix at the end of this chapter.

Note: Bonds will sell at a discount when the market rate of interest is higher than the stated rate.

To illustrate, assume that on January 1, 2014, New Brunswick Distribution Ltd. issued the following bonds:

Face value	$100,000
Stated rate....................................	6%
Interest paid semiannually on June 30 and December 31	
Term of bonds	5 years
Market rate	7%
Market price....................................	95.842[2]

2 The market price is calculated by using the present value concepts discussed in the Appendix at the end of this chapter.

Because the stated rate is less than the market rate, the bonds will sell at less than their principal amount. In this case, the bonds sold for 95.842% of the face value, or $95,842 ($100,000 × 0.95842). The entry to record the issuance of the bonds is as follows:

2014 Jan.	1	Cash	95,842	
		Discount on Bonds Payable	4,158	
		Bonds Payable		100,000
		Issued $100,000 bonds at a discount (100,000 × 0.95842).		

The $95,842 may be viewed as the amount investors are willing to pay for bonds that have a lower stated rate of interest (6%) than the market rate (7%). The discount is the market's way of adjusting the stated rate of interest to the higher market rate of interest.

The account, Discount on Bonds Payable, is a contra account to Bonds Payable and has a normal debit balance. It is subtracted from Bonds Payable to determine the carrying amount of the bonds payable. The **carrying amount**, or *book value*, of bonds payable is the face value of the bonds less any unamortized discount or plus any unamortized premium. Thus, after the preceding entry, the carrying amount of the bonds payable is $95,842 ($100,000 − $4,158).

Using T accounts, the $95,842 carrying amount of the bond is reflected in the two accounts, as follows:

Bonds Payable	Discount on Bonds Payable	
100,000	4,158	$ 95,842

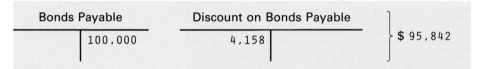

EXAMPLE EXERCISE 14-4 Issuing Bonds at a Discount   2

On the first day of the fiscal year, a company issues a $1,000,000, 6%, five-year bond that pays semi-annual interest of $30,000 ($1,000,000 × 6% × ½), receiving cash of $936,420. Journalize the entry to record the issuance of the bonds.

FOLLOW MY EXAMPLE 14-4

Cash..	936,420	
Discount on Bonds Payable..	63,580	
Bonds Payable..		1,000,000
Issued $1,000,000 bonds payable at a discount.		

For Practice: PE 14-4

Amortizing a Bond Discount

A bond discount must be amortized to interest expense over the life of the bond. Because the bond sold for less than its face value, the corporation is paying interest on a smaller amount, and the true cost of the bond is higher than the stated interest rate. If, for example, a bond paying interest of 5% sells at a discount, the cost to the corporation is more than 5%. This additional cost is reflected in the amortization of the bond discount, which transfers a portion of the discount to expense every interest period. The entry to amortize a bond discount is shown below.

	Interest Expense	XXX	
	Discount on Bonds Payable		XXX
	Amortized bond discount.		

The preceding entry may be recorded on its own, or it may be combined with the entry for the semiannual interest payment. In the latter case, the entry would be as follows:

Interest Expense	XXX	
Discount on Bonds Payable		XXX
Cash (amount of semiannual interest)		XXX
Paid interest and amortized bond discount.		

The two methods of computing the amortization of a bond discount are the following:

1. *Straight-line method*
2. *Effective interest method*, sometimes called the *interest method*

Businesses that report according to IFRS, under Part I of the *CICA Handbook*, must use the effective interest method to account for amortization of a bond discount or premium.[3] Businesses that report according to ASPE, under Part II of the *CICA Handbook*, may use either the straight-line method or the effective interest method.[4]

Straight-Line Method of Amortization

The **straight-line method** of amortization provides for a constant *amount* of amortization each period. To illustrate, amortization of the preceding bond discount of $4,158 is computed below.

Discount on bonds payable . . .	$4,158.00
Term of bonds	5 years
Semiannual amortization	$415.80 ($4,158/10 periods)

The combined entry to record the first interest payment and the amortization of the discount is as follows:

2014					
Jun.	30	Interest Expense		3,415.80	
		Discount on Bonds Payable			415.80
		Cash			3,000.00
		Paid semiannual interest and amortized 1/10 of bond discount.			

The June 30 interest payment adjusts the carrying amount of the bond to $96,257.80, as shown in the following T accounts:

Bonds Payable		Discount on Bonds Payable		
	100,000.00	4,158.00		$96,257.80
		Jun. 30	415.80	
		Bal. 3,742.20		

The preceding entry is made on each interest payment date. Thus, the amount of the semiannual interest expense on the bonds ($3,415.80) remains the same over the life of the bonds.

The effect of the discount amortization is to increase the interest expense from $3,000.00 to $3,415.80. In effect, this transaction increases the bond rate of interest from 6% to a rate of interest that approximates the market rate of 7%. In addition, as the discount is amortized, the carrying amount of the bonds increases until it equals the principal amount of the bonds on the maturity date.

---

3 *CICA Handbook—Accounting*, 2012 edition, Part I, IAS 39, para. 47.

4 *CICA Handbook—Accounting*, 2012 edition, Part II, S.3856.11 (c).

EXAMPLE EXERCISE 14-5 Discount Amortization—Straight-Line Method ②

Using the bond from Example Exercise 14-4, journalize the first interest payment and the amortization of the related bond discount, using the straight-line method for discount amortization.

FOLLOW MY EXAMPLE 14-5

Interest Expense.	36,358	
Discount on Bonds Payable		6,358[1]
Cash.		30,000[2]
Paid interest and amortized the bond discount ($63,580/10).		

[1]$6,358 = [$63,580 ÷ (5 × 2)].
[2]$30,000 = ($1,000,000 × 6% × 6/12).

For Practice: PE 14-5

Effective Interest Method of Amortization The **effective interest method**, or the **interest method**, of amortization provides for a constant *rate* of interest over the life of the bonds. Compared with the straight-line method, this method is a better reflection of reality because the interest expense reflects the constancy of interest costs over the bond's life. As the discount or premium is amortized, the carrying amount of the bonds changes. As a result, interest expense also changes each period, generating a changing interest expense but a constant rate of interest. This method produces conceptually superior results to the straight-line method, which provides for a constant *amount* of interest expense each period but a changing interest rate. Because this method provides superior results and better reflects the economic reality of the transaction, the effective interest method is required for companies reporting under IFRS.

Amortization of Discount by the Effective Interest Method To illustrate, the previously mentioned New Brunswick Distribution Ltd. bonds issued at a discount have the following data:

Face value of 6%, 5-year bonds, interest compounded semiannually	$100,000
Present value of bonds at effective (market) rate of interest of 7%	95,842
Discount on bonds payable	4,158

Exhibit 4 illustrates the effective interest method for the preceding bonds. Exhibit 4 was prepared as follows:

Step 1. List the interest payment dates in the first column. The New Brunswick Distribution Ltd. bonds have 10 interest payments (semiannual interest over five years). Also, list on the first line the initial amount of discount in Column D and the initial carrying amount of the bonds in Column E.

Step 2. List in Column A the semiannual interest payments. The New Brunswick Distribution Ltd. bonds issue semiannual interest payments of $3,000 ($100,000 × 3%).

Step 3. Compute the interest expense in Column B by multiplying the carrying amount at the beginning of each period times $3\frac{1}{2}\%$, which is the effective interest (market) rate of 7% divided by 2 because it is a semiannual rate.

Step 4. Compute the discount to be amortized each period in Column C by subtracting the interest payment in Column A ($3,000) from the interest expense for the period shown in Column B.

Step 5. Compute the remaining unamortized discount by subtracting the amortized discount for the period in Column C from the unamortized discount at the beginning of the period in Column D.

Step 6. Compute the bond's carrying amount at the end of the period by subtracting the unamortized discount at the end of the period from the principal amount of the bonds.

As shown in Exhibit 4, the interest expense increases each period as the carrying amount of the bond increases. Also, the unamortized discount decreases each period and is reduced to zero at the maturity date. Finally, the carrying amount of the bonds increases from $95,842 to $100,000 (the principal amount) at maturity, on December 31, 2018.

Exhibit 4

Amortization of Discount on Bonds Payable

Interest Payment Date	A Interest Paid (3% of Face Value)	B Interest Expense (3½% of Bond Carrying Amount)	C Discount Amortization (B – A)	D Unamortized Discount (D – C)	E Bond Carrying Amount ($100,000 – D)
				$4,158.00	$95,842.00
June 30, 2014	$3,000	$3,354.47 (3½% of $95,842.00)	$354.47	3,803.53	96,196.47
Dec. 31, 2014	3,000	3,366.88 (3½% of $96,196.47)	366.88	3,436.65	96,563.35
June 30, 2015	3,000	3,379.72 (3½% of $96,563.35)	379.72	3,056.93	96,943.07
Dec. 31, 2015	3,000	3,393.01 (3½% of $96,943.07)	393.01	2,663.92	97,336.08
June 30, 2016	3,000	3,406.76 (3½% of $97,336.08)	406.76	2,257.16	97,742.84
Dec. 31, 2016	3,000	3,421.00 (3½% of $97,742.84)	421.00	1,836.16	98,163.84
June 30, 2017	3,000	3,435.73 (3½% of $98,163.84)	435.73	1,400.43	98,599.57
Dec. 31, 2017	3,000	3,450.98 (3½% of $98,599.57)	450.98	949.45	99,050.55
June 30, 2018	3,000	3,466.77 (3½% of $99,050.55)	466.77	482.68	99,517.32
Dec. 31, 2018	3,000	3,483.10 (3½% of $99,517.32)	482.68[1]	—	100,000.00

[1]Adjusted so as to not exceed unamortized discount.

The entry to record the first interest payment on June 30, 2014, and the related discount amortization is as follows:

2014				
Jun.	30	Interest Expense	3,354.47	
		Discount on Bonds Payable		354.47
		Cash		3,000.00
		Paid semiannual interest and amortized bond discount for half a year.		

EXAMPLE EXERCISE 14-6 Discount Amortization—Effective Interest Method ②

A company issued a $2,000,000, 4%, five-year bond that pays semiannual interest of $40,000 ($2,000,000 × 4% × 1/2), receiving cash of $1,912,479, for an effective interest rate of 5%. Journalize the first interest payment.

FOLLOW MY EXAMPLE 14-6

Interest Expense.	47,811.98[1]	
Discount on Bonds Payable		7,811.98
Cash.		40,000.00
Paid semiannual interest and amortized bond discount for half a year.		

[1]($1,912,479 × 2.5%)

For Practice: PE 14-6

Adjusting Entry for Interest Expense

When the interest payment dates of bonds differ from the company's fiscal year-end, an adjusting entry is required to record interest expense for the period of time from the last payment to the year-end.

Using the example from page 713, on January 1, 2014, New Brunswick Distribution Ltd. issued a $100,000, 6%, five-year bond that pays semiannual interest, receiving cash of $95,842. The December 31, 2014, journal entry, under the two methods of discount amortization, is recorded as follows:

			Straight-Line		Effective Interest	
2014 Dec.	31	Interest Expense	3,415.80		3,366.88[1]	
		Discount on Bonds Payable		415.80		366.88
		Cash		3,000.00		3,000.00
		Paid semiannual interest and amortized bond discount for half a year.				
		[1]As per Exhibit 4.				

If New Brunswick Distribution Ltd.'s fiscal year-end is not the same as the interest payment date, then an adjusting entry is required. To illustrate, assume that New Brunswick Distribution has an August 31 year-end. Interest expense needs to be recorded for the two months from the last interest payment, June 30, to the August 31 year-end. Under both amortization methods, 2/6 of the amounts of the December 31 interest entry are recorded, with a credit to Interest Payable instead of to Cash, as follows:

			Straight-Line		Effective Interest	
2014 Aug.	31	Interest Expense	1,138.60[1]		1,122.29[2]	
		Discount on Bonds Payable		138.60		122.29
		Interest Payable		1,000.00		1,000.00
		Recorded interest expense and bond discount amortization for two months.				
		[1]$3,415.80 × 2/6.				
		[2]$3,366.88 × 2/6.				

At the time of the next interest payment, on December 31, 2014, the remaining 4/6 of the December 31 interest entry will be recorded with a debit to Interest Payable, as follows:

			Straight-Line		Effective Interest	
2014 Dec.	31	Interest Expense	2,277.20[1]		2,244.59[2]	
		Interest Payable	1,000.00		1,000.00	
		Discount on Bonds Payable		277.20		244.59
		Cash		3,000.00		3,000.00
		Recorded interest expense and bond discount amortization for four months.				
		[1]$3,415.80 − $1,138.60				
		[2]$3,366.88 − $1,122.29				

MID-CHAPTER ILLUSTRATIVE PROBLEM

On March 1, 2015, Apex Corporation, a wholesaler of mountain-climbing equipment, issued $1,000,000, three-year, 4% bonds at an effective interest rate of 5%, receiving cash of $972,459.37. Interest on the bonds is payable semiannually on August 31 and February 28 or 29. The fiscal year of the company is the calendar year.

Instructions

1. Journalize the cash proceeds from the sale of the bonds.
2. Prepare a bond discount amortization table for the bonds.
3. Journalize the August 31, 2015, entry to record payment of interest and amortization of the bond discount, using the effective interest method.
4. Journalize the December 31, 2015, adjusting entry pertaining to the bond.
5. Journalize the February 29, 2016, entry pertaining to the bond.

MID-CHAPTER ILLUSTRATIVE SOLUTION

1.

2015				
Mar.	1	Cash	972,459.37	
		Discount on Bonds Payable	27,540.63	
		Bonds Payable		1,000,000.00
		Issued $1,000,000 bonds payable at a discount.		

2.

Interest Payment Date	A Interest Paid (2% of Face Value)	B Interest Expense (2½% of Bond Carrying Amount)	C Discount Amortization (B – A)	D Unamortized Discount (D – C)	E Bond Carrying Amount ($1,000,000 – D)
				$27,540.63	$972,459.37
Aug. 31, 2015	$20,000	$24,311.48	$4,311.48	23,229.15	976,770.85
Feb. 29, 2016	20,000	24,419.27	4,419.27	18,809.88	981,190.12
Aug. 31, 2016	20,000	24,529.75	4,529.75	14,280.13	985,719.87
Feb. 28, 2017	20,000	24,643.00	4,643.00	9,637.13	990,362.87
Aug. 31, 2017	20,000	24,759.07	4,759.07	4,878.06	995,121.94
Feb. 28, 2018	20,000	24,878.05	4,878.06[1]	–	1,000,000.00

[1]rounded

3.

2015				
Aug.	31	Interest Expense	24,311.48	
		Discount on Bonds Payable		4,311.48
		Cash		20,000.00
		Paid six months' interest on bonds.		

4.

2015				
Dec.	31	Interest Expense	16,279.51[1]	
		Discount on Bonds Payable		2,946.18
		Interest Payable		13,333.33
		[1]($24,419.27 × 4/6)		
		Recorded adjusting entry for bond interest.		

(continued)

5.

2016					
Feb.	29	Interest Payable		13,333.33	
		Interest Expense		8,139.76[1]	
		Discount on Bonds Payable			1,473.09
		Cash			20,000.00
		[1]($24,419.27 − $16,279.51)			
		Paid six months' interest on bonds.			

Bonds Issued at a Premium

If the market rate is less than the stated rate, the bonds will sell for more than their principal amount. This is because investors are willing to pay more for bonds that pay a higher rate of interest (stated rate) than the rate they could earn on similar bonds (market rate).

Note: Bonds will sell at a premium when the market rate of interest is less than the stated rate.

To illustrate, assume that on January 1, 2014, Newfoundland Transportation Ltd. issued the following bonds:

Face value	$100,000
Stated rate.	6%
Interest paid semiannually on	
June 30 and December 31	
Term of bonds	5 years
Market rate	5%
Market price.	104.376[5]

Because the stated rate of interest is more than the market rate, the bonds will sell at more than their face value amount. Assuming the bonds sell for $104,376, the entry to record the issuance of the bonds is as follows:

2014					
Jan.	1	Cash		104,376	
		Bonds Payable			100,000
		Premium on Bonds Payable			4,376
		Issued $100,000 bonds at a premium.			

The $4,376 premium may be viewed as the extra amount investors are willing to pay for bonds that have a higher rate of interest (6%) than the market rate (5%). The premium is the market's way of adjusting the stated rate to the lower market rate.

The account, Premium on Bonds Payable, has a normal credit balance. It is added to Bonds Payable to determine the carrying amount of the bonds payable. Thus, after the preceding entry, the carrying amount of the bonds payable is $104,376 ($100,000 + $4,376).

Using T accounts, the $104,376 carrying amount of the bond is reflected in two accounts, as follows:

Bonds Payable		**Premium on Bonds Payable**		
	100,000		4,376	$104,376

5 The market price is calculated by using the present value concepts discussed in the Appendix at the end of this chapter.

EXAMPLE EXERCISE 14-7 Issuing Bonds at a Premium   (2)

A company issued a $2,000,000, 6%, five-year bond that pays semiannual interest of $60,000 ($2,000,000 × 6% × 1/2), receiving cash of $2,087,521. Journalize the bond issuance.

FOLLOW MY EXAMPLE 14-7

Cash...	2,087,521	
Premium on Bonds Payable.....................................		87,521
Bonds Payable		2,000,000
Issued $2,000,000 bonds payable at a premium.		

For Practice: PE 14-7

Amortizing a Bond Premium

Like bond discounts, a bond premium must be amortized over the life of the bond. The amortization can be computed using either the straight-line or the effective interest rate method. The entry to amortize a bond premium is shown below.

Premium on Bonds Payable	XXX	
Interest Expense		XXX
Amortized bond premium.		

The preceding entry may be made on its own, or it may be combined with the entry for the semiannual interest payment. In the latter case, the entry would be as follows:

Interest Expense	XXX	
Premium on Bonds Payable	XXX	
Cash (amount of semiannual interest)		XXX
Paid interest and amortized premium.		

Straight-Line Method of Amortization To illustrate, amortization of the preceding bond premium of $4,376 is computed using the straight-line method below.

Premium on bonds payable ..	$4,376
Term of bonds	5 years
Semiannual amortization.....	$437.60 ($4,376/10 periods)

The combined entry to record the first interest payment and the amortization of the premium is as follows:

2014				
Jun.	30	Interest Expense	2,562.40	
		Premium on Bonds Payable	437.60	
		Cash		3,000.00
		Paid semiannual interest and amortized 1/10 of bond premium.		

The June 30 interest payment adjusts the carrying amount of the bond to $103,938.40, as shown in the following T accounts:

Bonds Payable		Premium on Bonds Payable	
100,000.00			4,376.00
		Jun. 30 437.60	
		Bal.	3,938.40

$103,938.40

The preceding entry is made on each interest payment date. Thus, the amount of the semiannual interest expense on the bonds ($2,562.40) remains the same over the life of the bonds.

The effect of the premium amortization is to decrease the interest expense from $3,000.00 to $2,562.40. In effect, this transaction decreases the bond rate of interest from 6% to a rate of interest that approximates the market rate of 5%.

EXAMPLE EXERCISE 14-8 Premium Amortization—Straight-Line Method   (2)

Using the bond from Example Exercise 14-7, journalize the first interest payment and the amortization of the related bond premium, using the straight-line method of amortization.

FOLLOW MY EXAMPLE 14-8

Interest Expense.	51,247.90	
Premium on Bonds Payable.	8,752.10	
Cash.		60,000.00
Paid semiannual interest and amortized the bond premium ($87,521/10).		

For Practice: PE 14-8

Amortization of Premium by the Effective Interest Method To illustrate the effective interest method of amortizing bond premiums, we use the following data from Newfoundland Transportation Ltd.:

Present value of bonds at effective (market) rate of interest of 5%	$104,376
Face value of 6%, five-year bonds, interest compounded semiannually	100,000
Premium on bonds payable	$ 4,376

Exhibit 5 illustrates the effective interest method for the preceding bonds. Exhibit 5 was prepared as follows:

Step 1. List the interest payment dates in the first column. The Newfoundland Transportation Ltd. bonds have 10 interest payments (semiannual interest over five years). Also, list on the first line the initial amount of premium in Column D and the initial carrying amount of the bonds in Column E.

Step 2. List in Column A the semiannual interest payments. The Newfoundland Transportation Ltd. bonds issue semiannual interest payments of $3,000 ($100,000 × 3%).

Step 3. Compute the interest expense in Column B by multiplying the carrying amount at the beginning of each period times $2\frac{1}{2}$%, which is the effective interest (market) rate of 5%, divided by 2 because it is a semiannual rate.

Step 4. Compute the premium to be amortized each period in Column C by subtracting the interest expense in Column B from the interest payment for the period shown in Column A ($3,000).

Step 5.   Compute the remaining unamortized premium by subtracting the amortized premium for the period in Column C from the unamortized premium at the beginning of the period in Column D.

Step 6.   Compute the bond's carrying amount at the end of the period by adding the unamortized premium at the end of the period to the principal amount of the bonds.

As shown in Exhibit 5, the interest expense decreases each period as the carrying amount of the bond decreases. Also, the unamortized premium decreases each period and is reduced to zero at the maturity date. Finally, the carrying amount of the bonds decreases from $104,376 to $100,000 (the principal amount) at maturity, on December 31, 2018.

Exhibit 5

Amortization of Premium on Bonds Payable

Interest Payment Date	A Interest Paid (3% of Face Value)	B Interest Expense (2½% of Bond Carrying Amount)	C Premium Amortization (A – B)	D Unamortized Premium (D – C)	E Bond Carrying Amount ($100,000 + D)
				$4,376.00	$104,376.00
June 30, 2014	$3,000	$2,609.40 (2½% of $104,376.00)	$390.60	3,985.40	103,985.40
Dec. 31, 2014	3,000	2,599.64 (2½% of $103,985.40)	400.36	3,585.04	103,585.04
June 30, 2015	3,000	2,589.63 (2½% of $103,585.04)	410.37	3,174.67	103,174.67
Dec. 31, 2015	3,000	2,579.37 (2½% of $103,174.67)	420.63	2,754.04	102,754.04
June 30, 2016	3,000	2,568.85 (2½% of $102,754.04)	431.15	2,322.89	102,322.89
Dec. 31, 2016	3,000	2,558.07 (2½% of $102,322.89)	441.93	1,880.96	101,880.96
June 30, 2017	3,000	2,547.02 (2½% of $101,880.96)	452.98	1,427.98	101,427.98
Dec. 31, 2017	3,000	2,535.70 (2½% of $101,427.98)	464.30	963.68	100,963.68
June 30, 2018	3,000	2,524.09 (2½% of $100,963.68)	475.91	487.77	100,487.77
Dec. 31, 2018	3,000	2,512.19 (2½% of $100,487.77)	487.77	—	100,000.00

EXAMPLE EXERCISE 14-9   Premium Amortization—Effective Interest Method   ②

A company issued a $2,000,000, 6%, five-year bond that pays semiannual interest of $60,000 ($2,000,000 × 6% × ½), receiving cash of $2,087,521, for an effective interest rate of 5%. Journalize the first interest payment and premium amortization, using the effective interest method.

FOLLOW MY EXAMPLE 14-9

Interest Expense	52,188.03[1]	
Premium on Bonds Payable....................................	7,811.97	
Cash..		60,000.00

Paid semiannual interest and amortized premium for half a year.

[1]($2,087,521 × 2.5%)

For Practice: PE 14-9

Adjusting Entry for Interest Expense   Similar to when bonds are issued at a discount, an adjusting entry is required to record interest expense when the company's fiscal year-end differs from the interest payment dates.

Using the example from page 720, on January 1, 2014, Newfoundland Transportation Ltd. issued a $100,000, 6%, five-year bond that pays semiannual interest, receiving cash of $104,376. The December 31, 2014, journal entry, under the two methods of discount amortization, is recorded as follows:

			Straight-Line		Effective Interest	
2014 Dec.	31	Interest Expense	2,562.40		2,599.64[1]	
		Premium on Bonds Payable	437.60		400.36	
		Cash		3,000.00		3,000.00
		Paid semiannual interest and amortized bond premium for half a year.				
		[1]As per Exhibit 5.				

If Newfoundland Transportation Ltd.'s fiscal year-end is not the same as the interest payment date, then an adjusting entry is required. To illustrate, assume that Newfoundland Transportation Ltd. has an October 31 year-end. Interest expense needs to be recorded for the four months from the last interest payment, June 30, to the October 31 year-end. Under both amortization methods, 4/6 of the amounts of the December 31 interest entry are recorded, with a credit to Interest Payable, instead of to Cash, as follows:

			Straight-Line		Effective Interest	
2014 Oct.	31	Interest Expense	1,708.27[1]		1,733.09[2]	
		Premium on Bonds Payable	291.73		266.91	
		Interest Payable		2,000.00		2,000.00
		Recorded interest expense and bond premium amortization for four months.				
		[1]$2,562.40 × 4/6.				
		[2]$2,599.64 × 4/6.				

At the time of the next interest payment, on December 31, 2014, the remaining 2/6 of the December 31 interest entry will be recorded with a debit to Interest Payable, as follows:

			Straight-Line		Effective Interest	
2014 Dec.	31	Interest Expense	854.13[1]		866.55[2]	
		Interest Payable	2,000.00		2,000.00	
		Premium on Bonds Payable	145.87[3]		133.45[4]	
		Cash		3,000.00		3,000.00
		Recorded interest expense and bond premium amortization for two months.				
		[1]$2,562.40 − $1,708.27				
		[2]$2,599.64 − $1,733.09				
		[3]$437.60 − $291.73				
		[4]$400.36 − $266.91				

Bond Redemption

Bond Redemption at Maturity

When a bond matures, the carrying amount of the bond payable is the face value of the bond because any discount or premium has been amortized over the life of the bond. The principal of the bond will be repaid in full. Exhibits 4 and 5 both illustrate that the carrying amount of both bonds are equal to their principal amount, or face value, of $100,000, at maturity. The entry to record the maturity of the bond at maturity is as follows:

2018				
Dec.	31	Bonds Payable	100,000	
		Cash		100,000
		Maturity of bonds.		

Bond Redemption before Maturity

A corporation may redeem or call bonds before they mature. This is often done when the market rate of interest declines below the stated rate. In such cases, the corporation may issue new bonds at a lower interest rate and use the proceeds to redeem the original bond issue.

Callable bonds can be redeemed by the issuing corporation within the period of time and at the price stated in the bond indenture. Normally, the call price is above the face value. A corporation may also redeem its bonds by purchasing them on the open market.[6]

A corporation usually redeems its bonds at a price different from the carrying amount of the bonds. A gain or loss may be realized on a bond redemption as follows:

1. A *gain* is recorded if the price paid for the redemption is below the bond carrying amount.
2. A *loss* is recorded if the price paid for the redemption is above the bond carrying amount.

Gains and losses on the redemption of bonds are normally reported in the *Other income (loss)* section of the income statement.

To illustrate, assume that on June 1, 2014, a corporation has the following bond issue:

Face value of bonds	$100,000
Premium on bonds payable	4,000

On June 30, 2014, the corporation redeemed one-fourth ($25,000) of these bonds in the market for $24,000. The entry to record the redemption is as follows:

2014				
Jun.	30	Bonds Payable	25,000[1]	
		Premium on Bonds Payable	1,000[2]	
		Cash		24,000
		Gain on Redemption of Bonds		2,000
		Redeemed $25,000 bonds for $24,000.		
		[1]($100,000/4)		
		[2]($4,000/4)		

In the preceding entry, only the portion of the premium related to the redeemed bonds ($1,000) is written off. The difference between the carrying amount of the bonds redeemed, $26,000 ($25,000 + $1,000), and the redemption price, $24,000, is recorded as a gain.

---

6 Some bond indentures require the corporation issuing the bonds to transfer cash to a special cash fund, called a *sinking fund,* over the life of the bond. Such funds help assure investors adequate cash will be available to pay the bonds at their maturity date.

The June 30, 2014, redemption of one-fourth of these bonds adjusts the carrying amount of the bond to $78,000 ($75,000 + $3,000), as shown in the following T accounts:

Bonds Payable		Premium on Bonds Payable	
	100,000		4,000
Jun. 30 25,000		Jun. 30 1,000	
Bal.	75,000	Bal.	3,000

$78,000

Assume that the corporation calls the remaining $75,000 of outstanding bonds, which are held by a private investor, for $79,500 on July 1, 2014. The entry to record the redemption is as follows:

2014					
Jul.	1	Bonds Payable		75,000[1]	
		Premium on Bonds Payable		3,000[2]	
		Loss on Redemption of Bonds		1,500	
		Cash			79,500
		Redeemed $75,000 bonds for $79,500.			
		[1]($100,000 − $25,000)			
		[2]($4,000 − $1,000)			

The difference between the carrying amount of the bonds redeemed, $78,000, and the redemption price, $79,500, is recorded as a loss. The July 1, 2014, redemption of the remaining bonds adjusts the carrying amount of the bond to zero, as shown in the following T accounts:

Bonds Payable		Premium on Bonds Payable	
	75,000		3,000
Jul. 1 75,000		Jul. 1 3,000	
Bal.	0	Bal.	0

EXAMPLE EXERCISE 14-10 Redemption of Bonds Payable   2

A $500,000 bond with an unamortized discount of $40,000 is redeemed for $475,000. Journalize the redemption of the bonds.

FOLLOW MY EXAMPLE 14-10

Bonds Payable	500,000	
Loss on Redemption of Bonds.	15,000	
Discount on Bonds Payable		40,000
Cash.		475,000
Redeemed $500,000 bonds for $475,000.		

For Practice: PE 14-10

Installment Notes

Describe and illustrate the accounting for installment notes.

Corporations often finance their operations by issuing bonds payable. Corporations may also issue installment notes. An **installment note** is a debt that requires the borrower to make equal periodic payments to the lender for the term of the note. Unlike bonds, each note payment consists of the following:

1. Payment of a portion of the amount initially borrowed, called the *principal*
2. Payment of interest on the outstanding balance

At the end of the note's term, the principal will have been repaid in full. Installment notes, which are often used to purchase assets such as equipment, are usually issued by a bank. An installment note may be secured by a pledge of the borrower's assets. Such a note is called a **mortgage note**. If the borrower fails to repay a mortgage note, the lender has the right to take possession of the pledged asset and sell it to pay off the debt.

Issuing an Installment Note

When an installment note is issued, an entry is recorded by the issuer, debiting Cash and crediting Notes Payable. To illustrate, assume that Lewis Company issues the following installment note to TD Bank on January 1, 2013.

Principal amount of note..........	$24,000
Interest rate.....................	6%
Term of note.....................	5 years
Annual payments................	$5,698[7]

The entry to record the issuance of the note is as follows:

2013 Jan.	1	Cash	24,000	
		Notes Payable		24,000
		Issued installment note for cash.		

Annual Payments

The preceding note payable requires Lewis Company to repay the principal and interest in equal payments of $5,698 beginning December 31, 2013, for each of the next five years. Unlike bonds, however, each installment note payment includes an interest portion and a principal portion.

The interest portion of an installment note payment is computed by multiplying the interest rate by the carrying amount of the note at the beginning of the period. The principal portion of the payment is then computed as the difference between the total payment (cash paid) and the interest. These computations are illustrated in Exhibit 6 as follows:

1. The January 1, 2013, carrying amount (Column A) equals the amount borrowed from the bank. The January 1 balance in the following years equals the December 31 balance from the prior year.
2. The note payment (Column B) remains constant at $5,698, which represents the annual cash payments required by the bank.
3. The interest expense (Column C) is computed at 6% of the installment note carrying amount at the beginning of each year. As a result, the interest expense decreases each year.

---

7 The amount of the annual payment is calculated by using the present value concepts discussed in the Appendix at the end of this chapter. The annual payment of $5,698 is computed by dividing the $24,000 loan amount by the present value of an annuity of $1 for 5 periods at 6% (4.21236) from Exhibit 8 (rounded to the nearest dollar).

Exhibit 6

Amortization of Installment Notes

For the Year Ended:	A January 1 Carrying Amount	B Note Payment (Cash Paid)	C Interest Expense (6% of January 1 Note Carrying Amount)		D Decrease in Notes Payable (B − C)	E December 31 Carrying Amount (A − D)
December 31, 2013	$24,000	$ 5,698	$1,440	(6% of $24,000)	$ 4,258	$19,742
December 31, 2014	19,742	5,698	1,185	(6% of $19,742)	4,513	15,229
December 31, 2015	15,229	5,698	914	(6% of $15,229)	4,784	10,445
December 31, 2016	10,445	5,698	627	(6% of $10,445)	5,071	5,374
December 31, 2017	5,374	5,698	324[1]	(6% of $ 5,374)	5,374	0
		$28,490	$4,490		$24,000	

[1]Rounded.

4. Notes payable (Column D) decreases each year by the amount of the principal repayment. The principal repayment is computed by subtracting the interest expense (Column C) from the total payment (Column B). The principal repayment increases each year as the interest expense decreases (Column C).

5. The carrying amount on December 31 (Column E) of the note decreases from $24,000, the initial amount borrowed, to $0 at the end of the five years.

The entry to record the first payment on December 31, 2013, is as follows:

2013 Dec.	31	Interest Expense	1,440	
		Notes Payable	4,258	
		Cash		5,698
		Paid principal and interest on installment note.		

The entry to record the second payment on December 31, 2014, is as follows:

2014 Dec.	31	Interest Expense	1,185	
		Notes Payable	4,513	
		Cash		5,698
		Paid principal and interest on installment note.		

As the prior entries show, the cash payment is the same in each year. The interest and principal repayment, however, change each year. This is because the carrying amount of the note decreases each year as principal is repaid, which decreases the interest.

The entry to record the final payment on December 31, 2017, is as follows:

2017 Dec.	31	Interest Expense	324	
		Notes Payable	5,374	
		Cash		5,698
		Paid principal and interest on installment note.		

After the final payment, the carrying amount on the note is zero, indicating that the note has been paid in full. Any assets that secure the note would then be released by the bank.

EXAMPLE EXERCISE 14-11 Journalizing Installment Notes   ③

On the first day of the fiscal year, a company issues a $30,000, 10%, five-year installment note that has annual payments of $7,914.

  a. Journalize the entry to record the issuance of the installment note.

  b. Journalize the first annual note payment, which consists of both interest and principal repayment.

FOLLOW MY EXAMPLE 14-11

  a. Cash... 30,000
       Notes Payable...   30,000
       Issued $30,000 installment note for cash.

  b. Interest Expense.. 3,000[1]
       Notes Payable.. 4,914
         Cash   7,914
       Paid principal and interest on installment note.

[1]($30,000 × 10%)

For Practice: PE 14-11

---

④ # Reporting of Long-Term Liabilities

Describe and illustrate the reporting and analysis of long-term liabilities.

The reporting of long-term liabilities is the same under both IFRS and ASPE accounting standards. Bonds payable and notes payable are reported as liabilities on the balance sheet. Any portion of the bonds or notes that is due within one year is reported as a current liability. Any remaining bonds or notes are reported as a long-term liability.

Any unamortized premium is reported as an addition to the principal amount of the bonds. Any unamortized discount is reported as a deduction from the principal amount of the bonds. A description of the bonds and notes should also be reported either on the face of the financial statements or in the accompanying notes.

The reporting of bonds and notes payable for Morning Java is shown below.

Morning Java **Balance Sheet (Partial)** **December 31, 2015**		
Current liabilities:		
Accounts payable	$133,000	
Notes payable (current portion)	200,000	
Salaries and wages payable	42,000	
Source deductions payable	16,400	
Interest payable	40,000	
Total current liabilities		$ 431,400
Long-term liabilities:		
Bonds payable, 8%, due December 31, 2035	500,000	
Less unamortized discount	16,000	484,000
Notes payable		1,400,000
Total long-term liabilities		1,884,000
Total liabilities		$2,315,400

FINANCIAL ANALYSIS AND INTERPRETATION f·a·i

As we have discussed, the assets of a company are subject to (1) the claims of creditors and (2) the rights of owners. As creditors, bondholders are primarily concerned with the company's ability to make its periodic interest payment and repay the principal amount of the bonds at maturity.

Analysts assess the risk that bondholders will not receive their interest payments by computing the **times interest earned** during the year as follows:

Times Interest Earned =

$$\frac{\text{Income Before Income Taxes + Interest Expense}}{\text{Interest Expense}}$$

The ratio computes the number of times interest payments could be paid out of the company's current period earnings, which measures the company's ability to meet the obligation of its interest payments. Because interest payments reduce income taxes expense, the ratio is computed using income before income taxes. The higher the ratio, the greater the likelihood that interest payments will continue to be made.

To illustrate, the following data were taken from the 2011 annual report of WestJet Airlines Ltd., (in thousands):

	2011	2010
Interest expense	$ 60,911	$ 70,914
Income before income taxes	208,006	133,465

The times interest earned for WestJet Airlines Ltd. is computed as follows:

	2011	2010
Times Interest Earned	$\dfrac{\$208,006 + \$60,911}{\$60,911} = 4.41$	$\dfrac{\$133,465 + \$70,914}{\$70,914} = 2.88$

WestJet's times interest earned for 2011 is 4.41, which indicates that the company generates enough income before taxes to pay (meet the obligation of) its interest payments 4.41 times. As a result, debtholders have good protection in the event of an earnings decline. In addition, WestJet's times interest earned ratio has improved from 2010, increasing from 2.88 times to 4.41 times. WestJet's debtholders should have improved confidence in the company's ability to make its interest payments.

EXAMPLE EXERCISE 14-12 Times Interest Earned 4

Harris Industries reported the following on the company's income statement in 2015 and 2014:

	2015	2014
Interest expense	$ 200,000	$180,000
Income before income taxes	1,000,000	720,000

a. Determine the times interest earned for 2015 and 2014. Round to one decimal place.

b. Is the times interest earned improving or declining?

FOLLOW MY EXAMPLE 14-12

a. 2015:

$$\text{Times interest earned: } 6.0 = \frac{\$1,000,000 + \$200,000}{\$200,000}$$

2014:

$$\text{Times interest earned: } 5.0 = \frac{\$720,000 + \$180,000}{\$180,000}$$

b. The times interest earned has increased from 5.0 in 2014 to 6.0 in 2015. Thus, the debtholders have improved confidence in the company's ability to make its interest payments.

For Practice: PE 14-12

A P P E N D I X 1

Present Value Concepts and Pricing Bonds Payable

When a corporation issues bonds, the price that investors are willing to pay for the bonds depends on the following:

1. The face value of the bonds, which is the amount due at the maturity date
2. The periodic interest to be paid on the bonds
3. The market rate of interest

An investor determines how much to pay for the bonds by computing the present value of the bond's future cash receipts, using the market rate of interest. A bond's future cash receipts include its face value at maturity and the periodic interest.

Present Value Concepts

The concept of present value is based on the time value of money. The *time value of money concept* recognizes that cash received today is worth more than the same amount of cash to be received in the future.

To illustrate, which would you rather have: $1,000 today or $1,000 one year from now? You would rather have the $1,000 today because it could be invested to earn interest. For example, if the $1,000 could be invested to earn 10% per year, the $1,000 will accumulate to $1,100 ($1,000 plus $100 interest) in one year. In this sense, you can think of the $1,000 in hand today as the **present value** of $1,100 to be received a year from today. This present value is illustrated below.

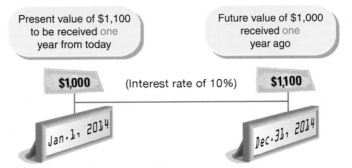

A related concept to present value is **future value**. To illustrate, using the preceding example, the $1,100 to be received on December 31, 2014, is the *future value* of $1,000 on January 1, 2014, assuming an interest rate of 10%.

Present Value of an Amount   To illustrate the present value of an amount, assume that $1,000 is to be received in one year. If the market rate of interest is 10%, the present value of the $1,000 is $909.09 ($1,000/1.10). This present value is illustrated below.

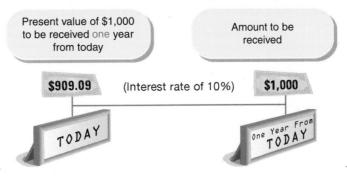

If the $1,000 is to be received in two years, with interest of 10% compounded at the end of the first year, the present value is $826.45 ($909.09/1.10).[8] This present value is illustrated below.

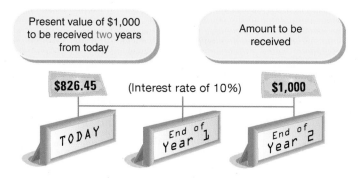

The present value of an amount to be received in the future can be calculated by a series of divisions such as illustrated above. In practice, however, it is easier to use a table of present values or a financial calculator.

The *present value of $1* table is used to find the present value factor for $1 to be received after a number of periods in the future. The amount to be received is then multiplied by this factor to determine its present value.

To illustrate, Exhibit 7 is a partial table of the present value of $1.[9] Exhibit 7 indicates that the present value of $1 to be received in two years with a market rate of interest of 10% a year is 0.82645. Multiplying $1,000 to be received in two years by 0.82645 yields $826.45 ($1,000 × 0.82645). This amount is the same amount computed earlier. In Exhibit 7, the Periods column represents the number of compounding periods, and the percentage columns represent the compound interest rate per period. Thus, the present value factor from Exhibit 7 for 12% for five years compounded semiannually is 0.55840. Since the interest is compounded semiannually, the interest rate is 6% (12% divided by 2), and the number of periods is 10 (5 years × 2 times per year). Some additional examples using Exhibit 7 are shown below.

Exhibit 7

Present Value of $1 at Compound Interest

Periods	2.5%	3%	3.5%	4%	5%	5.5%	6%	6.5%	7%	10%
1	0.97561	0.97087	0.96618	0.96154	0.95238	0.94787	0.94340	0.93897	0.93458	0.90909
2	0.95181	0.94260	0.93351	0.92456	0.90703	0.89845	0.89000	0.88166	0.87344	0.82645
3	0.92860	0.91514	0.90194	0.88900	0.86384	0.85161	0.83962	0.82785	0.81630	0.75132
4	0.90595	0.88849	0.87144	0.85480	0.82270	0.80722	0.79209	0.77732	0.76290	0.68301
5	0.88385	0.86261	0.84197	0.82193	0.78353	0.76513	0.74726	0.72988	0.71299	0.62092
6	0.86230	0.83748	0.81350	0.79031	0.74622	0.72525	0.70496	0.68533	0.66634	0.56447
7	0.84127	0.81309	0.78599	0.75992	0.71068	0.68744	0.66506	0.64351	0.62275	0.51316
8	0.82075	0.78941	0.75941	0.73069	0.67684	0.65160	0.62741	0.60423	0.58201	0.46651
9	0.80073	0.76642	0.73373	0.70259	0.64461	0.61763	0.59190	0.56735	0.54393	0.42410
10	0.78120	0.74409	0.70892	0.67556	0.61391	0.58543	0.55840	0.53273	0.50835	0.38554

8 Note that the future value of $826.45 in two years, at an interest rate of 10% compounded annually, is $1,000.

9 To simplify the illustrations and homework assignments, the tables presented in this chapter are limited to 10 periods for a small number of interest rates, and the amounts are carried to only five decimal places. Computer programs are available for determining present value factors for any number of interest rates, decimal places, or periods. More complete interest tables are presented in Appendix E of the text.

	Number of Periods	Interest Rate	Present Value of $1 Factor from Exhibit 7
10% for *two* years compounded *annually*	2	10%	0.82645
10% for *two* years compounded *semiannually*	4	5%	0.82270
10% for *three* years compounded *semiannually*	6	5%	0.74622
12% for *five* years compounded *semiannually*	10	6%	0.55840

Present Value of the Periodic Receipts A series of equal cash receipts at fixed intervals is called an **annuity**. The **present value of an annuity** is the sum of the present values of each cash receipt. To illustrate, assume that $100 is to be received annually for two years and that the market rate of interest is 10%. Using Exhibit 7, the present value of the receipt of the two amounts of $100 is $173.55, as shown below.

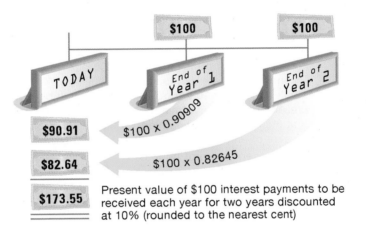

Present value of $100 interest payments to be received each year for two years discounted at 10% (rounded to the nearest cent)

Instead of using present value of $1 tables, such as Exhibit 7, separate present value tables are normally used for annuities. Exhibit 8 is a partial table of the **present value of an annuity of $1** at compound interest. It shows the present value of $1 to be received at the end of each period for various compound rates of interest.

Exhibit 8

Present Value of Annuity of $1 at Compound Interest

Periods	2.5%	3%	3.5%	4%	5%	5.5%	6%	6.5%	7%	10%
1	0.97561	0.97087	0.96618	0.96154	0.95238	0.94787	0.94340	0.93897	0.93458	0.90909
2	1.92742	1.91347	1.89969	1.88609	1.85941	1.84632	1.83339	1.82063	1.80802	1.73554
3	2.85602	2.82861	2.80164	2.77509	2.72325	2.69793	2.67301	2.64848	2.62432	2.48685
4	3.76197	3.71710	3.67308	3.62990	3.54595	3.50515	3.46511	3.42580	3.38721	3.16987
5	4.64583	4.57971	4.51505	4.45182	4.32948	4.27028	4.21236	4.15568	4.10020	3.79079
6	5.50813	5.41719	5.32855	5.24214	5.07569	4.99553	4.91732	4.84101	4.76654	4.35526
7	6.34939	6.23028	6.11454	6.00205	5.78637	5.68297	5.58238	5.48452	5.38929	4.86842
8	7.17014	7.01969	6.87396	6.73274	6.46321	6.33457	6.20979	6.08875	5.97130	5.33493
9	7.97087	7.78611	7.60769	7.43533	7.10782	6.95220	6.80169	6.65610	6.51523	5.75902
10	8.75206	8.53020	8.31661	8.11090	7.72174	7.53763	7.36009	7.18883	7.02358	6.14457

To illustrate, the present value of $100 to be received at the end of each of the next two years at 10% compound interest per period is $173.55 ($100 × 1.73554). This amount is the same amount computed above.

Pricing Bonds

The selling price of a bond is the present value, using the current market rate of interest, of the following:

1. The face value of the bonds due at the maturity date
2. The periodic interest to be paid on the bonds

To illustrate the pricing of bonds, assume that Fraser Valley Communications Ltd. issued the following bond on January 1, 2014:

Face value	$100,000
Stated rate of interest	6%
Interest paid semiannually on June 30 and December 31	
Term of bonds.	5 years

Market Rate of Interest of 6% Assuming a market rate of 6%, the bonds would sell for $100,000, their face value, as shown by the following present value computations.

Present value of principal of $100,000 due in 5 years, at 6%, compounded semiannually: $100,000 × 0.74409 (present value of $1 for 10 periods at 3% from Exhibit 7).	$ 74,409
Present value of 10 semiannual interest payments of $3,000, at 6% compounded semiannually: $3,000 × 8.53020 (present value of annuity of $1 for 10 periods at 3% from Exhibit 8)	25,591
Total present value of bonds.	$100,000

Market Rate of Interest of 7% Assuming a market rate of 7%, the bonds would sell at a discount. As shown by the following present value computations, the bonds would sell for $95,842.[10]

Present value of principal of $100,000 due in 5 years, at 7%, compounded semiannually: $100,000 × 0.70892 (present value of $1 for 10 periods at 3½% from Exhibit 7)	$70,892
Present value of 10 semiannual interest payments of $3,000, at 7% compounded semiannually: $3,000 × 8.31661 (present value of annuity of $1 for 10 periods at 3½% from Exhibit 8)	24,950
Total present value of bonds.	$95,842

Market Rate of Interest of 5% Assuming a market rate of 5%, the bonds would sell at a premium. As shown by the following present value computations, the bonds would sell for $104,376.

Present value of principal of $100,000 due in 5 years, at 5%, compounded semiannually: $100,000 × 0.78120 (present value of $1 for 10 periods at 2½% from Exhibit 7)	$ 78,120
Present value of 10 semiannual interest payments of $3,000, at 5% compounded semiannually: $3,000 × 8.75206 (present value of annuity of $1 for 10 periods at 2½% from Exhibit 8)	26,256
Total present value of bonds.	$104,376

As shown above, the present value of the bond varies with the present value of the bond's principal amount at maturity, the interest payments, and the market rate of interest.

---

10 Some corporations issue bonds called **zero-coupon bonds** that do not have periodic interest payments but pay the principal amount at maturity. Such bonds sell for large discounts. In this example, such a bond would sell for $70,892 but pay $100,000 at maturity.

At a Glance 14

1   Describe the characteristics and terminology of bonds payable, and the potential impact of borrowing on earnings per share.

Key Points

A corporation that issues bonds enters into a contract, or bond indenture. The characteristics of a bond depend on the type of bonds issued by a corporation.

When a corporation issues bonds, the price that buyers are willing to pay for the bonds depends on (1) the principal amount of the bonds, (2) the periodic interest to be paid on the bonds, and (3) the market rate of interest.

Corporations can finance their operations by issuing bonds or shares. This decision is partly influenced by the effect each alternative has on earnings per share.

Key Learning Outcomes	Page	Example Exercises
• Define the characteristics of a bond.	707	
• Describe the various types of bonds.	707	
• Calculate and compare the effect of alternative financing plans on earnings per share.	708	14-1
• Describe the factors that determine the price of a bond.	710	

2   Journalize entries for bonds payable.

Key Points

Bonds may be issued at amounts equal to, greater than, or less than the principal or face value of the bond. A discount or premium on bonds payable is amortized to interest expense over the life of the bonds. Businesses that report according to IFRS must use the effective interest method of amortization. Businesses that report according to ASPE may use either the straight-line method or the effective interest method of amortization.

Key Learning Outcomes	Page	Example Exercises
• Journalize the issuance of bonds at their principal amount and the related payment of interest.	711	14-2
• Journalize the issuance of bonds between interest dates.	712	14-3
• Journalize the issuance of bonds at a discount.	713	14-4
• Journalize the interest payment and bond discount amortization, using the straight-line method.	715	14-5
• Journalize the interest payment and bond discount amortization, using the effective interest method.	716	14-6
• Journalize the issuance of bonds at a premium.	720	14-7
• Journalize the interest payment and bond premium amortization, using the straight-line method.	721	14-8
• Journalize the interest payment and bond premium amortization, using the effective interest method.	722	14-9
• Describe bond redemptions.	724	
• Journalize the redemption of bonds payable.	725	14-10

3 Describe and illustrate the accounting for installment notes.

Key Points	Key Learning Outcomes	Page	Example Exercises
Companies issue installment notes as an alternative to issuing bonds. An installment note requires the borrower to make equal periodic payments to the lender for the term of the note. Unlike bonds, the annual payment in an installment note consists of both a principal portion and an interest portion.	• Describe the characteristics of an installment note.	727	
	• Journalize the issuance of installment notes.	727	14-11
	• Journalize the annual payment for an installment note.	727	14-11

4 Describe and illustrate the reporting and analysis of long-term liabilities.

Key Points	Key Learning Outcomes	Page	Example Exercises
Bonds payable and notes payable are usually reported as long-term liabilities. If the balance sheet date is within one year of their maturity date, the bonds and notes are reported as a current liability. The times interest earned measures the risk to bondholders that a company will not be able to make its interest payments.	• Illustrate the balance sheet presentation of bonds payable and notes payable.	729	
	• Describe, compute, and compare the times interest earned.	730	14-12

GLOSSARY

annuity – A series of equal cash receipts at fixed intervals. (p. 733)

bond – A form of an interest-bearing note used by corporations to borrow on a long-term basis. (p. 706)

bond indenture – The contract between a corporation issuing bonds and the bondholders. (p. 707)

carrying amount – The balance of the bonds payable account (face value of the bonds) less any unamortized discount or plus any unamortized premium. (p. 714)

contract rate – The periodic interest rate to be paid on the bonds that is identified in the bond indenture. (p. 710) Also known as *stated rate* or *coupon rate*.

coupon rate – The periodic interest rate to be paid on the bonds that is identified in the bond indenture. (p. 710). Also known as *stated rate* or *contract rate*.

discount – The interest deducted from the maturity value of a note or the excess of the face value of bonds over their issue price. (p. 710)

effective interest method – The method of amortizing discounts and premiums that provides for a constant rate of interest on the carrying amount of the bonds at the beginning of each period. (p. 716) Also known as *interest method*.

effective rate of interest – The rate determined from sales and purchases of similar bonds. (p. 710) Also known as *market rate of interest.*

face value – The amount due at the maturity date of the bonds. (p. 707) Also known as *principal.*

future value – The value of money in the future for money received today, taking into account the time value of money. (p. 731)

installment note – A debt that requires the borrower to make equal periodic payments to the lender for the term of the note. (p. 727)

interest method – The method of amortizing discounts and premiums that provides for a constant rate of interest on the carrying amount of the bonds at the beginning of each period. (p. 716) Also known as *effective interest method.*

market rate of interest – The rate determined from sales and purchases of similar bonds. (p. 710) Also known as *effective rate of interest.*

mortgage note – An installment note that may be secured by a pledge of the borrower's assets. (p. 727)

premium – The excess of the issue price of bonds over their face value. (p. 711)

present value – The value of money today for an amount to be received in the future, taking into account the time value of money. (p. 731)

present value of an annuity – The sum of the present values of each cash receipt of the annuity. (p. 733)

present value of an annuity of $1 – The sum of the present values of each $1 to be received at the end of each period for the life of the annuity. (p. 733)

principal – The amount due at the maturity date of bonds and notes. (p. 709) Also known as *face value.*

stated rate – The periodic interest rate to be paid on the bonds that is identified in the bond indenture. (p. 710) Also known as *contract rate* or *coupon rate.*

straight-line method – The method of amortizing discounts and premiums that provides for a constant amount of amortization each period. (p. 715)

times interest earned – A ratio that measures creditor margin of safety for interest payments, calculated as income before interest and taxes divided by interest expense. (p. 730)

zero-coupon bonds – Bonds that do not have periodic interest payments but pay the principal amount at maturity. (p. 734)

END-OF-CHAPTER ILLUSTRATIVE PROBLEM

The fiscal year of Russell Ltd., a manufacturer of acoustical supplies, ends December 31. Selected transactions for the period 2014 through 2021, involving bonds payable issued by Russell Ltd., are as follows:

2014
Jun. 30.   Issued $2,000,000 of 25-year, 7% callable bonds dated June 30, 2014, receiving cash of $1,909,468, for an effective interest rate of 7.4%. Interest is payable semiannually on June 30 and December 31.
Dec. 31.   Paid the interest on the bonds.

2015
Jun. 30.   Paid the interest on the bonds.
Dec. 31.   Paid the interest on the bonds.

2021
Jun. 30.   Recorded the redemption of the bonds, which were called at 101.5. The balance in the bond discount account is $78,878 after payment of interest has been recorded. (Record the redemption only.)

Instructions

1. Journalize entries to record the preceding transactions, using the effective interest method of amortization.
2. Determine the amount of interest expense for (a) 2014 and (b) 2015.
3. Determine the carrying amount of the bonds as at December 31, 2015.
4. Show the reporting of the bonds on the December 31, 2015, balance sheet.

Solution

1.

2014				
Jun.	30	Cash	1,909,468.00	
		Discount on Bonds Payable	90,532.00	
		Bonds Payable		2,000,000.00
Dec.	31	Interest Expense	70,650.32[1]	
		Discount on Bonds Payable		650.32
		Cash		70,000.00
		[1]($1,909,468 × 3.7%)		
2015				
Jun.	30	Interest Expense	70,674.38[2]	
		Discount on Bonds Payable		674.38
		Cash		70,000.00
		[2]($1,909,468 + $650.32) × 3.7%)		
Dec.	31	Interest Expense	70,699.33[3]	
		Discount on Bonds Payable		699.33
		Cash		70,000.00
		[3]($1,909,468 + $650.32 + $674.38) × 3.7%		
2021				
Jun.	30	Bonds Payable	2,000,000.00	
		Loss on Redemption of Bonds Payable	108,878.00	
		Discount on Bonds Payable		78,878.00
		Cash		2,030,000.00

2.
   a. 2014: $70,650.32
   b. 2015: $141,373.71

3.

Initial carrying amount of bonds	$1,909,468.00
Discount amortized in 2014	650.32
Discount amortized in 2015	1,373.71
Carrying amount of bonds, Dec. 31, 2015	$1,911,492.03

4.

Russell Ltd.
Balance Sheet (partial)
December 31, 2015

Long-term liabilities:	
Bonds payable, 7%, due Jun. 30, 2039	$2,000,000.00
Less unamortized discount	88,507.97
	$1,911,492.03

EYE OPENERS

1. Describe the two distinct obligations incurred by a corporation when issuing bonds.
2. Explain the meaning of each of the following terms as they relate to a bond issue: (a) convertible, (b) callable, and (c) debenture.
3. If you asked your broker to purchase for you a 4% bond when the market interest rate for such bonds was 5%, would you expect to pay more or less than the face value for the bond? Explain.
4. A corporation issues $9,000,000 of 5% bonds to yield interest at the rate of 3%. (a) Was the amount of cash received from the sale of the bonds greater or less than $9,000,000? (b) Identify the following terms related to the bond issue: (1) the principal amount, (2) the market or effective rate of interest, (3) the stated rate of interest, and (4) the maturity amount.
5. If bonds issued by a corporation are sold at a premium, is the market rate of interest greater or less than the stated rate?
6. How might a privately held company compute discount or premium amortization? How might a publicly traded company compute discount or premium amortization?
7. Assume that two 30-year, 10% bond issues are identical, except that one bond issue is callable at its face value at the end of five years. Which of the two bond issues will likely sell for a lower value?
8. Bonds Payable has a balance of $1,000,000, and Discount on Bonds Payable has a balance of $50,000. If the issuing corporation redeems the bonds at 98, does the corporation have a gain or loss on the bond redemption?
9. What is a mortgage note?
10. Fleeson Company needs additional funds to purchase equipment for a new production facility. The company is considering either issuing bonds or borrowing the money from a local bank in the form of an installment note. How does an installment note differ from a bond payable?
11. How would a bond payable be reported on the balance sheet if (a) it is payable within one year and (b) it is payable beyond one year?

PRACTICE EXERCISES

① PE 14-1
Effect of financing on earnings per share

Folmar Co. is considering the following alternative financing plans:

	Plan 1	Plan 2
Issue 5% bonds (at principal amount)	$2,000,000	$1,000,000
Issue common shares at $5 per share	2,000,000	3,000,000

EE 14-1 p. 709

Income taxes are estimated at 30% of income.

Determine the earnings per share under the two alternative financing plans, assuming income before bond interest and income taxes is $700,000.

② PE 14-2
Issuing bonds at face value

On January 1, when the market rate of interest was 5% for similar bonds, a company issued a $15,000,000, 5%, 10-year bond that pays semiannual interest on June 30 and December 31, receiving cash of $15,000,000. Journalize the entries to record (1) the issuance of the bonds and (2) the first interest payment.

EE 14-2 p. 712

PE 14-3

Bonds issued between interest dates

On June 1, a company issued at face value a $2,400,000, 4%, five-year bond that pays semiannual interest on April 30 and October 31. Journalize (a) the sale of the bond and (b) the interest payment on October 31.

EE 14-3 p. 713

PE 14-4

Issuing bonds at a discount

On the first day of the fiscal year, a company issues a $1,000,000, 6%, 10-year bond that pays annual interest of $60,000 ($1,000,000 × 6%), receiving cash of $964,060. Journalize the bond issuance.

EE 14-4 p. 714

PE 14-5

Discount amortization— straight-line method

Using the bond from Practice Exercise 14-4, journalize the first interest payment and the amortization of the related bond discount, using the straight-line method of amortization.

EE 14-5 p. 716

PE 14-6

Discount amortization— effective interest method

Using the bond from Practice Exercise 14-4, journalize the first interest payment and the amortization of the related bond discount, using the effective interest method. The bond was issued at an effective interest rate of 6.5%.

EE 14-6 p. 717

PE 14-7

Issuing bonds at a premium

A company issues a $10,000,000, 11%, five-year bond that pays semiannual interest of $550,000 ($10,000,000 × 11% × ½), receiving cash of $10,386,060 for an effective interest rate of 10%. Journalize the bond issuance.

EE 14-7 p. 721

PE 14-8

Premium amortization— straight-line method

Using the bond from Practice Exercise 14-7, journalize the first interest payment and the amortization of the related bond premium, using the straight-line method of amortization.

EE 14-8 p. 722

PE 14-9

Premium amortization— effective interest method

Using the bond from Practice Exercise 14-7, journalize the first interest payment and the amortization of the related bond premium, using the effective interest method.

EE 14-9 p. 723

2 **PE 14-10**
Redemption of bonds payable

EE 14-10 p. 726

A $500,000 bond issue with an unamortized discount of $50,000 is redeemed for $475,000. Journalize the redemption of the bonds.

3 **PE 14-11**
Journalizing inslment notes

EE 14-11 p. 729

On the first day of the fiscal year, a company issues a $65,000, 10%, six-year installment note that has annual payments of $14,924.
a. Journalize the entry to record the issuance of the installment notes.
b. Journalize the first annual note payment, which consists of both interest and principal repayment.

4 **PE 14-12**
Times interest earned

EE 14-12 p. 730

Katula Company reported the following on the company's income statement in 2015 and 2014:

	2015	2014
Interest expense	$ 250,000	$ 275,000
Income before income taxes	3,100,000	4,400,000

a. Determine the times interest earned for 2014 and 2015. Round to one decimal place.
b. Is the times interest earned improving or declining?

EXERCISES

1 **EX 14-1**
Financing with bonds versus shares

Wallace Contracting Ltd. is planning a new venture that is expected to generate $1,000,000 annual income before interest and taxes. Greenfield is considering the following alternative plans for financing its expansion:

	Plan 1	Plan 2
Issue common shares, at $40 per share	$4,000,000	$1,000,000
Issue 5% bonds	–	3,000,000

Determine the earnings per share under the two alternative financing plans, assuming income taxes of 30%.

1 **EX 14-2**
Effect of financing on earnings per share

✔ a. $0.35

Anders Co., which produces and sells skiing equipment, is financed as follows:

Bonds payable, 8% (issued at principal amount)	$10,000,000
Common shares, 400,000 issued and outstanding	10,000,000

Income taxes are estimated at 30% of income.

Determine the earnings per share, assuming that the income before bond interest and income taxes is (a) $1,000,000, (b) $2,000,000, and (c) $3,000,000.

1 **EX 14-3**
Evaluate alternative financing plans

Based on the data in Exercise 14-2, discuss the factors other than earnings per share that should be considered in evaluating such financing plans.

EX 14-4

Corporate financing

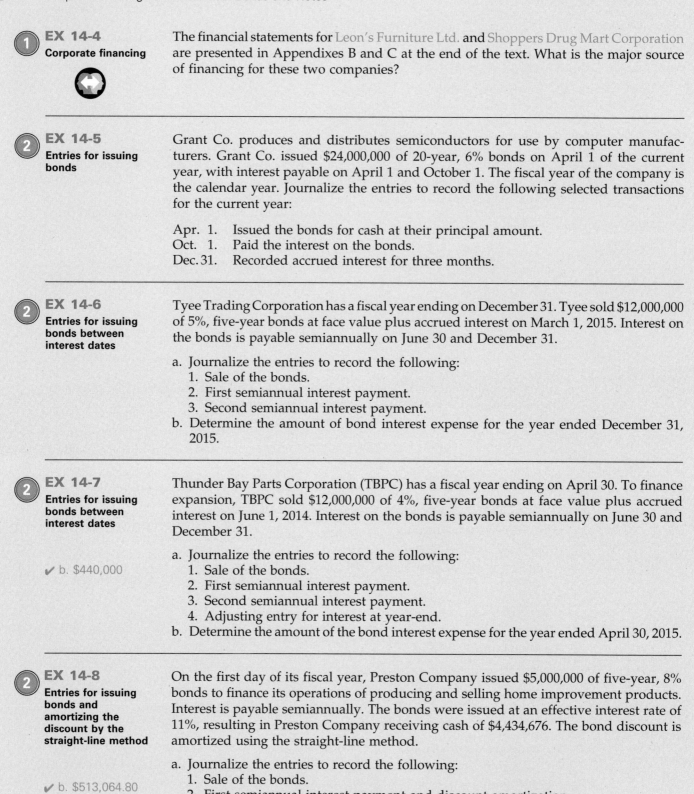

The financial statements for Leon's Furniture Ltd. and Shoppers Drug Mart Corporation are presented in Appendixes B and C at the end of the text. What is the major source of financing for these two companies?

EX 14-5

Entries for issuing bonds

Grant Co. produces and distributes semiconductors for use by computer manufacturers. Grant Co. issued $24,000,000 of 20-year, 6% bonds on April 1 of the current year, with interest payable on April 1 and October 1. The fiscal year of the company is the calendar year. Journalize the entries to record the following selected transactions for the current year:

Apr. 1.   Issued the bonds for cash at their principal amount.
Oct. 1.   Paid the interest on the bonds.
Dec. 31.   Recorded accrued interest for three months.

EX 14-6

Entries for issuing bonds between interest dates

Tyee Trading Corporation has a fiscal year ending on December 31. Tyee sold $12,000,000 of 5%, five-year bonds at face value plus accrued interest on March 1, 2015. Interest on the bonds is payable semiannually on June 30 and December 31.

a. Journalize the entries to record the following:
   1. Sale of the bonds.
   2. First semiannual interest payment.
   3. Second semiannual interest payment.
b. Determine the amount of bond interest expense for the year ended December 31, 2015.

EX 14-7

Entries for issuing bonds between interest dates

✔ b. $440,000

Thunder Bay Parts Corporation (TBPC) has a fiscal year ending on April 30. To finance expansion, TBPC sold $12,000,000 of 4%, five-year bonds at face value plus accrued interest on June 1, 2014. Interest on the bonds is payable semiannually on June 30 and December 31.

a. Journalize the entries to record the following:
   1. Sale of the bonds.
   2. First semiannual interest payment.
   3. Second semiannual interest payment.
   4. Adjusting entry for interest at year-end.
b. Determine the amount of the bond interest expense for the year ended April 30, 2015.

EX 14-8

Entries for issuing bonds and amortizing the discount by the straight-line method

✔ b. $513,064.80

On the first day of its fiscal year, Preston Company issued $5,000,000 of five-year, 8% bonds to finance its operations of producing and selling home improvement products. Interest is payable semiannually. The bonds were issued at an effective interest rate of 11%, resulting in Preston Company receiving cash of $4,434,676. The bond discount is amortized using the straight-line method.

a. Journalize the entries to record the following:
   1. Sale of the bonds.
   2. First semiannual interest payment and discount amortization.
   3. Second semiannual interest payment and discount amortization.
b. Determine the amount of the bond interest expense for the first year.
c. Will the interest expense in the second year be greater than, less than, or equal to the interest expense in the first year?

EX 14-9

② **Entries for issuing bonds and amortizing the premium by the straight-line method**

✔ b. Premium amortization, $204,724.90

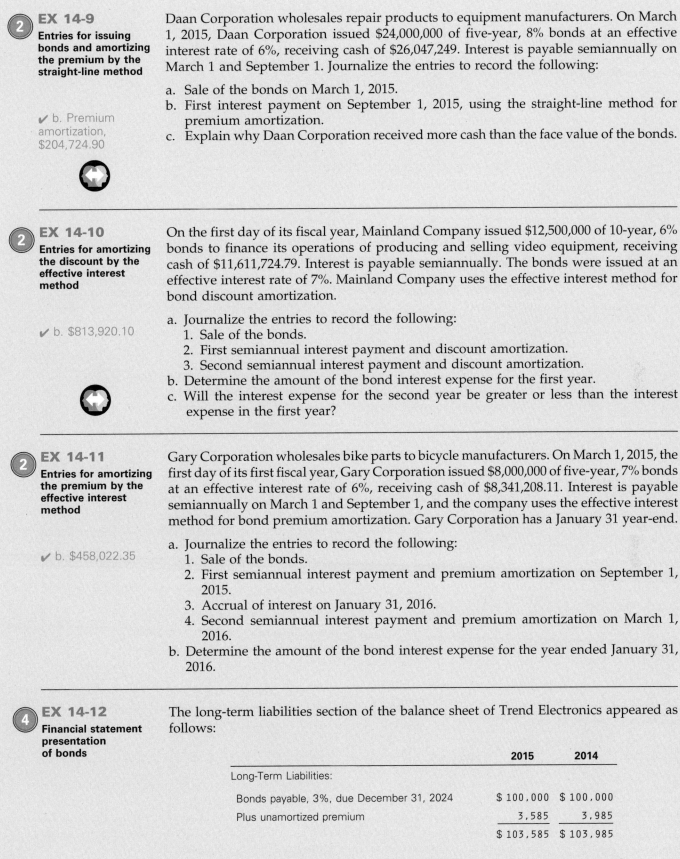

Daan Corporation wholesales repair products to equipment manufacturers. On March 1, 2015, Daan Corporation issued $24,000,000 of five-year, 8% bonds at an effective interest rate of 6%, receiving cash of $26,047,249. Interest is payable semiannually on March 1 and September 1. Journalize the entries to record the following:

a. Sale of the bonds on March 1, 2015.
b. First interest payment on September 1, 2015, using the straight-line method for premium amortization.
c. Explain why Daan Corporation received more cash than the face value of the bonds.

EX 14-10

② **Entries for amortizing the discount by the effective interest method**

✔ b. $813,920.10

On the first day of its fiscal year, Mainland Company issued $12,500,000 of 10-year, 6% bonds to finance its operations of producing and selling video equipment, receiving cash of $11,611,724.79. Interest is payable semiannually. The bonds were issued at an effective interest rate of 7%. Mainland Company uses the effective interest method for bond discount amortization.

a. Journalize the entries to record the following:
   1. Sale of the bonds.
   2. First semiannual interest payment and discount amortization.
   3. Second semiannual interest payment and discount amortization.
b. Determine the amount of the bond interest expense for the first year.
c. Will the interest expense for the second year be greater or less than the interest expense in the first year?

EX 14-11

② **Entries for amortizing the premium by the effective interest method**

✔ b. $458,022.35

Gary Corporation wholesales bike parts to bicycle manufacturers. On March 1, 2015, the first day of its first fiscal year, Gary Corporation issued $8,000,000 of five-year, 7% bonds at an effective interest rate of 6%, receiving cash of $8,341,208.11. Interest is payable semiannually on March 1 and September 1, and the company uses the effective interest method for bond premium amortization. Gary Corporation has a January 31 year-end.

a. Journalize the entries to record the following:
   1. Sale of the bonds.
   2. First semiannual interest payment and premium amortization on September 1, 2015.
   3. Accrual of interest on January 31, 2016.
   4. Second semiannual interest payment and premium amortization on March 1, 2016.
b. Determine the amount of the bond interest expense for the year ended January 31, 2016.

EX 14-12

④ **Financial statement presentation of bonds**

The long-term liabilities section of the balance sheet of Trend Electronics appeared as follows:

	2015	2014
Long-Term Liabilities:		
Bonds payable, 3%, due December 31, 2024	$ 100,000	$ 100,000
Plus unamortized premium	3,585	3,985
	$ 103,585	$ 103,985

1. Assuming interest is paid annually, what is the annual interest payment?
2. Will the interest expense be greater or lesser than the annual interest payment?
3. Journalize the 2015 interest payment and premium amortization.

EX 14-13

Entries for issuing bonds, straight-line discount amortization, and adjusting entries

✔ b. $975,503.33

On January 1, 2015, Crozier Company, a privately held company, sold $20,000,000 of five-year, 5% bonds to finance its expansion of operations. The bonds, which pay interest on June 30 and December 31, were issued at an effective interest rate of 6%, resulting in Crozier Company receiving cash of $19,146,980. The bond discount is amortized using the straight-line method of amortization.

a. Journalize the entries to record the following:
   1. Sale of the bonds.
   2. First semiannual interest payment and discount amortization.
   3. Adjusting entry for interest expense at the October 31 year-end.
   4. Second semiannual interest payment and discount amortization.
b. Determine the amount of bond interest expense for the fiscal year ended October 31, 2015.

EX 14-14

Entries for issuing bonds, effective-interest discount amortization, and adjusting entries

✔ b. $1,676,290.84

On April 1, 2015, Dot Equipment Ltd., a heavy equipment distributor, issued $50,000,000 of five-year, 5% bonds. The bonds, which pay interest on October 1 and April 1, were issued at an effective interest rate of 6%, resulting in Dot Equipment receiving cash of $47,867,449.29. The bond discount is amortized using the effective interest method of amortization.

a. Journalize the entries to record the following:
   1. Sale of the bonds.
   2. First semiannual interest payment and discount amortization.
   3. Adjusting entry for interest expense at the October 31 year-end. (Hint: take 1/6 of the amounts from the April 1, 2016 payment.)
   4. Second semiannual interest payment and discount amortization.
b. Determine the amount of bond interest expense for the fiscal year ended October 31, 2015.
c. Determine the carrying amount of the bonds at the October 31, 2015, year-end.

EX 14-15

Entries for issuing bonds, straight-line premium amortization, and adjusting entries

✔ b. $341,652.91

On March 1, 2015, Bruce Graham Corporation issued $10,000,000 of five-year, 6% bonds to finance its expansion of operations. The bonds, which pay interest on August 31 and February 28 or 29, were issued at an effective interest rate of 5%, resulting in Bruce Graham Corporation receiving cash of $10,437,603.20. Bruce Graham Corporation is a privately held company and has opted to use the straight-line method of amortization.

a. Journalize the entries to record the following:
   1. Sale of the bonds.
   2. First semiannual interest payment and premium amortization.
   3. Adjusting entry for interest expense at the October 31 year-end.
   4. Second semiannual interest payment and discount amortization.
b. Determine the amount of bond interest expense for the fiscal year ended October 31, 2015.
c. Show the reporting of the liabilities related to the bonds on the balance sheet at October 31, 2015, rounding to the nearest whole dollar. (Hint: Amounts related to the bonds will be reported in both the current liabilities and the long-term liabilities sections.)

EX 14-16

Entries for issuing bonds, effective interest premium amortization, and adjusting entries

✔ a. 2. Dec. 31, 2015; Interest expense $196,397.75

Mack Corporation produces and sells sporting equipment. To finance development of a wakeboard line, Mack Corporation issued $5,000,000 of 10-year, 7% bonds on June 1, 2015. The bonds pay interest on June 1 and were issued at an effective interest rate of 6.5%, resulting in Mack Corporation receiving cash of $5,179,720.76. The bond premium is amortized using the effective interest method of amortization.

a. Journalize the entries to record the following:
   1. Sale of the bonds on June 1, 2015.
   2. Adjusting entry for interest expense at the December 31 year-end.
   3. First annual interest payment and premium amortization.

b. Show the reporting of the liabilities related to the bonds on the balance sheet at December 31, 2015, rounding amounts to the nearest whole dollar. (Hint: Amounts related to the bonds will be reported in both the current liabilities and the long-term liabilities sections.)

---

② **EX 14-17**

Bond redemption at maturity, straight-line amortization

✔ a. 3. Dec. 31, 2015; Premium on bonds payable, $16,633.20

Solecki Corporation assembles and distributes fans. Solecki Corporation sold $4,000,000 five-year, 8% bonds on January 1, 2011. The bonds pay interest on June 30 and December 31 and were issued at an effective interest rate of 7%, resulting in Solecki Corporation receiving cash of $4,166,332. Solecki Corporation is a privately held company and has chosen to use the straight-line method of amortization.

Journalize the entries to record the following:

1. Sale of the bonds on January 1, 2011.
2. First semiannual interest payment and premium amortization.
3. Final semiannual interest payment and premium amortization on December 31, 2015.
4. Maturity of the bond on December 31, 2015.

---

② **EX 14-18**

Entries for issuing and calling bonds; loss

✔ Loss on bond redemption, $320,000

Potter Corp., a wholesaler of office equipment, issued $16,000,000 of 20-year, 8% callable bonds on April 1, 2015, with interest payable on April 1 and October 1. The fiscal year of the company is the calendar year.

a. Journalize the entries to record the following selected transactions:

2015
Apr. 1.   Issued the bonds for cash at their face value.
Oct. 1.   Paid the interest on the bonds.

2019
Oct. 1.   Called the bond issue at 102, the rate provided in the bond indenture. (Omit entry for payment of interest.)

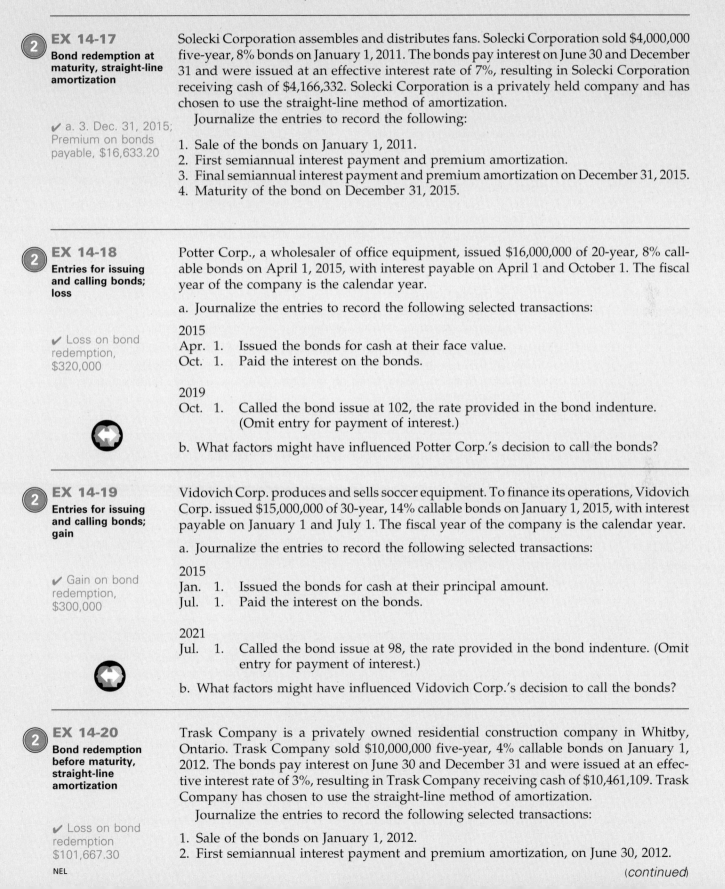

b. What factors might have influenced Potter Corp.'s decision to call the bonds?

---

② **EX 14-19**

Entries for issuing and calling bonds; gain

✔ Gain on bond redemption, $300,000

Vidovich Corp. produces and sells soccer equipment. To finance its operations, Vidovich Corp. issued $15,000,000 of 30-year, 14% callable bonds on January 1, 2015, with interest payable on January 1 and July 1. The fiscal year of the company is the calendar year.

a. Journalize the entries to record the following selected transactions:

2015
Jan. 1.   Issued the bonds for cash at their principal amount.
Jul. 1.   Paid the interest on the bonds.

2021
Jul. 1.   Called the bond issue at 98, the rate provided in the bond indenture. (Omit entry for payment of interest.)

b. What factors might have influenced Vidovich Corp.'s decision to call the bonds?

---

② **EX 14-20**

Bond redemption before maturity, straight-line amortization

✔ Loss on bond redemption $101,667.30

Trask Company is a privately owned residential construction company in Whitby, Ontario. Trask Company sold $10,000,000 five-year, 4% callable bonds on January 1, 2012. The bonds pay interest on June 30 and December 31 and were issued at an effective interest rate of 3%, resulting in Trask Company receiving cash of $10,461,109. Trask Company has chosen to use the straight-line method of amortization.

Journalize the entries to record the following selected transactions:

1. Sale of the bonds on January 1, 2012.
2. First semiannual interest payment and premium amortization, on June 30, 2012.

(continued)

3. Fifth semiannual interest payment and premium amortization, on June 30, 2014.
4. Trask Company called $6,000,000 of the bond issue at 104, the rate provided in the bond indenture, on June 30, 2014.
5. Sixth semiannual interest payment and premium amortization, on December 31, 2014.

EX 14-21

Bond redemption before maturity, effective interest amortization

✔ June 30, 2014; Interest expense, $342,098.66

Wakefield Construction Company sold $10,000,000 five-year, 6% callable bonds on June 30, 2011. The bonds pay interest on December 31 and June 30 and were issued at an effective interest rate of 7%, resulting in Wakefield receiving cash of $9,584,169.73. The company uses the effective interest method of amortization.

Journalize the entries to record the following selected transactions: (Hint: You may want to use a financial calculator.)

1. Sale of the bonds on June 30, 2011.
2. First semiannual interest payment and discount amortization on December 31, 2011.
3. Sixth semiannual interest payment and discount amortization on June 30, 2014.
4. Wakefield Company called $5,000,000 of the bond issue at 103, the rate provided in the bond indenture, on June 30, 2014.
5. Seventh semiannual interest payment and discount amortization, on December 31, 2014.

EX 14-22

Entries for installment note transactions

✔ b. Interest expense, $2,200

On the first day of the fiscal year, Hammond Company obtained a $44,000, seven-year, 5% installment note from TD Bank. The note requires annual payments of $7,604, with the first payment occurring on the last day of the fiscal year.

a. Journalize the entries to record the following:
    1. Issued the installment notes for cash on the first day of the fiscal year.
    2. Paid the first annual payment on the note, which consisted of interest and principal repayment.
b. Determine the amount of interest expense for the first year.

EX 14-23

Entries for installment note transactions

✔ Dec. 31, 2015, Interest expense, $15,400

On January 1, 2015, Guiado Company obtained a $140,000, 10-year, 11% installment note from Scotiabank. The note requires annual payments of $23,772, beginning on December 31, 2015. Journalize the entries to record the following:

2015
Jan. 1   Issued the notes for cash.
Dec. 31   Paid the annual payment on the note, which consisted of interest and principal repayment.

2024
Dec. 31   Paid the annual payment on the note, which consisted of interest of $2,353 and principal of $21,419.

EX 14-24

Entries for installment note transactions

✔ Dec. 31, 2018, Interest expense, $927

On January 1, 2015, Zinn Company obtained a $52,000, four-year, 6.5% installment note from RBC Royal Bank. The note requires annual payments of $15,179, beginning on December 31, 2015.

a. Prepare an amortization table for this installment note, similar to the one presented in Exhibit 6 on page 728.
b. Journalize the entries for the issuance of the note and the four annual note payments.

EX 14-25

Reporting bonds

Using the bond from Exercise 14-11, show the reporting of the bond on the balance sheet at January 31, 2016. Round to the nearest dollar. (Hint: Amounts related to the bonds will be reported in both the current liabilities and long-term liabilities sections.)

EX 14-26

Reporting bonds

Using the bond from Exercise 14-13, show the reporting of the bond on the balance sheet at October 31, 2015. Round to the nearest dollar.

EX 14-27

Times interest earned

f·a·i

The following data were taken from recent annual reports of TELUS Corporation, a leading national telecommunications company in Canada.

	Current Year (in millions of dollars)	Preceding Year (in millions of dollars)
Interest expense	$ 515	$ 582
Income before income taxes	1,366	1,205

a. Determine the times interest earned ratio for the current and preceding years. Round to one decimal place.
b. Is the times interest earned improving or declining?

EX 14-28

Appendix: Present value of amounts due

✔ b. $300,528

Determine the present value of $400,000 to be received in three years, using an interest rate of 10%, compounded annually, as follows:

a. By successive divisions.
b. By using the present value table in Exhibit 7.

EX 14-29

Appendix: Present value of an annuity

✔ b. $346,511

Determine the present value of $100,000 to be received at the end of each of four years, using an interest rate of 6%, compounded annually, as follows:

a. By successive computations, using the present value table in Exhibit 7.
b. By using the present value table in Exhibit 8.

EX 14-30

Appendix: Compute bond proceeds, amortizing the premium by the effective interest method

✔ a. $15,639,705
✔ c. $57,483.12

Motocar Co. produces and sells automobile parts. On the first day of its fiscal year, Motocar Co. issued $15,000,000 of five-year, 7% bonds at an effective rate of 6%, with interest payable semiannually. Compute the following, presenting the figures used in your computations.

a. The amount of cash proceeds from the sale of the bonds. (Use the tables of present values in Exhibits 7 and 8.)
b. The amount of premium to be amortized for the first semiannual interest payment period, using the effective interest method.
c. The amount of premium to be amortized for the second semiannual interest payment period, using the effective interest method.
d. The amount of the bond interest expense for the first year.

EX 14-31

Appendix: Compute bond proceeds, amortizing the discount by the effective interest method

✔ a. $36,755,480
✔ b. $270,219.20

Seward Co. produces and sells restaurant equipment. On the first day of its fiscal year, June 1, 2015, Seward Co. issued $40,000,000 of five-year, 6% bonds at an effective rate of 8%, with interest payable semiannually. Compute the following, presenting the figures used in your computations.

a. The amount of cash proceeds from the sale of the bonds. (Use the tables of present values in Exhibits 7 and 8.)
b. The amount of discount to be amortized for the first semiannual interest payment period, using the effective interest method.
c. The amount of discount to be amortized for the second semiannual interest payment period, using the effective interest method.
d. The amount of the bond interest expense for the first year.

EX 14-32

Appendix: Present value of an annuity

✔ $23,165,220

On January 1, 2015, you win $30,000,000 in the provincial lottery. The $30,000,000 prize will be paid in equal installments of $3,000,000 over 10 years. The payments will be made on December 31 of each year, beginning on December 31, 2015. If the current interest rate is 5%, determine the present value of your winnings. Use the present value tables in Exhibit 8.

EX 14-33

Appendix: Present value of an annuity

✔ $18,433,710

Assume the same data as in Exercise 14-32, except that the current interest rate is 10%. Will the present value of your winnings using an interest rate of 10% be one-half the present value of your winnings using an interest rate of 5%? Why or why not?

EX 14-34

Appendix: Present value of bonds payable; discount

✔ $9,573,450

Hi-Vis Co. produces and sells high-resolution, flat-panel televisions. To finance its operations, Hi-Vis Co. issued $10,000,000 of five-year, 5% bonds with interest payable semiannually at an effective interest rate of 6%. Determine the present value of the bonds payable, using the present value tables in Exhibits 7 and 8.

EX 14-35

Appendix: Present value of bonds payable; premium

✔ $65,251,326

Mason Co. issued $60,000,000 of five-year, 7% bonds with interest payable semiannually, at an effective interest rate of 5%. Determine the present value of the bonds payable, using the present value tables in Exhibits 7 and 8.

PROBLEMS SERIES A

① PR 14-1A

Effect of financing on earnings per share

✔ 1. Plan 3. $15.60

Three different plans for financing a $10,000,000 corporation are under consideration by its organizers. Under each of the following plans, the bonds will be issued at their principal amount or face value; the common shares will sell for $40 per share, and the income tax rate is estimated at 40% of income.

	Plan 1	Plan 2	Plan 3
5% bonds	—	$ 5,000,000	$ 7,500,000
Common shares	$10,000,000	5,000,000	2,500,000
Total	$10,000,000	$10,000,000	$10,000,000

Instructions

1. Determine for each plan the earnings per share, assuming that the income before bond interest and income taxes is $2,000,000.
2. Determine for each plan the earnings per share, assuming that the income before bond interest and income taxes is $950,000.
3. Discuss the advantages and disadvantages of each plan.

PR 14-2A

Bond discount, entries for bonds payable transactions, straight-line method

✔ 3. $1,073,692.80

On July 1, 2015, Brower Industries Ltd. issued $32,000,000 of 10-year, 6% bonds at an effective interest rate of 7%, receiving cash of $29,726,144. Interest on the bonds is payable semiannually on December 31 and June 30. The fiscal year of the company is the calendar year.

Instructions

1. Journalize the entry to record the amount of cash proceeds from the sale of the bonds.
2. Journalize the entries to record the following:
   a. The first semiannual interest payment on December 31, 2015, and the amortization of the bond discount, using the straight-line method.
   b. The interest payment on June 30, 2016, and the amortization of the bond discount, using the straight-line method.
3. Determine the total interest expense for 2015.
4. Will the bond proceeds always be less than the principal amount of the bonds when the stated rate is less than the market rate of interest?
5. (Appendix) Compute the price of $29,726,144 received for the bonds by using the tables of present value in Appendix E at the end of the text.

PR 14-3A

Bond premium, entries for bonds payable transactions, straight-line method, issued between interest dates, adjusting entries for interest

✔ c. Amortization, $35,009.45

On September 1, 2015, Grand Forks Ltd. issued $16,000,000 of five-year, 6% bonds at an effective interest rate of 5%, receiving cash of $16,700,189 plus accrued interest. Interest on the bonds is payable semiannually on December 31 and June 30. The fiscal year-end of the company is March 31.

Instructions

1. Journalize the entry to record the amount of cash proceeds from the sale of the bonds.
2. Journalize the entries to record the following:
   a. The first semiannual interest payment on December 31, 2015, and the amortization of the bond premium, using the straight-line method.
   b. The adjusting entry for interest expense at the March 31, 2016, year-end.
   c. The interest payment on June 30, 2016, and the amortization of the bond premium.
3. Prepare the long-term liabilities section of the balance sheet for Grand Forks Ltd. as at March 31, 2016, rounding to the nearest whole dollar.

PR 14-4A

Bond premium, entries for bonds payable transactions, straight-line method

✔ 3. $79,535.13

On July 1, 2015, Rashid Wholesalers Ltd. issued $3,000,000 of 15-year, 6% bonds at an effective interest rate of 5%, receiving cash of $3,313,946. Interest on the bonds is payable semiannually on December 31 and June 30. The fiscal year of the company is the calendar year.

Instructions

1. Journalize the entry to record the amount of cash proceeds from the sale of the bonds.
2. Journalize the entries to record the following:
   a. The first semiannual interest payment on December 31, 2015, and the amortization of the bond premium, using the straight-line method.
   b. The interest payment on June 30, 2016, and the amortization of the bond premium, using the straight-line method.
3. Determine the total interest expense for 2015.
4. Will the bond proceeds always be greater than the principal amount of the bonds when the stated rate is greater than the market rate of interest?
5. (Appendix) Compute the price of $3,313,946 received for the bonds by using the tables of present value in Appendix E at the end of the text.

PR 14-5A

Bond discount, entries for bonds payable transactions, effective interest method

✔ 3. $520,205.27

On July 1, 2015, Swift Current Industries Ltd. issued $16,000,000 of 10-year, 6% bonds at an effective interest rate of 7%, receiving cash of $14,863,007.74. Interest on the bonds is payable semiannually on December 31 and June 30. The fiscal year of the company is the calendar year.

Instructions

1. Journalize the entry to record the amount of cash proceeds from the sale of the bonds.
2. Journalize the entries to record the following:
   a. The first semiannual interest payment on December 31, 2015, and the amortization of the bond discount, using the effective interest method.
   b. The interest payment on June 30, 2016, and the amortization of the bond discount, using the effective interest method.
   c. The interest payment on December 31, 2016, and the amortization of the bond discount, using the effective interest method.
3. Determine the total interest expense for 2015.
4. Show the reporting of the bonds on the statement of financial position at December 31, 2015, and at December 31, 2016, rounding numbers to the nearest whole dollar.

PR 14-6A

Entries for notes payable, bonds payable, adjusting entries, straight-line method

✔ June 30, interest expense, $13,255.86

The following items were selected from among the transactions completed by Pot of Gold Coffee Ltd., a private coffee importing company with a May 31 year-end.

2015
Jul. 10.   Purchased merchandise on account from Hoffer Co., $220,000, terms 2/10, n/30. Pot of Gold Coffee Ltd. uses the perpetual inventory method.
Jul. 11.   Borrowed $150,000 from Capital Credit Union, issuing a 180-day, 5% note.
Jul. 15.   Paid Hoffer Co. for the amount owed on the July 10 transaction.

2016
Jan. 1.   Issued $3,000,000 of 15-year, 6% bonds at an effective interest rate of 5%, receiving cash of $3,313,946. Interest on the bonds is payable semiannually on December 31 and June 30.
Jan. 7.   Paid Capital Credit Union the interest due on the note of July 11 and renewed the loan by issuing a new 180-day, 6% note for $150,000.
May 31.   Recorded the year-end adjusting entry for the interest expense on the $3,000,000 bonds and the amortization of the bond premium, using the straight-line method.
            Recorded the year-end adjusting entry for the interest expense on the $150,000 note of January 7.
Jun. 30.   Recorded the interest payment and the amortization of the premium on the $3,000,000 bonds, using the straight-line method.

Instructions

1. Journalize the transactions.
2. Show the reporting of the liabilities for Pot of Gold Coffee Ltd. on the balance sheet at May 31, 2016, rounding to the nearest whole dollar. (Hint: Amounts related to the bonds will be reported in both the current liabilities and the long-term liabilities sections.)

PR 14-7A

Bond discount, entries for bonds payable transactions, effective interest method, adjusting entries for interest

✔ 3. $440,682.56

On April 1, 2015, GTI Industries Ltd. issued $10,000,000 of five-year, 5.5% bonds at an effective interest rate of 6%, receiving cash of $9,786,744.93. Interest on the bonds is payable semiannually on September 30 and March 31. The fiscal year-end of the company is December 31.

Instructions

1. Journalize the entry to record the amount of cash proceeds from the sale of the bonds.
2. Journalize the entries to record the following:
   a. The first semiannual interest payment on September 30, 2015, and the amortization of the bond discount, using the effective interest method.
   b. The adjusting entry for interest expense at the December 31, 2015, year-end.
   c. The interest payment on March 31, 2016, and the amortization of the bond discount, using the effective interest method.
3. Determine the total interest expense for the fiscal year ended December 31, 2015.

---

② ③ PR 14-8A

Entries for bonds payable and installment note transactions, reporting debt

✔ 1. Dec. 31, 2015, Interest expense on bonds, $516,968.45

The following transactions were completed by Hocking Inc., a publicly traded company, whose fiscal year is the calendar year:

2015

Jul.	1.	Issued $18,000,000 of five-year, 5% callable bonds dated July 1, 2015, at an effective rate of 6%, receiving cash of $17,232,281.74. Interest is payable semi-annually on December 31 and June 30.
Oct.	1.	Borrowed $800,000 as a 10-year, 7% installment note from Royal Bank. The note requires annual payments of $113,902, with the first payment occurring on September 30, 2016.
Dec.	31.	Accrued interest on the installment note. The interest is payable on the date of the next installment note payment.
	31.	Paid the semiannual interest on the bonds.

2016

Jun.	30.	Paid the semiannual interest on the bonds.
Sep.	30.	Paid the annual payment on the note, which consisted of interest of $56,000 and principal of $57,902.
Dec.	31.	Accrued interest on the installment note. The interest is payable on the date of the next installment note payment.
	31.	Paid the semiannual interest on the bonds.

2017

Jun.	30.	Paid the semiannual interest on the bonds. Recorded the redemption of the bonds, which were called at 97.

Instructions

1. Journalize the entries to record the foregoing transactions, using the effective interest method for amortization.
2. Show the reporting of the liabilities on the statement of financial position as at December 31, 2015, rounding numbers to the nearest whole dollar.

---

② PR 14-9A

Bond retirement before maturity, entries for bonds payable transactions, premium, straight-line method, issued between interest dates, adjusting entries for interest

✔ 2.c. Interest expense, $108,761.50

On March 1, 2015, Elden Distributors Ltd., a privately held company, sold $5,000,000 of 10-year, 6% callable bonds to finance its expansion of operations. The bonds, which pay interest on July 1 and January 1, were issued at an effective interest rate of 5%, resulting in Elden Distributors Ltd. receiving cash of $5,389,724 plus accrued interest. The bond premium is amortized using the straight-line method of amortization. The fiscal year-end of the company is July 31. On January 1, 2020, the bonds were called at 102, the rate provided in the bond indenture.

Instructions

1. Journalize the entry to record the amount of cash proceeds from the sale of the bonds.
2. Journalize the entries to record the following:
   a. The first semiannual interest payment on July 1, 2015, and the amortization of the bond premium, using the straight-line method.
   b. The adjusting entry for interest expense at the July 31, 2015, year-end.

(continued)

c. The interest payment on January 1, 2016, and the amortization of the bond premium, using the straight-line method.

d. The retirement of the bonds on January 1, 2020. (Omit entry for payment of interest.)

3. Identify possible reasons for Elden Distributors Ltd.'s decision to call the bonds.

---

② PR 14-10A

Bond retirement before maturity, entries for bonds payable transactions, discount, effective interest method

✔ 2.c. Interest expense, $384,427.78

On January 1, 2015, Grave Suppliers Ltd., a publicly traded company, sold $20,000,000 of five-year, 5% callable bonds to finance its expansion of operations. The bonds, which pay interest on June 30 and December 31, were issued at an effective interest rate of 6%, resulting in Grave Suppliers Ltd. receiving cash of $19,146,979.72. The bond discount is amortized using the effective interest method of amortization. The fiscal year-end of the company is August 31. On December 31, 2015, $10,000,000 of the bonds were called at 101, the rate provided in the bond indenture.

Instructions

1. Journalize the entry to record the amount of cash proceeds from the sale of the bonds.
2. Journalize the entries to record the following:
   a. The first semiannual interest payment on June 30, 2015, and the amortization of the bond discount, using the effective interest method.
   b. The adjusting entry for interest expense at the August 31, 2015, year-end.
   c. The interest payment on December 31, 2015, and the amortization of the bond discount, using the effective interest method.
   d. The retirement of the bonds on December 31, 2015.
   e. The interest payment on June 30, 2016, and the amortization of the bond discount, using the effective interest method.

PROBLEMS SERIES B

① PR 14-1B

Effect of financing on earnings per share

✔ 1. Plan 3. $9.84

Three different plans for financing a $60,000,000 corporation are under consideration by its organizers. Under each of the following plans, the bonds will be issued at their principal amount or face value, the common shares will sell for $20, and the income tax rate is estimated at 40% of income.

	Plan 1	Plan 2	Plan 3
6% bonds	—	$30,000,000	$45,000,000
Common shares	$60,000,000	30,000,000	15,000,000
Total	$60,000,000	$60,000,000	$60,000,000

Instructions

1. For each plan, determine the earnings per share, assuming that the income before bond interest and income taxes is $15,000,000.
2. For each plan, determine the earnings per share, assuming that the income before bond interest and income taxes is $7,000,000.
3. Discuss the advantages and disadvantages of each plan.

---

② PR 14-2B

Bond discount, entries for bonds payable transactions, straight-line method

✔ 3. $1,444,770

On July 1, 2015, Linux Corporation, a wholesaler of electronics equipment, issued $45,000,000 of 10-year, 5% bonds at an effective interest rate of 7%, receiving cash of $38,604,600. Interest on the bonds is payable semiannually on December 31 and June 30. The fiscal year of the company is the calendar year.

Instructions

1. Journalize the entry to record the amount of cash proceeds from the sale of the bonds.
2. Journalize the entries to record the following:
   a. The first semiannual interest payment on December 31, 2015, and the amortization of the bond discount, using the straight-line method.
   b. The interest payment on June 30, 2016, and the amortization of the bond discount, using the straight-line method.

3. Determine the total interest expense for 2015.
4. Will the bond proceeds always be less than the principal amount of the bonds when the contract rate is less than the market rate of interest?
5. (Appendix) Compute the price of $38,604,600 received for the bonds by using the tables of present value in Appendix E at the end of the text.

---

(2) **PR 14-3B**

(4) **Bond premium, entries for bonds payable transactions, straight-line method, issued between interest dates, adjusting entries for interest**

✔ c. Amortization, $109,684.79

On September 1, 2015, Bathurst Ltd. issued $30,000,000 of four-year, 7% bonds at an effective interest rate of 6%, receiving cash of $31,052,974 plus accrued interest. Interest on the bonds is payable semiannually on December 31 and June 30. The fiscal year-end of the company is January 31.

Instructions

1. Journalize the entry to record the amount of cash proceeds from the sale of the bonds.
2. Journalize the entries to record the following:
   a. The first semiannual interest payment on December 31, 2015, and the amortization of the bond premium, using the straight-line method.
   b. The adjusting entry for interest expense at the January 31, 2016, year-end.
   c. The interest payment on June 30, 2016, and the amortization of the bond premium.
3. Prepare the long-term liabilities section of the balance sheet for Bathurst Ltd. as at January 31, 2016, rounding to the nearest whole dollar.

---

(2) **PR 14-4B**

Bond premium, entries for bonds payable transactions, straight-line method

✔ 3. $1,566,165.60

Proust Corporation produces and sells hockey equipment. On July 1, 2015, Proust Corporation issued $60,000,000 of 10-year, 6% bonds at an effective interest rate of 5%, receiving cash of $64,676,688. Interest on the bonds is payable semiannually on December 31 and June 30. The fiscal year of the company is the calendar year.

Instructions

1. Journalize the entry to record the amount of cash proceeds from the sale of the bonds.
2. Journalize the entries to record the following:
   a. The first semiannual interest payment on December 31, 2015, and the amortization of the bond premium, using the straight-line method.
   b. The interest payment on June 30, 2016, and the amortization of the bond premium, using the straight-line method.
3. Determine the total interest expense for 2015.
4. Will the bond proceeds always be greater than the face amount of the bonds when the contract rate is greater than the market rate of interest?
5. (Appendix) Compute the price of $64,676,688 received for the bonds by using the tables of present value in Appendix E at the end of the text.

---

(2) **PR 14-5B**

(4) **Bond discount, entries for bonds payable transactions, effective interest method**

✔ 3. $450,384.88

On July 1, 2015, Lemer Corporation, a wholesaler of limited edition jewelry, issued $15,000,000 of 10-year, 5% bonds at an effective interest rate of 7%, receiving cash of $12,868,139.50. Interest on the bonds is payable semiannually on December 31 and June 30. The fiscal year of the company is the calendar year.

Instructions

1. Journalize the entry to record the amount of cash proceeds from the sale of the bonds.
2. Journalize the entries to record the following:
   a. The first semiannual interest payment on December 31, 2015, and the amortization of the bond discount, using the effective interest method.
   b. The interest payment on June 30, 2016, and the amortization of the bond discount, using the effective interest method.

                                                       (continued)

    c. The interest payment on December 31, 2016, and the amortization of the bond discount, using the effective interest method.

3. Determine the total interest expense for 2015.
4. Show the reporting of the bonds on the statement of financial position at December 31, 2015, and at December 31, 2016, rounding amounts to the nearest whole dollar.

---

2 **PR 14-6B**

4 **Entries for notes payable, bonds payable, adjusting entries, straight-line method**

✔ June 30, interest expense, $174,018.40

The following items were selected from among the transactions completed by Trainor Equipment Ltd., a company with a May 31 year-end.

2015

Jul. 10. Purchased equipment on account from Wholesalers Co., $225,000, terms 1/10, n/30. Trainor Equipment Ltd. uses the perpetual inventory method.

Jul. 16. Borrowed $550,000 from Central Credit Union, issuing a 180-day, 4% note.

Jul. 20. Paid Wholesalers Co. for the amount owed on the July 10 transaction.

2016

Jan. 1. Issued $40,000,000 of 10-year, 6% bonds at an effective interest rate of 5%, receiving cash of $43,117,792. Interest on the bonds is payable semiannually on December 31 and June 30.

Jan. 12. Paid Central Credit Union the interest due on the note of July 16 and renewed the loan by issuing a new 180-day, 6% note for $550,000.

May 31. Recorded the year-end adjusting entry for the interest expense on the $40,000,000 bonds and the amortization of the bond premium, using the straight-line method.

    Recorded the year-end adjusting entry for the interest expense on the $550,000 note of January 12.

Jun. 30. Recorded the interest payment and the amortization of the premium on the $40,000,000 bonds, using the straight-line method.

Instructions

1. Journalize the transactions.
2. Show the reporting of the liabilities for Trainor Equipment Ltd. on the balance sheet at May 31, 2016, rounding to the nearest whole dollar.

---

2 **PR 14-7B**

Bond discount, entries for bonds payable transactions, effective interest method, adjusting entries for interest

✔ 3. $866,940.94

On April 1, 2015, Tandem Corporation Ltd. issued $20,000,000 of 10-year 5.5% bonds at an effective interest rate of 6%, receiving cash of $19,256,126.26. Interest on the bonds is payable semiannually on September 30 and March 31. The fiscal year-end of the company is December 31.

Instructions

1. Journalize the entry to record the amount of cash proceeds from the sale of the bonds.
2. Journalize the entries to record the following:
   a. The first semiannual interest payment on September 30, 2015, and the amortization of the bond discount, using the effective interest method.
   b. The adjusting entry for interest expense at the December 31, 2015, year-end.
   c. The interest payment on March 31, 2016, and the amortization of the bond discount, using the effective interest method.
3. Determine the total interest expense for the fiscal year ended December 31, 2015.

PR 14-8B

Entries for bonds payable and installment note transactions, reporting debt

✔ 1. Dec. 31,2015; Interest expense on bonds, $288,972.91

The following transactions were completed by Hamilton Ltd., whose fiscal year is the calendar year:

2015
Jul.   1.   Issued $10,000,000 of 10-year, 7% callable bonds dated July 1, 2015, at an effective rate of 5%, receiving cash of $11,558,916.23. Interest is payable semi-annually on December 31 and June 30.

Oct.   1.   Borrowed $450,000 as a six-year, 8% installment note from CIBC. The note requires annual payments of $97,342, with the first payment occurring on September 30, 2016.

Dec. 31.   Accrued interest on the installment note. The interest is payable on the date of the next installment note payment.

     31.   Paid the semiannual interest on the bonds and recorded premium amortization.

2016
Jun. 30.   Paid the semiannual interest on the bonds and recorded premium amortization.

Sep. 30.   Paid the annual payment on the note, which consisted of interest of $36,000 and principal of $61,342.

Dec. 31.   Accrued interest on the installment note. The interest is payable on the date of the next installment note payment.

     31.   Paid the semiannual interest on the bonds and recorded premium amortization.

Instructions

1. Journalize the entries to record the foregoing transactions using the effective interest method for amortization.
2. Show the reporting of the liabilities on the statement of financial position as at December 31, 2015, rounding numbers to the nearest whole dollar.

PR 14-9B

Bond retirement before maturity, entries for bonds payable transactions, premium, straight-line method, issued between interest dates, adjusting entries for interest

✔ 2.c. Jan. 1, 2016; Interest expense, $256,238.20

On February 1, 2015, Landra Corp. Ltd., a privately held company, sold $15,000,000 of five-year, 6% callable bonds to finance its expansion of operations. The bonds, which pay interest on July 1 and January 1, were issued at an effective interest rate of 5%, resulting in Landra Corp. Ltd. receiving cash of $15,656,427 plus accrued interest. The bond discount is amortized using the straight-line method of amortization. The fiscal year-end of the company is August 31. On January 1, 2018, the bonds were called at 102, the rate provided in the bond indenture.

Instructions

1. Journalize the entry to record the amount of cash proceeds from the sale of the bonds.
2. Journalize the entries to record the following:
   a. The first semiannual interest payment on July 1, 2015, and the amortization of the bond premium, using the straight-line method.
   b. The adjusting entry for interest expense at the August 31, 2015, year-end.
   c. The interest payment on January 1, 2016, and the amortization of the bond premium, using the straight-line method.
   d. The retirement of the bonds on January 1, 2018. (Omit entry for payment of interest.)
3. Identify possible reasons for Landra Corp. Ltd.'s decision to call the bonds.

② **PR 14-10B**

Bond retirement before maturity, entries for bonds payable transactions, discount, effective interest method

✔ 2.e. Interest expense, $144,735.23

On April 1, 2015, Vital Suppliers Ltd, a publicly traded company, sold $10,000,000 of five-year, 5% callable bonds to finance its expansion of operations. The bonds, which pay interest on September 30 and March 31, were issued at an effective interest rate of 6%, resulting in Vital Suppliers Ltd. receiving cash of $9,573,489.86. The bond discount is amortized using the effective interest method of amortization. The fiscal year-end of the company is December 31. On March 31, 2016, $5,000,000 of the bonds were called at 101, the rate provided in the bond indenture.

Instructions

1. Journalize the entry to record the amount of cash proceeds from the sale of the bonds.
2. Journalize the entries to record the following:
   a. The first semiannual interest payment on September 30, 2015, and the amortization of the bond discount, using the effective interest method.
   b. The adjusting entry for interest expense at the December 31, 2015, year-end.
   c. The interest payment on March 31, 2016, and the amortization of the bond discount, using the effective interest method.
   d. The retirement of the bonds on March 31, 2016.
   e. The interest payment on September 30, 2016, and the amortization of the bond discount, using the effective interest method.

SPECIAL ACTIVITIES

① **SA 14-1**

General Electric bond issuance

General Electric Capital, a division of General Electric, uses long-term debt extensively. In 2002, GE Capital issued $11 billion in long-term debt to investors, then within days filed legal documents to prepare for another $50 billion long-term debt issue. As a result of the $50 billion filing, the price of the initial $11 billion offering declined (due to higher risk of more debt).

> Bill Gross, a manager of a bond investment fund, "denounced a 'lack in candor' related to GE's recent debt deal. 'It was the most recent and most egregious example of how bondholders are mistreated.' Gross argued that GE was not forthright when GE Capital recently issued $11 billion in bonds, one of the largest issues ever from a U.S. corporation. What bothered Gross is that three days after the issue the company announced its intention to sell as much as $50 billion in additional debt, warrants, preferred stock, guarantees, letters of credit and promissory notes at some future date."

In your opinion, did GE Capital act unethically by selling $11 billion of long-term debt without telling those investors that a few days later it would be filing documents to prepare for another $50 billion debt offering?

Source: Jennifer Ablan, "Gross Shakes the Bond Market; GE Calms It, a Bit," Barron's, March 25, 2002. Reprinted by permission of Barron's, Copyright © 2002 Dow Jones & Company, Inc. All Rights Reserved Worldwide. License number 2978250529294

SA 14-2

Ethics and professional conduct in business

Lachgar Industries develops and produces biodiesel, an alternative energy source. The company has an outstanding $200,000,000, 30-year, 12% bond issue dated July 1, 2010. The bond issue is due June 30, 2040. The bond indenture requires a bond sinking fund, which has a balance of $24,000,000 as at July 1, 2015. The company is currently experiencing a shortage of funds due to a recent acquisition. Abdou Hatch, the company's accountant, is considering using the funds from the bond sinking fund to cover payroll and other bills that are coming due at the end of the month. Abdou's brother-in-law is a trustee in the sinking fund, who has indicated a willingness to allow Abdou to use the funds from the sinking fund to temporarily meet the company's cash needs.

Discuss whether Abdou's proposal is appropriate.

SA 14-3
Present values

Finn Kilgallon recently won the jackpot in the BC 49 lottery while he was visiting his parents. When he arrived at the lottery office to collect his winnings, he was offered the following three payout options:

a.   Receive $10,000,000 in cash today.
b.   Receive $2,200,000 today and $1,050,000 per year for 15 years, with the first $1,050,000 payment being received one year from today.
c.   Receive $1,200,000 per year for 15 years, with the first payment being received one year from today.

Assuming that the effective rate of interest is 5%, which payout option should Finn select? Explain your answer and provide any necessary supporting calculations.

SA 14-4
Shares vs. bonds

Beacon Ltd. has decided to expand its operations to owning and operating retail clothing stores. The following is an excerpt from a conversation between the chief executive officer, Frank Forrest, and the vice president of finance, Rachel Tucker.

Frank: Rachel, have you given any thought to how we're going to finance the acquisition of the stores?

Rachel: Well, the two basic options, as I see it, are to issue either shares or bonds. The equity market is a little depressed right now. The rumour is that the Bank of Canada's going to increase the interest rates either this month or next.

Frank: Yes, I've heard the rumour. The problem is that we can't wait around to see what's going to happen. We'll have to move on this next week if we want any chance to complete the acquisition of the new clothing chain.

Rachel: Well, the bond market is strong right now. Maybe we should issue debt this time around.

Frank: That's what I would have guessed as well. The clothing chain financial statements look pretty good, except for the volatility of its income and cash flows. But that's characteristic of the industry.

Discuss the advantages and disadvantages of issuing shares versus bonds.

SA 14-5
Financing business expansion

You hold a 25% common share interest in the family-owned business, a vending machine company. Your sister, who is the manager, has proposed an expansion of plant facilities at an expected cost of $7,500,000. Two alternative plans have been suggested as methods of financing the expansion. Each plan is briefly described as follows:

Plan 1. Issue $7,500,000 of 10-year, 8% notes at principal amount.
Plan 2. Issue an additional 100,000 common shares at $40 per share and $3,500,000 of 10-year, 8% notes at principal amount.

The balance sheet as at the end of the previous fiscal year is as follows:

Thacker Ltd.
Balance Sheet
December 31, 2015

Assets	
Current assets	$ 4,000,000
Property, plant, and equipment	6,000,000
Total assets	$10,000,000

Liabilities and Shareholders' Equity	
Liabilities.	$ 3,000,000
Common shares, 200,000 issued and outstanding.	1,100,000
Retained earnings	5,900,000
Total liabilities and shareholders' equity	$10,000,000

Net income has remained relatively constant over the past several years. The expansion program is expected to increase yearly income before bond interest and income taxes from $750,000 in the previous year to $1,000,000 for this year. Your sister has asked you, as the company accountant, to prepare an analysis of each financing plan.

1.   Prepare a table indicating the expected earnings per share under each plan. Assume an income tax rate of 40%. Round to the nearest cent.

(continued)

2. a. Discuss the factors that should be considered in evaluating the two plans.
   b. Which plan offers the greater benefit to the present shareholders? Give reasons for your opinion.

SA 14-6
Bond ratings

Internet Project

Moody's Investors Service maintains a website at **www.moodys.ca**. One of the services offered at this site is a listing of announcements of recent bond rating changes. Visit this site and read over some of these announcements. Write down several of the reasons provided for rating downgrades and upgrades. If you were a bond investor or bond issuer, would you care whether Moody's changed the rating on your bonds? Why or why not?

SA 14-7
Times interest earned ratio

f·a·i

Using the financial statements of Shoppers Drug Mart Corporation in Appendix C:

1. Calculate the times interest earned ratio for the past two years (Use "finance expenses" for interest expense).
2. Has the ratio improved or declined over this time period?
3. Assess the company's ability to meet its interest payment obligations.
4. Because the company reports under IFRS, it uses the effective interest method for amortizing any discount or premium on long-term liabilities. Which note indicates that Shoppers Drug Mart Corporation is using the effective interest method?

Investments

SHAW COMMUNICATIONS INC.

You invest cash to earn more cash. For example, you can deposit cash in a bank account to earn interest. You can also invest cash in preferred or common shares or in corporate or government notes and bonds.

Preferred and common shares can be purchased through a stock exchange, such as the Toronto Stock Exchange (TSX). Preferred shares are purchased primarily with the expectation of earning dividends. Common shares are purchased with the expectation of earning dividends and/or realizing gains from a price increase in the shares.

Corporate and government bonds can also be purchased through a bond exchange. Bonds are purchased with the primary expectation of earning interest revenue.

Companies make investments for many of the same reasons that you, as an individual, make investments. For example, in October 2010, Shaw Communications Inc., a leader in the Canadian entertainment and communications industry, paid approximately $2 billion to acquire the broadcasting assets of Canwest Global Communications Corp., which includes the Global Television Network. In June 2011, Shaw Communications acquired the cable system assets of Sun Country Cablevision Ltd. in British Columbia. In addition, Shaw Communications has invested more than $29 million in other companies. It holds these investments to earn revenue from interest, dividends, expected price increases, and company growth.

However, unlike most individuals, companies also purchase significant amounts of the outstanding common shares of other companies for strategic reasons. For example, Shaw Communications' 2011 annual report indicated that the company purchased Canwest Global Communications to combine programming content with its cable and satellite distribution network to create a vertically integrated entertainment and communications company.

Investments in debt and equity securities give rise to many accounting issues. These issues are described and illustrated in this chapter.

After studying this chapter, you should be able to:

1 Describe why companies invest in debt and equity securities.

Why Companies Invest	Investing Cash in Current Operations	
	Investing Cash to Earn Additional Revenue	
	Investing Cash for Strategic Reasons	

2 Describe and illustrate the accounting for non-strategic investments.

Accounting for Non-Strategic Investments	Accounting for Held-for-Trading Investments	EXAMPLE EXERCISE 15-1 (page 764) EXAMPLE EXERCISE 15-2 (page 765)
	Accounting for Held-to-Maturity Investments, Loans, and Receivables	EXAMPLE EXERCISE 15-3 (page 768)
	Purchase of Bonds at a Discount or Premium	EXAMPLE EXERCISE 15-4 (page 770) EXAMPLE EXERCISE 15-5 (page 771)
	Accounting for Available-for-Sale Investments	EXAMPLE EXERCISE 15-6 (page 773)

3 Describe and illustrate the accounting for strategic investments.

Accounting for Strategic Investments	Classifications of Strategic Investments	
	Accounting for Investments in Associates	EXAMPLE EXERCISE 15-7 (page 779)
	Accounting for Joint Ventures	
	Accounting for Business Combinations	
	Reporting of Investments	
	Financial Analysis and Interpretation	EXAMPLE EXERCISE 15-8 (page 783)

APPENDIX 1 Accounting for Non-Strategic Investments Using International Financial Reporting Standards (IFRS) 9

For the chapter *At a Glance*, turn to page 785.

Why Companies Invest

Describe why companies invest in debt and equity securities.

Most companies generate cash from their operations. This cash can be used for the following purposes:

1. investing in current operations
2. investing to earn additional revenue
3. investing for strategic reasons

Investing Cash in Current Operations

Cash is often used to support the current operating activities of a company. For example, cash may be used to replace worn-out equipment or to purchase new, more efficient and productive equipment. In addition, cash may be reinvested in the company to expand its current operations. For example, a retailer based in Western Canada might decide to expand by opening stores in Ontario.

To support its current level of operations, a company also uses cash to pay suppliers or other creditors. For example, suppliers must be paid to ensure that the company will be able to continue to purchase merchandise on account. The company may also have issued notes or bonds payable to finance its current operations. The interest on the notes or bonds must be paid.

Cash is also used to pay dividends to preferred or common shareholders. In order for a company to maintain its ability to raise cash (capital), it must reward (pay) investors for the use of their funds. For preferred shareholders, this reward is primarily the payment of dividends on a regular basis. For common shareholders, this reward may also take the form of cash dividends, and/or it may be in the form of an increasing share price from improving prospects of the company.

The accounting for the use of cash in current operations has been described and illustrated in earlier chapters. For example, Chapter 9, "Property, Plant, and Equipment and Other Long-Term Assets," illustrated the use of cash for purchasing property, plant, and equipment. In this chapter, we describe and illustrate the use of cash for investing in debt (bonds) and equity (shares) of other companies.

Investing Cash to Earn Additional Revenue

A company may have excess cash that is not needed for use in its current operations. At times this excess cash may be temporary, such as when a company has a seasonal operating cycle. For example, a significant portion of the annual merchandise sales of a retailer occurs during the fall holiday season. As a result, retailers often experience a large increase in cash during this period, which is not needed until the spring buying season.

In other situations, companies may have excess cash for extended periods of time. For example, a company may be planning for a large plant expansion in the future that requires the setting aside of excess cash for use at a later date.

Instead of letting excess cash remain idle in a chequing account, most companies invest their excess cash in investments such as the following:

1. **Debt securities**, which are notes and bonds that pay interest and have a fixed maturity date.
2. **Equity securities**, which are preferred and common shares that pay dividends and do not have a fixed maturity date.

These types of investments have the following primary objectives:

1. to earn interest revenue
2. to receive dividends
3. to realize gains from increases in the market price of the securities

Investments in certificates of deposit and other securities that do not normally change in value are disclosed on the balance sheet as *cash and cash equivalents*. Such investments are held primarily for their interest revenue.

Investing cash to earn additional revenue is considered a **non-strategic investment**, much the same as when purchasing shares in, for example, Bell Canada. When making such an investment, you would not have any expectation of influencing the decisions made by the board of directors or top management; you would expect only a return on your investment in the form of dividends.

Investing Cash For Strategic Reasons

From time to time, companies make strategic investments through the purchase of large volumes of shares in other corporations. The purchase may be large enough to give the companies full control, or just enough to give them significant influence. This concept will be discussed later in the chapter.

Accounting for Non-Strategic Investments

Describe and illustrate the accounting for non-strategic investments.

International Financial Reporting Standards (IFRS) are continuously evolving. In 2010, the International Accounting Standards Board (IASB) issued IFRS 9—Financial Instruments, which replaces International Accounting Standard (IAS) 39, effective January 1, 2015. Should the effective date for IFRS 9 be delayed, IAS 39 will continue to be in effect. This chapter discusses IAS 39, the standard currently in effect at the time of writing. The differences between the two standards and the application of IFRS 9 are covered in the appendix to this chapter.

Under IFRS, non-strategic investments are categorized into one of four different classifications as follows:

1. **Held-for-Trading Investments**—Debt and equity securities that are purchased and sold to earn short-term profits from changes in their market price.
2. **Held-to-Maturity Investments**—Debt investments (bonds) that are purchased with the intent to hold them until their maturity date.
3. **Loans and Receivables**—Loans made for the purpose of receiving fixed interest revenue.
4. **Available-for-Sale Investments**—Debt and equity securities that are not classified as held-for-trading or held-to-maturity investments.

Which classification to use for a non-strategic investment is determined by management's intent when the investment is initially made.

Accounting for Held-for-Trading Investments

If management's intent is to sell the investment in the near future, IFRS require that it be recorded as a held-for-trading investment when initially purchased.

Held-for-trading investments are debt and equity securities that are purchased and sold to earn short-term profits from changes in their market prices. Held-for-trading investments are often held by banks, mutual funds, insurance companies, and other financial institutions.

Held-for-trading investments are held as a short-term investment, are reported as a current asset on the balance sheet, and are accounted for using the fair value through profit and loss (fair value) method. The **fair value through profit and loss method** adjusts the value of the investment to its market value at year-end, with any differences recorded as an **unrealized holding gain or loss** on the income statement. Since market value is used to revalue the asset at year-end, only securities traded in an open market can be classified as held-for-trading investments.

Purchase of Held-for-Trading Investments Any brokerage fees related to the purchase or sale of a held-for-trading investment should be expensed in the year in which the fees are incurred.

To illustrate held-for-trading investments, assume that on December 1, 2014, Maggie Inc. purchases 400 Armour Ltd. shares for $4,900, 500 Maven Ltd. shares for $10,700, and Polaris Corp. bonds with an $8,000 face value for $7,900, paying $23,500 plus a brokerage commission of $500. Maggie Inc. intends to report these securities as held-for-trading investments. The journal entry to record the purchase is as follows:

2014				
Dec.	1	Held-for-Trading Investments—Armour Ltd	4,900	
		Held-for-Trading Investments—Maven Ltd.	10,700	
		Held-for-Trading Investments—Polaris Corp.	7,900	
		Brokerage Fees Expense	500	
		Cash		24,000
		Purchased securities as held-for-trading investments.		

On December 31, 2014, the cost and fair values (market values) of the securities were as follows:

Name	Total Cost	Total Fair Value
Armour Ltd.	$ 4,900	$ 7,600
Maven Ltd.	10,700	9,400
Polaris Corp. Bonds	7,900	7,950
Total	$23,500	$24,950

Revaluing the Investments at Year-End The investments need to be adjusted to their fair values on December 31, 2014. When adjusting the investment accounts, two methods are acceptable: (1) the use of an allowance account that accumulates any increase or decrease in the value of the investment and (2) a direct increase or decrease in the investment. We will demonstrate the direct method for Maggie Inc.

On December 31, 2014, the cost and fair values (market values) of the held-for-trading investments were as follows:

Name	Total Cost	Total Fair Value	Change in Value
Armour Ltd. (400 shares)	$ 4,900	$ 7,600	$ 2,700
Maven Ltd. (500 shares)	10,700	9,400	(1,300)
Polaris Corp. ($8,000 bonds)	7,900	7,950	50
	$23,500	$24,950	$ 1,450

The entire portfolio (group) of investments has increased in value by $1,450 ($24,950 – $23,500). Since none of the investments has been sold, this increase is recorded as an unrealized holding gain and will appear as other revenue on the income statement. When the investments are sold, the difference between the recorded value and the selling price will be recognized as a gain or loss on sale of investments on the income statement.

The adjusting entry on December 31, 2014, to record the change in value of the investments is as follows:

2014				
Dec.	31	Held-for-Trading Investments—Armour Ltd.	2,700	
		Held-for-Trading Investments—Polaris Corp.	50	
		Held-for-Trading Investments—Maven Ltd.		1,300
		Unrealized Holding Gain		1,450
		To record increase in fair value of		
		held-for-trading investments.		

For illustrative purposes, we have listed each investment in its own account. In reality, companies would have one control account on the balance sheet supported by a subsidiary ledger for the individual investments. This concept is similar to other subsidiary ledgers discussed throughout the book for accounts receivable, accounts payable, and inventory. On December 31, 2014, Maggie Inc. would present its held-for-trading investments in the current assets section of the balance sheet as follows:

Maggie Inc.
Balance Sheet (Partial)
December 31, 2014

Current assets:	
Cash	$146,000
Held-for-trading investments—at fair value	24,950

EXAMPLE EXERCISE 15-1 Valuing Held-for-Trading Investments at Fair Value ②

On December 31, 2015, Complete Car Care Ltd. had the following costs and fair values for its held-for-trading investments:

Name	Total Cost	Total Fair Value
Amber Woods Inc.	$12,300	$ 8,700
Green Metals Corp.	8,200	10,500
Blue Moon Inc.	2,900	2,600

Journalize the adjusting entry required on December 31, 2015, to recognize these investments at fair value.

FOLLOW MY EXAMPLE 15-1

Name	Total Cost	Total Fair Value	Change in Value
Amber Woods Inc.	$12,300	$ 8,700	$(3,600)
Green Metals Corp.	8,200	10,500	2,300
Blue Moon Inc.	2,900	2,600	(300)
			$(1,600)

2015				
Dec.	31	Held-for-Trading Investments—Green Metals Corp.	2,300	
		Unrealized Holding Loss	1,600	
		Held-for-Trading Investments—Amber Woods Inc.		3,600
		Held-for-Trading Investments—Blue Moon Inc.		300
		To record decrease in fair value of held-for-trading investments.		

For Practice: PE 15-1

Receipt of Additional Revenue Although the main purpose of non-strategic investments is to earn profit through their increased market value, interest and dividends may also be received during the holding period. Assume the Polaris Corp. bonds have an $8,000 face value and pay 5% semi-annual interest on November 30 and May 31. On December 31, 2014, Maggie Inc. will record a journal entry to recognize the future receipt of interest as follows:

2014				
Dec.	31	Interest Receivable	33.33	
		Interest Revenue		33.33
		To record interest receivable.		
		($8,000 × 5% × 1/12)		

Also assume the Armour Ltd. shareholders received a $1.50 dividend on January 31, 2015. The dividend was declared on January 3 so Maggie Inc. did not record dividends receivable on December 31, 2014. The journal entry to record the receipt of the dividends on January 31, 2015, would be as follows:

2015				
Jan.	31	Cash	600	
		Dividend Revenue		600
		To record receipt of dividend revenue		
		(400 shares × $1.50).		

Accounting for Sale of Held-for-Trading Investments On February 24, 2015, Maggie Inc. sold 200 of the Maven Ltd. shares for $12 per share. The shares are valued at $18.80 ($9,400/500 shares) per share as a result of the revaluation on December 31, 2014.

Maggie Inc. was charged a brokerage fee of $200 on the sale and will recognize a loss on sale of investments of $1,360 [($18.80 − $12) × 200 shares] with the following entry:

2015					
Feb.	24	Cash		2,200	
		Brokerage Fees Expense		200	
		Loss on Sale of Investments		1,360	
		Held-for-Trading Investments—Maven Ltd.			3,760*
		To record sale of 200 shares of Maven Ltd.			
		*($9,400 × 200/500)			

EXAMPLE EXERCISE 15-2 JOURNALIZING THE SALE OF HELD-FOR-TRADING INVESTMENTS ②

Using the information from Example Exercise 15-1, journalize the entry required to record the sale on January 18, 2016, of one-half of the investment in Amber Woods Inc. for $5,000 less a $300 brokerage fee.

FOLLOW MY EXAMPLE 15-2

2016				
Jan.	18	Cash	4,700	
		Brokerage Fees Expense..	300	
		Held-for-Trading Investments—Amber Woods Inc.		4,350*
		Gain on Sale of Investments		650
		To record the sale of Amber Woods Inc. held-for-trading		
		investment.		
		*($8,700 × 0.5)		

For Practice: PE 15-2

INTEGRITY, OBJECTIVITY, AND ETHICS IN BUSINESS ❓

SUBPRIME WOES

Many of the largest U.S. banks provided mortgages to marginally qualified borrowers. Such loans were termed "subprime" loans. These loans were then packaged into investments that were sold to investors. Often, the banks earned attractive fees for creating these financial products. Unfortunately, many weak borrowers were unable to make their mortgage payments, which resulted in defaults on the mortgages. These defaults caused a fall in the value of the packaged investments that held these loans. As a result, many investors, including the banks themselves, were required to recognize large losses from declines in fair value of these investments. Some of these losses were as follows:

UBS	$37 billion
Merrill Lynch & Co.	34 billion
Citigroup	30 billion

These losses were some of the largest in the history of these companies. Because the losses were immediately disclosed and recognized, they were never hidden from company shareholders. The accounting principles require such losses to be recognized even if the investments are not sold. Canada has not had the same problem with subprime mortgages because Canadian banking legislation is stricter and Canadian housing prices have not declined as drastically as in the United States.

Accounting for Held-to-Maturity Investments, Loans, and Receivables

Held-to-maturity investments are debt investments, such as corporate or government bonds that a company intends to hold until their maturity date. Held-to-maturity investments also include notes receivable. The accounting for notes receivable is the same as for bonds. Held-to-maturity investments are purchased primarily to earn interest revenue.

Only securities with maturity dates, such as corporate notes and bonds, are classified as held-to-maturity investments. Equity securities are not held-to-maturity investments because they have no maturity date.

Held-to-maturity bond investments are reported on the balance sheet at their amortized cost. Management intends to hold these bonds to maturity, so reporting for changes in fair values of these securities is not meaningful.

The unrealized gains or losses reported for held-for-trading investments allow investors to evaluate management's short-term investing decisions. However, because management chooses held-to-maturity investments for their long-term interest revenue and not for short-term capital gains, the reporting of unrealized gains or losses does not provide relevant information.

If the market value of the held-to-maturity investment becomes impaired (declines), and evidence suggests that the impairment is permanent, the investment can be revalued to its lower market value and the unrealized loss is recorded under Other Expenses on the income statement. If the market value increases at a later date, the value of the investment can be increased, but not to a value higher than it was recorded at prior to the impairment. In this situation, the unrealized holding gain is recorded under Other Revenue on the income statement.

When the asset is sold, any gain or loss is recognized in the income statement in the same manner as described for the sale of held-for-trading investments.

Whereas Chapter 14 discussed notes and bonds from the issuer's point of view, Chapter 15 discusses notes and bonds from the investor's point of view.

The accounting for held-to-maturity investments includes recording the following:

1. purchase of held-to-maturity investments
2. interest revenue

Purchase of Held-to-Maturity Investments The purchase of bonds is recorded by debiting a held-to-maturity investments account for the purchase price of the bonds.

Bonds are purchased and sold in an open bond market, similar to a stock market, where their prices are quoted as a percentage of their face (par) value. For example, a $5,000 bond purchased at 103 is purchased for $5,150 ($5,000 × 103%). Brokerage commissions may be expensed or added to the cost of the investment. Because these investments are long term, it is more favourable, in terms of the conceptual framework, to capitalize the brokerage fees, so they can be applied to future revenues generated by the investment.

If the interest rate on the bonds differs from the market rate of interest, the bonds may be purchased at a premium or discount, as discussed in Chapter 14 with regard to the sale of bonds. In such cases, the premium or discount is amortized over the life of the bonds, as illustrated later in the chapter on page 768.

If the bonds are purchased between interest dates, the purchase price includes interest accrued since the last interest payment because the seller has earned the accrued interest, but the buyer receives the accrued interest when it is paid.

To illustrate, assume that Homer Inc. purchases $18,000 of bonds of Sakata Ltd. at their par value on April 14, 2015, plus accrued interest for 73 days. The bonds have an interest rate of 6%, payable on July 31 and January 31.

Because Homer Inc. purchased the bonds on April 14, it is also purchasing the accrued interest for 73 days (February 1 to April 14). The accrued interest of $216 is computed as follows:

$$\text{Accrued Interest} = \$18,000 \times 6\% \times (73/365) = \$216$$

The accrued interest is recorded by debiting Interest Receivable for $216. Held-to-Maturity Investments is debited for the purchase price of the bonds of $18,000.

The entry to record the purchase of the bonds is as follows:

2015				
Apr.	14	Held-to-Maturity Investments—Sakata Ltd. Bonds	18,000	
		Interest Receivable	216	
		Cash		18,216
		Purchased $18,000, 6% Sakata Ltd. bonds		

Receipt of Interest   On July 31, Homer Inc. receives a semiannual interest payment of $540 ($18,000 × 6% × ½). The $540 interest includes the $216 accrued interest that Homer purchased with the bonds on April 14. Thus, Homer has earned $324 ($540 − $216) of interest revenue since purchasing the bonds.

The receipt of the interest on July 31 is recorded as follows:

2015				
Jul.	31	Cash	540	
		Interest Receivable		216
		Interest Revenue		324
		Received semiannual interest		

Homer Inc's accounting period ends on December 31. Thus, an adjusting entry must be made to accrue interest for five months (August 1 to December 31) of $450 ($18,000 × 6% × 5⁄12). The adjusting entry to record the accrued interest is as follows:

2015				
Dec.	31	Interest Receivable	450	
		Interest Revenue		450
		Accrued interest.		

For the year ended December 31, 2015, Homer would report *Interest revenue* of $774 ($324 + $450) as part of *Other income* on its income statement.

The receipt of the semiannual interest of $540 on January 31, 2016, is recorded in the same manner as the receipt of interest is recorded on July 31, 2015.

If a held-to-maturity investment will mature within a year, it is reported as a current asset on the balance sheet. Held-to-maturity investments maturing beyond a year are reported as noncurrent assets. Homer Inc. will report its investment in Sakata Ltd. bonds as follows:

Homer Inc. Balance Sheet (Partial) December 31, 2015	
Current Assets:	
Interest receivable.	$ 450
Noncurrent Assets:	
Held-to-maturity investments—at amortized cost	18,000

EXAMPLE EXERCISE 15-3 Held-to-Maturity Transactions　②

Journalize the entries to record the following selected held-to-maturity investment transactions for Tristan Ltd.:

Oct. 24. Purchased for cash, $80,000 of Arcon Corp. 7% bonds at 100 plus 146 days of accrued interest and $450 of brokerage fees. Tristan capitalizes brokerage fees on held-to-maturity investments.
Nov. 30. Received the semiannual interest payment on the Arcon Corp. bonds.
Dec. 31. Accrued interest on the Arcon Corp. bonds.

FOLLOW MY EXAMPLE 15-3

Oct. 24	Held-to-Maturity Investments—Arcon Corp. Bonds	80,450.00	
	Interest Receivable	2,240.00	
	Cash		82,690.00
	Purchased $80,000 Arcon Corp. 7% bonds at 100 plus accrued interest and brokerage fees.		
Nov. 30	Cash	2,800.00*	
	Interest Receivable		2,240.00
	Interest Revenue		560.00
	Received semiannual interest.		
	*$80,000 × 7% × ½		
Dec. 31	Interest Receivable	466.67	
	Interest Revenue		466.67
	Accrued interest ($80,000 × 7% × ½)		

For Practice: PE 15-3

Purchase of Bonds at a Discount or Premium

As discussed in Chapter 14, the interest rate offered on bonds may differ from the market rate, which is the rate offered on similar bonds. If the interest rate on bonds differs from the market rate of interest, the bonds may be purchased at a premium or discount. Bonds are purchased at a premium or discount as follows:

1. If the bond rate of interest is *more than* the market rate of interest for equivalent investments, bonds are purchased at a *premium*. That is, the bonds are purchased for more than their face value.

2. If the bond rate of interest is *less than* the market rate of interest for equivalent investments, bonds are purchased at a *discount*. That is, the bonds are purchased for less than their face value.

The face value of the bond and the related premium or discount are normally not recorded in separate accounts. This procedure differs from the accounting for bonds payable, which uses separate premium and discount accounts. However, like bonds payable, any premium or discount on a bond investment is amortized over the remaining life of the bonds.

Amortization of Premium or Discount Any premium or discount on a bond investment should be amortized over the remaining life of the bond. The amortization affects the investment and interest revenue as follows:

1. Bond *Premium* Amortization: Decreases Held-to-Maturity Investment and decreases Interest Revenue.

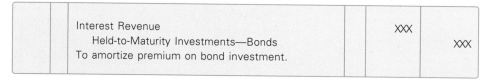

		Interest Revenue	XXX	
		Held-to-Maturity Investments—Bonds		XXX
		To amortize premium on bond investment.		

2. Bond *Discount* Amortization: Increases Held-to-Maturity Investment and increases Interest Revenue.

Held-to-Maturity Investments—Bonds	XXX	
Interest Revenue		XXX
To amortize discount on bond investment.		

The amortization on held-to-maturity investments is often recorded when the interest is received or accrued. IFRS require the amortization to be computed using the effective interest method, or *interest method*, but the straight-line method is acceptable under ASPE.

To illustrate the effective interest method, assume that on April 1, 2015, Crenshaw Ltd. purchases 10-year, 8% bonds on their issuance date directly from XPS Corporation as a long-term investment. The market rate on April 1 was 10%. The bonds pay semiannual interest on October 1 and April 1 and were purchased at 88 (88% of their face value).

The purchase price is $44,000 ($50,000 × 88%).

The entries related to the held-to-maturity investment during 2015 are as follows:

Purchase of bonds on April 1, 2015.

2015				
Apr.	1	Held-to-Maturity Investments—XPS Corporation Bonds	44,000	
		Cash		44,000
		Purchase of bonds as a held-to-maturity investment.		

Receipt of semiannual interest, and amortization of discount using the effective interest method on October 1.

Oct.	1	Cash	2,000*	
		Held-to-Maturity Investments—XPS Corporation Bonds	200	
		Interest Revenue		2,200**
		Receipt of semiannual interest and amortization		
		of discount.		
		*($50,000 × 8% × 6/12)		
		**($44,000 × 10%/2)		

Adjusting entry for accrued interest and amortization of discount on December 31, Crenshaw Ltd.'s year-end.

Dec.	31	Interest Receivable	1,000*	
		Held-to-Maturity Investments—XPS Corporation		
		Bonds	105	
		Interest Revenue		1,105**
		Accrued interest and amortization of discount on		
		held-to-maturity investment.		
		*($50,000 × 8% × 3/12)		
		**[($44,000 + $200) × 10%/2/2]		

To illustrate the straight-line method acceptable under ASPE, we will look at the accounting for the Crenshaw Ltd. purchase of the XPS Corporation bonds.

The entries related to the interest and discount amortization during 2015 are as follows:

Receipt of semiannual interest, and amortization of discount using the straight-line method on October 1.

Oct.	1	Cash	2,000*	
		Held-to-Maturity Investments—XPS Corporation Bonds	300**	
		Interest Revenue		2,300
		Receipt of semiannual interest and amortization		
		of discount on bond investment.		
		*($50,000 × 8% × 6/12)		
		**($6,000/20)		

Adjusting entry for accrued interest and amortization of discount on December 31, Crenshaw Ltd.'s year-end.

Dec.	31	Interest Receivable	1,000*	
		Held-to-Maturity Investments—XPS Corporation Bonds	150**	
		Interest Revenue		1,150
		Accrued interest and amortization of discount on		
		held-to-maturity investment.		
		*($50,000 × 8% × 3/12)		
		**($6,000/20 × 3/6)		

Receipt of Maturity Value of Bond At the maturity date of the bonds, any premium or discount will be fully amortized using either the effective interest method or straight-line method, and the book value (carrying value) of the held-to-maturity investment account will equal the face value of the bonds. At the maturity date, the investor will receive the face value of the bonds.

To illustrate, the XPS Corporation bonds mature on April 1, 2025. At that date, the $6,000 discount will have been totally amortized, and Held-to-Maturity Investments—XPS Corporation Bonds will have a balance of $50,000. The receipt of the face value of the bonds on April 1, 2025, is recorded as follows:

2025				
Apr.	1	Cash	50,000	
		Held-to-Maturity Investments—XPS Corporation Bonds		50,000
		Receipt of maturity value of bond investment.		

EXAMPLE EXERCISE 15-4 **Held-to-Maturity Transactions** ②

Journalize the entries to record the following selected held-to-maturity investment transactions for Cooper Ltd., using the effective interest method of amortization:

1. Purchased for cash $3,000,000 of XYZ Corp. 10-year, 6% bonds at 102.25 on their issuance date, January 1. The market rate was 5.7%. The bonds pay interest on July 1 and January 1.
2. Recorded receipt of the first semiannual interest payment and amortization of the premium on July 1.
3. Recorded the adjusting entry for accrued interest and amortization of the premium on December 31, Cooper Ltd.'s year-end.

FOLLOW MY EXAMPLE 15-4

Jan. 1	Held-to-Maturity Investments—XYZ Corp. Bonds	3,067,500.00	
	Cash..		3,067,500.00
	Purchase of $3,000,000 bonds at 102.25.		

(continued)

Jul. 1	Cash	90,000.00*	
	Interest Revenue		87,423.75**
	Held-to-Maturity Investments—XYZ Corp. Bonds....................		2,576.25
	Receipt of semiannual interest and amortization of premium.		
	*$3,000,000 × 6% × ⁶⁄₁₂ = $90,000		
	**$3,067,500 × 5.7%/2		

$*3{,}000{,}000 \times 6\% \times {}^{6}\!/_{12} = \$90{,}000$

Dec. 31	Interest Receivable	90,000.00	
	Interest Revenue		87,350.33*
	Held-to-Maturity Investments—XYZ Corp. Bonds....................		2,649.67
	Accrual of interest and amortization of premium at year-end.		
	*[(3,067,500 − 2,576.25) × 5.7%/2]		

For Practice: PE 15-4

EXAMPLE EXERCISE 15-5   Held-to-Maturity Transactions ②

Using the information from Example Exercise 15-4, journalize the following transactions using the straight-line method of amortization:

1. receipt of the first semiannual interest payment and amortization of the premium on July 1.
2. adjusting entry for accrued interest and amortization of the premium on December 31, Cooper Ltd.'s year-end.

FOLLOW MY EXAMPLE 15-5

Jul. 1	Cash..	90,000*	
	Interest Revenue..		86,625
	Held-to-Maturity Investments–XYZ Corp. Bonds		3,375**
	Receipt of semiannual interest and amortization of premium.		
	*$3,000,000 × 6% × ⁶⁄₁₂ = $90,000		
	**$67,500/20 = $3,375		

Dec. 31	Interest Receivable..	90,000	
	Interest Revenue..		86,625
	Held-to-Maturity Investments–XYZ Corp. Bonds		3,375
	Accrual of interest and amortization of premium at year-end.		

For Practice: PE 15-5

Accounting for Available-for-Sale Investments

Available-for-sale investments are debt and equity securities that are not classified as held-for-trading or held-to-maturity investments. For example, bonds that management

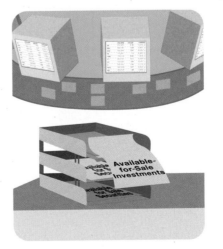

does not intend to hold to maturity may be classified as available-for-sale investments, if they are not held-for-trading.

The accounting for available-for-sale investments is similar to the accounting for held-for-trading investments except for the reporting of changes in fair values. Changes in the fair values of held-for-trading investments are reported as an unrealized holding gain or loss and are included in net income. In contrast, changes in the fair values of available-for-sale investments are excluded from net income but included in other comprehensive income.

Other comprehensive income is applicable only for corporations reporting under IFRS. Corporations reporting under ASPE include any gains or losses from the revaluation of available-for-sale investments in their income statements.

The other difference between held-for-trading investments and available-for-sale investments is that brokerage fees or commissions may be included in the initial cost of the available-for-sale investments, rather than expensed.

To illustrate, assume that on June 21, 2015, Montrose Inc., a publicly traded corporation using IFRS, purchased the following securities as available-for-sale investments, paying $200,000 plus a brokerage fee of $2,500:

Name	Shares	Cost
Carmon Ltd.	1,000	$ 60,000
Rasscom Inc.	1,500	66,000
Normandy Corp.	3,000	74,000
		$200,000

The brokerage fees can be allocated to the investments proportionately. For example, because the Carmon Ltd. investment was 30% ($60,000/$200,000) of the total portfolio, $750 ($2,500 × 30%) of the brokerage fees is allocated to the Carmon investment.

Following the same procedure, the brokerage fees are allocated as follows:

Name	Shares	Cost	Brokerage Fees	Total Cost
Carmon Ltd.	1,000	$ 60,000	$ 750	$ 60,750
Rasscom Inc.	1,500	66,000	825	66,825
Normandy Corp.	3,000	74,000	925	74,925
		$200,000	$2,500	$202,500

The journal entry to record the purchase is as follows:

2015					
Jun.	21	Available-for-Sale Investments—Carmon Ltd.		60,750	
		Available-for-Sale Investments—Rasscom Inc.		66,825	
		Available-for-Sale Investments—Normandy Corp.		74,925	
		Cash			202,500
		Purchased available-for-sale investments.			

On December 31, 2015 the cost and fair values of the securities are as follows:

Name	Shares	Total Cost	Total Fair Value	Change
Carmon Ltd.	1,000	$ 60,750	$ 70,250	$9,500
Rasscom Inc.	1,500	66,825	67,250	425
Normandy Corp.	3,000	74,925	70,500	(4,425)
		$202,500	$208,000	$5,500

The investments are revalued on December 31, 2015, to their fair values, using an adjusting entry. An allowance account can be used here as was discussed in held-for-trading investments. We will revalue the investments directly as follows:

2015					
Dec.	31	Available-for-Sale Investments—Carmon Ltd.		9,500	
		Available-for-Sale Investments—Rasscom Inc.		425	
		Available-for-Sale Investments—Normandy Corp.			4,425
		Unrealized Holding Gain on Available-for-Sale Investments—OCI			5,500
		To revalue available-for-sale investments to fair value.			

Other comprehensive income, which was discussed in Chapter 12, is not applicable for corporations reporting under ASPE. A closing entry is required at year-end to close Other Comprehensive Income (or Loss) to Accumulated Other Comprehensive Income. Accumulated Other Comprehensive Income appears in the shareholders' equity section of the statement of financial position (balance sheet) either immediately before or immediately after Retained Earnings.

Available-for-sale investments are reported as noncurrent assets on the statement of financial position in the same manner as held-to-maturity investments, shown on page 767.

EXAMPLE EXERCISE 15-6   Valuing Available-for-Sale Investments at Fair Value   ②

On December 31, 2015, Rockin' Lizards Ltd., a publicly traded corporation using IFRS, had the following costs and fair values for its available-for-sale investments:

Name	Total Cost	Total Fair Value
Park For You Inc.	$13,900	$ 8,700
Candy Carousel Corp.	8,500	8,900
Blue Meadow Ltd.	9,800	11,200

Journalize the adjusting entry required on December 31, 2015, to recognize these investments at fair value.

FOLLOW MY EXAMPLE 15-6

Name	Total Cost	Total Fair Value	Change in Value
Park For You Inc.	$13,900	$ 8,700	$(5,200)
Candy Carousel Corp.	8,500	8,900	400
Blue Meadow Ltd.	9,800	11,200	1,400
			$(3,400)

2015				
Dec.	31	Available-for-Sale Investments—Candy Carousel Corp.	400	
		Available-for-Sale Investments—Blue Meadow Ltd.	1,400	
		Unrealized Holding Loss on Available-for-Sale Investments—OCI	3,400	
		Available-for-Sale Investments—Park For You Inc.		5,200
		To record decrease in fair value of available-for-sale investments.		

For Practice: PE 15-6

MID-CHAPTER ILLUSTRATIVE PROBLEM

Vanderborg Corporation, a publicly traded corporation using IFRS, had the following transactions relating to securities during 2015. Vanderborg has a fiscal year ending on December 31:

2015

Jan. 10.   Purchased 5,000 Bell Direct Inc. shares for $21 per share as a held-for-trading investment. Brokerage fees of $300 were paid.

May   1.   Purchased $100,000, five-year, 6% ABC Corp. bonds for 90 as a held-to-maturity investment. The bonds pay semiannual interest on May 1 and November 1. The market interest rate on May 1 was 8.5%. Brokerage fees of $500 were paid.

Jun. 1.   Received a $1 cash dividend per Bell Direct Inc. share.

Oct. 3.   Purchased 1,500 Northern Lights Ltd. shares for $18 per share as an available-for-sale investment. Brokerage fees of $250 were paid. Vanderborg Corporation capitalizes brokerage fees on available-for-sale investments.

Nov. 1.   Received semiannual interest on the ABC Corp. bonds and recorded discount amortization.

Nov. 8.   Sold 2,000 Bell Direct Inc. shares for $19 per share and paid brokerage fees of $100.

Dec. 31.   Recorded the adjusting entry for bond interest and discount amortization.

Dec. 31.   The quoted market values of Vanderborg's investments were as follows:

Bell Direct Inc.	$17 per share
ABC Corp.	92
Northern Lights Ltd.	$21 per share

Instructions

1. Journalize the preceding transactions, rounding answers to the nearest dollar.
2. Which journal entries would differ if Vanderborg Corporation reported under ASPE?
3. Prepare the balance sheet disclosure for Vanderborg Corporation's investments on December 31, 2015.

MID-CHAPTER ILLUSTRATIVE SOLUTION

1.

2015				
Jan.	10	Held-for-Trading Investments—Bell Direct Inc.	105,000	
		Brokerage Fees Expense	300	
		Cash		105,300
		Purchased held-for-trading investment.		
May	1	Held-to-Maturity Investments—ABC Corp.	90,500	
		Cash		90,500
		Purchased held-to-maturity investments.		
Jun.	1	Cash	5,000	
		Dividend Revenue		5,000
		Received dividends from Bell Direct Inc.		
Oct.	3	Available-for-Sale Investment—Northern Lights Ltd.	27,250	
		Cash		27,250
		Purchased available-for-sale investment.		

2015					
Nov.	1	Cash		3,000	
		Held-to-Maturity Investments—ABC Corp.		846	
		Interest Revenue			3,846*
		Received semiannual interest on ABC Corp. bonds.			
		*$90,500 × 4.25%			
Nov.	8	Cash		37,900	
		Brokerage Fees Expense		100	
		Loss on Sale of Investment		4,000	
		Held-for-Trading Investments—Bell Direct Inc.			42,000
		Sold 2,000 shares of Bell Direct Inc.			
Dec.	31	Interest Receivable		1,000	
		Held-to-Maturity Investments—ABC Corp.		294	
		Interest Revenue			1,294*
		Accrued interest on ABC Corp. bond.			
		*($90,500 + $846) × 4.25% × 2/6			
Dec.	31	Available-for-Sale Investment—Northern Lights Ltd.		4,250	
		Unrealized Holding Gain on Available-for-Sale			
		Investment—OCI			4,250*
		Revalued available-for-sale investment.			
		*(1,500 shares × $21) − $27,250			
Dec.	31	Unrealized Holding Loss on Held-for-Trading			
		Investment		12,000	
		Held-for-Trading Investments—Bell Direct Inc.			12,000*
		Revalued held-for-trading investment.			
		*(3,000 shares × $17) − ($105,000 − $42,000)			

2.

If Vanderborg Corporation were reporting under ASPE, the journal entry to record the revaluation of the available-for-sale investment in Northern Lights Ltd. would not use Other Comprehensive Income because this account is applicable only under IFRS.

3.

Vanderborg Corporation
Statement of Financial Position (Partial)
December 31, 2015

Assets	
Current assets	
Interest receivable	$ 1,000
Held-for-Trading Investments—Bell Direct Inc.	51,000
Noncurrent assets	
Held-to-Maturity Investments—ABC Corp.	91,640
Available-for-Sale Investment—Northern Lights Ltd.	31,500

Accounting for Strategic Investments

③

Describe and
illustrate the
accounting for
strategic
investments.

A company may invest cash in the common equity of another company as a strategic investment. **Strategic investments** involve the purchase of a significant portion of the shares of another company. Such investments usually have a specific purpose, such as the following:

1. *Reduction of costs*: When one company buys another company, the combined company may be able to reduce administrative expenses. For example, a combined company may not need two chief executive officers (CEOs) or two chief financial officers (CFOs).

2. *Replacement of management*: If the purchased company has been mismanaged, the acquiring company may replace the company's management and, thus, improve operations and profits.

3. *Expansion*: The acquiring company may purchase a company because it has a complementary product line, territory, or customer base. The new combined company may be able to serve customers better than the two companies could separately.

4. *Integration*: A company may integrate operations by acquiring a supplier or customer. Acquiring a supplier may provide a more stable or uninterrupted supply of resources. Acquiring a customer may also provide a market for the company's products or services. For example, integration was Shaw Communication's motivation to purchase Canwest Global Communications.

The company investing in another company's shares is the **investor**. The company whose shares are purchased is the **investee**.

The percentage of the investee's outstanding shares purchased by the investor is considered when determining the investor's degree of control over the investee. An investor who holds 50% +1 voting common share in an investee is said to have control over the decisions made by the board of directors or top management. Such an investor would have more votes than all the other shareholders combined. An investor who holds between 20% and 50% of the common shares of an investee is considered to have significant influence, meaning this investor can sway or persuade, but not control the results of a vote. This percentage, in turn, determines the accounting method used to record the share investment, as shown in Exhibit 1.

The percentage of the investee's outstanding shares owned by the investor is not the only determinant of the degree of control the investor has over the investee. Another determinant of control is the distribution of the remaining outstanding shares. If the remaining shares are widely held, with no other shareholder holding a significant amount, the shareholder with more than 20% may be considered to have effective control. In addition, a shareholder could also own a major purchaser or supplier of the company's products, or have the ability to appoint members to the board of directors, giving such a shareholder effective control. Under IFRS, if one shareholder effectively controls the corporation, despite having less than 50% of the voting shares, the situation is treated as one of control, which is discussed later in the chapter.

Exhibit 1

Share Investments

Degree of Control of Investor over Investee	Percentage of Outstanding Shares Owned by Investor	Accounting Method
No control	Less than 20%	Fair value method
Significant influence	Between 20% and 50%	Equity method
Control	Greater than 50%	Consolidation

An investor may hold more than 20% of the common shares and not have significant influence. If, for example, the balance of the shares were held by one individual, the 20% investor may not have any involvement in the day-to-day operations or decisions of the company. Equally, an investor with less than 20% of the common shares could significantly influence an investee if, for example, the remaining shares were widely held.

The 20% measure is not a hard-and-fast ruling; instead, professional judgment should be used to determine whether an investor has significant influence over an investee, in which case the equity method should be used. If the investor has no significant influence, the investment is classified, and accounted for, as held-for-trading or available-for-sale. Because some investments, such as those in the 15% to 25% range, could be accounted for by various methods, we will identify the method to use in exercises and problems for this chapter.

Classifications of Strategic Investments

Under IFRS, strategic investments are categorized into one of three different classifications as follows:

1. **Investment in associate**—an investor that holds between 20% and 50% of the voting common equity of an investee.
2. **Joint venture**—two corporations that operate as one, with joint control, for the purpose of completing a project or operating a distinct aspect of their respective businesses.
3. **Business combination**—an investor that holds 50% or more of an investee's voting common shares.

Accounting For Investments in Associates

If the investor purchases between 20% and 50% of the outstanding voting common shares of the investee, the investor is usually considered to have a significant influence over the investee. In this case, the investor is assumed to have purchased the shares primarily for strategic reasons, such as developing a supplier relationship.

Because the investor can influence the investee, a more realistic reflection of the investor's ability to direct the company is to include the investor's share of the investee's earnings in the investor's income for the year, not just the dividends received.

Most investments of between 20% and 50% of the investee's outstanding shares are accounted for under the equity method.[1]

Under the **equity method**, the shares are recorded initially at cost, and then adjusted for the investor's share of the *net income* and *dividends* of the investee. These adjustments are as follows:

1. *Net Income:* The investor records its share of the net income of the investee as an increase in the investment account. Its share of any net loss is recorded as a decrease in the investment account.
2. *Dividends:* The investor's share of cash dividends received from the investee decreases the investment account.

Purchase of Shares To illustrate, assume that Simpson Inc. purchased a 40% interest in Flanders Corporation's common shares on January 2, 2015, for $350,000. The entry to record the purchase is as follows:

2015					
Jan.	2	Investment in Flanders Corporation Shares		350,000	
		Cash			350,000
		Purchased 40% of Flanders Corporation shares.			

---

1 ASPE allow an enterprise to account for significantly influenced investments using either the cost or equity method.

Recording Investee Net Income For the year ended December 31, 2015, Flanders Corporation reported net income of $105,000. Under the equity method, Simpson Inc. (the investor) records its share of Flanders net income as follows:

2015				
Dec.	31	Investment in Flanders Corporation Shares	42,000	
		Investment Revenue		42,000
		Record 40% share of Flanders Corporation net income ($105,000 × 40%).		

Investment Revenue is reported on Simpson Inc.'s income statement as part of *Other income.*

Recording Investee Dividends At the end of the year, Flanders declared and paid cash dividends of $45,000. Under the equity method, Simpson Inc. (the investor) records its share of Flanders dividends as follows:

2015				
Dec.	31	Cash	18,000	
		Investment in Flanders Corporation Shares		18,000
		Record 40% share of Flanders Corporation dividends ($45,000 × 40%).		

The effect of recording 40% of Flanders Corporation's net income and dividends is to increase the investment account by $24,000 ($42,000 − $18,000). Thus, Investment in Flanders Corporation Shares increases from $350,000 to $374,000, as shown below.

Investment and Dividends

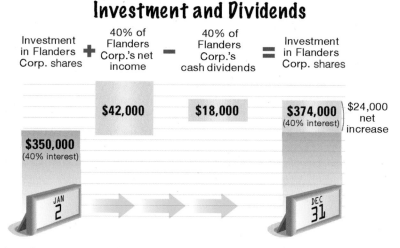

Under the equity method, the investment account reflects the investor's proportional changes in the net carrying value of the investee. For example, Flanders Corporation's net carrying value increased by $60,000 (net income of $105,000 less dividends of $45,000) during the year. As a result, Simpson's share of Flanders' net carrying value increased by $24,000 ($60,000 × 40%).

Reporting of Investments in Associates Investments in associates are reported as noncurrent assets on the balance sheet. On December 31, 2015, Simpson Inc. would report its investment in Flanders Corporation as follows:

Simpson Inc.
Statement of Financial Position (Partial)
December 31, 2015

Noncurrent assets
  Investment in Flanders Corporation Shares—at equity $374,000

Sale of Shares Under the equity method, a gain or loss is normally recorded from the sale of an investment. A gain is recorded if the proceeds exceed the *carrying value* of the investment. A loss is recorded if the proceeds are less than the *carrying value* of the investment. The gain or loss on sale is reported as other income or expense on the income statement.

To illlustrate, if Simpson Inc. sold Flanders Corporation's shares on January 1, 2016, for $400,000, a gain of $26,000 would be reported, as shown below.

Proceeds from sale	$400,000
Carrying value of share investment	374,000
Gain on sale	$ 26,000

The entry to record the sale is as follows:

2016				
Jan.	1	Cash	40,000	
		Investment in Flanders Corporation Shares		374,000
		Gain on Sale of Flanders Corporation Shares		26,000
		Sale of Flanders Corporation shares.		

EXAMPLE EXERCISE 15-7 Equity Method ③

On January 2, Olson Ltd. acquired 35% of the outstanding common shares of Bryant Corp. for $140,000. For the year ended December 31, Bryant Corp. earned income of $44,000 and paid dividends of $20,000. Using the equity method, prepare the entries for Olson Ltd. for the purchase of the shares, Olson's share of Bryant income, and the dividends received from Bryant Corp.

FOLLOW MY EXAMPLE 15-7

Jan. 2	Investment in Bryant Corp. Shares	140,000	
	Cash		140,000
	Purchased 35% of Bryant Corp. shares.		
Dec. 31	Investment in Bryant Corp. Shares	15,400*	
	Investment Revenue		15,400
	Record 35% of Bryant income.		
	*35% × $44,000		
Dec. 31	Cash	7,000**	
	Investment in Bryant Corp. Shares		7,000
	Record 35% share of Bryant Corp. dividends.		
	**35% × $20,000		

For Practice: PE 15-7

CRITICAL THINKING

Is it possible to own less than 50% of the common shares and still have control of a corporation?

Yes. It is possible that a shareholder holds less than 50% of the common shares but still effectively controls the corporation. One shareholder, for instance, could own 25% of the common shares while the remaining 75% are widely disbursed with no other shareholder holding a significant amount. A shareholder could also have control in other ways, such as owning a major purchaser or supplier of the company's products, or having the ability to appoint members to the board of directors. Under IFRS, the principle of representational faithfulness suggests the accounting treatment must reflect the substance of the situation more than the form. Thus, if one shareholder effectively controls the corporation, despite having less than 50% of the voting shares, the accounting would treat the situation as one of control.

Accounting for Joint Ventures

Often two or more corporations will enter into a contractual obligation for the purpose of a special project. Separately, each corporation may not have the resources required to complete the project, but they may be able to combine their resources. Two or more corporations may form a separate corporation to operate a joint venture. A unique aspect of joint ventures is the decision-making process. Decisions are made jointly, with equal votes for the venturers, regardless of the shareholding percentage held by the individual joint venturers. None of the individual venturers has control over the joint venture.

IFRS requires joint venturers to account for the joint venture using either the proportionate consolidation method or the equity method. ASPE requires joint ventures to be accounted for using either the proportionate consolidation method, the equity method, or the cost method. Proportionate consolidation requires the recognition of the joint venturer's proportionate share of the assets, liabilities, and net income of the joint venture. The accounting for joint ventures, including proportionate consolidation, is described and illustrated in advanced accounting courses and textbooks.

Accounting for Business Combinations

If an investor purchases more than 50% of the outstanding voting shares of an investee, the investor is considered to have control over the investee. In this case, it is assumed that the investor purchased the shares of the investee primarily for strategic reasons.

The purchase of more than 50% ownership of the investee's shares is termed a business combination. Companies may choose to combine to produce more efficiently, to diversify product lines, to expand geographically, or to acquire know-how.

It is possible for a shareholder to have effective control over a corporation with less than 50% ownership of the shares, if the remaining shares are widely held, as noted earlier in the chapter. Under IFRS, this situation would be accounted for using the same treatment as business combinations.

A corporation owning all or a majority of the voting shares of another corporation is called a **parent company**. The corporation that is controlled is called the **subsidiary company**.

Parent and subsidiary corporations often continue to maintain separate accounting records and prepare their own financial statements. In such cases, at the end of the year, the financial statements of the parent and subsidiary are combined and reported as a single company. These combined financial statements are called **consolidated financial statements**. Such statements are normally identified by adding *Consolidated* to the title of the parent corporation's statements.

To the external shareholders of the parent company, consolidated financial statements are more meaningful than separate statements for each corporation because the parent company, in substance, controls the subsidiaries. The accounting for business combinations, including preparing consolidated financial statements, is described and illustrated in advanced accounting courses and textbooks.

Reporting of Investments

Exhibit 2 summarizes the valuation and balance sheet reporting of held-for-trading, held-to-maturity, and available-for-sale investments, and loans and receivables.

Exhibit 2

Summary of Valuing and Reporting of Investments

	Held-for-Trading Investments	Held-to-Maturity Investments	Available-for-Sale Investments, Loans, and Receivables
Valued at	Fair value	Amortized cost	Fair value
Types of securities	Shares and bonds	Bonds only	Shares and bonds
Reporting of changes in valuation	Unrealized holding gain or loss is reported on income statement as *Other income (loss)*.	Premium or discount amortization is reported as part of interest revenue on the income statement using the effective interest method if reporting under IFRS, or the effective method or straight-line method if reporting under ASPE.	Under IFRS: Unrealized holding gain or loss is recorded as *Other comprehensive income* and reported in *Accumulated other comprehensive income* in the shareholders' equity. Under ASPE: Gains or losses resulting from year-end revaluations are reported on the income statement.
Reporting on the balance sheet	Fair value of investments	Amortized cost of investment	Fair value of investments
Classification on the balance sheet	A current asset	Either as a current or noncurrent asset, depending on time to maturity	Either as a current or noncurrent asset, depending on management's intent
Brokerage fees	Expensed	Included in cost of investment or expensed	Included in cost of investment or expensed
Treatment of impairment of investment	Loss is reported on income statement as *Other loss*.	Loss is reported on income statement as *Other loss*.	Loss is recorded as *Other comprehensive income* and reported as *Accumulated other comprehensive income* in the shareholders' equity.

The statement of financial position reporting for the investments of Morning Java International, using IFRS, is shown below.

Morning Java International invests in held-for-trading investments, shown as financial assets at fair value through profit or loss, and does not have held-to-maturity investments or available-for-sale investments. Morning Java International also owns 40% of AM Coffee Corporation, which is accounted for using the equity method. Morning Java intends to keep its investment in AM Coffee indefinitely for strategic reasons; thus, its investment in AM Coffee is classified as a noncurrent asset.

Morning Java International
Statement of Financial Position
December 31, 2015

Assets

Current assets:

Cash and cash equivalents....................................		$ 235,000
Financial assets at fair value through profit or loss		465,000
Accounts receivable, net		292,700
Inventory—at lower of cost (first-in, first-out) and realizable value		120,000
Prepaid insurance		24,000
Total current assets		$1,136,700

Noncurrent assets

Property, plant, and equipment....................................			
Land and buildings at fair value.............................	$4,500,000		
Less: Accumulated depreciation	375,200	4,124,800	
Office equipment at cost	350,000		
Less: Accumulated depreciation	102,000	248,000	
Patents at amortized cost		140,000	
Investment in AM Coffee (equity method)		565,000	
Total noncurrent assets			5,077,800
Total assets			$6,214,500

Morning Java International reported investment revenue from AM Coffee of $57,000 as Share in profit (loss) of associates, and an Unrealized Holding Gain on Held-for-Trading Investments of $5,000 as part of Other income (expenses) on its statement of comprehensive income as shown below:

For Morning Java financial statements reporting under ASPE, refer to Appendix A.

Morning Java International
Statement of Comprehensive Income
For the Year Ended December 31, 2015

Sales (net).....................................	$ 5,402,100
Cost of merchandise sold	(2,160,000)
Gross profit......................................	3,242,100
Selling expenses....................................	(1,654,700)
Administrative expenses	(954,000)
Loss on disposal of fixed asset	(23,000)
Other income (expenses)	23,000
Share in profit (loss) of associates	57,000
Operating profit....................................	690,400
Finance costs	(136,000)
Profit before income tax	554,400
Tax expense	(132,800)
Profit for the year.................................	421,600
Other comprehensive income	
Gain on revaluation of properties	44,800
Total comprehensive income for the year, net of tax	$ 466,400
Earnings per share, basic	$ 9.58

FINANCIAL ANALYSIS AND INTERPRETATION

The dividend yield indicates the rate of return to shareholders in terms of cash dividend distributions. Although the dividend yield can be computed for both preferred and common shares, it is more often computed for common shares. This is because most preferred shares have a stated dividend rate or amount. In contrast, the amount of common dividends normally varies with the profitability of the corporation.

The dividend yield is computed by dividing the annual dividends paid per common share by the market price per share at a specific date, as shown below.

$$\text{Dividend Yield} = \frac{\textbf{Annual Dividends per Share}}{\textbf{Market Price per Share}}$$

To illustrate, the market price of Shaw Communications Inc. common shares was $19.37 as at the close of business, June 27, 2012. During the past year, Shaw Communications Inc. has paid dividends of $0.90 per common share. Thus, the dividend yield of Shaw Communications Inc. common share is 4.65% ($0.90/$19.37). Because the market price of a corporation's shares will vary from day to day, its dividend yield

will also vary from day to day. Fortunately, the dividend yield is provided in the newspaper listings of market prices and by most Internet quotation services, such as from Yahoo!'s Finance website.

The recent dividend yields for some selected companies are as follows:

Company	Dividend Yield (%)
Enerflex Systems Income Fund	2.29
General Motors Corporation	None
Hewlett-Packard Development Company	2.73
Power Financial Corporation	5.51
Research In Motion	None
Suncor Energy Ltd.	1.88
Toronto-Dominion Bank	3.68

As can be seen, the dividend yield varies widely across firms. Growth companies often do not pay dividends but, instead, reinvest their earnings in research and marketing, which is the case with Research In Motion, the Canadian maker of BlackBerry® smartphones.

EXAMPLE EXERCISE 15-8   Dividend Yield
5

On September 25, 2015, Lucas Corporation had a market price per common share of $8. For the previous year, Lucas paid an annual dividend of $0.16. Compute the dividend yield for Lucas Corporation.

FOLLOW MY EXAMPLE 15-8

$$\text{Dividend Yield} = \frac{\text{Annual Dividends per Share}}{\text{Market Price per Share}}$$

$$= \frac{\$0.16}{\$8} = 2\%$$

For Practice: PE 15-8

A P P E N D I X   1

Accounting for Non-Strategic Investments Using International Financial Reporting Standard (IFRS) 9

As mentioned in the chapter, International Financial Reporting Standards are evolving. Until January 1, 2015, corporations can account for their non-strategic investments using International Accounting Standard (IAS) 39, which categorizes investments into one of four classifications. Effective January 1, 2015, International Financial Reporting Standard (IFRS) 9 will replace IAS 39, although this adoption date may be delayed until 2017. IFRS 9 classifies non-strategic investments into one of two classifications:

1. *Investments at amortized cost*—Investments that consist of the contractual receipt of principal and interest, when the company's intent is to hold the investment for the purpose of collecting interest.[2]
2. *Investments at fair value*—Debt and equity security purchases that are not classified as investments at amortized cost.[3]

The ASPE definition for investments at amortized cost (or at cost) includes unquoted equity investments and those investments not classified at fair value. Examples of unquoted equity instruments are shares of private corporations, which are not traded in an active market, treasury bills, and guaranteed investment certificates (GICs). Because these investments have no readily available fair value, they will be measured at cost, or the price originally paid for the investment.

Under ASPE, investments at fair value are quoted equity instruments only. These investments exclude bond investments, which are debt instruments.

Investments at Amortized Cost

Investments at amortized cost pay interest and repay principal at the end of the life of the instrument. Two examples are bonds and notes receivable. Because equity securities pay dividends and are never contractual, they are not measured at amortized cost.

Management's intent must be to hold the securities for the purpose of collecting interest. If management intends to sell the security quickly to recognize a gain on the change in market value, the security is not classified as an investment at amortized cost.

Investments at amortized cost are accounted for in the same manner as held-to-maturity investments. Brokerage fees paid to purchase the investments are capitalized at the time of the purchase. IFRS 9 requires corporations to use the effective interest method of amortizing the discount or premium.

Investments at Fair Value

Investments at fair value are all investments that are not classified as investments at amortized cost. Investments at fair value include equity investments and debt investments that are purchased with the intent of realizing a profit from the change in market value.

Investments at fair value are initially recorded at the price paid for the investment. They are adjusted to their market value at year-end, and any differences are recorded as an unrealized holding gain or loss. Because market value is used to revalue the asset at year-end, securities traded in an open market are classified as investments at fair value. Any brokerage fees paid to purchase the investments are expensed at the time of purchase.

Corporations reporting under IFRS 9 have two options when revaluing their investments at year-end. They can revalue them using either the fair value through profit and loss (fair value) method or the fair value through other comprehensive income (OCI) method. Fair value through profit and loss adjusts the value of the investment to its market value at year-end on the income statement, in the same manner as used for held-for-trading investments.

Corporations may purchase equity investments with the intent to hold them for earning dividends, rather than trading them quickly. Corporations may elect to revalue some or all of these investments using the fair value through other comprehensive income method, in the same manner as used for available-for-sale investments.

Corporations may elect to revalue all their investments using the same method, or they may elect different methods on an investment-by-investment basis. Whichever option the corporation elects to use, the decision is irrevocable. That is, corporations that elect to report the gain or loss through other comprehensive income may not later elect to report the gain or loss in the income statement, and vice versa.

2 *CICA Handbook—Accounting*, 2013, Part 1, IFRS 9, para. 4.1.2.

3 *CICA Handbook—Accounting*, 2013, Part 1, IFRS 9, para. 4.1.4.

At a Glance 15

1   Describe why companies invest in debt and equity securities.

Key Points	Key Learning Outcomes	Page	Example Exercises
Cash can be used to (1) invest in current operations, (2) invest to earn additional revenue, or (3) invest for strategic reasons. Strategic investments are made to reduce costs, replace management, expand, or integrate operations.	• Describe the ways excess cash is used by a business.	760	
	• Describe the purpose of non-strategic investments.	761	
	• Describe the strategic purpose of investments.	761	

2   Describe and illustrate the accounting for non-strategic investments.

Key Points	Key Learning Outcomes	Page	Example Exercises
Non-strategic investments are investments made for the purpose of earning additional revenues through the receipt of dividend or interest income. Depending on management's intent at the time of purchase, non-strategic investments are classified as held-for-trading investments, held-to-maturity investments, loans and receivables, or available-for-sale investments.	• Describe held-for-trading investments.	762	
	• Prepare journal entries to account for held-for-trading investments.	762	15-1 15-2
Held-for-trading invest-ments are debt and equity securities purchased and sold to earn short-term profits on the change in market price. Held-to-maturity investments are debt securities that are intended to be held until their maturity date. Loans and receivables are accounted for in much the same manner as held-to-maturity investments. Available-for-sale investments are debt and equity securities that are not classified as either held-for-trading investments or held-to-maturity investments.	• Describe held-to-maturity investments.	765	
	• Prepare journal entries to account for held-to-maturity investments.	767	15-3
	• Amortize the bond premium or discount on held-to-maturity investments using the effective, and straight-line methods.	768	15-4 15-5
	• Describe available-for-sale investments.	771	
	• Prepare journal entries to account for available-for-sale investments.	772	15-6

3 Describe and illustrate the accounting for strategic investments.

Key Points	Key Learning Outcomes	Page	Example Exercises
Strategic investments are made to reduce costs, replace management, expand operations, or integrate operations. Strategic investments are classified as investments in associates, joint ventures, or business combinations.	• Describe the accounting for investments of varying degrees of control.	776	
	• Prepare journal entries to account for investments in associates using the equity method.	777	15-7
Investments in associates involve the purchase of a significant portion of another company's outstanding common shares, usually 20% to 50% ownership. Joint ventures arise when two or more companies join together to complete a special project. Business combinations exist when one company, the parent, has control over another company, the subsidiary, through the purchase of more than 50% of the investee's common shares.	• Describe a joint venture.	780	
	• Describe a business combination, parent company, and subsidiary company.	780	
	• Describe and illustrate the reporting of investments on the balance sheet.	780	
	• Calculate and interpret a company's dividend yield.	783	15-8

GLOSSARY

available-for-sale investments – Debt and equity securities that are not classified as held-for-trading or held-to maturity investments. (p. 762)

business combination – One corporation's acquisition of a controlling share (greater than 50%) of the outstanding voting shares of another corporation, typically by paying cash or exchanging shares. (p. 777)

consolidated financial statements – Financial statements that result from combining the financial statements of the parent company with those of its subsidiary companies. (p. 780)

debt securities – Notes and bond investments that provide interest revenue over a fixed maturity. (p. 761)

equity method – A method of accounting for an investment in common shares in which the shares are first recorded at cost and then adjusted for the investor's share of periodic net income and for the cash dividends of the investee. (p. 777)

equity securities – The common and preferred shares of a firm. (p. 761)

fair value through profit and loss method – An accounting method used to revalue held-for-trading and available-for-sale investments to their market value at year-end. (p. 762)

held-for-trading investments – Debt and equity securities that are purchased and sold to earn short-term profits from changes in their market prices. (p. 762)

held-to-maturity investments – Investments in bonds or other debt securities that management intends to hold to their maturity. (p. 762)

investee – The company whose shares are purchased by the investor. (p. 776)

investment in associate – an investor that holds between 20% and 50% of the voting common equity of an investee. (p. 777)

investor – The company that invests in another company's shares. (p. 776)

joint venture – two corporations that operate as one, with joint control, for the purpose of completing a project

or operating a distinct aspect of their respective businesses. (p. 777)

loans and receivables – Loans made for the purpose of receiving fixed interest revenue. (p. 762)

non-strategic investment – An investment made for the purpose of gaining additional revenue through interest, dividends, or a change in market value. (p. 761)

parent company – The corporation owning all or a majority of the voting shares of the other corporation. (p. 780)

strategic investments – Investments involving the purchase of a significant portion of the shares of another company. (p. 776)

subsidiary company – The corporation that is controlled by a parent company. (p. 780)

unrealized holding gain or loss – Any difference resulting from changes in the fair value of held-for-trading investments and available-for-sale investments for a period. (p. 762)

ILLUSTRATIVE PROBLEM

The following selected investment transactions were completed by Rosewell Ltd. during 2015, its first year of operations:

2015

Jan. 11.   Purchased 800 Bryan Inc. shares as an available-for-sale investment at $23 per share plus an $80 brokerage commission.

Feb. 6.   Purchased $40,000 of 8% RTG Ltd. bonds at par value plus accrued interest for 36 days. The bonds pay interest on January 1 and July 1. The bonds were classified as held-to-maturity investments.

Mar. 3.   Purchased 1,900 Cohen Corp. shares as a held-for-trading investment at $48 per share plus a $152 brokerage commission.

Apr. 5.   Purchased 2,400 Lyons Ltd. shares as an available-for-sale investment at $68 per share plus a $120 brokerage commission.

May 12.   Purchased 200,000 Myers Inc. shares at $37 per share plus an $8,000 brokerage commission. Myers Inc. has 800,000 common shares issued and outstanding. The equity method was used for this investment.

Jul. 1.   Received semiannual interest on bonds purchased on February 6.

Aug. 29.   Sold 1,200 Cohen Corp. shares at $61 per share less a $90 brokerage commission.

Oct. 5.   Received an $0.80-per-share dividend on Bryan Inc. shares.

Nov. 11.   Received a $1.10-per-share dividend on Myers Inc. shares.

16.   Purchased 3,000 Morningside Ltd. shares as a held-for-trading investment for $52 per share plus a $150 brokerage commission.

Dec. 31.   Accrued interest on February 6 bonds.

31.   Recorded Rosewell's share of Myers Inc. earnings of $146,000 for the year.

31.   Prepared adjusting entries for the portfolios of held-for-trading and available-for-sale investments based upon the following fair values (share prices):

Bryan Inc.	$21
Cohen Corp.	43
Lyons Ltd.	88
Myers Inc.	40
Morningside Ltd.	45

Instructions

1. Journalize the preceding transactions, rounding answers to the nearest dollar.
2. Prepare the statement of financial position disclosure for Rosewell Ltd's. investments on December 31, 2015.

Solution

1.

2015				
Jan.	11	Available-for-Sale Investments—Bryan Inc.	18,480*	
		Cash		18,480
		Purchased 800 Bryan Inc. shares as an		
		available-for-sale investment.		
		*(800 shares × $23 per share) + $80		

Feb.	6	Held-to-Maturity Investments—RTG Ltd. Bonds	40,000	
		Interest Receivable	316*	
		Cash		40,316
		Purchased $40,000 RTG Ltd. bonds as a		
		held-to-maturity investment.		
		*$40,000 × 8% × (36 days/365 days)		

Mar.	3	Held-for-Trading Investments—Cohen Corp.	91,200*	
		Brokerage Fees Expense	152	
		Cash		91,352
		Purchased 1,900 Cohen Corp. shares as a		
		held-for-trading investment.		
		*(1,900 shares × $48 per share)		

Apr.	5	Available-for-Sale Investments—Lyons Ltd.	163,320*	
		Cash		163,320
		Purchased 2,400 Lyons Ltd. shares as an		
		avaliable-for-sale investment.		
		*(2,400 shares × $68 per share) + $120		

May	12	Investment in Myers Inc. Shares	7,408,000*	
		Cash		7,408,000
		Purchased 200,000 Myers Inc. shares as a strategic		
		investment.		
		*(200,000 shares × $37 per share) + $8,000		

Jul.	1	Cash	1,600*	
		Interest Receivable		316
		Interest Revenue		1,284
		Received semiannual interest on RTG bonds.		
		*($40,000 × 8% × ½)		

2015				
Aug.	29	Cash	73,110*	
		Held-for-Trading Investments—Cohen Corp.		57,600**
		Gain on Sale of Investments		15,510
		Sold 1,200 Cohen Corp. shares.		
		*(1,200 shares × $61 per share) − $90		
		**[1,200 shares × ($91,200/1,900 shares)]		

Oct.	5	Cash	640*	
		Dividend Revenue		640
		Received dividend on Bryan Inc. shares.		
		*(800 shares × $0.80 per share)		

Nov.	11	Cash	220,000*	
		Investment in Myers Inc. Shares		220,000
		Received dividend on Myers Inc. shares.		
		*(200,000 shares × $1.10 per share)		

Nov.	16	Held-for-Trading Investments—Morningside Ltd.	156,000*	
		Brokerage Fees Expense	150	
		Cash		156,150
		Purchased 3,000 Morningside Ltd. shares as a		
		held-for-trading investment.		
		*(3,000 shares × $52 per share)		

Dec.	31	Interest Receivable	1,600*	
		Interest Revenue		1,600
		Accrued interest on RTG Ltd. bonds.		
		*($40,000 × 8% × ½)		

Dec.	31	Investment in Myers Inc. Shares	36,500*	
		Investment Revenue		36,500
		Record equity income.		
		*[$146,000 × (200,000 shares/800,000 shares)]		

Dec.	31	Unrealized Holding Loss on Held-for-Trading Investment	24,500	
		Held-for-Trading Investments—Cohen Corp.		3,500
		Held-for-Trading Investments—Morningside Ltd.		21,000
		Record decrease in fair value of held-for-trading		
		investments.		

Name	Number of Shares	Total Cost	Total Fair Value	Change
Cohen Corp.	700	$ 33,600	$ 30,100	$ (3,500)
Morningside Ltd.	3,000	156,000	135,000	(21,000)
		$189,600	$165,100	$(24,500)

Note: Myers Inc. is valued using the equity method; thus, the fair value is not used.

2015				
Dec.	31	Available-for-Sale Investments—Lyons Ltd.	47,880	
		Available-for-Sale Investments—Bryan Inc.		1,680
		Unrealized Holding Gain on Available-for-Sale		46,200
		Investment—OCI		
		Record change in fair value of available-for-sale		
		investments.		

Name	Number of Shares	Total Cost	Total Fair Value	Change
Bryan Inc.	800	$ 18,480	$ 16,800	$ (1,680)
Lyons Ltd.	2,400	163,320	211,200	47,880
		$181,800	$228,000	$46,200

2.

Rosewell Ltd.
Statement of Financial Position (Partial)
December 31, 2015

Current assets:
Cash . . . . $ xxx,xxx
Interest receivable.   1,600
Held-for-trading investments—at fair value   165,100

Noncurrent assets:
Available-for-sale investments—at fair value   228,000
Held-to-maturity investments—at amortized cost.   40,000
Investment in Myers Inc. shares—at equity   7,224,500

Shareholders' Equity
Accumulated other comprehensive income   46,200

EYE OPENERS

1. Why might a business invest in another company's shares?
2. What are the four classifications of non-strategic investments?
3. How are brokerage commissions treated under the fair value method of accounting for equity investments?
4. If a bond is purchased between interest payment periods, how is the accrued interest treated?
5. Why does a gain or loss result from the sale of a bond investment?
6. What is the major difference in the accounting for a portfolio of held-for-trading investments and a portfolio of available-for-sale investments?
7. Are held-to-maturity investments (a) equity investments, (b) debt investments, or (c) both?
8. How is a debit balance in Unrealized Holding Gain (Loss) on Available-for-Sale Investments disclosed in the financial statements?
9. What would cause Unrealized Holding Gain (Loss) on Available-for-Sale Investments to change from a $12,000 debit balance at the beginning of the year to a $1,000 credit balance at the end of the year?
10. What are the three classifications of strategic investments?
11. When is the fair value method appropriate for accounting for equity investments?
12. How does the fair value method of accounting for a received dividend differ from the equity method?
13. How is the income of the investor affected by equity method investments?
14. If an investor owns more than 50% of an investee, how is this ownership treated on the investor's financial statements?
15. Google Inc. purchased all of the outstanding common shares of YouTube. Which is the parent company and which is the subsidiary company in this transaction?

PRACTICE EXERCISES

PE 15-1
②
Valuing
held-for-trading
investments at
fair value

On December 31, 2015, Cosmetics for Animals Ltd. had the following costs and fair values for its held-for-trading investments:

Name	Total Cost	Total Fair Value
Rock Bingo Inc.	$11,300	$13,500
Pebble Beech Corp.	4,500	6,000
Red Sun Inc.	1,000	800

EE 15-1 p. 764

Journalize the adjusting entry required on December 31, 2015, to recognize these investments at fair value.

PE 15-2
②
Journalizing the
sale of held-for-trading
investments

On January 18, 2016, Cosmetics for Animals Ltd. sold half of its investment in Pebble Beech Corp. The full investment was reduced to its fair value of $6,000 on December 31, 2015. Cosmetics for Animals received $2,500 less a $300 brokerage fee.

Journalize the entry required on January 18, 2016, to record the sale of this investment.

EE 15-2 p. 765

PE 15-3
②
Held-to-maturity
transactions

Journalize the entries to record the following selected held-to-maturity investment transactions for Oregon Technologies Inc:

Oct. 21.   Purchased for cash $100,000 of Krump Industries Ltd. 7% bonds at 100 plus accrued interest of $1,750.

Nov. 30.   Received the semiannual interest payment on the Krump Industries Ltd. bonds.

EE 15-3 p. 768

Dec. 31.   Accrued interest on the Krump Industries Ltd. bonds.

PE 15-4
②
Held-to-maturity
transactions

Journalize the entries to record the following selected held-to-maturity investment transactions for Green Corp.:

1. Purchased for cash $2,000,000 of ABC Corp. eight-year, 5% bonds at 98.98 on their issuance date, January 1. The market rate was 5.2%.
2. Recorded receipt of the first semiannual interest payment and amortization of the discount on July 1, using the effective interest method.
3. Recorded the adjusting entry for accrued interest and amortization of the discount on December 31, Green Corp.'s year-end.

EE 15-4 p. 770

✔ Jul. 1,
Held-to-maturity
investments, ABC
bonds, $1,470

PE 15-5
②
Held-to-maturity
transactions

Using the information from Practice Exercise 15-4, journalize the following transactions using the straight-line method of amortization:

1. Receipt of the first semiannual interest payment and amortization of the discount on July 1.
2. The adjusting entry for accrued interest and amortization of the discount on December 31, Green Corp.'s year-end.

EE 15-5 p. 771

✔ Jul. 1
Held-to-maturity
investments, ABC
bonds, $1,275

② PE 15-6

Valuing available-for-sale transactions at fair value

EE 15-6 p. 773

On December 31, 2015, Cookin' Pans Ltd., a publicly traded corporation using IFRS, had the following costs and fair values for its available-for-sale investments:

Name	Total Cost	Total Fair Value
BusIt Inc.	$11,100	$ 8,700
Caramel Dream Corp.	6,500	8,900
Black Shirt Ltd.	8,900	11,200

Journalize the adjusting entry required on December 31, 2015, to recognize these investments at fair value.

③ PE 15-7

Equity method

EE 15-7 p. 779

On January 2, Leonard Ltd. acquired 30% of the outstanding shares of Bristol Inc. for $350,000. For the year ended December 31, Bristol Inc. earned income of $90,000 and paid dividends of $28,000. Prepare the entries for Leonard Ltd. for the purchase of the shares, the portion of Bristol income, and dividends received from Bristol Inc., using the equity method.

③ PE 15-8

Dividend yield

f·a·i

EE 15-8 p. 783

On June 12, 2015, Eastern Power and Electric Ltd.'s common shares had a market price of $48 per share. For the previous year, Eastern Power and Electric paid an annual dividend of $2.88. Compute the dividend yield for Eastern Power and Electric Ltd.

EXERCISES

② EX 15-1

Entries for held-for-trading investments, receipt of dividends, and sale of shares

✔ c. Gain on sale of investments, $10,385

On March 13, Android Corporation acquired 4,500 shares of the 100,000 outstanding Tannis Inc. common shares at $32 per share plus brokerage fees of $250. On August 16, a cash dividend of $1.20 per share was received. On December 8, 1,500 shares were sold at $39 per share, less brokerage fees of $115.

Record the entries for (a) the purchase of shares, (b) the receipt of dividends, and (c) the sale of 1,500 shares. These shares were classified as held-for-trading investments.

② EX 15-2

Entries for held-for-trading investments, dividends, and sale of shares

✔ Nov. 14, Dividend revenue, $150

Plumbline Tech Corp. manufactures surveying equipment. Journalize the entries to record the following selected held-for-trading investment transactions completed by Plumbline during 2015:

Feb. 2. Purchased for cash 900 Devon Ltd. shares for $54 per share plus a $450 brokerage commission.

Apr. 16. Received dividends of $0.25 per Devon Ltd. share.

Jun. 17. Purchased 600 Devon Ltd. shares for $65 per share plus a $300 brokerage commission.

Aug. 19. Sold 1,000 Devon Ltd. shares for $70 per share less a $500 brokerage commission.

Nov. 14. Received dividends of $0.30 per Devon Ltd. share.

② EX 15-3

Entries for held-for-trading investment, interest, and sale of bonds

✔ Dec. 1, Loss on sale of investments, $20

Lance Co. purchased $36,000 of 6%, 10-year Flin Flon City bonds on March 12, 2014, directly from the city at face value as a held-for-trading investment. The bonds pay semiannual interest on May 1 and November 1. On December 1, 2014, Lance Co. sold $14,000 of the Flin Flon City bonds at 102 plus $69 accrued interest, less a $300 brokerage commission.

Provide the journal entries, rounding answers to the nearest dollar, for the following:

a. The purchase of the bonds on March 12, plus 131 days of accrued interest.
b. The semiannual interest on May 1 and November 1.
c. The sale of the bonds on December 1.
d. The adjusting entry for accrued interest of two months on December 31.

---

② EX 15-4

Interest on held-for-trading investments

✔ Total interest earned, 2015, $4,060.48

On May 20, 2015, Haist Inc. purchased $105,000 of 7%, 10-year Asher Corp. bonds at par plus 49 days' accrued interest. The bonds pay interest on April 1 and October 1. On November 1, 2015, Haist Inc. sold $40,000 of the Asher Corp. bonds acquired on May 20 at 98, plus 31 days' accrued interest. On December 31, 2015, 91 days' interest was accrued for the remaining bonds.

1. Journalize the transactions on May 20, October 1, November 1, and December 31.
2. Determine the interest earned by Haist Inc. on Asher Corp. bonds for 2015.

---

② EX 15-5

Fair value journal entries, held-for-trading investments

The investments of Commerce Co. Ltd. include 12,000 RadTek Ltd. common shares purchased on February 21, 2015, for $16 per share. These shares were classified as held-for-trading investments. As at the December 31, 2015, balance sheet date, assume that the share price increased to $21 per share. As at the December 31, 2016, balance sheet date, assume that the share price declined to $20 per share. The investment was held through December 31, 2016.

a. Journalize the entries to record the adjustment of the RadTek Ltd. investment to fair value on December 31, 2015, and December 31, 2016.
b. Where is the unrealized holding gain or unrealized holding loss for held-for-trading investments disclosed on the financial statements?

---

② EX 15-6

Fair value journal entries, held-for-trading investments

✔ c. Unrealized Holding Gain Dec. 31, 2015, $5,400

Rolf's Pets Inc. purchased a portfolio of held-for-trading securities during 2014. The cost and fair value of this portfolio on December 31, 2014, was as follows:

Name	Number of Shares	Total Cost	Total Fair Value
Anderson Ltd.	1,300	$14,000	$15,500
Monix Inc.	900	25,000	22,000
Paster Inc.	200	8,000	9,100
Total		$47,000	$46,600

On April 3, 2015, Rolf's Pets Inc. purchased 400 shares of Cookies Ltd., at $40.75 per share. On December 31, 2015, the trading security portfolio had the following cost and fair value:

Name	Number of Shares	Total Cost	Total Fair Value
Anderson Ltd.	1,300	$14,000	$14,200
Cookies Ltd.	400	16,300	18,500
Monix Inc.	900	25,000	24,000
Paster Inc.	200	8,000	11,600
Total		$63,300	$68,300

(continued)

Provide the journal entries to record the following:

a. The adjustment of the held-for-trading investments to fair value on December 31, 2014.
b. The April 3, 2015, purchase of Cookies Ltd. shares.
c. The adjustment of the held-for-trading investments to fair value on December 31, 2015.

---

② EX 15-7

Fair value journal entries, held-for-trading investments

✔ a. 2. Dec. 31, 2015, Unrealized holding loss on held-for-trading investments, $4,900

Union Financial Services Ltd. purchased the following held-for-trading securities during 2014, its first year of operations:

Name	Number of Shares	Cost
B&T Transportation Ltd.	3,400	$ 67,100
Citrus Foods Ltd.	1,800	29,700
Stuart Housewares Ltd.	800	19,700
Total		$116,500

There were no sales of securities during 2014 or 2015.

The market price per share for the held-for-trading security portfolio on December 31, 2014, and December 31, 2015, was as follows:

	Market Price per Share	
	Dec. 31, 2014	Dec. 31, 2015
B&T Transportation Ltd.	$25.00	$24.00
Citrus Foods Ltd.	17.50	18.00
Stuart Housewares Ltd.	23.00	20.00

a. Provide the journal entry to adjust the held-for-trading securities to fair value on:
   1. December 31, 2014
   2. December 31, 2015
b. Describe the income statement impact from the December 31, 2015, journal entry.

---

② EX 15-8

Entries for held-to-maturity investments, interest, and sale of investment

Mercer Investments acquired $120,000 Jericho Corp., 6% bonds at par value as a held-to-maturity investment on September 1, 2015. The bonds pay interest on September 1 and March 1. On March 1, 2016, Mercer sold $40,000 par value Jericho Corp. bonds at 102, after receipt of the interest.

Journalize the entries to record the following:

a. The initial acquisition of the Jericho Corp. bonds on September 1, 2015.
b. The adjusting entry for 121 days of accrued interest earned on the Jericho Corp. bonds on December 31, 2015.
c. The receipt of semiannual interest on March 1, 2016.
d. The sale of $40,000 Jericho Corp. bonds on March 1, 2016, at 102.

---

② EX 15-9

Entries for held-to-maturity investments, interest, and sale of investment

Cassidy Ltd. purchased $80,000 Stump Inc., 3% bonds at par value on October 1, 2015. Cassidy intends to hold the bonds to maturity in 2025. The bonds pay interest on October 1 and April 1. On April 1, 2016, Cassidy sold $30,000 par value Stump Inc. bonds at 97, after receipt of the interest.

Journalize the entries to record the following:

a. The initial acquisition of the Stump Inc. bonds on October 1, 2015.
b. The adjusting entry for 91 days of accrued interest earned on the Stump Inc. bonds on December 31, 2015.
c. The receipt of semiannual interest on April 1, 2016.
d. The sale of $30,000 Stump Inc. bonds on April 1, 2016, at 97.

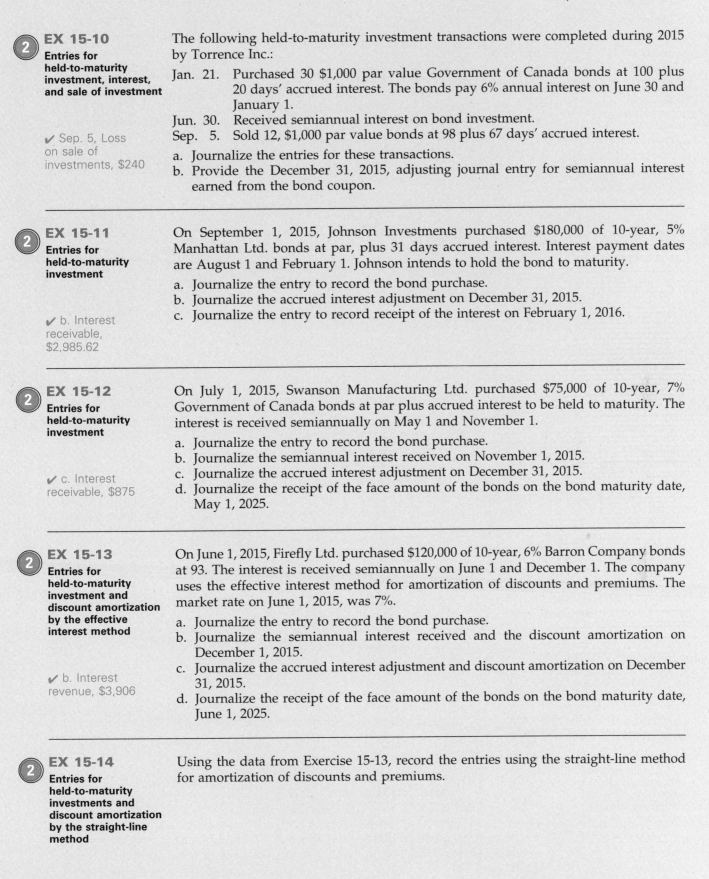

② EX 15-10

Entries for held-to-maturity investment, interest, and sale of investment

✔ Sep. 5, Loss on sale of investments, $240

The following held-to-maturity investment transactions were completed during 2015 by Torrence Inc.:

Jan. 21.   Purchased 30 $1,000 par value Government of Canada bonds at 100 plus 20 days' accrued interest. The bonds pay 6% annual interest on June 30 and January 1.

Jun. 30.   Received semiannual interest on bond investment.

Sep. 5.   Sold 12, $1,000 par value bonds at 98 plus 67 days' accrued interest.

a. Journalize the entries for these transactions.
b. Provide the December 31, 2015, adjusting journal entry for semiannual interest earned from the bond coupon.

---

② EX 15-11

Entries for held-to-maturity investment

✔ b. Interest receivable, $2,985.62

On September 1, 2015, Johnson Investments purchased $180,000 of 10-year, 5% Manhattan Ltd. bonds at par, plus 31 days accrued interest. Interest payment dates are August 1 and February 1. Johnson intends to hold the bond to maturity.

a. Journalize the entry to record the bond purchase.
b. Journalize the accrued interest adjustment on December 31, 2015.
c. Journalize the entry to record receipt of the interest on February 1, 2016.

---

② EX 15-12

Entries for held-to-maturity investment

✔ c. Interest receivable, $875

On July 1, 2015, Swanson Manufacturing Ltd. purchased $75,000 of 10-year, 7% Government of Canada bonds at par plus accrued interest to be held to maturity. The interest is received semiannually on May 1 and November 1.

a. Journalize the entry to record the bond purchase.
b. Journalize the semiannual interest received on November 1, 2015.
c. Journalize the accrued interest adjustment on December 31, 2015.
d. Journalize the receipt of the face amount of the bonds on the bond maturity date, May 1, 2025.

---

② EX 15-13

Entries for held-to-maturity investment and discount amortization by the effective interest method

✔ b. Interest revenue, $3,906

On June 1, 2015, Firefly Ltd. purchased $120,000 of 10-year, 6% Barron Company bonds at 93. The interest is received semiannually on June 1 and December 1. The company uses the effective interest method for amortization of discounts and premiums. The market rate on June 1, 2015, was 7%.

a. Journalize the entry to record the bond purchase.
b. Journalize the semiannual interest received and the discount amortization on December 1, 2015.
c. Journalize the accrued interest adjustment and discount amortization on December 31, 2015.
d. Journalize the receipt of the face amount of the bonds on the bond maturity date, June 1, 2025.

---

② EX 15-14

Entries for held-to-maturity investments and discount amortization by the straight-line method

✔ Dec. 31 interest revenue, $670

Using the data from Exercise 15-13, record the entries using the straight-line method for amortization of discounts and premiums.

2 **EX 15-15**

Entries for held-to-maturity investments and discount amortization by the effective interest method

✔ Dec. 31, Interest receivable, $240,000

Journalize the entries to record the following selected held-to-maturity investment transactions for ABC Company:

1. Purchased for cash $16,000,000 of Cummins Corporation eight-year, 6% bonds at 96.9 on their issuance date, April 1, 2015. ABC Company intends to hold these bonds to their maturity. The market rate was 6.5%.
2. Recorded receipt of the first semiannual interest payment and amortization of the discount on October 1, using the effective interest method.
3. Recorded accrued interest and amortization of discount at December 31, ABC Company's year-end.
4. Recorded receipt of cash for the bonds on their maturity date, April 1, 2023.

---

2 **EX 15-16**

Entries for held-to-maturity investments and discount amortization by the straight-line method

✔ Oct. 1 interest revenue, $511,000

Using the data from Exercise 15-15, record the entries using the straight-line method for amortization of discounts and premiums.

---

2 **EX 15-17**

Entries for held-to-maturity investments, interest, and premium amortization by the effective interest method

✔ b. Interest receivable, $5,600

On January 2, 2015, when the market interest rate was 6.5%, Maureen Company purchased $80,000, 10-year, 7% bonds at 103.6 with the intent to hold them to maturity. January 2 is the interest payment date.

a. Journalize the entry to record the bond purchase.
b. Journalize the accrued interest adjustment and premium amortization on December 31, 2015, using the effective interest method for amortization of discounts and premiums.
c. What is the relationship between the market rate of interest and the coupon rate on the bond investment acquisition date?

---

2 **EX 15-18**

Entries for held-to-maturity investments, interest, and premium amortization by the straight-line method

✔ Dec. 31, interest revenue, $5,312

Using the data from Exercise 15-17, record the entries using the straight-line method for amortization of discounts and premiums.

---

2 **EX 15-19**

Entries for held-to-maturity investments, interest, and premium amortization by the effective interest method

✔ Sept. 1 interest revenue, $569,520

Journalize the entries to record the following selected held-to-maturity investment transactions for XYZ Corp:

1. Purchased for cash $20,000,000 of Dognaught Corporation five-year, 6% bonds at 101.7 on their issuance date, March 1, 2015. XYZ Corp. intends to hold these bonds to their maturity. The market interest rate at the time of purchase was 5.6%.
2. Recorded receipt of the first semiannual interest payment and amortization of the premium on September 1, using the effective interest method.
3. Recorded accrued interest and amortization of premium at December 31, XYZ Corp.'s year-end.
4. Recorded receipt of cash for the bonds on their maturity date, March 1, 2020.

EX 15-20

Entries for held-to-maturity investments, interest, and premium amortization by the straight-line method

✔ Dec. 31, interest revenue, $5,312

Using the data from Exercise 15-19, record the entries using the straight-line method for amortization of discounts and premiums.

 EX 15-21

Entries for available-for-sale investments

✔ Oct. 3 Cash, $9,756.03

Crop Tech Corp. manufactures farming equipment. Journalize the entries to record the following selected available-for-sale investment transactions completed by Crop during 2015. Crop Tech Corp. includes brokerage fees as part of the cost of investments.

Feb. 2.   Purchased for cash $90,000 of 20-year, 8% Tronko Ltd. bonds at par plus accrued interest and a brokerage fee of $600. Interest is paid January 1 and July 1.

Jul. 1.   Received interest on the Tronko Ltd. bonds.

Oct. 3.   Sold $10,000 of the Tronko Ltd. bonds at 98 plus accrued interest, less brokerage fees of $250.

 EX 15-22

Entries for available-for-sale investments

✔ Aug. 1 interest revenue, $2,743.36

Montrose Corp. manufactures lawn care equipment. Journalize the entries to record the following selected available-for-sale investment transactions completed by Montrose Corp. during 2015. Montrose Corp. includes brokerage fees as part of the cost of investments.

Apr.   6.   Purchased for cash $130,000 of 10-year, 6.5% Cranberry Ltd. bonds at par plus accrued interest and a brokerage fee of $500. Interest is paid February 1 and August 1.

Aug.   1.   Received interest on the Cranberry Ltd. bonds.

Nov. 10.   Sold $20,000 of the Cranberry Ltd. bonds at 103 plus accrued interest, less brokerage fees of $200.

 EX 15-23

Entries for available-for-sale investments, receipt of dividends, and sale of shares

✔ Jun. 3, Loss on sale of investments, $12,725

The following available-for-sale investment-related transactions were completed by Lance Inc. in 2015. Lance Inc. includes brokerage fees as part of the cost of investments.

Jan.   12.   Purchased 1,800 shares of Baxter Ltd. for a price of $56.50 per share plus a brokerage commission of $90.

Apr.   10.   Received a quarterly dividend of $0.25 per share on the Baxter Ltd. investment.

Jun.   3.   Sold 1,200 shares for a price of $46 per share less a brokerage commission of $65.

Journalize the entries for these transactions.

 EX 15-24

Entries for available-for-sale investments and dividends

During 2015, its first year of operations, Gold North Corporation purchased the following available-for-sale investments. Brokerage fees are added to the cost of the investments.

Investment	Shares Purchased	Cost	Brokerage Fees Paid	Cash Dividends Received
Tree Life Ltd.	1,800	$57,600	$250	$1,170
Eastend Bakery Corp.	3,200	65,600	400	2,880

a. Record the purchase of the investments for cash.
b. Record the receipt of the dividends.
c. Record the sale of 900 Tree Life Ltd. shares for $32,000 less a $200 brokerage fee.

EX 15-25

2

Fair value
journal entries,
available-for-sale
investments

✔ 2. Unrealized
holding loss—OCI,
$15,100

Whitehorse Company purchased the following available-for-sale investments during 2014, its first year of operations:

Name	Number of Shares	Cost
Barns Electronics Ltd.	1,500	$ 42,500
Ryan Corp.	400	28,200
Muskrat Lake Inc.	2,200	66,100
Total		$136,800

The market price per share for the available-for-sale investment portfolio on December 31, 2014, and December 31, 2015 was as follows:

	Market Price per Share	
	Dec. 31, 2014	Dec. 31, 2015
Barns Electronics Ltd.	$31.00	$28.00
Ryan Corp.	77.00	67.00
Muskrat Lake Inc.	29.00	26.00

a. Provide the journal entry to adjust the available-for-sale investment portfolio to fair value on:
   1. December 31, 2014
   2. December 31, 2015
b. Describe the income statement impact from the December 31, 2015, journal entry.

EX 15-26

2

Balance sheet
presentation of
available-for-sale
investments

✔ a. Unrealized
holding gain, $5,900

During 2015, its first year of operations, Welland Ltd. purchased two available-for-sale investments as follows:

Security	Purchased	Cost
Kitchener Inc.	1,000 common shares	$32,000
Waterloo Ltd.	$5,000 bonds	5,000

Assume that as at December 31, 2015, the Kitchener shares had a market value of $38 per share, and the Waterloo bonds had a market value of 98. Welland Ltd. had net income of $428,000 and paid $20,000 in dividends on 100,000 common shares (500,000 authorized) for the year ended December 31, 2015. Welland's common shares had a value of $328,000.

a. Prepare the Current Assets section of the balance sheet presentation for the available-for-sale investments.
b. Prepare the Shareholders' Equity section of the balance sheet to reflect the earnings and unrealized holding gain (loss) for the available-for-sale investments.

EX 15-27

2

Balance sheet
presentation of
available-for-sale
investments

✔ 2. 2015 total,
$900,000

During 2015, Toney Corporation held a portfolio of available-for-sale investments having a cost of $190,000. There were no purchases or sales of investments during the year. The market values at the beginning and end of the year were $225,000 and $180,000, respectively. The net income for 2015 was $175,000, and no dividends were paid during the year. The Shareholders' Equity section of the balance sheet was as follows on December 31, 2014:

Toney Corporation
Shareholders' Equity
December 31, 2014

Common shares	$340,000
Retained earnings	395,000
Accumulated other comprehensive income	35,000
Total	$770,000

1. Journalize the entry to revalue the investments on December 31, 2015.
2. Prepare the Shareholders' Equity section of the balance sheet as at December 31, 2015.

EX 15-28
(2)
Fair value journal entries, available-for-sale investments

The investments of Charter Ltd. include 10,000 Wallace Ltd. common shares purchased on January 10, 2015, for $30 per share. These shares were classified as available-for-sale investments. As at the December 31, 2015, balance sheet date, assume that the share price declined to $23 per share. As at the December 31, 2016, balance sheet date, assume that the share price rose to $27 per share. The investment was held through December 31, 2016.

✔ b. Dec. 31, 2015, Accumulated other comprehensive income, $70,000 Dr.

a. Journalize the entries to record the adjustment of the Wallace Ltd. investment to fair value on December 31, 2015, and December 31, 2016.
b. What is the balance of accumulated other comprehensive income for December 31, 2015, and December 31, 2016?
c. Where is accumulated other comprehensive income disclosed on the financial statements?

EX 15-29
(3)
Equity method for share investment

At a total cost of $942,000, Randall Corporation acquired 40,000 shares of Banjo Corp. as a long-term investment. Randall Corporation uses the equity method of accounting for this investment. Banjo Corp. has 160,000 common shares outstanding, including the shares acquired by Randall Corporation.

Journalize the entries by Randall Corporation to record the following information:

a. Banjo Corp. reports net income of $2,430,000 for the current period.
b. A cash dividend of $1.75 per common share is paid by Banjo Corp. during the current period.

EX 15-30
(3)
Equity method for share investment

On January 15, 2015, National Star Ltd. purchased 80,000 shares of Krypton Labs Ltd. directly from one of the founders for $55 per share. Krypton has 250,000 shares outstanding, including the National Star shares. On July 2, 2015, Krypton paid $217,000 in total dividends to its shareholders. On December 31, 2015, Krypton reported a net income of $735,000 for the year. National Star uses the equity method in accounting for its investment in Krypton Labs.

✔ b. $4,565,760

a. Provide the National Star Ltd. journal entries for the transactions involving its investment in Krypton Labs Ltd. during 2015.
b. Determine the December 31, 2015, balance of Investment in Krypton Labs Ltd. Shares.

EX 15-31
(3)
Equity method for share investment

Corvis Ltd.'s balance sheet disclosed its long-term investment in Eastern Inc. under the equity method for comparative years as follows:

	Dec. 31, 2016	Dec. 31, 2015
Investment in Eastern Inc. shares (in millions)	$98	$90

In addition, the 2016 Corvis Ltd. income statement disclosed equity earnings in the Eastern Inc. investment as $10 million. Corvis Ltd. neither purchased nor sold Eastern Inc. shares during 2016. The fair value of the Eastern Inc. share investment on December 31, 2016, was $107 million.

Explain the change in the Investment in Eastern Inc. Shares balance sheet account from December 31, 2015, to December 31, 2016.

EX 15-32
(3)
Entries for equity investments

Excalibar Ltd. purchased 103,600 shares of Deerpark Ltd. on January 3, 2015, directly from one of the founders for $34 per share. Deerpark has 280,000 shares outstanding, including the Excalibar shares. On September 2, 2015, Deerpark paid $340,000 in total dividends to its shareholders. On December 31, 2015, Deerpark reported a net income of $842,000 for the year. Excalibar uses the equity method in accounting for its investment in Deerpark.

✔ July 2 cash, $125,800

a. Provide the Excalibar Ltd. journal entries for the transactions involving its investment in Deerpark Ltd. during 2015.
b. Determine the December 31, 2015, balance of Investment in Deerpark Ltd. Shares.

② EX 15-33
Comprehensive income

✔ Comprehensive income, $85,000

On April 23, 2015, Albert Co. purchased 1,500 shares of Jasper Ltd. for $55 per share including the brokerage commission. The Jasper Ltd. investment was classified as an available-for-sale investment. On December 31, 2015, the fair value of Jasper Ltd. was $65 per share. The net income of Albert Co. was $70,000 for 2015.

Prepare a statement of comprehensive income for Albert Co. for the year ended December 31, 2015. Albert Co. includes brokerage fees as part of the cost of investments.

---

② EX 15-34
Comprehensive income

✔ Unrealized holding loss, $19,000

On December 31, 2014, Battleford Co. had the following available-for-sale investment disclosure within the Current Assets section of the balance sheet:

Available-for-sale investments (at fair value)	$120,000

There were no purchases or sales of available-for-sale investments during 2015. On December 31, 2015, the fair value of the available-for-sale investment portfolio was $101,000. The net income of Battleford Co. was $135,000 for 2015.

Prepare a statement of comprehensive income for Battleford Co. for the year ended December 31, 2015.

EX 15-35
Dividend yield

f·a·i

✔ 5.0%

At the market close on December 30, 2011, Bank of Montreal had a closing share price of $55.88. In addition, Bank of Montreal had a dividend per share of $2.80.

Determine Bank of Montreal's dividend yield. (Round to one decimal place.)

EX 15-36
Dividend yield

f·a·i

✔ a. Dec. 31, 2010, 0.09%

The market price for Potash Corp. of Saskatchewan Inc. closed at $114.39 and $154.45 on December 31, 2009, and December 31, 2010, respectively. The dividends per share were $0.15 for 2009 and $0.14 for 2010.

a. Determine the dividend yield for Potash Corp. on December 31, 2009, and December 31, 2010. (Round percentages to two decimal places.)
b. Interpret these measures.

EX 15-37
Dividend yield

f·a·i

EBay Inc. developed a Web-based marketplace at **www.ebay.com**, in which individuals can buy and sell a variety of items. EBay also acquired PayPal, an online payments system that allows businesses and individuals to send and receive online payments securely. In a recent annual report, eBay published the following dividend policy:

We have never paid cash dividends on our stock and currently anticipate that we will continue to retain any future earnings for the foreseeable future.

Given eBay's dividend policy, why would an investor be attracted to its shares?

PROBLEMS SERIES A

② ③

PR 15-1A

Share investment transactions, equity method, and available-for-sale investments

✔ Dec. 31, 2015,
Unrealized holding
loss, $31,500

Greek Products Ltd. is a wholesaler of women's clothing. The company began operations on January 1, 2015. The following transactions relate to securities acquired by Greek Products Ltd., which has a fiscal year ending on December 31:

2015
Jan. 3. Purchased 5,000 shares of the 200,000 outstanding shares of Crossley Ltd. as an available-for-sale investment at $51 per share, plus a brokerage commission of $800.
Jul. 6. Crossley Ltd. shares split 2 for 1 and paid a cash dividend of $0.75 per new share, paid after the split.
Oct. 14. Sold 1,000 shares of Crossley Ltd. at $27 per share, less a brokerage commission of $300.
Dec. 9. Received a cash dividend of $0.75 per share.
31. The market value per share for Crossley Ltd. is $22 per share. Crossley Ltd. is classified as an available-for-sale investment and is adjusted to fair value.

2016
Jan. 5. Purchased a strategic interest in Eastdale Inc. for $780,000 by purchasing 75,000 shares directly from the estate of the founder of Eastdale Inc. There are 180,000 shares of Eastdale Inc. outstanding.
Jul. 8. Received a cash dividend of $0.90 per Crossley Ltd. share.
Dec. 8. Received a cash dividend of $0.90 per Crossley Ltd. share.
31. Received $20,000 of cash dividends on Eastdale Inc. shares. Eastdale Inc. reported net income of $94,000 in 2016. Greek Products uses the equity method of accounting for its investment in Eastdale Inc.
31. The market value per share for Crossley Ltd. is $28 per share.

Instructions

1. Journalize the entries to record the preceding share transactions. Greek Products Ltd. expenses brokerage fees. Round answers to the nearest dollar.
2. Prepare the investment-related asset and shareholders' equity statement of financial position disclosures for Greek Products Ltd. on December 31, 2016, assuming the Retained Earnings balance on December 31, 2016, is $785,000.

②

PR 15-2A

Held-for-trading investment transactions

✔ Dec. 31, 2016,
unrealized holding
loss, $11,600

Western Capital Inc. is an investment company that began operations on January 1, 2015. The following transactions relate to held-for-trading securities acquired by Western Capital Inc., which has a fiscal year ending on December 31:

2015
Feb. 3. Purchased 2,500 shares of Titan Inc. as a held-for-trading investment at $35 per share plus a brokerage commission of $500.
Mar. 12. Purchased 1,200 shares of Quick Tyme Inc. as a held-for-trading investment at $14 per share plus a brokerage commission of $240.
May 15. Sold 600 shares of Titan Inc. for $36 per share less an $80 brokerage commission.
Jun. 12. Received an annual dividend of $0.12 per share on Titan Inc. shares.
Dec. 31. The held-for-trading investments were adjusted to fair values of $15 and $39 per share for Quick Tyme Inc. and Titan Inc., respectively.

2016
Apr. 9. Purchased 1,100 shares of Aspire Inc. as a held-for-trading investment at $41 per share plus a $165 brokerage commission.
Jun. 15. Received an annual dividend of $0.15 per share on Titan Inc. shares.
Aug. 20. Sold 200 shares of Aspire Inc. for $35 per share less a $60 brokerage commission.

(continued)

Dec. 31. The held-for-trading investments were adjusted to fair value using the following fair values per share for the held-for-trading investments:

Aspire Inc.	$31
Quick Tyme Inc.	16
Titan Inc.	37

Instructions

1. Journalize the entries to record these transactions.
2. Prepare the investment-related current asset statement of financial position disclosures for Western Capital Inc. on December 31, 2016.
3. How are unrealized holding gains or losses on held-for-trading investments disclosed in the financial statements of Western Capital Inc.?

---

② PR 15-3A

Available-for-sale investment transactions, valuation

✔ 2. Available-for-sale investment (at fair value), $147,640

Dollar-Mart Inc. is a general merchandise retail company that began operations on January 1, 2015. The following transactions relate to debt investments acquired by Dollar-Mart Inc., which has a fiscal year ending on December 31:

2015

May 1. Purchased $60,000 of Brandon City 4%, 10-year bonds at par value plus accrued interest of $400. The bond is classified as an available-for-sale investment. The bonds pay interest semiannually on March 1 and September 1.

Jun. 16. Purchased $112,000 of Morgan Co. 6%, 12-year bonds at par value plus accrued interest of $280. The bond is classified as an available-for-sale investment. The bonds pay interest semiannually on June 1 and December 1.

Sep. 1. Received semiannual interest on the Brandon City bonds.

Oct. 1. Sold $24,000 of Brandon City bonds at 103 plus accrued interest of $80.

Dec. 1. Received semiannual interest on Morgan Co. bonds.

     31. Accrued $480 interest on Brandon City bonds.

     31. Accrued $560 interest on Morgan Co. bonds.

     31. The available-for-sale bonds were adjusted to fair values of 102 and 101 for Brandon City and Morgan Co. bonds, respectively.

2016

Mar. 1. Received semiannual interest on the Brandon City bonds.

Jun. 1. Received semiannual interest on the Morgan Co. bonds.
(Assume there are no purchases or sales of bonds during 2016. Also assume all subsequent interest transactions for 2016 have been recorded properly.)

Dec. 31. The available-for-sale bonds were adjusted to fair values of 99 and 100 for Brandon City and Morgan Co. bonds, respectively.

Instructions

1. Journalize the entries to record these transactions.
2. Prepare the investment-related current asset and shareholders' equity statement of financial position disclosures for Dollar-Mart Inc. on December 31, 2016, assuming the Retained Earnings balance on December 31, 2016, is $310,000.

---

② ③ PR 15-4A

Investment reporting

✔ 2. d. $53,500

Miranda Ltd. manufactures and sells commercial and residential security equipment. The comparative statement of financial position for December 31, 2016 and 2015, is provided below. Selected missing balances are shown by letters.

Miranda Ltd.
Statement of Financial Position
December 31, 2016 and 2015

	Dec. 31, 2016	Dec. 31, 2015
Current assets:		
Cash	$104,000	$ 98,000
Accounts receivable, net	71,000	67,500
Available-for-sale investments (fair value)—Note 1	a.	40,000
Interest receivable	b.	–
Total current assets	c.	205,500
Noncurrent assets:		
Investment in New Denver Co. shares—Note 2	d.	48,000
Office equipment (net)	60,000	65,000
Total noncurrent assets	e.	113,000
Total assets	$ f.	$318,500
Liabilities and Shareholders' Equity		
Current liabilities:		
Accounts payable	$ 56,900	$ 51,400
Shareholders' equity:		
Common shares	210,000	210,000
Retained earnings	g.	53,100
Accumulated other comprehensive income	h.	4,000
Total shareholders' equity	i.	267,100
Total liabilities and shareholders' equity	$ j.	$318,500

Note 1. Investments are classified as available-for-sale. The investments at cost and fair value on December 31, 2015, are as follows:

	No. of Shares	Cost per Share	Total Cost	Total Fair Value
Tyndale Inc. shares	600	$24	$14,400	$16,000
UR-Smart Inc. shares	1,200	18	21,600	24,000
			$36,000	$40,000

Note 2. The Investment in New Denver Co. shares is an equity-method investment representing 36% of the outstanding shares of New Denver Co.

Note 3. Miranda Ltd. treats brokerage fees as part of the investment cost.

The following selected investment transactions occurred during 2016:

2016

Apr. 21. Purchased 300 shares of Winkler Resorts Ltd. at $20 per share plus a $45 brokerage commission.

Jun. 12. Dividends of $1 per share are received on the UR-Smart Inc. share investment.

Sep. 9. Dividends of $8,900 are received on the New Denver Co. investment.

Oct. 1. Purchased $8,000 of Vita-Mighty Co. 7%, 10-year bonds at 100. The bonds are classified as available-for-sale. The bonds pay interest on October 1 and April 1.

Dec. 31. New Denver Co. reported a total net income of $40,000 for 2016. Miranda recorded equity earnings for its share of New Denver Co. net income.

31. Accrued interest on Vita-Mighty bonds purchased on October 1.

31. Adjusted the available-for-sale investment portfolio to fair value using the following fair value per share amounts:

Available-for-Sale Investments	Fair Value
Tyndale Inc. shares	$28 per share
UR-Smart Inc. shares	$20 per share
Winkler Resorts Ltd. shares	$24 per share
Vita-Mighty Co. bonds	102 per $1,000 of face value

31. Closed the Miranda Ltd. net income of $18,685 for 2016. Miranda paid no dividends during 2016.

(continued)

Instructions

1. Journalize the 2016 transactions.
2. Determine the missing letters in the unclassified statement of financial position. Provide appropriate supporting calculations.

PR 15-5A

Held-to-maturity investment transactions

✔ April 1, interest revenue, $426.26

Fleet Inc. is an athletic footware company that began operations on January 1, 2015. Fleet Inc. uses the effective interest method of amortizing discounts and premiums. The following transactions relate to held-to-maturity investments acquired by Fleet Inc., which has a fiscal year ending on December 31:

2015

Mar. 1. Purchased $36,000 of Madison Co. 5%, 10-year bonds at 95 plus accrued interest. The bonds pay interest semiannually on February 1 and August 1. The market interest rate was 5.6%.

Apr. 16. Purchased $45,000 of Westville 4%, 15-year bonds at 102.5 plus accrued interest. The bonds pay interest semiannually on April 1 and October 1. The market rate was 3.7%.

Aug. 1. Received semiannual interest on the Madison Co. bonds.

Sept. 1. Sold $12,000 of Madison Co. bonds at 98 plus accrued interest.

Oct. 1. Received semiannual interest on the Westville bonds.

Dec. 31. Accrued interest on the Madison Co. bonds.

31. Accrued interest on the Westville bonds.

2016

Feb. 1. Received semiannual interest on the Madison Co. bonds.

Apr. 1. Received semiannual interest on the Westville bonds.

Instructions

Journalize the entries to record these transactions.

PR 15-6A

Year-end valuation and statement of financial position presentation

✔ December 31, 2016, accumulated other comprehensive income, $7,000

Jessie Inc. had the following cost and fair market values for their investments:

	Initial Cost	Fair Value December 31, 2014	Fair Value December 31, 2015	Fair Value December 31, 2016	Recorded Carrying Value December 31, 2016
Held-for-trading					
Carruthers Brothers Inc.	$18,000	$16,500	$15,200	$17,500	
Jay Bird Ltd.	32,000	30,750	29,500	34,000	
Munchkins Ltd.	6,500	7,500	9,200	8,000	
	56,500	54,750	53,900	59,500	
Held-to-maturity					
Punky Sisters Ltd.	8,000	9,000	10,000	9,250	$ 9,300
Peanuts Inc.	19,000	18,300	18,500	18,000	23,500
Booper Corp.	26,000	32,000	33,750	35,000	23,750
	53,000	59,300	62,250	62,250	56,550
Available-for-sale— current					
Carrie's Carousel Ltd.	65,000	73,000	72,500	70,000	
Tracey Inc.	23,000	25,000	27,000	25,000	
	88,000	98,000	99,500	95,000	
Investment in associates					
Ian Investments Ltd.	32,000	34,500	36,000	37,000	53,750
DS Lochead Inc.	27,000	28,500	29,000	30,000	42,500
	59,000	63,000	65,000	67,000	96,250

Instructions

1. Journalize the year-end revaluation entries required by Jessie Inc.
2. Prepare the relevant current and noncurrent sections of the statement of financial position for Jessie Inc. on December 31, 2016.

PROBLEMS SERIES B

②③ PR 15-1B

Share investment transactions, equity method, and available-for-sale investments

✔ Dec. 31, 2015, Unrealized holding gain, $10,500

Hampton Ltd. produces and sells children's toys. The company began operations on January 1, 2015. The following transactions relate to securities acquired by Hampton Ltd., which has a fiscal year ending on December 31:

2015
Jan. 10. Purchased 2,000 shares of the 150,000 outstanding shares of Climbing Inc. as an available-for-sale investment at $48 per share, plus a brokerage commission of $1,500.
Mar. 12. Received the regular cash dividend of $0.90 per share.
Sep. 9. Climbing Inc. shares split 2 for 1 and paid a cash dividend of $0.45 per new Climbing Inc. share, paid after the split.
Oct. 14. Sold 500 shares of Climbing Inc. at $20 per share, less a brokerage commission of $200.
Dec. 31. Climbing Inc. is classified as an available-for-sale investment and is adjusted to a fair value of $27 per share.

2016
Jan. 5. Purchased a strategic interest in Roy Ball Inc. for $370,000 by purchasing 50,000 shares directly from the estate of the founder of Roy Ball Inc. There are 200,000 shares of Roy Ball Inc. outstanding.
Mar. 8. Received the regular cash dividend of $0.50 per Climbing Inc. share.
Sep. 10. Received the regular cash dividend of $0.50 per share plus an extra dividend of $0.15 per Climbing Inc. share.
Dec. 31. Received $42,000 of cash dividends on Roy Ball Inc. shares. Roy Ball Inc. reported net income of $154,000 in 2016. Hampton Ltd. uses the equity method of accounting for its investment in Roy Ball Inc.
31. Climbing Inc. is classified as an available-for-sale investment and is adjusted to a fair value of $22 per share.

Instructions

1. Journalize the entries to record these transactions. Hampton Ltd. expenses brokerage fees.
2. Prepare the investment-related asset and shareholders' equity statement of financial position disclosures for Hampton Ltd. on December 31, 2016, assuming the Retained Earnings balance on December 31, 2016, is $280,000.

② PR 15-2B

Share investment transactions, held-for-trading investments

✔ Dec. 31, 2015, Unrealized holding loss, $5,800

Jupiter Insurance Co. is an insurance company that began operations on January 1, 2015. The following transactions relate to held-for-trading investments acquired by Jupiter Insurance Co., which has a fiscal year ending on December 31:

2015
Feb. 21. Purchased 3,000 shares of Loral Ltd. as a held-for-trading investment at $25 per share plus a brokerage commission of $600.
Mar. 2. Purchased 900 shares of Monarch Inc. as a held-for-trading investment at $52 per share plus a brokerage commission of $180.
May 3. Sold 800 shares of Loral Ltd. for $23.50 per share less an $80 brokerage commission.
Jun. 8. Received an annual dividend of $0.18 per Loral Ltd. share.
Dec. 31. The held-for-trading investments were adjusted to fair values of $24 and $48 per share for Loral Ltd. and Monarch Inc., respectively.

 (continued)

2016

May 11. Purchased 1,600 shares of Echelon Co. as a held-for-trading investment at $18 per share plus a $160 brokerage commission.

Jun. 11. Received an annual dividend of $0.20 per Loral Ltd. share.

Aug. 14. Sold 400 shares of Echelon Co. for $20 per share less an $80 brokerage commission.

Dec. 31. The held-for-trading investments were adjusted to fair value using the following fair values per share for the held-for-trading securities:

Echelon Co.	$22
Loral Ltd.	23
Monarch Inc.	49

Instructions

1. Journalize the entries to record these transactions.
2. Prepare the investment-related current asset statement of financial position disclosures for Jupiter Insurance Co. on December 31, 2016.
3. How are unrealized holding gains or losses on held-for-trading investments disclosed in the financial statements of Jupiter Insurance Co.?

---

② **PR 15-3B**

Available-for-sale investment transactions, valuation

✔ 2. Available-for-sale investments (at fair value), $156,000

Eclipse Inc. is an athletic footware company that began operations on January 1, 2015. The following transactions relate to debt investments acquired by Eclipse Inc., which has a fiscal year ending on December 31:

2015

Mar. 1. Purchased $80,000 of Noble Co. 6%, 10-year bonds at par value plus accrued interest of $400. The bond is classified as an available-for-sale investment. The bonds pay interest semiannually on February 1 and August 1.

Apr. 16. Purchased $105,000 of Mason City 4%, 15-year bonds at par value plus accrued interest of $175. The bond is classified as an available-for-sale investment. The bonds pay interest semiannually on April 1 and October 1.

Aug. 1. Received semiannual interest on the Noble Co. bonds.

Sep. 1. Sold $30,000 of Noble Co. bonds at 99 plus accrued interest of $150.

Oct. 1. Received semiannual interest on Mason City bonds.

Dec. 31. Accrued $1,250 interest on Noble Co. bonds.

31. Accrued $1,050 interest on Mason City bonds.

31. The available-for-sale bonds were adjusted to fair values of 98 and 99 for Mason City and Noble Co. bonds, respectively.

2016

Feb. 1. Received semiannual interest on the Noble Co. bonds.

Apr. 1. Received semiannual interest on the Mason City bonds.

(Assume there are no purchases or sales of bonds during 2016. Also assume all subsequent interest transactions for 2016 have been recorded properly.)

Dec. 31. The available-for-sale bonds were adjusted to fair values of 100 and 102 for Mason City and Noble Co. bonds, respectively.

Instructions

1. Journalize the entries to record these transactions.
2. Prepare the investment-related current asset and shareholders' equity statement of financial position disclosures for Eclipse Inc. on December 31, 2016, assuming the Retained Earnings balance on December 31, 2016, is $490,000.

---

② ③ **PR 15-4B**

Investment reporting

✔ 2. i. $474,860

Scholar House Inc. is a book publisher. The comparative statement of financial position for December 31, 2016 and 2015, is provided below. Selected missing balances are shown by letters.

Scholar House Inc.
Statement of Financial Position
December 31, 2016 and 2015

	Dec. 31, 2016	Dec. 31, 2015
Current assets:		
Cash	$178,000	$157,000
Accounts receivable, net	106,000	98,000
Available-for-sale investments (fair value)—Note 1	a.	51,000
Interest receivable	b.	–
Total current assets	c.	306,000
Noncurrent assets:		
Investment in Nahum Co. shares—Note 2	d.	64,000
Office equipment (net)	90,000	95,000
Total noncurrent assets	e.	159,000
Total assets	$ f.	$465,000
Liabilities and Shareholders' Equity		
Current liabilities:		
Accounts payable	$ 56,900	$ 51,400
Shareholders' equity:		
Common shares	210,000	210,000
Retained earnings	g.	206,000
Accumulated other comprehensive income	h.	(2,400)
Total shareholders' equity	i.	413,600
Total liabilities and shareholders' equity	$ j.	$465,000

Note 1. Investments are classified as available-for-sale. The investments at cost and fair value on December 31, 2015, are as follows:

	No. of Shares	Cost per Share	Total Cost	Total Fair Value
Barns Co. shares	1,600	$12	$19,200	$18,000
Dynasty Co. shares	900	38	34,200	33,000
			$53,400	$51,000

Note 2. The investment in Nahum Co. shares is an equity-method investment representing 32% of the outstanding shares of Nahum Co.

Note 3. Scholar House Inc. treats brokerage fees as part of the investment cost.

The following selected investment transactions occurred during 2016:

2016
May 5.   Purchased 500 shares of High-Star Inc. at $29 per share plus a $100 brokerage commission.
Jun. 12.   Dividends of $1.25 per share are received on the Dynasty Co. investment.
Jul.   9.   Dividends of $5,700 are received on the Nahum Co. investment.
Sep.   1.   Purchased $18,000 of Opus Co. 5%, 10-year bonds at 100. The bonds are classified as available-for-sale. The bonds pay interest on September 1 and March 1.
Dec. 31.   Nahum Co. reported a total net income of $60,000 for 2016. Scholar House recorded equity earnings for its share of Nahum Co. net income.
        31.   Accrued 4 months of interest on the Opus bonds.
        31.   Adjusted the available-for-sale investment portfolio to fair value using the following fair value per share amounts:

Available-for-Sale Investments	Fair Value
Barns Co. shares	$10 per share
Dynasty Co. shares	$35 per share
High-Star Inc. shares	$30 per share
Opus Co. bonds	97 per $1,000 of face value

        31.   Closed the Scholar House Inc. net income of $64,900 for 2016. Scholar House paid no dividends during 2016.

(*continued*)

Instructions

1. Journalize the 2016 transactions.
2. Determine the missing letters in the unclassified statement of financial position. Provide appropriate supporting calculations.

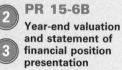

PR 15-5B

Held-to-maturity investment transactions

✔ March 1, Interest revenue, $360.49

Savers Mart Inc. is a general merchandise retail company that began operations on January 1, 2015. Savers Mart Inc. uses the effective interest method of amortizing discounts and premiums. The following transactions relate to held-to-maturity investments acquired by Savers Mart Inc., which has a fiscal year ending on December 31:

2015

May 1.   Purchased $80,000 of Northridge City 4.5%, 10-year bonds at 107.5 plus accrued interest. The bonds pay interest semiannually on March 1 and September 1. The market interest rate was 3.6%.

Jun. 16.   Purchased $38,000 of Hancock Co. 6%, 12-year bonds at 97.1 plus accrued interest. The bonds pay interest semiannually on June 1 and December 1. The market interest rate was 6.3%.

Sep. 1.   Received semiannual interest on the Northridge City bonds.
Oct. 1.   Sold $24,000 of Northridge City bonds at 102 plus accrued interest.
Dec. 1.   Received semiannual interest on the Hancock Co. bonds.
   31.   Accrued interest on the Northridge City bonds.
   31.   Accrued interest on the Hancock Co. bonds.

2016

Mar. 1.   Received semiannual interest on the Northridge City bonds.
Jun. 1.   Received semiannual interest on the Hancock Co. bonds.

Instruction

Journalize the entries to record these transactions.

PR 15-6B

Year-end valuation and statement of financial position presentation

✔ December 31, 2016, accumulated other comprehensive income, $2,750

Amore Inc. had the following cost and fair market values for their investments:

	Initial Cost	Fair Value December 31, 2014	Fair Value December 31, 2015	Fair Value December 31, 2016	Recorded Carrying Value December 31, 2016
Held-for-trading					
Ann's Doves Inc.	$ 7,000	$ 6,500	$ 7,800	$ 8,000	
Bryan's Computers Ltd.	22,000	24,000	21,500	23,000	
Pelham Inc.	4,900	6,500	7,000	7,200	
	33,900	37,000	36,300	38,200	
Held-to-maturity					
Nursery Ltd.	7,500	6,800	6,500	6,250	$ 12,500
Dogwood Ltd.	32,000	28,000	27,500	29,000	28,000
Beechnut Inc.	15,000	18,000	16,750	15,500	23,000
	54,500	52,800	50,750	50,750	63,500
Available-for-sale—current					
Vista Ltd.	63,000	65,000	61,700	63,250	
Meadows Corp.	45,000	48,000	49,000	47,500	
	108,000	113,000	110,700	110,750	
Investment in associates					
Longpoint Inc.	20,000	22,000	21,000	23,500	49,250
Canboro Ltd.	25,000	27,000	28,500	32,000	53,800
	45,000	49,000	49,500	55,500	103,050

Instructions

1. Journalize the year-end revaluation entries required by Amore Inc.
2. Prepare the relevant current and non-current sections of the statement of financial position for Amore Inc. on December 31, 2016.

COMPREHENSIVE PROBLEM 4

✔ g. Retained earnings, $148,200 Dr.

Selected transactions completed by Jordan Products Ltd. during the fiscal year ended December 31, 2015, are as follows:

a. Issued 14,500 common shares at $48 per share, receiving cash.
b. Issued 8,000 $7.20 cumulative preferred shares at $130 per share, receiving cash.
c. Issued $8,000,000 of 10-year, 7% bonds at 110, with interest payable semiannually.
d. Declared a dividend of $0.65 per common share and a quarterly dividend of $1.80 per preferred share. On the date of record, 120,000 common shares and 22,500 preferred shares were outstanding. Charge dividends directly to Retained Earnings.
e. Paid the cash dividends declared in (d).
f. Purchased 12,000 Avocado Corp. shares at $31 per share, plus a $2,400 brokerage commission. The investment is classified as an available-for-sale investment.
g. Purchased 9,500 common shares at $52 per share. The common shares had been issued at an average price of $36.40 per share.
h. Purchased 340,000 Amigo Co. shares directly from the founders for $21 per share. Amigo has 1,000,000 shares issued and outstanding. Jordan Products Ltd. treated the investment as an equity method investment.
i. Declared a 2% share dividend on the common shares and a $1.80 preferred share dividend. On the date of declaration, the market value of the common shares was $55 per share.
j. Issued the share dividends declared in (i) and paid the cash dividends to the preferred shareholders.
k. Received $272,000 dividend from the Amigo Co. investment in (h).
l. Purchased $86,000 of Game Gear Ltd. 10-year, 6% bonds, directly from the issuing company at par value, plus accrued interest of $950. The bonds are classified as a held-to-maturity long-term investment.
m. Issued 3,800 common shares at $59.50 per share, receiving cash.
n. Received a dividend of $1.45 per share from the Avocado Corp. investment in (f).
o. Sold 2,000 shares of Avocado Corp. at $32.80 per share, including commission.
p. Recorded the payment of semiannual interest and the premium amortization for six months on the bonds issued in (c), using the straight-line amortization method.
q. Accrued interest for three months on the Game Gear Ltd. bonds purchased in (l).
r. Amigo Co. reported total earnings of $478,000 for 2015. The equity earnings are recognized.
s. The market price for Avocado Corp. is $28.50 per share on December 31, 2015. The investment is adjusted to fair value.

Instructions

1. Journalize the selected transactions. Jordan Products Ltd. treats brokerage fees as part of the investment cost.
2. After all of the transactions for the year ended December 31, 2015, had been posted, the data below were taken from the records of Jordan Products Ltd.
   a. Prepare a multiple-step income statement for the year ended December 31, 2015, concluding with earnings per share. In computing earnings per share, assume that the average number of common shares outstanding was 120,000 and preferred dividends were $162,000. (Round earnings per share to the nearest cent.)
   b. Prepare a statement of changes in equity for the year ended December 31, 2015.
   c. Prepare a statement of financial position in report form as at December 31, 2015.

(continued)

Income statement data:

Advertising expense	$ 125,000
Cost of goods sold	3,240,000
Delivery expense	29,000
Depreciation expense—office buildings and equipment	26,000
Depreciation expense—store buildings and equipment	95,000
Dividend revenue	17,400
Gain on sale of investment	3,200
Income from Amigo Co. investment	162,520
Income taxes expense	306,700
Interest expense	384,000
Interest revenue	1,650
Miscellaneous administrative expense	7,500
Miscellaneous selling expense	13,750
Office rent expense	50,000
Office salaries expense	140,000
Office supplies expense	10,000
Sales	5,580,000
Sales commissions	182,000
Sales salaries expense	345,000
Store supplies expense	22,000

Retained earnings and statement of financial position data:

Accounts payable	$ 195,000
Accounts receivable	543,000
Accumulated depreciation—office buildings and equipment	1,580,000
Accumulated depreciation—store buildings and equipment	4,126,000
Allowance for doubtful accounts	8,150
Available-for-sale investments (at fair value)	285,000
Bonds payable, 7%, due 2025	8,000,000
Cash	240,000
Common shares (400,000 shares authorized; 116,510 issued and outstanding)	4,240,400
Dividends:	
Cash dividends for common shares	316,310
Cash dividends for preferred shares	162,000
Share dividends for common shares	121,550
Goodwill	510,000
Income taxes payable	40,000
Interest receivable	1,290
Investment in Amigo Co. shares (equity method)	7,030,520
Investment in Game Gear Ltd. bonds (long term)	86,000
Inventories (December 31, 2015), at lower of cost (FIFO) and NRV	780,000
Office buildings and equipment	4,320,000
$7.20 preferred 6% shares (30,000 shares authorized; 22,500 shares issued and outstanding)	2,850,000
Premium on bonds payable	760,000
Prepaid expenses	26,500
Retained earnings, January 1, 2015	4,569,000
Store buildings and equipment	12,560,000
Accumulated other comprehersive income	(27,000)

SPECIAL ACTIVITIES

SA 15-1

Why corporations invest excess cash

Refer to the financial statements for Leon's Furniture Limited in Appendix B. You will see that Leon's carried available-for-sale investments of $149.3 million at December 31, 2011, as current assets on its statement of financial position. Why would a corporation invest its excess cash in another corporation's debt and equity securities?

SA 15-2
Ethics and fair value measurement

Financial assets include shares and bonds. These are fairly simple securities that can often be valued using quoted market prices. However, Bay Street and Wall Street have created many complex and exotic securities that do not have quoted market prices. These securities, such as structured investment vehicles (SIVs), must still be valued on the balance sheet at fair value. IFRS require that the reporting entity use assumptions in valuing investments when market prices or critical valuation inputs are unobservable.

What are the ethical considerations in making subjective valuations of complex and exotic investments?

SA 15-3
Warren Buffett and "look-through" earnings

Berkshire Hathaway, the investment holding company of Warren Buffett, reports its "less than 20% ownership" investments according to generally accepted accounting principles. However, it also provides additional disclosures that it terms "look-through" earnings.

Warren Buffett states,

Many of these companies (in the less than 20% owned category) pay out relatively small proportions of their earnings in dividends. This means that only a small proportion of their earning power is recorded in our own current operating earnings. But, while our reported operating earnings reflect only the dividends received from such companies, our economic well-being is determined by their earnings, not their dividends.

The value to Berkshire Hathaway of retained earnings (of our investees) is not determined by whether we own 100%, 50%, 20%, or 1% of the businesses in which they reside. . . . Our perspective on such "forgotten-but-not-gone" earnings is simple: the way they are accounted for is of no importance, but their ownership and subsequent utilization is all-important. We care not whether the auditors hear a tree fall in the forest; we do care who owns the tree and what's next done with it.

I believe the best way to think about our earnings is in terms of "look-through" results, calculated as follows: Take $250 million, which is roughly our share of the operating earnings retained by our investees (<20% ownership holdings); subtract . . . incremental taxes we would have owed had that $250 million been paid to us in dividends; then add the remainder, $220 million, to our reported earnings of $371 million. Thus, our "look-through" earnings were about $590 million.

Source: Warren Buffett, *The Essays of Warren Buffett: Lessons for Corporate America*, edited by Lawrence A. Cunningham, pp. 180–183 (excerpted).

1. What are "look-through" earnings?
2. Why does Warren Buffett favour "look-through" earnings?

SA 15-4
Reporting investments

Group Project

Internet Project

In groups of three or four, find the latest annual report for BCE Inc. Notes 2, 8, and 15 to the financial statements include details of BCE's investments. From these disclosures, answer the following questions.

1. Where on the balance sheet are available-for-sale investments classified?
2. At what value are these investments recorded?
3. What is the total value of these investments?
4. What is the total income or expense on investments?
5. What is the total unrealized holding gain or loss on investments?

SA 15-5
Reporting investments

Group Project

Internet Project

Appendix B includes a set of financial statements for Leon's Furniture Limited for the year ended December 31, 2011, and the related disclosure notes.

From these statements and disclosures, answer the following questions.

1. Where on the balance sheet are portfolio investments classified?
2. At what value are these investments recorded?
3. What is the total value of these investments?
4. What is the total income or expense on investments?

Statement of Cash Flows

JONES SODA CO.

Suppose you were to receive $100 as a result of some event. Would it make a difference what the event was? Yes, it would! If you received $100 for your birthday, then it's a gift. If you received $100 as a result of working part time for a week, then it's the result of your effort. If you received $100 as a loan, then it's money that you will have to pay back in the future. If you received $100 as a result of selling your iPod, then it's the result of giving up something tangible. Thus, the same $100 received can be associated with different types of events, and these events have different meanings to you. You would much rather receive a $100 gift than take out a $100 loan. Likewise, company stakeholders would also view such events differently.

Companies are required to report information about the events causing a change in cash over a period of time. This information is reported in the statement of cash flows. One such company is Jones Soda Co. Jones began in the late 1980s in Vancouver, British Columbia, as an alternative beverage company, known for its customer-provided labels, unique flavours, and support for extreme sports. In 2000, Jones moved its headquarters to Seattle, Washington. You have probably seen Jones Soda at Starbucks or maybe sampled some of its unique flavours, such as Fufu Berry®, Blue Bubblegum®, or Lemon Drop®. As with any company, cash is important to Jones Soda. Without cash, Jones would be unable to expand its brands, distribute its product, support extreme sports, or provide a return for its owners. Thus, its managers are concerned about the sources and uses of cash.

In previous chapters, we have used the statement of income, statement of financial position, retained earnings statement, and other information to analyze the effects of management decisions on a business's financial position and operating performance. In this chapter, we focus on the events causing a change in cash by presenting the preparation and use of the statement of cash flows.

After studying this chapter, you should be able to:

1 Describe the cash flow activities reported in the statement of cash flows.

Reporting Cash Flows	Cash Flows from Operating Activities	
	Cash Flows from Investing Activities	
	Cash Flows from Financing Activities	
	Noncash Investing and Financing Activities	EXAMPLE EXERCISE 16-1 (page 818)

2 Prepare a statement of cash flows, using the indirect method.

Statement of Cash Flows— The Indirect Method	Operating Activities Section	EXAMPLE EXERCISE 16-2 (page 822) EXAMPLE EXERCISE 16-3 (page 824) EXAMPLE EXERCISE 16-4 (page 825)
	Investing Activities Section	EXAMPLE EXERCISE 16-5 (page 827)
	Financial Activities Section	
	Interpreting the Statement of Cash Flows	

3 Prepare the operating activities section, using the direct method.

Operating Activities Section—The Direct Method	Cash Received from Customers	EXAMPLE EXERCISE 16-6 (page 834)
	Cash Payments for Merchandise	EXAMPLE EXERCISE 16-7 (page 835)
	Cash Payments for Operating Expenses	
	Cash Payments for Interest Expense	
	Cash Payments for Income Taxes	
	Comparing the Operating Section—Direct to Indirect	
	Financial Analysis and Interpretation	EXAMPLE EXERCISE 16-8 (page 838)

APPENDIX 1 Spreadsheet (Worksheet) for Statement of Cash Flows—The Indirect Method

For the chapter *At a Glance*, turn to page 842.

1 # Reporting Cash Flows

Describe the cash flow activities reported in the statement of cash flows.

The **statement of cash flows**, also known as the **cash flow statement**, reports a company's cash inflows and outflows for a period. The statement of cash flows provides useful information about a company's ability to do the following:

1. generate cash from operations
2. maintain and expand its operating capacity
3. meet its financial obligations
4. pay dividends

The statement of cash flows is used by managers in evaluating past operations and in planning future investing and financing activities. It is also used by external users, such as investors and creditors, to assess a company's profit potential and ability to repay its debt and pay dividends.

For example, Ford Motor Company had a net loss of $12.6 billion but a positive cash flow from operating activities of $3.3 billion. This difference was mostly due to $16.5 billion of depreciation expense. This is because depreciation is a non-cash expense.

The statement of cash flows reports three types of cash flow activities as follows:

1. **Cash flows from operating activities** are cash flows from transactions that affect the operating income of the company.

Examples:
- purchase of merchandise by a retailer
- sale of merchandise by a retailer
- payment of operating expenses such as advertising, insurance, rent, salaries, supplies, and utilities
- payment of interest
- payment of taxes

2. **Cash flows from investing activities** are cash flows from transactions that affect investments in noncurrent assets of the company.
   Examples:
   - purchase of property, plant, and equipment
   - sale of property, plant, and equipment

3. **Cash flows from financing activities** are cash flows from transactions that affect the debt and equity of the company.
   Examples:
   - issuing common shares
   - retiring common shares
   - issuing debt securities such as notes payable
   - retiring debt securities such as notes payable

Note: Statement of cash flows order

O - Operating
I - Investing
F - Financing

The cash flows are reported in the cash flow statement as follows:

Cash flows from operating activities	$XXX
Cash flows from investing activities	XXX
Cash flows from financing activities	XXX
Net increase or decrease in cash for the period	$XXX
Cash at the beginning of the period	XXX
Cash at the end of the period	$XXX

The ending cash on the statement of cash flows equals the cash reported on the company's balance sheet.

Cash is considered to include both cash and cash equivalents. Examples of cash equivalents include short-term, highly liquid investments, such as money market accounts, bank certificates of deposit, and government bonds. When a company borrows from a bank, that transaction is generally considered to be part of financing activities. But when a company uses its bank overdraft as a way of dealing with day-to-day cash management, then the bank overdraft may be considered to be a cash equivalent.

Note: The statement of cash flows reports cash flows from operating, investing, and financing activities.

Exhibit 1 illustrates the sources (increases) and uses (decreases) of cash by each of the three cash flow activities. A *source* of cash causes the cash flow to increase and is called a *cash inflow*. A *use* of cash causes cash flow to decrease and is called a *cash outflow*.

Interest and dividends are treated differently under IFRS and ASPE. IFRS allows choices for reporting interest and dividends paid and received, depending on whether the interest and dividends were recorded in net income and whether the transaction was finance-related or investment-related.[1] Interest and dividends may be recorded in operating, investing, or financing, depending on the basis of the business transaction. ASPE is much more prescriptive in its approach. Dividends paid are classified as a financing activity. Dividends received and interest (both paid and received) are classified as operating activities.[2] For simplicity, in this textbook, interest both paid and received and dividends received are included in operating activities. Dividends paid are recorded in financing activities.

The statement of cash flows is an important financial statement. Users of the financial statements use the statement of cash flows to understand the statement

1 *CICA Handbook—Accounting*, 2011 edition, Part 1, IAS 7 para. 33.

2 *CICA Handbook—Accounting*, 2011 edition, Part II, 1540.31.

Cash Flows

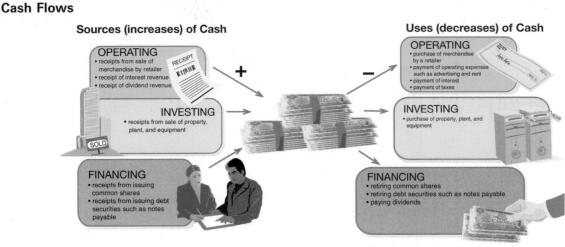

Note: Accounts for sections

O - net income
+/− current
assets and
current
liabilities

I - long-tem
assets

F - long-term debt
and equity

of income and the statement of financial position in relation to cash. Examining the net cash flow from operating activities as reported on the statement of cash flows is an important way of analyzing the health of a business. It's no wonder that many businesspeople say that "cash is king." For example, one business may report $100,000 of net income, most of which it generated through operating activities, while another business in the same industry may also report $100,000 of net income but most of it was generated through investing activities. The first business has a much stronger position, even though both businesses have the same overall net income. The operating activities reflect the purpose of the business. Thus, stronger cash numbers in the operating activities of the statement of cash flows indicate a healthier business. Analyzing the investing and financing sections will also inform users regarding the management philosophy toward investing in the business and financing the organization.

Cash Flows from Operating Activities

Two methods are used for reporting cash flows from operating activities in the cash flow statement:

1. Direct method
2. Indirect method

Both methods report the same amount of cash flow from operating activities but differ in how the cash flow is reported.

The **direct method** reports operating cash inflows (receipts) and cash outflows (payments) as follows:

Cash flows from operating activities		
Receipts:		
Cash received from customers	$ XXX	
Interest received on notes receivable	XXX	
Total cash receipts		$ XXX
Payments:		
Cash payments for merchandise	XXX	
Cash payments for operating expenses	XXX	
Cash payments for interest	XXX	
Cash payments for income taxes	XXX	
Total cash payments		XXX
Net cash flow from operating activities		$XXX

The primary operating cash inflow is cash received from customers. The primary operating cash outflows are cash payments for four items: merchandise, operating expenses, interest, and income taxes. The cash received less the cash payments is the net cash flow from operating activities.

The advantage of the direct method is that it *directly* reports cash receipts and payments in the cash flow statement. Users find this method easy to understand because it provides a picture of the sources and uses of cash. The direct method is encouraged for users of both ASPE and IFRS.[3]

The **indirect method** reports operating cash flows by beginning with net income and adjusting it for revenues and expenses that do not involve the receipt or payment of cash as follows:

Cash flows from operating activities:		
Net income	$XXX	
Adjustments to reconcile net income to net cash flow from operating activities	XXX	
Net cash flow from operating activities		$XXX

The adjustments to reconcile net income to net cash flow from operating activities include such items as depreciation and gains (or losses) on capital assets. Also added or deducted (depending on their effect on cash flows) are changes in current operating assets and liabilities such as accounts receivable or accounts payable. In effect, these additions and deductions adjust net income, which is reported on an accrual accounting basis, to cash flows from operating activities, which uses a cash basis.

An advantage of the indirect method is that it reconciles the differences between net income and net cash flows from operations. In doing so, the indirect method shows how net income is related to the ending cash balance that is reported on the balance sheet.

Exhibit 2 illustrates the Cash Flows from Operating Activities section of the statement of cash flows for NetSolutions. Exhibit 2 shows the direct and indirect methods using the NetSolutions data from Chapter 1. As Exhibit 2 illustrates, both methods report the same amount of net cash flow from operating activities, $2,900.

@netsolutions

Exhibit 2

Cash Flow from Operations: Direct and Indirect Methods—NetSolutions

Direct Method		**Indirect Method**	
Cash flows from operating activities:		Cash flows from operating activities:	
Cash received from customers	$7,500	Net income	$3,050
Cash payments for expenses and payments to creditors	4,600	Add increase in accounts payable	400
		Deduct increase in supplies	550
Net cash flow from operating activities	$2,900	Net cash flow from operating activities	$2,900

the same

In Chapter 1, the direct method was used to report NetSolutions' statement of cash flows.

Cash Flows from Investing Activities

Cash flows from investing activities are reported on the statement of cash flows as follows:

Cash flows from investing activities:		
Cash inflows from investing activities	$XXX	
Cash used for investing activities	(XXX)	
Net cash flow from investing activities		XXX

3 *CICA Handbook—Accounting*, 2011 edition, Part II, 1540.21 and Part I, IAS 7 para. 19.

Cash inflows from investing activities normally arise from
- selling property, plant, and equipment
- selling investments
- selling intangible assets

Cash outflows normally include
- payments to purchase capital assets
- payments to purchase investments
- payments to purchase intangible assets

Cash Flows from Financing Activities

Cash flows from financing activities are reported on the statement of cash flows as follows:

Cash flows from financing activities:		
Cash inflows from financing activities	$XXX	
Cash used for financing activities	(XXX)	
Net cash flow from financing activities		XXX

Cash inflows from financing activities normally arise from issuing debt or equity securities, such as
- bonds
- notes payable
- preferred shares
- common shares

Cash outflows from financing activities include
- paying cash dividends
- repaying debt
- repurchasing shares

Noncash Investing and Financing Activities

A company may enter into transactions involving investing and financing activities that do not *directly* affect cash. For example, a company may issue common shares to retire long-term debt. Although this transaction does not directly affect cash, it does eliminate future cash payments for interest and for paying the bonds when they mature. Because such a transaction does not involve cash, it is not included in the statement of cash flows. Instead, it is disclosed in the notes to the financial statements.

Examples include
- issuing common shares to retire long-term debt
- issuing share dividends
- purchasing land through a mortgage

EXAMPLE EXERCISE 16-1 Classifying Cash Flows　　　　　　　　　　　　　1

Identify whether each of the following would be reported as an operating, investing, or financing activity in the statement of cash flows.

a. Purchase of a patent
b. Payment of a cash dividend
c. Disposal of equipment

d. Cash sales
e. Receipt of interest on a note receivable
f. Payment of wages expense

(continued)

CRITICAL THINKING

Is it possible to have positive net income and not have enough cash to run the business?

Yes, having positive net income is no guarantee that a business will have cash on hand to operate. Not having enough cash to run a business can result from making sales on account, prepaying insurance, purchasing assets with cash, and paying cash for expenses.

 # Statement of Cash Flows—The Indirect Method

Prepare a statement of cash flows, using the indirect method.

The indirect method of reporting cash flows from operating activities uses the logic that a change in any statement of financial position account (including cash) can be analyzed in terms of changes in the other statement of financial position accounts. Thus, by analyzing changes in noncash statement of financial position accounts, any change in the cash account can be *indirectly* determined.

To illustrate, the accounting equation can be solved for cash as shown below.

$$\text{Assets} = \text{Liabilities} + \text{Shareholders' Equity}$$
$$\text{Cash} + \text{Noncash Assets} = \text{Liabilities} + \text{Shareholders' Equity}$$
$$\text{Cash} = \text{Liabilities} + \text{Shareholders' Equity} - \text{Noncash Assets}$$

Therefore, any change in the cash account can be determined by analyzing changes in the liability, shareholders' equity, and noncash asset accounts as shown below.

Change in Cash = *Change* in Liabilities + *Change* in Shareholders' Equity
   − *Change* in Noncash Assets

Under the indirect method, there is no order in which the statement of financial position accounts must be analyzed. However, net income (or net loss) is the first amount reported on the statement of cash flows. As you use the accounts in the statement of financial position and the statement of income, check them off to ensure that you have considered all the accounts when completing the statement of cash flows.

To illustrate the indirect method, we use the statement of income and the statement of financial position for Rundell Ltd. shown in Exhibit 3. Ledger accounts, T accounts, and other data supporting the statement of income and statement of financial position are presented as needed.[4]

Operating Activities Section

Adjustments to Net Income
The net income of $108,000 reported by Rundell Ltd. does not equal the cash flows from operating activities for the period. This is because net income is determined using the accrual method of accounting.

---

4 The use of a spreadsheet (work sheet) as an aid in assembling data for the statement of cash flows is presented in an appendix at the end of this chapter. This appendix illustrates the use of this spreadsheet in reporting cash flows from operating activities using the indirect method.

Exhibit 3

Statement of Income and Statement of Financial Position

Rundell Ltd. Statement of Income For the Year Ended December 31, 2015		
Sales		$1,180,000
Cost of goods sold.		790,000
Gross profit		390,000
Operating expenses:		
Depreciation expense	7,000	
Other operating expenses	196,000	
Total operating expenses.		203,000
Income from operations		187,000
Other income:		
Gain on sale of land	$ 12,000	
Other expense:		
Interest expense	8,000	4,000
Income before income taxes.		191,000
Income taxes expense		83,000
Net income		$ 108,000

Rundell Ltd. Statement of Financial Position December 31, 2015 and 2014			
	2015	2014	Increase Decrease*
Assets			
Cash.	$ 97,500	$ 26,000	$ 71,500
Accounts receivable (net)	74,000	65,000	9,000
Inventories	172,000	180,000	8,000*
Building	260,000	200,000	60,000
Accumulated depreciation—building.	(65,300)	(58,300)	7,000*
Land.	80,000	125,000	45,000*
Total assets	$618,200	$537,700	$ 80,500
Liabilities			
Accounts payable (merchandise creditors)	$ 43,500	$ 46,700	$ 3,200*
Accrued expenses payable (operating expenses) .	26,500	24,300	2,200
Income taxes payable.	7,900	8,400	500*
Dividends payable	14,000	10,000	4,000
Bonds payable	100,000	150,000	50,000*
Total liabilities.	191,900	239,400	47,500*
Shareholders' Equity			
Common shares	144,000	96,000	48,000
Retained earnings	282,300	202,300	80,000
Total shareholders' equity.	426,300	298,300	128,000
Total liabilities and shareholders' equity	$618,200	$537,700	$ 80,500

Under the accrual method of accounting, revenues and expenses are not always recorded when cash is received or paid. For example, merchandise may be sold on account and the cash received at a later date. Likewise, insurance premiums may be paid in the current period, but expensed in a following period.

Adjustments to Net Income (Loss) Using the Indirect Method

	Increase (Decrease)
Cash flows from operating activities	
Net income (loss).	$ XXX
Adjustments to reconcile net income to net cash flow from operating activities:	
Step 1 → Depreciation of capital assets.	XXX
Amortization of intangible assets	XXX
Step 2 → Losses on disposal of assets	XXX
Gains on disposal of assets	(XXX)
Step 3 → Changes in current operating assets and liabilities	
Increases in noncash current operating assets	(XXX)
Decreases in noncash current operating assets	XXX
Increases in current operating liabilities	XXX
Decreases in current operating liabilities	(XXX)
Net cash flow from operating activities.	$ XXX
	or
	$(XXX)

Subtract	**Add**
Increases in accounts receivable	Decreases in accounts receivable
Increases in inventories	Decreases in inventories
Increases in prepaid expenses	Decreases in prepaid expenses
Decreases in accounts payable	Increases in accounts payable
Decreases in accrued expenses payable*	Increases in accrued expenses payable
Decreases in income taxes payable	Increases in income taxes payable
Decreases in interest payable	Increases in interest payable
*this includes salaries payable	

Thus, under the indirect method, adjustments must be made to net income to determine cash flows from operating activities. The typical adjustments to net income are shown in Exhibit 4.[5]

Retained Earnings The comparative statement of financial position for Rundell Inc. shows that retained earnings increased $80,000 during the year. The retained earnings account shown below indicates how this change occurred.

Ledger					
Account Retained Earnings					Account No.
Date		**Item**	**Debit**	**Credit**	**Balance**
2015					
Jan.	1	Balance			202,300 CR.
Dec.	31	Net income		108,000	310,300 CR.
	31	Cash dividends	28,000		282,300 CR.

The retained earnings account indicates that the $80,000 ($108,000 – $28,000) change resulted from net income of $108,000 and cash dividends of $28,000. The net income of $108,000 is the first amount reported in the Cash Flows from Operating Activities

5 Other items that also require adjustments to net income to obtain cash flows from operating activities include amortization of bonds payable discounts (add), losses on debt retirement (add), amortization of bonds payable premiums (deduct), and gains on retirement of debt (deduct).

section, as discussed above. The net income figure can also be found in the statement of income.

Net income is normally adjusted to cash flows from operating activities using the following steps:

Step 1: Expenses that do not affect cash are added. Such expenses decrease net income but do not involve cash payments and, thus, are added to net income.

Examples: Depreciation of capital assets and amortization of intangible assets are added to net income.

Step 2: Losses and gains on disposal of assets are added or deducted. The disposal (sale) of assets is an investing activity, not an operating activity. However, such losses and gains are reported as part of net income. These losses and gains need to be removed from the operating activities section because they will be reported in the investing activities section. Thus, any losses need to be added back to net income in order to remove them. Equally, any gains need to be deducted from net income in order to remove them.

Example: Land costing $100,000 is sold for $90,000. The loss of $10,000 is added back to net income.

Step 3: Changes in current operating assets and liabilities are added or deducted as follows:

Increases in noncash current operating assets are deducted.
Decreases in noncash current operating assets are added.
Increases in current operating liabilities are added.
Decreases in current operating liabilities are deducted.

Example: A sale of $10,000 on account increases accounts receivable by $10,000. However, cash is not affected. Thus, an increase in accounts receivable of $10,000 is deducted. Similar adjustments are required for the changes in the other current asset and liability accounts such as inventory, prepaid expenses, accounts payable, accrued expenses payable, and income taxes payable, as shown in Exhibit 4.

EXAMPLE EXERCISE 16-2 Adjustments to Net Income—Indirect Method ⑵

O.M.I. Corporation's accumulated depreciation increased by $12,000, and $3,700 of patents were amortized between balance sheet dates. There were no purchases or sales of tangible or intangible assets during the year. In addition, the income statement showed a gain of $4,100 from the sale of land. Reconcile a net income of $62,000 to net cash flow from operating activities using the indirect method.

FOLLOW MY EXAMPLE 16-2

Net income.	$62,000
Adjustments to reconcile net income to net cash flow from operating activities:	
Depreciation.	12,000
Amortization of patents	3,700
Gain from sale of land	(4,100)
Net cash flow from operating activities.	$73,600

For Practice: PE 16-2

To illustrate, the statement of cash flows for Rundell Ltd. is used. The first part of the statement, the operating activities section, is shown in Exhibit 5. Rundell's net income of $108,000 is converted to cash flows from operating activities of $100,500.

Exhibit 5

Statement of Cash Flows, Operating Activities—Indirect Method

Rundell Ltd. Statement of Cash Flows (partial) For the Year Ended December 31, 2015		
Cash flows from operating activities:		
Net income		$108,000
Adjustments to reconcile net income to net		
cash flow from operating activities:		
Depreciation	7,000	
Gain on sale of land	(12,000)	
Changes in current operating assets and liabilities:		
Increase in accounts receivable	(9,000)	
Decrease in inventories	8,000	
Decrease in accounts payable	(3,200)	
Increase in accrued expenses payable	2,200	
Decrease in income taxes payable	(500)	
Net cash flow from operating activities . . .		$100,500

Step 1 →
Step 2 →
Step 3 →

Step 1.   Add depreciation of $7,000.

Analysis: The comparative statement of financial position sheet in Exhibit 3 indicates that the Accumulated Depreciation—Building account increased by $7,000. The T account, shown below, indicates that depreciation for the year was $7,000 for the building. The $7,000 depreciation is added to net income because depreciation is an expense that does not involve cash. Thus, the operating expenses (and net income) include $7,000 that was not spent in cash during the year.

Accumulated Depreciation—Building	
	58,300 opening
	7,000 depreciation
	65,300 balance

Step 2.   Deduct the gain on the sale of land of $12,000.

Analysis: The statement of income in Exhibit 3 reports a gain from the sale of land of $12,000. The proceeds, which include the gain, are reported in the Investing section of the statement of cash flows.[6] Thus, the gain of $12,000 is deducted from net income in determining cash flows from operating activities.

Step 3:   Add and deduct changes in current operating assets and liabilities.

Analysis: The increases and decreases in the current operating asset and current liability accounts are shown below.

| | December 31 | | Increase |
Accounts	2015	2014	Decrease*
Accounts Receivable (net)	$ 74,000	$ 65,000	$9,000
Inventories	172,000	180,000	8,000*
Accounts Payable (merchandise creditors)	43,500	46,700	3,200*
Accrued Expenses Payable (operating expenses)	26,500	24,300	2,200
Income Taxes Payable	7,900	8,400	500*

6 The reporting of the proceeds (cash flows) from the sale of land as part of investing activities is discussed later in this chapter.

Accounts receivable (net): The $9,000 increase is deducted from net income. This is because the $9,000 increase in accounts receivable indicates that sales on account were $9,000 more than the cash received from customers. Thus, sales (and net income) include $9,000 that was not received in cash during the year.

Inventory: The $8,000 decrease is added to net income. This is because the $8,000 decrease in inventories indicates that the cost of goods *sold* exceeds the cost of the goods *purchased* during the year by $8,000. In other words, cost of goods sold includes $8,000 that was not purchased (used cash) during the year.

Accounts payable (merchandise creditors): The $3,200 decrease is deducted from net income. This is because a decrease in accounts payable indicates that the cash *payments* to merchandise creditors exceeds the merchandise *purchased on account* by $3,200. Therefore, cost of goods sold is $3,200 less than the cash paid to merchandise creditors during the year.

Accrued expenses payable (operating expenses): The $2,200 increase is added to net income. This is because an increase in accrued expenses payable indicates that operating expenses exceed the cash payments for operating expenses by $2,200. In other words, operating expenses reported on the income statement include $2,200 that did not require a cash outflow during the year. This could include salaries payable and salaries expense.

Income taxes payable: The $500 decrease is deducted from net income. This is because a decrease in income taxes payable indicates that taxes paid exceed the amount of taxes incurred during the year by $500. In other words, the amount reported on the income statement for income taxes expense is less than the amount paid by $500.

Using the preceding analyses, Rundell's net income of $108,000 is converted to cash flows from operating activities of $100,500, as shown in Exhibit 5, on page 823.

EXAMPLE EXERCISE 16-3 Changes in Current Operating Assets and Liabilities—Indirect Method ②

Victor Corporation's statement of financial position data for current assets and liabilities for December 31, 2016 and 2015, are as follows:

	Dec. 31, 2016	Dec. 31, 2015
Accounts receivable	$ 6,500	$ 4,900
Inventory	12,300	15,000
Accounts payable	4,800	5,200
Dividends payable	5,000	4,000

Adjust net income of $70,000 for changes in operating assets and liabilities to arrive at cash flows from operating activities using the indirect method.

FOLLOW MY EXAMPLE 16-3

Net income.	$70,000
Changes in current operating assets and liabilities:	
Increase in accounts receivable.	(1,600)
Decrease in inventories.	2,700
Decrease in accounts payable	(400)
Net cash flow from operating activities.	$70,700

Note: The change in dividends payable affects the cash paid for dividends, which is disclosed under financing activities.

For Practice: PE 16-3

EXAMPLE EXERCISE 16-4 Cash Flows from Operating Activities—Indirect Method ②

Ideas Inc. reported the following data:

Net income	$120,000
Depreciation expense	15,000
Loss on disposal of equipment	17,000
Increase in accounts receivable	5,000
Decrease in accounts payable	2,500
Increase in dividends payable	3,000

Prepare the Cash Flows from Operating Activities section of the statement of cash flows using the indirect method.

FOLLOW MY EXAMPLE 16-4

Cash flows from operating activities:
Net income $120,000
    Adjustments to reconcile net income to net cash flow from
      operating activities:
        Depreciation expense... 15,000
        Loss on disposal of equipment............................... 17,000
    Changes in current operating assets and liabilities:
        Increase in accounts receivable .... (5,000)
        Decrease in accounts payable................................. (2,500)
            Net cash flow from operating activities $144,500

Note: The change in dividends payable affects the cash paid for dividends, which is disclosed under financing activities.

For Practice: PE 16-4

INTEGRITY, OBJECTIVITY, AND ETHICS IN BUSINESS

IN TIMES OF TROUBLE

We expect customers will pay for products and services sold on account. Unfortunately, that is not always the case. Most entrepreneurs would prefer to think about the exciting aspects of their business—such as product development, marketing, sales, and advertising—not credit collection or accounts receivable collectability. In times of economic trouble, businesses experience cash flow restrictions and downward pressure on sales. During these periods, an entrepreneur's attention may be diverted from the task of collecting on overdue accounts. However, just as financial statements need to reflect economic reality if they are to provide constructive information, an honest assessment of the collectability of accounts receivables is necessary to ensure an understanding of how net income relates to sales in a given period and how the firm's business plan, policies, and procedures are influencing business outcomes. Although accounts receivable balances are sometimes referred to as "money in the bank," savvy entrepreneurs know that collecting accounts receivable efficiently is the key to turning a current asset into positive cash flow.

Investing Activities Section

Refer to the property, plant, and equipment section of the statement of financial position for Rundell Ltd. on page 820 for the investing activities.

The accounts that are related to the investing activities section of the statement of cash flows are the long-term asset accounts, which include the contra account Accumulated Depreciation. The transactions may include additions or disposals of long-term assets. Disposals may include sales of long-term assets or retirement of assets without a sale.

When a long-term asset is purchased, consideration is given to both the amount paid for the asset and the method of payment, which may be cash and/or a liability, such as a note payable.

When a long-term asset is disposed of, the calculation involves removal of the cost of the asset from the asset account, removal of the accumulated depreciation related to the asset from the accumulated depreciation account, and consideration of the gain or loss recorded in the statement of income.

We now return to the Rundell Ltd. example.

Building Analysis: The Building account increased by $60,000, and the Accumulated Depreciation—Building account increased by $7,000, as shown below.

Building		Accumulated Depreciation—Building	
opening 200,000			58,300 opening
purchase 60,000			7,000 depreciation
balance 260,000			65,300 balance

The purchase of a building for cash of $60,000 is reported as an outflow of cash in the Investing Activities section as follows:

Cash flows from investing activities:
Cash paid for purchase of building . . . . ($60,000)

The credit in the Accumulated Depreciation—Building account represents depreciation expense for the year. This depreciation expense of $7,000 on the building was added to net income in determining cash flows from operating activities, as reported in Exhibit 5 on page 823.

Another Example In one year, a company may purchase and sell equipment using the same equipment account. In this case, both the accumulated depreciation and the year's annual depreciation will need to be considered. Because this situation did not occur with Rundell Ltd., an example is provided below. Using a T account may be needed to ensure that all aspects of the transaction are included. Alternatively, the journal entries themselves can be considered. For example, the following long-term asset accounts are recorded on the balance sheet.

Equipment	410,000	370,000
Accumulated depreciation	(150,000)	(158,000)

The depreciation for the year totals $57,000. Assume that equipment costing $125,000 was purchased for cash and that equipment costing $85,000 with accumulated depreciation of $65,000 was sold for a loss of $5,000.

Equipment		Accumulated Depreciation—Equipment	
opening 370,000			158,000 opening
purchase 125,000	85,000 sale	sale 65,000	57,000 yearly depreciation
closing 410,000			150,000 closing

The equipment purchase is a straight cash transaction, and the $125,000 purchase price is recorded in the T account. The sale of the equipment is considered next. The $85,000 credit is entered into the Equipment account and the balance is checked. The $65,000 in accumulated depreciation is then entered as a debit into the Accumulated Depreciation—Equipment account. This transaction removes the accumulated depreciation related to that equipment. When checking the final balance, the $57,000 yearly depreciation will balance the accounts correctly. The amount of cash related to the disposal is calculated on the basis of both the carrying value of the equipment and the loss recorded on the income statement. The cash involved with the disposal can be calculated by deducting the loss on sale of $5,000 from the carrying value at the time of disposal ($20,000 = $85,000 − $65,000). Total cash received from the sale of the equipment is $15,000 = $20,000 − $5,000.

Land The $45,000 decline in the land account of Rundell was from two transactions, as shown below.

When we create our T account, we might assume that the change of $45,000 was a result of the sale of land alone.

Land		
opening	125,000	
		45,000 sale?
closing	80,000	

But when we look into the Land account, we see two transactions.

Land		
opening	125,000	
		60,000 sale Jun. 8
Oct. 12 purchase	15,000	
closing	80,000	

The June 8 transaction is the sale of land with a cost of $60,000. How much cash was involved in the sale of the land? We can calculate the cash involved by identifying the gain or loss on the sale of the land. That amount is shown on the statement of income for Rundell Ltd. on page 820. Because the gain on the sale of land was $12,000, $72,000 ($60,000 + $12,000) must have been received for the sale of the land.

The entry would be as follows:

Jun.	8	Cash	72,000	
		Land		60,000
		Gain on Sale of Land		12,000
		Sale of land.		

The $72,000 proceeds from the sale are reported in the Investing Activities section, as follows:

Cash flows from investing activities:
Cash received from sale of land. $72,000

The proceeds of $72,000 include the $12,000 gain on the sale of land and the $60,000 cost (carrying value) of the land. As shown in Exhibit 5, the $12,000 gain is deducted from net income in the Cash Flows from Operating Activities section. This deduction is needed so that the $12,000 cash inflow related to the gain is not included twice as a cash inflow.

The October 12 transaction is the purchase of land for cash of $15,000. This transaction is reported as an outflow of cash in the Investing Activities section, as follows:

Cash flows from investing activities:
Cash paid for purchase of land . . . . $(15,000)

EXAMPLE EXERCISE 16-5   Land Transactions on the Statement of Cash Flows   2

Alpha Corporation purchased land for $125,000. Later in the year, the company sold land with a carrying value of $165,000 for $200,000. Show the effects of these transactions on the statement of cash flows, using the indirect method.

FOLLOW MY EXAMPLE 16-5

The gain on sale of land is deducted from net income as shown below.
Gain on sale of land . . . . $ (35,000)

The purchase and sale of land is reported as part of cash flows from investing activities as shown below.
Cash received for sale of land.   200,000
Cash paid for purchase of land . . . .   (125,000)

For Practice: PE 16-5

Financing Activities Section

Refer to the long-term liabilities and equity section of the statement of financial position on page 820 for financing activities.

Financing activities involve the Long-Term Liabilities and Equity section of the statement of financial position. Remember that when dividends are declared, no cash trades hands and so only dividends that have been paid are recorded on the statement of cash flows.

Dividends The retained earnings account of Rundell Ltd., shown on the next page, indicates cash dividends declared of $28,000 during the year. However, the dividends payable account, shown below, indicates that only $24,000 of the dividends was paid during the year. More information is available in the dividends payable account. The opening balance was $10,000, the amount that was paid on January 10. On June 20, dividends of $14,000 were declared, which were paid on July 10. On December 20, there was a dividend declaration of $14,000.

Dividends Payable		
	10,000	opening
Jan. 10 paid 10,000		
	14,000	declared Jun. 20
Jul. 10 paid 14,000		
	14,000	declared Dec. 20
	14,000	balance

These two debits to Dividends Payable will have matching credits to cash, resulting in an outflow of $24,000 ($10,000 + $14,000).

Because dividend payments are a financing activity, the dividend payment of $24,000 is reported in the Financing Activities section of the statement of cash flows, as shown below.

Cash flows from financing activities:
Cash paid for dividends $24,000

Common Shares The common shares account increased by $48,000. The opening and closing balances are known from the statement of financial position. This increase was generated from issuing 4,000 common shares for $12 per share.

Common Shares		
	96,000	opening
	48,000	issuance
	144,000	balance

This cash inflow is reported in the Financing Activities section as follows:

Cash flows from financing activities:
Cash received from sale of common shares $48,000

Bonds Payable The bonds payable account decreased by $50,000, as shown below. This decrease results from retiring the bonds by a cash payment for their face value.

Bonds Payable		
	150,000	opening
retired 50,000		
	100,000	balance

This cash outflow is reported in the Financing Activities section as follows:

Cash flows from financing activities:
    Cash paid to retire bonds payable . . . . $(50,000)

Retained Earnings The statement of financial position for Rundell Ltd. shown in Exhibit 3 indicates retained earnings increased by $80,000 during the year. The retained earnings account shown below illustrates how this change occurred.

Retained Earnings		
	202,300	opening
	108,000	net income
dividends 28,000		
	282,300	balance

The retained earnings account indicates that the $80,000 ($108,000 – $28,000) change resulted from net income of $108,000 and dividends declared of $28,000. The net income of $108,000 is the first amount reported in the Cash Flows from Operating Activities section.

However, as shown earlier, although $28,000 of dividends was declared, only $24,000 was paid.

Interpreting the Statement of Cash Flows

The statement of cash flows for Rundell Ltd. using the indirect method is shown in Exhibit 6. The statement of cash flows indicates that cash increased by $71,500 during the year. The most significant increase in net cash flows ($100,500) was from operating activities. The most significant use of cash ($26,000) was for financing activities. The ending balance of cash on December 31, 2015, is $97,500. This ending cash balance is also reported on the December 31, 2015, statement of financial position shown in Exhibit 3 on page 820.

CRITICAL THINKING

Where does Rundell Ltd. get its cash? Is it mostly from operating, which would be expected from a healthy business? **Summarize why Rundell Ltd.'s cash flow of $71,500 does not match its income of $108,000.**

As mentioned on page 819, not all net income is cash. Rundell Ltd.'s operating activities include two noncash items that are not reflected in cash flow—the gain on the sale of land and depreciation. Also, the amounts for current assets and current liabilities have changed for a total cash outflow of $2,500 (–$9,000 + $8,000 – $3,200 + $2,200 – $500), which needs to be reflected in the operating cash flow. In addition, investing activities resulted in changes to the land account and building account, resulting in $57,000 ($72,000 – $15,000) of cash inflow and $60,000 of cash outflow, respectively. Also, a $26,000 net outflow is related to the sale of common shares, the retirement of bonds, and cash paid for dividends.

Exhibit 6

Statement of Cash Flows Statement—Indirect Method

Rundell Ltd.
Statement of Cash Flows
For the Year Ended December 31, 2015

Cash flows from operating activities:
    Net income $108,000
           Adjustments to reconcile net income to net
           cash flow from operating activities:
                 Depreciation   7,000
                 Gain on sale of land . . . .   (12,000)
           Changes in current operating assets and liabilities:
                 Increase in accounts receivable . . . .   (9,000)
                 Decrease in inventories   8,000
                 Decrease in accounts payable . . . .   (3,200)
                 Increase in accrued expenses payable   2,200
                 Decrease in income taxes payable . . . .   (500)
                Net cash flow from operating activities $100,500

Cash flows from investing activities:
    Cash from sale of land   72,000
    Cash paid to purchase land . . . .   (15,000)
    Cash paid for purchase of building . . . .   (60,000)
        Net cash flow used for investing activities . . . .   (3,000)

Cash flows from financing activities:
    Cash received from sale of common shares   48,000
    Cash paid to retire bonds payable . . . .   (50,000)
    Cash paid for dividends . . . .   (24,000)
        Net cash flow used for financing activities . . . .   (26,000)
Increase in cash.   71,500
Cash at the beginning of the year   26,000
Cash at the end of the year . . . . $ 97,500

Step 4 →

Step 5 →

Step 6 →

MID-CHAPTER ILLUSTRATIVE PROBLEM

The statement of financial position and statement of income of Benjamin Corporation for December 31, 2015 and 2014, and related supplementary information are as follows:

Benjamin Corporation
Statement of Financial Position
As at December 31

Assets	2015	2014
Current Assets:		
Cash	$ 81,720	$ 35,000
Accounts receivable (net)	80,000	62,000
Inventories.	66,800	96,800
Prepaid expenses	5,400	5,200
Total current assets.	233,920	199,000
Property, Plant, and Equipment:		
Equipment.	130,000	120,000
Accumulated depreciation—equipment	(28,000)	(50,600)
Total property, plant, and equipment	102,000	69,400
Total assets	$335,920	$268,400

(*continued*)

Liabilities

Current Liabilities:		
Accounts payable.	$ 25,000	$ 34,000
Wages payable	7,000	14,000
Interest payable.	1,000	0
Income taxes payable	2,400	3,600
Total current liabilities	35,400	51,600
Long-Term Liabilities:		
Notes payable	40,000	70,000
Total liabilities	75,400	121,600

Shareholders' Equity

Common shares	230,000	139,400
Retained earnings	30,520	7,400
Total shareholders' equity	260,520	146,800
Total liabilities and shareholders' equity	$335,920	$268,400

Benjamin Corporation
Statement of Income
For the Year Ended December 31, 2015

Sales revenue		$655,000
Cost of goods sold.		399,000
Gross profit.		256,000
Operating expenses:		
Wages expense.	$43,000	
Depreciation expense	18,000	
Other operating expenses.	14,000	
		75,000
Income from operations.		181,000
Other revenues/gains and expenses/losses:		
Interest expense	(10,000)	
Gain on sale of equipment.	2,000	(8,000)
Income before taxes		173,000
Income taxes expense		(51,900)
Net Income		$121,100

Supplementary Information:

1. The company had no noncash investing or financing transactions during the year.
2. The only changes affecting retained earnings during the year were net income and cash dividends paid.
3. Equipment with a historical cost of $48,600 was sold during 2015. Its accumulated depreciation balance was $40,600 at the time of the sale.
4. New equipment was acquired during 2015 using cash.

Instructions

Prepare, in proper form, a statement of cash flows for Benjamin Corporation for the year ended December 31, 2015, using the indirect method.

MID-CHAPTER ILLUSTRATIVE SOLUTION

Benjamin Corporation
Statement of Cash Flows (Indirect Method)
For the Year Ended December 31, 2015

Cash flows from operating activities:

Net income...		$121,100
Adjustments to reconcile net income to net cash flow from operating activities:		
Depreciation expense	$ 18,000	
Gain on sale of equipment...............	(2,000)	
Changes in current operating assets and liabilities:		
Increase in accounts receivable...........	(18,000)	
Decrease in inventories	30,000	
Increase in prepaid expenses.............	(200)	
Decrease in accounts payable	(9,000)	
Decrease in wages payable	(7,000)	
Increase in interest payable..............	1,000	
Decrease in income taxes payable	(1,200)	
Net cash flow from operating activities		$132,700
Cash flows from investing activities:		
Cash received from sale of equipment	10,000*	
Cash paid for purchase of equipment	(58,600)**	
Net cash flow from investing activities		(48,600)
Cash flows from financing activities:		
Cash paid for note retirement..........................	(30,000)	
Cash received from common shares issue	90,600	
Cash paid for dividends...............................	(97,980)†	
Net cash flow from financing activities		(37,380)†
Net increase in cash......................................		46,720
Cash, January 1, 2015		35,000
Cash, December 31, 2015		$ 81,720
*Cash received for equipment....................	$ 10,000	
NBV of equipment.............................	8,000	
Gain on sale of equipment.....................	$ 2,000	

**

Equipment			
opening	120,000		
		48,600	sale
purchase	58,600		
closing	130,000		

From the above T account, the purchase price of the equipment can be identified by calculating the price needed to achieve a balance of $130,000.

†The retained earnings T account is used to identify the dividends. The net income of $121,100 is entered as a credit to Retained Earnings, and the $97,980 is used to achieve a balance of $30,520.

Retained Earnings			
		7,400	opening
		121,100	net income
dividends	97,980		
		30,520	closing

Operating Activities Section— The Direct Method

3

Prepare the operating activities section, using the direct method.

The direct method reports cash flows from operating activities as follows:

Cash flows from operating activities:		
Receipts:		
Cash received from customers..................	$XXX	
Interest received on notes receivable	XXX	
Total cash receipts		$XXX
Payments:		
Cash payments for merchandise	XXX	
Cash payments for operating expenses	XXX	
Cash payments for interest.....................	XXX	
Cash payments for income taxes................	XXX	
Total cash payments		XXX
Net cash flow from operating activities........		$XXX

The Cash Flows from Investing and Financing Activities sections of the statement of cash flows are the same under the direct and indirect methods. The amount of cash flows from operating activities is also the same.

Under the direct method, the statement of income is adjusted to cash flows from operating activities as follows:

Income Statement	Adjusted by the Change In	Cash Flows from Operating Activities
Sales	Accounts receivable	Cash received from customers
Cost of goods sold	Inventories and accounts payable	Cash payments for merchandise
Operating expenses:		
Depreciation expense	N/A	N/A
Other operating expenses	Accrued expenses payable (such as salaries) and prepaid expenses (such as insurance)	Cash payments for operating expenses
Gain on sale of land	N/A	N/A
Interest expense	Interest payable	Cash payments for interest
Income taxes expense	Income taxes payable	Cash payments for income taxes
Net income		Cash flows from operating activities

N/A—Not applicable

As shown above, depreciation and amortization expenses are not adjusted or reported as part of cash flows from operating activities. This is because depreciation and amortization expenses do not involve a cash outflow. The gain on sale of land is also not adjusted or reported as part of cash flows from operating activities. This is because the sale of land is reported as an investing activity, not an operating activity.

To illustrate the direct method, the statement of income and statement of financial position for Rundell Ltd. shown in Exhibit 3 on page 820 are used.

Cash Received from Customers

Rundell Ltd.'s statement of income (shown in Exhibit 3) reports sales of $1,180,000. To determine the *cash received from customers*, the $1,180,000 is adjusted for any increase or decrease in accounts receivable. The adjustment is summarized below.

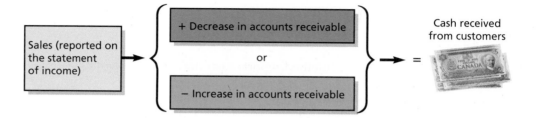

The cash received from customers is $1,171,000, computed as follows:

Sales	$1,180,000
Less increase in accounts receivable	9,000
Cash received from customers	$1,171,000

The increase of $9,000 in accounts receivable (shown in Exhibit 3) during 2015 indicates that sales on account exceeded cash received from customers by $9,000. In other words, sales include $9,000 that did not result in a cash inflow during the year. Thus, $9,000 is deducted from sales to determine the *cash received from customers*.

EXAMPLE EXERCISE 16-6   Cash Received from Customers—Direct Method   3

Sales reported on the statement of income were $350,000. The accounts receivable balance declined $7,200 over the year. Determine the amount of cash received from customers to be included in the operating section under the direct method.

FOLLOW MY EXAMPLE 16-6

Sales.	$350,000
Add decrease in accounts receivable.	7,200
Cash received from customers.	$357,200

For Practice: PE 16-6

Cash Payments for Merchandise

The statement of income for Rundell Ltd. (shown in Exhibit 3) reports cost of goods sold of $790,000. To determine the *cash payments for merchandise*, the $790,000 is adjusted for any increases or decreases in inventory and accounts payable. Assuming the accounts payable are owed to merchandise suppliers, the adjustment is summarized below.

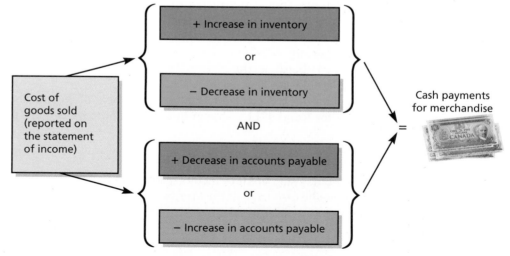

The cash payments for merchandise are $785,200, computed as follows:

Cost of goods sold	$790,000
Deduct decrease in inventory	(8,000)
Add decrease in accounts payable	3,200
Cash payments for merchandise	$785,200

The $8,000 decrease in inventory (from Exhibit 3) indicates that the merchandise sold exceeded the cost of the merchandise purchased by $8,000. In other words, cost of goods sold includes $8,000 that did not require a cash outflow during the year. Thus, $8,000 is deducted from the cost of goods sold in determining the *cash payments for merchandise*.

The $3,200 decrease in accounts payable (from Exhibit 3) indicates that cash payments for merchandise were $3,200 more than the purchases on account during 2012. Therefore, $3,200 is added to the cost of goods sold in determining *payments for merchandise*.

EXAMPLE EXERCISE 16-7   Cash Payments for Merchandise—Direct Method   **3**

Cost of goods sold reported on the statement of income was $145,000. The accounts payable balance increased $4,000, and the inventory balance increased by $9,000 over the year. Determine the amount of cash paid for merchandise to be included in the operating section under the direct method.

FOLLOW MY EXAMPLE 16-7

Cost of goods sold	$145,000
Add increase in inventories.	9,000
Deduct increase in accounts payable.	(4,000)
Cash paid for merchandise	$150,000

For Practice: PE 16-7

Cash Payments for Operating Expenses

The statement of income (from Exhibit 3) for Rundell Ltd. reports total operating expenses of $203,000, which includes depreciation expense of $7,000. Because depreciation expense does not require a cash outflow, it is omitted from *cash payments for operating expenses*.

To determine the *cash payments for operating expenses*, the other operating expenses (excluding depreciation) of $196,000 ($203,000 − $7,000) are adjusted for any increase or decrease in accrued expenses payable and prepaid expenses. Rundell Ltd. does not have any prepaid expenses, but prepaid expenses are included in the illustration below. Assuming that the accrued expenses payable are all operating expenses, this adjustment is summarized below.

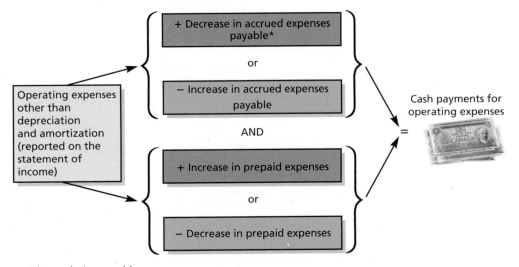

*such as salaries payable

The cash payments for operating expenses total $193,800, computed as follows:

Operating expenses other than depreciation	$196,000
Deduct increase in accrued expenses payable	(2,200)
Cash payments for operating expenses	$193,800

The increase in accrued expenses payable (from Exhibit 3) indicates that the cash payments for operating expenses were $2,200 less than the amount reported for operating expenses during the year. Thus, $2,200 is deducted from the operating expenses in determining the *cash payments for operating expenses*.

Cash Payments for Interest Expense

The statement of income for Rundell Ltd. (from Exhibit 3) reports interest expense of $8,000. To determine the *cash payments for interest*, the $8,000 is adjusted for any increases or decreases in interest payable. The adjustment is summarized below.

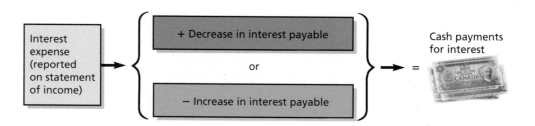

The statement of financial position of Rundell Ltd. in Exhibit 3 indicates no interest payable. This is because the interest expense on the bonds payable is paid on June 30 and December 31. Because there is no interest payable, no adjustment is necessary for the interest expense of $8,000.

Cash Payments for Income Taxes

The statement of income for Rundell Ltd. (from Exhibit 3) reports income taxes expense of $83,000. To determine the *Cash payments for income taxes*, the $83,000 is adjusted for any increases or decreases in income taxes payable. The adjustment is summarized below.

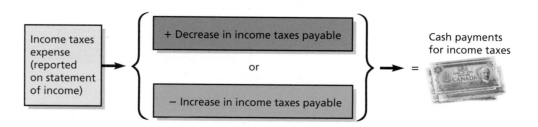

The cash payments for income taxes are $83,500, computed as follows:

Income taxes expense	$83,000
Add decrease in income taxes payable	500
Cash payments for income taxes	$83,500

The $500 decrease in income taxes payable (from Exhibit 3) indicates that the cash payments for income taxes were $500 more than the amount reported for income taxes expense during 2015. Thus, $500 is added to the income taxes expense in determining the *cash payments for income taxes*.

Comparing the Operating Section—Direct to Indirect

The statement of cash flows for Rundell Ltd. using the direct method for reporting cash flows from operating activities is shown in Exhibit 7. The only portion of the statement that differs from statements prepared using the indirect method is the operating section, which is highlighted in colour. The indirect method is shown in Exhibit 6 on page 830.

Exhibit 7

Statement of Cash Flows—Direct Method

Rundell Ltd.
Statement of Cash Flows
For the Year Ended December 31, 2015

Cash flows from operating activities:		
Receipts:		
Cash received from customers		$1,171,000
Payments:		
Cash payments for merchandise	$(785,200)	
Cash payments for operating expenses.	(193,800)	
Cash payments for interest	(8,000)	
Cash payments for income taxes.	(83,500)	(1,070,500)
Net cash flow from operating activities		100,500
Cash flows from investing activities:		
Cash from sale of land	72,000	
Cash paid to purchase land	(15,000)	
Cash paid for purchase of building	(60,000)	
Net cash flow used for investing activities		(3,000)
Cash flows from financing activities:		
Cash received from sale of common shares	48,000	
Cash paid to retire bonds payable	(50,000)	
Cash paid for dividends	(24,000)	
Net cash flow used for financing activities		(26,000)
Increase in cash.		71,500
Cash at the beginning of the year		26,000
Cash at the end of the year		$ 97,500

FINANCIAL ANALYSIS AND INTERPRETATION   (f·a·i)

A valuable tool for evaluating the cash flows of a business is free cash flow. **Free cash flow** is a measure of operating cash flow available for corporate purposes after providing sufficient capital asset additions to maintain current productive capacity. Thus, free cash flow can be calculated as follows:

Cash flow from operating activities	$XXX
Less: Investments in capital assets to	
maintain current production	XXX
Free cash flow	$XXX

Analysts often use free cash flow instead of cash flows from operating activities to measure the financial strength of a business. Many high-technology firms must aggressively reinvest in new technology to remain competitive. This investment can reduce free cash flow. For example, IBM's free cash flow was 76% of the cash flow from operating activities in a recent year. In contrast, Jones Soda Co.'s free cash flow was approximately 96% of the cash flow from operating activities in a recent year.

To illustrate, the cash flow from operating activities for IBM® was $19.85 billion in a recent fiscal year. The statement of cash flows indicated that the cash invested in property, plant, and equipment was $4.67 billion. Assuming that the amount invested in property, plant,

(continued)

and equipment maintained existing operations, free cash flow (in billions) would be calculated as follows:

Cash flow from operating activities	$19.85
Less: Investments in capital assets to maintain current production	4.67
Free cash flow	$15.18

During this period, IBM generated free cash flow in excess of $15 billion, which was 76% of cash flows from operations.

A company with no free cash flow is unable to maintain current productive capacity. Lack of free cash flow can be an early indicator of liquidity problems. On the other hand, a company that has free cash flow is able to fund internal growth, retire debt, retire shares, pay dividends, and enjoy financial flexibility.

EXAMPLE EXERCISE 16-8 Free Cash Flow   (3)

Omnicron Inc. reported the following on the company's statement of cash flows in 2014 and 2013:

	2014	2013
Net cash flow from operating activities	$ 140,000	$120,000
Net cash flow used for investing activities	(120,000)	(80,000)
Net cash flow used for financing activities	(20,000)	(32,000)

Seventy-five percent of the cash flow used for investing activities was used to replace existing capacity.

a. Determine Omnicron's free cash flow.

b. Has Omnicron's free cash flow improved or declined from 2013 to 2014?

FOLLOW MY EXAMPLE 16-8

a.

	2014	2013
Cash flow from operating activities	$140,000	$120,000
Less: Investments in fixed assets to maintain current production	90,000*	60,000**
Free cash flow	$ 50,000	$ 60,000

* $120,000 × 75%
** $80,000 × 75%

b. The change from $60,000 to $50,000 indicates an unfavourable trend.

For Practice: PE 16-8

A P P E N D I X 1

Spreadsheet (Work Sheet) for Statement of Cash Flows—The Indirect Method

A spreadsheet (work sheet) may be used in preparing the statement of cash flows. However, whether or not a spreadsheet (work sheet) is used, the concepts presented in this chapter are not affected.

Exhibit 8

End-of-Period Spreadsheet (Work Sheet) for Statement of Cash Flows—Indirect Method

Step 2

	A	B	C	D	E	F	G
1	Rundell Ltd.						
2	End-of-Period Spreadsheet (Work Sheet) for Statement of Cash Flows						
3	For the Year Ended December 31, 2015						
4	Accounts	Balance,		Transactions			Balance,
5		Dec. 31, 2014		Debit		Credit	Dec. 31, 2015
6	Cash	26,000	(o)	71,500			97,500
7	Accounts receivable (net)	65,000	(n)	9,000			74,000
8	Inventories	180,000			(m)	8,000	172,000
9	Land	125,000	(k)	15,000	(l)	60,000	80,000
10	Building	200,000	(j)	60,000			260,000
11	Accumulated depreciation—building	(58,300)			(i)	7,000	(65,300)
12	Accounts payable (merchandise creditors)	(46,700)	(h)	3,200			(43,500)
13	Accrued expenses payable (operating expenses)	(24,300)			(g)	2,200	(26,500)
14	Income taxes payable	(8,400)	(f)	500			(7,900)
15	Dividends payable	(10,000)			(e)	4,000	(14,000)
16	Bonds payable	(150,000)	(d)	50,000			(100,000)
17	Common shares	(96,000)			(c)	48,000	(144,000)
18	Retained earnings	202,300	(b)	28,000	(a)	108,000	(282,300)
19	Totals	0		237,200		237,200	0
20	Operating activities:						
21	Net income		(a)	108,000			
22	Depreciation of building		(i)	7,000			
23	Gain on sale of land				(l)	12,000	
24	Increase in accounts receivable				(n)	9,000	
25	Decrease in inventories		(m)	8,000			
26	Decrease in accounts payable				(h)	3,200	
27	Increase in accrued expenses payable		(g)	2,200			
28	Decrease in income taxes payable				(f)	500	
29	Investing activities:						
30	Sale of land		(l)	72,000			
31	Purchase of land				(k)	15,000	
32	Purchase of building				(j)	60,000	
33	Financing activities:						
34	Issued common shares		(c)	48,000			
35	Retired bonds payable				(d)	50,000	
36	Declared cash dividends				(b)	28,000	
37	Increase in dividends payable		(e)	4,000			
38	Net increase in cash				(o)	71,500	
39	Totals			249,200		249,200	
40							

Step 1 (rows 6–19)

Step 3 → (row 19) ← Step 3

Steps 4–7

The data for Rundell Ltd., presented in Exhibit 3, are used as a basis for illustrating the spreadsheet (work sheet) for the indirect method. The steps in preparing this spreadsheet (work sheet), shown in Exhibit 8, are as follows:

Step 1. List the title of each statement of financial position account in the Accounts column.

Step 2. For each statement of financial position account, enter its balance as at December 31, 2014, in the first column and its balance as at December 31, 2015, in the last column. Place the credit balances in parentheses.

Step 3. Add the December 31, 2014 and 2015, column totals, which should total to zero.

Step 4. Analyze the change during the year in each noncash account to determine its net increase (decrease) and classify the change as affecting cash flows from operating activities, investing activities, financing activities, or noncash investing and financing activities.

Step 5. Indicate the effect of the change on cash flows by making entries in the Transactions columns.

Step 6. After all noncash accounts have been analyzed, enter the net increase (decrease) in cash during the period.

Step 7. Add the Debit and Credit Transactions columns. The totals should be equal.

Analyzing Accounts

When analyzing the noncash accounts (step 4), try to determine the type of cash flow activity (operating, investing, or financing) that led to the change in the account. As each noncash account is analyzed, an entry (step 5) is made on the spreadsheet (work sheet) for the type of cash flow activity that caused the change. After all noncash accounts have been analyzed, an entry (step 6) is made for the increase (decrease) in cash during the period.

The entries made on the spreadsheet are not posted to the ledger. They are used only for preparing and summarizing the data on the spreadsheet.

The order in which the accounts are analyzed is not important. However, it is more efficient to begin with Retained Earnings and proceed upward in the account listing.

Retained Earnings

The spreadsheet (work sheet) shows a Retained Earnings balance of $202,300 at December 31, 2014, and $282,300 at December 31, 2015. Thus, Retained Earnings increased $80,000 during the year. This increase resulted from the following:

1. net income of $108,000
2. declaring cash dividends of $28,000

To identify the cash flows from these activities, two entries are made on the spreadsheet.

The $108,000 is reported on the statement of cash flows as part of "cash flows from operating activities." Thus, an entry is made in the Transactions columns on the spreadsheet as follows:

(a) Operating Activities—Net Income   108,000
         Retained Earnings   108,000

The preceding entry accounts for the net income portion of the change to Retained Earnings. It also identifies the cash flow in the bottom portion of the spreadsheet as related to operating activities.

The $28,000 of dividends is reported as a financing activity on the statement of cash flows. Thus, an entry is made in the Transactions columns on the spreadsheet as follows:

(b) Retained Earnings   28,000
         Financing Activities—Declared Cash Dividends.   28,000

The preceding entry accounts for the dividends portion of the change to Retained Earnings. It also identifies the cash flow in the bottom portion of the spreadsheet as related to financing activities. The $28,000 of declared dividends will be adjusted later for the actual amount of cash dividends paid during the year.

Other Accounts

The entries for the other noncash accounts are made in the spreadsheet in a manner similar to entries (a) and (b). A summary of these entries is as follows:

(c)	Financing Activities—Issued Common Shares	48,000	
	Common Shares		48,000
(d)	Bonds Payable	50,000	
	Financing Activities—Retired Bonds Payable		50,000
(e)	Financing Activities—Increase in Dividends Payable	4,000	
	Dividends Payable		4,000
(f)	Income Taxes Payable	500	
	Operating Activities—Decrease in Income Taxes Payable		500
(g)	Operating Activities—Increase in Accrued Expenses Payable	2,200	
	Accrued Expenses Payable		2,200
(h)	Accounts Payable	3,200	
	Operating Activities—Decrease in Accounts Payable		3,200
(i)	Operating Activities—Depreciation of Building	7,000	
	Accumulated Depreciation—Building		7,000
(j)	Building	60,000	
	Investing Activities—Purchase of Building		60,000
(k)	Land	15,000	
	Investing Activities—Purchase of Land		15,000
(l)	Investing Activities—Sale of Land	72,000	
	Operating Activities—Gain on Sale of Land		12,000
	Land		60,000
(m)	Operating Activities—Decrease in Inventory	8,000	
	Inventory		8,000
(n)	Accounts Receivable	9,000	
	Operating Activities—Increase in Accounts Receivable		9,000
(o)	Cash	71,500	
	Net Increase in Cash		71,500

After all the statement of financial position accounts have been analyzed and the entries have been made on the spreadsheet (work sheet), all the operating, investing, and financing activities are identified in the bottom portion of the spreadsheet. The accuracy of the entries is verified by totalling the Debit and Credit Transactions columns. The totals of the columns should be equal.

Preparing the Statement of Cash Flows

The statement of cash flows prepared from the spreadsheet is identical to the statement shown in Exhibit 6. The data for the three sections of the statement are obtained from the bottom portion of the spreadsheet.

At a Glance 16

1 Describe the cash flow activities reported in the statement of cash flows.

Key Points	Key Learning Outcomes	Page	Example Exercises
The statement of cash flows reports cash receipts and cash payments by three types of activities: operating activities, investing activities, and financing activities. Investing and financing for a business may be affected by transactions that do not involve cash. The effect of such transactions should be explained in the notes to the financial statements.	• Classify transactions that either provide or use cash into either operating, investing, or financing activities.	814	16-1

2 Prepare a statement of cash flows, using the indirect method.

Key Points	Key Learning Outcomes	Page	Example Exercises
The changes in the noncash statement of financial position accounts are used to develop the statement of cash flows, beginning with the cash flows from operating activities. Determine the cash flows from operating activities using the indirect method, which adjusts net income for expenses that do not require cash and for gains and losses from disposal of capital assets. Determine the cash flows from operating activities using the indirect method, which adjusts net income for changes in current operating assets and liabilities. Report cash flows from operating activities using the indirect method. Report investing and financing activities on the statement of cash flows.	• Use the steps to complete an indirect operating activities section.	819	
	• Adjust net income for noncash expenses and gains and losses from asset disposals using the indirect method.	819	16-2
	• Adjust net income for changes in current operating assets and liabilities using the indirect method.	823	16-3
	• Prepare the cash flows from operating activities using the indirect method in proper form.	823	16-4
	• Prepare the remainder of the statement of cash flows by reporting investing and financing activities.	825	16-5

3   Prepare the operating activities section, using the direct method.

Key Points	Key Learning Outcomes	Page	Example Exercises
The direct method reports cash flows from operating activities by major classes of operating cash receipts and cash payments. The difference between the major classes of total operating cash receipts and total operating cash payments is the net cash flow from operating activities. The investing and financing activities sections of the statement are the same as under the indirect method.	• Prepare the cash flows from operating activities and the remainder of the statement of cash flows using the direct method.	833	16-6 16-7

GLOSSARY

cash flow statement – A summary of the cash receipts and cash payments for a specific period of time, such as a month or a year. (p. 814) Also known as *Statement of cash flows* under IFRS.

cash flows from financing activities – The section of the statement of cash flows that reports cash flows from transactions affecting the debt and equity of the business. (p. 815)

cash flows from investing activities – The section of the statement of cash flows that reports cash flows from transactions affecting investments in noncurrent assets. (p. 815)

cash flows from operating activities – The section of the statement of cash flows that reports cash transactions affecting the determination of operating income. (p. 814)

direct method – A method of reporting the cash flows from operating activities as the difference between the operating cash receipts and the operating cash payments. (p. 816)

free cash flow – The amount of operating cash flow remaining after replacing current productive capacity. (p. 837)

indirect method – A method of reporting the cash flows from operating activities as the net income from operations adjusted for all deferrals of past cash receipts and payments and for all accruals of expected future cash receipts and payments. (p. 817).

statement of cash flows – A summary of the cash receipts and cash payments for a specific period of time, such as a month or a year. (p. 814) Also known as *cash flow statement*.

END-OF-CHAPTER ILLUSTRATIVE PROBLEM

Indirect and direct statement of cash flows

The statement of financial position of Dowling Company for December 31, 2015 and 2014, is as follows:

Dowling Company
Statement of Financial Position
December 31, 2015 and 2014

	2015	2014
Assets		
Cash.	$ 140,350	$ 95,900
Accounts receivable (net)	95,300	102,300
Inventories.	165,200	157,900
Prepaid expenses	6,240	5,860
Investments (long-term)	35,700	84,700
Buildings	375,000	260,000
Accumulated depreciation—buildings.	(71,300)	(58,300)
Machinery and equipment.	428,300	428,300
Accumulated depreciation—machinery and equipment	(148,500)	(138,000)
Land.	75,000	90,000
Patents	58,000	65,000
Total assets	$1,159,290	$1,093,660
Liabilities and Shareholders' Equity		
Accounts payable (merchandise creditors)	$ 43,500	$ 46,700
Accrued expenses payable (operating expenses)	14,000	12,500
Income taxes payable	7,900	8,400
Dividends payable	14,000	10,000
Mortgage note payable, due 2023.	40,000	0
Bonds payable	150,000	250,000
Common shares	516,250	416,250
Retained earnings	373,640	349,810
Total liabilities and shareholders' equity	$1,159,290	$1,093,660

The statement of income for Dowling Company is shown here.

Dowling Company Statement of Income For the Year Ended December 31, 2015		
Sales		$1,100,000
Cost of goods sold.		710,000
Gross profit		390,000
Operating expenses:		
Depreciation expense	$ 30,500	
Other operating expenses	196,000	
Total operating expenses.		226,500
Income from operations		163,500
Other income:		
Gain on sale of investments.	11,000	
Other expense:		
Interest expense	26,000	(15,000)
Inocme before income taxes.		148,500
Income taxes expense		50,000
Net income		$ 98,500

An examination of the accounting records revealed the following additional information applicable to 2015:

a.   Land costing $15,000 was sold for $15,000.

b.   A mortgage note was issued for $40,000.

c.   A building costing $115,000 was constructed.

d.   2,500 common shares were issued in exchange for bonds payable, when the shares had a market value of $40 per share.

e.   Cash dividends declared were $74,670.

Instructions

1.   Prepare a statement of cash flows, using the indirect method of reporting cash flows from operating activities.
2.   Prepare the operating activities section using the direct method.

Solution

1.

Dowling Company Statement of Cash Flows—Indirect Method For the Year Ended December 31, 2015		
Cash flows from operating activities:		
Net income.	$ 98,500	
Adjustments to reconcile net income to net		
cash flow from operating activities:		
Depreciation.	30,500	
Gain on sale of investments	(11,000)	
Changes in current operating assets and liabilities:		
Decrease in accounts receivable	7,000	
Increase in inventories.	(7,300)	
Increase in prepaid expenses	(380)	
Decrease in accounts payable	(3,200)	
Increase in accrued expenses payable	1,500	
Decrease in income taxes payable	(500)	
Net cash flow from operating activities.		$115,120
Cash flows from investing activities:		
Cash received from sale of investments	60,000	
Cash received from sale of land.	15,000	
Cash paid for construction of building	(115,000)	
Net cash flow used for investing activities . . .		(40,000)
Cash flows from financing activities:		
Cash received from issuing mortgage note payable	40,000	
Cash paid for dividends	(70,670)*	
Net cash flow used for financing activities . . .		(30,670)
Increase in cash.		44,450
Cash at the beginning of the year		95,900
Cash at the end of the year		$140,350
*$70,670 = $74,670 − $4,000 (increase in dividends payable)		

The noncash investing and financing activities related to the issuance of common shares to retire the bonds payable of $100,000 would appear in the notes to the financial statements.

2.

Dowling Company Statement of Cash Flows—Direct Method For the Year Ended December 31, 2015		
Cash flows from operating activities:		
Receipts:		
Cash received from customers*		$1,107,000
Payments:		
Cash paid for merchandise**	$(720,500)	
Cash paid for operating expenses†	(194,880)	
Cash paid for interest expense	(26,000)	
Cash paid for income taxes‡	(50,500)	(991,880)
Net cash flow from operating activities		115,120

The noncash investing and financing activities related to the issuance of common shares to retire the bonds payable of $100,000 would appear in the notes to the financial statements.

Computations:

*$1,100,000 + $7,000 = $1,107,000   †$196,000 + $380 − $1,500 = $194,880
**$710,000 + $3,200 + $7,300 = $720,500   ‡$50,000 + $500 = $50,500

EYE OPENERS

1. What is the principal advantage of the direct method of reporting cash flows from operating activities?
2. What is the major advantage of the indirect method of reporting cash flows from operating activities?
3. A corporation issued $300,000 of common shares in exchange for $300,000 of capital assets. Where is this transaction reported on the statement of cash flows?
4. A retail business, using the accrual method of accounting, owed merchandise creditors (accounts payable) $200,000 at the beginning of the year and $230,000 at the end of the year. How is the $30,000 increase used to adjust net income in determining the amount of cash flows from operating activities by the indirect method? Explain.
5. If salaries payable was $90,000 at the beginning of the year and $70,000 at the end of the year, should $20,000 be added to or deducted from income to determine the amount of cash flows from operating activities by the indirect method? Explain.
6. A long-term investment in bonds with a cost of $70,000 was sold for $84,000 cash. (a) What was the gain or loss on the sale? (b) What was the effect of the transaction on cash flows? (c) How is the transaction reported in the statement of cash flows if cash flows from operating activities are reported by the indirect method?
7. A corporation issued $6,000,000 of 20-year bonds for cash at 104. How is the transaction reported on the statement of cash flows?
8. Fully depreciated equipment costing $100,000 was disposed of. What was the effect of the transaction on cash flows if (a) $24,000 cash is received, (b) no cash is received?
9. For the current year, Coleman Company decided to align with IFRS direction by switching from the indirect method to the direct method for reporting cash flows from operating activities on the statement of cash flows. Will the change cause the amount of net cash flow from operating activities to be (a) larger, (b) smaller, or (c) the same as if the indirect method had been used? Explain.
10. Name five common major classes of operating cash receipts or operating cash payments presented on the statement of cash flows when the cash flows from operating activities are reported by the direct method.
11. In a recent annual report, eBay Inc. reported that during the year it issued shares of $18.4 million for acquisitions. How would this transaction be reported on the statement of cash flows?

PRACTICE EXERCISES

PE 16-1
Classifying cash flows

EE 16-1 p. 818

Identify whether each of the following would be reported in the statement of cash flows as an operating, investing, or financing activity.

a. Issuance of common shares
b. Purchase of land
c. Payment of accounts payable

d. Retirement of bonds payable
e. Payment for administrative expenses
f. Cash received from customers

PE 16-2
Adjustments to net income—indirect method

EE 16-2 p. 822

Cozy Corporation's accumulated depreciation—furniture increased by $5,000, and $1,300 of patents were amortized between balance sheet dates. Cozy had no purchases or sales of tangible or intangible assets during the year. In addition, the statement of income showed a gain of $12,000 from the sale of land. Reconcile a net income of $150,000 to net cash flow from operating activities using the indirect method.

② PE 16-3

Changes in current operating assets and liabilities—indirect method

EE 16-3 p. 824

Watson Corporation's statement of financial position data for current assets and liabilities were as follows:

	Dec. 31, 2015	Dec. 31, 2014
Accounts receivable	$30,000	$24,000
Inventories	58,000	49,500
Accounts payable	46,000	34,500
Dividends payable	14,000	18,000

Adjust net income of $320,000 for changes in operating assets and liabilities to arrive at net cash flow from operating activities using the indirect method.

② PE 16-4

Cash flows from operating activities—indirect method

EE 16-4 p. 825

Truly Inc. reported the following data:

Net income	$180,000
Depreciation expense	40,000
Loss on disposal of equipment	12,400
Increase in accounts receivable	12,100
Increase in accounts payable	5,900

Prepare the Cash Flows from Operating Activities section of the statement of cash flows using the indirect method.

② PE 16-5

Land transactions on the statement of cash flows

EE 16-5 p. 827

Slocum Corporation purchased land for $600,000. Later in the year, the company sold land with a cost of $360,000 for $410,000. How are the effects of these transactions reported on the statement of cash flows under the indirect method?

③ PE 16-6

Cash received from customers—direct method

EE 16-6 p. 834

Sales reported on the statement of income were $51,300. The accounts receivable balance decreased $4,100 over the year. Determine the amount of cash received from customers to be included in the operating section under the direct method.

③ PE 16-7

Cash payments for merchandise—direct method

EE 16-7 p. 835

Cost of goods sold reported on the statement of income was $130,000. Over the year, the accounts payable balance increased $6,200, and the inventory balance increased $11,400. Determine the amount of cash paid for merchandise to be included in the operating section under the direct method.

② PE 16-8

Free cash flow

f·a·i

EE 16-8 p. 838

Totson Inc. reported the following on the company's statement of cash flows in 2014 and 2013:

	2014	2013
Net cash flow from operating activities	$210,000	$200,000
Net cash flow used for investing activities	(160,000)	(180,000)
Net cash flow used for financing activities	(45,000)	(30,000)

Eighty percent of the cash flow used for investing activities was used to replace existing capacity.

a. Determine Totson's free cash flow.

b. Has Totson's free cash flow improved or declined from 2013 to 2014?

EXERCISES

EX 16-1

Cash flows from operating activities— net loss

On its statement of income for a recent year, Air Canada reported a net loss of $249 million. On its statement of cash flows, it reported $586 million of cash inflows from operating activities.

Explain the difference.

EX 16-2

Effect of transactions on cash flows

Consider each of the following transactions individually. State the amount of cash flow and whether the effect is a cash receipt or cash payment.

a. Sold a new issue of $300,000 of bonds at 89.
b. Purchased 2,500 common shares at $65 per share.
c. Sold 12,000 common shares for $40 per share.
d. Purchased a building by paying $70,000 cash and issuing a $120,000 mortgage note payable.
e. Retired $175,000 of bonds, on which there was $2,500 of unamortized discount, for $230,000.
f. Purchased land for $360,000 cash.
g. Paid dividends of $2.00 per common share. Throughout the year, 30,000 shares were issued and outstanding.
h. Sold equipment with a book value of $50,000 for $64,000.

EX 16-3

Classifying cash flows

For each of the following, identify the type of cash flow activity affected (operating, investing, or financing):

a. Issued common shares.
b. Redeemed bonds.
c. Issued preferred shares.
d. Purchased patents.
e. Net income.
f. Paid cash dividends.
g. Purchased shares.
h. Sold long-term investments.
i. Sold equipment.
j. Purchased buildings.
k. Issued bonds.

EX 16-4

Interest and dividends—ASPE and IFRS

Depending on whether a company uses ASPE or IFRS, interest and dividends may be recorded in different sections of the statement of cash flows. Summarize the sections for recording interest and dividends under ASPE and IFRS.

EX 16-5

Cash flows from operating activities— indirect method

Indicate whether each of the following would be added to or deducted from net income in determining net cash flow from operating activities by the indirect method:

a. Decrease in accounts receivable
b. Increase in notes payable to vendors, due in 90 days
c. Decrease in salaries payable
d. Decrease in prepaid expenses
e. Gain on retirement of long-term debt
f. Decrease in accounts payable
g. Increase in notes receivable from customers, due in 90 days
h. Depreciation of capital assets
i. Increase in inventory
j. Amortization of patent
k. Loss on disposal of capital assets

2 **EX 16-6**

Cash flows from operating activities— indirect method

The net income reported on the statement of income for the current year was $145,000. Depreciation recorded on store equipment for the year amounted to $23,900. Balances of the current asset and current liability accounts at the beginning and end of the year are as follows:

	End of Year	Beginning of Year
Cash	$52,300	$47,500
Accounts receivable (net)	37,700	35,600
Inventories	51,200	53,330
Prepaid expenses	6,100	4,600
Accounts payable (merchandise creditors)	51,000	45,600
Wages payable	26,800	30,400

✔ Net cash flow from operating activities, $169,230

Prepare the Cash Flows from Operating Activities section of the statement of cash flows using the indirect method.

---

2 **3** **EX 16-7**

Cash flows from operating activities— indirect method

The net income reported on the statement of income for the current year was $210,000. Depreciation recorded on equipment and a building amounted to $62,500 for the year. Balances of the current asset and current liability accounts at the beginning and end of the year are as follows:

	End of Year	Beginning of Year
Cash	$ 56,000	$ 59,500
Accounts receivable (net)	71,000	73,400
Inventories	140,000	126,500
Prepaid expenses	7,800	8,400
Accounts payable (merchandise creditors)	62,600	66,400
Salaries payable	9,000	8,250

✔ Cash flows from operating activities, $258,950

a. Prepare the Cash Flows from Operating Activities section of the statement of cash flows using the indirect method.
b. If the direct method had been used, would the net cash flow from operating activities have been the same? Explain.

---

2 **EX 16-8**

Cash flows from operating activities— indirect method

The statement of income disclosed the following items for 2015:

Depreciation expense	$ 32,000
Gain on disposal of equipment	20,500
Net income	319,500

Balances of the current asset and current liability accounts changed between December 31, 2014, and December 31, 2015, as follows:

✔ Cash flows from operating activities, $328,300

Accounts receivable	$4,500
Inventories	2,700*
Prepaid insurance	1,100*
Accounts payable	3,200*
Income taxes payable	1,200
Dividends payable	850

*Decrease

Prepare the Cash Flows from Operating Activities section of the statement of cash flows using the indirect method.

---

2 **3** **EX 16-9**

Determining cash payments to shareholders

The board of directors declared cash dividends totalling $152,000 during the current year. The statement of financial position indicates dividends payable of $42,000 at the beginning of the year and $38,000 at the end of the year. What was the amount of cash payments to shareholders during the year?

---

3 **EX 16-10**

Reporting changes in equipment on the statement of cash flows

Office equipment that cost $67,000 had accumulated depreciation of $22,500 when it sold for $38,600. Using this information, indicate the items to be reported on the statement of cash flows prepared using the direct method.

EX 16-11

Reporting changes in equipment on the statement of cash flows

Delivery equipment that cost $96,000 had accumulated depreciation of $42,100 when it sold for $46,500. Using this information, indicate the items to be reported on the statement of cash flows prepared using the direct method.

EX 16-12

Reporting changes in equipment on the cash flow statement

See the T accounts below. The equipment was sold for a gain of $5,000. Using this information, indicate the items to be reported on the statement of cash flows using the direct method.

Equipment		
opening 70,000		
purchase 25,000		
	50,000	sale
closing 45,000		

Accumulated Depreciation—Equipment		
	30,000	opening
sale 25,000		
	45,000	yearly depreciation
	50,000	closing

EX 16-13

Reporting changes in furniture on the statement of cash flows

Of the opening total balance in the office furniture account of $180,000, $40,000 was sold for a gain of $3,000. It was replaced with a new set of furniture costing $50,000, paid for in cash. The total furniture depreciation for the year was $45,000, and the closing balance for accumulated amortization was $166,000. Using this information and using T accounts, indicate the items to be reported on the cash flow statement using the direct method.

EX 16-14

Reporting changes in furniture on the statement of cash flows

Of the opening total balance in the office furniture account of $90,000, $20,000 was sold for a loss of $6,000. The final balance of the furniture account was $100,000. All transactions were made in cash. The total furniture depreciation for the year was $13,000, and the closing balance for accumulated amortization was $48,000. Using this information and using T accounts, indicate the items to be reported on the cash flow statement using the direct method.

EX 16-15

Reporting land transactions on the statement of cash flows

On the basis of the details of the following land account, and assuming cash was used, indicate the items to be reported on the statement of cash flows.

Land	
Jan. 1 opening 1,200,000	
Feb. 5 380,000	
	180,000 Oct. 30
closing 1,400,000	

The land was sold for $210,000.

EX 16-16

Reporting shareholders' equity items on the statement of cash flows

On the basis of the following shareholders' equity accounts, indicate the items, exclusive of net income, to be reported on the statement of cash flows. There were no unpaid dividends at either the beginning or the end of the year.

Common Shares	
	1,400,000 Jan. 1 opening
	680,000 Feb. 11
	123,200 Jun. 30
	2,203,200 closing

(continued)

On January 1, there were 60,000 shares.

On February 11, 15,000 shares were issued for cash.

On June 30, 2,200 shares were issued as a share dividend.

Retained Earnings			
		1,000,000	Jan. 1 opening
Jun. 30 share dividend	123,200		
Dec. 30 cash dividend	117,200		
		720,000	closing net income
		1,479,600	closing

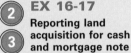

EX 16-17

Reporting land acquisition for cash and mortgage note on the statement of cash flows

On the basis of the details of the following land account, indicate the items to be reported on the statement of cash flows.

Land			
Jan. 1 opening	260,000		
Feb. 10	410,000		
Nov. 20	540,000		
closing	1,210,000		

The February 10 entry was a cash transaction.

The November 20 entry was completed with a long-term mortgage note.

EX 16-18

Reporting issuance and retirement of long-term debt on the statement of cash flows

On the basis of the details of the following bonds payable and related discount accounts, indicate the items to be reported in the Financing section of the statement of cash flows, assuming no gain or loss on retiring the bonds:

Bonds Payable			
		500,000	Jan. 1 opening
Jan. 3	100,000		
		300,000	Jul. 30
		700,000	closing

Discount on Bonds Payable			
Jan. 1 opening	22,500		
		8,000	Jan. 3
Jul. 30	20,000		
		1,750	Dec. 31
closing	32,750		

EX 16-19

Net cash flow from operating activities determining net income

✔ Net income, $159,150

Goodchild Inc. reported a net cash flow from operating activities of $165,500 on its statement of cash flows for the year ended December 31, 2015. The following information was reported in the Cash Flows from Operating Activities section of the statement of cash flows using the indirect method:

Decrease in income taxes payable	$ 3,500
Decrease in inventories	8,700
Depreciation	12,700
Gain on sale of investments	6,000
Increase in accounts payable	2,500
Increase in prepaid expenses	1,350
Increase in accounts receivable	6,700

Determine the net income reported by Goodchild Inc. for the year ended December 31, 2015.

2 **EX 16-20**

Cash flows from operating activities—indirect method

✔ Net cash outflow from operating activities, $7,118

Selected data derived from the statement of income and statement of financial position of Glennis Co. for a recent year are as follows:

Income statement data (in thousands):	
Net loss	$(6,106)
Depreciation expense	379
Balance sheet data (in thousands):	
Increase in accounts receivable	178
Increase in inventories	1,252
Increase in prepaid expenses	211
Decrease in accounts payable	549

a. Prepare the Cash Flows from Operating Activities section of the statement of cash flows using the indirect method for Glennis Co. for the year.
b. Interpret your results in part (a).

---

2 **EX 16-21**

Statement of cash flows—indirect method

✔ Net cash flow from operating activities, $30

The statement of financial position of Tru-Built Construction Inc. for December 31, 2015 and 2014 (all figures are in $000s), is as follows:

	Dec. 31, 2015	Dec. 31, 2014
Assets		
Cash.	$ 98	$ 32
Accounts receivable (net)	56	40
Inventories.	35	22
Equipment.	45	35
Accumulated depreciation—equipment	(12)	(6)
Land.	80	90
Total.	$302	$213
Liabilities and Shareholders' Equity		
Accounts payable (merchandise creditors).	$ 35	$ 32
Dividends payable	6	—
Common shares	70	35
Retained earnings	191	146
Total.	$302	$213

The following additional information is taken from the records:

a. Land was sold for $25.
b. Equipment was acquired for cash.
c. There were no disposals of equipment during the year.
d. The common shares were issued for cash.
e. There was a $65 credit to Retained Earnings for net income.
f. There was a $20 debit to Retained Earnings for cash dividends declared.

Prepare a statement of cash flows using the indirect method of presenting cash flows from operating activities.

---

2 **EX 16-22**

Statement of cash flows—indirect method

List the errors in the following statement of cash flows. The cash balance at the beginning of the year was $100,320. All other amounts are correct, except the cash balance at the end of the year.

(continued)

Devon Inc.
Statement of Cash Flows
For the Year Ended December 31, 2015

Cash flows from operating activities:		
Net income	$148,080	
Adjustments to reconcile net income to net cash flow		
from operating activities:		
Depreciation	42,000	
Gain on sale of investments	7,200	
Changes in current operating assets and liabilities:		
Increase in accounts receivable	11,400	
Increase in inventories	(14,760)	
Increase in accounts payable	(4,440)	
Decrease in accrued expenses payable	(1,080)	
Net cash flow from operating activities		$188,400
Cash flows from investing activities:		
Cash received from sale of investments	102,000	
Cash paid for purchase of land	(108,000)	
Cash paid for purchase of equipment	(180,200)	
Net cash flow used for investing activities		(186,200)
Cash flows from financing activities:		
Cash received from sale of common shares	128,400	
Cash paid for dividends	54,000	
Net cash flow provided by financing activities		182,400
Increase in cash		184,600
Cash at the end of the year		126,300
Cash at the beginning of the year		$310,900

---

② EX 16-23

Interpreting the statement of cash flows

An investor needs to decide which of two companies to invest in. Both companies are in the same industry and each has net income of $200,000. Which category on the statement of cash flows should the investor consider because it reveals important information relating to the quality of the net income.

---

③ EX 16-24

Cash flows from operating activities— direct method

✔ a. $728,500

The cash flows from operating activities are reported by the direct method on the statement of cash flows. Determine the following:

a. If sales for the current year were $685,000 and accounts receivable decreased by $43,500 during the year, what was the amount of cash received from customers?
b. If income taxes expense for the current year was $46,000 and income taxes payable decreased by $5,200 during the year, what was the amount of cash payments for income taxes?

---

③ EX 16-25

Cash paid for merchandise purchases

The cost of goods sold for Canadian Tire for a recent year was $7,326 million. The balance sheet showed the following current account balances (in millions):

	Balance, End of Year	Balance, Beginning of Year
Inventories	$1,449	$ 901
Accounts payable	1,641	1,180

Determine the amount of cash payments for merchandise.

---

③ EX 16-26

Determining selected amounts for cash flows from operating activities—direct method

✔ b. $77,870

Selected data taken from the accounting records of Lachgar Inc. for the current year ended December 31 are as follows:

	Balance, December 31	Balance, January 1
Accrued expenses payable (operating expenses)	$ 5,590	$ 6,110
Accounts payable (merchandise creditors)	41,730	46,020
Inventories	77,350	84,110
Prepaid expenses	3,250	3,900

During the current year, the cost of goods sold was $448,500, and the operating expenses other than depreciation were $78,000. The direct method is used for presenting the cash flows from operating activities on the statement of cash flows.

Determine the amount reported on the statement of cash flows for (a) cash payments for merchandise and (b) cash payments for operating expenses.

---

③ EX 16-27

Cash flows from operating activities— direct method

✔ Net cash flow from operating activities, $69,760

The statement of income of Kodiak Industries Inc. for the current year ended June 30 is as follows:

Sales		$364,800
Cost of goods sold		207,200
Gross profit		157,600
Operating expenses:		
Depreciation expense	$28,000	
Other operating expenses	73,920	
Total operating expenses		101,920
Income before income taxes		55,680
Income taxes expense		15,440
Net income		$ 40,240

Changes in the balances of selected accounts from the beginning to the end of the current year are as follows:

	Increase Decrease*
Accounts receivable (net)	$8,400*
Inventories	2,800
Prepaid expenses	2,720*
Accounts payable (merchandise creditors)	5,760*
Accrued expenses payable (operating expenses)	880
Income taxes payable	1,920*

Prepare the Cash Flows from Operating Activities section of the statement of cash flows using the direct method.

---

③ EX 16-28

Cash flows from operating activities— direct method

✔ Net cash flow from operating activities, $56,490

The statement of income for M2 Pizza Pie Company for the current year ended June 30 and balances of selected accounts at the beginning and the end of the year are as follows:

Sales		$202,400
Cost of goods sold		70,000
Gross profit		132,400
Operating expenses:		
Depreciation expense	$17,500	
Other operating expenses	52,400	
Total operating expenses		69,900
Income before income taxes		62,500
Income taxes expense		18,000
Net income		$ 44,500

(continued)

	End of Year	Beginning of Year
Accounts receivable (net).....................	$16,300	$14,190
Inventories	41,900	36,410
Prepaid expenses	6,600	7,260
Accounts payable (merchandise creditors).......	30,690	28,490
Accrued expenses payable (operating expenses) .	8,690	9,460
Income taxes payable........................	1,650	1,650

Prepare the Cash Flows from Operating Activities section of the statement of cash flows using the direct method.

EX 16-29
Free cash flow

Moroccan Marble Company has cash flows from operating activities of $300,000. Cash flows used for investments in property, plant, and equipment totalled $65,000, of which 75% of this investment was used to replace existing capacity.

Determine the free cash flow for Moroccan Marble Company.

EX 16-30
Free cash flow

The financial statements for Leon's are provided in Appendix B at the end of the text.

Determine the free cash flow for the year ended December 31, 2011. The $24,999,000 purchase of property, plant, and equipment from the investing section was used to maintain productive capacity.

PROBLEMS SERIES A

PR 16-1A
Statement of cash flows—indirect method (spreadsheet optional)

✔ Net cash flow from operating activities, $62,100

The statement of financial position of Maxim Tech. Inc. for December 31, 2015 and 2014, is shown as follows:

	Dec. 31, 2015	Dec. 31, 2014
Assets		
Cash......................................	$ 310,680	$ 290,290
Accounts receivable (net)	113,920	105,260
Inventories.................................	318,880	308,560
Investments................................	0	120,000
Equipment.................................	352,560	275,550
Accumulated depreciation.....................	(83,200)	(72,000)
Land......................................	166,000	0
	$1,178,840	$1,027,660
Liabilities and Shareholders' Equity		
Accounts payable (merchandise creditors).........	$ 214,240	$ 200,480
Accrued expenses payable (operating expenses) ...	21,120	26,320
Dividends payable	12,000	9,700
Common shares	303,000	188,000
Retained earnings	628,480	603,160
	$1,178,840	$1,027,660

The following additional information was taken from the records:

a. The investments were sold for $135,000 cash.
b. Equipment and land were acquired for cash.
c. There were no disposals of equipment during the year.
d. The common shares were issued for cash.
e. There was a $76,320 credit to Retained Earnings for net income.
f. There was a $51,000 debit to Retained Earnings for cash dividends declared.

Instructions

Prepare a statement of cash flows using the indirect method of presenting cash flows from operating activities. Use of the spreadsheet is optional.

 PR 16-2A
Statement of cash flows—indirect method (spreadsheet optional)

✔ Net cash flow from operating activities, $169,600

The statement of financial position of Amelia Enterprises Inc. at December 31, 2015 and 2014, is as follows:

	Dec. 31, 2015	Dec. 31, 2014
Assets		
Cash...	$ 73,300	$ 89,900
Accounts receivable (net)	112,300	121,000
Inventories..................................	160,800	149,600
Prepaid expenses	6,700	4,800
Equipment...................................	327,500	268,500
Accumulated depreciation—equipment	(85,400)	(66,100)
	$595,200	$567,700
Liabilities and Shareholders' Equity		
Accounts payable (merchandise creditors).........	$125,100	$118,800
Mortgage note payable........................	0	168,000
Common shares	312,000	172,000
Retained earnings	158,100	108,900
	$595,200	$567,700

Additional data obtained from the statement of income and from an examination of the accounts in the ledger for 2015 are as follows:

a. Net income, $126,000.
b. Depreciation reported on the income statement, $41,700.
c. Equipment was purchased at a cost of $81,400, and fully depreciated equipment costing $22,400 was discarded, with no salvage realized.
d. As the mortgage note payable was not due until 2018, but the terms permitted earlier payment without penalty, there is no current portion.
e. 7,000 shares of common shares were issued at $20 per share for cash.
f. Cash dividends declared and paid, $76,800.

Instructions

Prepare a statement of cash flows using the indirect method of presenting cash flows from operating activities. Use of the spreadsheet is optional.

 **PR 16-3A**
Statement of cash flows—indirect method (spreadsheet optional)

✔ Net cash flow from operating activities, $(103,510)

The statement of financial position of Morin Cycle Co. at December 31, 2015 and 2014, is as follows:

(continued)

	Dec. 31, 2015	Dec. 31, 2014
Assets		
Cash.	$ 512,000	$ 538,000
Accounts receivable (net)	460,500	424,400
Inventories.	702,500	640,060
Prepaid expenses	16,300	18,500
Buildings	810,500	500,500
Accumulated depreciation—buildings.	(225,000)	(212,000)
Equipment.	283,550	251,800
Accumulated depreciation—equipment	(78,500)	(86,100)
Land.	175,500	269,900
	$2,657,350	$2,345,060
Liabilities and Shareholders' Equity		
Accounts payable (merchandise creditors).	$ 520,000	$ 544,870
Bonds payable.	165,000	0
Common shares	602,000	400,150
Retained earnings	1,370,350	1,400,040
	$2,657,350	$2,345,060

The noncurrent asset, noncurrent liability, and shareholders' equity accounts for 2015 are as follows:

Land

Jan. 1	269,900		
		94,400	Apr. 20
	175,500		

The company realized $87,000 cash from the above sale transaction.

Buildings

Jan. 1 opening	500,500	
Apr. 20	310,000	
	810,500	

The above acquisition was completed with cash.

Accumulated Depreciation—Buildings

	212,000	Jan. 1
	13,000	Dec. 31
	225,000	

Equipment

Jan. 1 opening	251,800		
		19,100	Jan. 26
Aug. 11	50,850		
	283,550		

The January 26 transaction was retirement of equipment.

The August 11 purchase was a cash transaction.

Accumulated Depreciation—Equipment

		86,100	Jan. 1
Jan. 26	19,100		
		11,500	Dec. 31
		78,500	

Bonds Payable

	0	opening balance
	165,000	May 1
	165,000	

Common Shares

	400,150	Jan. 1
	201,850	Dec. 7
	602,000	

On December 7, Morin Cycle issued 11,000 common shares at $18.35 per share.

Retained Earnings

		1,400,040	Jan. 1
Dec. 31	14,200		
Dec. 31	15,490		
		1,370,350	

A loss of $14,200 was closed to the retained earnings at the end of the year. Cash dividends of $15,490 were paid in December.

Instructions

1. Prepare a statement of cash flows using the indirect method of presenting cash flows from operating activities. Use of the spreadsheet is optional.
2. How does Morin's cash flow compare to its net loss? Summarize the changes that caused the difference.

PR 16-4A

Statement of cash flows—indirect method

✔ Net cash flow from operating activities, $146,800

The statement of financial position of Rucker Photography Products Inc. for December 31, 2016 and 2015, is as follows:

	Dec. 31, 2016	Dec. 31, 2015
Assets		
Cash...........................	$ 321,700	$ 339,700
Accounts receivable (net)...............	283,400	273,700
Inventories.......................	505,500	491,400
Investments........................	0	120,000
Equipment.........................	440,000	340,000
Accumulated depreciation.................	(122,200)	(100,200)
Land.............................	260,000	0
	$1,688,400	$1,464,600
Liabilities and Shareholders' Equity		
Accounts payable (merchandise creditors).........	$ 385,900	$ 374,200
Accrued expenses payable (operating expenses) ...	31,700	35,400
Dividends payable.....................	4,400	3,200
Common shares......................	228,000	112,000
Retained earnings....................	1,038,400	939,800
	$1,688,400	$1,464,600

The statement of income for the year ended December 31, 2016, is as follows:

Sales		$2,990,000
Cost of goods sold		1,226,000
Gross profit		1,764,000
Operating expenses:		
Depreciation expense	$ 22,000	
Other operating expenses.............	1,550,000	
Total operating expenses............		1,572,000
Operating income		192,000
Other expense:		
Loss on sale of investments............		(32,000)
Income before income taxes		160,000
Income taxes expense		51,400
Net income		$ 108,600

The following additional information was taken from the records:
a. Equipment and land were acquired for cash.
b. There were no disposals of equipment during the year.
c. The investments were sold for $88,000 cash.
d. The common shares were issued for cash.
e. There was a $10,000 debit to Retained Earnings for cash dividends declared.
f. The income taxes expense was paid in cash.

Instructions

1. Prepare a statement of cash flows using the indirect method of presenting cash flows from operating activities.
2. How does Rucker's cash flow compare to its net income? Summarize the changes that caused the difference.

③ **PR 16-5A**

Statement of cash flows—direct method applied to PR 17-1A

✔ Net cash flow from operating activities, $62,100

The statement of financial position of Maxim Tech. Inc. for December 31, 2015 and 2014, as presented in Problem 16–1A, is as follows:

	Dec. 31, 2015	Dec. 31, 2014
Assets		
Cash.	$ 310,680	$ 290,290
Accounts receivable (net)	113,920	105,260
Inventories.	318,880	308,560
Investments.	0	120,000
Equipment.	352,560	275,220
Accumulated depreciation—equipment	(83,200)	(72,000)
Land.	166,000	0
	$1,178,840	$1,027,660
Liabilities and Shareholders' Equity		
Accounts payable (merchandise creditors).	$ 214,240	$ 200,480
Accrued expenses payable (operating expenses)	21,120	26,320
Dividends payable.	12,000	9,700
Common shares.	303,000	188,000
Retained earnings.	628,480	603,160
	$1,178,840	$1,027,660

The statement of income for the year ended December 31, 2015, is as follows:

Sales		$1,950,699
Cost of goods sold.		1,200,430
Gross profit.		750,269
Operating expenses:		
Depreciation expense	$ 11,200	
Other operating expenses.	635,202	
Total operating expenses		646,402
Operating income		103,867
Other income:		
Gain on sale of investments		15,000
Income before income taxes		118,867
Income taxes expense.		42,547
Net income.		$ 76,320

The following additional information was taken from the records:

a. The investments were sold for $135,000 cash.
b. Equipment and land were acquired for cash.
c. There were no disposals of equipment during the year.
d. The common shares were issued for cash.
e. There was a $51,000 debit to Retained Earnings for cash dividends declared.

Instructions

Prepare a statement of cash flows using the direct method of presenting cash flows from operating activities.

---

③ **PR 16-6A**

Statement of cash flows—direct method applied to PR 16-2A

The income statement of Amelia Enterprises Inc. for the year ended December 31, 2015, is as follows:

Sales		$901,250
Cost of goods sold		558,775
Gross profit		342,475
Operating expenses:		
Depreciation expense	$ 41,700	
Other operating expenses.	120,775	
Total operating expenses.		162,475
Income before income taxes		180,000
Income taxes expense		54,000
Net income		126,000

Instructions

Using the information from Problem 16-2A and the additional information provided, prepare a statement of cash flows using the direct method of presenting cash flows from operating activities.

---

3 **PR 16-7A**

Statement of cash flows—direct method applied to PR 16-3A

The statement of income of Morin Cycle Co. for the year ended December 31, 2015, is as follows:

Sales		$460,500
Cost of goods sold		345,375
Gross profit		115,125
Operating expenses:		
Depreciation expense	$24,500	
Other operating expenses	97,425	
Total operating expenses		121,925
Operating loss		(6,800)
Other expense:		
Loss on sale of land		(7,400)
Loss before income taxes		(14,200)
Income taxes expense		0
Net loss		$ (14,200)

Instructions

1. Using the information from Problem 16-3A and the additional information provided, prepare a statement of cash flows using the direct method of presenting cash flows from operating activities.
2. How does Morin's cash flow compare to its net income? Summarize the changes that caused the difference.

---

3 **PR 16-8A**

Statement of cash flows—direct method applied to PR 16-4A

Instructions

1. Using the information from Problem 16-4A, prepare a statement of cash flows for Rucker Photography Products Inc. using the direct method of presenting cash flows from operating activities.
2. How does Rucker's cash flow compare to its net income? Summarize the changes that caused the difference.

PROBLEMS SERIES B

2 **PR 16-1B**

Statement of cash flows—indirect method (spreadsheet optional)

✔ Net cash flow from operating activities, $86,600

The statement of financial position of House Construction Co. for June 30, 2015 and 2014, is as follows:

	June 30, 2015	June 30, 2014
Assets		
Cash	$ 41,600	$ 28,200
Accounts receivable (net)	121,900	110,700
Inventories	175,600	170,500
Investments	0	60,000
Equipment	258,000	210,600
Accumulated depreciation	(58,300)	(49,600)
Land	174,000	0
	$712,800	$530,400
Liabilities and Shareholders' Equity		
Accounts payable (merchandise creditors)	$121,000	$114,200
Accrued expenses payable (operating expenses)	18,000	15,800
Dividends payable	15,000	12,000
Common shares	331,200	180,000
Retained earnings	227,600	208,400
	$712,800	$530,400

(continued)

The following additional information was taken from the records of House Construction Co.:

a. Equipment and land were acquired for cash.
b. There were no disposals of equipment during the year.
c. The investments were sold for $54,000 cash.
d. The common shares were issued for cash.
e. There was a $79,200 credit to Retained Earnings for net income.
f. There was a $60,000 debit to Retained Earnings for cash dividends declared.

Instructions

Prepare a statement of cash flows using the indirect method of presenting cash flows from operating activities. The use of the spreadsheet is optional.

---

② PR 16-2B

Statement of cash flows—indirect method (spreadsheet optional)

✔ Net cash flow from operating activities, $200,500

The statement of financial position of TorMax Technology Inc. at December 31, 2015 and 2014, is as follows:

	Dec. 31, 2015	Dec. 31, 2014
Assets		
Cash.	$ 158,300	$ 128,900
Accounts receivable (net)	237,600	211,500
Inventories.	317,100	365,200
Prepaid expenses	11,300	9,000
Buildings	612,000	405,000
Accumulated depreciation—buildings.	(166,500)	(148,050)
Machinery and equipment	279,000	279,000
Accumulated depreciation—machinery and equipment.	(76,500)	(68,400)
Land.	108,000	108,000
Patents	38,200	43,200
	$1,518,500	$1,333,350
Liabilities and Shareholders' Equity		
Accounts payable (merchandise creditors).	$ 299,100	$ 331,100
Dividends payable	11,700	9,000
Salaries payable.	28,200	31,100
Mortgage note payable, due 2020	80,000	—
Bonds payable.	—	140,000
Common shares	203,000	63,000
Retained earnings	896,500	759,150
	$1,518,500	$1,333,350

An examination of the statement of income and the accounting records revealed the following additional information applicable to 2015:

a. Net income, $184,150.
b. Depreciation expense reported on the statement of income: buildings, $18,450; machinery and equipment, $8,100.
c. Patent amortization reported on the income statement, $5,000.
d. A building was constructed for $207,000.
e. A mortgage note for $80,000 was issued for cash. There is no current portion.
f. 5,000 common shares were issued at $28 per share in exchange for the bonds payable.
g. Cash dividends declared, $46,800.

Instructions

Prepare a statement of cash flows using the indirect method of presenting cash flows from operating activities.

PR 16-3B
Statement of cash flows—indirect method (spreadsheet optional)

✔ Net cash flow from operating activities, $7,800

The statement of financial position of Cantor Industries Inc. at December 31, 2015 and 2014, is as follows:

	Dec. 31, 2015	Dec. 31, 2014
Assets		
Cash.	$ 50,100	$ 56,300
Accounts receivable (net)	117,400	101,600
Inventories.	153,100	144,300
Prepaid expenses	3,100	4,400
Buildings	330,000	165,000
Accumulated depreciation—buildings.	(66,200)	(61,000)
Equipment.	110,100	88,300
Accumulated depreciation—equipment	(22,200)	(27,000)
Land.	165,000	231,000
	$840,400	$702,900
Liabilities and Shareholders' Equity		
Accounts payable (merchandise creditors).	$ 99,000	$105,200
Income taxes payable	4,400	3,600
Bonds payable.	55,000	0
Common shares	231,000	165,000
Retained earnings	451,000	429,100
	$840,400	$702,900

The noncurrent asset, noncurrent liability, and shareholders' equity accounts for 2015 are as follows:

Land

Jan. 1	231,000		
		66,000	Apr. 20
	165,000		

The company realized $76,000 cash from the above sale transaction.

Buildings

Jan. 1 opening	165,000		
Apr. 20	165,000		
	330,000		

The above acquisition was completed with cash.

Accumulated Depreciation—Buildings

		61,000	Jan. 1
		5,200	Dec. 31
		66,200	

Equipment

Jan. 1 opening	88,300		
		11,000	Jan. 26
Aug. 11	32,800		
	110,100		

On January 26, equipment was retired.
The August 11 purchase was a cash transaction.

Accumulated Depreciation—Equipment

		27,000	Jan. 1
Jan. 26	11,000		
		6,200	Dec. 31
		22,200	

Bonds Payable

		0	opening balance
		55,000	May 1
		55,000	

Common Shares

		165,000	Jan. 1
		66,000	Dec. 7
		231,000	

On December 7, Cantor Industries issued 66,000 common shares at $1 per share.

Retained Earnings

		429,100	Jan. 1
		35,100	Dec. 31
Dec. 31	13,200		
		451,000	

Net income of $35,100 was closed to the retained earnings at the end of the year. Cash dividends of $13,200 were paid in December.

(*continued*)

Instructions

1. Prepare a statement of cash flows using the indirect method of presenting cash flows from operating activities.
2. How does Cantor's cash flow compare to its net income? Summarize the changes that caused the difference.

---

② PR 16-4B

Statement of cash flows—indirect method

✔ Net cash flow from operating activities, $169,740

The statement of financial position of Lim Garden Supplies Inc. for December 31, 2016 and 2015, is as follows:

	Dec. 31, 2016	Dec. 31, 2015
Assets		
Cash...	$ 220,640	$ 227,700
Accounts receivable (net).......................	330,880	304,800
Inventories......................................	464,800	454,600
Investments.....................................	0	144,000
Equipment.......................................	408,000	328,000
Accumulated depreciation.......................	(160,500)	(122,800)
Land...	320,000	0
	$1,583,820	$1,336,300
Liabilities and Shareholders' Equity		
Accounts payable (merchandise creditors).........	$ 360,000	$ 322,200
Accrued expenses payable (operating expenses) ...	22,600	26,400
Dividends payable..............................	33,600	30,400
Common shares	336,000	168,000
Retained earnings	831,620	789,300
	$1,583,820	$1,336,300

The statement of income for the year ended December 31, 2016, is as follows:

Sales		$1,504,000
Cost of goods sold		784,000
Gross profit		720,000
Operating expenses:		
Depreciation expense	$ 37,700	
Other operating expenses.....................	448,280	
Total operating expenses....................		485,980
Operating income		234,020
Other income:		
Gain on sale of investments		52,000
Income before income taxes		286,020
Income taxes expense		99,700
Net income		$ 186,320

The following additional information was taken from the records:

a. Equipment and land were acquired for cash.
b. There were no disposals of equipment during the year.
c. The investments were sold for $196,000 cash.
d. The common shares were issued for cash.
e. There was a $144,000 debit to Retained Earnings for cash dividends declared.
f. The income taxes expense was paid in cash.

Instructions

1. Prepare a statement of cash flows using the indirect method of presenting cash flows from operating activities.
2. How does Lim Garden Supplies' cash flow compare to its net income? Summarize the changes that have caused the difference.

PR 16-5B

Statement of cash flows—direct method applied to PR 16-1B

✔ Net cash flow from operating activities, $86,600

The statement of financial position of House Construction Co. for June 30, 2015 and 2014, as presented in Problem 16–1B, is as follows:

	June 30, 2015	June 30, 2014
Assets		
Cash..	$ 41,600	$ 28,200
Accounts receivable (net).....................	121,900	110,700
Inventories...................................	175,600	170,500
Investments..................................	0	60,000
Equipment....................................	258,000	210,600
Accumulated depreciation.....................	(58,300)	(49,600)
Land...	174,000	0
	$712,800	$530,400
Liabilities and Shareholders' Equity		
Accounts payable (merchandise creditors).........	$121,000	$114,200
Accrued expenses payable (operating expenses)....	18,000	15,800
Dividends payable.............................	15,000	12,000
Common shares...............................	331,200	180,000
Retained earnings............................	227,600	208,400
	$712,800	$530,400

The statement of income for the year ended June 30, 2015, is as follows:

Sales..		$1,134,900
Cost of goods sold...........................		698,400
Gross profit..................................		436,500
Operating expenses:		
Depreciation expense........................	$ 8,700	
Other operating expenses....................	289,800	
Total operating expenses..................		298,500
Operating income............................		138,000
Other expenses:		
Loss on sale of investments..................		(6,000)
Income before income taxes..................		132,000
Income taxes expense........................		52,800
Net income..................................		$ 79,200

The following additional information was taken from the records:

a. Equipment and land were acquired for cash.
b. There were no disposals of equipment during the year.
c. The investments were sold for $54,000 cash.
d. The common shares were issued for cash.
e. There was a $60,000 debit to Retained Earnings for cash dividends declared.

Instructions

Prepare a statement of cash flows using the direct method of presenting cash flows from operating activities.

PR 16-6B

Statement of cash flows—direct method applied to PR 16-2B

The income statement of TorMax Technology Inc. for the year ended December 31, 2015, is as follows:

Sales..		$1,350,000
Cost of goods sold...........................		810,000
Gross profit..................................		540,000
Operating expenses:		
Depreciation expense........................	31,550	
Other operating expenses....................	245,379	
Total operating expenses..................		276,929
Income before income taxes..................		263,071
Income taxes expense........................		78,921
Net income..................................		$ 184,150

(*continued*)

Instructions

Using the information from Problem 16-2B and the additional information provided, prepare a statement of cash flows using the direct method of presenting cash flows from operating activities.

---

③ PR 16-7B

Statement of cash flows—direct method applied to PR 16-3B

The statement of income of Cantor Industries Ltd. for the year ended December 31, 2015, is as follows:

Sales		$388,888
Cost of goods sold		291,666
Gross profit		97,222
Operating expenses:		
Depreciation expense	$11,400	
Other operating expenses	47,192	
Total operating expenses		58,592
Operating income		38,630
Other income:		
Gain on sale of land		10,000
Income before income taxes		48,630
Income taxes expense		13,530
Net income		$ 35,100

Instructions

1. Using the information from Problem 16-3B and the additional information provided, prepare a statement of cash flows using the direct method of presenting cash flows from operating activities.
2. How does Cantor Industries' cash flow compare to its net income? Summarize the changes that caused the difference.

---

③ PR 16-8B

Statement of cash flows—direct method applied to PR 16-4B

Instructions

1. Using the information from Problem 16-4B, prepare a statement of cash flows for Lim Garden Supplies Inc. using the direct method of presenting cash flows from operating activities.
2. How does Lim Garden Supplies' cash flow compare to its net income? Summarize the changes that caused the difference.

SPECIAL ACTIVITIES

SA 16-1

Ethics and professional conduct in business

Lisa Maddick, president of Tu-Rock Industries Inc., believes that reporting free cash flow on the statement of income would be a useful addition to the company's just completed financial statements. The following discussion took place between Lisa Maddick and Tu-Rock's controller, Dean Kunz, in January, after the close of the fiscal year.

Lisa: I have been reviewing our financial statements for the last year. I am disappointed that our net income per share has dropped by 10% from last year. This is not going to look good to our shareholders. Is there anything we can do about this?

Dean: What do you mean? The past is the past, and the numbers are in. There isn't much that can be done about it. Our financial statements were prepared according to generally accepted accounting principles, and I don't see much leeway for significant change at this point.

Lisa: No, no. I'm not suggesting that we "cook the books." But look at the cash flow from operating activities on the statement of cash flows. The cash flow from operating activities has increased by 20%. This is very good news—and, I might add, useful information. The higher cash flow from operating activities will give our creditors comfort.

Dean: Well, the cash flow from operating activities is on the statement of cash flows, so I guess users will be able to see the improved cash flow figures there.

Lisa: This is true, but somehow I feel that this information should be given a much higher profile. I don't like this information being "buried" in the statement of cash flows. You know as well as I do that many users will focus on the statement of income. Therefore, I think we ought to include a free cash flow number on the face of the statement of income—someplace under the earnings per share number. In this way, users will get the complete picture of our operating performance. Yes, our earnings per share dropped this year, but our free cash flow improved! And all the information is in one place where users can see and compare the figures. What do you think?

Dean: I've never really thought about it like that before. I guess we could put the free cash flow on the statement of income, under the earnings per share. Users would really benefit from this disclosure. Thanks for the idea—I'll start working on it.

Lisa: Glad to be of service.

How would you interpret this situation? Is Dean behaving in an ethical and professional manner?

SA 16-2

Using the statement of cash flows

You are considering an investment in a new startup company, Steamboat IQ Inc., an Internet service provider. A review of the company's financial statements reveals negative retained earnings. In addition, the company appears to have been running a negative cash flow from operating activities since its inception.

How is the company staying in business under these circumstances? Could this company be a good investment?

SA 16-3

Analysis of the statement of cash flows

Jim Walker is the president and majority shareholder of Tech Trends Inc., a small retail store chain. Recently, Walker submitted a loan application for Tech Trends Inc. to Royal Bank. It called for a $200,000, 5%, 10-year loan to help finance the construction of a building and the purchase of store equipment, costing a total of $250,000. The funds will enable Tech Trends Inc. to open a store in Saskatoon. Land for this purpose was acquired last year. When Walker submitted the loan application, he included the company's most recent income statement, balance sheet, and retained earnings statement. The bank's loan officer then requested a statement of cash flows.

Because you are a close family friend, Walker asked you to prepare a statement of cash flows. From the records provided, you prepared the following statement:

Tech Trends Inc.
Statement of Cash Flows
For the Year Ended December 31, 2015

Cash flows from operating activities:		
Net income	$100,000	
Adjustments to reconcile net income to net cash flow from operating activities:		
Depreciation	28,000	
Gain on sale of investments	(10,000)	
Changes in current operating assets and liabilities:		
Decrease in accounts receivable	7,000	
Increase in inventories	(14,000)	
Increase in accounts payable	10,000	
Decrease in accrued expenses payable	(2,000)	
Net cash flow from operating activities		$119,000
Cash flows from investing activities:		
Cash received from investments sold	60,000	
Cash paid for purchase of store equipment	(40,000)	
Net cash flow provided by investing activities		20,000
Cash flows from financing activities:		
Cash paid for dividends	(42,000)	
Net cash flow used for financing activities		(42,000)
Increase in cash		97,000
Cash at the beginning of the year		36,000
Cash at the end of the year		$133,000
Noncash Financing and Investing Activities to be reported in notes to financial statements		
Issued common shares for land		$ 80,000

(continued)

After reviewing the statement, Walker telephoned you and commented, "Are you sure this statement is right?" He then raised the following questions:

1. "How can depreciation be a cash flow?"
2. "Issuing common shares for the land is not listed on the statement. Shouldn't users know about this transaction?"
3. "How can the gain on sale of investments be a deduction from net income in determining the cash flow from operating activities?"
4. "Why does the bank need this statement anyway? They can compute the increase in cash from the balance sheets for the past two years."

After jotting down Walker's questions, you assured him that this statement was "right." But to alleviate his concerns, you arranged a meeting for the following day.

a. How would you respond to each of Walker's questions?
b. Does the statement of cash flows enhance the chances of Tech Trends Inc. receiving the loan? Discuss.

SA 16-4

Analysis of cash flow from operations

The retailing division of Most Excellent Purchase Ltd. provided the following information on its cash flow from operations:

Net income	$ 540,000
Increase in accounts receivable	(648,000)
Increase in inventories	(720,000)
Decrease in accounts payable	(108,000)
Depreciation	120,000
Cash flow from operating activities	$(816,000)

The manager of the retailing division provided the accompanying memo with this report:

From: Senior Vice President, Retailing Division

I am pleased to report that we had earnings of $540,000 over the last period. This resulted in a return on invested capital of 10%, which is near our targets for this division. I have been aggressive in building the sales volume in the division. As a result, I am happy to report that we have increased the number of new credit card customers as a result of an aggressive marketing campaign. In addition, we have found some excellent merchandise opportunities. Some of our suppliers have made some of their apparel merchandise available at a deep discount. We have purchased as much of these goods as possible in order to improve profitability. I'm also happy to report that our vendor payment problems have improved. We are nearly caught up on our overdue payables balances.

Comment on the senior vice president's memo in light of the cash flow information.

SA 16-5

Statement of cash flows

f·a·i

This activity will require two teams to retrieve statement of cash flows information from the Internet. One team is to obtain the most recent year's statement of cash flows for TELUS Corporation and the other team the most recent year's statement of cash flows for Potash Corporation of Saskatchewan Inc.

The statement of cash flows is included as part of the annual report information that is a required disclosure to the Canadian Securities Administrators (CSA). CSA documents can be retrieved from the SEDAR (The System for Electronic Document Analysis and Retrieval) website, **www.sedar.com.**

To obtain annual report information, click on Search Database, then click on Public Company. Enter the company name where it is indicated. Under Document Type, select Annual Report or Financial Statements (if you do not want the whole report). If your search has no results, try changing the dates. The American version of this site is EdgarScan™ at **www.sec.gov/edgar/searchedgar/webusers.htm.**

As a group, compare the two statements of cash flow.

a. How are TELUS Corporation and Potash Corporation similar or different regarding cash flows?
b. Compute the free cash flow for each company, assuming additions to property, plant, and equipment replace current capacity.
c. Which company has the better free cash flow?

Financial Statement Analysis

© Francis Vachon/Alamy

POTASH CORPORATION OF SASKATCHEWAN, INC.

During a recent year, Potash Corporation of Saskatchewan, Inc. (PotashCorp) reported revenues of more than $8 billion and net income of more than $3 billion. The common shares of PotashCorp are traded on the Toronto Stock Exchange and on the New York Stock Exchange (symbol POT) and closed on December 16, 2011, at $40.58 per share. On the basis of current market values, PotashCorp is worth over $34 billion. Do you wish you could have invested in PotashCorp 10 years ago?

Headquartered in Saskatchewan, PotashCorp is the world's largest fertilizer company by capacity, producing the three primary crop nutrients—potash, phosphate, and nitrogen. Its five potash operations in Saskatchewan and one in New Brunswick are responsible for about 20 percent of global capacity and make PotashCorp the world's leading potash producer. The company's operations and business interests span seven countries, making PotashCorp both an international enterprise and a key player in meeting the growing challenge of feeding the world.

The achievements of PotashCorp show that reputation and demand for a company's product are important indicators of success. However, these are not the *only* factors that determine a company's success. A business needs to combine product offerings with proper financial, marketing, and sales strategies to be successful. Clearly, PotashCorp has achieved this winning combination. If you had invested in its common shares back in 2001, the share price would have risen from $3.41 per share to $40.58 per share 10 years later.

How, then, should you select companies in which to invest? Like any significant purchase, you should do some research to guide your investment decision. If you were buying a car, for example, you might go to www.autotrader.ca to obtain reviews, ratings, prices, specifications, options, and fuel economy across a number of vehicle alternatives. In deciding whether to invest in a company, you can use financial analysis to gain insight into a company's past performance and future prospects. This chapter describes and illustrates common financial data that can be analyzed to assist you in making investment decisions such as whether or not to invest in PotashCorp shares. The contents of corporate annual reports are also discussed.

After studying this chapter, you should be able to:

1 Describe basic financial statement analytical methods.

Basic Analytical Methods	Horizontal Analysis	EXAMPLE EXERCISE 17-1 (page 873)
	Vertical Analysis	EXAMPLE EXERCISE 17-2 (page 873)
	Common-Sized Statements	
	Ratio Analysis	

2 Use ratio analysis to assess the liquidity of a business.

Liquidity Analysis	Working Capital	
	Current Ratio	
	Quick Ratio	EXAMPLE EXERCISE 17-3 (page 878)

3 Use ratio analysis to assess the efficiency of a business.

Efficiency Analysis	Accounts Receivable Analysis	EXAMPLE EXERCISE 17-4 (page 880)
	Inventory Analysis	EXAMPLE EXERCISE 17-5 (page 881)
	Total Asset Turnover	

4 Use ratio analysis to assess the solvency of a business.

Solvency Analysis	Debt Ratio	EXAMPLE EXERCISE 17-6 (page 883)
	Times Interest Earned Ratio	EXAMPLE EXERCISE 17-7 (page 884)

5 Use ratio analysis to assess the profitability of a business.

Profitability Analysis	Profit Margin	
	Gross Margin	EXAMPLE EXERCISE 17-8 (page 886)
	Return on Assets	EXAMPLE EXERCISE 17-9 (page 887)
	Return on Common Shareholders' Equity	EXAMPLE EXERCISE 17-10 (page 889)
	Earnings per Share	EXAMPLE EXERCISE 17-11 (page 890)
	Price-Earnings Ratio	EXAMPLE EXERCISE 17-12 (page 891)
	Dividend Yield	
	Summary of Analytical Ratios	

6 Describe the contents of corporate annual reports.

Corporate Annual Reports	Notes to the Financial Statements	
	Management's Discussion and Analysis	
	Management Letter	
	Auditor's Report	

For the chapter *At a Glance*, turn to page 894.

1 # Basic Analytical Methods

Describe basic financial statement analytical methods.

Users analyze a company's financial statements using a variety of analytical methods. Four such methods are as follows:

1. horizontal analysis
2. vertical analysis

3. common-sized statements
4. ratio analysis

Horizontal Analysis

The percentage analysis of increases and decreases in related items in financial statements is called **horizontal analysis**. Each item on the most recent statement is compared with the related item on one or more earlier statements in terms of the following:

1. *amount* of increase or decrease
2. *percent* of increase or decrease

When comparing statements, the earlier statement is normally used as the base for computing increases and decreases.

Exhibit 1 illustrates horizontal analysis for the December 31, 2015 and 2014, balance sheets of Langley Company. In Exhibit 1, the December 31, 2014, balance sheet (the earliest year presented) is used as the base.

Exhibit 1 indicates that total assets decreased by $91,000 (7.4%), liabilities decreased by $133,000 (30.0%), and shareholders' equity increased by $42,000 (5.3%). Most of the decrease in long-term liabilities of $100,000 appears to have been achieved through the sale of long-term investments.

The balance sheet in Exhibit 1 may be expanded or supported by a separate schedule that includes the individual asset and liability accounts. For example, Exhibit 2 is a supporting schedule of Langley's current asset accounts.

Exhibit 2 indicates that although cash and temporary investments increased, accounts receivable and inventories decreased. The decrease in accounts receivable could be caused by improved collection policies, which would increase cash. The decrease in inventory could be caused by increased sales.

Exhibit 1

Balance Sheet—Horizontal Analysis

Langley Company
Balance Sheet
December 31, 2015 and 2014

	Dec. 31, 2015	Dec. 31, 2014	Increase (Decrease) Amount	Percent
Assets				
Current assets.	$ 550,000	$ 533,000	$ 17,000	3.2%
Long-term investments	95,000	177,500	(82,500)	(46.5%)
Property, plant, and equipment (net)	444,500	470,000	(25,500)	(5.4%)
Intangible assets.	50,000	50,000	—	—
Total assets.	$1,139,500	$1,230,500	$ (91,000)	(7.4%)
Liabilities				
Current liabilities	$ 210,000	$ 243,000	$ (33,000)	(13.6%)
Long-term liabilities.	100,000	200,000	(100,000)	(50.0%)
Total liabilities	310,000	443,000	(133,000)	(30.0%)
Shareholders' Equity				
$6 preferred shares, $1,500 issued and outstanding.	150,000	150,000	—	—
Common shares, 50,000 issued and outstanding.	500,000	500,000	—	—
Retained earnings	179,500	137,500	42,000	30.5%
Total shareholders' equity	829,500	787,500	42,000	5.3%
Total liabilities and shareholders' equity.	$1,139,500	$1,230,500	$ (91,000)	(7.4%)

Exhibit 2

Schedule of Current Assets—Horizontal Analysis

				Langley Company Schedule of Current Assets December 31, 2015 and 2014		

			2015	2014	Increase (Decrease) Amount	Increase (Decrease) Percent
Cash			$ 90,500	$ 64,700	$ 25,800	39.9%
Temporary investments			75,000	60,000	15,000	25.0%
Accounts receivable (net)			115,000	120,000	(5,000)	(4.2%)
Inventories			264,000	283,000	(19,000)	(6.7%)
Prepaid expenses			5,500	5,300	200	3.8%
Total current assets			$550,000	$533,000	$ 17,000	3.2%

Exhibit 3 illustrates horizontal analysis for the 2015 and 2014 income statements of Langley Company. Exhibit 3 indicates an increase in sales of $296,500, or 24.0%. However, the percentage increase in sales of 24.0% was accompanied by an even greater percentage increase in the cost of goods sold of 27.2%. Thus, gross profit increased by only 19.7%, not by the 24.0% increase in sales.

Exhibit 3 also indicates that selling expenses increased by 29.9%. Thus, the 24.0% increase in sales could have been caused by an advertising campaign, which increased selling expenses. Administrative expenses increased by only 6.8%, total operating expenses increased by 20.7%, and income from operations increased by 18.0%. Interest expense decreased by 50.0%. This decrease was probably caused by the 50.0% decrease in long-term liabilities (Exhibit 1). Overall, net income increased by 19.0%, a favourable result.

Exhibit 3

Income Statement—Horizontal Analysis

			Langley Company Income Statement For the Years Ended December 31, 2015 and 2014			

			2015	2014	Increase (Decrease) Amount	Increase (Decrease) Percent
Sales			$1,530,500	$1,234,000	$296,500	24.0%
Sales returns and allowances			32,500	34,000	(1,500)	(4.4%)
Net sales			1,498,000	1,200,000	298,000	24.8%
Cost of goods sold			1,043,000	820,000	223,000	27.2%
Gross profit			455,000	380,000	75,000	19.7%
Selling expenses			191,000	147,000	44,000	29.9%
Administrative expenses			104,000	97,400	6,600	6.8%
Total operating expenses			295,000	244,400	50,600	20.7%
Income from operations			160,000	135,600	24,400	18.0%
Other income			8,500	11,000	(2,500)	(22.7%)
			168,500	146,600	21,900	14.9%
Other expense (interest)			6,000	12,000	(6,000)	(50.0%)
Income before income taxes.			162,500	134,600	27,900	20.7%
Income taxes expense			71,500	58,100	13,400	23.1%
Net income			$ 91,000	$ 76,500	$ 14,500	19.0%

EXAMPLE EXERCISE 17-1 **Horizontal Analysis**   ①

The cash and accounts receivable balances for a company are provided below.

	Dec. 31, 2015	Dec. 31, 2014
Cash	$62,500	$50,000
Accounts receivable (net)	74,400	80,000

Based on this information, what is the amount and percentage of increase or decrease that would be shown in a balance sheet with horizontal analysis?

FOLLOW MY EXAMPLE 17-1

Cash	$12,500 increase ($62,500 – $50,000), 25%
Accounts receivable	$5,600 decrease ($74,400 – $80,000), 7%

For Practice: PE 17-1

Vertical Analysis

The percentage analysis of the relationship of each component in a financial statement to a total within the statement is called **vertical analysis**. Although vertical analysis is applied to a single statement, it may be applied on the same statement over time. This approach enhances the analysis by showing how the percentages of each item have changed over time.

In vertical analysis of the balance sheet, the percentages are computed as follows:

1. Each asset item is stated as a percent of the total assets.
2. Each liability and shareholders' equity item is stated as a percent of the total liabilities and shareholders' equity.

Exhibit 4 illustrates the vertical analysis of the December 31, 2015 and 2014, balance sheets of Langley Company. Exhibit 4 indicates that current assets have increased from 43.3% to 48.3% of total assets. Long-term investments decreased from 14.4% to 8.3% of total assets. Shareholders' equity increased from 64.0% to 72.8% with a comparable decrease in liabilities.

EXAMPLE EXERCISE 17-2 **Vertical Analysis**   ①

Income statement information for Lee Corporation is provided below.

Sales	$100,000
Cost of goods sold	65,000
Gross profit	$ 35,000

Prepare a vertical analysis of this income statement information for Lee Corporation.

FOLLOW MY EXAMPLE 17-2

	Amount	Percentage	
Sales	$100,000	100%	($100,000 ÷ $100,000)
Cost of goods sold	65,000	65	($65,000 ÷ $100,000)
Gross profit	$ 35,000	35%	($35,000 ÷ $100,000)

For Practice: PE 17-2

In a vertical analysis of the income statement, each item is stated as a percent of net sales. Exhibit 5 illustrates the vertical analysis of the 2015 and 2014, income statements of Langley Company.

Exhibit 4

Balance Sheet—Vertical Analysis

	Langley Company Balance Sheet December 31, 2015 and 2014			
	Dec. 31, 2015		Dec. 31, 2014	
	Amount	Percent	Amount	Percent
Assets				
Current assets	$ 550,000	48.3%	$ 533,000	43.3%
Long-term investments	95,000	8.3	177,500	14.4
Property, plant, and				
equipment (net)	444,500	39.0	470,000	38.2
Intangible assets	50,000	4.4	50,000	4.1
Total assets	$ 1,139,500	100.0%	$ 1,230,500	100.0%
Liabilities				
Current liabilities	$ 210,000	18.4%	$ 243,000	19.7%
Long-term liabilities	100,000	8.8	200,000	16.3
Total liabilities	310,000	27.2	443,000	36.0
Shareholders' Equity				
$6 preferred shares, 1,500 issued				
and outstanding	150,000	13.2	150,000	12.2
Common shares, 50,000 issued				
and outstanding	500,000	43.9	500,000	40.6
Retained earnings	179,500	15.7	137,500	11.2
Total shareholders' equity	829,500	72.8	787,500	64.0
Total liabilities and				
shareholders' equity.............	$ 1,139,500	100.0%	$ 1,230,500	100.0%

Exhibit 5

Income Statement—Vertical Analysis

	Langley Company Income Statement For the Years Ended December 31, 2015 and 2014			
	2015		2014	
	Amount	Percent	Amount	Percent
Sales	$1,530,500	102.2%	$1,234,000	102.8%
Sales returns and allowances	32,500	2.2	34,000	2.8
Net sales	1,498,000	100.0%	1,200,000	100.0%
Cost of goods sold	1,043,000	69.6	820,000	68.3
Gross profit	455,000	30.4%	380,000	31.7%
Selling expenses	191,000	12.8%	147,000	12.3%
Administrative expenses	104,000	6.9	97,400	8.1
Total operating expenses	295,000	19.7%	244,400	20.4%
Income from operations	160,000	10.7%	135,600	11.3%
Other income	8,500	0.6	11,000	0.9
	168,500	11.3%	146,600	12.2%
Other expense (interest)	6,000	0.4	12,000	1.0
Income before income taxes...........	162,500	10.9%	134,600	11.2%
Income taxes expense...............	71,500	4.8	58,100	4.8
Net income	$ 91,000	6.1%	$ 76,500	6.4%

Exhibit 5 indicates a decrease of the gross profit rate from 31.7% in 2014 to 30.4% in 2015. Although this is only a 1.3 percentage point (31.7% – 30.4%) decrease, in dollars of potential gross profit, it represents a decrease of about $19,500 (1.3% × $1,498,000). Thus, a small percentage decrease can have a large dollar effect.

Common-Sized Statements

In a **common-sized statement**, all items are expressed as percentages with no dollar amounts shown. Common-sized statements are a presentation form of vertical analysis. Common-sized statements allow for comparing two or more companies despite their size differences and for comparing a company against the industry averages.

Exhibit 6 illustrates common-sized income statements for Langley Company and Markham Corporation. Exhibit 6 indicates that Langley Company has a slightly higher rate of gross profit (30.4%) than Markham Corporation (30.0%). However, Langley has a higher percentage of selling expenses (12.8%) and administrative expenses (6.9%) than does Markham (11.5% and 4.1%). As a result, the income from operations of Langley (10.7%) is less than that of Markham (14.4%).

The unfavourable difference of 3.7 (14.4% – 10.7%) percentage points in income from operations would concern the managers and other stakeholders of Langley. The underlying causes of the difference should be investigated and possibly corrected. For example, Langley Company may decide to outsource some of its administrative duties so that its administrative expenses are more comparable with those of Markham Corporation.

Ratio Analysis

All users of financial statements are interested in learning the following:

1. A company's ability to meet its short-term financial obligations (debts), known as **liquidity**
2. A company's ability to use its assets to the best of its ability, known as **efficiency**
3. A company's ability to meet its long-term financial obligations (debts), known as **solvency**
4. A company's ability to earn income, known as **profitability**

Exhibit 6

Common-Sized Income Statement

	Langley Company	Markham Corporation
Sales	102.2%	102.3%
Sales returns and allowances	2.2	2.3
Net sales	100.0%	100.0%
Cost of goods sold	69.6	70.0
Gross profit	30.4%	30.0%
Selling expenses	12.8%	11.5%
Administrative expenses	6.9	4.1
Total operating expenses	19.7%	15.6%
Income from operations	10.7%	14.4%
Other income	0.6	0.6
	11.3%	15.0%
Other expenses	0.4	0.5
Income before income taxes	10.9%	14.5%
Income taxes expense	4.8	5.5
Net income	6.1%	9.0%

All these objectives are interrelated. For example, a company that cannot pay its debts will have difficulty obtaining credit. A lack of credit will, in turn, limit the company's ability to purchase merchandise or expand operations, which decreases its profitability. Ratio analysis provides investors and creditors with information on a business's financial health in terms of its liquidity, efficiency, solvency, and profitability.

Because there are no standard approved ratio calculations, ratios can vary slightly between textbooks and between companies in the industry. Thus, when reviewing ratios, it is important to be aware of these differences and to understand how a particular ratio is calculated.

The Langley Company financial statements presented earlier are used to illustrate the following analyses.

② Liquidity Analysis

Use ratio analysis to assess the liquidity of a business.

Evaluating a company's ability to pay its current liabilities is called liquidity analysis. It is of special interest to short-term creditors and includes the computation and analysis of the following:

1. working capital
2. current ratio
3. quick ratio

Working Capital

A company's **working capital** is computed as follows:

$$\text{Working Capital} = \text{Current Assets} - \text{Current Liabilities}$$

To illustrate, the working capital for Langley Company for 2015 and 2014 is computed below.

	2015	2014
Current assets	$550,000	$533,000
Less current liabilities	210,000	243,000
Working capital	$340,000	$290,000

The working capital is used to evaluate a company's ability to pay its current liabilities. A company's working capital is often monitored monthly, quarterly, or yearly by creditors and other debtors. However, it is difficult to use working capital to compare companies of different sizes. For example, working capital of $250,000 may be adequate for a local hardware store, but it would be inadequate for The Home Depot.

Current Ratio

The **current ratio**, sometimes called the **working capital ratio**, is computed as follows:

$$\text{Current Ratio} = \frac{\text{Current Assets}}{\text{Current Liabilities}}$$

To illustrate, the current ratio for Langley Company is computed below.

	2015	2014
Current assets	$550,000	$533,000
Current liabilities	210,000	243,000
Current ratio	2.6 ($550,000/$210,000)	2.2 ($533,000/$243,000)

The 2.6 current ratio means that Langley could pay off its current liabilities 2.6 times, or 260%, using its current assets. This is an improvement over the prior year's ratio of 2.2 times. The current ratio is a more reliable indicator of the ability to pay current

liabilities than is working capital. To illustrate, assume that as at December 31, 2015, the working capital of a competitor is much greater than $340,000, but its current ratio is only 1.3. Considering these facts alone, Langley Company, with its current ratio of 2.6, is in a more favourable position to obtain short-term credit than the competitor, which has the greater amount of working capital.

Quick Ratio

One limitation of working capital and the current ratio is that they do not consider the makeup of the current assets. Thus, two companies may have the same working capital and current ratios but differ significantly in their ability to pay their current liabilities.

To illustrate, the current assets and liabilities for Langley Company and Johnson Corporation as at December 31, 2015, are as follows:

	Langley Company	Johnson Corporation
Current assets:		
Cash	$ 90,500	$ 45,500
Temporary investments	75,000	25,000
Accounts receivable (net)	115,000	90,000
Inventories	264,000	380,000
Prepaid expenses	5,500	9,500
Total current assets	550,000	550,000
Less current liabilities	210,000	210,000
Working capital	$340,000	$340,000
Current ratio ($550,000/$210,000)	2.6	2.6

Langley and Johnson both have a working capital of $340,000 and current ratios of 2.6. Johnson, however, has more of its current assets in inventory. These goods in inventory must be sold and the receivables collected before all the current liabilities can be paid. This process takes time. In addition, if the market for its product declines, Johnson may have difficulty selling its inventory. This difficulty, in turn, could impair the company's ability to pay its current liabilities.

In contrast, Langley's current assets contain more cash, temporary investments, and accounts receivable, which can easily be converted to cash. Thus, Langley is in a stronger position than Johnson to pay its current liabilities.

A ratio that measures the "instant" debt-paying ability of a company is the **quick ratio**, sometimes called the **acid-test ratio**. The quick ratio is computed as follows:

$$\text{Quick Ratio} = \frac{\text{Quick Assets}}{\text{Current Liabilities}}$$

Quick assets are cash and other current assets that can be easily converted to cash. Quick assets normally include cash, temporary investments, and receivables and exclude prepaid expenses and inventories.

To illustrate, the quick ratio for Langley Company is computed below.

	2015	2014
Quick assets:		
Cash	$ 90,500	$ 64,700
Temporary investments	75,000	60,000
Accounts receivable (net)	115,000	120,000
Total quick assets	$280,500	$244,700
Current liabilities	$210,000	$243,000
Quick ratio	1.3[1]	1.0[2]

[1]1.3 = $280,500 ÷ $210,000
[2]1.0 = $244,700 ÷ $243,000

Again, this ratio shows an improvement over the prior year's ratio.

EXAMPLE EXERCISE 17-3   Liquidity Analysis   **2**

The following items are reported on a company's balance sheet:

Cash	$300,000
Temporary investments	100,000
Accounts receivable (net)	200,000
Inventories	200,000
Accounts payable	400,000

Determine (a) the current ratio and (b) the quick ratio.

FOLLOW MY EXAMPLE 17-3

a. Current Ratio = Current Assets ÷ Current Liabilities
   Current Ratio = ($300,000 + $100,000 + $200,000 + $200,000) ÷ $400,000
   Current Ratio = 2.0

b. Quick Ratio = Quick Assets ÷ Current Liabilities
   Quick Ratio = ($300,000 + $100,000 + $200,000) ÷ $400,000
   Quick Ratio = 1.5

For Practice: PE 17-3

Efficiency Analysis

Use ratio analysis to assess the efficiency of a business.

Efficiency ratios focus on the ability of a business to use its assets efficiently. This analysis includes the computation and analysis of the following ratios:

1. accounts receivable turnover
2. days' sales in receivables
3. inventory turnover
4. days' sales in inventory
5. total asset turnover

Accounts Receivable Analysis

Evaluation of a company's ability to collect its accounts receivable includes the computation and analysis of the following:

1. accounts receivable turnover
2. days' sales in receivables

Collecting accounts receivable as quickly as possible improves a company's cash position. In addition, the cash collected from receivables may be used to improve or expand operations. Quick collection of receivables also reduces the risk of uncollectible accounts.

Accounts Receivable Turnover   The **accounts receivable turnover** is computed as follows:

$$\text{Accounts Receivable Turnover} = \frac{\text{Net Sales[1]}}{\text{Average Net Accounts Receivable}}$$

Net accounts receivable equals accounts receivable less allowance for doubtful accounts. To illustrate, the accounts receivable turnover for Langley Company for 2015 and 2014 is computed below.

---

1 If known, *credit* sales should be used in the numerator. Because credit sales are not normally known by external users, we use net sales in the numerator.

	2015	**2014**
Net sales	$1,498,000	$1,200,000
Accounts receivable (net):		
Beginning of year	$ 120,000	$ 140,000
End of year	115,000	120,000
Total	$ 235,000	$ 260,000
Average accounts receivable	$117,500 ($235,000 ÷ 2)	$130,000 ($260,000 ÷ 2)
Accounts receivable turnover	12.7 times	9.2 times
	($1,498,000 ÷ $117,500)	($1,200,000 ÷ $130,000)

The increase in Langley's accounts receivable turnover from 9.2 times to 12.7 times indicates that the collection of receivables has improved during 2015. This improvement may be due to a change in how credit is granted, a change in collection practices, or both.

For Langley Company, the average accounts receivable was computed using the accounts receivable balance at the beginning and the end of the year. When sales are seasonal and, thus, vary throughout the year, monthly balances of receivables are often used. Also, if sales on account include both notes receivable and accounts receivable, notes and accounts receivable are normally combined for analysis.

Days' Sales in Receivables   The **days' sales in receivables** is computed as follows:

$$\text{Days' Sales in Receivables} = \frac{\text{Average Net Accounts Receivable}}{\text{Average Daily Sales}}$$

where

$$\text{Average Daily Sales} = \frac{\text{Net Sales}}{365 \text{ days}}$$

To illustrate, the days' sales in receivables for Langley Company is computed below.

	2015	**2014**
Average accounts receivable (net)	$117,500 ($235,000 ÷ 2)	$130,000 ($260,000 ÷ 2)
Average daily sales	$4,104 ($1,498,000 ÷ 365)	$3,288 ($1,200,000 ÷ 365)
Days' sales in receivables	28.6 days ($117,500 ÷ $4,104)	39.5 days ($130,000 ÷ $3,288)

Days' sales in receivables can also be calculated from the accounts receivable turnover ratio as follows:

$$\text{Days' Sales in Receivables} = \frac{365}{\text{Accounts Receivable Turnover}}$$

To illustrate, Langley Company's 2015 ratio can be calculated as follows:

Days' Sales in Receivables = 365 ÷ 12.7 = 28.7 days

The slight difference (28.6 versus 28.7 days) is due to rounding of the turnover ratio.

The days' sales in receivables is an estimate of the time (in days) that the accounts receivable have been outstanding. The days' sales in receivables is often compared with a company's credit terms to evaluate the efficiency of the collection of receivables.

To illustrate, if Langley's credit terms are 2/10, n/30, then Langley was very *inefficient* in collecting receivables in 2014. In other words, receivables should have been collected in 30 days or less but were being collected in 39.5 days. Although collections improved during 2015 to 28.6 days, there is probably still room for improvement. On the other hand, if Langley's credit terms are n/45, then there is probably little room for improving collections.

EXAMPLE EXERCISE 17-4 **Accounts Receivable Analysis** 3

A company reports the following:

Net sales	$960,000
Average accounts receivable (net)	48,000

Determine (a) the accounts receivable turnover and (b) the days' sales in receivables, using both methods for calculating the days' sales in receivables ratio. Round to one decimal place.

FOLLOW MY EXAMPLE 17-4

a. Accounts Receivable Turnover = Sales ÷ Average Accounts Receivable
   Accounts Receivable Turnover = $960,000 ÷ $48,000
   Accounts Receivable Turnover = 20.0 times

b. Days' Sales in Receivables = Average Accounts Receivable ÷ Average Daily Sales
   Days' Sales in Receivables = $48,000 ÷ ($960,000/365) = $48,000 ÷ $2,630
   Days' Sales in Receivables = 18.3 days
   Days' Sales in Receivables = 365 ÷ Accounts Receivable Turnover
   Days' Sales in Receivables = 365 ÷ 20.0
   Days' Sales in Receivables = 18.3 days

For Practice: PE 17-4

Inventory Analysis

Evaluation of a company's ability to manage its inventory effectively includes the computation and analysis of the following:

1. inventory turnover
2. days' sales in inventory

Excess inventory decreases working capital by tying up funds (cash) in inventory. In addition, excess inventory increases insurance expense, property taxes, storage costs, and other related expenses. These expenses further reduce funds that could be used elsewhere to improve or expand operations.

Excess inventory also increases the risk of losses because of price declines or obsolescence of the inventory. On the other hand, a company should keep enough inventory in stock so that it doesn't lose sales because of lack of inventory.

Inventory Turnover The **inventory turnover** is computed as follows:

$$\text{Inventory Turnover} = \frac{\text{Cost of Goods Sold}}{\text{Average Inventory}}$$

To illustrate, the inventory turnover for Langley Company for 2015 and 2014 is computed below.

	2015	2014
Cost of goods sold	$1,043,000	$820,000
Inventories:		
Beginning of year	$ 283,000	$311,000
End of year	264,000	283,000
Total	$ 547,000	$594,000
Average inventory	$273,500 ($547,000 ÷ 2)	$297,000 ($594,000 ÷ 2)
Inventory turnover	3.8 times ($1,043,000 ÷ $273,500)	2.8 times ($820,000 ÷ $297,000)

The increase in Langley's inventory turnover from 2.8 times to 3.8 times indicates that the management of inventory has improved in 2015. The inventory turnover improved because of an increase in the cost of goods sold, which indicates more sales, and a decrease in the average inventories.

What is considered a good inventory turnover varies by type of inventory, companies, and industries. For example, grocery stores have a higher inventory turnover than jewellers or furniture stores. Likewise, within a grocery store, perishable foods have a higher turnover than the soaps and cleaners.

Days' Sales in Inventory   The **days' sales in inventory** is computed as follows:

$$\text{Days' Sales in Inventory} = \frac{\text{Average Inventory}}{\text{Average Daily Cost of Goods Sold}}$$

where

$$\text{Average Daily Cost of Goods Sold} = \frac{\text{Cost of Goods Sold}}{365 \text{ days}}$$

To illustrate, the days' sales in inventory for Langley Company is computed below.

	2015	2014
Average inventory	$273,500 ($547,000 ÷ 2)	$297,000 ($594,000 ÷ 2)
Average daily cost of goods sold	$2,858 ($1,043,000 ÷ 365)	$2,247 ($820,000 ÷ 365)
Days' sales in inventory	95.7 days ($273,500 ÷ $2,858)	132.2 days ($297,000 ÷ $2,247)

The days' sales in inventory is a measure of the time it takes to purchase, sell, and replace the inventory. Langley's days' sales in inventory improved from 132.2 days to 95.7 days during 2015. This decrease represents a major improvement in managing inventory.

Days' sales in inventory can also be calculated from the inventory turnover ratio as follows:

$$\text{Days' Sales in Inventory} = \frac{365}{\text{Inventory Turnover}}$$

To illustrate, Langley Company's 2015 ratio can be calculated as follows:

Days' Sales in Inventory = 365 ÷ 3.8 = 96.1 days

The slight difference (96.1 versus 95.7 days) is due to rounding of the turnover ratio.

EXAMPLE EXERCISE 17-5   Inventory Analysis   ③

A company reports the following:

Cost of goods sold	$560,000
Average inventory	112,000

Determine (a) the inventory turnover and (b) the days' sales in inventory, using both methods for calculating the days' sales in inventory ratio. Round to one decimal place.

(continued)

a. Inventory Turnover = Cost of Goods Sold ÷ Average Inventory
   Inventory Turnover = $560,000 ÷ $112,000
   Inventory Turnover = 5.0 times

b. Days' Sales in Inventory = Average Inventory ÷ Average Daily Cost of Goods Sold
   Days' Sales in Inventory = $112,000 ÷ ($560,000/365) = $112,000 ÷ $1,534
   Days' Sales in Inventory = 73.0 days
   Days' Sales in Inventory = 365 ÷ Inventory Turnover
   Days' Sales in Inventory = 365 ÷ 5.0
   Days' Sales in Inventory = 73.0 days

For Practice: PE17-5

Total Asset Turnover

The **total asset turnover** ratio measures how effectively a company uses its assets to generate income. It is computed as follows:

$$\text{Total Asset Turnover} = \frac{\text{Net Sales}}{\text{Average Total Assets}}$$

To illustrate, the total asset turnover ratio for Langley Company is computed below.

	2015	2014
Net sales	$1,498,000	$1,200,000
Total Assets:		
Beginning of year	$1,230,500	$1,187,500
End of year	1,139,500	1,230,500
Total	$2,370,000	$2,418,000
Average total assets	$1,185,000 ($2,370,000 ÷ 2)	$1,209,000 ($2,418,000 ÷ 2)
Total asset turnover	1.3 times ($1,498,000 ÷ $1,185,000)	1.0 times ($1,200,000 ÷ $1,209,000)

Langley's total asset turnover increased from 1.0 times to 1.3 times during 2015. This increase represents an improvement in Langley's ability to generate sales through use of its assets.

④ Solvency Analysis

Use ratio analysis to assess the solvency of a business.

Solvency analysis focuses on the ability of a company to pay its long-term liabilities. It is normally assessed using the following ratios:

a. debt ratio
b. times interest earned ratio

Debt Ratio

The assets of a company can be financed by either the issuance of debt or the sale of shares, or equity. The **debt ratio** measures the percentage of assets that are financed with debt and is computed as follows:

$$\text{Debt Ratio} = \frac{\text{Total Liabilities}}{\text{Total Assets}}$$

To illustrate, the debt ratio for Langley Company is computed below.

	2015	**2014**
Total liabilities	$ 310,000	$ 443,000
Total assets	$1,139,500	$1,230,500
Debt ratio	27.2% ($310,000 ÷ $1,139,500)	36.0% ($443,000 ÷ $1,230,500)

Langley's debt ratio decreased from 36.0% to 27.2% during 2015. This decrease represents an improvement and indicates that Langley's assets are financed mainly by equity, which is less risky because fewer fixed payments, such as interest, are required.

EXAMPLE EXERCISE 17-6 Debt Ratio   **4**

The following information was taken from Acme Company's balance sheet:

Total assets	$1,960,000
Long-term liabilities	400,000
Total liabilities	560,000
Total shareholders' equity	1,400,000

Determine the company's debt ratio.

FOLLOW MY EXAMPLE 17-6

Debt Ratio = Total Liabilities ÷ Total Assets
Debt Ratio = $560,000 ÷ $1,960,000
Debt Ratio = 28.6%

For Practice: PE17-6

Times Interest Earned Ratio

The **times interest earned ratio** measures the likelihood of a company fulfilling its short-term interest obligations. It is computed as follows:

$$\text{Times Interest Earned} = \frac{\text{Income Before Income Taxes} + \text{Interest Expense}}{\text{Interest Expense}}$$

In financial reports, *income before interest and taxes* is often referred to as **EBIT**, an abbreviation of *earnings before interest and taxes*. The *higher* the ratio the more likely interest payments will be paid. To illustrate, the times interest earned ratio for Langley Company is computed below.

	2015	**2014**
Income before income taxes	$162,500	$134,600
Add interest expense	6,000	12,000
Amount available to pay interest	$168,500	$146,600
Times interest earned	28.1 times ($168,500 ÷ $6,000)	12.2 times ($146,600 ÷ $12,000)

The times interest earned ratio improved from 12.2 times to 28.1 times during 2015. This increase indicates that Langley Company has sufficient earnings to pay its interest expense.

This ratio is based on income as reported on the income statement. Because net income includes accrued revenues and expenses, it does not necessarily indicate the amount of cash available. While an improved times interest earned ratio is a helpful measure, it is no guarantee that a company will be able to meet its interest payments.

EXAMPLE EXERCISE 17-7   Times Interest Earned Ratio ④

A company reports the following:

Income before income taxes	$250,000
Interest expense	100,000

Determine the times interest earned ratio.

FOLLOW MY EXAMPLE 17-7

Times Interest Earned = (Income Before Income Taxes + Interest Expense) ÷ Interest Expense
Times Interest Earned = ($250,000 + $100,000) ÷ $100,000
Times Interest Earned = 3.5 times

For Practice: PE 17-7

MID-CHAPTER ILLUSTRATIVE PROBLEM

Partial information from the comparative financial statements of Barrington Foods Limited is as follows:

Barrington Foods Limited
Balance Sheet (Partial)
December 31, 2015 and 2014

	2015	2014
Assets		
Current assets:		
Cash	$ 504,000	$ 324,800
Temporary investments	764,400	657,600
Accounts receivable	557,600	422,400
Inventories	208,000	132,800
Prepaid expenses	104,000	46,400
Total current assets	2,138,000	1,584,000
Long-term investments	300,000	512,000
Property, plant, and equipment, net	3,338,100	1,952,000
Total assets	$5,776,100	$4,048,000

Barrington Foods Limited
Income Statement (Partial)
For Years Ended December 31, 2015 and 2014

	2015	2014
Sales, net	$3,364,400	$2,951,200
Cost of goods sold	1,008,500	998,400
Gross profit	$2,355,900	$1,952,800

Instructions:

1. Determine the following measures for 2015 and 2014, rounding the ratios to one decimal place. Assume the December 31, 2013 balances for Accounts Receivable, Inventory, and Total Assets were $380,000, $140,000, and $3,600,000, respectively.
   a. accounts receivable turnover
   b. days' sales in receivables
   c. inventory turnover
   d. days' sales in inventory
   e. total asset turnover
2. Comment on whether these ratios indicate an improvement or decline in efficiency.

MID-CHAPTER ILLUSTRATIVE SOLUTION

1.

		2015	2014
a.	Accounts receivable turnover	$3,364,400 ÷ (($422,400 + $557,600) ÷ 2) = 6.87 or 6.9 times	$2,951,200 ÷ (($380,000 + $422,400) ÷ 2) = 7.36 or 7.4 times
b.	Days' sales in receivables	(($422,400 + $557,600) ÷ 2) ÷ ($3,364,400 ÷ 365) = 53.15 or 53.2 days (or 365 ÷ 6.87 = 53.1 days)	(($380,000 + $422,400) ÷ 2) ÷ ($2,951,200 ÷ 365) = 49.6 days (or 365 ÷ 7.36 = 49.6 days)
c.	Inventory turnover	$1,008,500 ÷ (($132,800 + $208,000) ÷ 2) = 5.92 or 5.9 times	$998,400 ÷ (($140,000 + $132,800) ÷ 2) = 7.32 or 7.3 times
d.	Days' sales in inventory	(($132,800 + $208,000) ÷ 2) ÷ ($1,008,500 ÷ 365) = 61.67 or 61.7 days (or 365 ÷ 5.92 = 61.7 days)	(($140,000 + $132,800) ÷ 2) ÷ ($998,400 ÷ 365) = 49.87 or 49.9 days (or 365 ÷ 7.32 = 49.9 days)
e.	Total asset turnover	$3,364,400 ÷ (($4,048,000 + $5,776,100) ÷ 2) = 0.68 or 0.7 times	$2,951,200 ÷ (($3,600,000 + $4,048,000) ÷ 2) = 0.77 or 0.8 times

2. All the ratios indicate a slight decrease in efficiency. In 2015, the average collection period of accounts receivable increased from 49.6 days to 53.2 days, inventory turnover slowed from 7.3 times to 5.9 times, and the total asset turnover decreased from 0.8 times to 0.7 times.

Profitability Analysis

Use ratio analysis to assess the profitability of a business.

Profitability analysis focuses on the ability of a company to earn profits. This ability is reflected in the company's operating results, as reported in its income statement. The ability to earn profits also depends on the assets the company has available for use in its operations, as reported in its balance sheet. Thus, income statement and balance sheet relationships are often used in evaluating profitability.

Common profitability analyses include the following:

1. profit margin
2. gross margin

Note: Profitability analysis focuses on the relationship between operating results and the resources available to a business.

3. return on assets
4. return on common shareholders' equity
5. earnings per share
6. price-earnings ratio
7. dividend yield

Profit Margin

The **profit margin** measures the overall profitability of a company as a percentage of its net sales. It is computed as follows:

$$\text{Profit Margin} = \frac{\text{Net Income}}{\text{Net Sales}}$$

To illustrate, the profit margin for Langley Company is computed below.

	2015	2014
Net income	$ 91,000	$ 76,500
Net sales	1,498,000	1,200,000
Profit margin	6.1% ($91,000 ÷ $1,498,000)	6.4% ($76,500 ÷ $1,200,000)

Although sales and net income have both increased in 2015, the profit margin ratio indicates that Langley's overall profitability has decreased slightly from 6.4% to 6.1%.

Gross Margin

The **gross margin**, also referred to as the **gross profit margin**, is a comparison of sales and cost of goods sold. This ratio assesses a company's ability to earn a return on items sold before other expenses are considered. It is computed as follows:

$$\text{Gross Margin} = \frac{\text{Gross Profit}}{\text{Net Sales}}$$

To illustrate, the gross margin for Langley Company is computed below.

	2015	2014
Gross profit	$ 455,000	$ 380,000
Net sales	1,498,000	1,200,000
Gross margin	30.4% ($455,000 ÷ $1,498,000)	31.7% ($380,000 ÷ $1,200,000)

The gross margin decreased in 2015. In other words, the profit earned on each item sold decreased from 31.7% to 30.4%. This decrease contributed to the overall decline in profitability as measured by the profit margin.

EXAMPLE EXERCISE 17-8 Profit Margin and Gross Margin   ⑤

A company reports the following:

Net Sales	$1,450,000
Gross profit	754,000
Net income	101,500

Determine (a) the company's profit margin and (b) the company's gross margin.

a. Profit Margin = Net Income ÷ Net Sales
   Profit Margin = $101,500 ÷ $1,450,000
   Profit Margin = 7.0%

b. Gross Margin = Gross Profit ÷ Net Sales
   Gross Margin = $754,000 ÷ $1,450,000
   Gross Margin = 52.0%

For Practice: PE 17-8

Return on Assets

The **return on assets** ratio measures the profitability of total assets, without considering how the assets are financed. In other words, this rate is not affected by the portion of assets financed by creditors or shareholders. It is computed as follows:

$$\text{Return on Assets} = \frac{\text{Net Income}}{\text{Average Total Assets}}$$

Because net income includes any income earned from long-term investments, the average total assets includes both long-term investments and the net operating assets. To illustrate, the return on assets by Langley Company is computed below.

	2015	2014
Net income	$ 91,000	$ 76,500
Total assets:		
Beginning of year	$1,230,500	$1,187,500
End of year	1,139,500	1,230,500
Total	$2,370,000	$2,418,000
Average total assets	$1,185,000 ($2,370,000 ÷ 2)	$1,209,000 ($2,418,000 ÷ 2)
Return on assets	7.7% ($91,000 ÷ $1,185,000)	6.3% ($76,500 ÷ $1,209,000)

The return on assets improved from 6.3% to 7.7% during 2015.

The *return on operating assets* is sometimes computed when there are large amounts of nonoperating income and expense. Operating assets are assets used in the normal operations of a business. For example, accounts receivable, inventory, and property, plant, and equipment would be considered operating assets, whereas marketable securities would typically be considered nonoperating assets. The return on operating assets is computed as follows:

$$\text{Return on Operating Assets} = \frac{\text{Income from Operations}}{\text{Average Operating Assets}}$$

EXAMPLE EXERCISE 17-9   Return on Assets   ⑤

A company reports the following income statement and balance sheet information for the current year:

Net income	$ 125,000
Total assets, beginning of year	1,770,000
Total assets, end of year	2,000,000

Determine the return on assets.

FOLLOW MY EXAMPLE 17-9

Return on Assets = Net Income ÷ Average Total Assets
Return on Assets = $125,000 ÷ (($1,770,000 + $2,000,000) ÷ 2)
Return on Assets = $125,000 ÷ $1,885,000
Return on Assets = 6.6%

For Practice: PE 17-9

Return on Common Shareholders' Equity

The **return on common shareholders' equity** measures the rate of income earned on the amount invested by the common shareholders. It is computed as follows:

$$\text{Return on Common Shareholders' Equity} = \frac{\text{Net Income} - \text{Preferred Dividends}}{\text{Average Common Shareholders' Equity}}$$

Because preferred shareholders rank ahead of the common shareholders in their claim on earnings, any preferred dividends are subtracted from net income in computing the return on common shareholders' equity.

To illustrate, the return on common shareholders' equity for Langley Company is computed below.

	2015	**2014**
Net income	$ 91,000	$ 76,500
Less preferred dividends	9,000	9,000
Total	$ 82,000	$ 67,500
Common shareholders' equity:		
Beginning of year	$ 637,500	$ 600,000
End of year	679,500	637,500
Total	$1,317,000	$1,237,500
Average common shareholders' equity	$658,500 ($1,317,000 ÷ 2)	$ 618,750 ($1,237,500 ÷ 2)
Return on common shareholders' equity	12.5% ($82,000 ÷ $658,500)	10.9% ($67,500 ÷ $618,750)

Langley Company had 1,500 $6 preferred shares outstanding on December 31, 2015 and 2014. Thus, preferred dividends of $9,000 (1,500 × $6) were deducted from net income. Langley's common shareholders' equity was determined as follows:

		December 31	
	2015	**2014**	**2013**
Common shares	$500,000	$500,000	$500,000
Retained earnings	179,500	137,500	100,000
Common shareholders' equity	$679,500	$637,500	$600,000

The retained earnings on December 31, 2013, is $100,000. The remainder of the balances appear in Langley's balance sheets in Exhibit 1.

Langley Company's return on common shareholders' equity improved from 10.9% in 2014 to 12.5% in 2015.

Langley Company has financed its operations by issuing both debt and equity. The use of debt to finance operations is called **leverage**. When a firm uses debt to finance operations, the common shareholders may receive a higher return from the use of debt to expand the business. The interest payment on debt is fixed, and debtholders do not share in any corporate profits. If the company performs well, the common shareholders will benefit from the use of debt. Use of debt to leverage the company's operations, however, comes with greater risk. If the company does not perform well, the loss to common shareholders will be greater since leverage magnifies both gains and losses.

EXAMPLE EXERCISE 17-10 Return on Common Shareholders' Equity (5)

A company reports the following:

Net income	$ 125,000
Preferred dividends	5,000
Average shareholders' equity	1,000,000
Average common shareholders' equity	800,000

Determine the return on common shareholders' equity.

FOLLOW MY EXAMPLE 17-10

Return on Common Shareholders' Equity = (Net Income − Preferred Dividends) ÷ Average
Common Shareholders' Equity
Return on Common Shareholders' Equity = ($125,000 − $5,000) ÷ $800,000
Return on Common Shareholders' Equity = 15%

For Practice: PE 17-10

Earnings per Share

As discussed in Chapter 13, **earnings per share (EPS)** measures the share of profits that are earned by a common share. Companies preparing financial statements in accordance with IFRS, including companies with publicly traded shares, must report earnings per share in the statement of comprehensive income.[2] Privately held companies that choose to apply ASPE accounting policies are not required to report earnings per share. Earnings per share is often reported in the financial media. It is computed as follows:

$$\text{Earnings per Share (EPS)} = \frac{\text{Net Income} - \text{Preferred Dividends}}{\text{Weighted Average Number of Common Shares}}$$

When preferred and common shares are outstanding, preferred dividends are subtracted from net income to determine the income related to the common shares.

To illustrate, the earnings per share for Langley Company is computed below.

	2015	2014
Net income	$91,000	$76,500
Preferred dividends	9,000	9,000
Total	$82,000	$67,500
Number of common shares outstanding	50,000	50,000
Earnings per share	$1.64 ($82,000 ÷ 50,000)	$1.35 ($67,500 ÷ 50,000)

Langley Company had 1,500 of $6 preferred shares outstanding on December 31, 2015 and 2014. Thus, preferred dividends of $9,000 (1,500 × $6) are deducted from net income in computing earnings per share.

Langley did not issue any additional common shares in 2015. If Langley had issued additional shares in 2015, a weighted average of common shares outstanding during the year would have been used.

As shown above, Langley's earnings per share (EPS) improved from $1.35 to $1.64 during 2015.

Langley Company has a simple capital structure with only common shares and preferred shares outstanding. Many corporations, however, have complex capital structures with various types of equity securities outstanding, such as convertible preferred

2 *CICA Handbook—Accounting*, 2013 edition, IFRS, IAS 33, Earnings per Share.

shares, share options, and share warrants. In such cases, the possible effects of such securities on the common shares outstanding are considered in reporting earnings per share. These possible effects are reported separately as *diluted earnings per share*. This topic is described and illustrated in advanced accounting courses and textbooks.

Weighted Average Number of Common Shares If the number of common shares outstanding changes during the year, it is necessary to calculate the weighted average number of common shares. To illustrate, Norman Company started the year with 100,000 common shares, issued an additional 35,000 shares on July 1, and repurchased 12,000 shares on November 1. The number of shares outstanding is weighted by the portion of the year as follows:

Jan. 1 to Jul. 1	6/12 months × 100,000 shares	50,000
Jul. 1 to Nov. 1	4/12 months × 135,000 shares	45,000
Nov. 1 to Dec. 31	2/12 months × 123,000 shares	20,500
	12/12 months	115,500 shares

Assuming that Norman Company had net income of $1,246,200 and paid preferred dividends of $45,000, earnings per share is computed as follows:

$$\frac{\text{Net Income} - \text{Preferred Dividends}}{\text{Weighted Average Number of Common Shares}} = \frac{\$1,246,200 - \$45,000}{115,500 \text{ Shares}} = \$10.40$$

EXAMPLE EXERCISE 17-11 Earnings per Share ⑤

A company reports the following:

Net income	$ 1,000,000
Preferred dividends	$ 50,000
Number of common shares outstanding at December 31 year-end	20,000

a. Determine the weighted average number of shares, given that 4,000 shares were issued on October 3.
b. Determine the company's earnings per share, rounding to two decimal places.

FOLLOW MY EXAMPLE 17-11

a. Weighted average number of shares = 16,000 × 9/12 + 20,000 × 3/12
Weighted average number of shares = 12,000 + 5,000
Weighted average number of shares = 17,000

b. Earnings per Share = ($1,000,000 − $50,000) ÷ 17,000
Earnings per Share = $55.882, rounded to $55.88

For Practice: PE 17-11

Price-Earnings Ratio

The **price-earnings (P/E) ratio** on common shares measures a company's future earnings prospects. It is often quoted in the financial media and is computed as follows:

$$\text{Price-Earnings (P/E) Ratio} = \frac{\text{Market Price per Common Share}}{\text{Earnings per Share}}$$

To illustrate, the price-earnings (P/E) ratio for Langley Company is computed below.

	2015	2014
Market price per common share	$41.00	$27.00
Earnings per share	$1.64	$1.35
Price-earnings ratio	25 ($41 ÷ $1.64)	20 ($27 ÷ $1.35)

The price-earnings ratio improved from 20 to 25 during 2015. In other words, a common share of Langley Company was selling for 20 times earnings per share at the end of 2014. At the end of 2015, the common shares were selling for 25 times earnings per share. This indicates that the market expects Langley to experience favourable earnings in the future.

EXAMPLE EXERCISE 17-12 Earnings per Share and Price-Earnings Ratio (5)

A company reports the following:

Net income	$250,000
Preferred dividends	$ 15,000
Number of common shares outstanding	20,000
Market price per common share	$ 35.00

a. Determine the company's earnings per share.
b. Determine the company's price-earnings ratio. Round to one decimal place.

FOLLOW MY EXAMPLE 17-12

a. Earnings per Share = (Net Income − Preferred Dividends) ÷ Weighted Average Number of Common Shares Outstanding
   Earnings per Share = ($250,000 − $15,000) ÷ 20,000
   Earnings per Share = $11.75

b. Price-Earnings Ratio = Market Price per Share ÷ Earnings per Share
   Price-Earnings Ratio = $35.00 ÷ $11.75
   Price-Earnings Ratio = 3.0

For Practice: PE 17-12

Dividend Yield

The **dividend yield** measures the rate of return to common shareholders from cash dividends. It is of special interest to investors whose objective is to earn revenue (dividends) from their investment. It is computed as follows:

$$\text{Dividend Yield} = \frac{\text{Annual Dividends per Share}}{\text{Market Price per Share}}$$

To illustrate, the dividend yield for Langley Company is computed below.

	2015	2014
Dividends per share	$ 0.80	$ 0.60
Market price per share	$41.00	$27.00
Dividend yield	2.0% ($0.80 ÷ $41)	2.2% ($0.60 ÷ $27)

The dividend yield declined slightly from 2.2% to 2.0% in 2015. This decline was due primarily to the increase in the market price of Langley's common shares.

Summary of Analytical Ratios

Exhibit 7 shows a summary of the ratios discussed in this chapter. The type of industry and the company's operations usually affect which measures are used. In many cases, additional measures are used for a specific industry. For example, airlines use *revenue per passenger mile* and *cost per available seat* as profitability measures. Likewise, hotels use *occupancy rates* as a profitability measure.

The analytical measures shown in Exhibit 7 are a useful starting point for analyzing a company's liquidity, efficiency, solvency, and profitability. However, they are not a

Exhibit 7

Financial Statement Analysis Ratios

	Method of Computation	Use
Liquidity measures:		
Working Capital	Current Assets − Current Liabilities	To indicate the ability to meet currently maturing obligations
Current Ratio	$\dfrac{\text{Current Assets}}{\text{Current Liabilities}}$	
Quick Ratio	$\dfrac{\text{Quick Assets}}{\text{Current Liabilities}}$	To indicate instant debt-paying ability
Efficiency measures:		
Accounts Receivable Turnover	$\dfrac{\text{Net Sales}}{\text{Average Net Accounts Receivable}}$	To assess the efficiency in collecting receivables and in the management of credit
Days' Sales in Receivables	$\dfrac{\text{Average Net Accounts Receivable}}{\text{Average Daily Sales}}$	
Inventory Turnover	$\dfrac{\text{Cost of Goods Sold}}{\text{Average Inventory}}$	To assess the efficiency in the management of inventory
Days' Sales in Inventory	$\dfrac{\text{Average Inventory}}{\text{Average Daily Cost of Goods Sold}}$	
Total Asset Turnover	$\dfrac{\text{Net Sales}}{\text{Average Total Assets}}$	To assess the efficiency in the management of assets
Solvency measures:		
Debt Ratio	$\dfrac{\text{Total Liabilities}}{\text{Total Assets}}$	To indicate the percentage of assets financed with debt
Times Interest Earned Ratio	$\dfrac{\text{Income Before Income Taxes + Interest Expense}}{\text{Interest Expense}}$	To assess the risk to debtholders in terms of the times interest charges were earned
Profitability measures:		
Profit Margin	$\dfrac{\text{Net Income}}{\text{Net Sales}}$	To assess the overall profitability of a company
Gross Margin	$\dfrac{\text{Gross Profit}}{\text{Net Sales}}$	To assess the ability to earn a return on items sold
Return on Assets	$\dfrac{\text{Net Income}}{\text{Average Total Assets}}$	To assess the profitability of the assets
Return on Common Shareholders' Equity	$\dfrac{\text{Net Income − Preferred Dividends}}{\text{Average Common Shareholders' Equity}}$	To assess the profitability of the investment by common shareholders
Earnings per Share (EPS)	$\dfrac{\text{Net Income − Preferred Dividends}}{\text{Weighted Average Number of Common Shares}}$	
Price-Earnings Ratio	$\dfrac{\text{Market Price per Common Share}}{\text{Earnings per Share}}$	To indicate future earnings prospects, based on the relationship between the market value of common shares and earnings
Dividend Yield	$\dfrac{\text{Annual Dividends per Share}}{\text{Market Price per Share}}$	To indicate the rate of return to common shareholders in terms of dividends

substitute for sound judgment. For example, the general economic and business environment should always be considered in analyzing a company's future prospects. In addition, any trends and interrelationships among the measures should be carefully studied.

CRITICAL THINKING

Do ratios supply enough information to make good investment decisions?

No. Ratios supply useful information but additional information should be reviewed to make an informed investment decision. Ratios need to be compared against the prior year's results (horizontal analysis), the competition's ratios, and industry ratios. Investors should also consider information in the corporation's annual report, news items, and expected trends for both the industry and the economy.

Corporate Annual Reports

Describe the contents of corporate annual reports.

Public corporations issue annual reports summarizing their operating activities for the past year and their plans for the future. Such annual reports include the financial statements and the accompanying notes.

These reports provide additional information for potential and existing shareholders and other stakeholders. The Canadian Institute of Chartered Accountants (CICA) issues awards to encourage strong corporate reporting in Canada and to recognize leaders in financial reporting, corporate governance disclosure, and sustainable development reporting. PotashCorp., discussed at the start of this chapter, consistently wins awards for its clear, thorough, and informative reporting.

Notes to the Financial Statements

Notes are an integral and essential part of the financial statements. They provide much detail, which improves understandability of the information contained in the statements. Wherever accounting policy choices exist, a note explains the choice made. For example, Note 3 in the Leon's Furniture Limited financial statements in Appendix B, lists numerous choices made, including inventory valuation, depreciation, and revenue recognition. Notes can also provide information regarding items not shown on the statements, such as future lease payments and contingencies. The information provided in the notes allows for better comparability between statements prepared by different companies.[1]

In addition to the financial statements and accompanying notes, annual reports normally include the following sections:

1. management's discussion and analysis
2. management letter
3. auditor's report

3 Understandability and comparability are two qualitative characteristics of the conceptual framework.

Management's Discussion and Analysis

Management's Discussion and Analysis (MD&A) is required in annual reports filed with the Canadian Securities Administrators. It includes management's analysis of current operations and its plans for the future. Typical items included in the MD&A include the following:

1. Management's analysis and explanations of any significant changes between the current and prior years' financial statements.
2. Important accounting principles or policies that could affect interpretation of the financial statements, including the effect of changes in accounting principles or the adoption of new accounting principles.
3. Management's assessment of the company's liquidity and the availability of capital to the company.

4. Significant risk exposures that might affect the company.
5. Any "off-balance-sheet" arrangements, such as leases, not included directly in the financial statements. Such arrangements are discussed in advanced accounting courses and textbooks.

Management Letter

The report by management, entitled *Management Responsibility for Financial Reporting*, states management's responsibility for establishing and maintaining internal control. In addition, management's assessment of the effectiveness of internal controls over financial reporting is included in the report.

Auditor's Report

All publicly held corporations are required to have an independent audit (examination) of their financial statements. Audits can be performed in Canada by Chartered Accountants (CAs) and by Chartered Professional Accountants (CPAs) and, in some provinces and territories, by Certified General Accountants (CGAs) and by Certified Management Accountants (CMAs). The professional accounting firm that conducts the audit renders an opinion, called the *Auditor's Report*.

An opinion stating that the financial statements present fairly the financial position, results of operations, and cash flows of the company is said to be an *unqualified opinion*, sometimes called a *clean opinion*. Any report other than an unqualified opinion raises a "red flag" for financial statement users and requires further investigation as to its cause.

The audited consolidated financial statements of Leon's Furniture Limited are shown in Appendix B, along with the auditor's report and the management letter from the annual report.

At a Glance 17

1 Describe basic financial statement analytical methods.

Key Points	Key Learning Outcomes	Page	Example Exercises
The basic financial statements provide much of the information users need to make economic decisions. Analytical procedures are used to compare items on a current financial statement with related items on earlier statements or to examine relationships within a financial statement.	• Prepare a horizontal analysis from a company's financial statements.	871	17-1
	• Prepare a vertical analysis from a company's financial statements.	873	17-2
	• Prepare common-sized financial statements.	875	

2 Use ratio analysis to assess the liquidity of a business.

Key Points	Key Learning Outcomes	Page	Example Exercises
Liquidity, the ability of a business to pay its short-term debt, is normally assessed by examining (1) the working capital, (2) the current ratio, and (3) the quick ratio.	• Determine working capital.	876	
	• Compute and interpret the current ratio.	876	
	• Compute and interpret the quick ratio.	877	17-3

3 | Use ratio analysis to assess the efficiency of a business.

Key Points	Key Learning Outcomes	Page	Example Exercises
Efficiency, the ability of a business to use its assets effectively, is normally assessed by analyzing (1) the accounts receivable, (2) the inventory, and (3) the total asset turnovers.	• Compute and interpret accounts receivable turnover.	878	
	• Compute and interpret days' sales in receivables.	879	17-4
	• Compute and interpret inventory turnover.	880	
	• Compute and interpret days' sales in inventory.	881	17-5
	• Compute and interpret total asset turnover.	882	

4 | Use ratio analysis to assess the solvency of a business.

Key Points	Key Learning Outcomes	Page	Example Exercises
Solvency analysis focuses mainly on the ability of a company to meet its long-term debt obligations and is normally assessed by examining (1) the debt ratio and (2) the times interest earned ratio.	• Compute and interpret the debt ratio.	882	17-6
	• Compute and interpret the times interest earned ratio.	883	17-7

5 | Use ratio analysis to assess the profitability of a business.

Key Points	Key Learning Outcomes	Page	Example Exercises
Profitability analysis focuses mainly on the relationship between operating results (on the income statement) and resources available (on the balance sheet). Major analyses include (1) the profit margin, (2) the gross margin, (3) the return on assets, (4) the return on common shareholders' equity, (5) the earnings per share, (6) the price-earnings ratio, and (7) the dividend yield.	• Compute and interpret the profit margin.	886	
	• Compute and interpret the gross margin.	886	17-8
	• Compute and interpret the return on assets.	887	17-9
	• Compute and interpret the return on common shareholders' equity.	888	17-10
	• Compute and interpret the earnings per share.	889	
	• Compute the weighted average number of common shares.	890	17-11
	• Compute and interpret the price-earnings ratio.	890	17-12
	• Compute and interpret the dividend yield.	891	
	• Describe the uses and limitations of analytical measures.	892	

6 | Describe the contents of corporate annual reports.

Key Points	Key Learning Outcomes	Page	Example Exercises
Corporations normally issue annual reports to their shareholders and other interested parties. Such reports summarize the corporation's operating activities for the past year and plans for the future.	• Describe the elements of a corporate annual report.	893	

GLOSSARY

accounts receivable turnover – The relationship between net sales and accounts receivable that measures how frequently during the year the accounts receivable are being converted to cash, computed by dividing the net sales by the average net accounts receivable. (p. 878)

acid-test ratio – A financial ratio that measures the ability to pay current liabilities with quick assets (cash, marketable securities, accounts receivable). (p. 877) Also known as *quick ratio*.

common-sized statement – A financial statement in which all items are expressed only in percentages. (p. 875)

current ratio – A financial ratio that is computed by dividing current assets by current liabilities. (p. 876) Also known as *working capital ratio*.

days' sales in inventory – The relationship between the volume of sales and inventory, computed by dividing the average inventory at the end of the year by the average daily cost of goods sold. (p. 881)

days' sales in receivables – The relationship between sales and accounts receivable, computed by dividing the average accounts receivable at the end of the year by the average daily sales. (p. 879)

debt ratio – A measure of the percentage of assets that are financed with debt, computed by dividing total liabilities by total assets. (p. 882)

dividend yield – A ratio that indicates the rate of return to shareholders in terms of cash dividend distributions, computed by dividing the annual dividends paid per common share by the market price per share at a specific date. (p. 891)

EBIT – An abbreviation of *earnings before interest and taxes*. (p. 883)

earnings per share (EPS) – The profitability ratio of net income available to common shareholders to the weighted average number of common shares outstanding. (p. 889)

efficiency – The ability of a company to utilize its assets efficiently, normally assessed by analyzing accounts receivable, inventory, and total asset turnover. (p. 875)

gross margin – A measure of a company's ability to earn a return on items sold before other expenses are considered, computed by dividing gross profit by net sales. (p. 886) Also known as *gross profit margin*.

gross profit margin – A measure of a company's ability to earn a return on items sold before other expenses are considered, computed by dividing gross profit by net sales. (p. 886) Also known as *gross margin*.

horizontal analysis – Financial analysis that compares an item in a current statement with the same item in prior statements. (p. 871)

inventory turnover – The relationship between the volume of goods sold and inventory, computed by dividing the cost of goods sold by the average inventory. (p. 880)

leverage – The use of debt to potentially generate a higher return to common shareholders. (p. 888)

liquidity – the ability of a firm to pay its current liabilities. (p. 875)

Management's Discussion and Analysis (MD&A) – An annual report disclosure that provides management's analysis of the results of operations and its financial condition. (p. 893)

price-earnings (P/E) ratio – The ratio of the market price per common share to the annual earnings per share on a specific date. (p. 890)

profit margin – A measure of the overall profitability of a company, computed by dividing net income by net sales. (p. 886)

profitability – A company's ability to earn income. (p. 875)

quick assets – Cash and other current assets that can be quickly converted to cash, such as marketable securities and receivables. (p. 877)

quick ratio – A financial ratio that measures the ability to pay current liabilities with quick assets (cash, marketable securities, accounts receivable). (p. 877) Also known as *acid-test ratio*.

return on assets – A measure of the profitability of assets, without regard to the equity of creditors and shareholders in the assets, computed by dividing net income by average total assets. (p. 887)

return on common shareholders' equity – A measure of profitability computed by dividing net income, reduced by preferred dividend requirements, by average common shareholders' equity. (p. 888)

solvency – The ability of a firm to pay its debts as they come due. (p. 875)

times interest earned ratio – A ratio that measures creditor margin of safety for interest payments, calculated as income before interest and taxes divided by interest expense. (p. 883)

total asset turnover – A measure of how effectively a company uses its assets to generate sales, computed by dividing net sales by average total assets. (p. 882)

vertical analysis – An evaluation that compares each item in a current statement with a total amount within the same statement. (p. 873)

working capital – The excess of the current assets of a business over its current liabilities. (p. 876)

working capital ratio – A financial ratio that is computed by dividing current assets by current liabilities. (p. 876) Also known as *current ratio*.

END-OF-CHAPTER ILLUSTRATIVE PROBLEM

Rainbow Paint Co.'s income statement and statement of financial position for the years ended December 31, 2015 and 2014, are as follows. The market price of Rainbow Paint Co.'s common shares was $30 per share on December 31, 2014, and $25 per share on December 31, 2015. For both years, the company paid dividends of $40,000 to preferred shareholders. The company paid dividends of $45,000 and $30,000 to common shareholders in 2015 and 2014, respectively.

Rainbow Paint Co. Income Statement For the Years Ended December 31, 2015 and 2014	2015	2014
Sales	$ 5,125,000	$ 3,257,600
Sales returns and allowances	125,000	57,600
Net sales	5,000,000	3,200,000
Cost of goods sold	3,400,000	2,080,000
Gross profit	1,600,000	1,120,000
Selling expenses	650,000	464,000
Administrative expenses	325,000	224,000
Total operating expenses	975,000	688,000
Income from operations	625,000	432,000
Other income	25,000	19,200
	650,000	451,200
Other expense (interest)	105,000	64,000
Income before income taxes	545,000	387,200
Income taxes expense	300,000	176,000
Net income	$ 245,000	$ 211,200

Rainbow Paint Co.
Statement of Financial Position
December 31, 2015 and 2014

	2015	2014
Assets		
Current assets:		
Cash	$ 175,000	$ 125,000
Short-term investments	150,000	50,000
Accounts receivable (net)	425,000	325,000
Inventories	720,000	480,000
Prepaid expenses	30,000	20,000
Total current assets	1,500,000	1,000,000
Long-term investments	250,000	225,000
Property, plant, and equipment (net)	2,093,000	1,948,000
Total assets	$ 3,843,000	$ 3,173,000
Liabilities		
Current liabilities	$ 750,000	$ 650,000
Long-term liabilities:		
Mortgage note payable, 10%, due 2018	410,000	---
Bonds payable, 8%, due 2021	800,000	800,000
Total long-term liabilities	1,210,000	800,000
Total liabilities	1,960,000	1,450,000
Shareholders' Equity		
$8 preferred shares, 5,000 shares issued and outstanding	500,000	500,000
Common shares, 50,000 shares issued and outstanding	500,000	500,000
Retained earnings	883,000	723,000
Total shareholders' equity	1,883,000	1,723,000
Total liabilities and shareholders' equity	$ 3,843,000	$ 3,173,000

Instructions

1. Calculate all liquidity, efficiency, solvency, and profitability ratios for 2015 and 2014, rounding to one decimal place. (The 2013 year-end balances were Accounts receivable, $300,000; Inventories, $630,000; Total assets, $3,450,000; Common shareholders' equity, $1,300,000.)
2. Indicate whether each ratio has improved or declined from 2014 to 2015.

Solution

	2015	2014	
	(Calculations in thousands)		
Liquidity ratios:			
1. Working capital	$750,000 ($1,500 − $750)	$350,000 ($1,000 − $650)	Improved
2. Current ratio	2.0 ($1,500 ÷ $750)	1.5 ($1,000 ÷ $650)	Improved
3. Quick ratio	1.0 ($175 + $150 + 425) ÷ $750	0.8 ($125 + $50 + $325) ÷ $650	Improved
Efficiency ratios:			
4. Accounts receivable turnover	13.3 times [$5,000 ÷ (($425 + $325) ÷ 2)]	10.2 times [$3,200 ÷ (($325 + $300) ÷ 2)]	Improved

5. Days' sales in receivables	27.4 days ($5,000 ÷ 365 = $13.699; $375 ÷ $13.699) (or 365 ÷ 13.3 = 27.4 days)	35.6 days ($3,200 ÷ 365 = $8.767; $312.5 ÷ $8.767) (or 365 ÷ 10.2 = 35.8 days)	Improved
6. Inventory turnover	5.667 or 5.7 times [$3,400 ÷ (($720 + $480) ÷ 2)]	3.748 or 3.7 times [$2,080 ÷ (($480 + $630) ÷ 2)]	Improved
7. Days' sales in inventory	64.4 days ($3,400 ÷ 365 = $9,315; $600 ÷ $9,315) (or 365 ÷ 5.667 = 64.4 days)	97.4 days ($2,080 ÷ 365 = $5,699; $555 ÷ $5,699) (or 365 ÷ 3.748 = 97.4 days)	Improved
8. Total asset turnover	1.4 times [$5,000 ÷ (($3,843 + $3,173) ÷ 2)]	1.0 times [$3,200 ÷ (($3,173 + $3,450) ÷ 2)]	Improved

Solvency ratios:

9. Debt ratio	51.0% ($1,960 ÷ $3,843)	45.7% ($1,450 ÷ $3,173)	Declined
10. Times interest earned ratio	6.2 times [($545 + $105) ÷ $105]	7.1 times [($387.2 + $64) ÷ $64]	Declined

Profitability ratios:

11. Profit margin	4.9% ($245 ÷ $5,000)	6.6% ($211.2 ÷ $3,200)	Declined
12. Gross margin	32% ($1,600 ÷ $5,000)	35% ($1,120 ÷ $3,200)	Declined
13. Return on assets	7.0% [$245 ÷ (($3,843 + $3,173) ÷ 2)]	6.4% [$211.2 ÷ (($3,173 + $3,450) ÷ 2)]	Improved
14. Return on common shareholders' equity	15.7% [($245 − $40) ÷ (($1,383 + $1,223) ÷ 2)]	13.6% [($211.2 − $40) ÷ (($1,223 + $1,300) ÷ 2)]	Improved

(Calculations in dollars)			
15. Earnings per share	$4.10 [($245,000 − $40,000) ÷ 50,000]	$3.42 [($211,200 − $40,000) ÷ 50,000]	Improved
16. Price-earnings ratio	6.1 ($25 ÷ $4.10)	8.8 ($30 ÷ $3.42)	Declined
17. Dividend yield	3.6% [($45,000 ÷ 50,000) ÷ $25]	2.0 [($30,000 ÷ 50,000) ÷ $30]	Improved

EYE OPENERS

1. What is the difference between horizontal and vertical analysis of financial statements?
2. What is the advantage of using comparative statements for financial analysis instead of statements for a single date or period?
3. The current year's net income is 20% larger than the net income of the preceding year. How will you determine whether this increase is due to an improved operating performance? What other events could have caused this increase?
4. How would you respond to a horizontal analysis that showed an expense increasing by more than 80%? Would such an increase always warrant investigation?
5. How would the current and quick ratios of a service business compare? Would you expect them to be very different from each other? Explain.
6. A company grants terms of n/45 on all sales. Based on monthly averages, the company has a yearly accounts receivable turnover of 5. Is this a satisfactory turnover? Discuss.
7. a. Why is it advantageous to have a high inventory turnover?
   b. Is it possible for the inventory turnover to be too high? Discuss.
   c. Is it possible to have a high inventory turnover and a high ratio for days' sales in inventory? Discuss.

8. The following data are taken from a comparative balance sheet. What do the data indicate about the company's ability to borrow additional funds on a long-term basis in the current year as compared with the preceding year?

	Current Year	Preceding Year
Total assets	$480,000	$540,000
Total long-term liabilities	120,000	180,000

9. a. How does the return on assets differ from the return on common shareholders' equity?
   b. Which ratio is normally higher? Explain.
10. a. How does the profit margin differ from the gross margin?
    b. Is it possible for the gross margin for a company to improve while the profit margin decreases from the previous year? Explain.
11. Describe the report provided by independent auditors in the annual report to shareholders.

PRACTICE EXERCISES

1

PE 17-1
Horizontal analysis

EE 17-1 p. 873

The comparative accounts payable and long-term debt balances of a company are provided below.

	2015	2014
Accounts payable	$ 78,400	$70,000
Long-term debt	101,760	96,000

Based on this information, what is the amount and percentage of increase or decrease that would be shown in a balance sheet with horizontal analysis?

1

PE 17-2
Vertical analysis

EE 17-2 p. 873

Income statement information for Shand Corporation is provided below.

Sales	$700,000
Gross profit	196,000
Net income	60,000

Prepare a vertical analysis of the income statement for Shand Corporation.

2

PE 17-3
Liquidity analysis

EE 17-3 p. 878

The following items are reported on a company's balance sheet:

Cash	$190,000
Temporary investments	150,000
Accounts receivable (net)	260,000
Inventories	300,000
Accounts payable	600,000

Determine (a) the current ratio and (b) the quick ratio. Round to one decimal place.

3

PE 17-4
Accounts receivable analysis

EE 17-4 p. 880

A company reports the following:

Net sales	$1,120,000
Average accounts receivable (net)	72,000

Determine (a) the accounts receivable turnover and (b) the days' sales in receivables, using both methods for calculating the days' sales in receivables ratio. Round to one decimal place.

③ PE 17-5
Inventory analysis

A company reports the following:

Cost of goods sold	$510,000
Average inventory	60,000

EE 17-5 p. 881

Determine (a) the inventory turnover and (b) the days' sales in inventory, using both methods for calculating the days' sales in inventory ratio. Round to one decimal place.

---

④ PE 17-6
Debt ratio

The following information was taken from Gordon Company's balance sheet:

Total assets	$500,000
Long-term liabilities	200,000
Total liabilities	300,000
Total shareholders' equity	200,000

EE 17-6 p. 883

Determine the company's debt ratio.

---

④ PE 17-7
Times interest earned ratio

A company reports the following:

Income before income taxes	$2,000,000
Interest expense	80,000

Determine the times interest earned ratio.

EE 17-7 p. 884

---

⑤ PE 17-8
Profitability analysis

A company reports the following:

Net sales	$2,760,000
Gross profit	975,000
Net income	238,000

EE 17-8 p. 886

Determine (a) the company's profit margin and (b) the company's gross margin.

---

⑤ PE 17-9
Return on assets

A company reports the following income statement and balance sheet information for the current year:

Net income	$ 400,000
Total assets, beginning of year	3,450,000
Total assets, end of year	3,700,000

EE 17-9 p. 887

Determine the return on assets.

---

⑤ PE 17-10
Return on common shareholders' equity

A company reports the following:

Net income	$120,000
Preferred dividends	20,000
Average shareholders' equity	600,000
Average common shareholders' equity	500,000

EE 17-10 p. 889

Determine the return on common shareholders' equity. Round to one decimal place.

---

⑤ PE 17-11
Earnings per share

A company reports the following at its December 31 fiscal year-end:

Net income	$1,830,000
Preferred dividends	$ 50,000
Number of common shares outstanding	19,680

EE 17-11 p. 890

a. Determine the weighted average number of shares, given that 9,000 shares were repurchased on March 1.
b. Determine the company's earnings per share, rounding to two decimal places.

5 **PE 17-12**

Earnings per share and price-earnings ratio

EE 17-12 p. 891

A company reports the following:

Net income	$340,000
Preferred dividends	$ 40,000
Common shares outstanding	40,000
Market price per common share	$ 60.00

a. Determine the company's earnings per share.
b. Determine the company's price-earnings ratio. Round to one decimal place.

EXERCISES

1 **EX 17-1**

Vertical analysis of income statement

✔ a. 2015 net income: $14,400; 1.8% of sales

Revenue and expense data for Mandell Technologies Co. are as follows:

	2015	2014
Sales	$800,000	$740,000
Cost of goods sold	504,000	407,000
Selling expenses	120,000	140,600
Administrative expenses	128,000	125,800
Income taxes expense	33,600	48,100

a. Prepare an income statement in comparative form, stating each item for both 2015 and 2014 as a percent of sales. Round to one decimal place.
b. Comment on the significant changes disclosed by the comparative income statement.

1 **EX 17-2**

Vertical analysis of income statement

✔ a. 2014 operating income, 3.9% of revenues

Income statement data (in thousands of dollars) for Collingwood Productions Corporation, a production company involved in the production of motion pictures and home entertainment, for the years ended December 31, 2015 and 2014, are as follows:

	2015	2014
Revenues	$1,587,600	1,582,700
Expenses:		
Direct operating	908,400	795,700
Distribution and marketing	483,500	547,200
General and administration	168,900	171,400
Gain on sale of video production group	(11,000)	
Depreciation and amortization	4,200	5,900
Total expenses	1,554,000	1,520,200
Operating income	$ 33,600	$ 62,500

a. Prepare a comparative income statement for fiscal years 2015 and 2014 in vertical form, stating each item as a percent of revenues. Round to one decimal place.
b. Comment on the significant changes.

1 **EX 17-3**

Common-sized income statement

✔ a. Shoesmith net income: $144,000; 3.6% of net sales

Revenue and expense data for the current calendar year for Shoesmith Electronics Company and for the electronics industry are as follows. The Shoesmith Electronics Company data are expressed in dollars. The electronics industry averages are expressed in percentages.

	Shoesmith Electronics Company	Electronics Industry Average
Sales	$4,200,000	105.0%
Sales returns and allowances	200,000	5.0
Net sales	4,000,000	100.0%
Cost of goods sold	2,120,000	59.0
Gross profit	1,880,000	41.0%
Selling expenses	1,160,000	24.0%
Administrative expenses	480,000	10.5
Total operating expenses	1,640,000	34.5%
Operating income	240,000	6.5%
Other income	84,000	2.1
	324,000	8.6%
Other expense	60,000	1.5
Income before income taxes	264,000	7.1%
Income taxes expense	120,000	6.0
Net income	$ 144,000	1.1%

a. Prepare a common-sized income statement comparing the results of operations for Shoesmith Electronics Company with the industry average. Round to one decimal place.

b. As far as the data permit, comment on significant relationships revealed by the comparisons.

EX 17-4

Vertical analysis of balance sheet

✔ Retained earnings, Dec. 31, 2015, 33.0%

Balance sheet data for Bryant Company on December 31, the end of the fiscal year, are shown below.

	2015	2014
Current assets	$ 775,000	$ 585,000
Property, plant, and equipment	1,425,000	1,597,500
Intangible assets	300,000	67,500
Current liabilities	525,000	360,000
Long-term liabilities	900,000	855,000
Common shares	250,000	270,000
Retained earnings	825,000	765,000

Prepare a comparative balance sheet for 2015 and 2014, stating each asset as a percent of total assets and each liability and shareholders' equity item as a percent of the total liabilities and shareholders' equity. Round to one decimal place.

EX 17-5

Horizontal analysis of the income statement

✔ a. Net income increase, 95.0%

Income statement data for Grendel Images Company for the years ended December 31, 2015 and 2014, are as follows:

	2015	2014
Sales	$196,000	$160,000
Cost of goods sold	170,100	140,000
Gross profit	25,900	20,000
Selling expenses	12,200	10,000
Administrative expenses	9,750	8,000
Total operating expenses	21,950	18,000
Income before income taxes	3,950	2,000
Income taxes expense	2,000	1,000
Net income	$ 1,950	$ 1,000

a. Prepare a comparative income statement with horizontal analysis, indicating the increase (decrease) for 2015 when compared with 2014. Round to one decimal place.

b. What conclusions can be drawn from the horizontal analysis?

EX 17-6

Horizontal analysis of income statement

The following data (in millions) is taken from the financial statements of RONA inc. for years ended 2011 and 2010.

	2011	2010
Net sales (revenues)	$4,805	$4,820
Total operating expenses	4,648	4,597

a. For RONA, comparing 2011 with 2010, determine the amount of change in millions and the percent of change for:
   1. Net sales (revenues)
   2. Total operating expenses
b. What conclusions can you draw from your analysis of the net sales and the total operating expenses?

EX 17-7

Horizontal analysis of income statement

The following data were adapted from the financial statements of Kmart Corporation, prior to its filing for bankruptcy:

	In millions	
For years ended January 31	2000	1999
Sales	$ 37,028	$ 35,925
Cost of sales (expense)	(29,658)	(28,111)
Selling, general, and administrative expenses	(7,415)	(6,514)
Operating income (loss)	$ (45)	$ 1,300

a. Prepare a horizontal analysis for the income statement showing the amount and percent of change in each of the following:
   1. Sales
   2. Cost of sales
   3. Selling, general, and administrative expenses
   4. Operating income (loss)
b. Comment on the results of your horizontal analysis in part (a).

EX 17-8

Liquidity analysis

✔ 2015 working capital, $1,342,000

The following data were taken from the balance sheet of Beatty Company:

	Dec. 31, 2015	Dec. 31, 2014
Cash	$ 330,000	$ 238,000
Temporary investments	465,000	385,000
Accounts and notes receivable (net)	425,000	295,000
Inventories	420,000	291,000
Prepaid expenses	312,000	141,000
Total current assets	$1,952,000	$1,350,000
Accounts and notes payable (short-term)	$ 420,000	$ 400,000
Accrued liabilities	190,000	140,000
Total current liabilities	$ 610,000	$ 540,000

a. Determine for each year (1) the working capital, (2) the current ratio, and (3) the quick ratio. Round ratios to one decimal place.
b. What conclusions can be drawn from these data as to the company's ability to meet its currently maturing debts?

EX 17-9

Liquidity analysis

PepsiCo., Inc., whose brands include Frito-Lay snack foods and Pepsi beverages, had the following current assets and current liabilities at the end of two recent years*:

* © 2012 PepsiCo, Inc. Used with permission.

	December 25, 2010 (in millions except per share amounts)	December 26, 2009 (in millions except per share amounts)
Cash and cash equivalents	$ 4,067	$ 5,943
Short-term investments	358	426
Accounts and notes receivable, net	6,912	6,323
Inventories	3,827	3,372
Prepaid expenses and other current assets	2,277	1,505
Short-term obligations	6,205	4,898
Accounts payable and other current liabilities	11,757	10,923
Income taxes payable	192	71

a. Determine (1) the current ratio and (2) the quick ratio for both years. Round to one decimal place.

b. What conclusions can you draw from these data?

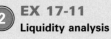

EX 17-10

Liquidity analysis

For Gray Corporation, the working capital at the end of the current year is $10,000 more than the working capital at the end of the preceding year, reported as follows:

	Current Year	Preceding Year
Current assets:		
Cash, temporary investments, and receivables.....................	$ 80,000	$ 84,000
Inventories	120,000	66,000
Total current assets..................	200,000	150,000
Current liabilities.......................	100,000	60,000
Working capital	$100,000	$ 90,000

Has the current position improved? Explain.

EX 17-11

Liquidity analysis

The bond indenture for the 10-year, 10% debenture bonds dated January 2, 2014, required working capital of $142,000, a current ratio of 1.7, and a quick ratio of 1.2 at the end of each calendar year until the bonds mature. At December 31, 2015, the three measures were computed as follows:

1. Current assets:		
Cash	$170,000	
Temporary investments	80,000	
Accounts and notes receivable (net)	200,000	
Inventories...........................	60,000	
Prepaid expenses	40,000	
Intangible assets.....................	208,000	
Property, plant, and equipment	92,000	
Total current assets (net)		$850,000
Current liabilities:		
Accounts and short-term notes payable....	$160,000	
Accrued liabilities	340,000	
Total current liabilities		500,000
Working capital.........................		$350,000
2. Current Ratio..........................	1.7	$850,000 ÷ $500,000
3. Quick Ratio...........................	1.2	$192,000 ÷ $160,000

a. List the errors in the determination of the three measures of liquidity analysis.

b. Is the company satisfying the terms of the bond indenture?

EX 17-12

Accounts receivable analysis

The following data are taken from the financial statements of McKee Technology Inc. Terms of all sales are 2/10, n/60.

	2015	2014	2013
Accounts receivable, end of year	$147,500	$158,000	$165,000
Net sales on account	975,000	900,000	

a. Determine for years 2015 and 2014 (1) the accounts receivable turnover and (2) the number of days' sales in receivables. Round to nearest dollar and one decimal place.
b. What conclusions can be drawn from these data concerning accounts receivable and credit policies?

EX 17-13

Accounts receivable analysis

Xavier Stores Company and Lestrade Stores Ltd. are large retail department stores. Both companies offer credit to their customers through their own credit card operations. Information from the financial statements for both companies for two recent years is as follows (all numbers are in thousands):

	Xavier	Lestrade
Merchandise sales	$28,000	$65,000
Credit card receivables—beginning	2,750	15,000
Credit card receivables—ending	2,250	11,000

a. Determine (1) the accounts receivable turnover and (2) the days' sales in receivables for both companies. Round to one decimal place.
b. Determine which company is more efficient in collecting its accounts receivable.

EX 17-14

Inventory analysis

The following data were extracted from the income statement of Brecca Systems Ltd.:

	Current Year	Preceding Year
Sales	$1,139,600	$1,192,320
Beginning inventories	80,000	64,000
Cost of goods sold	569,800	662,400
Ending inventories	74,000	80,000

a. Determine for each year (1) the inventory turnover and (2) the days' sales in inventory. Round to nearest dollar and one decimal place.
b. What conclusions can be drawn from these data concerning the inventories?

EX 17-15

Inventory analysis

Dell Inc. and Hewlett-Packard Company (HP) compete with each other in the personal computer market. Dell's primary strategy is to assemble computers to customer orders, not for inventory. For example, Dell will build and deliver a computer within four days of a customer entering an order on a Web page. Hewlett-Packard, on the other hand, builds some computers prior to receiving an order, then sells from this inventory after an order is received. Below is selected financial information for both companies from a recent year's financial statements (in millions):

	Dell Inc.	Hewlett-Packard Company
Sales	$62,071	$127,245
Cost of goods sold	48,260	97,223
Inventories, beginning of period	1,301	6,466
Inventories, end of period	1,404	7,490

a. Determine for both companies (1) the inventory turnover and (2) the days' sales in inventory. Round to one decimal place.
b. Interpret the inventory ratios by considering Dell's and Hewlett-Packard's operating strategies.

EX 17-16

Debt ratio and times interest earned ratio

The total liabilities and shareholders' equity of Weal Construction Ltd. for December 31, 2015 and 2014, are as follows:

	2015	2014
Accounts payable	$ 300,000	$ 280,000
Current maturities of serial bonds payable	400,000	400,000
Serial bonds payable, 10% issued 2010, due 2020	2,000,000	2,400,000
Total shareholders' equity	4,500,000	3,850,000

The income before income taxes was $720,000 and $560,000 for the years 2015 and 2014, respectively.

a. Determine the debt ratio for both years. Round the percentage to one decimal place.
b. Determine the times interest earned ratio during the year for both years. Round to one decimal place.
c. What conclusions can be drawn from these data regarding the company's ability to meet its currently maturing debts?

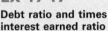

EX 17-17

Debt ratio and times interest earned ratio

Toys in a Box is a retail toy company. Financial data from the December 31, 2015, and December 31, 2014, financial statements are shown as follows (in thousands):

	2015	2014
Current liabilities	$1,038,900	$1,350,300
Long-term debt	1,500,000	950,000
Other liabilities	522,100	488,800
Total liabilities	3,061,000	2,789,100
Total shareholders' equity	2,610,600	2,628,600
Total liabilities and shareholders' equity	$5,671,600	$5,417,600

The income from operations and interest expense from the income statement for both years are as follows:

	2015	2014
Income from operations	$970,700	$846,800
Interest expense	75,300	64,800

a. Determine the debt ratio for 2015 and 2014. Round the percentage to one decimal place.
b. Determine the times interest earned ratio for 2015 and 2014. Round to one decimal place.
c. Have the 2015 ratios determined above improved or declined since 2014? Review the financial information presented in the exercise. What might have caused the change in the ratios?

EX 17-18

Debt ratio

Canadian Tire Corporation, Limited, has been operating in Canada since 1922. It consists of five businesses in different sectors, including general merchandise, automotive parts, clothing retail, gas bars, and financial services. Canadian Tire has more than 400 stores across Canada offering automotive, sports, leisure, and home products.

For the years ended December 31, 2011, and January 1, 2011, Canadian Tire reported the following balance sheet data (in millions):

	2011	2010
Total assets	$12,339	$11,049
Total equity	4,409	4,005

a. Determine the total liabilities as at December 31, 2011, and January 1, 2011.
b. Determine the debt ratios for 2011 and 2010. Round the percentages to one decimal place.
c. Has the margin of protection for debtholders increased or declined during this time period?

EX 17-19
Debt ratio

4

RONA, inc., a major competitor in the home improvement business, operates more than 600 stores in Canada. For the years ended December 25, 2011, and December 26, 2010, RONA reported the following statement of financial position data (in millions):

	2011	2010
Total assets	$2,780	$2,921
Total liabilities	825	1,010

a. Determine the total equity as at December 25, 2011 and December 26, 2010.
b. Determine the debt ratios for 2011 and 2010. Round the percentages to one decimal place.
c. What conclusions can you draw from (b) regarding the margin of protection to the creditors?
d. Using the balance sheet data for Canadian Tire Corporation from Exercise 17-18, how does RONA's debt ratio compare with that of Canadian Tire?

EX 17-20
Profitability analysis

5

The following selected data were taken from the financial statements of two grocery chains, GoodFood Corp. and Tasty's Ltd., for 2015 (in thousands):

	GoodFood Corp.	Tasty's Ltd.
Sales	$5,402	$12,369
Sales returns	43	49
Cost of goods sold	4,321	9,276
Net income	162	446

a. Determine the gross margins for both companies. Round the percentage to one decimal place.
b. Determine the profit margins for both companies. Round the percentage to one decimal place.
c. Interpret the ratio differences between the two companies.

EX 17-21
Return on assets

5

Three major segments of the transportation industry are airlines, such as WestJet; railroads, such as Canadian National Railway (CNR); and transportation arrangement services, such as TransForce Inc. Recent financial statement information for these three companies is shown as follows (in millions of dollars):

	WestJet	CNR	TransForce
Net income	$ 149	$ 2,457	$ 102
Average total assets	3,429	25,616	1,875

a. Determine the return on assets for all three companies. Round to one decimal place.
b. Assume that the return on asset ratio for each company represents each company's respective industry segment. Interpret the differences in the return on assets in terms of the operating characteristics of each of the respective segments.

EX 17-22
Profitability ratios

5

The following selected data were taken from the financial statements of The Sigemund Group Inc. for December 31, 2013, 2014, and 2015:

	December 31		
	2015	2014	2013
Total assets.................	$3,000,000	$2,700,000	$2,400,000
Notes payable (10% interest)...	1,000,000	1,000,000	1,000,000
$6 preferred shares, 2,000 issued			
and outstanding............	200,000	200,000	200,000
Common shares, 40,000 issued			
and outstanding............	400,000	400,000	400,000
Retained earnings............	1,126,000	896,000	600,000

The 2015 net income was $242,000, and the 2014 net income was $308,000. No dividends on common shares were declared between 2013 and 2015.

a. Determine the return on assets, the return on common shareholders' equity, and the earnings per share for the years 2014 and 2015. Round to one decimal place.

b. What conclusions can be drawn from these data regarding the company's profitability?

EX 17-23

⑤ **Profitability ratios**

Reitmans (Canada) Limited operates a network of clothing stores specializing in women's fashions and accessories. Recent financial information for Reitmans is provided below (all numbers in thousands).

	Fiscal Year Ended		
	Jan. 28, 2012	Jan. 29, 2011	Jan. 30, 2010
Net income	$ 47,539	$ 88,985	$ 67,236
Total assets	$ 633,861	$659,357	$632,731
Total shareholders' equity	492,852	512,800	498,252

The apparel industry average return on assets is 4.6%, and the average return on common shareholders' equity is 10.5% for fiscal 2012.

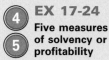

a. Determine the return on total assets for Reitmans for the fiscal years ended January 28, 2012, and January 29, 2011. Round to one decimal place.

b. Determine the return on common shareholders' equity for Reitmans for the fiscal years ended January 28, 2012, and January 29, 2011. Round to one decimal place.

c. Evaluate the two-year trend for the profitability ratios determined in (a) and (b).

d. Evaluate Reitmans' profit performance relative to the industry.

EX 17-24

④
⑤ **Five measures of solvency or profitability**

The following data were taken from the financial statements of Heremod Enterprises Inc. for the current fiscal year. Assuming that total assets were $4,000,000 at the beginning of the year, determine (a) the debt ratio, (b) the profit margin, (c) the return on assets, (d) the earnings per share, and (e) the return on common shareholders' equity. Round to one decimal place except earnings per share, which should be rounded to two decimal places.

Total assets..		$ 4,200,000
Liabilities:		
Current liabilities	$ 200,000	
Mortgage note payable, 10%, issued 2002, due 2020	1,000,000	
Total liabilities		$ 1,200,000
Shareholders' Equity:		
$10 preferred shares, 10,000 issued and outstanding (no change during year).....................		$ 1,000,000
Common shares, 100,000 issued and outstanding (no change during year).....................		1,000,000
Retained Earnings:		
Balance, beginning of year	$ 800,000	
Net income....................................	400,000	
Less dividends	(200,000)	
Balance, end of year...........................		1,000,000
Total shareholders' equity......................		$ 3,000,000
Net sales.......................................		$10,000,000

EX 17-25

⑤ **Profitability ratios**

The balance sheet for Fitela Industries Ltd. at the end of the current fiscal year indicated the following:

Bonds payable, 10% (issued in 2002, due in 2022)	$4,000,000
$5 preferred shares, 10,000 shares issued and outstanding	1,000,000
Common shares, 200,000 shares issued and outstanding	2,000,000

(continued)

Income before income taxes was $1,000,000, and income taxes were $150,000 for the current year. Cash dividends paid on common shares during the current year totalled $200,000. The common shares were selling for $40 per share at the end of the year. Determine (a) the earnings per share, (b) the price-earnings ratio, and (c) the dividend yield. Round to one decimal place except earnings per share, which should be rounded to two decimal places.

---

⑤ EX 17-26
Profitability ratios

The following information was taken from the financial statements of Finn Resources Ltd. for December 31 of the current fiscal year:

$10 preferred shares, 20,000 shares issued and outstanding	$ 800,000
Common shares, 250,000 shares issued and outstanding	5,000,000

The net income was $600,000, and the declared dividends on the common shares were $125,000 for the current year. The market price is $20 per common share. For the common shares, determine (a) the earnings per share, (b) the price-earnings ratio, and (c) the dividend yield. Round to one decimal place except earnings per share, which should be rounded to two decimal places.

---

⑤ EX 17-27
Price-earnings ratio; dividend yield

The table below shows the share price, earnings per share, and dividends per share for three banks as at May 2012:

	Price	Earnings per Share	Dividends per Share
Bank of Montreal	$ 58.67	$ 5.28	$ 0.70
Bank of Nova Scotia	54.80	4.74	0.55
Royal Bank of Canada	57.81	3.12	0.57

a. Determine the price-earnings ratio and dividend yield for the three banks. Round to one decimal place.
b. Which bank is viewed most favourably by the market in terms of its future earnings prospects?
c. Which bank's shares would you prefer to own if you were interested mainly in receiving income?

---

② EX 17-28
③ Analysis of ratios
④
⑤

A clothing retailer has the following statistical information calculated from its financial statements for the past three years:

	2015	2014	2013
Current ratio	1.1:1	1.3:1	1.4:1
Accounts receivable turnover	18 times	20.2 times	30 times
Inventory turnover	35 times	28 times	23 times
Debt ratio	64%	58%	49%
Return on shareholders' equity	10%	9.5%	8.5%
Annual sales revenue	$8,754,000	$8,810,000	$8,792,000

Using the information above, answer each of the following questions and explain your answer.

a. Are current assets increasing or decreasing in relation to current liabilities?
b. Is the retailer becoming more or less efficient in the collection of its accounts receivable?
c. Over the three-year period, has more or less money been tied up in inventory?
d. From the shareholders' point of view, is profitability improving or not improving?
e. Suppose the retailer needs to borrow capital through long-term debt. Would it be easier to find a lender now, or would it have been easier three years earlier?
f. Has the retailer been using leverage to the advantage of the shareholders over the three-year period?

PROBLEMS SERIES A

PR 17-1A

Horizontal analysis
for income
statement

For 2015, Eurie Company reported its most significant decline in net income in years. At the end of the year, H. Finn, the president, is presented with the following condensed comparative income statement:

✔ 1. Net sales,
14.4% increase

Eurie Company
Income Statement
For the Years Ended December 31, 2015 and 2014

	2015	2014
Sales..	$928,000	$800,000
Sales returns and allowances	70,000	50,000
Net sales.....................................	858,000	750,000
Cost of goods sold	640,000	500,000
Gross profit..	218,000	250,000
Selling expenses	85,800	65,000
Administrative expenses	43,400	35,000
Total operating expenses.....................	129,200	100,000
Income from operations	88,800	150,000
Other income	16,000	10,000
Income before income taxes.....................	104,800	160,000
Income taxes expense..........................	15,700	24,000
Net income	$ 89,100	$136,000

Instructions

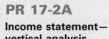

1. Prepare a comparative income statement with horizontal analysis for the two-year period, using 2014 as the base year. Round to one decimal place.
2. To the extent the data permit, comment on the significant relationships revealed by the horizontal analysis prepared in (1).

PR 17-2A

Income statement—
vertical analysis

For 2015, Ottawa Technology Company initiated a sales promotion campaign that included the expenditure of an additional $20,000 for advertising. At the end of the year, George Wallace, the president, is presented with the following condensed income statement:

✔ 1. Net income,
2015, 16.0%

Ottawa Technology Company
Income Statement
For the Years Ended December 31, 2015 and 2014

	2015	2014
Sales.....................................	$714,000	$612,000
Sales returns and allowances.............	14,000	12,000
Net sales.....................................	700,000	600,000
Cost of goods sold...................	322,000	312,000
Gross profit........................	378,000	288,000
Selling expenses..........................	154,000	120,000
Administrative expenses	70,000	66,000
Total operating expenses.................	224,000	186,000
Income from operations...................	154,000	102,000
Other income...........................	28,000	24,000
Income before income taxes...............	182,000	126,000
Income taxes expense...................	70,000	60,000
Net income.............................	$112,000	$ 66,000

Instructions

1. Prepare an income statement for the two-year period, presenting an analysis of each item in relationship to net sales for each of the years. Round to one decimal place.
2. Was the advertising campaign successful? Did the additional cost result in a proportionate increase in net income?

PR 17-3A

Effect of transactions on liquidity analysis

✔ 2. c.
Current ratio, 2.2

Data pertaining to the liquidity of Brin Company are as follows:

Cash	$520,000
Temporary investments	380,000
Accounts and notes receivable (net)	700,000
Inventories	720,000
Prepaid expenses	80,000
Accounts payable	300,000
Notes payable (short-term)	360,000
Accrued expenses	340,000

Instructions

1. Compute (a) the working capital, (b) the current ratio, and (c) the quick ratio. Round to one decimal place.
2. List the following captions on a sheet of paper:

Transaction	Working Capital	Current Ratio	Quick Ratio

Compute the working capital, the current ratio, and the quick ratio after each of the following transactions and record the results in the appropriate columns. *Consider each transaction separately* and assume that only that transaction affects the data given above. Round to one decimal place.

a. Sold temporary investments at no gain or loss, $90,000.
b. Paid accounts payable, $175,000.
c. Purchased goods on account, $125,000.
d. Paid notes payable, $200,000.
e. Declared a cash dividend, $160,000.
f. Declared a common share dividend on common shares, $45,000.
g. Borrowed cash from bank on a long-term note, $300,000.
h. Received cash on account, $140,000.
i. Issued additional shares for cash, $700,000.
j. Paid cash for prepaid expenses, $80,000.

PR 17-4A

Ratio analysis

✔ Days' sales in receivables, 53.7

Some of the financial statements of Optical Solutions Inc. are as follows. The market price of Optical Solutions Inc. common shares was $60.00 on December 31, 2015. For both years, the company paid dividends of $4,000 and $12,000 to the preferred shareholders and the common shareholders, respectively.

Optical Solutions Inc.
Income Statement
For the Years Ended December 31, 2015 and 2014

	2015	2014
Sales	$1,608,000	$1,481,600
Sales returns and allowances.	5,920	6,000
Net sales.	1,602,080	1,475,600
Cost of goods sold	480,200	499,200
Gross profit.	1,121,880	976,400
Selling expenses.	324,000	352,000
Administrative expenses	234,000	211,200
Total operating expenses	558,000	563,200
Income from operations.	563,880	413,200
Other income	24,000	19,200
	587,880	432,400
Other expense (interest)	110,720	80,000
Income before income taxes	477,160	352,400
Income taxes expense	49,160	38,400
Net income	$ 428,000	$ 314,000

Optical Solutions Inc.
Statement of Financial Position
December 31, 2015 and 2014

	2015	2014
Assets		
Current assets:		
Cash	$ 240,000	$ 162,400
Temporary investments	364,000	328,800
Accounts receivable (net)	260,000	211,200
Inventories.	208,000	66,400
Prepaid expenses	44,000	23,200
Total current assets.	1,116,000	792,000
Long-term investments	204,800	256,000
Property, plant, and equipment (net)	1,539,200	976,000
Total assets	$2,860,000	$2,024,000
Liabilities		
Current liabilities.	$ 360,000	$ 320,000
Long-term liabilities:		
Mortgage note payable, 8%, due 2020 . . .	384,000	—
Bonds payable, 10%, due 2024	800,000	800,000
Total long-term liabilities	1,184,000	800,000
Total liabilities	1,544,000	1,120,000
Shareholders' Equity		
$2 preferred shares, 2,000 issued and outstanding	100,000	100,000
Common shares, 20,000 issued and outstanding	200,000	200,000
Retained earnings.	1,016,000	604,000
Total shareholders' equity	1,316,000	904,000
Total liabilities and shareholders' equity	$2,860,000	$2,024,000

Instructions

Calculate all possible liquidity, efficiency, solvency, and profitability ratios for 2015, rounding to one decimal place, except for earnings per share, which is rounded to two decimal places.

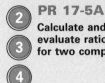

PR 17-5A

2

Calculate and
evaluate ratios
for two companies

3

4

5

Andrew Peller Limited and Magnotta Winery Corporation are two producers of quality wines in Canada. Selected financial data (in thousands) for these two competitors for a recent year are as follows:

	Andrew Peller	Magnotta Winery
Statement of Earnings		
Sales	$276,883	$ 23,224
Cost of sales	174,452	14,156
Gross profit	102,431	9,068
Operating and other expenses	78,538	5,211
Interest expense	5,354	419
Income before income taxes	18,539	3,438
Income taxes	5,538	1,116
Net income	$ 13,001	$ 2,322
Balance Sheet		
Current assets		
Accounts receivable	$ 24,937	$ 617
Inventories	110,256	30,810
Other current assets	2,219	836
Total current assets	137,412	32,263
Property, plant, and equipment	84,490	20,085
Other assets	63,650	252
Total assets	$ 285,552	$ 52,600
Current liabilities	$ 102,543	$ 8,116
Long-term liabilities	62,457	5,415
Shareholders' equity	120,552	39,069
Total liabilities and shareholders' equity	$ 285,552	$ 52,600
Additional Information		
Average accounts receivable	$ 24,164	$ 604
Average inventories	102,474	30,344
Average total assets	276,774	52,139
Average total shareholders' equity	117,425	37,849

Instructions

1. For each company, determine the following measures, rounding to one decimal place. Industry averages are provided in parentheses after each ratio.
   a. current ratio (2.4:1)
   b. accounts receivable turnover (11.3 times)
   c. inventory turnover (3.2 times)
   d. total asset turnover (0.6 times)
   e. debt ratio (63%)
   f. times interest earned ratio (3.8 times)
   g. profit margin (2.8%)
   h. return on assets (1.7%)
   i. return on shareholders' equity (4.6%)
2. Compare the liquidity, efficiency, solvency, and profitability of the two companies to each other and to the industry.
3. Which company would be more appealing to an investor? Explain your decision.

PR 17-6A

Calculate and evaluate ratios, trend analysis

② ③ ④ ⑤

Corby Distilleries Limited is a leading Canadian manufacturer and marketer of spirits and imported wines. Corby's portfolio of owned-brands includes some of the most renowned brands in Canada, including Wiser's Canadian whiskies, Lamb's rum, Polar Ice vodka, and McGuinness liqueurs.

Selected financial data (in thousands) for recent years are as follows:

	2011	2010	2009
Statement of Earnings			
Sales	$158,790	$162,230	
Cost of sales	71,336	73,061	
Gross profit	87,454	89,169	
Operating and other expenses	47,457	46,144	
Other expenses	1,112	11,543	
Income before income taxes	38,885	31,482	
Income taxes	11,462	10,807	
Net income	$ 27,423	$ 20,675	
Balance Sheet			
Current assets			
Cash	$ 96,636	$ 74,685	
Accounts receivable	31,005	28,340	28,640
Inventories	59,654	60,502	53,987
Other current assets	2,492	2,756	
Total current assets	189,787	166,283	
Property, plant, and equipment	15,646	15,238	
Other assets	78,504	89,720	
Total assets	$283,937	$271,241	
Current liabilities	$ 19,607	$ 18,285	
Long-term liabilities	11,889	11,994	
Shareholders' equity	252,441	240,962	236,231
Total liabilities and shareholders' equity	$283,937	$271,241	

Instructions

1. Determine the following measures for 2011 and 2010, rounding to one decimal place. Industry averages are provided in parentheses after each ratio.
   a. current ratio (2.4:1)
   b. accounts receivable turnover (11.3 times)
   c. inventory turnover (3.2 times)
   d. total asset turnover (0.6 times)
   e. debt ratio (63%)
   f. profit margin (2.8%)
   g. return on assets (1.7%)
   h. return on shareholders' equity (4.6%)
2. Identify whether the liquidity, efficiency, solvency, and profitability ratios have improved or declined since 2010.
3. How does Corby Distillers compare to the industry averages?

PR 17-7A

Solvency and profitability trend analysis

④ ⑤

✔ I.c. 2014, 5.7

Lancelot Company has provided the following information:

	2015	2014	2013	2012	2011
Net income	$ 1,930,500	$ 1,287,000	$ 975,000	$ 650,000	$ 500,000
Interest expense	400,200	345,000	300,000	240,000	200,000
Income taxes expense	477,360	318,240	244,800	163,200	120,000
Total assets (ending balance)	11,498,760	8,845,200	6,804,000	5,040,000	4,200,000
Total shareholders' equity (ending balance)	6,742,500	4,812,000	3,525,000	2,550,000	1,900,000
Average total assets	10,171,980	7,824,600	5,922,000	4,620,000	3,600,000
Average shareholders' equity	5,777,250	4,168,500	3,037,500	2,225,000	1,650,000

(continued)

You have been asked to evaluate the historical performance of the company over the past five years. Lancelot has no preferred shareholders.

Selected industry ratios have remained relatively steady at the following levels for the past five years:

	2011–2015
Return on assets	15%
Return on common shareholders' equity	23%
Times interest earned ratio	3.5 times
Debt ratio	40%

Instructions

1. Prepare four line graphs with the ratio on the vertical axis and the years on the horizontal axis for the following four ratios (rounded to one decimal place):
   a. Return on assets
   b. Return on common shareholders' equity
   c. Times interest earned ratio
   d. Debt ratio
   Display both the company ratio and the industry benchmark on each graph so that each graph shows two lines.
2. Prepare an analysis of the graphs in (1).

PROBLEMS SERIES B

PR 17-1B
Horizontal analysis for income statement

For 2015, McFadden Inc. reported its most significant increase in net income in years. At the end of the year, Jane Mayer, the president, is presented with the following condensed comparative income statement:

✔ 1. Net sales, 26.1% increase

McFadden Inc.
Income Statement
For the Years Ended December 31, 2015 and 2014

	2015	2014
Sales.	$516,600	$410,000
Sales returns and allowances	12,200	10,000
Net sales.	504,400	400,000
Cost of goods sold	240,000	200,000
Gross profit	264,400	200,000
Selling expenses.	69,600	60,000
Administrative expenses	44,800	40,000
Total operating expenses.	114,400	100,000
Income from operations	150,000	100,000
Other income	12,600	10,000
Income before income taxes.	162,600	110,000
Income taxes expense.	24,400	16,500
Net income	$138,200	$ 93,500

Instructions

1. Prepare a comparative income statement with horizontal analysis for the two-year period, using 2014 as the base year. Round to one decimal place.
2. To the extent the data permit, comment on the significant relationships revealed by the horizontal analysis prepared in (1).

1 **PR 17-2B**

**Income statement—
vertical analysis**

✔ 1. Net income,
2014, 10.0%

For 2015, Engels Industries Inc. initiated a sales promotion campaign that included the expenditure of an additional $40,000 for advertising. At the end of the year, Diane Heaney, the president, is presented with the following condensed income statement:

Engels Industries Inc.
Income Statement
For the Years Ended December 31, 2015 and 2014

	2015	2014
Sales.	$525,000	$420,000
Sales returns and allowances.	25,000	20,000
Net sales.	500,000	400,000
Cost of goods sold.	280,000	220,000
Gross profit.	220,000	180,000
Selling expenses.	130,000	80,000
Administrative expenses	65,000	56,000
Total operating expenses.	195,000	136,000
Income from operations.	25,000	44,000
Other income.	30,000	24,000
Income before income taxes.	55,000	68,000
Income taxes expense.	35,000	28,000
Net income.	$ 20,000	$ 40,000

Instructions

1. Prepare an income statement for the two-year period, presenting an analysis of each item in relationship to net sales for each of the years. Round to one decimal place.
2. Was the advertising campaign successful? Did the additional cost result in a proportionate increase in net income?

---

2 **PR 17-3B**

**Effect of transactions
on liquidity analysis**

✔ 2. e.
Quick ratio, 0.9

Data pertaining to the liquidity of Dancey Industries Inc. are as follows:

Cash	$560,000
Temporary investments	520,000
Accounts and notes receivable (net)	800,000
Inventories	900,000
Prepaid expenses	100,000
Accounts payable	800,000
Notes payable (short-term)	700,000
Accrued expenses	300,000

Instructions

1. Compute (a) the working capital, (b) the current ratio, and (c) the quick ratio. Round to one decimal place.
2. List the following captions on a sheet of paper:

Transaction	Working Capital	Current Ratio	Quick Ratio

Compute the working capital, the current ratio, and the quick ratio after each of the following transactions and record the results in the appropriate columns. *Consider each transaction separately* and assume that only that transaction affects the data given above. Round to one decimal place.

a. Sold temporary investments at no gain or loss, $200,000.
b. Paid accounts payable, $400,000.
c. Purchased goods on account, $150,000.
d. Paid notes payable, $380,000.
e. Declared a cash dividend, $220,000.
f. Declared a common share dividend on common shares, $200,000.
g. Borrowed cash from bank on a long-term note, $680,000.
h. Received cash on account, $110,000.
i. Issued additional shares for cash, $1,400,000.
j. Paid cash for prepaid expenses, $50,000.

2

PR 17-4B
Ratio analysis

3

4 ✔ Times interest
earned, 4.5

5

The financial statements of Caylay Technologies Inc. are as follows. The market price of Caylay Technologies Inc. common shares was $40 per share on December 31, 2015. For both years, the company paid dividends of $24,000 an $48,000 to the preferred shareholders and the common shareholders, respectively.

Caylay Technologies Inc.
Income Statement
For the Years Ended December 31, 2015 and 2014

	2015	2014
Sales	$4,245,000	$3,675,000
Sales returns and allowances	35,000	22,500
Net sales	4,210,000	3,652,500
Cost of goods sold	1,866,150	1,725,000
Gross profit	2,343,850	1,927,500
Selling expenses	907,500	862,500
Administrative expenses	607,500	570,000
Total operating expenses	1,515,000	1,432,500
Income from operations	828,850	495,000
Other income	60,000	45,000
	888,850	540,000
Other expense (interest)	196,000	90,000
Income before income taxes	692,850	450,000
Income taxes expense	210,000	142,500
Net income	$ 482,850	$ 307,500

Caylay Technologies Inc.
Statement of Financial Position
December 31, 2015 and 2014

	2015	2014
Assets		
Current assets:		
Cash	$ 400,000	$ 180,000
Temporary investments	614,000	240,000
Accounts receivable (net)	390,000	283,600
Inventories	631,000	500,000
Prepaid expenses	45,000	52,500
Total current assets	2,080,000	1,256,100
Long-term investments	324,450	375,000
Property, plant, and equipment (net)	3,780,000	3,000,000
Total assets	$6,184,450	$4,631,100
Liabilities		
Current liabilities	$ 520,000	$ 427,500
Long-term liabilities:		
Mortgage note payable, 10%, due 2020	1,000,000	—
Bonds payable, 12%, due 2024	800,000	750,000
Total long-term liabilities	1,800,000	750,000
Total liabilities	2,320,000	1,177,500
Shareholders' Equity		
$3 preferred shares, 8,000 issued and outstanding	800,000	800,000
Common shares, 120,000 issued and outstanding	1,200,000	1,200,000
Retained earnings	1,864,450	1,453,600
Total shareholders' equity	3,864,450	3,453,600
Total liabilities and shareholders' equity	$6,184,450	$4,631,100

Instructions

Calculate all possible liquidity, efficiency, solvency, and profitability ratios for 2015, rounding to one decimal place, except for earnings per share, which is rounded to two decimal places.

PR 17-5B

Calculate and evaluate ratios for two companies

② ③ ④ ⑤

Reitmans (Canada) Limited and Danier Leather Inc. are two companies with clothing stores within Canada. Selected financial data (in thousands) for these two companies for a recent year are as follows:

	Danier Leather	Reitmans
Statement of Earnings		
Sales	$157,621	$1,019,397
Cost of sales	71,352	363,333
Gross profit	86,269	656,064
Operating and other expenses	75,458	588,683
Interest expense	103	1,509
Income before income taxes	10,708	65,872
Income taxes	3,140	18,333
Net income	$ 7,568	$ 47,539
Statement of Financial Position		
Current assets		
Cash	$ 28,698	$ 196,835
Accounts receivable	385	3,033
Inventories	28,964	78,285
Other current assets	901	88,830
Total current assets	58,948	366,983
Property, plant, and equipment	14,404	184,221
Other assets	2,732	82,657
Total assets	$ 76,084	$ 633,861
Current liabilities	$ 12,838	$ 89,132
Long-term liabilities	1,318	51,877
Shareholders' equity	61,928	492,852
Total liabilities and shareholders' equity	$ 76,084	$ 633,861
Additional Information		
Average accounts receivable	464	2,950
Average inventories	27,617	75,743
Average total assets	74,833	646,609
Average total shareholders' equity	58,097	502,826

Instructions

1. For each company, determine the following measures, rounding to one decimal place. Industry averages are provided in parentheses after each ratio.
   a. current ratio (1.9:1)
   b. accounts receivable turnover (13.6 times)
   c. inventory turnover (5.8 times)
   d. total asset turnover (1.5 times)
   e. debt ratio (56%)
   f. times interest earned ratio (7.4 times)
   g. profit margin (3.1%)
   h. return on assets (4.6%)
   i. return on shareholders' equity (10.5%)
2. Compare the liquidity, efficiency, solvency, and profitability of the two companies to each other and to the industry.
3. Which company would be more appealing to an investor? Explain your decision.

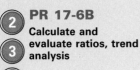

PR 17-6B

2

3

Calculate and evaluate ratios, trend analysis

4

5

Design Extravaganza Ltd. designs and retails formal wear sold in stores in North America, Asia, and Europe. Selected financial data (in thousands) for recent years are as follows:

	2015	2014	2013
Income Statement			
Sales	$ 711,704	$ 452,898	
Cost of sales	316,757	229,812	
Gross profit	394,947	223,086	
Operating and other expenses	211,670	136,376	
Income before income taxes	183,277	86,710	
Income taxes	61,080	28,429	
Net income	$ 122,197	$ 58,281	
Statement of Financial Position			
Current assets			
Cash	$ 316,286	$ 159,573	
Accounts receivable	9,116	8,238	$ 4,029
Inventories	57,469	44,070	52,051
Other current assets	6,408	4,529	
Total current assets	389,279	216,410	
Property, plant, and equipment	70,954	61,591	
Other assets	39,069	29,257	
Total assets	$ 499,302	$ 307,258	211,636
Current liabilities	$ 85,364	$ 58,678	
Long-term liabilities	19,645	15,472	
Shareholders' equity	394,293	233,108	154,842
Total liabilities and shareholders' equity	$ 499,302	$ 307,258	

Instructions

1. Determine the following measures for 2015 and 2014, rounding to one decimal place. Industry averages are provided in parentheses after each ratio.
   a. current ratio (1.9:1)
   b. accounts receivable turnover (13.6 times)
   c. inventory turnover (5.8 times)
   d. total asset turnover (1.5 times)
   e. debt ratio (56%)
   f. profit margin (3.1%)
   g. return on assets (4.6%)
   h. return on shareholders' equity (10.5%)
2. Identify whether the liquidity, efficiency, solvency, and profitability ratios have improved or declined since 2014.
3. How does Design Extravaganza Ltd. compare to the industry averages?

PR 17-7B

4

5

Solvency and profitability trend analysis

✔ c. 2015, 1.5

Merlin Company has provided the following information:

	2015	2014	2013	2012	2011
Net income	$ 129,868	$ 174,788	$ 299,809	$ 419,900	$ 380,000
Interest expense	280,021	260,001	240,075	225,000	200,000
Income taxes expense	20,002	33,617	67,234	100,800	126,000
Total assets (ending balance)	4,417,178	4,124,350	3,732,443	3,338,500	2,750,000
Total shareholders' equity (ending balance)	1,904,365	1,774,497	1,599,709	1,299,900	880,000
Average total assets	4,270,764	3,928,397	3,535,472	3,044,250	2,475,000
Average shareholders' equity	1,839,431	1,687,103	1,449,805	1,089,950	690,000

You have been asked to evaluate the historical performance of the company over the past five years. Merlin has no preferred shareholders.

Selected industry ratios have remained relatively steady at the following levels for the past five years:

	2011–2015
Return on assets	12%
Return on common shareholders' equity	20%
Times interest earned ratio	2.8 times
Debt ratio	40%

Instructions

1. Prepare four line graphs with the ratio on the vertical axis and the years on the horizontal axis for the following four ratios (rounded to one decimal place):
   a. return on assets
   b. return on common shareholders' equity
   c. times interest earned ratio
   d. debt ratio
   Display both the company ratio and the industry benchmark on each graph so that each graph shows two lines.
2. Prepare an analysis of the graphs in (1).

THE SHOPPERS DRUG MART CORP. PROBLEM

Financial statement analysis

✔ c. 2011, 22.6

The financial statements for Shoppers Drug Mart Corporation are presented in Appendix C at the end of the text.

Instructions

1. Determine the following measures for the fiscal years ended December 31, 2011, and January 1, 2011, rounding to one decimal place. Industry averages are provided in parentheses after each ratio.
   a. current ratio (1.35:1)
   b. quick ratio (0.65:1)
   c. accounts receivable turnover (13.6 times)
   d. inventory turnover (11.4 times)
   e. total asset turnover (1.9 times)
   f. debt ratio (48%)
   g. times interest earned ratio (6.6 times)
   h. profit margin (3.0%)
   i. return on assets (5.7%)
   j. return on shareholders' equity (11.1%)
2. Compare the liquidity, efficiency, solvency, and profitability of Shoppers Drug Mart Corporation to the prior year and to the industry averages.
3. Assess whether Shoppers Drug Mart Corporation's financial situation is improving or declining from the prior year.

SPECIAL ACTIVITIES

SA 17-1

Analysis of financing corporate growth

Assume that the president of Garden Isle Brewery made the following statement in the Annual Report to Shareholders:

"The founding family and majority shareholders of the company do not believe in using debt to finance future growth. The founding family learned from hard experience during Prohibition and the Great Depression that debt can cause loss of flexibility and eventual loss of corporate control. The company will not place itself at such risk. As such, all future growth will be financed either by selling shares to the public or by internally generated resources."

As a public shareholder of this company, how would you respond to this policy? What are the potential risks and rewards of using debt to finance future growth?

SA 17-2

Receivables and inventory turnover

Tylee Industries Ltd. has completed its fiscal year on December 31, 2015. The auditor, Holly Marcum, has approached the CFO, Doug Bliss, regarding the year-end receivables and inventory levels of Tylee Industries. The following conversation takes place:

Holly: We are beginning our audit of Tylee Industries and have prepared ratio analyses to determine if there have been significant changes in operations or financial position. This helps us guide the audit process. This analysis indicates that the inventory turnover has decreased from 4.5 to 2.1, while the accounts receivable turnover has decreased from 10 to 6. I was wondering if you could explain this change in operations.

Doug: There is little need for concern. The inventory represents computers that we were unable to sell during the holiday buying season. We are confident, however, that we will be able to sell these computers as we move into the next fiscal year.

Holly: What gives you this confidence?

Doug: We will increase our advertising and provide some very attractive price concessions to move these machines. We have no choice. Newer technology is already out there, and we have to unload this inventory.

Holly: . . . and the receivables?

Doug: As you may be aware, the company is under tremendous pressure to expand sales and profits. As a result, we lowered our credit standards to our commercial customers so that we would be able to sell products to a broader customer base. As a result of this policy change, we have been able to expand sales by 35%.

Holly: Your responses have not been reassuring to me.

Doug: I'm a little confused. Assets are good, right? Why don't you look at our current ratio? It has improved, hasn't it? I would think that you would view that very favourably.

Why is Holly concerned about the inventory and accounts receivable turnover ratios and Doug's responses to them? What action may Holly need to take? How would you respond to Doug's last comment?

SA 17-3

Vertical analysis

✔ Gross profit, 2012, 22.3%

The condensed income statements through income from operations for Dell Inc. are reproduced below for the years ended February 3, 2012, and January 28, 2011 (numbers in millions of dollars).

	2012	2011
Sales (net)	$62,071	$61,494
Cost of sales	48,260	50,098
Gross profit	13,811	11,396
Selling, general, and administrative expenses	8,524	7,302
Research and development	856	661
Operating expenses	9,380	7,963
Income from operations	$ 4,431	$ 3,433

Prepare common-sized statements, rounding percents to one decimal place. Interpret the analyses.

SA 17-4
Profitability and shareholder ratios

✔ 1. (c) 2010, $0.63

Harley-Davidson, Inc., is a leading motorcycle manufacturer in the United States. The company manufactures and sells a number of different types of motorcycles, a complete line of motorcycle parts, and brand-related accessories, clothing, and collectibles. In recent years, Harley-Davidson has attempted to expand its dealer network and product lines internationally.

The following information is available for three recent years (in millions except per share amounts):

	2011	2010	2009
Net income (loss)	$ 599	$ 147	$ (55)
Interest expense	45	90	22
Average number of shares outstanding	235	235	234
Cash dividend per share	0.475	0.40	0.40
Average total assets	9,552	9,293	8,492
Average shareholders' equity (no preferred shareholders)	2,314	2,157	2,112
Market price per share	52.33	34.89	25.20

1. Calculate the following for each year:
   a. return on assets
   b. return on common shareholders' equity
   c. earnings per share
   d. dividend yield
   e. price-earnings ratio
2. Explain the direction of the dividend yield and price-earnings ratio in light of Harley-Davidson's profitability trend.
3. Based on these data, evaluate Harley-Davidson's strategy to expand to international markets.

SA 17-5
Comprehensive profitability and solvency analysis

Canadian National Railway Company (CNR) and Canadian Pacific Railway Limited (CPR) are the two major rail companies in Canada. They cross the continent east to west and north to south; serve ports on the Atlantic, Pacific, and Gulf coasts; and link customers to all three NAFTA nations. For a recent year, abstracted income statement information for the two companies is as follows:

	CPR (in millions)	CNR (in millions)
Operating profit before other expenses and interest	$ 967	$3,296
Other income (expense)	(18)	401
Interest expense	(252)	(341)
Income before income taxes	697	3,356
Income taxes expense	127	899
Net income	$ 570	$2,457

Balance sheet information and analysis is as follows (neither company has any preferred shares):

	CPR (in millions)	CNR (in millions)
Total liabilities	$ 9,461	$15,346
Total shareholders' equity	4,649	10,680
Total liabilities and shareholders' equity	$14,110	$26,026
Average total liabilities	$ 9,157	$14,634
Average total shareholders' equity	4,737	10,982
Average total assets	13,893	25,616

(continued)

1. Determine the following for both companies (round to one decimal place):
    a. return on assets
    b. return on common shareholders' equity
    c. times interest earned ratio
    d. debt ratio
2. Analyze and compare the two companies, using the information in (1).

SA 17-6

Notes to the financial statements

The financial statements for Leon's Furniture Limited are presented in Appendix B at the end of the text. Locate the notes to the financial statements that do the following:

1. describe the accounting policies
2. provide additional information about items in the statements
3. provide information about items not in the statements

APPENDICES

 Financial Statements Information for Morning Java (ASPE) and Morning Java International

 Leon's Furniture Limited, 2011 Financial Statements

 Shoppers Drug Mart Corporation, 2011 Financial Statements Information

 Financial Statements Analysis Ratios

E Interest Tables

APPENDIX A

Financial Statements Information for Morning Java (ASPE) and Morning Java International

Morning Java is planning to expand operations to various places around the world. Financing for this expansion will come from foreign banks. While financial statements prepared under ASPE may be appropriate for Canadian operations, financial statements prepared for foreign bankers should be prepared using international accounting standards.

The following pages illustrate the financial statements of Morning Java International using IFRS and the financial statements of Morning Java using ASPE. Note that both sets of statements exclude the Statement of Cash Flows. This illustration highlights reporting and terminology differences between IFRS and ASPE.

IFRS Financial Statements

The following Morning Java International financial statements are simplified and illustrate only those portions of IFRS that are appropriate for introductory accounting. Throughout the illustration, call-outs and end notes to each statement are used to highlight the differences between financial statements prepared under IFRS and under ASPE.

Morning Java International
Statement of Comprehensive Income
For the Year Ended December 31, 2015

Sales (net)*	$5,402,100
Cost of goods sold	(2,160,000)
Gross profit	3,242,100
Selling expenses	(1,654,700)
Administrative expenses	(954,000)
Loss on disposal of property, plant, and equipment	(23,000)
Other income (expenses)	23,000
Share in profit (loss) of associates*	57,000
Operating profit	690,400
Finance costs*	(136,000)
Profit before income taxes	554,400
Income taxes expense*	(132,800)
Profit for the year*	421,600
Other comprehensive income	
Gain on revaluation of properties, net of tax*	44,800
Total comprehensive income for the year, net of tax*	$ 466,400
Earnings per share basic* ($421,600 − $30,000)/[(40,500 × 11/12) + (45,000 × 1/12)]	$ 9.58

*A required disclosure on the face of the statement of comprehensive income

Title includes the word "Comprehensive."

This is a common term for an equity method investment.

The term "Finance costs" is used, rather than "Interest expense."

The term "Profit for the year" is used, rather than "Net income."

Expenses are organi by their function. See Note 2.

Diversity is allow with regard to subtotal definitio

Other comprehensiv income is repor only under IFR

Earnings per sh is not require under ASPE.

IFRS allows latitu on how statemen are organized, but does list minimum disclosu requirements. Se Note 1.

1. IFRS statements are often more summarized than ASPE statements. To compensate, IFRS require specific disclosures on the face of the financial statements (denoted*) and additional disclosures in the footnotes to the financial statements.

2. Expenses in an IFRS income statement are classified by either their nature or function. The nature of an expense is how the expense would naturally be recorded in a journal entry. Examples include salaries, depreciation, advertising, and utilities. The function of an expense identifies the purpose of the expense, such as a selling expense or an administrative expense. IFRS does not permit the natural and functional classifications to be mixed together on the same statement. That is, all expenses must be classified by either nature or function. However, if a functional classification of expenses is used, a footnote to the income statement must show the natural classification of expenses. Because Morning Java International uses the

	Morning Java International		
	Statement of Financial Position		
	December 31, 2015		
Assets			
Current assets:			
Cash and cash equivalents*		$235,000	
Financial assets at fair value through profit or loss*		465,000	
Accounts receivable, net		292,700	
Inventory		120,000	
Prepaid insurance		24,000	
Total current assets			$1,136,700
Non-current assets:			
Property, plant, and equipment:			
Land and buildings at fair value	$4,500,000		
Less accumulated depreciation	375,200	4,124,800	
Office equipment at cost	350,000		
Less accumulated depreciation	102,000	248,000	
Patents at amortized cost*		140,000	
Investment in *AM Coffee* (equity method)*		565,000	
Total non-current assets			5,077,800
Total assets*			$6,214,500
Liabilities and Shareholders' Equity			
Current liabilities:			
Accounts payable*		$133,000	
Employee provisions		58,400	
Loans*		200,000	
Interest payable		40,000	
Total current liabilities			$ 431,400
Non-current liabilities:			
Bonds payable, 8%, due December 31, 2035 (net of discount)			484,000
Notes payable			1,400,000
Total non-current liabilities			1,884,000
Total liabilities			2,315,400
Shareholders' equity			
$5 preferred (6,000 shares authorized, issued, and outstanding)*			350,000
Common shares (50,000 shares authorized,			
45,000 shares issued)*			2,350,000
Accumulated other comprehensive income.			44,800
Retained earnings*			1,154,300
Total shareholders' equity			3,899,100
Total liabilities and equity			$6,214,500

Side annotations:

- Preferred title for the "Balance Sheet." → (points to Statement of Financial Position title)
- IFRS terminology for "trading investments." Same accounting treatment as ASPE. → (points to Financial assets at fair value through profit or loss)
- Some PP&E may be valued at fair value. See Note 3. → (points to Land and buildings at fair value)
- Employee provisions are wages, salaries, and payroll taxes payable. See Note 4. → (points to Employee provisions)

Morning Java International
Statement of Changes in Equity
For the Year Ended December 31, 2015

	Preferred Shares	Common Shares	Accum. Other Comp. Income	Retained Earnings	Total
Balance, January 1, 2015	$350,000	$2,075,000	$ 0	$806,700	$3,231,700
Net income.				421,600	421,600
Unrealized gain on revaluation of land and building.			44,800		44,800
Dividends on preferred shares				(30,000)	(30,000)
Dividends on common shares				(44,000)	(44,000)
Issuance of additional common shares.		275,000			275,000
Balance, December 31, 2015	$350,000	$2,350,000	$44,800	$1,154,300	$3,899,100

    functional classification of expenses in its income statement, it must also show the natural classification of expenses in a footnote.

3. Under IFRS, property, plant, and equipment (PP&E) may be measured at historical cost or fair value. If fair value is used, the revaluation must be for similar classifications of PP&E, but need not be for all PP&E. This departs from ASPE, which requires PP&E to be measured at historical cost. Morning Java International restated its Land and Buildings, shown together, to fair value since the café sites have readily available real estate market prices. The office equipment remains at historical cost since it does not have a readily available market price. The increase in fair value is recorded by reducing accumulated depreciation and recognizing the gain as other comprehensive income. This increase, $44,800, is the only difference between Morning Java's ASPE net income, and Morning Java's IFRS comprehensive income.

4. The term "provision" is used to denote a liability under IFRS.

ASPE Financial Statements

A "Cost of goods sold" line indicates this is a merchandising business.

ASPE requires an inventory expense line, which may be called "Cost of goods sold"; IFRS does not.

"Gross profit" subtotal is not required by ASPE or IFRS.

IFRS includes the word "Comprehensive" in the statement title.

This is a multiple-step presentation.

The term "Profit for the year" may be used in IFRS.

Morning Java
Income Statement
For the Year Ended December 31, 2015

Revenue from sales:			
Sales			$5,450,000
Less: Sales returns and allowances	$ 26,500		
Sales discounts	21,400	47,900	
Net sales			$5,402,100
Cost of goods sold			2,160,000
Gross profit			3,242,100
Operating expenses:			
Selling expenses:			
Wages expense	825,000		
Advertising expense	678,900		
Depreciation expense—buildings	124,300		
Miscellaneous selling expense	26,500		
Total selling expenses		1,654,700	
Administrative expenses:			
Office salaries expense	325,000		
Rent expense	425,600		
Source deductions expense	110,000		
Depreciation expense—office equipment	68,900		
Bad debt expense	14,000		
Amortization expense—intangibles	10,500		
Total administrative expenses		954,000	
Total operating expenses			2,608,700
Income from operations			633,400
Other income and expense:			
Interest revenue		18,000	
Interest expense		(136,000)	
Loss on disposal of property, plant, and equipment		(23,000)	
Unrealized gain on trading investments		5,000	
Investment revenue		57,000	(79,000)
Income before income taxes			554,400
Income tax expense			132,800
Net income			$ 421,600

Title of statement may be "Statement of Financial Position" under IFRS.

"Allowance for doubtful accounts" line is not required by ASPE or IFRS. It is often included because it provides additional information to users.

Inventory requires a note to describe the method of determining cost. IFRS also requires the method of valuation, whether write-down has occurred, and whether inventory is pledged as security.

Under ASPE, cc is used to valu property, plant, a equipment. Und IFRS, a compar may choose to report some or a its PPE at fair val

This is a report form of the balan sheet using a classified method presentation.

Morning Java
Balance sheet
December 31, 2015

Assets

Current assets:		
Cash and cash equivalents.....................................		$ 235,000
Trading investments (at fair value).............................		465,000
Accounts receivable	$ 305,000	
Less allowance for doubtful accounts....................	12,300	292,700
Inventory		120,000
Prepaid insurance		24,000
Total current assets		$1,136,700
Investments:		
Investment in *AM Coffee* (equity method)		565,000
Property, plant, and equipment:		
Buildings...	2,650,000	
Less accumulated depreciation..............................	420,000	2,230,000
Office equipment	350,000	
Less accumulated depreciation..............................	102,000	248,000
Land	1,850,000	
Total property, plant, and equipment		4,328,000
Intangible assets:		
Patents...	160,000	
Less accumulated amortization..............................	20,000	140,000
Total assets		$6,169,700

Liabilities

Current liabilities:		
Accounts payable..		$ 133,000
Notes payable (current portion)................................		200,000
Salaries and wages payable		42,000
Source deductions payable		16,400
Interest payable..		40,000
Total current liabilities		$ 431,400
Long-term liabilities:		
Bonds payable, 8%, due December 31, 2035	500,000	
Less unamortized discount.....................................	16,000	484,000
Notes payable		1,400,000
Total long-term liabilities......................................		1,884,000
Total liabilities..		2,315,400

Shareholders' Equity

Contributed capital:		
$5 preferred shares (6,000 shares authorized, issued, and outstanding)		350,000
Common shares (50,000 shares authorized, 45,000 shares issued and outstanding)		2,350,000
Total contributed capital		2,700,000
Retained earnings..		1,154,300
Total shareholders' equity..		3,854,300
Total liabilities and shareholders' equity		$6,169,700

This statement replaces the "Statement of Changes in Equity" presented under IFRS.

Morning Java
Statement of Retained Earnings
For the Year Ended December 31, 2015

Retained earnings, January 1, 2015			$ 806,700
Net income.		$421,600	
Less dividends:			
Preferred.	$30,000		
Common.	44,000	74,000	
Increase in retained earnings			347,600
Retained earnings, December 31, 2015			$1,154,300

A complete set of financial statements would also include a Statement of Cash Flows.

Leon's Furniture Limited, 2011 Financial Statements

MANAGEMENT'S DISCUSSION & ANALYSIS

Financial Review

The following Management's Discussion and Analysis ("MD&A") is prepared as at February 23, 2012 and is based on the consolidated financial position and operating results of Leon's Furniture Limited/Meubles Leon Ltée (the "Company") as of December 31, 2011, and for the year ended December 31, 2011. It should be read in conjunction with the fiscal year 2011 consolidated financial statements and the notes thereto. For additional details and information relating to the Company, readers are referred to the fiscal 2011 quarterly financial statements and corresponding MD&As, which are published separately and available at www.sedar.com.

Cautionary Statement Regarding Forward-Looking Statements

This MD&A is intended to provide readers with the information that management believes is required to gain an understanding of Leon's Furniture Limited's current results and to assess the Company's future prospects. This MD&A, and in particular the section under the heading "Outlook", includes forward-looking statements, which are based on certain assumptions and reflect Leon's Furniture Limited's current plans and expectations. These forward-looking statements are subject to a number of risks and uncertainties that could cause actual results and future prospects to differ materially from current expectations. Some of the factors that can cause actual results to differ materially from current expectations are: a continuing slowdown in the Canadian economy; a further drop in consumer confidence; and dependency on product from third-party suppliers. Given these risks and uncertainties, investors should not place undue reliance on forward-looking statements as a prediction of actual results. Readers of this report are cautioned that actual events and results may vary.

Financial Statements Governance Practice

The consolidated financial statements of the Company have been prepared in accordance with International Financial Reporting Standards ("IFRS") as issued by the International Accounting Standards Board ("IASB"). These consolidated financial statements represent the first annual financial statements of the Company prepared in accordance with IFRS. The Company adopted IFRS in accordance with International Financial Reporting Standards 1, *First time Adoption of International Financial Reporting Standards* ("IFRS 1"). Further details, including the effects of the transition from the previous Canadian generally accepted accounting principles ("Canadian GAAP") to IFRS, are explained in Note 22 to these accompanying consolidated financial statements. Certain comparative figures have been reclassified to conform to the basis of presentation adopted in fiscal 2010.

Leon's Furniture Limited 2010 financial results included in this MD&A have been restated to be in accordance with IFRS.

The Audit Committee of the Board of Directors of the Company reviewed the MD&A and the consolidated financial statements, and recommended that the Board of Directors approve them. Following review by the full Board, the consolidated financial statements and MD&A were approved on February 23, 2012.

Introduction

Leon's Furniture Limited has been in the furniture retail business for over 100 years. The Company's 43 corporate and 32 franchise stores can be found in every province across Canada except British Columbia. Main product lines sold at retail include furniture, appliances and electronics.

14

LEON'S FURNITURE LIMITED
Management's Discussion & Analysis

Revenues and Expenses

For the year ended December 31, 2011, total Leon's sales were $879,561,000 including $196,725,000 of franchise sales ($907,497,000 including $197,062,000 of franchise sales in 2010), a decrease of 3.1%.

The decrease in sales for the year compared to the prior year reflected a continuation of waning consumer confidence and a decrease in housing starts. These factors also resulted in downward pressure on retail pricing. In particular electronics have experienced declines in same product pricing for the past four years. Overall same store sales decreased by 6.4% (see section on "Non-IFRS Financial Measures").

Leon's franchise sales for 2011 were flat compared to 2010. Overall store for store franchise sales decreased by 1.8%. The sales difference in 2011 was the result of the successful opening of two new franchise stores in Bathurst, New Brunswick and Drummondville, Quebec.

Our gross margin for the year 2011 of 42.3% was up approximately 0.3% from the prior year 2010. The increase in gross margin was mainly attributable to the conscientious effort to reduce damaged and discounted product sales and a reduction in our sales finance expenses, which are deducted from sales.

For the year, net operating expenses of $213,395,000 were up $1,159,000, or 0.55% as compared to 2010. General and administrative expenses decreased $2,646,000 from the prior year. The decrease was mainly the result of lower depreciation cost on buildings. Under IFRS, buildings are now being depreciated over a useful life of 30 years, which resulted in a depreciation expense reduction of approximately $2,600,000 compared to the prior year. Sales and marketing expenses were basically flat with the prior year. We did see lower sales commission costs as a result of decreased sales for the year. This cost reduction was offset by the increase of advertising expenses of $1,400,000 or 4.5% from the prior year. Additional marketing dollars were spent during the year to increase consumer traffic into our stores and to promote the opening of four new corporate stores in 2011 being Guelph, Ontario; Mississauga, Ontario; Rosemère, Quebec; and Regina, Saskatchewan. These new stores plus some significant increases in existing store property assessments led to higher property and business taxes in 2011. As a result, we saw occupancy expenses increase by $3,180,000 or 10.8% as compared to 2010.

As a result of the above, net income for the year ended 2011 was $56,666,000, $0.81 per common share ($63,284,000, $0.90 per common share in 2010), a decrease of 10% per common share.

For the three months ended December 31, 2011, total Leon's sales were $254,989,000 including $61,166,000 of franchise sales ($257,708,000 including $59,820,000 of franchise sales in 2010), a decrease of 1.1%.

Leon's corporate sales of $193,823,000 in the fourth quarter of 2011, decreased by $4,065,000, or 2.1%, compared to the fourth quarter of 2010. Same store corporate sales decreased by 7.4% compared to the prior year's quarter.

Leon's franchise sales of $61,166,000 in the fourth quarter of 2011 increased by $1,346,000, or 2.25% compared to 2010. The sales increase is mainly attributable to the two new franchise stores opened during 2011.

Net income for the fourth quarter of 2011 was $19,872,000, $0.28 per common share ($21,360,000, $0.30 per common share in 2010), a decrease of 6.7% per common share.

Annual Financial Information

($ in thousands, except earnings per share and dividends)	**2011**	2010	2009
Net corporate sales	$ **682,836**	$ 710,435	$ 703,180
Leon franchise sales	**196,725**	197,062	194,290
Total Leon's sales	$ **879,561**	$ 907,497	$ 897,470
Net income	**56,666**	63,284	56,864
Earnings per share			
Basic	$ **0.81**	$ 0.90	$ 0.80
Diluted	$ **0.78**	$ 0.87	$ 0.78
Total assets	$ **595,339**	$ 566,674	$ 529,156
Common share dividends declared	$ **0.37**	$ 0.32	$ 0.28
Special common share dividends declared	$ **0.15**	$ –	$ 0.20
Convertible, non-voting shares dividends declared	$ **0.20**	$ 0.18	$ 0.14

The year ended 2010 has been restated to IFRS while the year ended 2009 is as originally reported under Canadian GAAP. Furthermore, the year ended 2010 figures have been revised, from previously reported IFRS amounts, to reflect an immaterial adjustment to the amount of foreign exchange that is required to be recorded within comprehensive income as it relates to the Company's foreign denominated non-monetary available-for-sale financial assets. Any foreign denominated monetary available-for-sale financial assets were appropriately recorded in the consolidated income statement.

Liquidity and Financial Resources

($ in thousands, except dividends per share)	**Dec 31, 2011**	Dec 31, 2010	Dec 31, 2009
Cash, cash equivalents, available-for-sale financial assets	$ **221,823**	$ 211,813	$ 170,726
Trade and other accounts receivable	**28,937**	28,569	31,501
Inventory	**87,830**	85,423	83,957
Total assets	**595,339**	566,674	529,156
Working capital	**204,649**	200,826	164,759

For the 3 Months Ended	**Current Quarter Dec 31, 2011**	Prior Quarter Sept 30, 2011	Prior Quarter June 30, 2011
Cash flow provided by operations	$ **26,230**	$ 26,857	$ 12,770
Purchase of property, plant and equipment	**6,336**	9,386	6,401
Repurchase of capital stock	**219**	1,615	3,785
Dividends paid	**6,292**	6,305	6,317
Dividends paid per share	$ **0.09**	$ 0.09	$ 0.09

In the third quarter of 2011, the Company celebrated a grand opening of a new corporate store in Guelph, Ontario. That was followed by grand openings in the fourth quarter of 2011 of three additional corporate stores in Mississauga, Ontario; Rosemère, Quebec; and Regina, Saskatchewan. As well, during the fourth quarter of 2011, new Leon's franchise locations had grand openings in Bathurst, New Brunswick; and Drummondville, Quebec, our first franchise located in Quebec.

In addition to these new locations, the Company and our existing franchisees continue to replace, renovate and expand existing stores in order to serve our customers better. Renovations are well underway in our Sudbury and Sault Ste. Marie, Ontario corporate stores. Our Trenton, Ontario franchise recently completed a renovation of their store and a renovation and expansion will commence shortly at our Simcoe, Ontario franchise. Our Kentville franchise has recently completed construction of a new and larger replacement store in Coldbrook, Nova Scotia. Finally, construction has started for a brand new franchise store to replace our existing St. John, New Brunswick store.

16
LEON'S FURNITURE LIMITED
Management's Discussion & Analysis

The Company continues to explore new opportunities across Canada. The Company has recently secured sites for four new corporate stores in: Orangeville and Brantford, Ontario; Sherbrooke, Quebec; and Rocky View County, which is just north of Calgary, Alberta. Our current plan is to open these locations during 2012 and 2013. All funding for new store projects and renovations is planned to come from our existing cash resources.

Common Shares

At December 31, 2011, there were 69,815,734 common shares issued and outstanding. During 2011, 484,727 shares were repurchased at an average cost of $13.07 and then cancelled by the Company through its Normal Course Issuer Bid. In addition, during the year ended December 31, 2011, 145,583 convertible, non-voting series 2002 shares and 79,545 convertible, non-voting series 2005 shares were converted into common shares. There were 53,017 convertible, non-voting series 2009 shares cancelled. For details on the Company's commitments related to its redeemable shares, please refer to Note 13 to the accompanying consolidated financial statements.

Commitments

($ in thousands)   Payments Due by Period

CONTRACTUAL OBLIGATIONS		Total		Less than 1 Year		2-3 Years		4-5 Years		After 5 Years
Operating Leases[1]	$	44,131	$	5,860	$	10,329	$	9,660	$	18,282
Purchase Obligations		4,407		4,407		–		–		–
Total Contractual Obligations	$	48,538	$	10,267	$	10,329	$	9,660	$	18,282

(1) The Company is obligated under operating leases to future minimum rental payments for various land and building sites across Canada.

Recent Accounting Pronouncements

Please refer to Note 3 to the accompanying consolidated financial statements for the accounting standards and amendments issued but not yet adopted.

Impact of New Accounting Policies – Adoption of IFRS

Leon's Furniture Limited was required to prepare financial statements in accordance with IFRS starting with the unaudited interim condensed consolidated financial statements for the quarter ended March 31, 2011. These statements required the 2010 results to be presented in accordance with IFRS.

Further details, including the effects of the transition from the previous Canadian GAAP to IFRS, are explained in Note 22 to the accompanying consolidated financial statements.

Critical Accounting Estimates

Please refer to Note 4 to the accompanying consolidated financial statements for the Company's critical accounting estimates and assumptions.

Related Party Transactions

Please refer to Note 21 to the accompanying consolidated financial statements for the Company's related party transactions.

Risks and Uncertainties

For a complete discussion of the risks and uncertainties that apply to the Company's business and operating results, please refer to the Company's Annual Information Form dated March 31, 2011 available on www.sedar.com.

Quarterly Results (2011, 2010)

Quarterly Income Statement

($ in thousands, except per share data)	Quarter Ended December 31		Quarter Ended September 30		Quarter Ended June 30		Quarter Ended March 31	
	2011	2010	**2011**	2010	**2011**	2010	**2011**	2010
Leon's corporate sales	**$ 193,823**	$ 197,888	**$ 174,373**	$ 182,125	**$ 163,857**	$ 168,952	**$ 150,783**	$ 161,470
Leon's franchise sales	**61,166**	59,820	**49,273**	49,421	**45,477**	45,493	**40,809**	42,328
Total Leon's sales	**254,989**	257,708	**223,646**	231,546	**209,334**	214,445	**191,592**	203,798
Net income per share	**$ 0.28**	$ 0.30	**$ 0.22**	$ 0.26	**$ 0.16**	$ 0.17	**$ 0.15**	$ 0.17
Fully diluted per share	**$ 0.27**	$ 0.29	**$ 0.21**	$ 0.25	**$ 0.15**	$ 0.16	**$ 0.14**	$ 0.16

Net income per share and fully diluted per share amounts presented in the above table, with the exception of the fourth quarter ended December 31, 2011, have been revised from previously reported IRFS reports to reflect an immaterial adjustment to the amount of foreign exchange that is required to be recorded within comprehensive income as it relates to the Company's foreign denominated non-monetary available-for-sale financial assets. Any foreign denominated monetary available-for-sale financial assets were appropriately recorded in the consolidated income statement.

The following table provides selected 2010 results by quarter.

IFRS 2010 Results by Quarter

($ in thousands, except per share data)	First Quarter	Second Quarter	Third Quarter	Fourth Quarter	Full Year 2010
Revenue	$ 161,470	$ 168,952	$ 182,125	$ 197,888	$ 710,435
Cost of sales	93,498	100,187	106,564	112,130	412,379
Gross profit	67,972	68,765	75,561	85,758	298,056
Operating expenses					
General and administrative expenses	23,293	25,432	24,484	25,475	98,684
Sales and marketing expenses	18,572	18,008	19,297	22,344	78,221
Occupancy expenses	7,630	7,490	7,214	7,217	29,551
Other operating expenses	1,558	1,281	1,464	1,477	5,780
	51,053	52,211	52,459	56,513	212,236
Operating profit	16,919	16,554	23,102	29,245	85,820
Gain on sale of capital property	–	–	1,231	–	1,231
Finance income	691	663	789	991	3,134
Profit before income tax	17,610	17,217	25,122	30,236	90,185
Income tax expense	5,640	5,344	7,041	8,876	26,901
Profit for the period attributable to the shareholders of the Company	$ 11,970	$ 11,873	$ 18,081	$ 23,360	$ 63,284
Earnings per share					
Basic	$ 0.17	$ 0.17	$ 0.26	$ 0.30	$ 0.90
Diluted	$ 0.16	$ 0.16	$ 0.25	$ 0.29	$ 0.87

The Full Year 2010 and Quarters ended March 31, 2010, June 30, 2010, September 30, 2010 and December 31, 2010 figures above have been revised, from previously reported IFRS amounts, to reflect an immaterial adjustment to the amount of foreign exchange that is required to be recorded within comprehensive income as it relates to the Company's foreign denominated non-monetary available-for-sale financial assets. Any foreign denominated monetary available-for-sale financial assets were appropriately recorded in the consolidated income statement.

18

LEON'S FURNITURE LIMITED
Management's Discussion & Analysis

Disclosure Controls and Procedures

Management is responsible for establishing and maintaining a system of disclosure controls and procedures to provide reasonable assurance that all material information relating to the Company is gathered and reported on a timely basis to senior management, including the Chief Executive Officer and Chief Financial Officer so that appropriate decisions can be made by them regarding public disclosure. Based on the evaluation of disclosure controls and procedures, the CEO and CFO have concluded that the Company's disclosure controls and procedures were effective as at December 31, 2011.

Internal Controls Over Financial Reporting

Management is also responsible for establishing and maintaining adequate internal control over financial reporting to provide reasonable assurance regarding the reliability of financial reporting and the preparation of consolidated financial statements for external purposes in accordance with IFRS. The Company's internal control over financial reporting may not prevent or detect all misstatements because of inherent limitations. The Company assessed the effectiveness of its internal control over financial reporting as of December 31, 2011, based on the framework established in the publications, Internal Control – Integrated Framework and specifically in Internal Control over Financial Reporting – Guidance for Smaller Public Companies published by the Committee of Sponsoring Organizations of the Treadway Commission. Based on this assessment, the CEO and the CFO concluded that the Company maintained effective internal control over financial reporting as of December 31, 2011.

Changes in Internal Control Over Financial Reporting

Management has also evaluated whether there were changes in the Company's internal control over financial reporting that occurred during the period beginning on October 1, 2011 and ended on December 31, 2011 that have materially affected, or are reasonably likely to materially affect, the Company's internal control over financial reporting. The Company has determined that no material changes in internal controls have occurred during this period.

Outlook

We have been experiencing a slowdown in our economy, which began in 2009, and we don't see any signs of any major improvement moving into 2012. As such, we anticipate that consumer discretionary spending will remain soft in 2012. To help counter this, we plan an even more robust marketing and merchandising campaign for 2012. The recent opening of four new stores in the latter part of 2011 should also aid our sales in 2012. Even with these measures in place, growing profits in 2012 will be challenging. Despite this, our strong financial position coupled with our experience in adjusting to changing market conditions, provide us with the confidence to adapt to the prevailing economic conditions.

Non-IFRS Financial Measures

In order to provide additional insight into the business, the Company has provided the measure of same store sales, in the revenue and expenses section above. This measure does not have a standardized meaning prescribed by IFRS but it is a key indicator used by the Company to measure performance against prior period results. Comparable store sales are defined as sales generated by stores that have been open or closed for more than 12 months on a yearly basis. The reconciliation between total corporate sales (an IFRS measure) and comparable store sales is provided below:

($ in thousands)	2011	2010
Net corporate sales	$ 682,836	$ 710,435
Adjustments for stores not in both fiscal periods	(20,555)	(2,516)
Comparable store sales	$ 662,281	$ 707,919

MANAGEMENT'S RESPONSIBILITY FOR FINANCIAL REPORTING

The accompanying consolidated financial statements are the responsibility of management and have been approved by the Board of Directors.

The accompanying consolidated financial statements have been prepared by management in accordance with International Financial Reporting Standards ("IFRS") and incorporate the requirements of IFRS 1, *First time adoption of IFRS*. Financial statements are not precise since they include certain amounts based upon estimates and judgments. When alternative methods exist, management has chosen those it deems to be the most appropriate in the circumstances.

Leon's Furniture Limited/Meubles Leon Ltee ("Leon's" or the "Company") maintains systems of internal accounting and administrative controls, consistent with reasonable costs. Such systems are designed to provide reasonable assurance that the financial information is relevant and reliable and that Leon's assets are appropriately accounted for and adequately safeguarded.

The Board of Directors is responsible for ensuring that management fulfils its responsibilities for financial reporting and is ultimately responsible for reviewing and approving the financial statements. The Board carries out this responsibility through its Audit Committee.

The Audit Committee is appointed by the Board and reviews these consolidated financial statements; considers the report of the external auditors; assesses the adequacy of the internal controls of the Company; examines the fees and expenses for audit services; and recommends to the Board the independent auditors for appointment by the shareholders. The Committee reports its findings to the Board of Directors for consideration when approving these consolidated financial statements for issuance to the shareholders.

These consolidated financial statements have been audited by Ernst & Young, the external auditors, in accordance with Canadian generally accepted auditing standards on behalf of the shareholders. Ernst & Young has full and free access to the Audit Committee.

Terrence T. Leon
President and CEO

Dominic Scarangella
Vice President and CFO

20

LEON'S FURNITURE LIMITED

INDEPENDENT AUDITORS' REPORT

To the Shareholders of

Leon's Furniture Limited/Meubles Leon Ltée

We have audited the accompanying consolidated financial statements of Leon's Furniture Limited/Meubles Leon Ltée, which comprise the consolidated statements of financial position as at December 31, 2011 and 2010, and January 1, 2010, and the consolidated income statements, comprehensive income, changes in equity and cash flows for the years ended December 31, 2011 and 2010, and a summary of significant accounting policies and other explanatory information.

Management's Responsibility for the Consolidated Financial Statements

Management is responsible for the preparation and fair presentation of these consolidated financial statements in accordance with International Financial Reporting Standards, and for such internal control as management determines is necessary to enable the preparation of consolidated financial statements that are free from material misstatement, whether due to fraud or error.

Auditors' Responsibility

Our responsibility is to express an opinion on these consolidated financial statements based on our audits. We conducted our audits in accordance with Canadian generally accepted auditing standards. Those standards require that we comply with ethical requirements and plan and perform the audit to obtain reasonable assurance about whether the consolidated financial statements are free from material misstatement.

An audit involves performing procedures to obtain audit evidence about the amounts and disclosures in the consolidated financial statements. The procedures selected depend on the auditors' judgment, including the assessment of the risks of material misstatement of the consolidated financial statements, whether due to fraud or error. In making those risk assessments, the auditors consider internal control relevant to the entity's preparation and fair presentation of the consolidated financial statements in order to design audit procedures that are appropriate in the circumstances, but not for the purpose of expressing an opinion on the effectiveness of the entity's internal control. An audit also includes evaluating the appropriateness of accounting policies used and the reasonableness of accounting estimates made by management, as well as evaluating the overall presentation of the consolidated financial statements.

We believe that the audit evidence we have obtained in our audits is sufficient and appropriate to provide a basis for our audit opinion.

Opinion

In our opinion, the consolidated financial statements present fairly, in all material respects, the financial position of Leon's Furniture Limited/Meubles Leon Ltée as at December 31, 2011 and 2010, and January 1, 2010, and its financial performance and its cash flows for the years ended December 31, 2011 and 2010 in accordance with International Financial Reporting Standards.

Ernst & Young LLP

Chartered Accountants
Licensed Public Accountants

Toronto, Canada
February 23, 2012

CONSOLIDATED STATEMENTS OF FINANCIAL POSITION

Leon's Furniture Limited / Meubles Leon Ltée Incorporated under the laws of Ontario	As at **December 31**	As at December 31	As at January 1
($ in thousands)	**2011**	2010	2010
		(Note 22)	(Note 22)
Assets			
Current			
Cash and cash equivalents (Notes 5 and 7)	$ **72,505**	$ 71,589	$ 58,301
Available-for-sale financial assets (Notes 5 and 19(e))	**149,318**	140,224	112,425
Trade receivables (Note 5)	**28,937**	28,569	31,501
Income taxes receivable	**5,182**	–	–
Inventories	**87,830**	85,423	83,957
Total current assets	$ **343,772**	$ 325,805	$ 286,184
Other assets	**1,431**	1,574	1,560
Property, plant and equipment, net (Note 8)	**214,158**	201,492	203,653
Investment properties (Note 9)	**8,366**	8,417	8,545
Intangible assets, net (Note 10)	**3,958**	4,902	5,334
Goodwill (Note 10)	**11,282**	11,282	11,282
Deferred income tax assets (Note 17)	**12,372**	13,202	12,598
Total assets	$ **595,339**	$ 566,674	$ 529,156
Liabilities and Shareholders' Equity			
Current			
Trade and other payables (Notes 5 and 11)	$ **75,126**	$ 71,724	$ 72,603
Provisions (Note 12)	**11,231**	12,341	11,277
Income taxes payable	**–**	524	1,958
Customers' deposits	**19,157**	17,198	15,632
Dividends payable (Note 14)	**17,457**	6,310	4,938
Deferred warranty plan revenue	**16,152**	16,882	16,150
Total current liabilities	$ **139,123**	$ 124,979	$ 122,558
Deferred warranty plan revenue	**19,445**	21,392	22,248
Redeemable share liability (Notes 5 and 13)	**382**	172	383
Deferred income tax liabilities (Note 17)	**10,928**	9,845	8,829
Total liabilities	$ **169,878**	$ 156,388	$ 154,018
Shareholders' equity attributable to the shareholders of the Company			
Common shares (Note 14)	$ **20,918**	$ 19,177	$ 17,704
Retained earnings	**404,647**	390,629	357,576
Accumulated other comprehensive income (loss)	**(104)**	480	(142)
Total shareholders' equity	$ **425,461**	$ 410,286	$ 375,138
	$ **595,339**	$ 566,674	$ 529,156

Commitments and contingencies (Note 19)

The accompanying notes are an integral part of these consolidated financial statements.

On behalf of the Board:

Mark Leon
Director

Peter Eby
Director

22
LEON'S FURNITURE LIMITED
Consolidated Financial Statements

CONSOLIDATED INCOME STATEMENTS

Years ended December 31 ($ in thousands, except shares outstanding and earnings per share)	2011	2010
Revenue (Notes 15 and 22)	$ 682,836	$ 710,435
Cost of sales	394,099	412,379
Gross profit	$ 288,737	$ 298,056
Operating expenses (Notes 16 and 22)		
General and administrative expenses	96,038	98,684
Sales and marketing expenses	78,387	78,221
Occupancy expenses	32,731	29,551
Other operating expenses	6,260	5,785
	$ 213,416	$ 212,241
Operating profit	75,321	85,815
Gain on sale of capital property	21	1,236
Finance income	3,506	3,134
Profit before income tax	78,848	90,185
Income tax expense (Note 17)	22,182	26,901
Profit for the year attributable to the shareholders of the Company	$ 56,666	$ 63,284
Weighted average number of common shares outstanding		
Basic	69,969,417	70,371,744
Diluted	72,305,424	73,133,906
Earnings per share		
Basic	$ 0.81	$ 0.90
Diluted	$ 0.78	$ 0.87
Dividends declared per share		
Common	$ 0.52	$ 0.32
Convertible, non-voting	$ 0.20	$ 0.18

The accompanying notes are an integral part of these consolidated financial statements.

CONSOLIDATED STATEMENTS OF COMPREHENSIVE INCOME

Year ended December 31 ($ in thousands)	2011	2011 Tax Effect	2011
Profit for the year	$ 56,666	$ –	$ 56,666
Other comprehensive loss, net of tax			
Unrealized (losses) on available-for-sale financial assets arising during the year	(621)	(87)	(534)
Reclassification adjustment for net gains and losses included in net income	(58)	(8)	(50)
Change in unrealized gains on available-for-sale financial assets arising during the year	(679)	(95)	(584)
Comprehensive income for the year	$ 55,987	$ (95)	$ 56,082

Year ended December 31 ($ in thousands)	2010	2010 Tax Effect	2010
Profit for the year	$ 63,284	$ –	$ 63,284
Other comprehensive income, net of tax			
Unrealized gains on available-for-sale financial assets arising during the year	917	144	773
Reclassification adjustment for net gains and losses included in net income	(178)	(27)	(151)
Change in unrealized gains on available-for-sale financial assets arising during the year	739	117	622
Comprehensive income for the year	$ 64,023	$ 117	$ 63,906

The accompanying notes are an integral part of these consolidated financial statements.

24

LEON'S FURNITURE LIMITED
Consolidated Financial Statements

CONSOLIDATED STATEMENTS OF CHANGES IN EQUITY

($ in thousands)	Common Shares	Accumulated Other Comprehensive Income (Loss)	Retained Earnings	Total
At January 1, 2010	$ 17,704	$ (142)	$ 357,576	$ 375,138
Comprehensive income				
Profit for the period	–	–	63,284	63,284
Change in unrealized gains on available-for-sale financial assets arising during the period	–	622	–	622
Total comprehensive income	–	622	63,284	63,906
Transactions with shareholders				
Dividends declared	–	–	(22,492)	(22,492)
Management share purchase plan (Note 13)	1,768	–	–	1,768
Repurchase of common shares (Note 14)	(295)	–	(7,739)	(8,034)
Total transactions with shareholders	1,473	–	(30,231)	(28,758)
At December 31, 2010	$ 19,177	$ 480	$ 390,629	$ 410,286
At January 1, 2011	$ 19,177	$ 480	$ 390,629	$ 410,286
Comprehensive income				
Profit for the period	–	–	56,666	56,666
Change in unrealized (losses) on available-for-sale financial assets arising during the period	–	(584)	–	(584)
Total comprehensive income	–	(584)	56,666	56,082
Transactions with shareholders				
Dividends declared	–	–	(36,371)	(36,371)
Management share purchase plan (Note 13)	1,798	–	–	1,798
Repurchase of common shares (Note 14)	(57)	–	(6,277)	(6,334)
Total transactions with shareholders	1,741	–	(42,648)	(40,907)
At December 31, 2011	$ 20,918	$ (104)	$ 404,647	$ 425,461

The accompanying notes are an integral part of these consolidated financial statements.

CONSOLIDATED STATEMENTS OF
CASH FLOWS

Years ended December 31 ($ in thousands)	**2011**	2010
Operating Activities		
Profit for the year	$ **56,666**	$ 63,284
Add (deduct) items not involving an outlay of cash		
Depreciation of property, plant and equipment and investment properties (Note 16)	**12,705**	15,354
Amortization of intangible assets (Note 16)	**880**	802
Amortization of deferred warranty plan revenue	**(17,271)**	(16,838)
Gain on sale of property, plant and equipment (Note 16)	**(21)**	(1,236)
Deferred income taxes	**2,008**	295
Gain (loss) on sale of available-for-sale financial assets	**35**	(337)
Cash received on warranty plan sales	**14,594**	16,714
	69,596	78,038
Net change in non-cash working capital balances related to operations (Note 20)	**(4,426)**	1,391
Cash provided by operating activities	**65,170**	79,429
Investing Activities		
Purchase of property, plant and equipment (Note 8)	**(24,999)**	(13,567)
Purchase of intangible assets (Note 10)	**64**	(370)
Proceeds on sale of property, plant and equipment (Note 8)	**39**	2,117
Purchase of available-for-sale financial assets	**(569,050)**	(524,414)
Proceeds on sale of available-for-sale financial assets	**559,242**	497,691
Decrease in employee share purchase loans (Note 13)	**2,008**	1,556
Cash used in investing activities	**(32,696)**	(36,987)
Financing Activities		
Dividends paid	**(25,224)**	(21,120)
Repurchase of common shares (Note 14)	**(6,334)**	(8,034)
Cash used in financing activities	**(31,558)**	(29,154)
Net increase in cash and cash equivalents during the year	**916**	13,288
Cash and cash equivalents, beginning of year	**71,589**	58,301
Cash and cash equivalents, end of year	$ **72,505**	$ 71,589

The accompanying notes are an integral part of these consolidated financial statements.

26
LEON'S FURNITURE LIMITED

NOTES TO THE CONSOLIDATED FINANCIAL STATEMENTS

For the years ended December 31, 2011 and 2010
(Tabular amounts in thousands of Canadian dollars except shares outstanding and earnings per share)

1. General Information

Leon's Furniture Limited/Meubles Leon Ltée was incorporated by Articles of Incorporation under the Business Corporations Act on February 28, 1969. Leon's Furniture Limited/Meubles Leon Ltée and its subsidiaries ("Leon's" or the "Company") is a public company with its common shares listed on the Toronto Stock Exchange and is incorporated and domiciled in Canada. The address of the Company's head and registered office is 45 Gordon Mackay Road, Toronto, Ontario, M9N 3X3.

Leon's is a retailer of home furnishings, electronics and appliances across Canada from Alberta to Newfoundland and Labrador. The Company owns a chain of forty-one retail stores operating as Leon's Home Furnishings Super Stores, two retail stores operating under the brand of Appliance Canada and operates an ecommerce internet site www.leons.ca. In addition, the Company has twenty-seven franchisees operating thirty-two Leon's Furniture franchise stores.

2. Basis of Preparation and Adoption of IFRS

The consolidated financial statements of the Company have been prepared in accordance with International Financial Reporting Standards ("IFRS") as issued by the International Accounting Standards Board ("IASB"). These consolidated financial statements represent the first annual financial statements of the Company prepared in accordance with IFRS. The Company adopted IFRS in accordance with International Financial Reporting Standards 1 First-time Adoption of International Financial Reporting Standards ("IFRS 1"). The first date at which IFRS was applied was January 1, 2010. Further details, including the effects of the transition from the previous Canadian generally accepted accounting principles ("Canadian GAAP") to IFRS, are explained in Note 22 to these consolidated financial statements. The accounting policies were consistently applied to all periods presented unless otherwise noted.

Use of Judgment and Estimates

Management has exercised judgment in the process of applying the Company's accounting policies. The preparation of consolidated financial statements in accordance with IFRS requires management to make estimates and assumptions that affect the reported amounts of assets and liabilities and disclosure of contingent assets and liabilities at the consolidated balance sheet date and the reported amounts of revenue and expenses during the reporting period. Key areas where management has made estimates include allowance for doubtful accounts, valuation of inventory, fair values and impairment of financial assets, investment properties, goodwill and intangible assets, income taxes, and useful lives of capital assets and intangible assets. Actual results could differ from those estimates.

These consolidated financial statements were approved by the Board of Directors for issuance on February 23, 2012.

3. Summary of Significant Accounting Policies

The significant accounting policies used in the preparation of these consolidated financial statements are as follows:

Basis of Measurement

The consolidated financial statements have been prepared under the historical cost convention, except for available-for-sale financial assets, which are measured at fair value.

Consolidation

The financial statements consolidate the accounts of the Company and its wholly owned subsidiaries, Murlee Holdings Limited, Leon Holdings (1967) Limited and Ablan Insurance Corporation. Subsidiaries are all those entities over which the Company has the power to govern the financial and operating policies generally accompanying a shareholding of more than one half of the voting rights. The existence and effect of potential voting rights that are currently exercisable or convertible are considered when assessing whether the Company controls another entity. Subsidiaries are fully consolidated from the date on which control is transferred to the Company and de-consolidated from the date that control ceases. Intercompany transactions, balances, income and expenses, and profits and losses are eliminated.

Segment Reporting

Operating segments are reported in a manner consistent with the internal reporting provided to the chief operating decision-maker. The chief operating decision-maker, who is responsible for allocating resources and assessing performance of the operating segments, has been identified as the President and Chief Executive Officer. The Company operates in one geographical segment (Canada) and one industry (sale of home furnishings, appliances and electronics). Accordingly, no segment information has been provided in these consolidated financial statements.

Foreign Currency Translation

Functional and Presentation Currency

Items included in the consolidated financial statements are measured using the currency of the primary economic environment in which the Company operates (the functional currency). These consolidated financial statements are presented in Canadian dollars, which is the Company's functional and presentation currency and is also the functional currency of each of the Company's subsidiaries.

Foreign Currency Transactions

Foreign currency transactions are translated into the respective functional currencies of the Company's subsidiaries using the exchange rate at the dates of transactions. Merchandise imported from the United States and South East Asia, paid for in U.S. dollars, is recorded at its equivalent Canadian dollar value upon receipt. U.S. dollar trade payables are translated at the year-end exchange rate. The Company is subject to gains and losses due to fluctuations in the U.S. dollar. Foreign exchange gains and losses resulting from translation of U.S. dollar accounts payable are included in the consolidated income statement within cost of sales.

Any foreign exchange gains and losses on monetary available-for-sale financial assets are recognized in the consolidated income statement, and other changes in the carrying amounts are recognized in other comprehensive income. For available-for-sale assets that are not monetary items, the gain or loss that is recognized in other comprehensive income includes any related foreign exchange component.

Financial Assets and Liabilities

A financial asset or liability is recognized if the Company becomes a party to the contractual provisions of the asset or liability. A financial asset or liability is recognized initially (at trade date) at its fair value plus, in the case of a financial asset or liability not at fair value through profit or loss, transaction costs that are directly attributable to the acquisition or issue of the instrument. Financial assets and liabilities carried at fair value through profit or loss are initially recognized at fair value and transaction costs are expensed in the consolidated income statement.

After initial recognition, financial assets are measured at their fair values except for loans and receivables, which are measured at amortized cost using the effective interest method. After initial recognition, financial liabilities are measured at amortized cost except for financial liabilities at fair value through profit or loss, which are measured at fair value.

The Company classifies its financial assets and liabilities according to their characteristics and management's choices and intentions related thereto for the purposes of ongoing measurement.

Classifications that the Company has used for financial assets include:

(a) **Available-for-sale** – financial assets that are non-derivatives that are either designated in this category or not classified in any other category and include marketable securities, which consist primarily of quoted bonds, equities and debentures. These assets are measured at fair value with changes in fair value recognized in other comprehensive income for the current period until realized through disposal or impairment; and

(b) **Loans and receivables** – are non-derivative financial assets with fixed or determinable payments that are not quoted in an active market. Loans and receivables include trade receivables and recorded at amortized cost with gains and losses recognized in the consolidated income statement in the period that the asset is no longer recognized or impaired.

28

LEON'S FURNITURE LIMITED
Notes to the Consolidated Financial Statements

Classification choice that the Company has used for financial liabilities includes:

Other financial liabilities – measured at amortized cost with gains and losses recognized in the consolidated income statement in the period that the liability is no longer recognized.

Financial assets are derecognized if the Company's contractual rights to the cash flows from the financial assets expire or if the Company transfers the financial asset to another party without retaining control or substantially all risks and rewards of the asset. Financial liabilities are derecognized if the Company's obligations specified in the contract expire or are discharged or cancelled.

Impairment of Financial Assets

The Company assesses at the end of each reporting period whether there is objective evidence that a financial asset or group of financial assets is impaired. A financial asset or group of financial assets is impaired and impairment losses are incurred only if there is objective evidence of impairment as a result of one or more events that occurred after the initial recognition of the asset (a loss event) and that loss event has an impact on the estimated future cash flows of the financial asset or group of financial assets that can be reliably estimated.

The amount of the loss is measured as the difference between the asset's carrying amount and the present value of estimated future cash flows discounted at the financial asset's original effective interest rate. The asset's carrying amount is reduced and the amount of the loss is recognized in the consolidated income statement.

If, in a subsequent period, the amount of the impairment loss decreases and the decrease can be related objectively to an event occurring after the impairment was recognized, the reversal of the previously recognized impairment is recognized in the consolidated income statement.

Cash and Cash Equivalents

Cash and cash equivalents include cash on hand, balances with banks and short-term market investments with a remaining term to maturity of less than 90 days from the date of purchase.

Trade Receivables

Trade receivables are amounts due for goods sold in the ordinary course of business. If collection is expected in one year or less, they are classified as current assets. If not, they are presented as non-current assets.

Trade receivables are initially recognized at fair value and subsequently measured at amortized cost using the effective interest method, less provision for impairment.

Inventories

Inventories are valued at the lower of cost, determined on a first-in, first-out basis, and net realizable value.

The Company receives vendor rebates on certain products based on the volume of purchases made during specified periods. The rebates are deducted from the inventory value of goods received and are recognized as a reduction of cost of sales upon sale of the goods. Incentives received for a direct reimbursement of costs incurred to sell the vendor's products such as marketing and advertising funds are recorded as a reduction of those related costs in the consolidated income statement, provided certain conditions are met.

Property, Plant and Equipment

Property, plant and equipment are initially recorded at cost. Historical cost includes expenditure that is directly attributable to the acquisition of items. Subsequent costs are included in the asset's carrying amount or recognized as a separate asset, as appropriate, only when it is probable that future economic benefits associated with the asset will flow to the Company and the cost can be measured reliably. When significant parts of property, plant and equipment are required to be replaced at intervals, the Company derecognizes the replaced part, and recognizes the new part with its own associated useful life and depreciation. Normal repair and maintenance expenditures are expensed as incurred.

Land and construction in progress are not depreciated. Depreciation on other assets is provided over the estimated useful lives of the assets using the following annual rates and methods:

Buildings	30 years straight-line
Equipment	20% to 30% declining balance
Vehicles	30% declining balance
Computer hardware	5 years straight-line
Building improvements	Over the estimated useful life to a maximum of 15 years

The Company allocates the amount initially recognized in respect of an item of property, plant and equipment to its significant parts and depreciates separately each such part. The Company reviews the condition and consistently maintains items of property, plant and equipment to maximize the useful life of these items. However, residual values, method of depreciation and useful lives of items of property, plant and equipment are reviewed annually by the Company and adjusted if appropriate.

Gains and losses on disposals of property, plant and equipment are determined by comparing the proceeds with the carrying amount of the asset and are included as part of other expenses in the consolidated income statement.

Leases

The determination of whether an arrangement is, or contains, a lease is based on the substance of the arrangement at the inception date, whether fulfillment of the arrangement is dependent on the use of a specific asset or assets or the arrangement conveys a right to use the asset, even if that right is not explicitly specified in an arrangement.

Leased Assets – Leon's is the Lessee
Leases that are not finance leases are classified as operating leases and the assets are not recognized on the Company's consolidated statements of financial position. Operating lease payments are recognized as an expense in the consolidated income statement on a straight-line basis over the period of the lease.

Leased Assets – Leon's is the Lessor
Assets leased to third parties under operating leases are classified as investment property in the consolidated statements of financial position. They are depreciated over their expected useful lives on a basis consistent with similar owned investment property. Rental income (net of any incentives given to lessees) is recognized on a straight-line basis over the period of the lease.

Investment Properties

Assets that are held for long-term rental yields or for capital appreciation or both, and that are not occupied by either the Company or any of its subsidiaries, are classified as investment properties. Investment properties are measured initially at cost, including related transaction costs. Subsequent to initial recognition, investment properties are carried at cost and depreciated over the estimated useful lives of the properties using the following annual rates and methods:

Buildings	30 years straight-line
Building improvements	Over the estimated useful life to a maximum of 15 years

Land held by the Company and classified as investment property is not depreciated.

Subsequent expenditures on investment properties are capitalized to the properties' carrying amount only when it is probable that future economic benefits associated with the expenditures will flow to the Company and the cost of the item can be measured reliably. All other repairs and maintenance costs are expensed when incurred. When part of an investment property is replaced, the carrying amount of the replaced part is derecognized.

If an investment property becomes owner-occupied, it is reclassified as property, plant and equipment.

Goodwill and Intangible Assets

Goodwill
Goodwill is the residual amount that results when the purchase price of an acquired business exceeds the sum of the amounts allocated to the tangible and intangible assets acquired, less liabilities assumed, based on their fair value. Goodwill is assigned as of the date of the business acquisition. The Company assesses at least annually, or at any time if an indicator of impairment exists, whether there has been an impairment loss in the carrying value of goodwill and it is carried at cost less accumulated impairment losses. Impairment losses on goodwill are not reversed.

30

LEON'S FURNITURE LIMITED
Notes to the Consolidated Financial Statements

Goodwill is allocated to cash-generating units ("CGUs"), or groups of CGUs, that are expected to benefit from the business combination for the purpose of impairment testing. A group of CGUs represents the lowest level within the Company at which goodwill is monitored for internal management purposes.

Finite-Lived Intangible Assets

Intangible assets with finite useful lives are amortized on a straight-line basis over their estimated useful lives using the following annual rates:

Customer relationships	8 years
Brand name	10 years
Non-compete agreement	8 years
Computer software	7 years

The Company identifies and measures intangible assets acquired in business acquisitions and accounts for these assets separately from goodwill.

Impairment of Non-Financial Assets

Property, plant and equipment and finite lived intangible assets are reviewed quarterly for impairment and whenever events or changes in circumstances indicate that the carrying amount may not be recoverable. If the estimated recoverable amount of an asset is less than its carrying amount, the asset is written down to its estimated recoverable amount and an impairment loss is recognized. The recoverable amount of an asset is the higher of its fair value less costs to sell and value in use. For the purposes of assessing impairment, assets are grouped at the lowest level for which there are separately identifiable cash inflows (CGU). The Company has identified the CGU to be at the store level. Non-financial assets, other than goodwill, that suffered impairment are reviewed for possible reversal of the impairment at each reporting date.

Income Taxes

Income tax expense for the period comprises current and deferred income tax. Income tax is recognized in the consolidated income statement except to the extent it relates to items recognized in other comprehensive income or directly in equity, in which case the related tax is recognized in equity. Levies other than income taxes, such as taxes on real estate, are included in occupancy expenses.

Current Income Tax

Current income tax expense is based on the results of the period as adjusted for items that are not taxable or not deductible. Current tax is calculated using tax rates and laws that were substantively enacted at the end of the reporting period. Management periodically evaluates positions taken in tax returns with respect to situations in which applicable tax regulation is subject to interpretation. It establishes provisions where appropriate on the basis of amounts expected to be paid to the tax authorities.

Deferred Income Tax

Deferred income tax is recognized, using the liability method, on temporary differences arising between the tax bases of assets and liabilities and their carrying amounts in the consolidated statement of financial position. Deferred income tax is determined using tax rates (and laws) that have been enacted or substantively enacted by the consolidated statement of financial position date and are expected to apply when the related deferred income tax asset is realized or the deferred income tax liability is settled.

Deferred income tax assets are recognized only to the extent that it is probable that future taxable profit will be available against which the temporary differences can be utilized.

Deferred income tax assets and liabilities are offset when there is a legally enforceable right to offset current income tax assets against current income tax liabilities and when the deferred income tax assets and liabilities relate to income taxes levied by the same taxation authority where there is an intention to settle the balances on a net basis.

Trade and Other Payables

Trade and other payables are obligations to pay for goods or services that have been acquired in the ordinary course of business from suppliers. Trade and other payables are classified as current liabilities if payment is due within one year or less.

Provisions

Provisions are recognized only in those circumstances where the Company has a present legal or constructive obligation as a result of a past event, when it is probable that an outflow of resources will be required to settle the obligation, and a reliable estimate of the amount can be made.

Provisions are measured at the present value of the expenditures expected to be required to settle the obligation using a pre-tax discount rate that reflects current market assessments of the time value of money and the risks specific to the obligation.

Share Capital

Common shares are classified as equity. Incremental costs directly attributable to the issuance of new shares are shown in equity as a deduction, net of income tax, from the proceeds.

Revenue Recognition

Revenue comprises the fair value of consideration received or receivable for the sale of goods and services in the ordinary course of the Company's activities. Revenue is shown net of sales tax and financing charges. The Company recognizes revenue when the amount of revenue can be reliably measured and it is probable that future economic benefits will flow to the Company.

In addition to the above general principles, the Company applies the following specific revenue recognition policies:

Sale of Goods
Revenue from the sale of goods is recognized either when the customer picks up the merchandise ordered or when merchandise is delivered to the customer's home. Any payments received in advance of delivery are deferred and recorded as customers' deposits.

Extended Warranty
The Company recognizes extended warranty plan revenue on a straight-line basis over the contract period. The service costs associated with the warranty obligations are expensed as incurred.

Franchise Fees
Leon's franchisees operate principally as independent owners. The Company charges each franchisee a royalty fee based on a percentage of the franchisee's gross revenue. This royalty income is recorded by the Company on an accrual basis and presented within revenue.

Rent on Investment Properties
Rental income arising on investment properties is accounted for on a straight-line basis over the lease term and is presented within revenue.

Sale of Gift Cards
Revenue from the sale of gift cards is recognized when the gift cards are redeemed (the customer purchases merchandise), or when the gift cards are no longer expected to be redeemed, based on an analysis of historical redemption rates, if any. Revenue from unredeemed gift cards is deferred and included in trade and other payables.

Store Pre-Opening Costs

Store pre-opening costs are expensed as incurred.

Earnings per Share

Basic earnings per share have been calculated using the weighted average number of common shares outstanding during the year. Diluted earnings per share are calculated using the "if converted" method. The dividends declared on the redeemable share liability under the Company's Management Share Purchase Plan (the Plan) are included in net income for the year. The redeemable shares convertible under the Plan are included in the calculation of diluted number of common shares to the extent the redemption price was less than the average annual market price of the Company's common shares.

Accounting Standards and Amendments Issued But Not Yet Adopted

Unless otherwise noted, the following revised standards and amendments are effective for annual periods beginning on or after January 1, 2013, with earlier application permitted. The Company has not yet assessed the impact of these standards and amendments or determined whether it will early adopt them.

i.   IFRS 7, *Financial Instruments: Disclosures*, has been amended to include additional disclosure requirements in the reporting of transfer transactions and risk exposures relating to transfers of financial assets and the effect of those risks on an entity's financial position, particularly those involving securitization of financial assets. The amendment is applicable for annual periods beginning on or after July 1, 2011, with earlier application permitted.

32

LEON'S FURNITURE LIMITED
Notes to the Consolidated Financial Statements

ii.   IFRS 9, *Financial Instruments,* was issued in November 2009 and addresses classification and measurement of financial assets. It replaces the multiple category and measurement models in IAS 39 for debt instruments with a new mixed measurement model having only two categories: amortized cost and fair value through profit or loss. IFRS 9 also replaces the models for measuring equity instruments. Such instruments are either recognized at fair value through profit or loss or at fair value through other comprehensive income. Where equity instruments are measured at fair value through other comprehensive income, dividends are recognized in profit or loss to the extent that they do not clearly represent a return of investment; however, other gains and losses (including impairments) associated with such instruments remain in accumulated other comprehensive income (loss) indefinitely.

Requirements for financial liabilities were added to IFRS 9 in October 2010 and they largely carried forward existing requirements in IAS 39, *Financial Instruments – Recognition and Measurement*, except that fair value changes due to credit risk for liabilities designated at fair value through profit and loss are generally recorded in other comprehensive income.

iii.   IFRS 10, *Consolidated Financial Statements*, requires an entity to consolidate an investee when it has power over the investee, is exposed, or has rights, to variable returns from its involvement with the investee and has the ability to affect those returns through its power over the investee. Under existing IFRS, consolidation is required when an entity has the power to govern the financial and operating policies of an entity so as to obtain benefits from its activities. IFRS 10 replaces SIC-12, *Consolidation – Special Purpose Entities* and parts of IAS 27, *Consolidated and Separate Financial Statements*.

iv.   IFRS 11, *Joint Arrangements*, requires an entity to classify its interest in a joint arrangement as a joint operation or a joint venture. The standard eliminates the use of the proportionate consolidation method to account for joint ventures. Joint ventures will be accounted for using the equity method of accounting, while for a joint operation the entity will recognize its share of the assets, liabilities, revenues and expenses of the joint operation. IFRS 11 supersedes SIC-13, *Jointly Controlled Entities – Non-Monetary Contributions by Venturers* and IAS 31 *Joint Ventures*.

v.   IFRS 12, *Disclosure of Interests in Other Entities*, establishes disclosure requirements for interests in other entities, such as subsidiaries, joint arrangements, associates, and unconsolidated structured entities. The standard carries forward existing disclosures and also introduces significant additional disclosure that address the nature of, and risks associated with, an entity's interests in other entities.

vi.   IFRS 13, *Fair Value Measurement*, is a comprehensive standard for fair value measurement and disclosure for use across all IFRS standards. The new standard clarifies that fair value is the price that would be received to sell an asset, or paid to transfer a liability in an orderly transaction between market participants, at the measurement date. Under existing IFRS, guidance on measuring and disclosing fair value is dispersed among the specific standards requiring fair value measurements and does not always reflect a clear measurement basis or consistent disclosures.

vii.   There have been amendments to existing standards, including IAS 27, *Separate Financial Statements* (IAS 27), and IAS 28, *Investments in Associates and Joint Ventures* (IAS 28). IAS 27 addresses accounting for subsidiaries, jointly controlled entities and associates in non-consolidated financial statements. IAS 28 has been amended to include joint ventures in its scope and to address the changes in IFRS 10-13.

viii.   IAS 1, *Presentation of Financial Statements*, has been amended to require entities to separate items presented in OCI into two groups, based on whether or not items may be recycled in the future. Entities that choose to present OCI items before tax will be required to show the amount of tax related to the two groups separately. The amendment is effective for annual periods beginning on or after July 1, 2012, with earlier application permitted.

ix.   IFRS 1, *First-time Adoption of International Financial Reporting Standards*, has been amended for two changes. The first replaces references to a fixed date of January 1, 2004 with 'the date of transition to IFRSs'. This eliminates the need for entities adopting IFRSs for the first time to restate derecognition transactions that occurred before the date of transition to IFRS. The second amendment provides guidance on how an entity should resume presenting financial statements in accordance with IFRSs after a period when the entity was unable to comply with IFRSs because its functional currency was subject to severe hyperinflation. The amendment is effective for annual periods beginning on or after July 1, 2011, with earlier application permitted.

x.   IAS 12, *Income Taxes*, was amended to introduce an exception to the existing principle for the measurement of deferred tax assets or liabilities arising on investment property measured at fair value. As a result of the amendment, there is a rebuttable presumption that the carrying amount of the investment property will be recovered through sale when considering the expected manner or recovery or settlement. SIC-21, *Income Taxes – Recovery of Revalued Non-Depreciable Assets*, will no longer apply to investment properties carried at fair value. The amendment also incorporates into IAS 12 the remaining guidance previously contained in SIC-21, which is withdrawn. The amendment is effective for annual periods beginning on or after January 1, 2012, with earlier application permitted.

4. Critical Accounting Estimates and Assumptions

The preparation of consolidated financial statements requires management to use judgment in applying its accounting policies and estimates and assumptions about the future. Estimates and other judgments are continuously evaluated and are based on management's experience and other factors, including expectations about future events that are believed to be reasonable under the circumstances. The following discusses the most significant accounting judgments and estimates that the Company has made in the preparation of the consolidated financial statements:

Revenue Recognition

Revenue is recognized for accounting purposes upon the customer either picking up the merchandise or when merchandise is delivered to the customer's home. The Company offers the option to finance purchases through various third-party financing companies. In situations where a customer elects to take advantage of delayed payment terms, the costs of financing this revenue are deducted from revenue.

Inventories

The Company estimates the net realizable value as the amount at which inventories are expected to be sold by taking into account fluctuations of retail prices due to prevailing market conditions. If required, inventories are written down to net realizable value when the cost of inventories is estimated to not be recoverable due to obsolescence, damage or declining sales prices.

Reserves for slow moving and damaged inventory are deducted in the Company's evaluation of inventories. The reserve for slow moving inventory is based on many years of historic retail experience. The reserve is calculated by analyzing all inventory on hand older than one year. The amount of reserve for damaged inventory is determined by specific product categories.

The amount of inventory recognized as an expense for the year ended December 31, 2011 was $385,495,000 (year ended December 31, 2010 – $402,685,000), which is presented within cost of sales in the consolidated income statements. There were $535,000 inventory write-downs (2010 – $67,000) recognized as an expense during 2011.

As at December 31, 2011, the inventory markdown provision totalled $4,846,000 (as at December 31, 2010 – $4,311,000 and as at January 1, 2010 – $4,244,000). None of the Company's inventory has been pledged as security for any liabilities of the Company.

Extended Warranty Revenue

Extended warranty revenue is deferred and taken into revenue on a straight-line basis over the life of the extended warranty period.

Franchise Royalties

Leon's franchisees operate as independent owners. The Company charges the franchisee a royalty fee based primarily on a percentage of the franchisee's gross revenues. This royalty revenue is recorded by the Company on an accruals basis and is classified as revenue within the consolidated income statements.

Volume Rebates

The Company receives vendor rebates on certain products based on the volume of purchases made during specified periods. The rebates are deducted from the inventory value of goods received and are recognized as a reduction in cost of goods sold as revenue is recognized.

Income Taxes

The Company computes an income tax provision. However, actual amounts of income tax expense only become final upon filing and acceptance of the tax return by the relevant taxation authorities, which occur subsequent to the issuance of the annual consolidated financial statements. Additionally, estimation of income taxes includes evaluating the recoverability of deferred income tax assets based on an assessment of the ability to use the underlying future tax deductions before they expire against future taxable income. The assessment is based upon existing tax laws and estimates of future taxable income. To the extent estimates differ from the final tax return, earnings would be affected in a subsequent period.

Impairment

The Company reviews goodwill at least annually and other non-financial assets when there is any indication that the asset might be impaired. The Company has estimated the recoverable amount of Appliance Canada, a division of the Company, to which goodwill is allocated using a discounted cash flow model that required assumptions about future cash flows, margins, and discount rates.

34

LEON'S FURNITURE LIMITED
Notes to the Consolidated Financial Statements

5. Financial Risk Management

Classification of Financial Instruments and Fair Value

The classification of the Company's financial instruments, as well as their carrying amounts and fair values are disclosed in the table below.

Financial Instrument	Designation	Measurement	December 31 2011	December 31 2010	January 1 2010
Cash and cash equivalents	Available-for-sale	Fair value	$ 72,505	$ 71,589	$ 58,301
Available-for-sale financial assets	Available-for-sale	Fair value	$ 149,318	$ 140,224	$ 112,425
Trade receivables	Loans and receivables	Amortized cost	$ 28,937	$ 28,569	$ 31,501
Trade and other payables	Other financial liabilities	Amortized cost	$ 75,126	$ 71,724	$ 72,603
Redeemable share liability	Other financial liabilities	Amortized cost	$ 382	$ 172	$ 383

Fair Value Hierarchy

The following table classifies financial assets and liabilities that are recognized on the consolidated statements of financial position at fair value in a hierarchy that is based on significance of the inputs used in making the measurements. The levels in the hierarchy are:

Level 1:   Quoted prices (unadjusted) in active markets for identical assets or liabilities.
Level 2:   Inputs other than quoted prices included within level 1 that are observable for the asset or liability, either directly (that is, as prices) or indirectly (that is, derived from prices).
Level 3:   Inputs for the asset or liability that are not based on observable market data (that is, unobservable inputs).

Financial Instruments at Fair Value

	Fair Value Measurement at December 31, 2011		
	Level 1	Level 2	Level 3
Cash and cash equivalents	$ 72,505	$ –	$ –
Available-for-sale financial assets – Bonds	–	118,171	–
Available-for-sale financial assets – Equities	31,147	–	–
	$ 103,652	$ 118,171	$ –

	Fair Value Measurement at December 31, 2010		
	Level 1	Level 2	Level 3
Cash and cash equivalents	$ 71,589	$ –	$ –
Available-for-sale financial assets – Bonds	–	117,817	–
Available-for-sale financial assets – Equities	22,407	–	–
	$ 93,996	$ 117,817	$ –

	Fair Value Measurement at January 1, 2010		
	Level 1	Level 2	Level 3
Cash and cash equivalents	$ 58,301	$ –	$ –
Available-for-sale financial assets – Bonds	–	92,884	–
Available-for-sale financial assets – Equities	19,541	–	–
	$ 77,842	$ 92,884	$ –

Financial Risks Factors

The Company's activities expose it to a variety of financial risks: market risk (including foreign currency risk, interest rate risk and other price risk), credit risk and liquidity risk. Risk management is carried out by the Company by identifying and evaluating the financial risks inherent within its operations. The Company's overall risk management activities seek to minimize potential adverse effects on the Company's financial performance.

(a) Market Risk

i.   **Foreign exchange risk** – The Company is exposed to foreign currency risk. Certain merchandise is paid for in U.S. dollars. This foreign exchange cost is included in the inventory cost. The Company does not believe it has significant foreign currency risk with respect to its trade payables in U.S. dollars.

The Company is also exposed to foreign currency risk on its foreign currency denominated portfolio of available-for-sale financial assets, primarily related to actively traded international equities. As at December 31, 2011, the Company's investment portfolio included 10% of foreign currency denominated assets (as at December 31, 2010 – 8% and as at January 1, 2010 – 8%). This risk is monitored by the Company's investment managers in an effort to reduce the Company's exposure to foreign currency exchange rate risk.

ii. **Interest rate risk** – The Company is exposed to interest rate risk through its portfolio of available-for-sale financial assets by holding cash, cash equivalents and actively traded Canadian and international Bonds. At December 31, 2011, 86% of the Company's investment portfolio was made up of cash, cash equivalents and Canadian and international Bonds (as at December 31, 2010 – 89% and as at January 1, 2010 – 89%). This risk is monitored by the Company's investment managers in an effort to reduce the Company's exposure to interest rate risk. The exposure to this risk is minimal due to the short-term maturities of the bonds held. The Company is not subject to any other interest rate risk.

iii. **Price risk** – The Company is exposed to fluctuations in the market prices of its portfolio of available-for-sale financial assets. Changes in the fair value of the available-for-sale financial assets are recorded, net of income taxes, in accumulated other comprehensive income as it relates to unrecognized gains and losses. The risk is managed by the Company and its investment managers by ensuring a conservative asset allocation of bonds and equities.

(b) Credit Risk

Credit risk arises from cash and cash equivalents, available-for-sale financial assets and trade receivables. The Company places its cash and cash equivalents and available-for-sale financial assets with institutions of high credit worthiness. Maximum credit risk exposure represents the loss that would be incurred if all of the Company's counterparties were to default at the same time.

The Company has some credit risk associated with its trade receivables as it relates to the Appliance Canada division that is partially mitigated by the Company's credit management practices.

The Company's trade receivables total $28,937,000 as at December 31, 2011 (as at December 31, 2010 – $28,569,000 and as at January 1, 2010 – $31,501,000). The amount of trade receivables that the Company has determined to be past due (which is defined as a balance that is more than 90 days past due) is $191,000 as at December 31, 2011 (as at December 31, 2010 – $158,000 and as at January 1, 2010 – $431,000), which relates entirely to the Appliance Canada division. The Company's provision for impairment of trade receivables, established through ongoing monitoring of individual customer accounts, was $500,000 as at December 31, 2011 (as at December 31, 2010 – $470,000 and as at January 1, 2010 – $300,000).

The majority of the Company's sales are paid through cash, credit card or non-recourse third-party finance. The Company relies on one third-party credit supplier to supply financing to its customers.

(c) Liquidity Risk

The Company has no outstanding borrowings and does not rely upon available credit facilities to finance operations or to finance committed capital expenditures. The portfolio of available-for-sale financial assets consists primarily of actively traded Canadian and international bonds. There is no immediate need for cash by the Company from its investment portfolio.

The Company expects to settle its trade and other payables within 30 days of the period end date. The redeemable share liability does not have any fixed terms of repayment.

36

LEON'S FURNITURE LIMITED
Notes to the Consolidated Financial Statements

6. Capital Risk Management

The Company defines capital as shareholders' equity. The Company's objectives when managing capital are to:

- ensure sufficient liquidity to support its financial obligations and execute its operating and strategic plans; and
- utilize working capital to negotiate favourable supplier agreements both in respect of early payment discounts and overall payment terms.

The Company is not subject to any externally imposed capital requirements.

7. Cash and Cash Equivalents

	As at December 31 2011	As at December 31 2010	As at January 1 2010
Cash at bank and on hand	$ 2,181	$ 19,642	$ 7,620
Short-term investments	70,324	51,947	50,681
	$ 72,505	$ 71,589	$ 58,301

8. Property, Plant and Equipment

	Land	Buildings	Equipment	Vehicles	Computer Hardware	Building Improvements	Total
At January 1, 2010							
Cost	$ 56,156	$ 163,680	$ 34,730	$ 20,853	$ 8,604	$ 78,175	$ 362,198
Accumulated depreciation	–	86,277	23,112	16,726	7,297	25,133	158,545
Net book value	$ 56,156	$ 77,403	$ 11,618	$ 4,127	$ 1,307	$ 53,042	$ 203,653
Year ended December 31, 2010							
At January 1, 2010	$ 56,156	$ 77,403	$ 11,618	$ 4,127	$ 1,307	$ 53,042	$ 203,653
Additions	45	11,685	1,323	484	347	98	13,982
Disposals	870	–	–	10	–	–	880
Depreciation	–	6,484	1,880	1,253	537	5,109	15,263
Closing net book value	55,331	82,604	11,061	3,348	1,117	48,031	201,492
At December 31, 2010							
Cost	55,331	175,365	36,053	20,900	8,951	78,273	374,873
Accumulated depreciation	–	92,761	24,992	17,552	7,834	30,242	173,381
Net book value	$ 55,331	$ 82,604	$ 11,061	$ 3,348	$ 1,117	$ 48,031	$ 201,492
Year ended December 31, 2011							
At January 1, 2011	$ 55,331	$ 82,604	$ 11,061	$ 3,348	$ 1,117	$ 48,031	$ 201,492
Additions	100	9,165	4,403	2,253	164	9,253	25,338
Disposals	–	–	–	18	–	–	18
Depreciation	–	3,563	2,029	1,271	538	5,253	12,654
Closing net book value	55,431	88,206	13,435	4,312	743	52,031	214,158
At December 31, 2011							
Cost	55,431	184,530	40,456	23,051	9,115	87,526	400,109
Accumulated depreciation	–	96,324	27,021	18,739	8,372	35,495	185,951
Net book value	$ 55,431	$ 88,206	$ 13,435	$ 4,312	$ 743	$ 52,031	$ 214,158

Included in the above balances at December 31, 2011 are assets not being amortized with a net book value of approximately $2,638,000 (as at December 31, 2010 – $2,400,000 and as at January 1, 2010 – $Nil) being construction-in-progress.

The Company assessed for an indicator of impairment of each CGU by comparing the CV (carrying value)/EBITDA (earnings before interest, depreciation and amortization) multiple to that of comparable public companies. Where the impairment indicator existed, the carrying value of the assets within a CGU was compared with its estimated recoverable value, which was generally considered to be the CGU's value-in-use.

When determining the CGU's value-in-use, the Company estimated the future cash flows and discounted them at an appropriate pre-tax rate for the individual CGU. Where the carrying value of the CGU's assets exceeded the recoverable amounts, as represented by the CGU's value-in-use, the store's property and equipment assets were written down.

For the year ended December 31, 2011 and 2010, there has been no impairment loss recognized.

9. Investment Properties

	Land	Buildings	Building Improvements	Total
At January 1, 2010				
Cost	$ 8,286	$ 8,039	$ 1,494	$ 17,819
Accumulated depreciation	–	8,039	1,235	9,274
Net book value	$ 8,286	$ –	$ 259	$ 8,545
Year ended December 31, 2010				
At January 1, 2010	$ 8,286	$ –	$ 259	$ 8,545
Additions	–	–	–	–
Disposals	–	–	37	37
Depreciation	–	–	91	91
At December 31, 2010	8,286	–	131	8,417
As at December 31, 2010				
Cost	8,286	8,039	1,457	17,782
Accumulated depreciation	–	8,039	1,326	9,365
Net book value	$ 8,286	$ –	$ 131	$ 8,417
Year ended December 31, 2011				
At January 1, 2011	$ 8,286	$ –	$ 131	$ 8,417
Additions	–	–	–	–
Disposals	–	–	–	–
Depreciation	–	–	51	51
Closing net book value	8,286	–	80	8,366
As at December 31, 2011				
Cost	8,286	8,039	1,457	17,782
Accumulated depreciation	–	8,039	1,377	9,416
Net book value	$ 8,286	$ –	$ 80	$ 8,366

The fair value of the investment property portfolio as at December 31, 2011 was $29,750,000 (as at December 31, 2010 – $29,750,000 and as at January 1, 2010 – $29,750,000). The fair value was compiled internally by management based on available market evidence.

38

LEON'S FURNITURE LIMITED
Notes to the Consolidated Financial Statements

10. Intangible Assets and Goodwill

	Customer Relationships		Brand Name		Non-Compete Agreement		Computer Software		Total
At January 1, 2010									
Cost	$	2,000	$	2,500	$	1,000	$	3,896	$ 9,396
Accumulated amortization		500		500		250		2,812	4,062
Net book value	$	1,500	$	2,000	$	750	$	1,084	$ 5,334
Year ended December 31, 2010									
At January 1, 2010	$	1,500	$	2,000	$	750	$	1,084	$ 5,334
Additions		–		–		–		370	370
Disposals		–		–		–		–	–
Amortization for the year		250		250		125		177	802
Closing net book value		1,250		1,750		625		1,277	4,902
As at December 31, 2010									
Cost		2,000		2,500		1,000		4,266	9,766
Accumulated amortization		750		750		375		2,989	4,864
Net book value	$	1,250	$	1,750	$	625	$	1,277	$ 4,902
Year ended December 31, 2011									
At January 1, 2011	$	1,250	$	1,750	$	625	$	1,277	$ 4,902
Additions		–		–		–		(64)	(64)
Disposals		–		–		–		–	–
Amortization for the year		250		250		125		255	880
Closing net book value		1,000		1,500		500		958	3,958
At December 31, 2011									
Cost		2,000		2,500		1,000		4,202	9,702
Accumulated amortization		1,000		1,000		500		3,244	5,744
Net book value	$	1,000	$	1,500	$	500	$	958	$ 3,958

Impairment Test of Goodwill

The Company performed impairment tests of goodwill at December 31, 2011, December 31, 2010 and January 1, 2010 in accordance with the accounting policy as described in note 3 and IFRS transitional provisions. The recoverable amount of the Appliance Canada CGU, where all goodwill is allocated, was determined based on value-in-use calculations. These calculations used cash flow projections based on financial budgets approved by management covering a one-year period. Cash flows beyond the one-year period are extrapolated using the estimated growth rates stated below. The key assumptions used for the value-in-use calculation at December 31, 2010 and January 1, 2010 were as follows:

	Growth Rate %	After-Tax Discount Rate %
December 31, 2011	3.0	10.0
December 31, 2010	2.0	9.7
January 1, 2010	3.0	9.9

The impairment tests performed resulted in no impairment of the goodwill as at December 31, 2011, December 31, 2010 or January 1, 2010.

11. Trade and Other Payables

	As at December 31 2011	As at December 31 2010	As at January 1 2010
Trade payables	$ **62,485**	$ 60,127	$ 69,495
Other payables	**12,641**	11,597	3,108
	$ **75,126**	$ 71,724	$ 72,603

12. Provisions

	Profit Sharing and Bonuses	Vacation Pay	Totals
As at January 1, 2010	$ 10,775	$ 502	$ 11,277
Additional provisions	11,880	3,302	15,182
Unused amounts reversed	(598)	–	(598)
Utilized during the year	(10,057)	(3,463)	(13,520)
As at December 31, 2010	$ 12,000	$ 341	$ 12,341
Additional provisions	**10,860**	**3,365**	**14,225**
Unused amounts reversed	**(1,019)**	**–**	**(1,019)**
Utilized during the year	**(10,981)**	**(3,335)**	**(14,316)**
As at December 31, 2011	$ **10,860**	$ **371**	$ **11,231**

(a)   The provision for profit sharing and bonuses is payable within the first half of the following fiscal year.

(b)   The provision for vacation pay represents employee entitlements to vacation time not taken at each reporting date.

13. Redeemable Share Liability

	As at December 31 2011	As at December 31 2010	As at January 1 2010
Authorized			
2,284,000 convertible, non-voting, series 2002 shares			
806,000 convertible, non-voting, series 2005			
1,224,000 convertible, non-voting, series 2009 shares			
Issued and fully paid			
667,748 series 2002 shares			
(December 31, 2010 – 813,331 and January 1, 2010 – 969,033)	$ **4,799**	$ 5,846	$ 6,965
541,248 series 2005 shares			
(December 31, 2010 – 620,793 and January 1, 2010 – 689,513)	**5,111**	5,862	6,511
1,115,107 series 2009 shares			
(December 31, 2010 – 1,168,124 and January 1, 2010 – 1,207,000)	**9,869**	10,339	10,683
Less employee share purchase loans	**(19,397)**	(21,875)	(23,776)
	$ **382**	$ 172	$ 383

Under the terms of the Plan, the Company advanced non-interest bearing loans to certain of its employees in 2002, 2005 and 2009 to allow them to acquire convertible, non-voting, series 2002 shares, series 2005 shares and series 2009 shares, respectively, of the Company. These loans are repayable through the application against the loans of any dividends on the shares, with any remaining balance repayable on the date the shares are converted to common shares. Each issued and fully paid for series 2002, 2005 and

40

LEON'S FURNITURE LIMITED
Notes to the Consolidated Financial Statements

2009 share may be converted into one common share at any time after the fifth anniversary date of the issue of these shares and prior to the tenth anniversary of such issue. Series 2002 shares may also be redeemed at the option of the holder or by the Company at any time after the fifth anniversary date of the issue of these shares and must be redeemed prior to the tenth anniversary of such issue. The series 2005 and series 2009 shares are redeemable at the option of the holder for a period of one business day following the date of issue of such shares. The Company has the option to redeem the series 2005 and series 2009 shares at any time after the fifth anniversary date of the issue of these shares and must redeem them prior to the tenth anniversary of such issue. The redemption price is equal to the original issue price of the shares adjusted for subsequent subdivisions of shares plus accrued and unpaid dividends. The purchase prices of the shares are $7.19 per series 2002 share, $9.44 per series 2005 share and $8.85 per series 2009 share.

Dividends paid to holders of series 2002, 2005 and 2009 shares of approximately $470,000 (2010 – $401,000) have been used to reduce the respective shareholder loans.

During the year ended December 31, 2011, 145,583 series 2002 shares (year ended December 31, 2010 – 155,702) and 79,545 series 2005 shares (year ended December 31, 2010 – 68,720) were converted into common shares with a stated value of approximately $1,047,000 (year ended December 31, 2010 – $1,119,000) and $751,000 (year ended December 31, 2010 – $475,000), respectively.

During the year ended December 31, 2011, the Company cancelled 53,017 series 2009 shares (year ended December 31, 2010 – 38,876) in the amount of $470,000 (year ended December 31, 2010 – $344,000).

Employee share purchase loans have been netted against the redeemable share liability as the Company has the legally enforceable right of offset and the positive intent to settle on a net basis.

The Plan represents a compensatory plan under IFRS 2 as the terms of the series 2002, 2005 and 2009 shares and related employee share purchase loans collectively give the employees that ability, but not the obligation, to acquire common shares of the Company.

14. Common Shares

	As at December 31 2011	As at December 31 2010	As at January 1 2010
Authorized Unlimited common shares **Issued** 69,815,734 common shares (December 31, 2010 – 70,075,333 and January 1, 2010 – 70,477,611)	**20,918**	19,177	17,704

During the year ended December 31, 2011, 145,583 series 2002 shares (year ended December 31, 2010 – 155,702) and 79,545 series 2005 shares (year ended December 31, 2010 – 68,720) were converted into common shares with a stated value of approximately $1,047,000 (year ended December 31, 2010 – $1,119,000) and $751,000 (year ended December 31, 2010 – $475,000), respectively.

During the year ended December 31, 2011, the Company repurchased 484,727 (year ended December 31, 2010 – 626,700) of its common shares on the open market pursuant to the terms and conditions of Normal Course Issuer Bid at a net cost of approximately $6,334,000 (year ended December 31, 2010 – $8,034,000). All shares repurchased by the Company pursuant to its Normal Course Issuer Bid have been cancelled. The repurchase of common shares resulted in a reduction of share capital in the amount of approximately $57,000 (year ended December 31, 2010 – $295,000). The excess net cost over the average carrying value of the shares of approximately $6,277,000 (year ended December 31, 2010 – $7,739,000) has been recorded as a reduction in retained earnings.

As at December 31, 2011, the dividends payable were $17,457,000 ($0.25 per share) and December 31, 2010, $6,310,000 ($0.09 per share) and as at January 1, 2010 $4,938,000 ($0.07 per share).

15. Revenue

	Year Ended December 31 2011	Year Ended December 31 2010
Sale of goods by corporate stores	$ 663,607	$ 691,079
Royalty income from franchisees	10,434	10,663
Extended warranty revenue	8,055	8,007
Rental income from investment property	740	686
	$ 682,836	$ 710,435

16. Operating Expenses by Nature

	Year Ended December 31 2011	Year Ended December 31 2010
Depreciation of property, plant and equipment and investment properties	$ 12,705	$ 15,354
Amortization of intangible assets	$ 880	$ 802
Operating lease payments	$ 3,631	$ 3,300
Gain on disposal of property, plant and equipment	$ 21	$ 1,236

17. Income Tax Expense

(a) The Major Components of Income Tax Expense for the Year Ended are:

INCOME STATEMENT	December 31 2011	December 31 2010
Current income tax expense:		
Based on taxable income of the current year	$ 20,636	$ 26,606
Adjustments in respect of prior years	(368)	–
	20,268	26,606
Deferred income tax expense (benefit):		
Origination and reversal of temporary differences	1,758	(2)
Impact of change in tax rates/new tax laws	156	297
	1,914	295
Income tax expense reported in the income statement	$ 22,182	$ 26,901

(b) Reconciliation of Effective Tax Rate:

	2011		2010	
Income before income taxes	$ 78,848		$ 90,185	
Income tax expense based on statutory rate	22,219	28.18%	27,507	30.50%
Increase (decrease) in income taxes resulting from non-taxable items or adjustments of prior year taxes:				
Non-deductible items	86	0.11%	(158)	(0.17%)
Rate differences related to origination and reversal of temporary differences	156	0.20%	298	0.33%
Remeasurement of deferred tax asset for rate changes	66	0.08%	(286)	(0.32%)
Other	(345)	(0.44%)	(460)	(0.51%)
Total income tax expense	$ 22,182	28.13%	$ 26,901	29.83%

42

LEON'S FURNITURE LIMITED
Notes to the Consolidated Financial Statements

(c) Deferred Taxes:

i.   DEFERRED TAX RELATES TO THE FOLLOWING:

	December 31 2011	December 31 2010	January 1 2010
Deferred income tax assets			
Deferred warranty plan revenue	$ 4,245	$ 4,739	$ 4,644
Unrealized gains/losses on available-for-sale investments	(25)	(38)	42
Fixed assets	8,152	8,501	7,912
	12,372	13,202	12,598
Deferred income tax liabilities			
Deferred warranty plan direct costs	(617)	–	–
Fixed assets	(10,311)	(9,845)	(8,829)
	(10,928)	(9,845)	(8,829)
Net deferred tax asset position	1,444	3,357	3,769
Reported in:			
Deferred income tax assets	12,372	13,202	12,598
Deferred income tax liabilities	$ (10,928)	$ (9,845)	$ (8,829)

ii.   DEFERRED TAX MOVEMENT IN THE INCOME STATEMENT IS AS FOLLOWS:

	2011	2010
Expense (benefit)		
Deferred warranty plan revenue	$ 494	$ (95)
Unrealized gains/losses on available-for-sale investments	(13)	81
Fixed assets	815	426
Deferred warranty plan direct costs	617	–
Net deferred income tax expense	$ 1,913	$ 412

iii.   RECONCILIATION OF NET DEFERRED TAX ASSET:

	2011	2010
Opening balance as of January 1	$ 3,357	$ 3,769
Tax expense during the period recognized in profit or loss	(1,913)	(412)
Closing balance as of December 31	$ 1,444	$ 3,357

18. Earnings per Share

Earnings per share are calculated using the weighted average number of shares outstanding. The weighted average number of shares used in the basic earnings per share calculations amounted to 69,969,417 for the year ended December 31, 2011 (year ended December 31, 2010 – 70,371,744).

The following table reconciles the profit for the period and the number of shares for the basic and diluted earnings per share calculations:

Year Ended December 31, 2011	Profit for the Period Attributed to Common Shareholders	Weighted Average Number of Shares	Per Share Amount
Basic	$ 56,666	69,969,417	$ 0.81
Dilutive effect (Note 13)	–	2,336,007	–
Diluted	$ 56,666	72,305,424	$ 0.78

Year Ended December 31, 2010	Profit for the Period Attributed to Common Shareholders	Weighted Average Number of Shares	Per Share Amount
Basic	$ 63,284	70,371,744	$ 0.90
Dilutive effect (Note 13)	–	2,762,162	–
Diluted	$ 63,284	73,133,906	$ 0.87

19. Commitments and Contingencies

(a) The cost to complete all construction-in-progress as at December 31, 2011 totals $4,407,000 at two locations (December 31, 2010 – to complete at two locations at an approximate cost of $9,609,000).

(b) The Company is obligated under operating leases for future minimum annual rental payments for certain land and buildings as follows:

No later than 1 year	$ 5,860
Later than 1 year and no later than 5 years	19,989
Later than 5 years	18,282
	$ 44,131

(c) The future minimum lease payments receivable under non-cancellable operating leases for certain land and buildings classified as investment property are as follows:

No later than 1 year	$ 712
Later than 1 year and no later than 5 years	2,027
Later than 5 years	427
	$ 3,166

(d) The Company has issued approximately $255,000 in letters of credit primarily with respect to buildings under construction (as at December 31, 2010 – $2,400,000).

(e) Pursuant to a reinsurance agreement relating to the extended warranty sales, the Company has pledged available-for-sale financial assets amounting to $20,257,000 (as at December 31, 2010 – $19,498,000) and provided a letter of credit of $1,500,000 (as at December 31, 2010 – $1,500,000) for the benefit of the insurance company.

44

LEON'S FURNITURE LIMITED
Notes to the Consolidated Financial Statements

20. Consolidated Statements of Cash Flows

(a)   The net change in non-cash working capital balances related to operations consists of the following:

	Year Ended December 31 2011	Year Ended December 31 2010
Trade receivables	$ (368)	$ 2,932
Inventory	(2,407)	(1,466)
Other assets	143	(14)
Trade, other payables and provisions	1,953	(193)
Income taxes payable	(5,706)	(1,434)
Customers' deposits	1,959	1,566
	$ (4,426)	$ 1,391

(b)   Supplemental cash flow information:

	Year Ended December 31 2011	Year Ended December 31 2010
Income taxes paid	$ 26,076	$ 28,541
Interest paid	$ –	$ 24

(c)   During the year, property, plant and equipment were acquired at an aggregate cost of $25,338,000 (2010 – $13,946,000), of which $874,000 (2010 – $536,000) is included in trade and other payables as at December 31, 2011.

21. Related Party Transactions

Key Management Compensation
Key management includes the Directors and the five senior executives of the Company. The compensation expense paid to key management for employee services during each period is shown below:

	Year Ended December 31 2011	Year Ended December 31 2010
Salaries and other short-term employee benefits	$ 3,416,188	$ 3,706,894

22. Transition to IFRS

The effect of the Company's transition to IFRS, described in note 2, is summarized in this note as follows:

(a)   Transition elections

The Company has applied the following transition exceptions and exemptions to full retrospective application of IFRS:

Business combinations – In accordance with IFRS transitional provisions, the Company elected to apply IFRS relating to business combinations prospectively from January 1, 2010. As such, Canadian GAAP balances relating to the acquisition of Appliance Canada Ltd. on January 2, 2008, including goodwill, have been carried forward without adjustment.

Share-based payments – In accordance with IFRS transitional provisions, the Company elected not to apply IFRS 2, *Share-based Payments*, to convertible shares issued under the Management Share Purchase Plan that were still outstanding at January 1, 2010 but had fully vested.

Estimates – Hindsight is not used to create or revise estimates. The estimates previously made by the Company under Canadian GAAP were not revised for application of IFRS except where necessary to reflect any difference in accounting policies.

(b)   Effect of material transition adjustments on the consolidated statements of financial positions, consolidated income statements, consolidated statements of comprehensive income and consolidated statements of cash flows:

i.   Consolidated Statements of Financial Position

	As at December 31, 2010			As at January 1, 2010		
	Cdn. GAAP	Adj. (revised*)	IFRS	Cdn. GAAP	Adj. (revised*)	IFRS
Assets						
Cash and cash equivalents	$ 71,589	$ –	$ 71,589	$ 58,301	$ –	$ 58,301
Available-for-sale financial assets	140,224	–	140,224	112,425	–	112,425
Trade receivables	28,569	–	28,569	31,501	–	31,501
Inventory	85,423	–	85,423	83,957	–	83,957
Deferred income tax assets (Note (a))	1,251	(1,251)	–	1,133	(1,133)	–
Total current assets	$ 327,056	$ (1,251)	$ 325,805	$ 287,317	$ (1,133)	$ 286,184
Other assets	1,574	–	1,574	1,560	–	1,560
Property, plant and equipment (Note (b))	209,909	(8,417)	201,492	212,198	(8,545)	203,653
Investment properties (Note (b))	–	8,417	8,417	–	8,545	8,545
Intangible assets	4,902	–	4,902	5,334	–	5,334
Goodwill	11,282	–	11,282	11,282	–	11,282
Deferred income tax assets (Note (a))	11,951	1,251	13,202	11,465	1,133	12,598
Total assets	$ 566,674	$ –	$ 566,674	$ 529,156	$ –	$ 529,156
Liabilities and Shareholders' Equity						
Trade and other payables (Note (c))	$ 84,065	$ (12,341)	$ 71,724	$ 83,880	$ (11,277)	$ 72,603
Provisions (Note (c))	–	12,341	12,341	–	11,277	11,277
Income taxes payable	524	–	524	1,958	–	1,958
Customers' deposits	17,198	–	17,198	15,632	–	15,632
Dividends payable	6,310	–	6,310	4,938	–	4,938
Deferred warranty plan revenue	16,882	–	16,882	16,150	–	16,150
Total current liabilities	$ 124,979	$ –	$ 124,979	$ 122,558	$ –	$ 122,558
Deferred warranty plan revenue	21,392	–	21,392	22,248	–	22,248
Redeemable share liability	172	–	172	383	–	383
Deferred income tax liabilities (Note (a))	9,845	–	9,845	8,829	–	8,829
Total liabilities	$ 156,388	$ –	$ 156,388	$ 154,018	$ –	$ 154,018
Common shares	19,177	–	19,177	17,704	–	17,704
Retained earnings	390,629	–	390,629	357,576	–	357,576
Accumulated other comprehensive income (loss)	480	–	480	(142)	–	(142)
Total shareholders' equity	$ 410,286	$ –	$ 410,286	$ 375,138	$ –	$ 375,138
Total liabilities and shareholders' equity	$ 566,674	$ –	$ 566,674	$ 529,156	$ –	$ 529,156

*   *The above figures have been revised, from previously reported IFRS amounts, to reflect an immaterial adjustment to the amount of foreign exchange that is required to be recorded within comprehensive income as it relates to the Company's foreign denominated non-monetary available-for-sale financial assets. Any foreign denominated monetary available-for-sale financial assets were appropriately recorded in the consolidated income statement.*

46

LEON'S FURNITURE LIMITED
Notes to the Consolidated Financial Statements

ii. Consolidated Statement of Comprehensive Income

	As at December 31, 2010		
	Cdn. GAAP	Reclasses (revised*)	IFRS
Revenue (Note (e))	$ 699,772	$ 10,663	$ 710,435
Cost of sales	412,379	–	412,379
Gross profit	$ 287,393	$ 10,663	$ 298,056
Operating expenses (Note (f))			
General and administrative expenses	–	98,684	98,684
Sales and marketing expenses	–	78,221	78,221
Occupancy expenses	–	29,551	29,551
Other operating expenses	–	5,780	5,780
Salaries and commissions	105,368	(105,368)	–
Advertising	31,565	(31,565)	–
Rent and property taxes	14,000	(14,000)	–
Amortization	16,156	(16,156)	–
Employee profit-sharing plan	4,746	(4,746)	–
Other operating expenses	41,495	(41,495)	–
Interest income	(3,134)	3,134	–
Other income	(12,988)	12,988	–
	$ 197,208	$ 15,028	$ 212,236
Operating profit	90,185	(4,365)	85,820
Gain on disposal	–	1,231	1,231
Finance income	–	3,134	3,134
Profit before income tax	90,185	–	90,185
Income tax expense	26,901	–	26,901
Profit for the period attributable to the shareholders of the Company	$ 63,284	$ –	$ 63,284
Other comprehensive income, net of tax			
Unrealized gains on available-for-sale financial assets arising during the period (Note (d))	773	–	773
Reclassification adjustment for net gains and losses included in profit for the period	(151)	–	(151)
Change in unrealized gains on available-for-sale financial assets arising during the period	622	–	622
Comprehensive income for the period attributable to the Shareholders of the Company	$ 63,906	$ –	$ 63,906

* The above figures have been revised, from previously reported IFRS amounts, to reflect an immaterial adjustment to the amount of foreign exchange that is required to be recorded within comprehensive income as it relates to the Company's foreign denominated non-monetary available-for-sale financial assets. Any foreign denominated monetary available-for-sale financial assets were appropriately recorded in the consolidated income statement.

Shoppers Drug Mart Corporation, 2011 Financial Statements Information

Consolidated Statements of Earnings

For the 52 weeks ended December 31, 2011 and January 1, 2011
(in thousands of Canadian dollars, except per share amounts)

	Note	2011	2010[1]
Sales		$ 10,458,652	$ 10,192,714
Cost of goods sold	9	(6,416,208)	(6,283,634)
Gross profit		4,042,444	3,909,080
Operating and administrative expenses	10, 11, 13	(3,131,539)	(3,011,758)
Operating income		910,905	897,322
Finance expenses	12	(64,038)	(60,633)
Earnings before income taxes		846,867	836,689
Income taxes	14		
Current		(208,696)	(238,779)
Deferred		(24,237)	(6,059)
		(232,933)	(244,838)
Net earnings		$ 613,934	$ 591,851
Net earnings per common share			
Basic	25	$ 2.84	$ 2.72
Diluted	25	$ 2.84	$ 2.72
Weighted average common shares outstanding (millions):			
Basic	25	216.4	217.4
Diluted	25	216.5	217.5
Actual common shares outstanding (millions)	24	212.5	217.5

[1] In preparing its 2010 comparative information, the Company has adjusted amounts reported previously in financial statements prepared in accordance with Canadian Generally Accepted Accounting Principles ("previous Canadian GAAP"). See Note 30 to these consolidated financial statements for an explanation of the transition to International Financial Reporting Standards ("IFRS").

The accompanying notes are an integral part of these consolidated financial statements.

Consolidated Statements of Comprehensive Income

For the 52 weeks ended December 31, 2011 and January 1, 2011
(in thousands of Canadian dollars)

	Note	2011	2010[1]
Net earnings		$ 613,934	$ 591,851
Other comprehensive income (loss), net of tax			
Effective portion of changes in fair value of hedges on interest rate derivatives (net of tax of $nil (2010: $525))	18	–	1,120
Effective portion of changes in fair value of hedges on equity forward derivatives (net of tax of $12 (2010: $205))	18	(39)	(521)
Net change in fair value of hedges on interest rate and equity forward derivatives transferred to earnings (net of tax of $163 (2010: $13))	18	411	33
Retirement benefit obligations actuarial losses (net of tax of $7,433 (2010: $2,905))	21	(21,943)	(8,150)
Other comprehensive loss, net of tax	7	(21,571)	(7,518)
Total comprehensive income		$ 592,363	$ 584,333

[1] In preparing its 2010 comparative information, the Company has adjusted amounts reported previously in financial statements prepared in accordance with previous Canadian GAAP. See Note 30 to these consolidated financial statements for an explanation of the transition to IFRS.

The accompanying notes are an integral part of these consolidated financial statements.

Source: Used with permission of Shoppers Drug Mart.

Consolidated Balance Sheets

As at December 31, 2011, January 1, 2011 and January 3, 2010
(in thousands of Canadian dollars)

	Note	December 31, 2011	January 1, 2011[1]	January 3, 2010[1]
Current assets				
Cash		$ 118,566	$ 64,354	$ 44,391
Accounts receivable		493,338	432,089	470,935
Inventory		2,042,302	1,957,525	1,852,441
Income taxes recoverable		–	20,384	–
Prepaid expenses and deposits		41,441	68,468	74,206
Total current assets		2,695,647	2,542,820	2,441,973
Non-current assets				
Property and equipment	15	1,767,543	1,677,340	1,541,841
Investment property	15	16,372	12,770	5,884
Goodwill	16	2,499,722	2,493,108	2,483,430
Intangible assets	17	281,737	272,217	258,766
Other assets		18,214	19,678	16,716
Deferred tax assets	14	21,075	26,264	28,456
Total non-current assets		4,604,663	4,501,377	4,335,093
Total assets		$ 7,300,310	$ 7,044,197	$ 6,777,066
Liabilities				
Bank indebtedness	19	$ 172,262	$ 209,013	$ 270,332
Commercial paper	19	–	127,828	260,386
Accounts payable and accrued liabilities	18	1,109,444	990,244	970,831
Income taxes payable		26,538	–	17,046
Dividends payable	24	53,119	48,927	46,748
Current portion of long-term debt	20	249,971	–	–
Provisions	22	12,024	12,562	11,009
Associate interest		152,880	138,993	130,189
Total current liabilities		1,776,238	1,527,567	1,706,541
Long-term debt	20	695,675	943,412	946,098
Other long-term liabilities	23	520,188	442,124	386,262
Provisions	22	1,701	1,852	1,062
Deferred tax liabilities	14	38,678	26,607	25,219
Total long-term liabilities		1,256,242	1,413,995	1,358,641
Total liabilities		3,032,480	2,941,562	3,065,182
Shareholders' equity				
Share capital	24	1,486,455	1,520,558	1,519,870
Treasury shares	24	(4,735)	–	–
Contributed surplus	26	10,246	11,702	10,274
Accumulated other comprehensive loss	7	(30,214)	(8,643)	(1,125)
Retained earnings		2,806,078	2,579,018	2,182,865
Total shareholders' equity		4,267,830	4,102,635	3,711,884
Total liabilities and shareholders' equity		$ 7,300,310	$ 7,044,197	$ 6,777,066

[1] In preparing its 2010 comparative information, the Company has adjusted amounts reported previously in financial statements prepared in accordance with previous Canadian GAAP. See Note 30 to these consolidated financial statements for an explanation of the transition to IFRS.

The accompanying notes are an integral part of these consolidated financial statements

On behalf of the Board of Directors:

Domenic Pilla
Director

Holger Kluge
Director

Consolidated Statements of Changes in Shareholders' Equity

For the 52 weeks ended December 31, 2011 and January 1, 2011
(in thousands of Canadian dollars)

	Note	Share Capital	Treasury Shares	Contributed Surplus	Accumulated Other Comprehensive Loss (Notes 18 and 21)	Retained Earnings	Total
Balance as at January 1, 2011[1]		$ 1,520,558	$ –	$ 11,702	$ (8,643)	$ 2,579,018	$ 4,102,635
Total comprehensive income		–	–	–	(21,571)	613,934	592,363
Dividends	24	–	–	–	–	(215,671)	(215,671)
Share repurchases	24	(35,576)	(4,735)	–	–	(171,203)	(211,514)
Share-based payments	26	–	–	(1,210)	–	–	(1,210)
Share options exercised	26	1,466	–	(246)	–	–	1,220
Repayment of share-purchase loans		7	–	–	–	–	7
Balance as at December 31, 2011		**$ 1,486,455**	**$ (4,735)**	**$ 10,246**	**$ (30,214)**	**$ 2,806,078**	**$ 4,267,830**
Balance as at January 3, 2010[1]		$ 1,519,870	$ –	$ 10,274	$ (1,125)	$ 2,182,865	$ 3,711,884
Total comprehensive income		–	–	–	(7,518)	591,851	584,333
Dividends	24	–	–	–	–	(195,698)	(195,698)
Share-based payments	26	–	–	1,592	–	–	1,592
Share options exercised	26	655	–	(164)	–	–	491
Repayment of share-purchase loans		33	–	–	–	–	33
Balance as at January 1, 2011[1]		$ 1,520,558	$ –	$ 11,702	$ (8,643)	$ 2,579,018	$ 4,102,635

[1] In preparing its 2010 comparative information, the Company has adjusted amounts reported previously in financial statements prepared in accordance with previous Canadian GAAP. See Note 30 to these consolidated financial statements for an explanation of the transition to IFRS.

The accompanying notes are an integral part of these consolidated financial statements.

Consolidated Statements of Cash Flows

For the 52 weeks ended December 31, 2011 and January 1, 2011
(in thousands of Canadian dollars)

	Note	2011	2010[1]
Cash flows from operating activities			
Net earnings		$ 613,934	$ 591,851
Adjustments for:			
Depreciation and amortization	13, 15, 17	296,464	278,421
Finance expenses	12	64,038	60,633
Loss on sale or disposal of property and equipment, including impairments	15, 17	2,015	3,880
Share-based payment transactions	26	(1,210)	1,592
Recognition and reversal of provisions, net	22	9,218	12,160
Other long-term liabilities	23	296	18,491
Income tax expense	14	232,933	244,838
		1,217,688	1,211,866
Net change in non-cash working capital balances	27	32,166	(34,824)
Provisions used	22	(9,907)	(9,817)
Interest paid		(63,853)	(62,916)
Income taxes paid		(202,256)	(276,108)
Net cash from operating activities		973,838	828,201
Cash flows from investing activities			
Proceeds from disposition of property and equipment and investment property		55,459	60,538
Business acquisitions	8	(10,496)	(11,779)
Deposits		105	1,534
Acquisition or development of property and equipment	15	(341,868)	(415,094)
Acquisition or development of intangible assets	17	(53,836)	(56,625)
Other assets		1,464	(3,249)
Net cash used in investing activities		(349,172)	(424,675)
Cash flows from financing activities			
Repurchase of own shares	24	(206,779)	–
Proceeds from exercise of share options	26	1,220	491
Repayment of share-purchase loans	24	7	33
Repayment of bank indebtedness, net	19	(36,714)	(61,319)
Repayment of commercial paper, net	19	(128,000)	(133,000)
Revolving term debt, net	20	152	(1,298)
Payment of transaction costs for debt refinancing	20	(575)	(2,792)
Repayment of financing lease obligations	23	(2,173)	(1,436)
Associate interest		13,887	9,277
Dividends paid	24	(211,479)	(193,519)
Net cash used in financing activities		(570,454)	(383,563)
Net increase in cash		54,212	19,963
Cash, beginning of the year		64,354	44,391
Cash, end of the year		$ 118,566	$ 64,354

[1] In preparing its 2010 comparative information, the Company has adjusted amounts reported previously in financial statements prepared in accordance with previous Canadian GAAP. See Note 30 to these consolidated financial statements for an explanation of the transition to IFRS.

The accompanying notes are an integral part of these consolidated financial statements.

Notes to the Consolidated Financial Statements

December 31, 2011 and January 1, 2011 (in thousands of Canadian dollars, except per share data)

> In order to save space, only notes that are referenced in the textbook are included.

1. GENERAL INFORMATION

Shoppers Drug Mart Corporation (the "Company") is a public company incorporated and domiciled in Canada, whose shares are publicly traded on the Toronto Stock Exchange. The Company's registered address is 243 Consumers Road, Toronto, Ontario M2J 4W8, Canada.

The Company is a licensor of 1,199 Shoppers Drug Mart®/Pharmaprix® full-service retail drug stores across Canada. The Shoppers Drug Mart®/Pharmaprix® stores are licensed to corporations owned by pharmacists ("Associates"). The Company also licenses or owns 58 Shoppers Simply Pharmacy®/Pharmaprix Simplement Santé® medical clinic pharmacies and eight Murale™ beauty stores. In addition, the Company owns and operates 63 Shoppers Home Health Care® stores. In addition to its store network, the Company owns Shoppers Drug Mart Specialty Health Network Inc., a provider of specialty drug distribution, pharmacy and comprehensive patient support services, and MediSystem Technologies Inc., a provider of pharmaceutical products and services to long-term care facilities in Ontario and Alberta.

The majority of the Company's sales are generated from the Shoppers Drug Mart®/Pharmaprix® full-service retail drug stores and the majority of the Company's assets are used in the operations of these stores. As such, the Company presents one operating segment in its consolidated financial statement disclosures. The revenue generated by Shoppers Drug Mart®/Pharmaprix Simplement Santé®, MediSystem Technologies Inc. and Shoppers Drug Mart Specialty Health Network Inc. is included with prescription sales of the Company's retail drug stores. The revenue generated by Shoppers Home Health Care® and Murale™ is included with the front store sales of the Company's retail drug stores.

These consolidated financial statements of the Company as at and for the financial year ended December 31, 2011 include the accounts of Shoppers Drug Mart Corporation, its subsidiaries, and the Associate-owned stores that comprise the majority of the Company's store network. The financial year of the Company consists of a 52 or 53 week period ending on the Saturday closest to December 31. The current financial year is the 52 weeks ended December 31, 2011. The comparative financial year is the 52 weeks ended January 1, 2011. The Company has also presented the consolidated balance sheet as at January 3, 2010, the Company's date of transition to International Financial Reporting Standards ("IFRS").

2. BASIS OF PREPARATION

(a) Statement of Compliance

These consolidated financial statements have been prepared in accordance with Canadian Generally Accepted Accounting Principles ("Canadian GAAP"). These consolidated financial statements also comply with International Financial Reporting Standards ("IFRS") as issued by the International Accounting Standards Board ("IASB").

These are the Company's first consolidated financial statements prepared in accordance with IFRS. IFRS 1, "First-time Adoption of International Financial Reporting Standards", has been applied in the preparation of these financial statements. Consolidated financial statements of the Company had been prepared under previous Canadian GAAP, which differs in certain respects from IFRS. When preparing the Company's 2011 consolidated financial statements, management has amended certain accounting methods in order to comply with IFRS. The comparative consolidated financial statements reflect the adoption of IFRS.

An explanation of how the transition from previous Canadian GAAP to IFRS has affected the reported financial position, financial performance and cash flows of the Company is provided in Note 30 to these consolidated financial statements.

These consolidated financial statements were authorized for issuance by the Board of Directors of the Company on February 9, 2012.

(b) Use of Estimates and Judgements

The preparation of these consolidated financial statements in conformity with IFRS requires management to make certain judgements, estimates and assumptions that affect the application of accounting policies and the reported amounts of assets and liabilities and disclosure of contingent assets and liabilities at the date of these consolidated financial statements and the reported amounts of revenues and expenses during the reporting period.

2. BASIS OF PREPARATION (continued)

Judgement is commonly used in determining whether a balance or transaction should be recognized in the consolidated financial statements and estimates and assumptions are more commonly used in determining the measurement of recognized transactions and balances. However, judgement and estimates are often interrelated.

The Company has applied judgement in its assessment of the appropriateness of the consolidation of the Associate-owned stores, classification of items such as leases and financial instruments, the recognition of tax losses and provisions, determining the tax rates used for measuring deferred taxes, determining cash-generating units, identifying the indicators of impairment for property and equipment and intangible assets with finite useful lives, and the level of componentization of property and equipment.

Estimates are used when estimating the useful lives of property and equipment and intangible assets for the purpose of depreciation and amortization, when accounting for or measuring items such as inventory provisions, Shoppers Optimum® loyalty card program deferred revenue, assumptions underlying the actuarial determination of retirement benefit obligations, income and other taxes, provisions, certain fair value measures including those related to the valuation of business combinations, share-based payments and financial instruments and when testing goodwill, indefinite useful life intangible assets and other assets for impairment. Actual results may differ from these estimates.

Estimates and underlying assumptions are reviewed on an ongoing basis. Revisions to accounting estimates are recognized in the period in which the estimates are revised and in any future periods affected.

3. SIGNIFICANT ACCOUNTING POLICIES

The accounting policies set out in these consolidated financial statements have been applied consistently to all periods presented in these consolidated financial statements.

(a) Basis of Consolidation

(i) Subsidiaries

Subsidiaries are entities controlled by the Company. Control exists where the Company has the power to govern the financial and operating policies of an entity so as to obtain benefits from its activities. All of the Company's subsidiaries are wholly-owned. The financial statements of subsidiaries are included in the Company's consolidated financial statements from the date that control commences until the date that control ceases.

(ii) Associate-owned Stores

Associate-owned stores comprise the majority of the Company's store network. The Company does not have any direct or indirect shareholdings in these Associates' corporations. The Associates' corporations remain separate legal entities. The Company consolidates the Associate-owned stores under IAS 27, "Consolidated and Separate Financial Statements" ("IAS 27"). The consolidation of the stores under IAS 27 was determined based on the concept of control under IAS 27 and determined primarily through the agreements with Associates ("Associate Agreements") that govern the relationship between the Company and the Associates.

(iii) Transactions Eliminated on Consolidation

Intra-company balances and transactions and any unrealized earnings and expenses arising from intra-company transactions, including those of the Associate-owned stores, are eliminated in preparing the consolidated financial statements.

(b) Basis of Measurement

These consolidated financial statements have been prepared on the historical cost basis except for certain financial instruments, deferred revenue related to the Shoppers Optimum® loyalty card program and the liabilities for the Company's long-term incentive plan and restricted share unit plan, which are measured at fair value (see Note 26 to these consolidated financial statements for further information on the long-term incentive plan and the restricted share unit plan). Any recognized impairment losses will also impact the historical cost of certain balances.

The methods used to measure fair values are discussed further in Note 4 to these consolidated financial statements.

(c) Revenue

(i) Sale of Goods and Services

Revenue is comprised primarily of retail sales, including prescription sales. Retail sales are recognized as revenue when the goods are sold to the customer. Revenue is net of returns and amounts deferred related to the issuance of points under the Shoppers Optimum® Loyalty Card Program (the "Program"). Where a sales transaction includes points awarded under the Program, revenue allocated to the Program points is deferred based on the fair value of the awards and recognized as revenue when the Program points are redeemed and the Company fulfills its obligations to supply the awards.

Revenue is measured at the fair value of the consideration received or receivable from the customer for products sold or services supplied.

(ii) Shoppers Optimum® Loyalty Card Program

The Shoppers Optimum® Loyalty Card Program allows members to earn points on their purchases in Shoppers Drug Mart®, Pharmaprix®, Shoppers Simply Pharmacy®, Pharmaprix Simplement Santé®, Shoppers Home Health Care® and Murale™ stores at a rate of 10 points for each dollar spent on eligible products and services, plus any applicable bonus points. Members can then redeem points, in accordance with the Program rewards schedule or other offers, for qualifying merchandise at the time of a future purchase transaction.

When points are earned by Program members, the Company defers revenue equal to the fair value of the awards. The Program's deferred revenue is recognized within accounts payable and accrued liabilities in the Company's consolidated balance sheets. When awards are redeemed by Program members, the redemption value of the awards is charged against the deferred revenue balance and recognized as revenue.

The estimated fair value per point is determined based on the expected weighted average redemption levels for future redemptions based on the program reward schedule, including special redemption events. The trends in redemption rates (points redeemed as a percentage of points issued) are reviewed on an ongoing basis and the estimated fair value per point is adjusted based upon expected future activity.

(d) Vendor Rebates

The Company classifies rebates and other consideration received from vendors as a reduction to the cost of inventory. These amounts are recognized in cost of goods sold when the associated inventory is sold. Certain exceptions apply where the consideration received from the vendor is a reimbursement of a selling cost or a payment for services delivered to the vendor, in which case the consideration is reflected in cost of goods sold or operating and administrative expenses dependent on where the related expenses are recorded.

(e) Finance Expenses

Finance expenses are comprised of interest expense on borrowings and the amortization of transaction costs incurred in conjunction with debt transactions. All borrowing costs are recognized in earnings on an accrual basis using the effective interest method, net of amounts capitalized as part of the cost of qualifying property and equipment.

The Company's finance income is not significant.

(f) Borrowing Costs

Borrowing costs that are directly attributable to the acquisition, construction or development of a qualifying asset are recognized as part of the cost of that asset. Qualifying assets are those that require a substantial period of time to prepare for their intended use. All other borrowing costs are recognized as finance expenses in the period in which they are incurred.

The Company capitalizes borrowing costs at the weighted average interest rate on borrowings outstanding for the period. The Company commences capitalization of borrowing costs as part of the cost of a qualifying asset when activities are undertaken to prepare the asset for its intended use and when expenditures, including borrowing costs, are incurred for the asset. Capitalization of borrowing costs ceases when substantially all of the activities necessary to prepare the asset for its intended use are complete.

3. SIGNIFICANT ACCOUNTING POLICIES (continued)

(g) Income Taxes

Income tax expense is comprised of taxes currently payable on earnings and changes in deferred tax balances, excluding those changes related to business acquisitions. Income tax expense is recognized in net earnings except to the extent that it relates to items recognized either in other comprehensive income (loss) or directly in equity, in which case it is recognized in other comprehensive income (loss) or in equity respectively.

Current tax expense is comprised of the tax payable on the taxable income for the current financial year using tax rates enacted or substantively enacted at the reporting date, and any adjustment to income taxes payable in respect of previous years.

Deferred tax is recognized using the balance sheet method in respect of taxable temporary differences arising from differences between the carrying amount of assets and liabilities for tax purposes and their carrying amounts in the financial statements. Deferred tax is calculated at the tax rates that are expected to apply to temporary differences in the year they are expected to reverse and are based on the tax legislation that has been enacted or substantively enacted by the reporting date. Deferred tax is not recognized for the following temporary differences: the initial recognition of goodwill and the initial recognition of assets or liabilities in a transaction that is not a business acquisition and that affects neither accounting nor taxable earnings; and, differences relating to investments in subsidiaries to the extent that it is probable that they will not reverse in the foreseeable future. Deferred tax assets and liabilities are offset if there is a legally enforceable right to offset the recognized amounts and the Company intends to settle on a net basis or to realize the asset and settle the liability simultaneously.

A deferred tax asset is recognized to the extent that it is probable that future taxable earnings will be available against which the temporary difference can be utilized. Deferred tax assets are reviewed at each reporting date and are reduced to the extent that it is no longer probable that all or part of the related tax benefit will be realized.

(h) Earnings per Common Share

The Company presents basic and diluted earnings per share ("EPS") amounts for its common shares. Basic EPS is calculated by dividing the net earnings attributable to common shareholders of the Company by the weighted average number of common shares outstanding during the period. Diluted EPS is determined by dividing the net earnings attributable to common shareholders of the Company by the weighted average number of common shares outstanding after adjusting both amounts for the effects of all potential dilutive common shares, which are comprised of share options granted to employees. Anti-dilutive options are not included in the calculation of diluted EPS.

(i) Financial Instruments

(i) Classification of Financial Instruments

Financial instruments are recognized when the Company becomes a party to the contractual provisions of a financial instrument. Financial instruments are classified into one of the following categories: held for trading, held-to-maturity investments, loans and receivables, available-for-sale financial assets or financial liabilities. The classification determines the accounting treatment of the instrument. The classification is determined by the Company when the financial instrument is initially recorded, based on the underlying purpose of the instrument.

The Company's financial instruments are classified and measured as follows:

Financial Asset/Liability	Category	Measurement
Cash	Loans and receivables	Amortized cost
Accounts receivable	Loans and receivables	Amortized cost
Deposits[1]	Loans and receivables	Amortized cost
Long-term receivables[2]	Loans and receivables	Amortized cost
Bank indebtedness	Financial liabilities	Amortized cost
Commercial paper	Financial liabilities	Amortized cost
Accounts payable and accrued liabilities	Financial liabilities	Amortized cost
Dividends payable	Financial liabilities	Amortized cost
Long-term debt	Financial liabilities	Amortized cost
Other long-term liabilities	Financial liabilities	Amortized cost

Derivatives	Classification	Measurement
Interest rate derivatives[3]	Effective cash flow hedge	Fair value through other comprehensive income (loss)
Equity forward derivatives[3][4]	Derivative financial instrument	Fair value through earnings
Equity forward derivatives[3][4]	Effective cash flow hedge	Fair value through other comprehensive income (loss)

[1] The carrying value of deposits is recognized within prepaid expenses and deposits in the consolidated balance sheets.

[2] The carrying value of long-term receivables is recognized within other assets in the consolidated balance sheets.

[3] The carrying values of the Company's derivatives are recognized within other assets, accounts payable and accrued liabilities and other long-term liabilities in the consolidated balance sheets.

[4] The portion of the equity forward derivative agreements relating to the earned long-term incentive plan units and earned restricted share unit plan units is considered a derivative financial instrument. The portion of the equity forward derivative agreements relating to the unearned long-term incentive plan units and unearned restricted share unit plan units is considered an effective cash flow hedge. See Note 26 to these consolidated financial statements for further discussion of the long-term incentive plan and the restricted share unit plan.

Financial instruments measured at amortized cost are initially recognized at fair value and then subsequently at amortized cost using the effective interest method, less any impairment losses, with gains and losses recognized in earnings in the period in which the gain or loss occurs. Changes in the fair value of the Company's derivative instruments designated as effective cash flow hedges are recognized in other comprehensive income (loss) and changes in derivative instruments not designated as effective hedges are recognized within operating and administrative expenses in the Company's consolidated statements of earnings in the period of the change.

The Company categorizes its financial assets and financial liabilities that are recognized in the consolidated balance sheets at fair value using the fair value hierarchy. The fair value hierarchy has the following levels:

- Level 1 – quoted market prices in active markets for identical assets or liabilities;
- Level 2 – inputs other than quoted market prices included in Level 1 that are observable for the asset or liability, either directly (as prices) or indirectly (derived from prices); and
- Level 3 – unobservable inputs such as inputs for the asset or liability that are not based on observable market data.

The level in the fair value hierarchy within which the fair value measurement is categorized in its entirety is determined on the basis of the lowest level input that is significant to the fair value measurement in its entirety.

3. SIGNIFICANT ACCOUNTING POLICIES (continued)

(ii) Transaction Costs

Transaction costs are added to the initial fair value of financial assets and liabilities when those financial assets and liabilities are not measured at fair value subsequent to initial measurement. Transaction costs are amortized to net earnings, within finance expenses, using the effective interest method.

(iii) Derivative Financial Instruments and Hedge Accounting

The Company is exposed to fluctuations in interest rates by virtue of its borrowings under its bank credit facilities, commercial paper program and financing programs available to its Associates. Increases and decreases in interest rates will negatively or positively impact the financial performance of the Company. The Company may use, from time to time, interest rate derivatives to manage this exposure. The earnings or expense arising from the use of these instruments is recognized within finance expenses for the financial year.

The Company uses cash-settled equity forward agreements to limit its exposure to future price changes in the Company's share price for share unit awards under the Company's long-term incentive plan ("LTIP") and restricted share unit plan ("RSU Plan"). The earnings or expense arising from the use of these instruments is included in other comprehensive income (loss) and in operating and administrative expenses, based on the amounts considered to be a hedge or a derivative, respectively, for the financial year. See Note 26 to these consolidated financial statements for further discussion of the LTIP and RSU Plan.

The Company formally identifies, designates and documents all relationships between hedging instruments and hedged items, as well as its risk assessment objective and strategy for undertaking various hedge transactions. The Company assesses, both at the inception of the hedge and on an ongoing basis, including on re-designation, whether the derivatives that are used in hedging transactions are highly effective in offsetting changes in fair values or cash flows of hedged items. When such derivative instruments cease to exist or to be effective as hedges, or when designation of a hedging relationship is terminated, any associated deferred gains or losses are recognized in earnings in the same period as the corresponding gains or losses associated with the hedged item. When a hedged item ceases to exist, any associated deferred gains or losses are recognized in earnings in the period the hedged item ceases to exist.

(iv) Embedded Derivatives

Embedded derivatives (elements of contracts whose cash flows move independently from the host contract) are required to be separated and measured at their respective fair values unless certain criteria are met. The Company does not have any significant embedded features in contractual arrangements that require separate accounting or presentation from the related host contracts.

(v) Share Capital

Common Shares   Common shares issued by the Company are recorded in the amount of the proceeds received, net of direct issue costs.

Repurchase of Share Capital   The Company, from time to time, will repurchase its common shares under a Normal Course Issuer Bid. When common shares are repurchased, the amount of the consideration paid which includes directly attributable costs and is net of any tax effects, is recognized as a deduction from share capital. Any repurchased common shares are cancelled. The premium paid over the average book value of the common shares repurchased is charged to retained earnings. At the end of a reporting period, if there are shares that have not yet been cancelled, they are recognized as treasury shares at the purchase price of the transaction.

(j) Business Combinations

The Company applies the acquisition method in accounting for business combinations.

On acquisition, the assets, including intangible assets, and any liabilities assumed are measured at their fair value. Purchase price allocations may be preliminary when initially recognized and may change pending finalization of the valuation of the assets acquired. Purchase price allocations are finalized within one year of the acquisition and prior periods are restated to reflect any adjustments to the purchase price allocation made subsequent to the initial recognition.

The determination of fair values, particularly for intangible assets, is based on management's estimates and includes assumptions on the timing and amount of future cash flows. The Company recognizes as goodwill the excess of the purchase price of an acquired business over the fair value of the underlying net assets, including intangible assets, at the date of acquisition. Transaction costs are expensed as incurred. The date of acquisition is the date on which the Company obtains control over the acquired business.

(k) Inventory

Inventory is comprised of merchandise inventory, which includes prescription inventory, and is valued at the lower of cost and estimated net realizable value. Cost is determined on the first-in, first-out basis. Cost includes all direct expenditures and other appropriate costs incurred in bringing inventory to its present location and condition. The Company classifies rebates and other consideration received from a vendor as a reduction to the cost of inventory unless the rebate relates to the reimbursement of a selling cost or a payment for services.

Net realizable value is the estimated selling price in the ordinary course of business, less the estimated selling expenses.

(l) Property and Equipment and Investment Property

(i) Recognition and Measurement

Items of property and equipment are carried at cost less accumulated depreciation and any recognized impairment losses (see (p) Impairment).

Cost includes expenditures that are directly attributable to the acquisition of the asset. The cost of self-constructed assets includes the cost of materials and direct labour, any other costs directly attributable to bringing the assets to a working condition for their intended use, and, where applicable, the costs of dismantling and removing the items and restoring the site on which they are located. Borrowing costs are recognized as part of the cost of an asset, where appropriate.

Purchased software that is integral to the functionality of the related equipment is capitalized as part of that equipment.

When components of property and equipment have different useful lives, they are accounted for as separate items of property and equipment.

Gains and losses on disposal of an item of property and equipment are determined by comparing the proceeds from disposal with the carrying amount of property and equipment and are recognized net, within operating and administrative expenses, in net earnings.

Fully-depreciated items of property and equipment that are still in use continue to be recognized in cost and accumulated depreciation.

(ii) Subsequent Costs

The cost of replacing part of an item of property and equipment is recognized in the carrying amount of the item if it is probable that the future economic benefits embodied within the part will flow to the Company and its cost can be measured reliably. The carrying amount of the replaced part is de-recognized. The costs of repairs and maintenance of property and equipment are recognized in earnings as incurred.

Notes to the Consolidated Financial Statements (continued)
December 31, 2011 and January 1, 2011 (in thousands of Canadian dollars, except per share data)

3. SIGNIFICANT ACCOUNTING POLICIES (continued)

(iii) Depreciation

Depreciation is recognized in earnings on a straight-line basis over the estimated useful lives of each component of an item of property and equipment. Land is not depreciated. The Company commences recognition of depreciation in earnings when the item of property and equipment is ready for its intended use.

The estimated useful lives for the current and comparative periods are as follows:

Buildings and their components	10 to 40 years
Equipment and fixtures	3 to 10 years
Computer equipment	2 to 10 years
Leasehold improvements	Lesser of term of the lease and useful life
Assets under financing leases	Lesser of term of the lease and useful life

Depreciation methods and useful lives are reviewed at each reporting date.

(iv) Investment Property

Investment property is carried at cost less accumulated depreciation and any recognized impairment losses.

(m) Goodwill

(i) Recognition and Measurement

The Company recognizes goodwill as the excess amount of the purchase price of an acquired business over the fair value of the underlying net assets, including intangible assets, at the date of acquisition. Goodwill is not amortized but is tested for impairment on an annual basis or more frequently if there are indicators that goodwill may be impaired (see (p) Impairment).

(ii) Acquisitions Prior to January 3, 2010

As described in Note 30 to these consolidated financial statements, as part of its transition to IFRS, the Company elected to apply IFRS 3, "Business Combinations" ("IFRS 3"), only to those business combinations that occurred on or after January 3, 2010. In respect of acquisitions prior to January 3, 2010, goodwill represents the amount recognized under previous Canadian GAAP.

(iii) Subsequent Measurement

Goodwill is measured at cost less any accumulated impairment losses.

(n) Intangible Assets

(i) Computer Software

The Company acquires computer software through purchases from vendors and internal development. Computer software that is an integral part of computer equipment is presented in property and equipment. All other computer software is treated as an intangible asset. The Company includes computer software under development in intangible assets. The assessment of whether computer software is an integral part of computer hardware is made when the software development project is complete and placed into use. Costs for internally developed computer software include directly attributable costs including direct labour and overheads associated with the software development project. Expenditures on research activities as part of internally developed computer software are recognized in earnings when incurred.

(ii) Other Intangible Assets

Other intangible assets that are acquired by the Company, other than as a result of a business acquisition, which have finite useful lives, are measured at cost less accumulated amortization and any accumulated impairment losses (see (p) Impairment). Other intangible assets that are acquired by the Company as a result of a business acquisition are measured at their fair values as at the date of acquisition.

(iii) Amortization

Amortization is recognized in earnings on a straight-line basis over the estimated useful lives of intangible assets from the date that they are available for their intended use. The estimated useful lives are as follows:

Prescription files	7 to 12 years
Customer relationships	5 to 25 years
Computer software	3 to 10 years
Other	Term of the lease or 3 years

Computer software under development is not amortized. Amortization methods and useful lives are reviewed at each reporting date.

(o) Leases

The Company leases most of its store locations and office space. Terms vary in length and typically permit renewal for additional periods. Leases for which substantially all the benefits and risks of ownership are transferred to the Company based on certain criteria are recorded as financing leases and classified as property and equipment, accounts payable and accrued liabilities and other long-term liabilities. All other leases are classified as operating leases under which minimum rent, including scheduled escalations, is expensed on a straight-line basis over the term of the lease, including any rent-free periods. Landlord inducements are deferred and amortized as reductions to rent expense on a straight-line basis over the same period.

In the normal course of business, the Company sells certain real estate properties and enters into leaseback arrangements for the area occupied by the Associate-owned stores. The leases are assessed as financing or operating in nature as applicable, and are accounted for accordingly. The gains realized on the disposal of the real estate properties related to sale-leaseback transactions, which are financing in nature, are deferred and amortized on a straight-line basis over the shorter of the lease term and the estimated useful life of the leased asset. The gains realized on the disposal of real estate properties related to sale-leaseback transactions, which are transacted at fair value and are operating in nature, are recognized within operating and administrative expenses in the consolidated statements of earnings. In the event the fair value of the asset at the time of the sale-leaseback transaction is less than its carrying value, the difference would be recognized within operating and administrative expenses in the consolidated statements of earnings.

Leases may include additional payments for real estate taxes, maintenance and insurance. These amounts are expensed in the period to which they relate.

(p) Impairment

(i) Financial Assets

A financial asset is assessed at each reporting date to determine whether there is any objective evidence that it is impaired. A financial asset is considered to be impaired if objective evidence indicates that one or more events, which have a negative effect on the estimated future cash flows of that asset, have occurred.

An impairment loss in respect of a financial asset measured at amortized cost is calculated as the difference between its carrying amount and the present value of the estimated future cash flows, discounted at the original effective interest rate.

Individually significant financial assets are tested for impairment on an individual basis. The remaining financial assets are assessed collectively in groups that share similar credit risk characteristics.

All impairment losses are recognized in the consolidated statements of earnings.

An impairment loss is reversed if the reversal can be objectively related to an event occurring after the impairment loss was recognized. For financial assets measured at amortized cost, the reversal is recognized in earnings.

December 31, 2011 and January 1, 2011 (in thousands of Canadian dollars, except per share data)

3. SIGNIFICANT ACCOUNTING POLICIES (continued)

(ii) Property and Equipment and Intangible Assets with Finite Useful Lives

The carrying amount of property and equipment and intangible assets with finite useful lives is reviewed at each reporting date to determine whether there are any indicators of impairment. If any such indicators exist, then the recoverable amount of the asset is estimated as the higher of the fair value of the asset less costs to sell, or value-in-use. An impairment loss is recognized in net earnings for the amount by which the carrying amount of the asset exceeds its recoverable amount. For the purposes of assessing impairment, when an individual asset does not generate cash flows in and of itself, assets are then grouped and tested at the lowest level for which there are separately identifiable cash flows, called a cash-generating unit. The Company has determined that its cash generating units are primarily its retail stores.

(iii) Goodwill and Intangible Assets with Indefinite Useful Lives

For goodwill and intangible assets that have indefinite useful lives or that are not yet available for use, the carrying value is reviewed for impairment on an annual basis, or more frequently if there are indicators that impairment may exist.

Goodwill is allocated to cash-generating units expected to benefit from the synergies created from a business combination and to the lowest level at which management monitors goodwill. To review for impairment, the recoverable amount of each cash-generating unit to which goodwill is allocated is compared to its carrying value, including goodwill.

(iv) Recoverable Amount

The recoverable amount of an asset or cash-generating unit is the greater of its value-in-use and its fair value less costs to sell. In assessing value-in-use, the estimated future cash flows are discounted to their present value using a pre-tax discount rate that reflects current market assessments of the time value of money and the risks specific to the asset.

(v) Impairment Losses

An impairment loss is recognized if the carrying amount of an asset or its cash-generating unit exceeds its estimated recoverable amount. Impairment losses are recognized in operating and administrative expenses in the consolidated statements of earnings. Impairment losses recognized in respect of cash-generating units are allocated first to reduce the carrying amount of any goodwill allocated to the cash-generating units and, then, to reduce the carrying amounts of the other assets in the cash-generating unit (group of cash-generating units) on a pro rata basis.

An impairment loss in respect of goodwill is not reversed. In respect of other assets, impairment losses recognized in prior periods are assessed at each reporting date for any indicators that the loss has decreased or no longer exists. An impairment loss is reversed if there has been a change in the estimates used to determine the recoverable amount. An impairment loss is reversed only to the extent that the carrying amount of the asset does not exceed the carrying amount that would have been determined, net of depreciation or amortization, if no impairment loss had been recognized.

(q) Bank Indebtedness

Bank indebtedness is comprised of corporate bank overdraft balances, corporate and Associate-owned store bank lines of credit and outstanding cheques.

5. FINANCIAL RISK MANAGEMENT OBJECTIVES AND POLICIES RELATED TO FINANCIAL INSTRUMENTS

Financial Risk Management Objectives and Policies

In the normal course of business, the Company is exposed to financial risks that have the potential to negatively impact its financial performance. The Company may use derivative financial instruments to manage certain of these risks. The Company does not use derivative financial instruments for trading or speculative purposes. These risks are discussed in more detail below.

Interest Rate Risk

Interest rate risk is the risk that fair value or future cash flows associated with the Company's financial assets or liabilities will fluctuate due to changes in market interest rates.

The Company, including its Associate-owned store network, is exposed to fluctuations in interest rates by virtue of its borrowings under its bank credit facilities, commercial paper program and financing programs available to its Associates. Increases or decreases in interest rates will positively or negatively impact the financial performance of the Company.

The Company monitors market conditions and the impact of interest rate fluctuations on its fixed and floating rate debt instruments on an ongoing basis and may use interest rate derivatives to manage this exposure. Until December 2010, the Company used interest rate derivatives to manage a portion of the interest rate risk on its commercial paper. The Company was party to an agreement converting an aggregate notional principal amount of $50,000 of floating rate commercial paper debt into fixed rate debt at a rate of 4.18%, which expired in December 2010. Throughout 2011, the Company no longer had interest rate derivative agreements to convert its floating rate debt into fixed rate debt. See Note 18 to these consolidated financial statements for further discussion of the derivative agreement.

As at December 31, 2011, the Company had $166,592 (2010: $304,410) of unhedged floating rate debt. During the current financial year, the Company's average outstanding unhedged floating rate debt was $386,193 (2010: $538,243). Had interest rates been higher or lower by 50 basis points during the current financial year, net earnings for the financial year would have decreased or increased, respectively, by approximately $1,396 (2010: $1,885) as a result of the Company's exposure to interest rate fluctuations on its unhedged floating rate debt.

Credit Risk

Credit risk is the risk that the Company's counterparties will fail to meet their financial obligations to the Company, causing a financial loss.

Accounts receivable arise primarily in respect of prescription sales billed to governments and third-party drug plans and, as a result, collection risk is low. There is no concentration of balances with debtors in the remaining accounts receivable. The Company does not consider its exposure to credit risk to be material.

Liquidity Risk

Liquidity risk is the risk that the Company will be unable to meet its obligations relating to its financial liabilities.

The Company prepares cash flow budgets and forecasts to ensure that it has sufficient funds through operations, access to bank facilities and access to debt and capital markets to meet its financial obligations, capital investment program requirements and fund new investment opportunities or other unanticipated requirements as they arise. The Company manages its liquidity risk as it relates to financial liabilities by monitoring its cash flow from operating activities to meet its short-term financial liability obligations and planning for the repayment of its long-term financial liability obligations through cash flow from operating activities and/or the issuance of new debt or equity.

December 31, 2011 and January 1, 2011 (in thousands of Canadian dollars, except per share data)

5. FINANCIAL RISK MANAGEMENT OBJECTIVES AND POLICIES RELATED TO FINANCIAL INSTRUMENTS (continued)

The contractual maturities of the Company's financial liabilities in the consolidated balance sheet as at December 31, 2011 are as follows:

	Carrying Amount	Payments Due in the Next 90 Days	Payments Due Between 90 Days and Less Than a Year	Payments Due Between 1 Year and Less Than 2 Years	Payments Due After 2 Years	Total Contractual Cash Flows
Bank indebtedness	$ 172,262	$ 172,262	$ –	$ –	$ –	$ 172,262
Accounts payable and accrued liabilities	1,055,891	1,032,431	23,460	–	–	1,055,891
Derivatives	915	–	793	122	–	915
Dividends payable	53,119	53,119	–	–	–	53,119
Medium-term notes	945,494	262,488	28,943	474,202	256,487	1,022,120
Revolving-term debt	152	–	–	–	152	152
Other long-term liabilities	231,970	–	–	18,478	213,492	231,970
Total	**$ 2,459,803**	**$ 1,520,300**	**$ 53,196**	**$ 492,802**	**$ 470,131**	**$ 2,536,429**

The contractual maturities of the Company's financial liabilities in the consolidated balance sheet as at January 1, 2011, were as follows:

	Carrying Amount	Payments Due in the Next 90 Days	Payments Due Between 90 Days and Less Than a Year	Payments Due Between 1 Year and Less Than 2 Years	Payments Due After 2 Years	Total Contractual Cash Flows
Bank indebtedness	$ 209,013	$ 209,013	$ –	$ –	$ –	$ 209,013
Commercial paper	127,828	128,000	–	–	–	128,000
Accounts payable and accrued liabilities	930,910	920,384	10,526	–	–	930,910
Derivatives	2,257	–	674	1,583	–	2,257
Dividends payable	48,927	48,927	–	–	–	48,927
Medium-term notes	946,641	12,488	34,943	291,430	730,690	1,069,551
Other long-term liabilities	167,709	–	–	19,207	148,502	167,709
Total	$ 2,433,285	$ 1,318,812	$ 46,143	$ 312,220	$ 879,192	$ 2,556,367

The accounts payable and accrued liabilities and other long-term liabilities amounts exclude certain liabilities that are not considered financial liabilities. The medium-term note amounts, which are recognized within long-term debt in the consolidated balance sheets, include principal and interest liabilities.

9. COST OF GOODS SOLD

During the current financial year, the Company recorded $39,943 (2010: $37,884) as an expense for the write-down of inventory as a result of net realizable value being lower than cost in cost of goods sold in the consolidated statements of earnings.

During the financial years ended December 31, 2011 and January 1, 2011, the Company did not reverse any significant inventory write-downs recognized in previous years.

15. PROPERTY AND EQUIPMENT AND INVESTMENT PROPERTY

	Properties Under Development	Land	Buildings	Equipment, Fixtures and Computer Equipment	Leasehold Improvements	Assets Under Financing Leases (Note 23)	Total
Cost							
Balance at January 1, 2011	$ 72,035	$ 70,411	$ 206,472	$1,135,805	$1,179,795	$ 83,082	$2,747,600
Additions:							
– Asset acquisitions	9,979	–	–	–	–	43,952	53,931
– Development	9,990	3,688	25,738	168,204	131,667	–	339,287
Transfers	(20,662)	6,147	8,791	752	320	–	(4,652)
Computer software transfers from intangible assets	–	–	–	1,330	–	–	1,330
Disposals	–	(14,768)	(26,958)	(23,563)	(20,337)	–	(85,626)
Retirements	–	–	–	534	–	–	534
Balance at December 31, 2011	**$ 71,342**	**$ 65,478**	**$ 214,043**	**$1,283,062**	**$1,291,445**	**$ 127,034**	**$3,052,404**
Depreciation							
Balance at January 1, 2011	$ –	$ –	$ 16,102	$ 655,467	$ 355,523	$ 11,446	$1,038,538
Depreciation for the financial year	–	–	11,542	140,537	92,423	4,965	249,467
Transfers	–	–	(216)	375	(123)	–	36
Computer software transfers from intangible assets	–	–	–	(18)	–	–	(18)
Disposals	–	–	(3,103)	(19,792)	(11,807)	–	(34,702)
Retirements	–	–	–	(182)	–	–	(182)
Balance at December 31, 2011	**$ –**	**$ –**	**$ 24,325**	**$ 776,387**	**$ 436,016**	**$ 16,411**	**$1,253,139**
Impairment losses							
Balance at January 1, 2011	$ –	$ –	$ –	$ 16,257	$ 15,465	$ –	$ 31,722
Impairment loss	–	–	–	–	–	–	–
Balance at December 31, 2011	**$ –**	**$ –**	**$ –**	**$ 16,257**	**$ 15,465**	**$ –**	**$ 31,722**
Net book value							
At December 31, 2011	**$ 71,342**	**$ 65,478**	**$ 189,718**	**$ 490,418**	**$ 839,964**	**$ 110,623**	**$1,767,543**
Cost							
Balance at January 3, 2010	$ 113,478	$ 57,683	$ 144,515	$1,048,056	$1,022,868	$ 59,382	$2,445,982
Additions:							
– Asset acquisitions	11,139	531	695	–	–	23,700	36,065
– Development	94,745	327	5,206	135,454	166,986	–	402,718
Transfers	(143,302)	27,880	97,365	(1,223)	11,943	–	(7,337)
Computer software transfers from intangible assets	–	–	–	1,395	–	–	1,395
Disposals	(4,025)	(16,010)	(41,309)	(45,515)	(22,002)	–	(128,861)
Retirements	–	–	–	(2,362)	–	–	(2,362)
Balance at January 1, 2011	**$ 72,035**	**$ 70,411**	**$ 206,472**	**$1,135,805**	**$1,179,795**	**$ 83,082**	**$2,747,600**
Depreciation							
Balance at January 3, 2010	$ –	$ –	$ 24,412	$ 561,691	$ 288,519	$ 8,135	$ 882,757
Depreciation for the financial year	–	–	8,759	136,933	85,487	3,311	234,490
Transfers	–	–	732	(439)	(293)	–	–
Disposals	–	–	(17,801)	(41,255)	(18,190)	–	(77,246)
Retirements	–	–	–	(1,463)	–	–	(1,463)

15. PROPERTY AND EQUIPMENT AND INVESTMENT PROPERTY (continued)

	Properties Under Development	Land	Buildings	Equipment, Fixtures and Computer Equipment	Leasehold Improvements	Assets Under Financing Leases (Note 23)	Total
Balance at January 1, 2011	$ −	$ −	$ 16,102	$ 655,467	$ 355,523	$ 11,446	$ 1,038,538
Impairment losses							
Balance at January 3, 2010	$ −	$ −	$ −	$ 10,502	$ 10,882	$ −	$ 21,384
Impairment loss	−	−	−	5,755	4,583	−	10,338
Balance at January 1, 2011	$ −	$ −	$ −	$ 16,257	$ 15,465	$ −	$ 31,722
Net book value							
At January 1, 2011	$ 72,035	$ 70,411	$ 190,370	$ 464,081	$ 808,807	$ 71,636	$ 1,677,340
At January 3, 2010	$ 113,478	$ 57,683	$ 120,103	$ 475,863	$ 723,467	$ 51,247	$ 1,541,841

During the financial year ended December 31, 2011, the Company recognized depreciation expense of $249,467 (2010: $234,490), an impairment loss on store assets of $nil (2010: $10,338) and a loss on disposal of property and equipment of $1,498 (2010: a net gain of $6,818) within operating and administrative expenses in the consolidated statements of earnings.

Impairment Loss

During the financial year ended December 31, 2011, the Company reviewed its long-lived assets for indicators of impairment at the cash-generating unit level and determined that an impairment test was not necessary.

During the financial year ended January 1, 2011, the Company reviewed its long-lived assets for indicators of impairment at the cash-generating unit level and determined that a test for impairment was necessary on certain of its store assets. This resulted in the identification of an impairment charge of $7,554, which is net of taxes of $2,784. The impaired assets consist primarily of equipment, fixtures, computer equipment and leasehold improvements at certain of the Company's newer stores. The recoverable amount of the impaired assets was determined through a value-in-use methodology using a pre-tax discount rate of 8 percent.

During the financial years ended December 31, 2011 and January 1, 2011, the Company did not record any reversals of previously recorded impairment charges.

Property under Development

During the financial year ended December 31, 2011, the Company acquired properties with the intention of developing retail stores on the sites. The cost of acquisition was $9,979 (2010: $11,139).

Investment Property

		2011			2010	
	Land	**Building**	**Total**	Land	Building	Total
Cost						
Balance, beginning of financial year $	**8,084** $	**5,995** $	**14,079** $	3,729 $	3,044 $	6,773
Transfers	**4,325**	**327**	**4,652**	4,386	2,951	7,337
Disposals	**(723)**	**(2)**	**(725)**	(31)	–	(31)
Balance, end of financial year $	**11,686** $	**6,320** $	**18,006** $	8,084 $	5,995 $	14,079
Amortization						
Balance, beginning of financial year $	**–** $	**1,309** $	**1,309** $	– $	889 $	889
Amortization for the financial year	**–**	**325**	**325**	–	420	420
Transfers	**–**	**–**	**–**	–	–	–
Balance, end of financial year $	**–** $	**1,634** $	**1,634** $	– $	1,309 $	1,309
Net book value		$	**16,372**		$	12,770
Net book value at January 3, 2010					$	5,884

The fair value of investment property approximates its carrying value.

24. SHARE CAPITAL

Share Capital and Contributed Surplus

Authorized

Unlimited number of common shares

Unlimited number of preferred shares, issuable in series without nominal or par value

Outstanding

	2011		2010	
	Number of Common Shares	**Stated Value**	Number of Common Shares	Stated Value
Beginning balance	**217,452,068** $	**1,520,558**	217,431,898 $	1,519,870
Shares issued for cash	**109,729**	**1,220**	20,170	491
Shares repurchased in cash	**(5,086,200)**	**(35,576)**	–	–
Repayment of share purchase loans	**–**	**7**	–	33
Exercise of share options	**–**	**246**	–	164
Ending balance	**212,475,597** $	**1,486,455**	217,452,068 $	1,520,558

The Company also has issued share options. See Note 26 to these consolidated financial statements for further details on the Company's issued share options.

24. SHARE CAPITAL (continued)

Individual shareholder agreements address matters related to the transfer of certain shares issued to the Company's management and Associates, including shares issued under certain options granted to management. In particular, each provides, subject to certain exceptions, for a general prohibition on any transfer of a member of management's or Associate's shares for a period of five years from the date that the individual entered into the shareholder agreement.

The holders of common shares are entitled to receive dividends as declared from time to time and are entitled to one vote per share at meetings of the Company.

Normal Course Issuer Bid

On February 10, 2011, the Company implemented a normal course issuer bid to repurchase, for cancellation, up to 8,700,000 of its common shares, representing approximately 4.0% of the Company's then outstanding common shares. Repurchases will be effected through the facilities of the Toronto Stock Exchange (the "TSX") and may take place over a 12-month period ending no later than February 14, 2012. Repurchases will be made at market prices in accordance with the requirements of the TSX.

From February 10, 2011 to December 31, 2011, the Company purchased and cancelled 5,086,200 common shares under the normal course issuer bid at a cost of $206,779. The premium paid over the average book value of the common shares repurchased of $171,203 has been charged to retained earnings. The Company purchased an additional 115,900 shares at the end of the financial year at a cost of $4,735. These shares were cancelled subsequent to the end of the financial year. The cost of this latter purchase is recorded as treasury shares in Shareholders' Equity as at December 31, 2011.

Dividends

The following table provides a summary of the dividends declared by the Company:

Declaration Date	Record Date	Payment Date	Dividend per Common Share
February 10, 2011	March 31, 2011	April 15, 2011	$ 0.250
April 27, 2011	June 30, 2011	July 15, 2011	$ 0.250
July 21, 2011	September 30, 2011	October 14, 2011	$ 0.250
November 9, 2011	December 30, 2011	January 13, 2012	$ 0.250
February 11, 2010	March 31, 2010	April 15, 2010	$ 0.225
April 28, 2010	June 30, 2010	July 15, 2010	$ 0.225
July 22, 2010	September 30, 2010	October 15, 2010	$ 0.225
November 9, 2010	December 31, 2010	January 14, 2011	$ 0.225

On February 9, 2012, the Board of Directors declared a dividend of 26.5 cents per common share payable April 13, 2012 to shareholders of record as of the close of business on March 30, 2012.

25. EARNINGS PER COMMON SHARE

Basic Net Earnings per Common Share

The calculation of basic net earnings per common share at December 31, 2011 was based on net earnings for the financial year of $613,934 (2010: $591,851) and a weighted average number of shares outstanding (basic) of 216,420,096 (2010: 217,435,868). The weighted average number of shares outstanding (basic) is calculated as follows:

Weighted Average Shares Outstanding (Basic)

	Note	2011	2010
Issued shares, beginning of the financial year	24	217,452,068	217,431,898
Effect of share options exercised		52,350	8,094
Effect of shares repurchased		(1,082,326)	–
Effect of share purchase loans		(1,996)	(4,124)
Weighted average number of shares outstanding (basic), end of the financial year		216,420,096	217,435,868

Diluted Net Earnings per Common Share

The calculation of diluted net earnings per common share at December 31, 2011 was based on net earnings for the financial year of $613,934 (2010: $591,851) and a weighted average number of shares outstanding, after adjustment for the effects of all potentially dilutive shares, of 216,504,784 (2010: 217,537,709). The weighted average number of shares outstanding (diluted) is calculated as follows:

Weighted Average Shares Outstanding (Diluted)

	2011	2010
Weighted average number of shares outstanding (basic), end of the financial year	216,420,096	217,435,868
Potentially dilutive share options	84,688	101,841
Weighted average number of shares outstanding (diluted), end of the financial year	216,504,784	217,537,709

The average market value of the Company's shares for purposes of calculating the effect of dilutive share options was based on quoted market prices for the period that the stock options were outstanding. Anti-dilutive stock options have been excluded.

Financial Statements Analysis Ratios

Exhibit

Financial Statement Analysis Ratios

	Method of Computation	Use
Liquidity measures:		
Working Capital	Current Assets − Current Liabilities	To indicate the ability to meet currently maturing obligations
Current Ratio	$\dfrac{\text{Current Assets}}{\text{Current Liabilities}}$	
Quick Ratio	$\dfrac{\text{Quick Assets}}{\text{Current Liabilities}}$	To indicate instant debt-paying ability
Efficiency measures:		
Accounts Receivable Turnover	$\dfrac{\text{Net Sales}}{\text{Average Net Accounts Receivable}}$	To assess the efficiency in collecting receivables and in the management of credit
Days' Sales in Receivables	$\dfrac{\text{Average Net Accounts Receivable}}{\text{Average Daily Sales}}$	
Inventory Turnover	$\dfrac{\text{Cost of Goods Sold}}{\text{Average Inventory}}$	To assess the efficiency in the management of inventory
Days' Sales in Inventory	$\dfrac{\text{Average Inventory}}{\text{Average Daily Cost of Goods Sold}}$	
Total Asset Turnover	$\dfrac{\text{Net Sales}}{\text{Average Total Assets}}$	To assess the efficiency in the management of assets
Solvency measures:		
Debt Ratio	$\dfrac{\text{Total Liabilities}}{\text{Total Assets}}$	To indicate the percentage of assets financed with debt
Times Interest Earned Ratio	$\dfrac{\text{Income Before Income Taxes} + \text{Interest Expense}}{\text{Interest Expense}}$	To assess the risk to debtholders in terms of number of times interest charges were earned
Profitability measures:		
Profit Margin	$\dfrac{\text{Net Income}}{\text{Net Sales}}$	To assess the overall profitability of a company
Gross Margin	$\dfrac{\text{Gross Profit}}{\text{Net Sales}}$	To assess the ability to earn a return on items sold
Return on Assets	$\dfrac{\text{Net Income}}{\text{Average Total Assets}}$	To assess the profitability of the assets
Return on Common Shareholders' Equity	$\dfrac{\text{Net Income} - \text{Preferred Dividends}}{\text{Average Common Shareholders' Equity}}$	To assess the profitability of the investment by common shareholders
Earnings per Share (EPS)	$\dfrac{\text{Net Income} - \text{Preferred Dividends}}{\text{Weighted Average Number of Common Shares}}$	
Price-Earnings Ratio	$\dfrac{\text{Market Price per Common Share}}{\text{Earnings per Share}}$	To indicate future earnings prospects, based on the relationship between market value of common shares and earnings
Dividend Yield	$\dfrac{\text{Annual Dividends per Share}}{\text{Market Price per Share}}$	To indicate the rate of return to common shareholders in terms of dividends

Interest Tables

Present Value of $1 at Compound Interest Due in n Periods						
Periods	**2.5%**	**3%**	**3.5%**	**4%**	**5%**	**5.5%**
1	0.97561	0.97087	0.96618	0.96154	0.95238	0.94787
2	0.95181	0.94260	0.93351	0.92456	0.90703	0.89845
3	0.92860	0.91514	0.90194	0.88900	0.86384	0.85161
4	0.90595	0.88849	0.87144	0.85480	0.82270	0.80722
5	0.88385	0.86261	0.84197	0.82193	0.78353	0.76513
6	0.86230	0.83748	0.81350	0.79031	0.74622	0.72525
7	0.84127	0.81309	0.78599	0.75992	0.71068	0.68744
8	0.82075	0.78941	0.75941	0.73069	0.67684	0.65160
9	0.80073	0.76642	0.73373	0.70259	0.64461	0.61763
10	0.78120	0.74409	0.70892	0.67556	0.61391	0.58543
11	0.76214	0.72242	0.68495	0.64958	0.58468	0.55491
12	0.74356	0.70138	0.66178	0.62460	0.55684	0.52598
13	0.72542	0.68095	0.63940	0.60057	0.53032	0.49856
14	0.70773	0.66112	0.61778	0.57748	0.50507	0.47257
15	0.69047	0.64186	0.59689	0.55527	0.48102	0.44793
16	0.67362	0.62317	0.57671	0.53391	0.45811	0.42458
17	0.65720	0.60502	0.55720	0.51337	0.43630	0.40245
18	0.64117	0.58740	0.53836	0.49363	0.41552	0.38147
19	0.62553	0.57029	0.52016	0.47464	0.39573	0.36158
20	0.61027	0.55368	0.50257	0.45639	0.37689	0.34273
21	0.59539	0.53755	0.48557	0.43883	0.35894	0.32486
22	0.58086	0.52189	0.46915	0.42196	0.34185	0.30793
23	0.56670	0.50669	0.45329	0.40573	0.32557	0.29187
24	0.55288	0.49193	0.43796	0.39012	0.31007	0.27666
25	0.53939	0.47761	0.42315	0.37512	0.29530	0.26223
26	0.52623	0.46369	0.40884	0.36069	0.28124	0.24856
27	0.51340	0.45019	0.39501	0.34682	0.26785	0.23560
28	0.50088	0.43708	0.38165	0.33348	0.25509	0.22332
29	0.48866	0.42435	0.36875	0.32065	0.24295	0.21168
30	0.47674	0.41199	0.35628	0.30832	0.23138	0.20064
31	0.46511	0.39999	0.34423	0.29646	0.22036	0.19018
32	0.45377	0.38834	0.33259	0.28506	0.20987	0.18027
33	0.44270	0.37703	0.32134	0.27409	0.19987	0.17087
34	0.43191	0.36604	0.31048	0.26355	0.19036	0.16196
35	0.42137	0.35538	0.29998	0.25342	0.18129	0.15352
40	0.37243	0.30656	0.25257	0.20829	0.14205	0.11746
45	0.32917	0.26444	0.21266	0.17120	0.11130	0.08988
50	0.29094	0.22811	0.17905	0.14071	0.08720	0.06877

Present Value of $1 at Compound Interest Due in n Periods

Periods	6%	6.5%	7%	8%	9%	10%
1	0.94334	0.93897	0.93458	0.92593	0.91743	0.90909
2	0.89000	0.88166	0.87344	0.85734	0.84168	0.82645
3	0.83962	0.82785	0.81630	0.79383	0.77218	0.75132
4	0.79209	0.77732	0.76290	0.73503	0.70842	0.68301
5	0.74726	0.72988	0.71290	0.68058	0.64993	0.62092
6	0.70496	0.68533	0.66634	0.63017	0.59627	0.56447
7	0.66506	0.64351	0.62275	0.58349	0.54703	0.51316
8	0.62741	0.60423	0.58201	0.54027	0.50187	0.46651
9	0.59190	0.56735	0.54393	0.50025	0.46043	0.42410
10	0.55840	0.53273	0.50835	0.46319	0.42241	0.38554
11	0.52679	0.50021	0.47509	0.42888	0.38753	0.35049
12	0.49697	0.46968	0.44401	0.39711	0.35554	0.31863
13	0.46884	0.44102	0.41496	0.36770	0.32618	0.28966
14	0.44230	0.41410	0.38782	0.34046	0.29925	0.26333
15	0.41726	0.38883	0.36245	0.31524	0.27454	0.23939
16	0.39365	0.36510	0.33874	0.29189	0.25187	0.21763
17	0.37136	0.34281	0.31657	0.27027	0.23107	0.19784
18	0.35034	0.32189	0.29586	0.25025	0.21199	0.17986
19	0.33051	0.30224	0.27651	0.23171	0.19449	0.16351
20	0.31180	0.28380	0.25842	0.21455	0.17843	0.14864
21	0.29416	0.26648	0.24151	0.19866	0.16370	0.13513
22	0.27750	0.25021	0.22571	0.18394	0.15018	0.12285
23	0.26180	0.23494	0.21095	0.17032	0.13778	0.11168
24	0.24698	0.22060	0.19715	0.15770	0.12640	0.10153
25	0.23300	0.20714	0.18425	0.14602	0.11597	0.09230
26	0.21981	0.19450	0.17211	0.13520	0.10639	0.08390
27	0.20737	0.18263	0.16093	0.12519	0.09761	0.07628
28	0.19563	0.17148	0.15040	0.11591	0.08955	0.06934
29	0.18456	0.16101	0.14056	0.10733	0.08216	0.06304
30	0.17411	0.15119	0.13137	0.09938	0.07537	0.05731
31	0.16426	0.14196	0.12277	0.09202	0.06915	0.05210
32	0.15496	0.13329	0.11474	0.08520	0.06344	0.04736
33	0.14619	0.12516	0.10724	0.07889	0.05820	0.04306
34	0.13791	0.11752	0.10022	0.07304	0.05331	0.03914
35	0.13010	0.11035	0.09366	0.06764	0.04899	0.03558
40	0.09722	0.08054	0.06678	0.04603	0.03184	0.02210
45	0.07265	0.05879	0.04761	0.03133	0.02069	0.01372
50	0.05429	0.04291	0.03395	0.02132	0.01345	0.00852

Present Value of Ordinary Annuity of $1 per Period

Periods	2.5%	3.0%	3.5%	4.0%	5%	5.5%
1	0.97561	0.97087	0.96618	0.96154	0.95238	0.94787
2	1.92742	1.91347	1.89969	1.88609	1.85941	1.84632
3	2.85602	2.82861	2.80164	2.77509	2.72325	2.69793
4	3.76197	3.71710	3.67308	3.62990	3.54595	3.50515
5	4.64583	4.57971	4.51505	4.45182	4.32948	4.27028
6	5.50813	5.41719	5.32855	5.24214	5.07569	4.99553
7	6.34939	6.23028	6.11454	6.00205	5.78637	5.68297
8	7.17014	7.01969	6.87396	6.73274	6.46321	6.33457
9	7.97087	7.78611	7.60769	7.43533	7.10782	6.95220
10	8.75206	8.53020	8.31661	8.11090	7.72174	7.53763
11	9.51421	9.25262	9.00155	8.76048	8.30641	8.09254
12	10.25776	9.95400	9.66333	9.38507	8.86325	8.61852
13	10.98318	10.63496	10.30274	9.98565	9.39357	9.11708
14	11.69091	11.29607	10.92052	10.56312	9.89864	9.58965
15	12.38138	11.93794	11.51741	11.11839	10.37966	10.03758
16	13.05500	12.56110	12.09412	11.65230	10.83777	10.46216
17	13.71220	13.16612	12.65132	12.16567	11.27407	10.86461
18	14.35336	13.75351	13.18968	12.65930	11.68959	11.24607
19	14.97889	14.32380	13.70984	13.13394	12.08532	11.60765
20	15.58916	14.87747	14.21240	13.59033	12.46221	11.95038
21	16.18455	15.41502	14.69797	14.02916	12.82115	12.27524
22	16.76541	15.93692	15.16712	14.45112	13.16300	12.58317
23	17.33211	16.44361	15.62041	14.85684	13.48857	12.87504
24	17.88499	16.93554	16.05837	15.24696	13.79864	13.15170
25	18.42438	17.41315	16.48151	15.62208	14.09394	13.41393
26	18.95061	17.87684	16.89035	15.98277	14.37518	13.66250
27	19.46401	18.32703	17.28536	16.32959	14.64303	13.89810
28	19.96489	18.76411	17.66702	16.66306	14.89813	14.12142
29	20.45355	19.18845	18.03577	16.98371	15.14107	14.33310
30	20.93029	19.60044	18.39205	17.29203	15.37245	14.53375
31	21.39541	20.00043	18.73628	17.58849	15.59281	14.72393
32	21.84918	20.38877	19.06887	17.87355	15.80268	14.90420
33	22.29188	20.76579	19.39021	18.14765	16.00255	15.07507
34	22.72379	21.13184	19.70068	18.41120	16.19290	15.23703
35	23.14516	21.48722	20.00066	18.66461	16.37420	15.39055
40	25.10278	23.11477	21.35507	19.79277	17.15909	16.04612
45	26.83302	24.51871	22.49545	20.72004	17.77407	16.54773
50	28.36231	25.72976	23.45562	21.48218	18.25592	16.93152

Present Value of Ordinary Annuity of $1 per Period

Periods	6%	6.5%	7%	8%	9%	10%
1	0.94340	0.93897	0.93458	0.92593	0.91743	0.90909
2	1.83339	1.82063	1.80802	1.78326	1.75911	1.73554
3	2.67301	2.64848	2.62432	2.57710	2.53130	2.48685
4	3.46511	3.42580	3.38721	3.31213	3.23972	3.16986
5	4.21236	4.15568	4.10020	3.99271	3.88965	3.79079
6	4.91732	4.84101	4.76654	4.62288	4.48592	4.35526
7	5.58238	5.48452	5.38923	5.20637	5.03295	4.86842
8	6.20979	6.08875	5.97130	5.74664	5.53482	5.33493
9	6.80169	6.65610	6.51523	6.24689	5.99525	5.75902
10	7.36009	7.18883	7.02358	6.71008	6.41766	6.14457
11	7.88688	7.68904	7.49867	7.13896	6.80519	6.49506
12	8.38384	8.15873	7.94269	7.53608	7.16072	6.81369
13	8.85268	8.59974	8.35765	7.90378	7.48690	7.10336
14	9.29498	9.01384	8.74547	8.22424	7.78615	7.36669
15	9.71225	9.40267	9.10791	8.55948	8.06069	7.60608
16	10.10590	9.76776	9.44665	8.85137	8.31256	7.82371
17	10.47726	10.11058	9.76322	9.12164	8.54363	8.02155
18	10.82760	10.43247	10.05909	9.37189	8.75562	8.20141
19	11.15812	10.73471	10.33560	9.60360	8.95012	8.36492
20	11.46992	11.01851	10.59401	9.81815	9.12855	8.51356
21	11.76408	11.28498	10.83553	10.01680	9.29224	8.64869
22	12.04158	11.53520	11.06124	10.20074	9.44242	8.77154
23	12.30338	11.77014	11.27219	10.37106	9.58021	8.88322
24	12.55036	11.99074	11.46933	10.52876	9.70661	8.98474
25	12.78336	12.19788	11.65358	10.67478	9.82258	9.07704
26	13.00317	12.39237	11.82578	10.80998	9.92897	9.16094
27	13.21053	12.57500	11.98671	10.93516	10.02658	9.23722
28	13.40616	12.74648	12.13711	11.05108	10.11613	9.30657
29	13.59072	12.90749	12.27767	11.15841	10.19828	9.36961
30	13.76483	13.05868	12.40904	11.25778	10.27365	9.42691
31	13.92909	13.20063	12.53181	11.34980	10.34280	9.47901
32	14.08404	13.33393	12.64656	11.43500	10.40624	9.52638
33	14.23023	13.45909	12.75379	11.51389	10.46444	9.56943
34	14.36814	13.57661	12.85401	11.58693	10.51784	9.60858
35	14.49825	13.68696	12.94767	11.65457	10.56682	9.64416
40	15.04630	14.14553	13.33171	11.92461	10.75736	9.77905
45	15.45583	14.48023	13.60552	12.10840	10.88118	9.86281
50	15.76186	14.72452	13.80075	12.23348	10.96168	9.91481

SUBJECT INDEX

Page references followed by "n" refer to footnotes.

COMPANY INDEX

Account Title	Account Classification	Normal Balance	Financial Statement
Accounts Payable	Current liability	Credit	Statement of Financial Position
Accounts Receivable	Current asset	Debit	Statement of Financial Position
Accumulated Amortization	Contra asset	Credit	Statement of Financial Position
Accumulated Depreciation	Contra asset	Credit	Statement of Financial Position
Accumulated Other Comprehensive Income	Shareholders' equity	Credit	Statement of Financial Position
Advertising Expense	Operating expense	Debit	Statement of Comprehensive Income
Allowance for Doubtful Accounts	Contra current asset	Credit	Statement of Financial Position
Amortization Expense	Operating expense	Debit	Statement of Comprehensive Income
Available-for-Sale Investments	Current asset/Noncurrent asset	Debit	Statement of Financial Position
Bad Debt Expense	Operating expense	Debit	Statement of Comprehensive Income
Bonds Payable	Long-term liability	Credit	Statement of Financial Position
Building	Property, plant, and equipment	Debit	Statement of Financial Position
Canada Pension Plan (CPP) Expense	Operating expense	Debit	Statement of Comprehensive Income
Canada Pension Plan (CPP) Payable	Current liability	Credit	Statement of Financial Position
(Owner's name), Capital	Owner's equity	Credit	Statement of Changes in Equity/ Statement of Financial Position
Cash	Current asset	Debit	Statement of Financial Position
Cash Dividends	Shareholders' equity	Debit	Retained earnings statement
Cash Dividends Payable	Current liability	Credit	Statement of Financial Position
Common Shares	Shareholders' equity	Credit	Statement of Financial Position
Common Share Dividend Distributable	Shareholders' equity	Credit	Statement of Financial Position
Contributed Capital from Retirement of Common Shares	Shareholders' equity	Credit	Statement of Financial Position
Cost of Goods Sold	Cost of goods sold	Debit	Statement of Comprehensive Income
Current Portion of Long-Term Debt	Current liability	Credit	Statement of Financial Position
Delivery Expense	Operating expense	Debit	Statement of Comprehensive Income
Depreciation Expense	Operating expense	Debit	Statement of Comprehensive Income
Discount on Bonds Payable	Contra long-term liability	Debit	Statement of Financial Position
Discount on Notes Payable	Contra long-term liability	Debit	Statement of Financial Position
Dividend Revenue	Other income	Credit	Statement of Comprehensive Income
Dividends	Shareholders' equity	Debit	Retained earnings statement
Dividends Payable—Common	Current liability	Credit	Statement of Financial Position
Dividends Payable—Preferred	Current liability	Credit	Statement of Financial Position
Employment Insurance (EI) Expense	Operating expense	Debit	Statement of Comprehensive Income
Employment Insurance (EI) Payable	Current liability	Credit	Statement of Financial Position
Equipment	Property, plant, and equipment	Debit	Statement of Financial Position
Federal Income Taxes Payable	Current liability	Credit	Statement of Financial Position

Classification of Accounts-IFRS

Account Title	Account Classification	Normal Balance	Financial Statement
Fees Earned	Revenue	Credit	Statement of Comprehensive Income
Freight In	Cost of goods sold	Debit	Statement of Comprehensive Income
Freight Out	Operating expense	Debit	Statement of Comprehensive Income
Gain on Disposal of Property, Plant, and Equipment	Other income	Credit	Statement of Comprehensive Income
Gain on Sale of Investments	Other income	Credit	Statement of Comprehensive Income
Goodwill	Intangible asset	Debit	Statement of Financial Position
GST Charged on Sales	Current liability	Credit	Statement of Financial Position
GST Paid on Purchases	Contra current liability	Debit	Statement of Financial Position
Held-to-Maturity Investments	Current asset/Noncurrent asset	Debit	Statement of Financial Position
Impairment Loss	Other expense	Debit	Statement of Comprehensive Income
HST Charged on Sales	Current liability	Credit	Statement of Financial Position
HST Paid on Purchases	Contra current liability	Debit	Statement of Financial Position
Income Taxes Expense	Income tax	Debit	Statement of Comprehensive Income
Income Taxes Payable	Current liability	Credit	Statement of Financial Position
Insurance Expense	Operating expense	Debit	Statement of Comprehensive Income
Interest Expense	Other expense	Debit	Statement of Comprehensive Income
Interest Payable	Current liability	Credit	Statement of Financial Position
Interest Receivable	Current asset	Debit	Statement of Financial Position
Interest Revenue	Other income	Credit	Statement of Comprehensive Income
Inventory	Current asset/Cost of goods sold	Debit	Statement of Financial Position/ Statement of Comprehensive Income
Investment in Bonds	Investment	Debit	Statement of Financial Position
Investment in Shares	Investment	Debit	Statement of Financial Position
Investment Revenue	Other income	Credit	Statement of Comprehensive Income
Land	Property, plant, and equipment	Debit	Statement of Financial Position
Loss on Disposal of Property, Plant, and Equipment	Other expense	Debit	Statement of Comprehensive Income
Loss on Sale of Investments	Other expense	Debit	Statement of Comprehensive Income
Notes Payable	Current liability/Long-term liability	Credit	Statement of Financial Position
Notes Receivable	Current asset/Investment	Debit	Statement of Financial Position
Other Benefits Expense	Operating expense	Debit	Statement of Comprehensive Income
Other Benefits Payable	Current liability	Credit	Statement of Financial Position
Patents	Intangible asset	Debit	Statement of Financial Position
Pension Expense	Operating expense	Debit	Statement of Comprehensive Income
Petty Cash	Current asset	Debit	Statement of Financial Position
Preferred Shares	Shareholders' equity	Credit	Statement of Financial Position
Premium on Bonds Payable	Contra long-term liability	Credit	Statement of Financial Position
Prepaid Insurance	Current asset	Debit	Statement of Financial Position
Prepaid Rent	Current asset	Debit	Statement of Financial Position
Product Warranty Expense	Operating expense	Debit	Statement of Comprehensive Income
Product Warranty Liability	Current liability	Credit	Statement of Financial Position
Provincial Income Taxes Payable	Current liability	Credit	Statement of Financial Position
PST Payable	Current liability	Credit	Statement of Financial Position
Purchases	Cost of goods sold	Debit	Statement of Comprehensive Income
Purchases Discounts	Cost of goods sold	Credit	Statement of Comprehensive Income

Account Title	Account Classification	Normal Balance	Financial Statement
Purchases Returns and Allowances	Cost of goods sold	Credit	Statement of Comprehensive Income
Rent Expense	Operating expense	Debit	Statement of Comprehensive Income
Rent Revenue	Other income	Credit	Statement of Comprehensive Income
Retained Earnings	Shareholders' equity	Credit	Statement of Financial Position/ Retained earnings statement
Salaries Expense	Operating expense	Debit	Statement of Comprehensive Income
Salaries Payable	Current liability	Credit	Statement of Financial Position
Sales	Revenue from sales	Credit	Statement of Comprehensive Income
Sales Discounts	Revenue from sales	Debit	Statement of Comprehensive Income
Sales Returns and Allowances	Revenue from sales	Debit	Statement of Comprehensive Income
Share Dividends	Shareholders' equity	Debit	Retained earnings statement
Supplies	Current asset	Debit	Statement of Financial Position
Supplies Expense	Operating expense	Debit	Statement of Comprehensive Income
Trading Investments	Current asset	Debit	Statement of Financial Position
Unearned Rent	Current liability	Credit	Statement of Financial Position
Unrealized Gain (Loss) on Trading Investments	Other income (loss)	Credit (Debit)	Statement of Comprehensive Income
Unrealized Gain (Loss) on Available-for-Sale Investments	Shareholders' equity	Credit (Debit)	Statement of Financial Position
Utilities Expense	Operating expense	Debit	Statement of Comprehensive Income
Vacation Pay Expense	Operating expense	Debit	Statement of Comprehensive Income
Vacation Pay Payable	Current liability/Long-term liability	Credit	Statement of Financial Position
Wages Expense	Operating expense	Debit	Statement of Comprehensive Income
Wages Payable	Current liability	Credit	Statement of Financial Position
(Owner's name), Withdrawals	Owner's equity	Debit	Statement of Changes in Equity

The Basics

1. Accounting Equation (page 10):

Assets = Liabilities + Owner's Equity

2. T Account (page 47):

Account Title	
Left side *debit*	Right side *credit*

3. Rules of Debit and Credit (page 51):

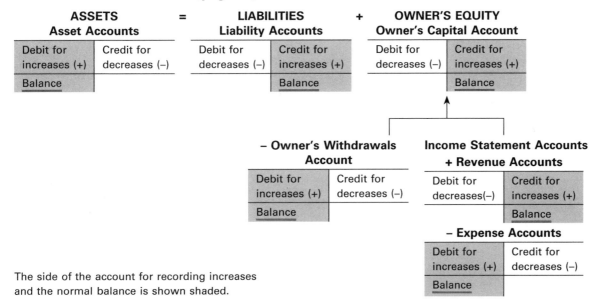

The side of the account for recording increases and the normal balance is shown shaded.

Net income or net loss

4. Analyzing and Journalizing Transactions (page 53)

A. Carefully read the description of the transaction to determine whether an asset, a liability, an owner's equity, a revenue, an expense, or a withdrawals account is affected.

B. For each account affected by the transaction, determine whether the account increases or decreases.

C. Determine whether each increase or decrease should be recorded as a debit or a credit, following the rules of debit and credit.

D. Record the transaction using a journal entry.

E. Periodically post journal entries to the accounts in the ledger.

F. Prepare an unadjusted trial balance at the end of the period.

5. Financial Statements—ASPE (page 16):

INCOME STATEMENT

A summary of the revenues and expenses of a business entity for a specific period of time, such as a month or a year.

STATEMENT OF OWNER'S EQUITY

A summary of the changes in the owner's equity of a business entity that have occurred during a specific period of time, such as a month or a year.

BALANCE SHEET

A list of the assets, liabilities, and owner's equity of a business entity as of a specific date, usually at the close of the last day of a month or a year.

CASH FLOW STATEMENT

A summary of the cash receipts and cash payments of a business entity for a specific period of time, such as a month or a year.

6. Accounting Cycle (page 52):

1. Source documents arrive.
2. Journal entries are recorded.
3. Transactions are posted to accounts.
4. Unadjusted trial balance is prepared.
5. Optional worksheet is prepared.
6. Adjusting entries are journalized and posted.
7. Adjusted trial balance is prepared.
8. Financial statements are prepared.
9. Closing entries are journalized and prepared.
10. Post-closing trial balance is prepared.

7. Types of Adjusting Entries (page 102):

1. Prepaid expenses
2. Unearned revenues
3. Accrued revenues
4. Accrued expenses
5. Depreciation of property, plant, and equipment

Each entry will always affect both a balance sheet and an income statement account.

8. Closing Entries (page 175):

1. Revenue account balances are transferred to an account called Income Summary.
2. Expense account balances are transferred to an account called Income Summary.
3. The balance of Income Summary (net income or net loss) is transferred to the owner's capital account.
4. The balance of the owner's withdrawals account is transferred to the owner's capital account.

9. Format for Bank Reconciliation (page 366):

```
Cash balance according to bank                              $XXX
Add: Debits to cash not on bank statement
      (deposits in transit, etc.)                    $XX
Add or Deduct: bank errors                            XX
Deduct: Credits to cash not on bank statement
      (outstanding cheques, etc.)                     XX     XXX
Adjusted balance                                            $XXX
```

```
Cash balance according to company                          $XXX
Add: Unrecorded bank credits (notes collected
      by bank)                                       $XX
Add or Deduct: company errors                         XX
Deduct: Unrecorded bank debits (NSF cheques,
      service charges, etc.)                          XX     XXX
Adjusted balance                                            $XXX
```

Must be equal

10. Interest Computations (page 429):

$$\text{Interest} = \text{Principal} \times \text{Interest Rate} \times (\text{Term}/365 \text{ days})$$

11. Methods of Determining Annual Depreciation (page 465):

STRAIGHT-LINE: $\dfrac{\text{Cost} - \text{Residual Value}}{\text{Useful Life}}$

DOUBLE-DECLINING-BALANCE: Rate* × Carrying Amount at Beginning of Period

*Rate is commonly twice the straight-line rate (100%/Estimated Life).

12. Payroll Steps (page 519):

1. Calculating gross pay, deductions, and resulting net pay.
2. Recording distribution of gross pay.
3. Recording employer's portion of payroll expenses.
4. Recording payment of net pay to employees.
5. Recording remittance of payroll deductions.